~~~~Flood~Legends~Sorted~~~~
~~~~~~~~Global from Local~~~~~
~~~~~~~~And some evidence for each~~~~~~~~

R. Pilotte

Order this book online at www.trafford.com
or email orders@trafford.com

Most Trafford titles are also available at major online book retailers.

Print information available on the last page.

ISBN: 978-1-4907-9564-5 (sc)
ISBN: 978-1-4907-9565-2 (e)

Library of Congress Control Number: 2019907790

Trafford rev. 07/03/2019

North America & international
toll-free: 1 888 232 4444 (USA & Canada)
fax: 812 355 4082

CONTENTS

FOREWORD

Sometimes the reason for writing something is as important, as what is written, and gives the reader a grasp of the motivation behind the work. So let me start this with a bit of my personal history that led to realizing this book needed to be written.

I was given up for adoption soon after I turned 5 and when I met my parents again shortly before I turned 12, I was led to believe it was because of my dad's alcoholism that my sister and I were given up, for our well being and protection. This apparently slapped a bit of sense into dad and he stopped drinking for over seven years. During my absence he got into a different branch of Christian beliefs via Garner Ted Armstrong's (GTA) TV broadcasts and the accompanying literature. Formerly Dad had Catholic background which he and his brother Joe/Roger rebelled against, so this appears to have been his way to break free and search his personal own way. When I came onto the scene again we watched this GTA TV program and I saw some GTA literature such as The Plain Truth magazines. I remember dad showing me graphic pictures of huge earthquakes that were 12, 13 or more on the Richter scale (same source?) which he said would come in the future (He also explained the Richter scale to me). I guess he was a bit of a salesman so one day I asked to borrow a bible to read some of this stuff for myself. In the bible I borrowed was a bookmark showing how long it had taken Dad to read it, a little over 7 months: I had that bible for many years and I once even beat the time it took him to read it on one occasion. Shortly after starting it at age 12, I of course came to the creation story and the story of Noah and the flood. It was clear to me in the creation narrative that it spoke of water being up in the sky, though not in clouds, but different. I went outside and looked up and stared intently at the sky trying to see if I could detect something watery about the blue sky, but couldn't. I came back in and asked dad if there was water in the sky...not the clouds but way up. He understood and said it had all come down in the flood and wasn't up there anymore. The way he said it matter-of-factly made it appear to me to be that this was probably common knowledge.

So, whatever held it up there and made it come down was one of the early mysteries of my life. I didn't really have any reason to doubt the flood story, but I wanted to understand the mechanics and the causes for it all. I did eventually figure it out and wrote the solution in my first book *Earth, Man, & Devolution*. With the myriad of mysteries solved in that book I thought that would be my one and only book, but on New year's eve 2017/18, soon after I'd completed the more polished 3rd edition of my book I realized *this* book had to be written. I continue with the history as to why.

Dad's searches didn't end with Garner Ted Armstrong, and I noticed over the years an increasing scepticism in his outlook that made him willing to turn in spirit, against some of the authorities in the world like government rules, and religious axioms or specific religions with a more worldly or secular investigative nature to him, and some of the things he dug into or accepted came from this ongoing search. He often would tell me to not just believe what I believe but prove and search, as he knew I had started going to church after I had gotten out on my own. He would quote the Tibetans, The Quran, Readers Digest, the bible, Buddhists, and all sorts of things I've forgotten; anything he thought had a "grain of truth" in it. His experiences with whatever churches he went to seemed to harden his overall outlook on organized religion. Early on during his searches after GTA, I knew he was reading the Urantia book; I couldn't miss or forget it as it took him so long to read, and he often had it with him when I visited my parents on weekends. Several years later I was visiting some friends of my Uncle living on the same property and one of them knowing I was a believer of the bible said to me out of the blue, that the Urantia said "The Flood" was just a local flood. Knowing my dad had read this book, and that this friend of my uncle's statement referring to it, still never got me curious enough to read the Urantia book. Nonetheless this statement that the flood was a local flood made me begin to realize that many people believed, for whatever reason, in a different flood.

On the surface this appeared to contradict the bible and my "beliefs", so I assumed such ideas came from people who say this don't like the bible and try to break people's faith this way, or it is their defence for a contrary belief system or some such reasoning. I've come to realize that the very earliest books we've read seem to determine in the future what we continue to like to read and maintain an interest in and often forms our beliefs. And people tend to gravitate toward the beliefs of whoever they come across first that is a kindred spirit or is the most convincing. Various authors whether they are right or wrong will slant your opinions for years to come if not for the rest of your life, and even if what you believe or learned is completely wrong and even ludicrous, it can sometimes take a mountain of evidence to change your mind if it changes it at all. It can even be harder to overcome if the people you learned stuff from were dear to you, and looked up to. If as a child we read about explorers of new lands we want to follow their footsteps or see what they saw. If we read detective novels we may want to be a detective. I wonder how much we really chose our careers and how much chance of what we happen to read first determined what we become.

OK back at it. Knowing about the flood for years I hadn't done a lot of digging into the science and evidence of the flood, and I was convinced enough with the evidence I *did* come across that there was indeed a worldwide flood, and thus people out there were either living in denial, or a self delusion to insist there was just legends of a local flood, or maybe they were just misinformed. This mindset / belief seemed particularly strange to me because there are such a vast number of ancient flood legends out there. I've read there are more than 300 and as many as 600 ancient flood legends, myths and stories that originate from every corner of the globe. This universality of the flood legends seemed an obvious proof all by itself that the flood they must be talking about was a universal one. I mean after all, the flood legends were universal, why wouldn't the flood itself have been so? I mean consider, if a flood only happened in one little location like say, Oklahoma, would people in Germany be telling tales of it thousands of years later? Seriously?! No way! So the concept that the sheer bulk of flood legends were just talking about local floods just seemed silly, and it seemed to me that the overabundance of flood legends could only be referring to a universal flood. Some flood legends were of course possibly narrated from a local standpoint, to give the impressions of a "local" flood to some of us who read or hear about them in the present day. Consider this quote from *Earth Magic* by Francis Hitching for example. "Sudden catastrophes such as floods and earthquakes also seem much more likely to have local explanations, rather than tying together neatly into one great event that reshaped the history of the world." (Book 13 page 252) Clearly he's aware that there exist a lot of flood legends, but he presumed them to be all local in nature, not interconnected or simultaneous. But as far as I was concerned, my stance was, whatever hole people wanted to hide their heads in, I was content that the legends had to be talking about a world flood.

Then I researched my first book.

Part of my research was digging into the flood and I noticed that the flood legends were inconsistent. Some were very similar or even identical to the biblical version of the flood, which is a global universal flood. But some were definitely different…and apparently very local with very different narratives. When I matched up some of these other floods and looked more closely at the biblical narrative I realized even the bible directly or at least indirectly, spoke of more than one flood and indeed more than one *kind* of flood. It was a general separating of the kinds of floods that helped me solve so many ancient mysteries in the book length chapter 6 of my first book. The suspicion that there were global flood legends and local flood legends became inescapable when I realized the Hopi flood legend, so very different from the biblical legend was actually provable. It also became clear that the different flood legends speak of different parts of history and not the same part of history, but since they are so far removed from today, mythologists have lumped them all into one single category: the "flood legends". I've determined they fall into at least three categories: 1) is the global flood legends, 2a) is either the indistinct Mumbo jumbo sort of flood legend which may be of little value, at least to someone not well versed in local culture to make any sense of it all, or 2b) the mixing of local and worldwide flood legends into the same story as though time has made the distinction unclear even to the tellers of the tales, and3)local type of flood legends.

Looking for books on flood legends didn't help. I found they seem to focus primarily on proving the apparent biblical point of view of a global flood, so any "local" floods legends that exist are either absent or played down and lumped into the ancient flood legend category which ergo must prove the universal flood simply by their massive numbers, something like my conclusions spoken of above. They also pick through them and find parts that match up with the biblical global flood as if it's the only flood to match up with. All flood legends will have some things that match with other floods, mainly lots of water. We could compare a Québec flood from a few years ago and the flood of Noah and find things in common. Consider this quote I found on the internet.

"There are at least 500 legends of a worldwide deluge. Many of these show remarkable similarities, with many aspects similar to the details about Noah's Flood in the Bible.

"We are left with a few options. Perhaps all the peoples of these remote civilisations had different flood experiences that, by chance, had all these features in common, on which they based their stories. However, the more reasonable alternative is that these legends all find their root in *the same one global Flood experience* that Genesis records." (Italics in the original)

This assumes that ALL of the Flood legends must be speaking of the same flood, even though it suggests some have had different flood experiences. Examination of the flood legends shows that clearly there are different flood experiences and thus quite probably different floods, so to presume the tellers of the tales are all just not quite remembering the story right is not entirely correct. Furthermore to assume they are, is doing geological history a disservice. The assumption the 500 + legends are ALL about a "worldwide deluge" is just not correct and they have only read them with the world flood of Noah in mind, automatically discarding the local nature based on the global flood bias. On the other hand the fact that so many flood legends do exist, local and / or universal, has built a bit of a fortress for the biblical belief too, such as this quote found on line. "If there were no near-universal distribution of world-destroying flood legends, sceptics would no doubt attack the Bible, credibility on this basis, questioning how the memory of such an awesome account could be lost in so many cultures."

As much of a boon to faith in the biblical version the multitude of flood legends are, it's still important to distinguish between local and world flood legends. The local flood legends that exist direct us to discover something that virtually everyone has missed, because they are either too intent on proving the biblical flood, or conversely, too intent on disproving the same. But the fact of the matter is both sides of the argument are correct...there was the universal flood, and there were also many major local floods, that when you piece the local floods together like pieces of a big puzzle, you discover a very different chunk of ancient history that everyone missed...well almost everyone. In rereading some of Immanuel Velikovsky's work I realized he was aware of the two types of flood legends. For example he mentions that the historic flood during the time of Yahou was originally thought to be the Chinese version of the universal flood, but this deduction had to be abandoned, and he determined that the flood in the days of Fo-hi had the needed similarities to the flood of Noah. (Book 14 page 116-117) However he didn't really clue into what the extra flood legends meant.

I had originally intended to just write an article on the differing flood legends and indeed started to write it, but it soon became clear it couldn't be done as just an article and do the subject matter justice in just 2500 words. Though I thought I would just rework it, it never seemed to click on how to do it. Then I realized this was way too big and important a topic for just a single article hidden in some magazine that might get short notice. People that research the flood needed something else that just wasn't available to them to see past the incomplete approach. This needed a full blown effort and I determined this book was in order. Though I did briefly cover the topic when I first realized that there was a difference between global and local flood legends in my first book, it is far from the focus of the book and people buying that book would not have picked that as a reason for getting it, as it was only one of the pieces of the puzzle of the big picture presented in that work. It slowly dawned on me that this subject was indeed a whole new puzzle that needed a primary focus and work all its own. If you bought my first book, some of the substance here will be familiar to you, and there will even be some review and reiterating some of the points of my first book. But even I was surprised at some of the material I was finding and often found myself experiencing new eureka moments as I delved deeper into this topic.

I intend to do primarily three things in this book. 1) Sort and lump many of the universal flood legends together and show the evidence that substantiates the universal flood. 2) Sort and lump the local flood legends together to show what they mean and then 3) show the evidence that points to just what these so called "local floods" did to the globe, long after the universal flood was ancient history. The conclusions will fly in the face of what we have all been taught by geologists, archaeologists and evolutionists, and yes, even creationists of which I will say right up front that I am one. As you can perceive I had to re-evaluate some of what I believed based on the evidence to get by my ingrained biases and get at the truth. It's never easy to challenge your own walls and tear down the weak points, so keep your wits about you as I present the legends and the following evidence; it won't be easy for you either. Some of my points at first and as you go through the work will seem contrived or even preposterous, some of which I established in my first work so I won't explain some of them in any length. But I'm sure as you forge ahead through this work, these "preposterous" claims will slowly become more and more plausible until you realise in the end, there is no escaping these conclusions. I dare say that you are in for a bumpy ride.

Chapter 1

Worldwide or, Global Flood legends (type 1)

In this chapter we will explore a number of legends, myths, or histories that speak of a global worldwide flood. I won't present them all of course, but I will also try to find flood legends that represent every major global area, that is, each continent and a few places within each continent and people groups to show that not only do worldwide flood legends exist that mirror or at least to a great extent confirm the biblical account, they are completely widespread and indeed confirm each other. If only 8 people survived the world flood then all their descendants on down through the ages, no matter where they went on earth and what people group they became, we would expect to find this history in common with all people which would naturally account for the widespread knowledge of the flood. Showing that global flood legends exist worldwide would be a predictable possibility confirming the legends by working backwards so to speak. But strangely with the permeation of the evolution theory and the increased belief in a world that is not less than 10,000 years old but rather millions, or billions of years old, and the conflicting flood legends that suggest local floods or a world flood, one could expect to find a smattering of (local) flood legends throughout the globe anyway, but not necessarily any synchronicity between them. I mean if the world is 4.5 billion years old and mankind / civilization is what…400 million, 3 million, 70,000, or 50,000 years old, we would assume, nay expect that every area on the globe had some major flooding at some point in their history and thus not be particularly impressed with the number of flood legends, but only that the legends survived this long, as entropic reality simply means legends, written or verbal, slowly change and eventually disintegrate over the aeons. Indeed many are already virtually incomprehensible today. We could also loosely assume that a "worldwide flood" legend could even be interpreted as a local flood, as it might be assumed that it only flooded that people's entire world (ergo 'worldwide') and expect a smattering of survivors from each area to live and tell the tale, making it appear similar to a world flood. Indeed some people have used this explanation to marginalize the flood legend. Thus the biblical narrative would consequently become just one of many worldwide flood legends and apparently of little significance. If this were the case, few people would want to dig any deeper than this assumption.

Some people just don't get or grasp how the legend of the universal flood and even the name of Noah could spread throughout the world. For example Peter Kolosimo suggests that the Hawaiian legends main character is Nu-u, along with the Chinese legend of a man named Nu Wah, and a dead city called "Ma-Noa, signifying "the waters of Noah", in between Brazil and Venezuela were not influenced by a global event. Instead he suggests that the agreement of names over such a vast distance around the globe means it can only be explained "…by supposing men were able to communicate over long distances immediately after the flood." (Book 21 pg 143) He assumes this spread of Noah's name wasn't based on the experience of a universal flood and that an advanced civilization wasn't affected by it, but it was a local flood that became news to the point people were naming places after the event. No! It means the direct descendants of Noah told the story to their children who told it to their children as they slowly migrated around the world. For example completely contradicting Kolosimo's premise, the Hawaiians repeat the legend as though their ancestors experienced it and not like it was part of someone else's experience far away affecting people who they've never met. All legends clearly indicate their ancestors experienced the flood they speak of, and it wasn't just news from a far away land. Indeed many people speak of the flood as what caused them to be how they were or how to clarify some detail of their environment such as explaining shells on mountains. Such narrations tend to give the appearance that it was a local flood, because the flood was somehow personal to them and their own history. When people spread out across the globe the story continued to be told no matter where they moved to. Why isn't this conclusion obvious to some people? It is because people just find it so hard to believe that the flood could possibly be a universal one. Well based on what the earth looks like today, that's understandable.

However if we can first see that the universal flood legend is indeed universal and common to all people and places on earth, then just as importantly we need to date the event of the flood reasonably well. Why? Because when we do this, not only do we show that the physical, geological and archaeological evidence for a global flood matches the legends: but once we see that there really was a global flood, this automatically places the "local" flood legends that would have of necessity come after the global flood into a much tighter time frame and makes their importance suddenly much more significant.

Now believe it or not, the main thrust of this book is not the proving of the global world flood A.K.A. the flood of Noah. This has been done adequately by a few authors. However I need to illustrate that there are clearly two types of flood legends: global and very drastic 'local' floods, which were also significant enough to become part and parcel of ancient legends. However the significance of the local flood stories does not become apparent until we separate them from the global flood. We can't just focus on the local floods and ignore the global one, as this route might falsely give the impression that the flood legends were just local. We have to demonstrate clearly that there are two kinds of floods and each type were equally significant to all aspects of history. To the best of my knowledge no one has ever done this or realized the significance of the many local flood legends, as to date they have only been lumped in with flood legends as a whole, or considered as merely useful in disproving the global flood, so, first things first.

THE BIG PICTURE FIRST.

To help you understand my interpretations of some of the flood legends it might help you if I tell you beforehand what I feel caused the flood. This will seem really off the wall, but if you want to know how I came to these conclusions you'll just have to check out my earlier work. Here we go...

Man before the flood was vastly superior to we...or us... of the post flood generations because their genetics were so close to perfect they could marry their sisters. They were mentally, physically and physiologically far superior to us, where even angels thought them almost on a par and they married some of our daughters and lived on earth with man seemingly most of the preflood era. Preflood man's grasp of science and technology was complete; they knew everything. Between man, the angels and the hybrids, they built at least one and possibly three man-made moons. These were no ordinary orbiting space labs; these were monstrously huge moons that we have actually spotted in our telescopes from at least as far away as Jupiter and inside the orbit of Mercury. It was even thought Venus had a moon because they orbited that planet off and on. Yes man-made moons just like the "death star" of Star Wars" fame. Richard Hoagland suspects the story of Star Wars may be based on forgotten or 'in the know' material, and I wouldn't be surprised if this is the case. It would seem they colonised the planets and there is a lot of evidence they colonized Mars, and may still have bases on our moon. At some point there appears to have been friction between the Men, and the hybrids, (or at least that's my guess) so there was a war in space or "in the heavens". The planet between Mars and Jupiter also appears to have been colonised and it was the target of one of the man-made moons and the planet was destroyed creating what we know as the asteroid belt. The destruction of this planet spread chaos throughout the solar system and blasted Mars and Venus out of their normal orbits, nearly destroyed some moons of planets, probably tipped Uranus on its side, and worst of all, a giant asteroid got by the people trying to obliterate them and it hit the earth, smashing though the water shell, collapsing it onto the earth drowning everyone. At the same time, this asteroid knocked earth out of its normal orbit too, just as they did to Venus and Mars. As I say, if you want to find out how the heck I came up with this and a whole bunch of other stuff, you'll just have to read my fist book. For the biblically learned you may be wondering how I can infer man caused the flood if God said he would destroy the earth? The Bible says "Except God keeps the city, the watchmen watch in vain." Man was guarding the earth blasting asteroids before they hit the earth, but God let one get by them.

OK you're basically up to speed.

As you might expect we start with the flood legend as described in the Bible. It all appears to start with the sons of god marrying the daughters of men, because immediately after this occurs, God prophesies that man's days shall be 120 years. (Before the flood people were living to around 950 years. After the flood, man's life span steadily drops from 600 to about 120, and then on down to our modern standard of 70) Only exposure to a more harmful environment would vastly reduce the lifespan of man, so this marrying of sons of god and daughters of men sets something in motion. (Genesis 6:2-3) It has been determined that from these marriages were born giants and as a result two things start to proliferate...wickedness and the imagination of the thoughts of man's heart become evil continually. The children of these marriages became 'men of renown'...that is famous, and setting the habits of mankind in a downward spiral of increased infamy. I think it's fair to say that in today's world famous people have led many astray too. Many people have done copycat crimes based on TV shows, movies, or newscasts and even simple newspapers stories have been behind some terrible behaviour. When Leon Czolgosz was captured after shooting President McKinley, there was found in his pockets several inflammatory newspaper editorials denouncing the president by irresponsible publishers to boost circulation. (Book 62 pg. 248)

A lot of people equate wickedness and evil as the same thing but this is incorrect. Consider, God's only rule to Adam and Eve was not to eat from the tree of the knowledge of good and evil...only God was to eat from this tree. So, does that mean God is wicked? No. But he knows 'evil'. So what is evil? It is defined as the ability to cause calamity, hurt or destruction. God can create good and cause destruction. The serpent said to Eve if you eat "...ye shall be as gods, knowing good and evil." But the problem became with a disobedient mankind not accepting God at his word, so that consequently after man ate the food from this tree his nature fell, and thus with this fallen nature, "good and evil" become tilted with a natural leaning toward evil or destruction proliferating. Admittedly suggesting "good and evil" means the ability to create and destroy is a bit of a narrow definition as indeed much more than just destructive ability is implied. However this excess is likely linked to man's fallen nature, and to be sure the bible adds that the wickedness of man was great in the earth. (6:5) So God, after deciding to spare Noah and his sons (and their wives), says he will destroy the other living beings with the earth (6:13). This is something people miss or gloss over: the flood destroyed the earth. What we are living on is a destroyed creation, it doesn't support life like it did before the flood where we lived to over 900 years old, but we were only going to live to 120. But now even this isn't the case anymore, as few if anyone reaching this advanced age any more. So not only do we not live to 900 anymore, we don't even live to 120, but average about 70. So we can decipher that something additional had to have occurred to the earth to cause man's average age to drop from what was supposed to be around 120 down to just 70 years. We will see that these other so called "local" floods have a part in this further decline. Many theologians miss this and assume when God said man's days would be 120 years, he meant this was how long it would be until the flood. But clues show that the sons of the angels and the daughters of man were living a very long time. Indeed it appears they lived longer than man, and this makes sense because eternal angels were mingling with finite humans. So, if this is the case, the angels had to have been here long before Methuselah was born.

On with the biblical flood story. God tells Noah to build an ark and gives him specific dimensions: 300 cubits long, 50 cubits wide and 30 cubits high, (Multiply these measurements by about 1 ½ to 1 ¾ to get measurements in feet. Metric? You're on your own.) and what sort of wood to make it with (gopher wood; a wood some say hasn't been identified, and some say is supposed to be Cyprus, and some say it's known to grow only in the plains of the Euphrates.) and to coat it all in pitch (also translated as bitumen) inward and outwardly. The ark is to house Noah and family and 2 of every creature, and 7 of every 'clean' creature (Genesis 7:2). And there appears to have been 7 of each kind of bird too (7:3). Later it mentions some of the clean fowl were sacrificed so presumably there were just 2 of each unclean fowl, similar to the beasts. (Clean and unclean creatures were something Noah understood... but this detail had to be explained to the Israelites when Moses gave them the law many years later, indicating a grasp of what was common knowledge declined over the centuries.)

After the flood, not only was man not living as long, but his mental grasp was diminishing. Man's mind was becoming veiled. A few researchers have come across references to man's mind becoming fogged or existing now with a veil over our minds. A Mayan legend from the Popul Vuh tells us that visitors from above that knew the secrets of the universe, used a compass and knew the earth was round, were upset because man was also learning these secrets. This quote is given: the "Eyes of the first men were covered and they could only see what was close" so that "the "wisdom and all knowledge of the first men were destroyed." (Book 29 Pg 52, Book 11 pg162) Brad Steiger summarises this way "The "sky people knew the secrets of the universe, and when the tribesmen became determined to steal these secrets, the visitors fogged the earthmen's minds." (Book 35 pg 181) "The gods took council and clouded the sight of men, destroying their wisdom and knowledge" (book 23 pg 110 quoting Popul Vuh). So if you think you are Mister Know-it-all... you're in good company because so does Bullwinkle the Moose. Jeffrey Goodman notes that after the return of Jesus Christ, with many helpers, the veils are lifted from men's mind. (book 19 pg 54) Though I recall reading this somewhere, I couldn't for the life of me find it, even with a Strong's concordance. But thankfully at least Mister Goodman has confirmed it. I did eventually find this lost to me verse in my normal nightly reading and realized why I couldn't find it with a concordance: the KJV spells the word ''veil' in this instance "vail" in II Corinthians 3: 14 which reads "But their minds were blinded: for until this day remaineth the same vail untaken away in the reading of the old testament; which vail is done away in Christ." So it seems a few veils are covering the minds of men. One put there by the gods, one which could be called a spiritual veil. And, it would seem another fogging of men's minds occurred at the tower of Babel and other legends even link the two events which also stopped men from becoming like the gods, or like the bible says in Genesis 11:6 about their building the tower ":and now nothing will be restrained from them, which they have imagined to do." So God confuses their languages and supposedly fogs their minds at the same time as part of the action that caused diversity of language.

I had initially concluded that the earth's degraded environment, the direct sunlight and the reduced atmosphere from so much of it escaping into space after the flood was the only cause of the fogging of men's minds. Though it appears it is not, I'm still certain this has a part in the big picture. Consider these clues in this regard.

Madame David-Neel when staying with the Tibetans was told that the best time for people using the power of "Lung-gom-pa" (where Tibetans levitated while walking at incredibly fast speeds while sleeping) was in the morning, evening and night. These were said to be more favourable for this than from noon on. (Book 11 pg. 105-106)

Nikola Tesla hated the direct sun and said it caused pressure on his brain.

Some of the gods wore "firmaments" on their heads, which were probably solar radiation and UV filtering helmets. These "firmaments" or clear globes are often drawn in religious art as halos around the heads of saint's and Christ.

Too weird for you?... OK, try these... Through time it's been correlated that sun spot maximums have coincided with the French and Russian revolutions, both world wars and the Korean conflict. The number of car accidents increases four times on the second day after solar flare-ups compared to when the sun is calm, and suicide rates quintuple the normal rate during explosive solar activity. (Book 11 pg 71) I quote my first book here...

"Biologist Martha Adam's experiments with embryo chick hearts showed something in the environment was affecting biological processes because the results periodically swung from a positive stimulation to a depression. After much detective work it was realized these downturns in biological variability were found to originate during increased solar activity, which also precluded or seemed linked to large magnetic earthquakes, showing not only was solar activity affecting living creatures biologically in a negative way, with increased sickness for at least short terms; it may also be linked to increased geologic activity. Symptoms such as fatigue, vertigo, chills, headaches, nausea, ringing in the ears, and excessive bleeding were found to be linked to the increased solar activity.

"A medical center was not in the least surprised by her findings, and corroborated her findings by saying their patients had these symptoms just prior to earthquakes. To prove the point they then predicted the next earthquake. (Science Digest October 1982 page 73-74)

"If increased solar activity is affecting us negatively, obviously one can only conclude that **any** solar activity is affecting us this way, and thus our lives are shorter since the advent of the protective water shell's collapse during the flood. Thus it seems as our environment diminishes its capacity to protect biological beings on earth then as a result, those biological beings suffer with shorter and less healthy life spans."

Still, these legends suggest the gods did something additional, though I've not found any clues as to what exactly they did. However one of the "sky people" recently showed that to a degree they can unfog men's minds too. (Don't worry; I'll get to the flood legends in a sec.) On December 30th 1972 a farmer in Argentina named Ventura Macceiras was sitting in his cabin and listening to the radio when it suddenly went dead. In the ensuing quiet he could hear a humming overhead so he left his cabin to investigate. The source of the humming turned out to be a glowing red-orange UFO about 80 feet across hovering about 35 feet from the ground above some eucalyptus trees: so low in fact that he could distinguish humanlike occupants along with machinery visible inside through large portholes. Suddenly the UFO flashed a ray on him, changed colour, and then blasted the trees while it took off leaving a scent of sulphur. The ray made Maceiras feel a tingling all over as he saw the UFO fly off, but afterwards he started to feel vertigo and severe headaches. Within a week or so much of his hair fell out and he developed a series of skin rashes and experienced some difficulty talking. However as the effects wore off he found to his and his doctors amazement that his overall physical condition improved beyond his previous state. His hair grew back, but black instead of grey, his mouth grew a number of new teeth, and he appeared more youthful, with faster reaction times. And though he was still illiterate, "he began with unaccustomed fluency to discuss with his interviewers matters concerning sociology, philosophy, and his concept of the cosmos." It was like part of the veil of his mind had been lifted and his body had grown notably younger. (Book 24 pg. 184-185)

Where were we? Oh yeah Noah takes all the creatures onto the ark. God gets Noah to move into the ark and caused it to rain 40 days and nights.

Now there are some curious descriptions about the causes of the flood...it doesn't just 'rain', but when God closes the ark door, "The same day were all the fountains of the great deep broken up, and the windows of heaven were opened."(7:11). and the rain happened for 40 days...and nights. ("windows in heaven" means holes in the sky. The water canopy had holes punctured in it from meteors. The description continues...) And the waters prevailed exceedingly upon the earth: and all the high hills that were under the whole heaven were covered. Fifteen cubits and upward did the waters prevail: and the mountains were covered. (Genesis 7:19-20) I say this is positively wild! I just noticed something I should have spotted years ago! After writing the first book and going to great pains to make a point which I now see is plainly contained in that verse, and now after writing this book and indeed now on my final proofread, I finally see two words in that verse I completely glossed over even after typing it verbatim from the bible. I can hardly believe it. I just saw that this verse says "high hills" rather than "mountains". If you've read my first book that will be funny to you and if not, as you read on you will see why this is simply uproarious. I won't tell you why...you'll figure it out. Remember, this book is completely written as I write this and I'm just proof reading it for the last time.

Once the flood has done its work killing all of man and the animals and "prevailing" for 150 days, the way the water leaves the surface of the earth is considered something of a mystery. Many assume the earth swallowed it back up, from where the fountains of the deep came from. That works for the water that came from below, but there's all that water that came from above still to deal with. The water came from above the earth, and once it falls back to earth, the earth becomes like the earth was before the waters of the earth were separated with a firmament between the waters above and the waters here below as seen in (Genesis 1:6-7) 6: "And God said let there be a firmament in the midst of the waters, and let it divide the waters from the waters. 7: And God made the firmament and divided the waters which *were* under the firmament from the waters which were above the firmament: and it was so." Firmament means the 'visible arch of the sky'. And in verse 8 God calls the firmament "heaven". (One of the heavens, as later indications indicate there are more 'heavens' above that) Subduction reaches a saturation or equilibrium point, and the earth cannot 'swallow' any more water. (A truncated Egyptian legend notes this very thing where it says the flood 'return[ed] the earth to the Primordial Water which was its original state.' So where did all that extra water go? The bible only says "...God made a wind to pass over the earth, and the waters asswaged." It took a lot of figuring but that mystery is solved in my first book, and I'll recap the solution here soon.

After the waters receded enough (17th day of the 7th month of the flood) the ark lands on the mountains of Ararat and on first day of tenth month the tops of the mountains were seen. Forty days later Noah sends out a raven which kept going back and forth until the waters were dried up. This is a bit indistinct and it sounds like it keeps coming back to the ark or flying around until the waters dry? Afterwards Noah also sends out a dove that finds no rest so it returns to the ark. A week later he sends her out again and she comes back with an olive leaf. After yet another week he sends the dove out again and it never returns. I count a total of 11 months 24 days from the start of the flood to the day he opens the ark, 1 year 1 month and ten days from the time he enters to the time the earth is said to be dried (8:14). Noah enters the ark when he's 600 years 1 month and 17 days old (7:11), and when Noah is 601...apparently on his birthday (or the day after?) he takes off the ark covering, and on the 27th day of the second month he leaves the ark, builds an sacrifice altar that burns up the 7th clean fowls and7th clean beasts on it. God subsequently takes the curse off the ground. Animals start to fear man, which I suspect is somehow connected to the solar rays now coming directly to earth, and the thinner atmosphere. The promise of no flood wiping out all of mankind again is specified with the rainbow given as a reminder to God and us of his promise. Soon after Noah makes a vineyard and makes wine from it.

These are the major points of the Genesis flood story. If by chance I find any material of interest mixed in with other flood legends that I've not covered in this recap I'll mention them too. Clearly with all the mountains being covered by a minimum of 15 cubits of water, this can only depict a world flood. If that seems impossible, bear in mind geology shows that the average height of land above sea level was about 1/3 that of today or about 1000 feet above sea level, whereas today the average is about 3,000 feet. This is a huge difference in the amount of water that came from above and below on a global basis. There were no mountain ranges as we know them today; these were made in recent geologic history: preflood land masses were more like hilly plains. That's right; the mountain ranges we see around the globe today were created, as we shall see, during historic times. Though many a geologist or evolutionist would have us believe mountains were made millions of years ago, some are forced to acknowledge that many ancient civilizations had to have been built before the mountains rose.

Furthermore many geologists are forced to admit the mountains are young, as no erosion is visible on them. They also often admit they rose suddenly, as if overnight. Though I go into this a bit in my first book, we will see this is the case later on by some more evidence linked directly to the local flood legends that come well after the global flood. Anyway this is the biblical version of the global flood legend on a major point by point basis.

Whether the biblical version sounds fantastic or not, the point here is to gather many flood legends together that are clearly global in nature to compare...whether we believe them or not. We'll work on proving them later. It's noteworthy that some biblical scholars, even from the 19th century, had a hard time believing in the universal flood. For example one suggests that "It is natural to suppose that the writer, when he speaks of "all in whose nostrils is the breath of life" refers only to his own locality". The editor then goes on to find examples of great depressions where water could rise for 40 days or where channels such as the Gulf of Finland could be considered "fountains of the great deep". (Dictionary of the Bible by William Smith 1884) Such minimalization of the scriptures basically attempts to negate any belief in the more dramatic biblical record or tries to make it easier to believe by somehow explaining away anything that otherwise seems hard to confirm or too fantastic compared to how the world works as we see it today. It completely overlooks the fact that the way the earth was initially created is completely different than what we see today. This mindset contrasts sharply with the recent discoveries in near and Middle East including the Dead Sea scrolls. "...not even the most sceptical can any longer dismiss the Bible as a poetic recounting of old fantasies. Scholars now agree that the Old and New testaments are for the most part accurate records of events that really happened between 3000 B.C. and A.D. 100." (Book 8 page 51) I assume the parts they are not sure about are when miraculous or fantastic events occurred....like floods and plagues and parting seas and the sun standing still...that sort of thing. Well, we'll deal with all this later. So let's look at some other flood legends that are decidedly global in nature.

Now the mountains of Ararat (where the ark landed) are roughly 40°N 44°E. And Israel (where we get the biblical version of the flood) isn't extremely far away from Mount Ararat at roughly 32°N 35°E. So as a start, let's look as far away from these places to see if any global flood legends similar to the biblical one exist. Now there are not any islands on the exact opposite side of the world, but let's see what some Pacific islands roughly on the other side of the world have to offer by way of global flood legends. Feel free to track the locations on a globe to verify the widespread remembrance of the global flood around the world. I include the approximate co-ordinates of all global flood legends.

All these legends have been paraphrased, summarised, very briefly quoted or stated in my own words. To read them as originally worded by the original authors check internet or follow sources. Some of my explanation of legends details will seem so fantastic you will just have to press on until you see the inescapable similarities in so many legends that no other conclusion is really possible. But keep the 'fantastic' in mind so you can see that maybe these legends really do indicate these conclusions. When I first read some of the legends that existed while researching my first book, I would just shake my head, ignore them and keep reading on to get back to the saner stuff. Somewhere along the line I suddenly clued in that there was something to these legends that I needed to pay attention to. So I hope you will consider this and not discount my explanations as the big picture of the legends get slowly put together piece meal in the background as more legends offer more corroborating pieces. OK carry on and remember...that water's deep out there.

Non Continental Flood legends.

Hawaiian Flood legend (20°N, 155°E) Hawaii has a global flood legend very similar to the biblical one. Kane (Their name for the 'originator', one of the godhead which was a trinity, the other two being Ku (Architect and builder) and Lono (executer and director of the elements) saw the world had turned evil and so Kane decided to destroy the world with a flood. Nuu (pronounced Nu-U) and his family would be spared and he was told to build (or was given) an ark or a great canoe to carry his wife and three sons and male and female of all breathing things. Nuu was just 13 generations from the first man. (Biblical version put Noah at the just the 10th generation from the first man Adam.) The Hawaiian name for the first man is Kumu-honua who was formed by spittle of Kane mixed with red earth. This is interesting because Adam means red. One of this first man's ribs was taken out and the first woman was made from it. Nuu's new wife name was Ivi pronounced Eve-y...virtually identical to the biblical version. Once Nuu and all were in the ark the waters came and covered the earth, and eventually subsided to leave the ark resting on some mountains overlooking a beautiful valley. Nuu sacrificed a pig, some coconuts and some Awa (an intoxicating drink made from a plant of the same name) to a moon he mistook for Kane. Kane later descends on a rainbow to correct Nuu but left the rainbow as a perpetual sign of his forgiveness. (Legends and Myths of Hawaii by King David Kalakaua 1888, compared with internet sources)

So here we see half way around the globe in the middle of the Pacific Ocean, a global flood legend almost identical to the Biblical version. I don't think it will get any better than that. But one might ask, how could Nuu mistake Kane for a moon? My previous research shows the origin of this moon was probably the blue moon Elysia which confused Nuu. This is of course not mentioned in the bible and I've not seen it in any other flood legend. However if this is the case, it means at least one manmade moon returned to earth right after the flood.

NEW ZEALAND MAORI FLOOD LEGENDS. (40°S, 175°E)

The Maori seem to have a couple world flood legends.

1) Many tribes quarrelled and the worship of God was neglected, and those that did so were mocked. The mocked became angry and built a raft and a house on it at the source of the Tohinga River. Two men and some women were on the raft, and it was supplied with fern roots, sweet potatoes and dogs. It rained for 4 or 5 days until the raft priest Tiu prayed for it to stop, and though the rain stopped, the water continued to rise and took the raft down the river out into the sea, where they were for 8 months until the water began to thin. The earth was much changed by the flood and the people on the raft were the only survivors. Though this flood legend sounds a bit like a world flood, it could in fact be a local flood or a mixing of the two. The short duration"4 or 5 days " is clearly from local flood legends but the two types of flood legends could have been meshed together, something that became quite common once the local floods started devastating many areas of the planet.

2) Another Maori flood legend has two versions and a combining of the two might give a more complete picture...such as it is. Two brothers-in-law of Tawhaki attacked him leaving him for dead, but he recovered and took his warriors and their families to a high mountain and built a fortified village. He prayed for revenge and stamped his feet on the floor of heaven and the floods of heaven descended and killed everyone on earth.

One version suggests, as a result of praying to the gods, they let the flood descend from heaven, the other version included the stamping the floor of heaven. This might be a mix up confusing stamping the ground releasing the waters from below as well as the waters from above. But that's only how I interpret it knowing the more complete biblical version, and the other legends and the evidence which we will get more familiar with as we go along. However I don't want you thinking I'm forcing things toward the biblical version. We'll come across what appear to be local flood and world flood legends fused to emerge to be one single flood legend. But even with this Maori legend combined it sounds a bit like a threading together of scattered parts remembered to patch together a legend after some event caused much of the context to be forgotten.

With the benefit of hindsight of previous research I discovered what both types of floods did to the planet and in some cases the integration of both types of legends into a single legend appears to have been the result caused by the complete chaos for those who survived the later 'local' floods. Furthermore when stories got told over and over people tend to make the stories a bit more concise for expediency. If this sounds like I'm making excuses to you for apparently unclear legends or my interpretation of them as I see them, consider this quote. "For instance, Philo of Alexandria (20B.C. - A.D. 54) wrote: By reason of the constant and repeated destructions by water and fire, the later generations did not receive from the former the memory of the order and sequence of events." (Book 11 Pg 162) So, as we'll see more clearly as we go on, some flood legends are a bit garbled and need a deciphering based on seeing a fairly complete picture viewed from the panorama of the many to get what the individual legends appear to be trying to convey.

Some flood legends are very brief compared to others about the same event...like the Maori one. (Summary of internet references Gaster, pp. 110-112; Kelsen, p. 133)

Polynesia (165°W, 15°S)

They say at one time the earth was submerged in the ocean, but [the ocean] was drawn by Tefaafanau (or Taafanua...Typhon!). (Book 14 pg 83)

When I realized this had to be the Polynesian name for Typhon I had to check the legend behind the name Tefaafanau ...by shortcutting and looking...online. It was worth it!

The story of "Tefaafanau: Accompanying the hurricane was a piercing noise so terrifying and prolonged it is *reminiscent* of the testimony of "noise" recorded by the Egyptian scribe Ipuwer, and the Book of Exodus. The Polynesians talk of a deluge of *water which was drawn away by the mighty pull of a hurricane called "Tefaafanau."* To commemorate the event, the natives of this scenic paradise celebrate a feast of the same name in March -- the very time when the Exodus took place! (Williamson)"(*Italics mine*) Though this legend and assumption, places the event during the Exodus because it is *reminiscent* of that event, I had to place it here as well as in the local flood section because it's initial description matches that of a global flood ("*at one time the earth was submerged in the ocean* ") and how the water vanished confirming my deduction in my first book. It could be a combining of the two types of floods or it may be this 'Williamson' assuming the noise heard is one and the same noise as that of the time of the exodus because it is *reminiscent* of that time and event. It may be the same noise, but as we shall see this "same noise" event appears to have happened more than once. Or of course it could also just be a local flood legend as Polynesia isn't exactly surrounded by desserts.

Though in my first work, the mystery of where the flood water went and how it got there is a secret I leave as a surprise revelation for those who buy the book, in this book about the floods, I have to reveal it. I just won't go into how I figured it out and the proof...much... so catch the cat as it escapes the bag...

Here we have a very good clue...no...virtually an exact description as to exactly what Typhon is and what it did. I wish I'd found this in time for my first book but it's nice to find this confirmation for us here. More confirming clues will follow.

Some basic mechanics of gravitational pull. The moon pulls up the water towards itself as it passes overhead and causes tides. Directly "under" the moon the water is actually a hill as the surface of the ocean and even the land itself is literally pulled upwards towards the moon. If the moon was closer tides would be pretty drastic, and if the moon was significantly closer tides would be fearsome, and local earthquakes would be a daily phenomena. We all know how much noise water makes in your taps while it's running. Tefaafanau or Typhon is the drawing or tidal pulling of water from the ocean up into space by a very large and nearby source of strong gravity. Ancient legends tell how a 'star' fished islands out of the sea and, such a star, would be Mars, or Venus knocked from their orbit and coming close to the earth. Fishing the islands out of the sea would be gravitational pulling of the actual land masses closest towards the source of gravity and, if it pulls land from beneath the waves, water too would literally be siphoned off the planet. Indeed the Polynesians also say that new islands were baited by a star, which is exactly the same cause and effect creating Typhon, that is the gravity of a planet coming close to the earth and pulling water and land upwards towards it by gravitational pull, creating a very noisy cyclonic stream or water leaving the earth towards the planet or "star" and the islands being formed by the same action. This phenomenon has been termed or equated with a snake with many heads in many legends because of the hissing sound and because it had the appearance of many watery branches as it spread outward towards space and the nearby source of gravity. I can't explain why I say water went to Mars here as I spent a good deal of effort proving this in the updated version my first book. However I will deal with Venus later on. (If you bought an earlier version of my first book, {It would have no interior artwork illustrations and the Pyramid waves higher than the mountains front cover} feel free to contact me for a free emailed version of the updates and illustrations. Include the number of pages your version of my first book has so I can send the correct update version. There is one third more information added to the book in this update which increased the words count from about 250K words to about 338K words, and the update also includes the 19 illustrations and the new cover art as well)

Borneo, flood legend (1°S, 113°E)

A man named Trow made a boat out of a wooden vessel that was used for making rice flour when a flood came. He took with him his wife, and his dog, a pig, a cat, birds and other animals and was carried around in the flood. When the flood was over, to help repopulate the earth he made more wives out of a log, a stone and anything he could get his hands on. The large family he created became the ancestors of the various Dyak tribes. (Native to Borneo) [Internet based on Gaster, p. 102]

Asian World Flood Legends

China

There are a few Chinese legends about the flood, some of a local nature and some of a global nature. The Bahnars of the **Cochin tribe in China** (105°E 10°N), have a legend which goes like this: A kite once quarrelled with the crab and pecked a hole in its skull (which hole can still be seen today). In revenge, the crab caused the sea and rivers to swell until the waters reached the sky, and all living beings perished except two, which were a brother and sister, who were saved in a huge chest in which they saved a pair of all kinds of animals. They floated for an entire week. When the brother heard a cock crowing outside, he knew it was sent by the spirits to let them know the flood had subsided. Everyone and all the animals got out of the box shaped ship, first the birds, the animals, and then the two people. The brother and sister had eaten all the rice stored in the chest and were unsure how they would survive. But a black ant brought them two grains of rice which the brother planted. Soon, that is the next morning; the plain was covered with rice that had grown. [Paraphrasing Internet source quoting Gaster, p. 98]

Before the flood, mankind's genes were far less devolved from radiation. Little or no radiation from the sun entered earth's atmosphere to degrade mans genetics. It's therefore quite possible that Noah *did* marry a sister. Cain had to have married a sister and even Abraham married a half sister. It took 1000 years or so after the flood before the earth and man became affected enough by radiation degrading our genetics to make marrying a sister unsafe for the next generation: thus God's handing down the law forbidding sibling marriages to Moses.

Interestingly this story includes a crab. The legend of Typhon is occasionally linked with a crab and a large crab like object has been photographed on Mars. This story is undoubtedly a Typhon related legend, by the inclusion of the crab in relation to the waters swelling to reach the sky and not a more conventional flood description. This legend gives a clear picture of the water being pulled upwards to the sky by the gravity of a nearby object though the legend doesn't mention a nearby source of this gravity. It also described the ark as a box shaped ship, which as will become clearer as we go is a good description of the Ark's shape.

China Nu-wah 1

Knowing there was a Chinese flood legend that had a Noah (Nu Wa, or Nu-Wah) in it, I had to find it and in doing so discovered something very interesting by stumbling on the fact that Chinese history or legends contain two different Nu-Wah's but are very linked via the events they deal with, which people that study Chinese legends are probably unaware of; but my previous research has clued me into.

The first story of the flood of Nu-Wah is summarised from early in the book *Secret of Lost Races* by Rene Noorbergen. He notes that the legend says all Chinese are descendents of Nu-Wah who was saved and thus saved mankind from a great flood along with his wife, three sons and three daughters by riding out the flood in a boat. This flood is said to have happened around 2300 BC. This date would mesh fairly well with Usher's date for the flood being 2348 B.C. Indeed '2300' B.C. is probably a rounding approximation and thus this could be considered an astonishing match. By saying this I'm of course a bit conflicted because I date the flood around 3410 B.C., though I admit there are some variables which would could end up confirming the younger date. My only real blocks are so many events are connected with 3100 B.C. not to mention some Chinese history exists that predates this flood. Anyway, Noorbergen also notes that the Chinese character for' boat are two characters used together; one which means the number '8' and the other means 'mouths'; which of course equals the 8 mouths to feed on the ark, not counting the thousands of animals of course.

This legend meshes so well with the flood legend in the bible I'm sure it must be a shock to some. It's also very interesting that the three wives are also said to be his daughters, which strongly suggests his three sons married three sisters.

China Nu-wah 2

Now the other very curious legend concerns the other Nu-wah: 'Nu' means woman, and 'Wah' means flowery; thus it's a female name! I thought I had this wrong or there had to be some confusion, so I dug a little deeper.

"She" is described as a woman that is half dragon and her bottom half appears snakelike or like the tail of a fishlike entity, and her role was to try and repair the wall of heaven. The sky had been broken and tilted by the water god Gong Gong and she tried to fix it with seven different coloured stones (Rainbow?). But a more important version is where Nu-Wah or Nüwa rose up to heaven and filled a gap in heaven with her body, described as half human and half serpent, and so she stopped the flood. Thus she can only be the Chinese version of Typhon, described in other legends as a Multi headed snake or serpent that reaches to the sky, which in turn describes Nu-Wah. So, how does Nüwa stop a flood or more properly put an end to the flooded earth? With her being clearly the local version of Typhon I can only surmise "she" did so by pulling the water off the planet in the form of a snake or serpent or more exactly a column of water going up to the sky, which could be interpreted by observers two ways. With her taking the water off, the water level of the earth dropped and the world was flooded no more. And secondly by trying to put the water back up into the sky where it came from like it was before the flood (repair the sky, or wall of heaven) thus saying she was attempting to repair heaven, but though this never worked and all that happened was a rainbow (?) of seven coloured stones, thus her actions did end the flooded nature of the planet by taking the water off the earth up to the sky and making it go away. But an additional detail in this legend is the parts of the sky being depicted as falling rocks of the seven colours suggesting that as the water was being pulled off, part of heaven was still falling: what could that be? It has to be rocks from Mars being pulled to earth while the water of earth was being pulled to Mars, thus her link with stones she's trying to put back up into the sky. It is real neat finding this legend and having the clues from before that clears up this very intriguing legend. It may not make sense to you yet, but as you continue deductions like this will become plainer. I have to start somewhere in this book and these fantastic explanations are in virtually every legend, and only the weight of a lot of similar legends related to us slightly different ways by the ancients will make it all clear in the end.

The date, for the flood of Nu-wah, said to be 2300 B.C. is in all likelihood a date that is supposed to be linked with a different or more "local" flood. This would be one of the massive local ones that overtopped the mountains and flooded the mountains for years, as you'll read about later. Much of Chinese history was destroyed by Emperor Tsin-chi-hoang (246-209 B.C.) so events prior to this are considered as the mythical period. (Book 14 pg. 114) Some was rewritten and hidden by older people who remembered the history later on, But Nu-wah's flood story probably has managed to survive all attempts to obliterate history simply because of the vastness and importance of the event. Donnelly in Atlantis quoting a Sir William Jones (*Asiatic Researches 1788)* states "The Chinese believe the Earth to have been wholly covered with water, which, in works of undisputed authenticity, they describe as flowing abundantly, then subsiding and separating the higher from the lower ages of mankind". This shows not only that the Chinese also have the universal flood history which is Nu-wah's flood, and also speaks of a higher and lower age of mankind, referring to ages of relative advancement and civilization, the pre-flood era being the more advanced. This universal flood would have destroyed ALL records, if there were any, so if this date of 2300 B.C were for the Flood of Nu-wah, then a record showing there were ten suns in the sky in 2346 B.C. (book 34 pg. 79) wouldn't exist. Thus different floods have been mixed up and the date of 2300 B.C. is likely attributed to the wrong flood. Ten suns of course would be an event where the gods visited in flying craft that shone like the sun some time after the flood. Japanese also have a legend of ten suns in the sky.

There is a very similar legend in India.

Munda (north-central India) (84°E, 22°N)

God, locally called "Sing Bonga" created man from the dust of the ground but soon after creation they became lazy, wicked and wouldn't wash and they spent all their time dancing and singing. So bad did man become that Sing Bonga regretted creating man and decided to destroy mankind with a flood. He sent a stream of fire water down from heaven to the ground and all the people on earth died except a brother and sister who hid under a Tirlil tree, which is why this tree looks black and charred today. After a while God reassessed the situation and so created the snake Lurbing to stop the fiery rain. Lurbing did this by holding up the showers by puffing up himself into the shape of a rainbow. Today the Munda's connect the rainbow with Lurbing destroying the rain. [Internet based on Frazer, p. 196]

As we will see there are post flood legends that speak of the sky being like fire and this burning of the Tirlil tree, so this legend does appear to blend certain post flood events with that of the global flood. An asteroid crashing through the water shell would be burning up at the same time as water rushing down so this may just be another global flood legend. This seems like a good place to put this legend because it might help you see this is the same story we just read with almost identical allegorical symbolism.

When the flood occurred caused by an asteroid smashing through the water shell, I had previously deduced the flood wasn't caused just by rain, but by the water from the shell literally pouring down onto the earth with similar visuals to that of a plug in a sink being pulled and the water spiralling down the drain. This legend adds substantiation to that deduction.

Like the female Nuwah of the above legend, we have a snake reaching the sky and holding it up in some fashion with a rainbow as a result. This snake is also the same as Typhon pulling water off the planet or like this legend says, holding it up and spreading out. Other legends of Typhon use this spreading out to suggest a many headed snakes whereas this one has the same snake fanning outward and linking the escaping water directly with the rainbow, which we all know that a rainbow is simply refracting of water droplets to reflect back to us parts of the spectrum. Other parts of this legend also reflect the same story told in the bible such as man created from the dirt, and wickedness running rampant, but it's curious to see how this post-flood legend interprets the wickedness of that time with laziness, not washing and too much dancing and singing, very tame almost juvenile offences used as moral direction for this people, suggesting a period in time where at least a small part of mankind was a much gentler kinder people.

Tuvinian (Soyot) (north of Mongolia) (approx 100°E, 53°N)

A giant turtle (or frog) which is said to hold the world on its back, and it moved, causing the ocean to begin flooding the earth. An old man who had deduced something like this might happen built an iron-reinforced raft, for him and his family, which they lived on and were saved from the flood. When the waters finally withdrew, the raft was left on a high forested mountain, where it remains to this day. When the flood was over, Kezer-Tshingis-Kaira-Khan created everything around us, and he even taught people how to make strong liquor. [Internet based on Holmberg, p. 366]

It's interesting to find the belief of the world resting on a turtle in an ancient legend. The turtle's motion clearly indicates a huge earthquake as would be caused by a huge asteroid pounding and sinking into the core of the earth. Much of the story parallels the biblical version even down to the detail of Noah building a vineyard. Interesting that the craft was iron reinforced is stated in this legend. Though the ark as found has been said to consist of wood now petrified, some witnesses did mention there was a lot of iron in the cages. So it's quite possible there is more iron in it not as yet found.

Babylonian. (There appears to be more than one Babylon. I'll assume this is the Babylon in or near Syria in Iraq) (32°N, 45°E) This legend is attributed to a priest of Babylon, named Berosus 330-250 B.C. Writers from his time and afterwards quote him, but his complete writings to date were either destroyed or have not yet surfaced.

The antediluvians were giants who became irreverent and degenerate, except one named Noa who was wise and reverenced the gods. He lived in Syria with his three sons Sem, Japet, Chem, (very comparable to the biblical Shem, Japheth and Ham) and their wives whose names were Tidea, Pandora, Noela, and Noegla. He saw signs in the stars, which foretold the coming destruction, so he spent 78 years building an ark. When finished, violent rain began and lasted many days while the oceans, inland seas, and rivers burst forth from beneath. The waters overflowed all the mountains, and the human race was drowned except Noa and his family on his ship. The ship eventually came to rest at last on the top of a mountain. Parts of the boat still exist, which people take bitumen from to make talismans. [based on internet quoting H. Miller, pp. 291-292]

This bit about making charms from the wood coated in pitch or bitumen demonstrates this story was written some time after the flood as eventually people made pilgrimages to the ark and took samples of the wood of the ark to make charms out of, and as we'll see, this fits with other stories about the ark from this and later periods. We'll get back to this. This notation that Noa lived in a place named Syria before the flood is the first I've seen a place with this name from before the flood. If we assume it's in the same location as Syria today, the ark would have drifted only about 3-400 miles in the space of about 7 months. The names of 'Noa' and the three sons are so similar; that we could assume the names of the wives are correct too which are never mentioned in the bible. It'd be interesting to know what their names meant. Generally speaking Biblical scholars assume it took 120 years to build the ark, so the difference in the time it took to build the ark might be acceptable if we consider it might have taken Noah 42 years just to obtain enough wood, pitch, supplies, creating the blueprints, have some down time and whatnot so that the actual building might not have taken the presumed 120 years to build the ark, but just the 78 mentioned in this legend. The bible doesn't actually say how long it took to build the ark. When God says the days of man shall be 120 years, some people think this is how much time was left before the flood, though God apparently talked to Noah when he was 500 so the math doesn't work. Interestingly some have said 120 years (or 100) wasn't enough time to build such a big ark with just four men, assuming the women didn't help, which is probably a bad assumption. Even so to refute this claim, people have worked out that the ark would have been built using a total of about 0.38×10^6 cubic feet of wood. And they've determined that 4 men could utilize 15 cubic feet of wood a day, meaning the ark could have been built in 81 years (Book 71 Pg 264) this is curiously close the 78 years mentioned in this legend. But be that as it may, the bible also says God was patient waiting for Noah to finish the ark, meaning if he needed 121 years or whatever God can wait. One thing that this figuring doesn't account for is the superior strength, size and technology at Noah's disposal. If they were conquering space before the flood, building a wooden boat, no matter how big, would have been child's play for Noah. One thing this legend has in common with the biblical flood is the waters bursting forth out of the ground, which this legend indicates instantly created oceans, seas and rivers, which might be ones that exist now. Often under the sea and watery places there are springs that come from underground, which this legend is probably referring to.

Buryat (eastern Siberia) (135°E, 47°N)

A Siberian name for God is Burkhan and he told a man to build a great ship to save him, his family and the animals from a flood. So the man worked on the boat in the forest for very many days, keeping his great project secret from his wife by telling her he was chopping wood. The devil, Shitkur, clued the wife in about her husband's secret project saying it would be ready soon. Then the devil persuaded her to refuse to embark, so that if the husband angrily struck her, she was to ask him, "Why do you strike me, Shitkur?" The wife did as suggested which allowed the devil to come on the boat with her when she boarded the boat. Burkhan helps get all the animals onto the boat except Argalan-Zan, the Prince of animals which thought they were too tall to drown. The flood drowned all animals not on the boat, including Argalan-Zan considered the Prince of animals. The bones of this animal can still be found. When the devil got on the boat he turned into a mouse chewing holes in the boat. Burkhan nipped this in the bud by creating a cat to catch it. [Based on Internet quoting Holmberg, pp. 361-362]

We have another legend where some estrangement occurs between "Noah" and his wife, where she refers to Noah as Shitku, the devil. So did she follow the devils advice and not board or just the advice to refuse then be forced on? Or is this a possible legend that infers a second wife confused as just one? This legend could be deduced to be a mixing of flood legends because later floods caused animals to go extinct, not the first one. As second Siberian legends ads more...or...?

Sagaiye (eastern Siberia)

Noj was told by God to build a ship. The devil urged the wife to find out what Noj was building in the forest and when she figured out what it was she told the devil it was a boat. So the devil would wreck at night what Noj built in the daytime, causing the boat not to be finished in time for the flood. So God sent down an iron vessel to save Noj, his wife and children, as well as all kinds of animals. [Ibid]

The name Noj is very similar to Noah and sometimes the 'h' dropped and is silent anyway as could be the 'j'. Now this legend strangely suggests that a ship from above or space came and saved Noj and the animals, and that's pretty odd, or is it...well consider this next bit.

Some famous astronomers have seen a manmade planet at various times since the reinvention of the telescope, around Jupiter, Venus and inside the orbit of Mercury, even giving the objects names such as "Vulcan" in 1859 for when it was spotted inside the orbit of Mercury. But there is a group that refers to this space sphere as "The Great Ark". Dr. M. K. Jessup wrote a book called *The Case for the UFO* and it seems to have hit a nerve or two. Three people apparently 'in the know' put notes in the margins in a copy of his book. One of these people in the margins also had corresponded with Jessup previously by mail, though they had never met. Somehow the government got this copy of the book and red lights started flashing in the minds of U.S. officials and they quickly made reprint copies of the book which included the notes in the margins. In his book, Jessup had commented on a dark spot seen moving over the surface of Jupiter. This garnered some comments by "Mister "A" in the margin. "The Great Ark! To have seen the Great Ark would humble or terrify any human. I wish even so, that I could have seen it, the greatest structure ever built by Humanoids." (book 30 pg 165) Humanoids would refer to the offspring of women and the Sons of God which would include some of the giants. Further research has identified this planet or great ark is named Elysia. Supposedly a spaceman said that an Elysian world blasted a planet named "Lucifer" which was situated between Mars and Jupiter. (Book 47 pg. 34) Ancient legends also speak of this ship, which we'll get to in the bonus section. Whether or not this Siberian legend is actually referring to this space ship is debatable, but it seemed like a good place to mention it. Once a person is lifted off the earth, they are no longer on dry ground, and if rescued they could be considered as not in the flood. Did this moonlike "Great Ark" also grab some vestiges of earth to save some animals and a few people...maybe even Noah's other wife and her family...just in case? Or is this legend blurring lines of one flood with another with this ship coming down from the heavens? At least one "local" flood has a similar event in it as well.

Hindu Flood legend. (approx. 27°N, 77°E)

There are three very similar Hindi world flood legends all with the same basic story and the same man named Manu. (Manu is the Hindu Lawgiver who received laws from the Deity.) I have therefore combined the three into one with the excerpts from the slightly different version in italics. Parts from one or the other were missing in the others so it seems a bit more complete using all three to compensate each other. Two of the versions were missing the part where the creatures were placed in a ship so I went with this version and adding extra bits from the other two to this one.

King Manu, son of the Sun, was abstinent and unselfish to the point his spirit was in union with the Deity. Thus Brahma's favour rested on Manu and asked him if there was something he would like to have. Manu asked for the power to preserve all existing things upon the dissolution of the universe. Later, while offering oblations in his possessions, a carp (fish) fell in his hands, which Manu preserved. *The fish asked to be protected from the larger fishes, and in return it would save Manu.* The fish grew and asked Manu to preserve it, and in doing so Manu moved it to progressively larger vessels, eventually moving it to the river Ganga and then to the ocean. *Upon being released into the ocean, the fish told Manu that soon all earthly objects would be destroyed in a coming time of purification. The fish told Manu to build a strong ship with a cable attached and to embark with the seven sages (rishis) and certain seeds, and to then watch for the fish, since the waters could not be crossed without it.* When it filled the ocean, Manu recognized the fish as the god Janardana, (another name for Vishnu or God or Brahma). It told Manu that the end of the yuga (end of a world age) was approaching, and soon all would be covered with water. He was to preserve all creatures and plants aboard a ship which had been prepared. It said that a hundred years of drought and famine would begin this day, which would be followed by fires from the sun and from underground that would consume the earth and the ether, destroying this world, the gods, and the planets. Seven clouds from the steam of the fire will inundate the earth, and the three worlds will be reduced to one ocean. Manu's ship alone will remain, fastened by a rope to the great fish's horn. Having announced all this, the great being vanished. The deluge occurred as stated; Janardana appeared in the form of a horned fish, and the multi headed serpent Ananta came in the form of a rope. Manu, by contemplation, drew all creatures towards him and stowed them in the ship and, after making obeisance to Janardana, attached the ship to the fish's horn with the serpent-rope. *Manu, alone of all creatures, survived. He made offerings of clarified butter, sour milk, whey, and curds. From these, a woman arose, calling herself Manu's daughter. Whatever blessings he invoked through her were granted him. Through her, he generated this race.* [Internet quoting H. Miller, pp. 289-290; Howey, pp. 389-390; Frazer, pp. 191-193]

Ananta or Anant means infinite, limitless, or unending, and refers to the infinite multi headed snake so this has to be the Hindu name for Typhon, that is, the stream of water being drawn off the earth that reached up to the heavens onto a nearby celestial body. This ancient Hindu association and presence of Ananta with the flood is important as it lends credence to the deduction of it being a stream of water being taken off the earth to cause the water level of the earth to drop.

Several legends refer to Noah or the apparent translation for this name of the person who survived the flood as a king. It would seem that Noah was thus considered the ruler of all after the flood and so in preflood terms they simply refer to him as a king. This is somewhat ironic as in all likelihood before the flood he was ridiculed for building the ark. But then it's common for Biblical people who were considered the least to be elevated to leader status, Saul: least of the tribe of Benjamin, David: youngest brother not considered worth inviting to dinner, Gideon, Mordecai, and on and on.

Noah was on the boat with seven other people...his three sons, their wives and his wife, so these may have been exalted in stature after the flood too and referred to as the "seven sages" in the Hindu legend. He also brought seeds and plants onto the boat: the biblical version omits this detail.

A hundred years of drought following Manu's order to build a boat might have something to do with how long it took to build the boat, followed soon after by the events that caused the flood, or it could be a detail of a precursor to a later 'local' flood. Who can say?

Fires from the sun might be the direct rays or solar eruptions that now penetrate the earth's atmosphere which did not do so previously or a meteor shower (such as occurred when Mars "threw" rocks at us which would appear as flame during their descent from the apparent direction of the sun), or this detail could be a mixture of post flood legends creeping in as well.

The gods destroyed spoken of could be the people who were 'like gods' because they ate the fruit. This is an interesting note if it refers to the people from before the flood as the gods. Planets destroyed appear to refer to the destroyed planet between Jupiter and Mars called by various names such as Marduk, and Krypton. The use of the word "planets" being plural might refer to a moon of Saturn that turned into the ring. Or it could be these asteroids blasted other planets destroying the colonization work on them. Richard Hoagland in a meticulous study of every planet and moon photo of our solar system he could get his hands on, concluded that our solar system was something of a wasteland of former civilizations and development on them. He saw a lot of signs that many of these places appeared to have been developed and subsequently laid flat from some catastrophe. For example some of the moon pictures were destroyed because they had evidence of structures on them and some moon pictures were airbrushed to hide details we were not allowed to see, but a few got out of Nasa's hands which show very suspicious details in them, such as details that could be broken domed structures. Similarly pictures of Mars as seen on the internet show obvious signs of smearing details as though they took colour from one area and brushed over other areas with that colour to hide something. Occasionally they miss stuff and I've seen a picture of Mars' surface with definite geometric structures on the surface.

"Seven clouds from the steam of the fire will inundate the earth". This could refer to the environment that occurred long after the world flood where worldwide many volcanoes erupting simultaneously evaporating the oceans to the point they nearly dried up causing massive flooding and snowfalls. So again some hints that this legend could be a mixing of details from the great flood, and the many local floods to come occurring globally much later on.

"Three worlds will be reduced to one ocean", a curious sentence...could it mean land, sky and sea, places where men roamed before the flood reduced to just one ocean? Or three colonised planets that were commonly traveled to by those of earth cut off from travel by the flood. I'm not sure what to make of that sentence.

Though Noah made sacrifices and this version has (different) sacrifices mentioned, the bit about a woman arising from the sacrifice is myth language I don't pretend to get, particularly when we consider his wife and his three sons and their wives were also on the boat.

Obviously a fish isn't going to pull an ark (though I suppose a whale could) and a snake isn't going to stand the stress of the pulling, Then again there have been seen 100 foot long snakes with 5 food heads in South America that had to be hunted down because they kept eating soldiers. So this obviously has to be metaphorical. The Snake Ananta is part of Hindu cosmology referring to Vishnu floating on the snake Ananta on the primeval waters, which I assume refers to earth before the land appeared or after the flood when the earth was a water planet. Interestingly legends say the 'snake' that reaches up to the sky is also something that appeared over Atlantis when it sunk. This Ananta almost certainly has to be another name for Typhon which is in many legends and is said to be a giant that hissed and coiled whose head was of a hundred snakes which reached to the stars. The description of Typhon is in reality a pillar of cyclonic water and atmosphere escaping the earth by being drawn off by a nearby celestial body with its gravity.

Hindu

Here is another Hindu legend with some elements of the previous one but with a few differences. A merging of the two could be considered, but I've left them as separate legends.

The demon Hayagriva stole Brahma's sacred books during the last kalpa, causing all of the mankind except for seven Nishis, and Satyavrata the prince of a naval district, to forget God and became corrupt. One day when Satyavrata was washing in the river, a fish visited him and begged for protection. Satyavrata took charge of the fish and when it grew larger he transferred it into progressively larger containers. After a long while he recognised the fish as the god Vishnu, Lord of the Universe". Vishnu warned Satyavrata that in a week the corrupted creatures would be drowned in a great flood, but that Satyavrata would be saved in a large vessel. He was told to take all kinds of medicinal herbs, food, grains, the seven Nishis and their wives aboard the boat, as well as pairs of animals. When the week was over, the oceans began to rise and overflowed the coasts while constant rain flooded the earth. The rising waters lifted the boat, and Satyavrata along with the Nishis who entered with their wives and cargo. During the flood, Vishnu saved the ship by turning into a fish again and tying himself to the ark along with a huge sea serpent. When the flood was over and the water level dropped again, he killed the demon that stole the holy books and then related the contents to Satyavrata. [based on Internet referring to this legend as mentioned by H. Miller, pp. 289-290; Howey, pp. 389-390; and Frazer, pp. 191-193]

A Kalpa is the duration of a world age said to be 4.32 million years; much longer than a 'yuga' of the previous Hindu legend. Many ancient civilizations like to be considered the oldest civilization so their ages were artificially lengthened almost as part of a competition. It's also plausible the gods explained stuff to men about space, the stars, time dilation and their ages or life spans that confused us and so interpretations of their words got a bit creative or even silly. Obviously there were not multiple complete global floods caused by a collapsing water shell; it can only collapse once, so any ages attributed to the global flood no matter how extreme have to be talking about the same incident. Some people justify belief in an old earth based on these extreme dates included in legends such as this. But if many legends date the flood around 3000 BC and then one dates it at millions of years ago, the Millions of years date has to be suspect, as well as any other dated myths by the same people group.

Man before the flood did not need to read as they grasped everything, but the legend suggests this as a plausible explanation for the corruption of man and probably to encourage the people to read and treasure such material after the flood and beyond. It also appears to suggest the gods taught men after the flood to write as Egyptian legends do, thus alluding to the coming of the gods after the flood. Also, this legend, like the Masai, doubles the 8 of Noah's family, but this time actually places them all on the large vessel. I put this out as a suggestion. A title once acceptable or given to both men and women, later on only given to men, could confuse people later on. If there were thus 7 Nishis on the boat, later on it could be assumed the title was only a masculine title so it was supposed they had wives, when in fact some of those Nishis *were* the wives, thus possibly accounting for the doubling of the number of people on the ark in this legend.

Kashmir North India (77°W, 35°N)

Thought to be the earliest Hindu flood legend is the Kashmir version found in the *Satapatha Brahmana*. A holy man named Manu, by prayers and determined self improvements won the favour of the lord of Heaven. Manu had three sons named Charma, Sharma, and Yapeti which are strikingly similar to Noah's three sons named Ham, Shem, and Japheth.

While he was meditating thousands and thousands of years passed and after all this time Brahma showed himself to Manu and told him to ask for something. Manu said sooner or later there is going to be a coming destruction when the world doesn't exist anymore, and I would like to be the person who saves the world when the time of destruction comes. Brahma granted him his wish and then said indeed the world will end soon so you need to build a strong ark and put a strong rope on it. Take seven sages with you who existed since the beginning of time, along with seeds of all things and pairs of each animal. When you are ready I will appear to you as a fish with horns on my head for you to throw your rope around so I can pull you to safety, and without me you cannot escape from the flood.

You'll pardon my sceptical mind, but I suspect that someone meditating for thousands and thousands of years might be a slight exaggeration.

Altaic (central Asia) (90E°, 52°N)

At one time the ocean covered the world; this is how it happened. A good man named Nama, ruled with three sons, Sozun-uul, Sar-uul, and Balyks. Ülgen commanded Nama to build a large boat but since Nama's eyesight was diminishing, he got his sons to do the building. (Ülgen is a Turkic and Mongolian name for the creator) They built the ark on a mountain, and they hung eight 80-fathom cables from it to determine the waters depth. When it was finished Nama and his family boarded the ark along with the animals and birds which had been forced toward them by the rising waters. After a week, the cables gave way from the earth, indicating that the flood attained 80 fathoms. After another week, Nama told his firstborn son to open the window to see what he could see, and all he saw was the tops of mountains. The next time the son looked all that could be seen was water and sky: now the ocean ruled the world. Eventually the ark grounded in a group of eight mountains. Several days in a row, Nama released a raven, a rook, and a crow, none of which returned. The fourth day, he sent out a dove, which came back with a birch twig and the dove told Nama why the other birds hadn't returned; because they had found carcasses of a deer, dog, and a horse and had stayed there living off them.

The rest of the legend is a bit strange and I'll include it here after some thoughts on the above. Once again a rope or cable(s) extending from the ark are mentioned, but a real rope and not a snake. Ripley's believe it or not, who has never been proven wrong, says that an incredibly huge metal anchor (about 12 feet tall) found in Kairouan, Tunisia was once the anchor used by Noah. (Book 72 Photo section) If this is true this anchor has traveled about 2000 miles from where Noah landed on Mount Ararat, or about 4,250 miles from the Altai Mountains where this legend stems from. Since this legend comes from the Altaic region which is a mountain range, the legend apparently localizes the flood and likely refers to the mountains on which the ark rested as being their Altai Mountains, and may even have localized the building of the ark on the same mountains for this reason. It's interesting that this legend mentions a Raven, Crow and Rook, all the same <u>kind</u> of birds, which never return, just as the Raven (only) is mentioned in the biblical story which is never declared to have returned, however this legend includes insight into why they may not have returned. And now for the rest of the story...

Nama angry at hearing why the raven, rook and crow didn't return, he cursed them to behave like this until the end of the world. When Nama was very old, his wife urged him to kill all the men and animals he had saved from the flood so when they were all transferred to the next world, they would be his to rule forever. Nama didn't know what to do. Sozun-uul, afraid to go against his mother in the open, told his father a story about coming across a blue-black cow eating a human with only the legs still showing. Nama grasped the meaning of the story and cut his wife in two with a sword. When Nama went to heaven, he took Sozun-uul and changed him into a constellation of five stars. [based on Internet quoting Holmberg, pp. 364-365]

OK I don't pretend to know what that last bit is all about, but I included it for your reading displeasure.

European World Flood Legends

Celtic: (A location for the Celts is a bit hard to pin point but we'll go with Brittany as a central point at (48°N, 2°W)

Flood legends like this one that follows sometimes get me scratching my head. Though apparently a global flood legend, some of it's difficult to decipher. I've left it as found.

Heaven and Earth were great giants, and Heaven lay upon the Earth so that their children were crowded between them, and the children and their mother were unhappy in the darkness. The boldest of the sons led his brothers in cutting up Heaven into many pieces. From his skull they made the firmament. His spilling blood caused a great flood which killed all humans except a single pair, who were saved in a ship made by a beneficent Titan. The waters settled in hollows to become the oceans. The son who led in the mutilation of Heaven was a Titan and became their king, but the Titans and gods hated each other, and the king titan was driven from his throne by his son, who was born a god. That Titan at last went to the land of the departed. The Titan who built the ship, whom some consider to be the same as the king Titan, went there also. (Internet source referring to a work by Paul Cantave, Shana Fitzmaurice, and Samantha Maris)

I will just dissect and try to decipher the above as best as I can. If after reading this you wonder what I've been taking, you might be able to piece a bit of it together as we go along through the many legends. This is what I pull from this legend: In the heavens and on earth there were giants. The giants attained to the heavens {by their technology}. There was a war in heaven and some of these giants or a particular Titan wreaked havoc and destruction in the heavens ("cutting up Heaven into many pieces") including blowing up a moon of Saturn and the planet between Mars and Jupiter creating the asteroid belt. This action caused the great flood of which only a pair were saved in a boat.

The continual use of the name / word Titan is confusing, so that's the best I can muster. Titans being hated by men (the gods) sound like the giants here were particularly nasty offspring of angels and women. However there were wars in the heavens after the flood too, which means this could be a combining of pre and post flood details. We'll get to these references of wars in the heavens near the end of this work.

Welsh (53°N, 3°W)

The lake of Llion burst, flooding all lands. Dwyfan and Dwyfach escaped in a "mastless" ship [sounds like an ark to me] with pairs of every sort of living creature. They landed in a place in Britain called Prydain and repopulated the world. [Internet quoting Gaster, pp. 92-93]

Pretty short and to the point and obviously localized, and only superficially parallels the biblical account.

It even hints it might be a local flood legend indicated by a lake bursting which would happen when land suddenly shifted causing a lake to jump out of its bed and rush across land, so I'm guessing this is a merging of local and global flood legends.

Greek (22°E, 38°N)

The first race of people was completely destroyed because they were excessively wicked. They were destroyed when the fountains of the deep opened, and rain fell in torrents, causing seas and rivers to rise and cover the earth to drown everyone. Deucalion survived due to his foresight and faith and becoming the only link between the first and second race of men. Into a great ark he packed his wives and children and all animals. The animals came to him, by God's help, and they remained friendly for the duration of the flood. [Mirroring the note that they become afraid of man after the flood] The flood waters escaped down a chasm opened in Hierapolis. (Book 14 pg 159 and Internet quoting Frazer, pp. 153-154)

This Greek version is not too distant from Turkey (where the Ararat mountains are), or Israel, and the story is very similar but with Greek names inserted making the legends appear localized. This mention of a chasm in Hierapolis, which is in Phrygia of Asia Minor (which is now Turkey) is interesting, as indeed there is a hole called the Plutonium there that reaches deep into the earth from which exudes a nasty smelling vapour. This is quite possibly one of the many fountains of the deep where water could have burst forth and later receded back into after the flood. Another older version of the story told by Hellanicus has Deucalion's ark landing on Mount Othrys in Thessaly. This older version is more complete as it mentions a resting place on top of a mountain, though once again a Greek location is substituted. Another version has the ark landing on a mountain in Argolis (possibly Nemea, previously called Phouka), which is yet another Greek location. With of course no hope of finding the remains of such an ark in these locations this would marginalize such a legend's validity to hearers. Except for the localized name places, it does mirror the biblical version pretty well. This however must be a mixing of local and world flood legends because the people of Athens drink or toast to the remembering the Flood of Deucalion, the flood that ended the Bronze Age. The Greek Bronze age as we'll see later was one of the later world ages the world experienced meaning there is some mixing of global and local flood legends in this tale even though the distinctions are not obvious.

Interestingly this legend refers to Deucalion as the only link between the first and second race of men. Noah would be a preflood man living in a post flood world. The first race of men would be preflood, and we the second race of men. But distinguishing these as a different race of men alludes to a difference that is distinguishable between them. Keep your eyes peeled to see what that difference is in this work.

Gypsy legend of Transylvania (24°E, 46°N)

Men originally lived forever with no troubles. The earth grew all kinds of fine fruits, flesh grew on trees, and milk and wine flowed in many of the rivers. One day, an old man came by and asked to sleep overnight, and a couple let him sleep in their small house. When he left the next day, he promised he would return in nine days and asked the couple to take care of a fish for him. He would reward them if they didn't eat the fish and returned it to him when he returned. The wife looked at the fish only as a potential meal but the husband said to her to leave it alone as he had promised the old man to preserve it for him and made the wife swear not to eat it. But after just two days, the wife couldn't stop thinking about it and the temptation overcame her and she threw the fish on the hot coals. No sooner had she done so when she was struck dead by lightning, and it started to rain causing the rivers to surge and flood the country. When the old man returned [no doubt wearing hip waders] and told the widower that all living things were to be drowned, but since he had kept his promise, he and a wife he had to find and marry would be saved. He was to then gather his relatives, build a very large boat for them, animals, along with seeds of trees and herbs. The man found a woman, married her, built the boat and got the family, animals and stuff onto the boat. It rained an entire year, and the waters covered everything. After a year, the waters sank, and the people and animals came off the boat. Life now was harder and they had to work to survive, and now sickness and death came. The population slowly grew and after thousands of years the people reached the same number as there were before the flood. [Based on Internet quotes of Frazer, pp. 177-178]

The time to build a boat in anticipation of a flood is before it starts, not seven days after it starts raining, so this legend seems a bit quirky here... if the fish story isn't. Man was meant to live forever before they ate the fruit and the fish appears to be equated with the fruit of the tree of the knowledge of good and evil and the woman with that of Eve. Saying trees grew meat, and rivers flowed milk and wine suggests some fantasizing of what a perfect world might have been like by the Gypsies at some point. This suggests the tellers of the tale got a bit carried away. When the lady kills the fish and is immediately killed by lightning echoes the biblical version of eating the fruit of the tree of knowledge of good and evil: "In the day that you eat the fruit you shall surely die". But that death was a spiritual death and Adam didn't physically die till about 950 years of age, and Eve probably lived as long too, so this appears to be a way to move the story along from creation to the flood quickly. Again the idea of the faithful man re-marrying, building a boat, gathering trees, herbs and animal during the start of the flood seems odd. It easily would have taken the year it rained to do a portion of this and others on earth in the same predicament could have done the same, and would have probably concentrated on the boat part first without worry about finding a wife. I mean just finding a woman to take time out from saving herself from the rain so she could marry a stranger during an obvious catastrophe might have been hard enough to accomplish in a year all by itself. So it is probably a way to condense through the generations of man from Adam to Noah. But this legend is probably merging post flood legends or mixing up details from these floods in this story for it to be raining while he's about looking for a wife, stuff to build a boat with, and a few thousand animals. The mentioning of the diminished ages and strength of man after the flood is reflected here and the water remaining a year also links it more closely with the global flood rather than a local one. Though lightning now often starts a downpour, saying this occurred to start the flood in the legend appears to be grasping at what they knew in the post flood world to tell of the time they did not fully comprehend in Earth's geological preflood history. You see, it had never rained before the flood so lightning was certainly never experienced during this time either. This legend appears to have been told long after the flood to the point that one can see why some of the details were blurred and merged with other flood occurrences over that time. Curiously it is another legend that suggests Noah had two wives, possibly at the same time. But with bigamy apparently taboo in some people's minds, suggesting the saviour of all animals and flesh was a bigamist might have urged the tellers of the tale to alter this bit.

African Flood legends

Egyptian. (27°N 30°E)

Egyptian flood legends apparently are rare and one Egyptian universal flood legend that *does* exist is incomplete, but it has a key piece in what little remains.-

People had become rebellious. Atum (Egyptian name for the creator) said he will destroy all he made and return the earth to the Primordial Water which was its original state. Atum will remain, in the form of a serpent, with Osiris. [Internet quoting Faulkner, plate 30]

That is about as much of the flood legend that remains as the telling of flood story on this papyrus is damaged and unclear. However, as we mentioned before, noteworthy is how it speaks of the earth returning to its 'original state'. This of course would be before the waters were separated above and below by a firmament, thus returning the earth to a complete water planet. There is another mention of an Egyptian flood legend worthy of note here. "An Egyptian Copt historian, Masudi, writing during the middle ages, recounted a tradition that the Great Pyramid was build during the Reign of the Gods*, before the Flood, to safeguard ancient knowledge. There is evidence that the Great Pyramid has experienced one or more floods, since the shells and fossils from the sea have been found around its base, and indications of a salt deposit have been noted in the Queen's Chamber within the pyramid. Masudi wrote the Great Pyramid was not a tomb, but a book in stone, a book that could be read when generations far in the future possessed enough scientific knowledge to understand its implications." (Book 6 pg. 146- * capital 'G' used in original)

I've determined that there was indeed more than one flood that occurred in Egypt. Masudi referring to the pyramid being built before the flood could refer to it being built before the world flood, however with the reference to the "Reign of the Gods", this more than likely refers to the reign of the gods immediately preceding the first dynasty. I've determined in my first book this is probably the period from just after the world flood to the time when the gods left, around 3100 B.C. We'll get to the Egyptian local flood in chapter 3, and the period of the gods in the bonus section. Also noteworthy is the mention of the serpent in relation to the flood. Though this was not explained, so many links with the many headed serpent Typhon and the escape of water from the planet exist that this is probably another partial reference to this phenomena.

Masai (East Africa): (4°S, 33°E)

A righteous man named Tumbainot, his wife Naipande and three sons named, Oshomo, Bartimaro, and Barmao. When his brother died, Tumbainot, married the widow Nahaba-logunja, who had with him three more sons. However they argued about her refusal to give him a drink of milk in the evening, so she set up her own homestead. The world was very populated in those days, and the people were sinful and forgot God. One day a man named Nambija hit another named Suage on the head killing him. At this, God resolved to destroy all mankind, except Tumbainot who found grace in God's eyes. God told Tumbainot to build a wooden ark for his two wives, six sons and their wives, and some of every sort of animals. Once aboard and their store cupboard set up, God caused a great long rain which flooded the earth, so that all other men and animals drowned. The ark drifted for a long time, and food began to run out. When the rain ceased, Tumbainot sent a dove to determine the state of the earth after the flood. The tired dove returned, so Tumbainot knew the earth was still flooded. After several days he let vulture loose again to try to find some dry ground. This time he attached an arrow to the tail feathers of the vulture so that, if the bird landed somewhere, the arrow would hook on something and be lost. The vulture returned at the end of the day but without the arrow, so Tumbainot figured it must have found a carcass to nibble on, so the flood must be receding. When the water receded enough, the ark ran aground on a steppe, and its seafarers left the ark and soon after Tumbainot saw four rainbows, north east, south and west demonstrating that God's wrath was over. [based on Internet quoting Frazer, pp. 330-331]

I imagine, with Noah living another 350 years after the flood, he was visited by many descendants to hear the story of the flood in person. Geniuses, as all pre flood people would have been, and that's probably an insult as they were all staggeringly gifted compared to us, do not like to say the same thing over and over and do not make good production line employees. It's entirely possible Noah told a slightly different pre flood life story to everyone who came to him. He may even have used allegory as some of the global flood legends seem anything but plausible unless they are allegorical in nature, and probably suited or tailored to the individual listening. That factored with the retelling of the story generation after generation who may even have tailored the story some more, has no doubt led to some convoluted tales of the flood.

We see the problem of extreme population again in this legend linked with growing sinfulness and alienation from God. It also sounds like the story of Abel and Cain being equated for all the problems that came afterwards. Possibly the story of the sons of God marrying the daughters of men sounded too fantastic and that part was dropped over the centuries. Interestingly there are two wives and twice as many kids supposedly on the ark. Noah's dad Lamech had two wives so this little tidbit of Noah and a second wife is certainly plausible and this legend once again suggests this occurred. Thus one might suggest half of them missed the boat because they were alienated from Tumbainot sometime after Noah got the word about the impending doom. Maybe Nahaba-logunja thought she was well rid of a nut building a big boat, especially if he was building it on a mountain like some legends state.

Southwest Tanzania (Rukwa Region) (18°S, 33°E)

When the rivers began flooding, God told two men to go into a ship, and take with them all sorts of seed and animals. The flood got worse and even covered the mountains. Checking to find out if the water had gone away, the man sent a dove to see, but it came back to the ship. He waited a while then sent out a hawk, which did not return because the land had dried. The men then left the boat with the animals and seeds. [Internet quoting Gaster, pp. 120-121]

Though short and mostly reflecting the Noah flood in many aspects, with the rivers already starting to flood suggests it was too late to warn and build a boat, so this is probably a mixing up of a local flood legend and the global one. Obviously two men surviving the global flood doesn't work. It's possible women in this narrative were just not mentioned as a matter of course based on the assumption than men would obviously have women with them. This would be similar to how when the bible tells of when Jesus fed the five thousand men and we assume there were women and children there too, as what man wouldn't have a woman: possibly in the context that after marriage two shall become one flesh. Oddly, mid story, it refers to just "the man" sending out birds.

Now think about this. Before the flood the earth had a far more rolling plain kind of topography. Real mountains such as we have today were nonexistent. The mountains before the flood were little more than hills. Don't take my word for it ... geologists have already figured out that there was a time when the land around the world was far smoother. So mountains were probably all roughly the same height as no upheavals had shoved the land around. Now think how many legends you've already read that state that the mountains were covered, and there will be more to come. So, if the flood covered one mountain...it had to have covered them all. There's no escaping it.

Australian Flood legends

Fitzroy River area, Western Australian:
Though the Aborigines of this area have a world flood legend, they distrust the version of Noah's ark that says the ark landed in the Middle East because they say this version is the white man's way to keep them in subservience. (I'm not sure how that would accomplish this.) They have localized the flood legend to say Noah's Ark which carried the aborigines, and animals drifted south and came to rest in the flood plain of Djilinbadu where they say it can still be seen today. (Djilinbadu is about 70 km south of Noonkanbah Station, just south of the Barbwire Range and east of the Worral Range, but I've not been able to find it on the net) [Internet based on Kolig, pp. 242-245]

There are enough differences that this could be a later local flood that has been meshed and somewhat confused with the global flood. One wonders if such a boat is really there. The Squamish of British Columbia say the canoe that saved people from the flood landed on Mount Baker and can still be seen there half way up. Washington tribes such as Spokane, Yakima, Nez Perce, and Cayuse each tell of a different mountain the life saving raft landed on, similar to how the Greeks do too.

Another Australian Flood legend
Some traveled south and started to do a nyalaidj (?) ceremony dance. During the dance a girl climbed a Palm tree and noticed an orphan boy crying and tried to get him attended to by calling out, yet the people just kept dancing. The child's crying began to upset the land and water came out of the ground. Suddenly the people cried in fear, but they couldn't escape the water because the ground became soft and so the water covered them up, and then the Rainbow serpent Ngalyod ate the people and then the boy. This happened at Gaalbaraya and so people still consider the place taboo. [Internet based on Berndt & Berndt, pp. 96-97]

The water coming out of the ground to flood and destroy man can only be referring to the global flood, and by ignoring a child in distress this appears to be equating man wickedness as the grounds for the flood. This has some similarities to the Indian Munda legend where people were lazy and just danced sang and wouldn't wash being the cause for the flood. Very interesting in this legend is that the Rainbow serpent ate the people. We've seen that the rainbow serpent is the same as Typhon that was a pillar of water reaching to the sky but here we have an indication that this gravitationally caused pillar of water reaching to the sky, took not only water, but actually took people off the planet with it too. This would mean that there would be remains of people on Mars, as well as fish and crabs and whatever else was caught up.

Victoria Australia

Some legends used pretty nasty graphic, even disturbing imagery and I don't really enjoy reading them and have not included them; but to include at least three global flood legends per continent I include this slightly distasteful one, but for a good reason too.

To Victorian natives the name of God is Bunjil who created the world and man, but he became angry with the people because of how they had turned to evil ways, so he caused the oceans to flood by urinating into the oceans. This killed all people except a man and a woman who Bunjil loved which he allowed to escape the flood by having them climb and live in a tall tree on a mountain. Later he put them in the heavens as stars. From these two all the human race now alive comes from. [Internet based on Gaster, p. 114]

I went with this particular legend, which although short, has the imagery of water descending from the heavens likened to the world's oceans rising by being peed in by this legend. The water sphere was broken and destabilized by the asteroid to the point it just collapsed onto the earth. More than one asteroid likely hit as legends refer to windows (plural) in heaven being opened up, though an argument could be made that the impact of the asteroid on the shell rippled around its spherical nature breaking it in several places also causing several windows in heaven to be opened up. Anyway water draining down to the surface of the earth, likened to a stream of urine, from the water sphere or canopy is retained in this legend, identifying it with the global flood. A few legends have mentioned that Noah or the local name for this man and his wife being placed as stars in the heavens, presumably meaning that constellations were named for them sometime after the flood by their children. My guesses would be the twins and Aquarius might be a couple. The crab legends fighting Typhon is one named as "Cancer". I guess some study could be made to show that even the names we've given to the constellations which are common to many people's around the globe is also evidence of the flood.

South American Flood legends.

The Inca's of Peru (75°W, 10°S)

The Inca's have an almost identical flood legend as Cochin. They say that the water came and flooded above the highest mountains in the world, so that all people and creatures drowned. Before the flood many of the people were giants. Two famous giants were Atlan (Atlas?) and Theitani (Titan). No living thing escaped the flood except a man and a woman, who floated in a box on the face of the waters and so were saved. Incan Pictorial records also show a flood that rose above even the highest mountains. All living things died in it, except for a man and woman who were saved by floating in a box. When the flood dropped back, the floating box was carried by the wind to Tiahuanacu, about 200 miles from Cuzco, where the Creator said they should live. The Creator fashioned new people from clay on which he painted dress and hair style, gave to the people of each nation their own language, songs, and seeds to plant. When they came to life he sent them into the earth to travel underground and come forward from caves, springs, tree trunks, etc. in their various homes. While this happened He created the sun, moon, and stars. (Book 4 pg. 34 and Internet quoting Bierhorst, 1988, pp. 200,202; Gaster, p. 127; Frazer, p. 271)

This story seems to have forgotten to add that a few creatures must have been in the 'box', for them to be here now. But that might have been considered obvious and not needed for inclusion. Once again the ark is referred to as a "box". After all, it wasn't built for going anywhere; all it had to do was float. And if it had a traditional under belly it would be less stable and harder to build and accommodate more animals.

Though this is at least partially the legend of the world flood, they've added second flood details that include local landmarks and details which were about a local flood they averted by going underground. (We'll cover this aspect in the local floods section) As you the reader this is important as it is much clearer in this legend that this is a splicing together of both global and local flood legends. The note about the sun moon and stars being created and seen after they emerged indicates how the sun, moon and stars looked different than from before the flood, and these differences seen in the sky were heralded as a new heaven. As time went on after following cataclysms these new slightly different heavens were numbered. This flood also appears to infer three of the gods that are thought to be post flood beings, Titan, Atlas and probably Quetzalcoatl not named but said to be the creator of different races, which is also important as it indicates the different races were a result of genetic mastery and not environmental or whatever other reasons evolutionists, anthropologists and creationists have attributed to the differing races.

Macusi (British Guyana)

The creator of heaven and earth, called Makunaima by the Macusi meaning "He who works in the night", after creating plants and trees, he came down from his mansion in heaven and chopped off some bark from a tree from which all kinds of animals sprung when they hit the water. After this Makunaima made a man who when he fell asleep found a woman beside him when he woke. After a time the evil spirit became predominant on the earth so Makunaima sent a great flood. Only one man survived in a canoe. After the flood was over and the water had gone down, he sent a rat out to see if the flood had dried up. The rat came back with a corn cob. When the flood was over the man threw stones behind him which turned into people. [Based on internet quote of Frazer, pp. 255-256]

This is clearly a condensed rendition of the time from creation to the flood and much of the biblical version is encapsulated in it. Since man was made from red earth, why couldn't animals *be* made from tree bark? Same as the biblical version of creation we see Man created first then woman next, and evil overtaking the world. And though it might seem odd to call God by a name meaning "He who works in the night", this too meshes with the biblical version of creation when creation in the bible mentions "darkness was upon the face of the deep". And this concept is reiterated when Moses was on the mount and God came down in the thick darkness. It's odd that they mention a rat was sent to scout as I would think it would drown if dispatched from a canoe, though it shows here that this was no ordinary canoe but a canoe with limited vision in order that, like the biblical version he needed to send out an animal emissary to scout the situation. So either someone got a rat and a raven mixed up or the significance of the rat is cultural. I'm not sure what's behind so many legends speaking of people coming from stones and inanimate objects. Well, there are some oddball clues that would take too long to piece together and hypothesise, and it's really not central to the theme here so I'll just pass over these curious legend particulars. Were the random people picked up before the flood by this moon and replaced on the earth afterwards? Yeah it's an out there hypothetical question, but some of the legends make you scratch your head wondering just what is behind them, and how does one explain them. Details aside, this is another clearly global flood legend.

Eastern Brazil (Rio de Janiero region):

There was a great wizard that had twin sons, one good and one evil who were always arguing. During one heated argument the good brother was so frustrated he stamped his foot and the earth cracked open causing water to shoot out of the ground so high it hit the clouds and flooded the entire world. The two brothers escaped the flood by climbing trees (or survived in canoes as another version says) until the waters were gone and they could come back to the ground. From these two brothers came the Tupinambas and Tominus tribes which have never gotten along well. [Based on internet quoting Gaster, pp. 124-125; Vitaliano, p. 175]

This legend has the interesting detail about water shooting out of the ground (or as the bible says the fountains of the great deep were broken up) as caused by some great impact on the earth, indicated by the brother's stamping his foot. And it's noted that it was caused by the struggle of good and evil, similar to how this struggle caused the destruction of earth in the biblical version. This struggle between a good and bad brother could be interpreted many different ways and that might be the point of the legend being told this way.

Eastern Brazil

I include this legend here because of something I clued into just dawned on me.

God, named Tupi by the Brazilians, warned Tamanduare the medicine man that there was a flood coming that would cover the entire earth so he told him to live in a palm tree on top of a lofty peak. So he and his family heeded the warning and as soon as they got to the top of the mountain it started to rain, and continued to rain until the whole earth was flooded. The water even covered the summit of the mountains including the one Tamanduare was on so they climbed the Palm tree and lived there eating the tree's fruit until the water subsided. When the flood was over they came down and repopulated the world. [Internet based on Frazer, pp. 255-256]

Though many flood legends are similar to the biblical flood legend of a family of 8 people surviving on a boat with many animals, I also noticed that a lot of flood legends not only mentioned that all the mountains were covered with water, just like the bible says, but that some legends also added that people climbed the trees on top of the mountains to escape the flood. Many legends said the same thing that people climbed the trees when the flood covered the mountains. Some mentioned that the trees eventually were submerged too, but not all. I had discounted these for a long time until it dawned on me that this was theoretically possible. The bible states all the mountains were covered with water to '15 cubits and upward'. And all the people 'on the face of the ground' were destroyed. "Upward" of course indicates that not all the mountains were the same height and some would be submerged by considerably more than 15 cubits. We've seen that the earth before the flood was a more modest terrain where huge mountains didn't exist. This would signify there were probably trees on the entire mountains with no "tree lines". 15 cubits is only about 22 feet, and even doubling that to 30 cubits would only be about 45 feet: trees could easily be taller than this. So it would be very possible, indeed probable, that even though the mountains were all covered, there would be trees sticking out of the water! This never dawned on me before. So the legends talking about people surviving in trees on the tops of mountains is plausible and for bible purists, it doesn't contradict the bible because they were not "on the face of the ground". Could a few people survive a year in tree tops eating fruit and maybe the odd monkey that might have been in them? There are enough of these types of legends that it makes you wonder. For example an eastern Ecuador legend mentions a boy fleeing to the top of a palm tree on a mountain top, returning many days later when the waters had subsided. Another Eastern Brazilian legend says that two brothers ran to the highest mountains and climbed a couple trees, helping their wives up with them and the legend continues on after they survived the flood.

How soon did the water subside to reveal the tops of the mountain ground surface again? Noah's ark grounded about 3000 feet below the peak of Mount Ararat. How much of Ararat was showing and for how long before he landed? Did a few wary people grab seeds, stuff them in their pockets and grab armfuls of food and run for the hills? Could they have survived long enough to plant a few crops and live to survive on them? Couldn't some mountain tops have been covered with fruit trees? Could they have made fishing poles and fished from the trees and live off fish too? I can't say no. Perhaps it wasn't likely as it would be difficult to live 6 months to almost an entire year in a tree on almost no resources, but not impossible. If only a few people managed to get to the mountains in time as the water initially would have come pouring down very fast, some mountains with trees would have no one on them and within sight of one that did have a survivor or two. One could float on a log back and forth to another treed topped mountain for more fruit. Indeed some legends even suggest this sort of thing happened. A long time ago someone suggested this idea of people surviving the flood in trees to me and I discounted it out of hand...now I'm not so sure. This puts another possibility out there and I must admit this is eye opening for me.

North American Flood legends

Aztec Valley of Mexico (20°N, 100°W)

"In the valley of Mexico there lived a pious man named Tapi. One day the Creator of all things appeared to him and said: 'Build a boat to live in, and take your wife with you, and a pair of every animal there is. Make haste for your time is at hand!' Tapi did as he was told, despite the insults and mockery of his neighbours, who thought him mad. Hardly had he finished when it began to rain. It rained without ceasing, the valley was flooded, men and animals fled to the mountains, but they too were submerged. The earth became one great ocean, and the only creatures left alive were those in Tapi's boat."

When it stopped raining, the waters began to sink and the sun came out again. Tapi sent forth a dove: it did not return and Tapi rejoiced because he understood that the dove had found a patch of dry ground to rest on" (Book 21 pg 142) Clearly another global flood legend like the biblical one though not as expressive or detailed. It does note that the builder of the boat was ridiculed, as one might guess was the case.

Michoacan (Mexico) (19°N 102°W)

A flood began, and when the waters started to rise, a man named Tezpi along with his wife, children, seeds and animals got into a great craft to survive the flood. Once the waters receded, the man sent out a vulture to check if the land had emerged, but the vulture found lots of dead creatures to live off of and never returned. So later he sent out a humming bird and it did return with a fresh twig in its mouth. [Based on Gaster, p. 122] The song the bird hummed was not mentioned.

Bella Coola (British Columbia) (52°30'N, 127°W)

Masmasalanich, the Creator of Man, attached the earth firmly by a strong rope to keep the sun at the proper distance and to the keep the earth from sinking. One day Masmasalanich stretched the rope, causing a fierce storm and the earth sank and was overrun by water, which eventually covered over the tops of the mountains. Many people who had boats were out in the water but were still drowned, and others were driven far away. Finally Masmasalanich shortened the rope and the earth emerged again from the water and man spread out all over it again. Different languages happened from the people being scattered, whereas before the flood there was only one speech. [Based on internet excerpts of Frazer, p. 320]

This is actually quite interesting. Short and tight but has a lot of clues in it. It indicates the earth had shifted out of its normal orbit by something that caused the great flood. It also indicates that some of the people before the flood besides Noah had some boats but the year on the waters either drowned them or they starved to death. It also mirrors the biblical note that before the flood all men spoke one language and an incident not really alluded to in this legend spread man out across the globe which is tied to the cause of the diversity of languages.

Tsimshian (British Columbia) (53°N, 129°W)

There's another short B.C. flood legend that has some telling bits.

A flood was sent because man had taken to "ill behaviour" and nearly everyone died in this flood except for a few. Sometime after the flood, people were overwhelmed by fire. Before the flood there were no mountains or trees, but they were created after the flood. [Based on internet story by Frazer, p. 319]

This short legend unwittingly speaks of two catastrophes, water and fire. Although Noah made an ark and many other legends speak of him in a boat, a box or an ark made of wood from TREES before the first global flood, this clearly indicates there is some mistake in this legend, but based on what, I can't be positive. As we'll see in coming sections there were flood incidences that were caused by cataclysms that included a lot of heat and fire, which is probably the cause of the destruction of trees, sometime after the global flood, but remembered after a subsequent flood, and so they've mixed the two up. We'll see how this could happen later on. We know vast amounts of coal exist throughout the world and something had to have happened to destroy this immeasurable number of trees, and then bury them to form coal. However this legend also mentioned there were no mountains before the flood which geologists have realized is the case at some point in earths past. So it's neat to find this interesting confirmation in this out of the way legend.

Squamish B.C.

I found this one while reading an old Beaver magazine during the time this book was being proofread and I had to include it.

Chief Mathias Joe Capilano, whose Father met Edward VII and who himself met George VI, and whose forefathers met Captain Vancouver, and I believe has a bridge named after the family in Vancouver somewhere, is quoted in the June 1939 edition of the Beaver (page 37). Chief Joe teaching to his son of the centuries old story of the flood is quoted. "The Great Man flooded the earth because the man he created was getting too smart for his own good. After the Flood, the Great Man took away the common language and made the survivors learn a new language of their own. This is true now, for a few miles from here live tribes whose language we do not understand. The Great Man did this so that men would not be so smart again. The Squamish knew the flood was coming. The bears became striped and the fish from the sea changed colour. The leaves on the trees and the grass were different in the year before the flood."

This particular flood legend is a great find, as not only does it speak of the changed languages that occurred after the Tower of Babel incident, but it speaks specifically of the declined intelligence of man that I spent a long chapter in my first book establishing, and is one of the few legends that refers to this decline or devolving of mankind. I'm not certain what the striped bears, changed fish and altered grass and trees have to do with the flood but include it here as I've not seen these bits mentioned in any other legends and so I include them in this book.

Great Lake tribes (83°W, 42°N)
Before any missionaries came to the Great Lakes area the tribes told of a time when their Great Father was warned in a dream that an enormous flood would soon cover the earth. He built a large raft and saved himself and all the animals. (Book 35 pg 20) Short and sweet.

When the story of a great event gets old and well known, maybe even a bit worn out when people get tired of hearing it from it being told time and time again, often you might cut it short, if you're not one of the people that like to hear the sound of your own voice. When you think about it, there really isn't much to the flood story of Noah, so that if I was to condense it in a 'Readers Digest version': Man became immoral and destructive, so God chose a man and his family who hadn't turned his back on God to save and told him the earth was going to be flooded, so he needed to build a boat for him and all the animals which will come to him. The flood lasted a year, covered all the mountains, then the boat finally landed on a mountain. The man sent out a few birds to check for dry land and when it was safe the world starts fresh. And even that is long winded compared to some legends of the flood. I must like the sound of hunting and pecking.

Yurok (North California coast) (41°30'N, 123°30'W)
There was a great flood that was caused by the sky falling and hitting the water which created huge waves. This is why seashells and redwood logs can be found on the highest points in the land. Only two women and men were saved as they saw the flood coming and jumped into a boat. The owner of the sky gave these people a song and when they sung it Sky-Owner sent them a rainbow as a promise the world would never be covered by water again. [based on Internet citing a book by Bell, p. 68]

Here we see an obvious reference to the flood being caused by an asteroid and it is the same flood of Noah as the rainbow gift is also included in this legend. It even states some evidence that was easily found by people such as shells on mountains which we still see today. Maybe the kids asked why there were sea shells on the mountains, and so the answer stuck with the legend.

Twana (Puget Sound, Washington) (47°30'N, 123°W)
All mankind was wicked, so to punish man, a flood happened that covered all the land except one mountain. People that had canoes escaped to the highest peak in their country, which they called "Fastener." They fastened their canoes with long ropes to the tallest tree on this mountain but it was still not enough as the water rose over this mountain too and submerged the tree. Some of the canoes broke their moorings and drifted west; those people formed a tribe to the west which speaks a language like that of the Twanas. Because those people drifted away, the present Twana tribe is small. [Based on an Internet quote of Frazer, p. 324]

This appears to be combining the world flood legend that drowned even the tallest mountains with later flood legends where they afterwards met other survivors much later with the same language but changed in some ways due to separation, Like France and Quebec...sorta.

Caddo (Oklahoma, Arkansas) (33°N, 94°W)
Before the waters covered the world there was a woman who was told to kill the four children she had given birth to because they were monsters, but she refused and let them grow. But being monsters they

turned out evil and as they grew they became impossible to kill. To be safe one day while they were in the camp they stood with their backs together and grew together into one single powerful monster that could reach the sky. People then lived at the base of the monsters because they couldn't bend down to kill them while the monsters grabbed other people with their long arms and ate them.

A man who saw the future heard a voice saying to plant a hollow reed and then was told when he saw all the birds fly south he and his wife should climb naked into the reed along with pairs of good animals. Once in the reed the rain and rising waters submerged everything except the monster's heads and the top of the reed. Turtle destroyed the monster by digging under it, uprooting it so that it fell apart and has now become the four directional corners of the earth.

Once the waters subsided and winds dried the earth, there was little left except barren earth and the wife wondered how they would survive. The man just told her to go to sleep and after four nights in their grass hut they woke to see corn grown all around them. A voice told them corn was their holy food and if the day comes when they plant corn and something else comes up, the world would end. After this the voice was heard no more. [Internet based on Erdoes & Ortiz, p. 120-122]

In the light of some of the events today this is something of an eerie flood legend. With the known biblical flood as a backdrop we can assume the monstrous children of the woman were the giants that changed the course of history and set man on the path to destruction. The reed like the gourd of the Burmese flood legend is obviously the ark. And this is another legend with a turtle playing a major part which makes me truly wonder what the origin of this parallel is. But the eerie part I think is the corn legend that says when you plant it and something else comes up this will indicate the world will end. There has been a lot of genetic tinkering with crops in general and corn specifically, and many patented corn types exist along with laws to protect the patent. Meaning that if you planted corn in your field and happen to have any of these patented types of corn planted and grown found in your crop, your crop can be seized. With corn mutations and genetic alterations being done so much on corn, it makes perfect sense that someone could plant corn and have something weird and monstrous grow that would definitely not be corn in its place. Interestingly enough the origin of corn is unknown, nor are the original plants used to create corn known. It's entirely plausible that genetic tinkering at some point could cause corn to revert to its original state, which of course would not be corn. The Hopi tribe of America have lately been preparing for the end of the world and much of their civilization centers around corn. It makes one scratch your head and wonder.

Ye Olde Grigori

Though this legend doesn't talk about the flood it does match up with the prelude to the flood

The book of Enoch says "...the Grigori" broke through their vows on the shoulder of the hill, Ermon, and saw the daughters of men how good they are, and took to themselves wives, and befouled the earth with their deeds, who in all times of their age made lawlessness and mixing, and the giants were born and marvellous big men of great hostility."

This quite mirrors the biblical reference to giants and seems more clearly to state they were the result of the intermarriage. I looked up "Grigori" and it means 'watcher' and or 'fallen angel' watcher angel or angel watcher. (Book 12 page 135)

Satisfactory Sampling.

If you were to take the time to plot the global flood legends from the samples covered here using the longitudes and latitudes I provided, you would see that at least three widely dispersed locations from every continent (except Antarctica) are represented as well as vast open waters that contain a few islands such as Hawaii, Polynesian and New Zealand. There may be Antarctic flood legends that exist, but we probably know them more as Lemurian or some other lost civilization that few if any connect with Antarctica because people assume Antarctic's placement and ice coverage are older than civilized man. We'll chat about Antarctica later on.

It is clear that the global flood stories are told in ancient legends from around the globe and are not limited to just the Middle East, or bible lands and Hebrew texts. This was just a sampling of global flood legends to illustrate they exist everywhere. For more complete collections of such legends check out books or follow reference leads. This has to stand as very strong evidence that such a flood occurred. As to what caused the flood, there is some debate, but the ancient legends also indicate how it happened. Not all of them give clues to the cause, but enough of them do to be able to piece it together, as mentioned in my opening section. But here's something I found later.

Cause of the Global flood: The Aztecs believed that Atonatiuh (their word meaning "Water-sun" the first world civilization) was destroyed by a deluge caused by the planet Maldek between Mars and Jupiter, which exploded into asteroids producing the great floods on earth. (Book 23 pg 149) It felt pretty good to find that confirmation, and some of these flood legends mentioned above, which I might add I read after my first book was published also had this clue contained in them. Well I did read book 23 of my bibliography, but I must have missed this tidbit or it was a subconscious note I fell in line with as I read more.

Whether or not you believe my deduction of the cause of the flood or someone else's is immaterial; the flood happened as enough witnesses testimony exists that it would stand up in court as an event that happened, despite the diversity of ways this event has been conveyed to us down through the ages. Every jury would have to say that beyond a reasonable doubt that a global flood occurred. You the reader thankfully did not witness it, but when we read in the newspaper or hear on the radio that a jury convicts someone, we usually take their word and say that so and so did such and such, and we are no longer told to say the incident is "alleged" to have occurred. It is not an 'alleged' global flood, it happened.

I understand the bias against the Bible and it's version of the flood. Many people have become alienated from the Bible and the religions that promote it and stand on its principles because 'bible thumpers' have sometimes been something of a 'in your face lot'. I myself have sincerely urged people to 'see' things that appeared painfully obvious to me and consequently have actually pushed some people further away from the thing I wanted them to see. I'm pretty lame at 'witnessing'. Not everyone has the gift of evangelism like Billy Graham had at one time. The September 1955 issue of Readers Digest showed not only how many hundreds of thousands of people flocked to hear him preach, it showed that about 90% of people who took a hold of the values and life he promoted stayed with it as surveys showed from two years after his crusades concluded. Sometimes bible promoters can tend to be less than great at sharing our discoveries without guilt trips. The bible say Christians are to be ready on the drop of a hat to explain their hope if someone asked, and not shove it down people's throats. What's somewhat ironic is that today many people are turning to other religions and ancient philosophies and are finding the flood legend repeated in their new beliefs. Well like they say…"you aint seen nuthin yet!"… wait till you get a load of the local flood legends.

Anyway since it is safe to assume the global flood happened, let's dig around and see what evidence we can find that confirms this event happened.

Chapter 2

The Evidence of the Great Flood

Though many biblical writers and scholars have found countless evidences of a flood in geological backdrops, they have virtually always understood the evidence to be of a global flood. They have assumed that the bible speaks of one flood and therefore all extensive flood evidence must be attributed to this flood. This is something I try to undo in this book. There was NOT just one flood and indeed the bible itself speaks specifically of at least two. However ancient legends from around the world indicate there were as many as four major floods, which were apparently almost worldwide in scope, so it's understandable they could be assumed to be evidence of the global flood. If your basement had a habit of flooding in stormy weather, after four or five floods could you remember what got damaged in which flood? Would an expert be able to tell you had five floods and be able to distinguish there were five floods if you just told him there'd been a flood? I have to admit, I am not a geologic expert, and though my finding of known evidence will be ample, I can't be absolutely positive of my conclusions as to which flood the evidence points to, as I simply don't have the resources to do field work, travel and accompany experts who might be supportive with my conclusions to assist in analysing the physical locations. Perhaps this book will be a groundwork that opens eyes of some branches of science to look closer once they realize there were more floods. The 19th century geologists knowing and usually accepting of the biblical story of the flood were confused by what appeared to them to be evidences of multiple floods. If nothing else this book should at least clear that question up: there *were* multiple floods, they just had to look a little deeper in ancient legends, folklore, and biblical sources, and realize that, if for example the legends and the bible say the sun moved backwards ten degrees, then this must be doing something besides just the sun's apparent position in the sky altering its course. The earth had to have moved in an extraordinary fashion to give this impression, and if the earth moved, so did the water and the air. My assessments of the flood evidences, whether they be global or local, will for the most part be based on logical assumptions of what evidence I find in conjunction with the legends I have become aware of which indicate floods and continental shifts took place in recorded history. That combined with knowing the general direction that the continental drift took, and an elementary grasp of mechanics of motions will aid my conclusions. These as you might guess are little more than basic needs for solid analysis, but because of a predisposition to solving puzzles with a high degree of 3-d space perception as found in tests I've taken, I think it will at least provide a good starting point. No doubt anyone who takes my newly lit torch for another lap will find flaws and much improve this ground breaking work. So, I will look at flood evidence and try and sort though the puzzle simply by these tools at my disposal, and hopefully a little clearer picture of the past will arise from the pieces I *do* manage to put together.

EVEREST UNDER WATER

One of the favourite proofs of a global flood for creationists is the fact that on Mount Everest has been found skeletons of "Marine animals, Ocean fishes, and shells and mollusks." That should clinch it for most people and indeed evolutionary scientists of the 19th century were "dismayed" when this fact was discovered. Jeffery Goodman asks the unavoidable question "How are we to explain the sea floor of remote times becoming lofty highlands of today? Instead of slowly creeping up, were the Himalayas born when the Indian subcontinent *slammed*, not pushed, into the Asian mainland? Were colossal upheavals and uplifts triggered? Did it take millions of years or just a few centuries to create the Himalayas? Two opposing geological schools of thought confront each other here: uniformitarianism versus catastrophism." (Book 19 pg 96)

One thing I didn't find with references to global flood and shells found on Everest was whether the shells found on Everest were open, closed or both. Opened ones only would indicate they died there before the flood then the ground rose slowly afterwards giving living examples a chance to migrate, or if the shells were closed signifying the mountains were suddenly thrust upwards sometimes after the global flood: Or both. Meaning Everest before the flood was a nonexistent underwater location where clams lived and died, and then suddenly the mountains thrust via horizontal movement slamming into India catching and burying living clams, which could not be opened due to surrounding dirt solidifying. But any way you slice it, marine remains on Mount Everest has to be eye opening to the harshest of critics of the global flood story. So I dug a little and found that the shells on Everest are all closed. Creationists assume this means it proves the global flood, but there's a 99% chance it doesn't. Why? Because the global flood was mainly water pouring/ raining down from the water shell making the water level around the globe rise. That would not suddenly enclose the clams; they would live a normal life then die and the shell would open. But with the clams being found closed means a sudden burial, death, then probably a subsequent unearthing in successive continental shifts for them to be found near the surface.

One thing is certain; Everest as it exists today did not exist at the time of the global flood. Geologic evidence clearly shows the world at one time was a much less exiting landscape, where the average height of land above sea level since the flood has tripled. This is almost counter intuitive; as you would think the land after the flood would be on average lower altitude above sea level with so much flood waters still remaining on the earth. This also clearly indicates that forces after the flood created mountains in a far shorter period than geologists would have us believe, particularly when you consider dates attributed to the global flood range from about 2400 BC to about 3500 BC. So that brings me to my next point.

TREES SPEAK OF THE FLOOD OCCURRING IN 3410 BC

Around 1988 dendrochronology (tree ring dating), the most accurate dating method in existence (because you can date global events to a specific year) had its 5400 birthday. From what I've read in all my sources, from the 1950's to the early 1990's, they noted that dendrochronology was good for nearly, to over 5400 years. Virtually all sources agree that this is as far back as you can reliably use tree rings to date events. Though some sources indicate there could be more rings, these extra rings appear to exist from times when unusually long winters, summers or more than one winter occurred during a single year. (You'll be able to deduce why we might have long winters, summers or more than one winter occurring during a single year affecting tree rings when you read chapter 4)

As a youth of about 18 and for years afterwards, I determined to double-check Ussher's date for creation which he stated as being 4004 BC, so I independently charted the dates in the bible to see what I would come up with for the date of creation and the flood. My date for creation varied from Ussher's as I came up with a date for the creation at 5066 BC and the flood occurring in 3410 BC. I included possible variables for the age of the earth, one of which, (assuming there could be something wrong with the Dendrochronology record) came to within just 24 years of Ussher's date. Doing the math with my chart, I realized that the date of the flood and the date for the initiation for tree rings both occurred in 3410 BC. That was a staggering discovery. Trees before the flood grew at extremely even rates as the climate during the antediluvian period was extremely consistent all year round, making tree rings difficult to spot and count or virtually nonexistent. Trees from this period could be said to have no rings at all, though evidence from pieces of wood pulled from the ark indicate wide tree rings did exist. So what 5400 years worth of tree rings proves is there had to be something that occurred to initiate the beginning of tree rings which we use for zeroing on exact dates for climate conditions and such. There are only two events that could initiate the beginning of tree rings as we know them: the flood and creation. But creation as the initiation for clear tree rings has to be eliminated, because if creation occurred in 3410 B.C. that would mean the flood occurred at 1754 B.C. (3410-1656 years from creation to the flood as preflood genealogy indicates). But no one would ever put the flood at such a recent date, so it has to be eliminated as a cause. Thus the flood could be the only event that initiates the existence of nice solid dateable tree rings ...and the dates match to the year. For those of you with their eye burning and seeing red because I assume creation here and a young earth, you'll have to read my first work where I disprove evolution in chapter 1 and disprove the old earth theory in chapter 5. It's easier to do than you might think. However I will include some new information I found while researching this work.

FORMATION AND BREAKDOWN OF RADIOACTIVE CARBON 14 NOT AT EQUILIBRIUM.

Evidence for the flood is the very air we breathe. I repeat a few paragraphs from my first book.

[RADIOACTIVE]CARBON 14 EQUILIBRIUM NOT YET ACHIEVED.

By one account it is said that [Radioactive] Carbon 14 forms in the atmosphere at the rate of 18.4 atoms per gram per minute and the decay of C14 is at the rate of 13.3 atoms per gram per minute. This is a huge point! The C14 in the atmosphere is not at a point of equilibrium!

If the air was at a point of equilibrium the C14 formation rate would equal the rate of decay!!! The point of equilibrium has been worked out and determined that the atmosphere would need to be 30,000 years old for the point of equilibrium to be met! This means the atmosphere cannot possibly be thirty thousand years old! It's been worked out that at this stage the present atmosphere can be no older than 10,000 years old! It's felt that this is also the upper limit of the age of the earth, but this in fact is only the upper limit of the age of the atmosphere[in its present state]. There's more!

Robert Whitelow found an error in the calculations of the rate of formation of C14 in the atmosphere mentioned above and he came up with the figure of 27 atoms of C14 per gram formed every minute! That means over twice as much C14 is being formed than is being broken down! This too has been extrapolated and it means the present atmosphere is only around 5000 years old! Doctor Henry Morris appeared to feel that this gave a low figure because he felt that this C14 reading in the atmosphere was an indication of the age of the earth, on the apparent assumption that the atmosphere was the same before the flood as after. However the atmosphere could NOT have been the same before the flood as it is now because a water sphere stopped radiation from the sun making any radioactive carbon 14 in the atmosphere. It only started to form AFTER the flood.

We have shown by dating the flood that the present atmosphere is about 5429 years old (as of 2019). This lines up with Robert Whitelow's figures for the formation of C14 exceptionally well as his figures thus indicate the atmosphere in its present state to be only about 5000 years old, exactly as is shown by the biblical date for the flood. (Book 9 pg 164-165) A variation of just 400 odd years, an extremely close match up considering how much play has been seen in some of these dating methods.

Whale skeleton found in the Himalayan Mountains. (Book 7 pg. 159).

This is another favourite of Creationists to parade out as evidence for the global flood. Perhaps, but, believe it or not, there is just as good a reason for it to indicate a local flood, which will become evident in Chapter 4. Now I could get silly and say that this was one of those whales evolutionists say hadn't yet gone back to the water on its legs and decided to do a bit of mountain climbing before it returned to the water and got lost in the mountains, but then who'd believe that; Whales walking...silly, silly, silly.

Similarly whale bones have been found in Minnesota in such numbers the farmers were making fences out of them. Whale skeletons are also found in Vermont and Montreal (Book 23 pg 108). This too indicates a flood, but once again it's not clear which type of flood, as there are good reasons to suspect both types of flood. In a global flood a few pods of whales could have been stranded in a large sea above North America while it was still partially submerged then as the temporary sea lost mass as the water was absorbed back into the ground or taken off to Mars or Venus, the whales had less and less area to swim and feed and perished. We'll suggest why this is just as good a piece of evidence for a local flood in chapter 5. Bones tend to disintegrate after few hundred years in more humid rainy climates so I'm surprised there were enough in good enough shape to make fences out of. This would suggest these bones weren't all that old, maybe 2 or 3000 years old at most.

AND YOU THOUGHT YOUR WIFE WAS SCARED OF A FEW CUTE LITTLE SPIDERS.

My favourite spider is the little black jumping spiders. I mentioned this once to a girlfriend who was freaked out by spiders and she said "you mean there's spiders that jump!?!...brrr". The first time I saw a cockroach I thought it was cool looking bug and it was about an inch long. I grabbed it and showed it to a girl at work thinking she would think it was cool too. Wow what a reaction! She ran from me screaming! Well these girls aint seen nothing yet!

Giant bugs found in the fossils indicate possibly 4-8 or more times the atmospheric pressure before the flood at sea level than we have today. Bugs can only grow to the size allowed by the amount of air they can absorb through their exterior. The amount of air they can absorb is the limiting factor in their size which is directly linked to the atmospheric pressure. Some have suggested extreme moist mists existed before the flood was the source for enough water to have existed for the flood. This has at least two flaws. The bible and other legends indicate there was a moon and stars visible before the flood. You could not see stars and the moon or even the sun from a globe enshrouded in dense mists. Earth would be like Venus if that had been the case. And huge amounts of mist would not increase the air pressure at sea level enough to create giant bugs that have been found in the fossil record such as 18 inch cockroaches, 6 foot long centipedes, 2 foot grasshoppers, three foot tarantulas, and dragon flies with a 50 inch wingspan. Only a complete water sphere surrounding the earth allows you to see the stars, can account for all the water on the earth to cover the mountains, and would force the atmospheric pressure at sea level to produce giant bugs. So oddly enough giant bugs found in the fossil record indicate there had to have been a flood for them to shrink to the size we find bugs at today. It'd be fun to find and show some of these giant bug fossils to the girls. I'm such a brat...

THE LIGHT DAWNS

Something just occurred to me as I proofread this last point. I had previously deduced few if any fossils would be created by the global flood due to the nature of the mechanics of water simply pouring and raining onto the globe. This would mean creatures just rotted and no fossil formation was possible. But obviously large preflood bug fossils exist. Though the atmospheric pressure for a few hundred years after the flood was still high enough that it might have created larger bugs than we have today, I doubt they'd reach those proportions. Fossils form from sudden encapsulation along with salt water and slurry providing hardening agents which would be abundant in tsunamis caused floods due to continental shifting. We appear to have two ways fossils can form here. Distinguishing how a particular fossil formed would help decipher which flood they point to. My guess is when water burst from the deep forcing dirt upwards and falling back down burying some creatures might have formed some of the preflood fossils.

THICK LAYERS OF CLAY

Often cited as evidence for the flood is the 9-12 foot layer of a specific type of "clay" or "mud" found in the excavations of Ur just like the Epic of Gilgamesh said occurred. The epic of Gilgamesh specifically notes that after the flood there was a layer of clay over the surface similar to a roof that was brought in from the direction of the south, clearly indicating a tsunami type of flood that brought the clay in, probably leaving behind ocean bottom deposits on the land. However, different sources call this layer found under Ur different things "A type of <u>clay</u> that could only have been left by water" (Book 1 pg 107) which contrasts with…"But after digging through eleven feet of <u>silted, dry mud</u>, …" (Book 17 pg 387) It's almost the tomayto / tomahto syndrome…is it clay or is it mud? Similar layers of clay or mud have been found buried under Kish, mud under Erech and at Shuruppak and 60 feet under Nineveh was found 13 layers and river sand. (Book 17 pg 388, book 6 pg 216, book 8 pg 75) All these places confirm if not a global flood, at least a vast local flood covering each of these areas. These layers of mud and sand are considered deep at a thickness of about 9, or 10 or 14 feet, but I can't quite decide if these sites indicate a local flood or the global flood.

As we'll see there were a handful of times the ocean literally burst forth onto land in many places all over the globe, which could really confuse the picture if during these instances the ocean deposited any sizable amount of ocean sediment onto the land. The layers of sediment on the ocean floors are said to be thousands of feet thick. There is a universal layer of clay around the globe which does confirm the existence of a universal flood because such a flood would deposit layers of clay as the sediments settled. What confuses me a little is if after the global flood occurred and there was left a universal layer of clay all over the planet (and there is) why isn't clay often found right at the surface and why are things growing? One can dig down in many places maybe as little as a foot and you hit clay. Clay is heavier than normal dirt so what I think occurred is the layers of clay settled first accounting for the universal layer of clay, then the mud settled, and mud is just wet dirt. Clay wouldn't be as deep over vast expanses of land whereas mud that settled later would make up the top soil when the land finally dried. But I'm guessing here, Hydraulic specialist could decipher how that works.

Bear in mind, the tumultuous action that accompanied the end of the three ages some time after the global flood where mountains formed, land folded, continents sunk and shifted, mixed up, overturned, slanted, and jumbled the layers of vast expanses of real estate would really mix up the puzzle. (See chapter 4)

WHAT ABOUT THAT BOAT OR ARK OR BOX OR WHATEVER YOU WANNA CALL IT?

Probably the most important evidence for the occurrence of a global flood as stated in many legends and the bible is the ongoing existence of Noah's ark. This single item is so validating to the flood legend and indeed the bible as a whole, that there is evidence to indicate there is actually a struggle to keep the arks existence unknown to the general world population. Between its nearly inaccessible location and the forces trying to keep its existence a secret, the reality of the ark is little known but to the few who actively search for the ark and attempt to substantiate its existence. But interestingly the accounts of sightings not only confirm its initial formation and survival, but the narratives of each sighting often creates corroboration for other accounts because no collusion between witnesses is possible, or so remote as to be statistically zero.

As we've read there are several named resting places for the ark suggested by legends of people who attempted to convert the global flood legend to give it a localised flavour; whereas the bible contrary to the trend, named a mountain remote from the people who wrote the historical sections of the bible. That location was the mountains of Ararat, fully 700 miles and two or three countries to the north east of Israel. If not for the story in the bible, few if any Hebrews would even know of that's mountains existence, so it's odd they would pick some mountain at random unless there was something to the story worth checking out.

Much of the following information is found in Tim. F. LaHaye and John D. Morris' book *The Ark On Ararat* and another ark book called *In Search of Noah's Ark* by Dave Balsiger and Charles E. Sellier. I've condensed the information they've found which covers over half their books into a few pages leaving out proofs and much background information and recommend these books for further reading if the following rouses up your interest. (Some brief more condensed ark information can be found in Book 1 pgs 101-103. Other books either ignore the sightings or refer to the inconclusive sightings such as wood found on Ararat, but ignore the sightings of the boat itself)

If one went to the base of the mountains of Ararat and talked to the people of the area from time immemorial to about 1910, the existence of the ark on the mountain was considered common knowledge.

Though the mountain access to the site of the ark is daunting even to the most accomplished of mountaineers, a few of the local people around Mount Ararat would know of someone who saw or touched the ark, and even relics from the ark were talked and known about. So we appear to be on the right track. Let's look at the history of sightings of the ark through the ages because even though these might be discounted by some as wishfully thinking stories, or possibly slanted by biblical biases, they offer interesting correlations to each other that can't be ignored, and actually confirm each other, just like two witnesses in a court can give similar testimony to substantiate and event.

Case in point: Berosus, a Babylonian historian whose writings at present have not been found, or worse have been destroyed during ancient library destructions, has been quoted by people whose writings *do* still exist and at the time of their works had access to the writings of Berosus. Alexander Polyhistor (c. 50 B.C.) quoted Berosus: "But of this ship that grounded in Armenia, some part still remain in the mountain of Gordyaeans (one of the local names for the mountains of Ararat) in Armenia, and some get pitch from the ship by scraping it off and use it for amulets. ... But the vessel in Armenia furnished the inhabitants with wooden amulets to ward off evil." (Book 71 Pgs 12-14.)

Now here's our second witness to these statements. The Armenians have traditions that they are direct descendants of Noah and lived in the area of Mount Ararat continuously even until now, though since the early 20th century they have been somewhat dispersed around the world. The Armenians maintained that the Ark still exists and during ancient times they used to make regular pilgrimages to the ark to worship there and they would take small pieces of the ark and make talismans and good luck charms from the wood. They say this practice continued until God began to prevent even the righteous to visit the ark and eventually the ark became buried in the snow.

It has been established that Mount Ararat was at one time a significantly lower mountain of not more than 12,000 feet. (It's now in excess of 17,000 feet) It may be hard to accept right now that this mountain could climb 5,000 feet during the time the Armenians lived here since the flood, but you will see as we go, that this was part and parcel of things that were happening around the globe during three intervals the ancients referred to as 'world ages'. So we'll leave the proof of that for a later chapter. This belief of the Armenians that God made access to the ark difficult would seem to me to be their interpretations of whatever caused mount Ararat to rise 5000 feet in tandem with the earth's total mass of atmosphere being reduced here on earth as occasional upheavals and catastrophes, along with Venus and Mars stealing our atmosphere made the higher elevation around the globes inhospitable, colder and less accessible.

Now consider, it's highly unlikely Berosus' history which briefly includes mention of the Armenians would be widely read by the Armenians to the point that the Armenians would make up an ancient tradition about their people based on someone else's biographical assumptions. (For example The Inuit Eskimos don't say they crossed over the Bering strait because they've been told by anthropologists this is how they got to America...no, they say 'silly' stories like the gods flew them to the north in giant birds. That's their story and they are sticking to it.) People aren't going to compromise their history to satisfy some historian's erroneous historical accounts, they are going to stick with what they know to be true and if some historian gets it wrong, well they keep their history regardless until someone gets it right. Berosus' history verifies the Armenians histories in two ways, by telling of their proximity and access to the ark, and by mentioning the curious practice of making amulets from pitch and wood from the ark. Thus this tandem of two sets of histories about the same thing that substantiate each other can at least be set down here as one verified story of a significantly important ship sitting on a mountain which appears to be linked to the story of Noah, his ark and the global flood. I mean ask yourself how many ships are going to be found sitting on a mountain. Well actually that's not a very good question because as we will see, there have been a few. But this one in particular matches up with the stories of the legends and the biblical story of the flood exactly.

Josephus made a more whitewashed version of Hebrew history, concentrating on the glories of the Jews past while passing over some of the darker aspects of Jewish history. For example he conveniently ignored Moses' faults like his killing of the Egyptian, but went on at length about his Egyptian military history of which the bible makes no mention. The bible is virtually nonexistent in India because they have other holy books, so few in India have ever even heard of the bible. Similarly few people of the western world except biblical scholars or long time Christians have heard of the history of Josephus, let alone read this daunting work. Josephus wrote his histories around 70 A.D. but he too had access to some documents and histories that have since been lost. His written work is so enormous, that standard college text books have nothing on him. My copy is so small and the text so tiny I still have not been able to finish my copy because eye strain limits me to about two pages at a time.

In his work entitled the *Antiquities of the Jews* Josephus', states "After this the ark rested on the top of a certain mountain in Armenia; "..."However, the Armenians call this place (Αποβατήρον) *The Place of Descent*; for the ark being saved in that place, its remains are shown there by the inhabitants to this day.

"Now all the writers of barbarian histories make mention of this flood and of the ark; among whom is Berosus the Chaldean; for when he is describing the circumstances of the flood, he goes on thus:-'It is said there is still some part of this ship in Armenia, at the mountain of the Cordyæans; and that some people carry off pieces of the bitumen, which they take away, and use chiefly as amulets for the averting of mischief's.' Hieronynus, the Egyptian, who wrote the Phoenician Antiquities, and Mnaseas, and a great many more, also make mention of the same. Nay, Nicolaus of Damascus, in his ninety-sixth book, hath a particular relation about them where he speaks thus:- 'There is a great mountain in Armenia, over Minyas, called Baris, upon which it is reported that many who fled at the time of the Deluge were saved: and that one who was carried in an ark came to shore upon the top of it: and that the remains of the timber were a great while preserved." (Josephus Antiquities of the Jews, Chapter III, Section 5, 6)

In the days when religious values were placed higher in society in general than materialism, it was considered common knowledge that the Ark still existed. For example Theophilus of Antioch wrote in 180 A.D. "And the Ark, the remains are to this day to be seen in the Arabian mountains." (Book 71 pg 16) One might ask 'How could a wooden boat survive to as late as 180 A.D. and not rot away?' A fair question because the time that had elapsed ...well by my reckoning was about 3500 years in 180 A.D. The bible says it was covered with pitch inside and out, and the higher elevation put it out of reach of harm's way from most of the casual vandalism, and the rarefied cold air probably kept it preserved with minimal if any microbial or insect infestation, if the pitch all by itself didn't prevent its demise in the first place.

But the ark has been seen even later than 180 AD. In the fourth century Bishop of Medzpin set out for the mountains of Armenia, in particular Mount Ararat to see if he could find the ark. The mountain almost finished him but he somehow was refreshed and beside him he found a wooden plank from the ark. True, that's not very convincing, but he was at the summit and no trees grow above the tree line well below where he was situated, so where did the hand hewn wooden plank come from?

Though not the ark, in the latter half of the fourth century, the altar where Noah sacrificed some clean animals was mentioned as still existing at the base of Mount Ararat by Bishop Epiphanius. Around the same time John Chrysostom wrote "Do not the mountains of Armenia testify to it, where the ark rested? And are not the remains of the Ark preserved there to this very day for our admonition?" Again the ark's presence and continued existence was considered common knowledge and easily verifiable, even in the late fourth century (Book 71 pg 21)

Around 610 A.D. Isidore of Seville is quoted: "Ararat is a mountain in Armenia, where the historians testify that the Ark came to rest after the Flood. So even to this day wood remains of it are to be seen there."

The Ark keeps popping up in unexpected references. In the seventh century the East Roman emperor Heraclius after conquering the Persian city of Thamanin near the base of Mount Ararat, used the opportunity to climb Mount Ararat to visit the remains of the Ark.

Marco Polo mentions that in his travels while passing through Armenia he happened on information from the locals about the large high mountain that was called "the mountain of the Ark" because it is said the Ark of Noah rested up there. Though he didn't see it, his noting this local record by such a famous person is worth mentioning.

In around the time of 1254 it seems snow coverage of the mountain wasn't a problem, and it was noted that there was always visible a black speck which was known to be the Ark, as mentioned by a monk named Jehan Haithon (Book 71 pg 22)

The mountain at some point must have had some readjustments because in 1316 another monk named Odoric wanted to go visit the ark but was told by the folks of the country no one could ever climb the mountain. Not being a mountaineer, he was not willing to risk his neck and accepted the existence of the Ark on the mountain as taken for granted. (Ibid)

An interesting detail about the ark pops up in 1647. Adam Olearius in his book *Voyages and travels of the Ambassadors* states he lived near Mount Ararat in 1633 and was told that time had hardened the wood of the Ark into almost stone. He was shown a cross made of very hard black wood which the people told him was made from wood from the Ark. True, it's just an unusual piece of wood, but it is clearly related to the early stories of the Armenians making relics out of the ark; this apparently was just one of the many relics of the ark around in Armenia at the time, and not considered particularly extraordinary. Another cross made from the wood of the Ark was given to Jan Janzoon Struys in 1670 by a person who lived on the mountain. He noted that though the trip up the mountain was bad like the locals stated, he said it was not inaccessible.

The Ark's existence came to the attention of an American in the early 1800's when Claudius James Rich came in contact with a Persian named Aga Hussein. Hussein stated that he had climbed Mount Ararat at one time and actually saw the Ark. (book 71 pg. 28)

On June 20th 1840 a gigantic earthquake hit Mount Ararat that opened up a massive cleft section of the upper region of the mountain by creating a massive gorge apparently making the path to the higher parts of the mountain a little bit more accessible, because from this point on there have been an increasing number of sightings of the Ark recorded. Unfortunately the earthquake destroyed and buried an 8 century old monastery built on the mountain where the gorge now exists, which housed several relics from the Ark along with ancient manuscripts and books. The earthquake also devastated the town of Ahora situated at the foot of the mountain at the 5000 foot level.

WHAT MOTIVATES YOU?

If someone went through a hospital and miraculously healed everyone in the hospital and anyone who came afterwards, he'd put nurses and doctors out of a job: he might not be popular with them afterwards. In the bible Paul cast a familiar spirit out of a girl who was a source of gain to the people she lived with, and when they realized their meal ticket had evaporated, they took it out on Paul. They didn't care for the wellbeing of the girl, they cared about their pocket and how she helped fill it. Once people build up an empire they have an incentive to keep that empire, whatever it is, to keep it going. Drug pushers have motivation for keeping junkies hooked, and evolutionists apparently have a motivation for discrediting anything that validates the bible. Some people will go to extreme lengths to keep the status quo, and some evolutionists have freely admitted they don't like the idea of a God directing their sexual freedoms, or moral choices. Gambling houses want suckers to place their bets, whore houses want johns to bleed dry, and whoever is a source of easy money is wanted by someone who cares for little else. The world sadly is filled with people who have no wish for a world to suddenly turn to the bible or God, even if it just means they don't want someone preaching at them or making them feel guilty. Pubs would go broke and police would get bored like they did after the Welsh revival around 1905. Whatever the motivation for these presumed evolutionists in this next sighting was, clearly they were extremely antagonistic towards any proof of God and the bible.

In 1856 15 year old Haji Yearman and his father were visited by three "vile men" who did not believe in the bible or God and were scientists and apparently evolutionist, though Darwin's book wouldn't be published for another 3 years, so this may be an assumption presumed later on simply by it being the only alternative. Anyway these men were atheists and came to Armenia specifically to debunk the bible story and wanted a guide to take them to whatever it was that was supposed to be the Ark which was apparently confusing the superstitious locals to believe in this myth: at least that's my guess from reading the story; and I'm sure they probably thought something along these lines. They wanted to prove the existence of the ark was a fraud and that this boat or whatever it was on the mountain, was a fake. Well Haji's Dad was picked out, and hired to take these people to the ark, probably because they were told he knew where the ark was. He did, because he and his son with no guess work took the three men right to the ark. Normally Armenians were reluctant to show the ark to people fearing it would displease God figuring the ark shouldn't be disturbed until the end of the world. The father thought proving its existence to three atheists would help the world finally believe the bible was true. It had been a very hot summer and the ark was showing very clearly, exposing a good portion of the prow resting partially in a glacial lake. Haji described the Ark as being a little way down from the top of the mountain, in a little valley surrounded by some small peaks. The ark had a no windows and a large door was missing but the door's entrance was of immense size, and the ark appeared to be built like a huge house set on the hull of a ship. The entire ship was covered with a varnish or lacquer that was incredibly strong, both outside and inside. They went inside the ark and did a lot of exploring. It appeared to Hadji to have several floors, stages and compartments which had bars on them like animal cages do.

The Scientists were 'dumbstruck' but soon found their tongue... and their rage. They were furious, because what they had set out to disprove as a pathetic myth was staring them in the face as true as the sun in the sky. But instead of realizing "gosh maybe we were wrong" and making some life altering decisions, they almost unbelievably decided to try and destroy the ark. They tried hacking at it but the wood was like stone, so they tried burning it but it was so hard it just simply wouldn't burn. So they turned their wrath onto Hadji and his father and said that if they ever told anyone about what they had found here they would be tortured and murdered and they took a solemn oath of the pair and said they would be keeping track of them. For fear of their lives they held the secret to themselves except between their most trusted family and friends.

When Hadji was old and nearly dying he felt he had to tell someone about this event before he died, and felt reasonably safe in doing so because he thought the three scientists must be dead by then, as he was considerably younger than them at the time of the event. Curiously about three years after he told his story to Harold H. Williams, one of the three atheists that tried to destroy the ship made a deathbed confession of his part of the story in London, which confirmed Hadji's story. It appeared as a very small newspaper story, even as far away as the States. Strangely since then no one has been able to track down the small newspaper story, but looking into this 'keep the ark a secret' business, I'm not entirely surprised. I knew someone who saw a story in a newspaper she did not want a certain party to know about or see any time ever, so she advertised to buy copies of that particular paper, and then she would burn them. She was charged with tampering with public records because she even destroyed the microfilm that contained the newspaper story. Years later a copy of that paper was found and was shown to her and she grabbed it and threw it in the fire. Though the microfilm missing page was replaced using a distant library's copies of the records, it again disappeared, but was cleverly replaced so as not to be noticed and has never been replaced since. It wouldn't surprise me if something like this happened with this news story. This sort of thing happens again and again with credible Ark stories and pictures as you will see. One interesting corroboration in this story is his description of the wood being hard as rock. Hadji could not have come across other stories of the ark mentioning the state of the wood, so it becomes another confirming piece of evidence of the Ark's existence. (Book 71 pgs 46-52)

In 1883 Mount Ararat made worldwide news when it experienced another major earthquake and avalanche that sent tons of rock and ice down the slopes burying villages on the slopes of the mountains. The seriousness of the event prompted a Turkish scientific expedition which happened to include a member of the British diplomatic corps. The Constantinople news release containing this story has never been found, but the story exists in the British *Prophetic Messenger* using the Levant *Herald* as its source. Apparently in an effort to secure the slide area from further incidences for the villages below, they stumbled on a "gigantic structure of very dark wood, embedded at the foot of one of the glaciers, with one end protruding, and which they believe to be none other than the old Ark in which Noah and his family navigated the waters of the Deluge." They estimated the height of the ark to be between 40 and 50 feet. The article gave a rough description of the location of the ark. The ark was described as being painted with a dark brown pigment and constructed of great strength. It noted that the ark had been "a good deal broken at the angles", possibly from the slow descent of the glacier. I'm not entirely sure what "broken at the angles" means, and I thought maybe the ark had cracked from under its own weight. But one of the corners was broken so that might be what they refer to. The interior was almost filled with Ice, but they were able to explore a few compartments which were between 12 and 15 feet high. This would indicate the ark probably had four stories.

Sometimes a story is just too big to hide and this is one time the news of the ark's discovery hit the headlines...around the world. The news of the ark did initiated some humorous remarks by the New York herald on August 10th 1883, suggesting Jules Verne could come up with a way to bring the Ark to America, and the cost of the transfer could be paid by the value of ice which the Ark contained. The Navy was suggested as a good buyer of the ark because they could learn some lessons in how to make a boat that doesn't rot. It was also suggested that the government could make some extra money from the wood the navy got rid of from the ark, because they would no doubt try to improve the boat, and by selling the 'extra' wood they cut off from the ark for making canes and Church pews, presumably to seat all the new churchgoers and converts to the bible's way of life when they heard the news about the Ark being found, proving the bible. The Chicago Tribune of the same date noted that the length of the boat was not discernable but if it ended up being 300 cubits that this would go hard with disbelievers.

As huge as the news about the Ark's discovery was, there were some people who found ways to disparage the event. Some suggested that just like the 'syndicate' that tried to sell relics promoting the existence of a missing link by planting bones of the Cardiff Giant, and another 'syndicate' that tried to sell a copy of the bible signed by Moses to the British Museum, another such syndicate would no doubt go to Persia and break into the Ark and 'find' the original log book written by Noah. They suggested that Philology (the love of learning), ethnology and archaeology can fight it out among themselves and the newspaper can only report on the events.

That these news stories exist from 1883 which broke the secular barrier concerning the existence, the uncovering and discovery of the Ark, pro and con, should give sceptics pause.

The news of the Ark's discovery in 1883 appears to have rekindled an exploration movement because in 1887 John Joseph, Prince of Nouri (a Chaldean title of some kind) who was prone to exploring things like the source of the Euphrates (which starts at or near Mount Ararat) also said he made three attempts to find the ark for himself, the third of which proved successful. He found the ark almost completely exposed except for the central section which was covered in snow. He noted the beams were very thick and a dark reddish brown. He said he had made measurements of the ark and they coincided with those mentioned in Genesis chapter six. He was a constantly active person and seems in some ways more interested in adding another notch or experience to his impressive resume, or ticking off things on his "bucket list": been there, done that, time to move on. For example later on he discovered gold on Moon Mountain, but he doesn't appear to have even profited by the discovery. He did try to "promote love, harmony, and cooperation between religions by trying to get the Ark displayed at the Chicago World Fair of 1893 and he had actually convinced a group of Belgian financers to go ahead with the project when the Turkish officials refused permission. Though he had a ton of accomplishments and titles from his home land, and was something of a successful evangelist, his lofty titles and such seemed to mean nothing to some people in the west. So much so that strangely in 1892, just nine years after the Ark made world news, Keslo Carter, a supposed defender of the bible and an early propagator of the "canopy theory" completely discounted "Dr. Nouri" and his claim to finding the ark because he "failed to produce any satisfactory credentials or indorsements." (sic) and said "There is, however, certainly no objection ...to the possibility of the ark being found by someone if it were ever there." (Book 71 pg 67-69) So did he or didn't he believe in the flood story? That seems to me like a strange position to take for someone who supposedly believes in the bible and the brotherhood of others who do and hold to the principles it promotes, such as 'honesty'. Nouri's attempts to promote the ark met with enthusiasm by most of those who heard him, but eventually it just led to disappointments as he just couldn't get any real action going on some sort of Ark project. He felt it would be a great attraction but he finally had to let the matter rest. So the Ark continues to reside at #1 Ararat Way, Turkey: Postal Code 00-00-01. But what would make a man go out of his way and spend so much effort in promoting something if it doesn't exist? He had to have been urged and encouraged by its existence and his personal sighting of the boat, because if he hadn't found it there is *no* motivation.

20TH CENTURY.

Every summer Georgie Hagopian was taken by his uncle to graze his flock on the Ararat Mountain. In 1908 and 1910, they would approach the mountain from the south as usual then walk around it to get to an access and start the ascent from the north and then climb for the grazing areas; but during these two years his uncle took him on an extra little detour. His uncle knew exactly where to go and on these occasions the mountain was more hospitable, so the trip was doable in one day and they could get back to the villages by nightfall; so they went right to the ark. This sort of thing was quite common for the Armenians and there were plenty of fathers who would take their sons to see the relic.

When some political strife between Turkey and Russia occurred, the Armenians sided with the patriot Russians. But these Russians were suddenly influenced by the revolution and had to abandon Turkey and the Armenians, to fight in the rebellion, leaving the Armenians in the Turks now very unfriendly glare. Most Armenians fled Turkey to Russia, but some came to America and their stories were found out like Georgie's story was. Though no one doubted his story, his thick accent, poor English and inability to translate his story to a map to guide 'Arkaeologist' to the site of the ark, limited his ability to aid modern Ark hunters to the spot. He was able to be of some aid when he was shown mountain pictures, and he was able to give several clues which are relied on by many Ark hunters, when they got the chance to climb the mountain. That is, if they could get past the mountain of red tape the Turks put all tourists through. The problem they had with people who want to climb Mount Ararat is because the mountain is within sight of the Russian border.

Georgie stated that 1908 was a very warm year and the ark was resting on a bluish green rock. He gave the definitive description of the ark as he appears to have seen it in its entirety. When he first saw it he thought it might have been made of stone. One side of the ark was resting on the edge of a steep cliff, which was inaccessible from that side. The ark was very long and rectangular and part of the bottom was exposed and he could see that it was flat under there. The roof was nearly flat except for a row of about 50 windows that were each about 18 inches by 30 inches. There were no windows or doors on the side, just one large hole with something of a staircase leading partway down, but he was unsure if it was part of the boat or placed there by the many pilgrims had would come to the ark in times past. The ark's wood was entirely petrified. He stated that his uncle had brought a musket and shot a few shots at the ark and they barely left a dent, and he couldn't even carve a piece of the ark off with a knife. Though he could clearly see the joints of the wood, nowhere could he actually feel the joints as the entire boat was completely smooth. Though he saw no nails he could discern dowels. The top was covered in moss but where he peeled it off he found more soft smooth dark brown wooden surface. His uncle piled loose stones till he could lift Georgie to the ladder or steps. His grandfather told him visiting the ark was a good start to becoming a holy man in the future. When he went home and chatted with his friends he found that many of them had also been to see the Ark. This was the story he told about two years before he died, and an artist painted a picture of the ark based on his descriptions which Georgie approved of as a good representation of the ark. I've based part of my cover art on this drawing. (Book 71 pg -76) One thing that strikes me about this ark is that it was no rush job, it was built with exceptional care and with an eye for quality. It's like the builder knew this wasn't just to save him, his family and the animals, but the ark itself would serve as an ongoing witness after he was gone.

One of the most striking ironies of Ark history is the discovery of the ark by Russian pilots during the latter part of the First World War. In 1916 on a very hot August day while watching lizards pant in the heat and looking out across the distance to the snow capped tip of mount Ararat and wishing for some of that snow, a captain suddenly walked in and gave two pilots permission to test a new supercharged high altitude engine that had been installed on a couple planes. In no time they had their gear, parachutes on, oxygen in place and were on their way into the blue. As they slowly climbed, one of the pilots looked at Mount Ararat 25 miles away beckoning him to that snow and in 15 minutes both pilots flew a beeline toward the mountain and were acting more like sightseers than pilots as they looked at the stone battlement surrounding part of the lower mountain.

One of the pilots had heard of the legend of Armenian pilgrims looking for a boat on the mountain to make good luck emblems out of to hang around their necks, but he laughed to himself thinking how nutty it was for people past and present to look for a boat on a mountain. They circled the mountain a few times and saw a small emerald blue lake when the other pilot shouted out to the other to look, and the pilot who had just moments before been laughing at the idea of a boat on a mountain nearly fainted when he saw what he thought was a submarine at the outflow end of the little lake. They flew in as near to it as was safe and were stunned at the immensity of the boat, being about a city block long, and thought it would compare in size to modern battle ships. It was grounded on the shore of the lake with about a quarter of the length running out onto the water and the other end was about three quarters under water. Part of the front had been partly dismantled, and on the other side there was a big gaping door about 20 feet square but with the door missing. The door seemed unusually large as they noted that even in their day few ships had doors even half that size. Then they raced back to the airport to tell their story and were laughed at soundly as apparently none of the other pilots had ever heard the story of the ark. But the captain who sent them out asked lots of questions then said "Take me up there; I want to look at it." Apparently the pilots had no idea what they had discovered other than a huge boat completely out of its element. The captain after they got back asked them what they made of the thing and they just thought it was astounding. The captain asked them "Do you know what that ship is?" And the two pilots had no idea. He asked them if they had ever heard of Noah's ark. They said yes but didn't understand what that had to do with the boat 14,000 feet up the side of a mountain. Finally the captain spelled it out for them telling them it WAS Noah's ark.

The Captain wasted no time sending this information to the Russian government and Tsar Nicholas sent three special companies of fifty soldiers to climb the mountain, taking opposite ways to reach the Ark. Fifty of the soldiers got to a point where they could see the ark but the way was blocked by a swamp, masses of insects and puff adders. For the other 100 well equipped soldiers it still took nearly a month of trail blazing to reach the ark. But reach it they did and they took pictures and documented the entire relic. They even drew up an entire floor plan map of the ark. The ark contained many very large rooms with high ceilings and hundreds of small rooms. The large rooms usually had large timbers across them as thick as two feet apparently meant for animals ten times as large as an elephant. There were rooms lined with rows of small cages which were protected by wrought iron bars along the fronts. Every bit of the wood was coated with a wax-like paint that resembled shellac. They determined the wood to be similar to the cypress family, which is a type of wood that never rots. The type of wood along with the shellac and the cold storage explained its perfect state of preservation. The expedition also found near the ark some timbers that had been burned which were deduced to have come from one side of the ship. There was also found a small one room shrine like the Hebrews used for sacrificial altars. They couldn't explain the burnt timbers. (This would be the wood from the ark the three atheist scientist tried to burn, thus ironically being a confirmation of that story.) The expedition sent its report to the Tsar within days of the Bolshevik revolution overthrowing of the Russian government. (Book 71 pg 77-84, book 72 pg 102-104, Crusader Comic #7 "The Ark")

The irony I find in this is the government was overthrown by a leader named Lenin that had his faith undermined by the evolutionary belief of Darwinism which ended up being the ideology of his new government within days of the proof of the bible they had lost faith in within their grasp. What would Lenin's reaction have been had he seen the proof, and what would the world be like today if he had?

Many WWII pilots claimed to have seen the ark on Mount Ararat during the war. A 1943 edition of the U.S. armed force newspaper called the *Stars and Stripes* contained an article told by two pilots who saw the ark on the mountains several times so they finally invited a professional photographer on one of their flights to photograph the ark on the mountain and this picture was on the front page of the paper. Files of the paper though were not kept and no copy of this war news paper is known to exist. Many veterans recalled the story and even remember keeping clippings but tossed them out eventually.

It's around this time the stories of Ark pictures seem to take a mysterious and even a sinister twist.

Investigators while looking for this Stars and Stripes issue found out that many veterans recall seeing not only pictures of the ark in this newspaper, the ark was also photographed by a few other pilots including some taken by a couple Australians and shown to people in an English Pub. Several vets also recall seeing a movie with the ark in it, and in fact some recalled seeing footage of the ark taken from a helicopter in an ongoing newscast serial seen in the movie theatres for years all across America called the *March of Time*. The ark was plainly visible in these newscasts. I've seen these old *March of Time* newscast reels and they are saved for historical purposes. While the March of Time newsreel used the helicopter footage, it appears that same footage or more footage was shown to high school students in Los Angeles, but again attempts to track down these footages have come up empty. Again in Philadelphia a class of about a dozen boys on the campus of the Faith Theological Seminary were also shown footage of the Ark taken from a helicopter. They note that the film also showed several men exploring the ark! Who those people are no one knows and attempts to track down all these films have turned up empty. No one has been able to track down this particular *March of Time* newsreel or any of these other known footages showing the ark. Are they lost, forgotten in some attic, or have people like those atheists / evolutionists that tried to destroy the ark, tracked down, found and destroyed all copies of the movies showing the Ark?

The identification of the people exploring the Ark as seen in the footages of the ark taken from the helicopter may very well have been Russians. In 1940 a Russian airman in a reconnaissance aircraft looked for the ark because, he had heard about the Russians who found it during WWI and wanted to see if he could see it too. He did, and he reported that he had seen the ark to Major Jasper Maskelyn, a Russian military camouflage chief. What the pilot saw was the ark partly submerged in an ice lake, just like Georgie Hagopian had described. So arctic climbers were sent to investigate the sighting and said they found it very rotted, over 400 feet long, and composed of Fossilized wood similar to coal. Ark hunters digging for clues and traces of the ark have discovered that apparently the Russians maintain considerable files on the existence of the ark and they are unwilling to share them because it contradicts their "basic assumption of atheistic evolution".

Post War

After WW II in 1947, a Dr. Liedmann became a friend and acquaintance of a Russian Air Force major with whom he had many shared interests. During the war the Russians were allies so such friendships weren't uncommon, and they discovered they were both squadron leaders near the end of the war, and they both had Ukrainian roots. Over dinner one time the Russian airman mentioned Mount Ararat was inspected each summer during a good weather period and on one of these flights at least three pictures were taken at the 14,000 foot level of the ark from different angles and he had them with him to show the Doctor. They had been taken sometime before 1938 and showed the ark sticking out of a glacier about 80 or 90 feet, tilted slightly downwards with a little melted pond near the bottom. He couldn't give the doctor the pictures or copies of them because they were property of the USSR. Even if he wanted to, had these pictures leaked, the Russians no doubt could trace who had access to the pictures, so he didn't dare. Not to mention each of the pictures showed at least one more airplanes with a Russian insignia on the wings: so no way could he give him copies. The two met again about a year later and once again the Russian had about a dozen pictures with him that had been taken since their 1947 meeting. This time they showed only about a 12 or 15 foot tip of the ark protruding from the snowy ice with some of the length of the ark visible through the glassy clear ice. All these pictures showed in them another Russian aircraft and once again he could not give the Doctor any copies. On a third occasion he met with his friend but he had some of his Russian companions with him. The doctor tried to bring up the subject of the ark but the Russian Air force major acted like he had no idea what he was talking about, no doubt because of the men with him. (Book 71 pgs 116-120)

So now we've seen that the Russian Communists clearly know of the arks existence as do at least some evolutionists and thus we can deduce from their hiding this fact from the general public, that truth is not their aim but power and control over people's minds is. What other reason could there be for hiding this global treasure from the masses?

A key photograph of the ark was known to at one time be in the hands of Sister Bertha Davis of Holtville California, who would teach kids bible stories with the aid of several pictures she had in a portfolio. The picture she had of Mount Ararat clearly showed the ark partially protruding from the ice which appeared to have a 'catwalk' along the top, and the planking of the ark was clearly visible. But the key in the picture was they showed a stone bench and a partially burned wooden roof. (Book 71 pg 122) Again confirmation of the atheists attempts to burn the ark. It's almost funny, and the ultimate irony; for the reason that their attempt to burn the ark has in fact created confirmation of the existence of the ark, the very thing they tried to avoid, because other ark sightings after their excursion mentioned the burned wood, something never mentioned in sightings predating their visit!

In the hunt for pictures existing showing the ark, it was heard that a traveling evangelist that visited the Los Angeles district had one, a New York state geography book circa 1950 had one in it, and a Turkish calendar had one on it. A lady who read an article about John Joseph Nouri wrote the magazine saying she was a friend of Nouri's and she had a picture of the ark he had taken and given to her. But none of these pictures or copies could be obtained as they had all disappeared. (Book 71 pg 123)

On November 13th 1948 once again news of the Ark's continued existence hit the headlines. During another warm year a Muslim Kurdish farmer simply known as Resit apparently just liked to climb the mountain a lot as he had been up it many times. On one occasion he had climbed much higher than usual and looked down to observe the view and on this occasion he saw something he had never seen before. It looked like a ship sticking out in a canyon, the rest of which was covered by snow and ice. He climbed down to it and what was visible was clearly the prow of a ship the size of a house. He tried to pry some of the wood out which was blackened with age, but it was as hard as a rock; but he insisted it was not a rock formation. When he climbed down the mountain he spread the news about the odd thing on the mountain and several of the village peasants climbed the northern slope to see this curious item. After they reached it and came back each person who saw it said it was a ship. Oddly enough they knew of no folklore to indicate just what this ship was or how it could have gotten up the mountain so it appears to have been the reason the story was told by Resit or someone else to associated press correspondent Edwin Greenwald, who *did* realize what the ship was and submitted the story which was then published.

This story inspired Christian circles around the globe and the rush was on to organize expeditions up the mountain, all they needed was a guide to take them to the ship. But there was a snag. No one could find Resit, even though a reward was offered, he never came forth, and peculiarly neither did any of the other people who had seen the ark on the mountain. When questioned, they all said nothing and they "know nothing", probably because of their fear and distrust based on a history of fighting between Russian Catholics and Moslem Turks. So it's presumed that because of this adversarial history linked to these religions, that no one wanted to aid the American Christian inquires about the ark. Nevertheless the story was out once again and the hunt was on. Though a few expeditions were organized, any that actually made it to the mountain were unsuccessful in locating the ark. It is in fact a huge double mountain of lesser and greater Ararat of about a hundred square miles, so that even as big an item as the ark is, it is little more than a needle in a haystack if you don't know where to look.

In 1937 Ferdinand Navarra once climbed a mountain with his friend Alim, who became worn out and rested part way up unable to complete the climb. Navarra continued to the peak of Mount Hermon at 9000 feet and came back to his friend and they continued on back down the mountain. On the way down Nahim talked about his grandfather who tried to climb Mount Ararat because he knew the ark was up there but could never find it and told Alim he should find it and bring a piece of its wood back. Alim said he would climb it for his grandfather but stated to Navarra, I clearly am unable to climb such a mountain if I can't climb this one...and encouraged Navarra to find the ark, so Navarra took up the torch.

Navarra tried in 1952 with a companion and though they didn't see the ark they found a strangely dark patch of ice with no explanation for its darkness. So they traced it out and they even measured the length of the dark patch and it measured out to 300 cubits. This was when they realized they were standing on top of the ark which was now completely covered in ice. Unfortunately they had no equipment that could get them into the ice and the ark so they had to leave. They tried again in 1953 but severe weather and altitude sickness got the better of Navarra and he had to abandon the effort. He tried again in 1955 and this time went up with his eleven year old son. Once again they found the place where the ark was, which now had less ice, but the ice and snow was configured all differently which made access to the ark somewhat treacherous. Possible access existed over a cliff of ice but they couldn't get close without fear of the ice breaking sending them hurling down a cliff. The son Raphael came up with the solution: wrap a rope around him and lower him down. Navarra found a secure foothold and the boy was lowered down until he declared "There, I can see it now. Yes the boat is there, papa. I can see it distinctly." Navarra spurred on, now lowered himself and after much cold and struggle managed with his pickaxe to pull out a very heavy 5 foot length of stone hard hewn lumber. (Book 71 pg 135-144)

The wood Navarra pulled from the ark had a surprise for me. It had grain and annual rings that were between 2 and 4 mm, showing "active growth". (Book 72 pg 183) I had previously deduced wood before the flood had no rings due to a global even climate year round. Trees with no rings do exist which I still think is safe to presume are antediluvian. This discovery of rings on the wood of the ark means the climate before the flood did have seasons with enough variation to create rings in at least some trees. Geologists do know that there was a time when the world's climate was a universal greenhouse, though they have been unable to decipher what conditions on earth would create this environment. They even turn back the clock on continental drift and admit no rearranging of the continents can account for the known fact that the world was in a state, where both poles and equatorial regions experienced a period when the climate was like that of a green house. That in itself is evidence that there was a flood. I had interpreted this evidence to account for all trees having no rings. Obviously a few dots were connected wrong by me, but it doesn't change the overall picture, in fact it probably clarifies it a bit more.

This next Ark substantiation is a grim reminder that the world is divided into people with extremes dispositions like that of sheep and wolves. George Greene was working in eastern Turkey as a representative of an oil company and had a helicopter at his disposal for the purpose of searching for mineral and oil deposits. Since he was scouring the northern section of the Mountains of Ararat anyway, the news of the ark may have prompted him to take a small detour to the higher elevations to take a peek. His family confirms that he not only found the ark at the 13,000-14,000 foot elevation of the mountain, he filmed it and located it on a good geological map of the mountain, something no one had done before. Once again the description of the ark matches and verifies previous sightings. About one third of it was visible protruding from a snow or glacier shelf, sitting on the edge of a cliff. Planking was easily distinguishable running parallel to the roof. The bottom part of the ark was submerged in ice and mud.

This fact that the ark is sitting by a cliff is mentioned in most sightings, by people who don't know of the other sightings, as are other details by those who actually get to the ark itself.

Knowing what he had in his possession, George enlarged the photographs and presented them to a business associate and other potentially interested parties to try to get an expedition together to get to the ark for a closer examination, with the map pointing to the location in his possession, this would have shortened the duration of any expedition immensely by not having to search blindly for the ark. He tried many people in many locations, east to west and from USA to Canada, to try and get something off the ground, but just couldn't get anyone to commit. He had to continue with his mining work during the '50's so he dropped off the pictures and stuff with a friend and continued his work. He obtained them again in 1961, did a bit more exploration in British Guiana and came back to the States in December 1962 and checked into a hotel in Georgetown.* (*which one not noted) He was found face down in the swimming pool apparently having been thrown into it from his room several floors up. His room had not been ransacked and the only thing missing was the contents of his briefcase. What did it hold, a map to a great gold mine, or maybe all the pictures and maps...of the ark? No one is sure, but an uncompleted search of George's files, never turned up any pictures, maps, or the movie of the ark. (Book 71 pgs 145-148)

Was Greene once again trying to drum up interest in an expedition to the ark with the proof in his hands only to rankle opposition to the proof spurring them to grab his pictures and shut this man up permanently? Some people can be very resourceful in their attempts to hide the truth. I knew one person that managed to somehow have access to cross police lines and cut out and steal some pages from a photo album that contained incriminating pictures, almost as if they had the aid of the police. Whatever happened, once again photos, a movie and proof of the Ark's existence have disappeared from circulation when all instincts would suppose these would or should be world news. The forces of darkness continually battle those of the light, making faith in witness's accounts all people have to go on, just like those witnesses of the resurrection of Christ couldn't produce the body and just their testimony to the world leaving it up to the hearer or the reader to decide by faith alone.

Turkey, due to political pressures, has made it virtually impossible to climb Mount Ararat or fly nearby because of the mountain's proximity to Russia, based on the theoretical reason these mountain climbers might be spying. Perhaps the ark will not be found in our lifetime but it doesn't change its existence.

In case you were wondering, though the Ark could be photographed from space satellites, two kinds of satellite cameras exists, high resolution satellites used for gleaning intelligence and more normal cameras that are used for weather. Access to intelligence satellite images are virtually impossible because of the close proximity of Mount Ararat to Russia which if certain photographs were released, could compromise security should certain images fall into the wrong hands. Images of the ark on normal satellite cameras would take up about one pixel making positive identification impossible.

The evidence of the flood and the ark are recorded in ancient and recent history, but you may never ever see a picture of it to convince you of its existence. But the ancients told of the flood and they told of visiting the relic of the flood that being the Ark of Noah and it appears to still exist. I've discovered lies told to me by people about essential things that made me not believe when something important came up that some of their associates tried to make me believe, which sadly affected the rest of my life and some significant people in my life have been separated from me as a result of those lies, some even to this day. Don't let the lies of some people discourage you from believing the most important truth you'll ever encounter. There is no such thing as evolution, it's a lie made up to keep people from believing in a Creator that calls himself your father, if only you'll believe and turn back to him.

Well though this book on the floods does have some very important religious life impacting implication, it also has some important historical and geological and anthropological and whatever otherological repercussion it entails, so we'll continue on with flood legends that are at first a bit indistinct, and then move onto the central focus of this book, the local flood legends, their proof and implications.

Chapter 3

THE INDISTINCT FLOOD LEGENDS (TYPE 2A): INCOMPREHENSIBLE...TO ME.

Though we are told there are more than 300 to as many as 600 different flood legends, some of these 'flood legends' are obscure at best. Some of the flood legends, as far as I'm concerned, hardly qualify as flood legends at all. Some are so strange or convoluted and indistinct they seem to have little or no flood research value. But I'm not an expert so it's possible some of these may mean more to cultural experts or people from the specific locations these legends come from. Since it's impractical to really list every last flood legends as it would be tedious to read through all 600 or so legends, I think it's best to focus on the understandable ones anyway. But in reading through many all at once from around the world, there does appear some common themes that though the particulars don't seem to have much in common with world or local flood legends; they do seem to have some connection with each other and some sort of historic events. We'll start with Type 2a which are just legends that make you scratch your head wondering why such a weird legend would exist at all and what the mindset was to have this legends repeated endlessly down through the ages.

Keep in mind what Solon the Egyptian high priest said about survivors of large tragic events "...when the stream from heaven, descends like a pestilence and leaves only those of you who are destitute of letters and education...you have to begin all over again as children and know nothing about what happened in ancient times, either among us or among yourselves."

Imagine if you will what civilization would look like if a vast disaster overcame your location for hundreds of miles in every direction wiping out gas stations, TV reception, computer access, libraries, grocery stores, and gasp...elevators and comic books, not to mention killing out all the genius', leaving just the odd beer drinking truck driving dude who can't read or doesn't like reading cuz books don't got no pictures in them. (We won't ask how they got their licenses) Or a small population of people that just like to shoot things because they like to shoot things that survived. How would they explain what happened to their grandchildren, if they couldn't drive far enough on what gas they had left to get a scientific explanation of the events that occurred? What sort of story would they pass down to their children? And what would that remnant of civilization look like in a hundred years if no influence from other parts of the world, not affected by the disaster, ever entered into that region? Pockets of isolated population can tend to degenerate into a more primitive state fairly quickly. The Tasaday of the interior of Mindanao in the Philippines somehow became isolated 500-1000 years ago. At that time they were practicing agriculture, and producing a variety of tools and weapons. When rediscovered they had no knowledge of agriculture or weapons and only used crude stone or bamboo tools. (Book 54 pg 144) Our civilization has become so reliant on computers to answer their important questions, like who starred in the 1948 version of The King and I or how many hotdogs did Johnny Sugarbean eat in ten minutes, that they would be at a loss as to how to boil water or start a fire if a disaster struck.

Professor Fredrick Soddy seems to have deduced this decline in man's civilization in ancient times too, when he wrote in 1909, "The legend of the Fall of Man, possibly, may be all that survived of such a time before, for some unknown reason, the whole world was plunged back again under the undisputed sway of nature to begin once more its upward toilsome journey through the ages." (Book 11 pg 161)

Well I've got to start somewhere so we'll start small.

PYGMY FLOOD LEGEND:

Chameleon heard a strange noise, like water running, in a tree, but at that time there was no water in the world. He cut open the trunk, and water came out in a great flood that spread all over the earth. The first human couple emerged with the water.

This almost sounds like a creation of mankind legend, mixed with a flood legend, and tapping trees for maple syrup.

SCANDINAVIAN:

Oden, Vili, and Ve being mighty men fought and killed the Great ice giant named Ymir, but instead of bleeding, icewater emptied from his cuts drowning most of the Rime Giants, except one named Bergelmir who escaped with his wife and children, in a boat created from a tree trunk. His descendants became frost ogres. What was left of Ymir became the oceans filled by his blood. [Internet based on Sturluson, p. 35] You're on your own with that one.

AFRICA

AN AFRICAN BOTHERSOME RAIN LEGEND
Komililo Nandi (of Uganda)
Ilet, the spirit of lightning, came to live on earth in human form, and chose to live in a cave high on a mountain named Tinderet. This action caused it to rain incessantly and killed most of the hunters that lived in the forest below. Surviving hunters decided to search for the cause of the rain, and found Ilet in his mountain cave and wounded him with poison arrows. Ilet fled and died in a neighbouring country. When he died, the rain stopped.

Let the head scratching begin.

KWAYA (LAKE VICTORIA)

There once was a time when the oceans were all pent up in a single pot which was kept by a family including husband, wife and a son and daughter-in-law. They used this pot containing the oceans to fill up other pots in the hut when they needed water. With the daughter-in-law being new to the family, the father told her to never touch the pot because it contained their sacred ancestors, but apparently not mentioning the important water business. She became curious, touched it and somehow it shattered causing a flood that drowned everything. (Internet: source not noted)

BENA-LULUA (CONGO RIVER, SOUTHEAST ZAIRE):

There was an old water woman who had many sores and she promised she would give people water if they sucked them. One man did so and she poured out so much water that almost everyone drowned. But the man kept up his vile task and eventually the water stopped running. [Based on internet quoting Kelsen, p. 136] Ewww! Son...I want you to pass this story down to your sons and their sons for endless generations so we don't forget this all important time in the world's history. Ok dad...what did they taste like anyway? Ugh, don't ask me!

EKOI (NIGERIA):

The first people on the earth came from the sky and their name was Etim 'Ne (meaning Old Person), and his wife Ejaw. When they arrived there was no water on the earth so they asked the god Obassi Osaw for water. The god gave them a calabash with seven clear stones in it. (A calabash is a gourd that grows on trees, the shell of which is used to make bottles and pots when dried.) When Old Person put one of the stones in the ground water came out of the hole and became a lake. After the couple had seven sons and daughters which married and had their own children Old Person gave each household a river and a lake of their own. Three of the sons were poor hunters, and with what little they did get they never shared so to make matter worse Old Person took away their rivers, but relented when they begged him. When his grandchildren grew up and established households of their own, Old Person sent for all of them and told them to each take seven stones from their parent's streams and plant them at intervals to create their own streams. They all did this except one grandson who filled up a basket with stones and emptied all his stones in one place. The waters gushed and flooded his entire farm and beyond and threatened to flood the entire earth. Everyone ran from the flood to Old Man and he prayed to Obassi Osaw who stopped the flood but let the water on the bad grandson's farm remain. Old Person gave them the names of the rivers and streams and told them to remember him as the bringer of water to the world then he died two days later. (No source noted)

...scratch scratch scratch...

One thing suggests this is a post flood legend because it talks of the first people coming down from the sky. You'll see why I say this later on.

MANDINGO (IVORY COAST):

There once was a very generous man who gave away all he had to feed the animals. His family deserted him because of this. The man gave his last meal to a god named Ouende who rewarded him with three handfuls of flour that automatically replenished itself when used, and even produced better riches than he had. He was advised by Ouende to leave the area, and when he did so he sent six months of rain to destroy the selfish neighbours. All the people that live today are the descendants of the generous man who later became rich. [Based on internet source quoting Kelsen, pp. 135-136]

MONGOLIA:

A man named Hailibu rescued a white snake that was being attacked by a crane. He happened upon the snake again the next day and the snake told him she was the Dragon King's daughter who wanted to reward him. The white snake suggested he ask for a stone that was inside the Dragon King's mouth as it would let him be able to understand the animal's language. However she warned him if he took this stone to never to tell anyone this secret. When Halibu met the Dragon King he was offered many gifts but Hailibu refused them all until he was finally given the stone. Some years later he heard some birds talking about a flood that would come the next day when the mountains would erupt water and flood the land. He went home and warned everyone and of course they didn't believe him so he told them about the stone that let him understand animal's speech and when he did so he turned to stone. This convinced the villagers and they fled. It rained the next day and the mountain burst out with water causing a great flood. The people that escaped came back after the flood was over and found the stone man and put him on a mountain top. They offered sacrifices to the stone man to honor Hailibu's memory for generations afterwards. [Internet based on Elder & Wong, pp. 75-77] People turning to stone and stones into people in myths are surprisingly common, and one myth from Central America turns some of these people that turned to stone back into flesh and alive.

This sounds more like a local flood, though it does have some elements of Noah's story along with elements of the preflood environment such as water bursting out of the ground, so it could be a composite. One might equate the white snake as the serpent that beguiled Eve but a lot doesn't really fit to be sure of this link. One could say the snake's gift is linked with the flood here as is the snake's urging Eve to take the fruit that leads to the flood, but this connection too is feeble. Before the flood it appears man could communicate with the animals on some level, but most of this legend causes itchy scalp syndrome if you ask me. It's odd though how many legends connected with the flood have animals associated to the story in some way, suggesting more allegorical connections that need to be understood through cultural understandings I would guess.

KOREA:

When a fairy and a laurel tree had a son, the fairy returned to heaven when the son reached seven years old. One day it started to rain and the rain lasted for many months flooding the earth which became a raging sea as a result. The flood endangered the laurels strength so that it knew it would soon fall, so it told his son to reside with him so when he fell he could ride out the waves. Once the tree fell and floated for a while with the boy, they came upon a group of ants which asked to be saved, and the tree when asked by the boy, gave them permission to ride on the tree. Likewise so did some mosquitoes and they were saved. Then another boy floated by and when the son asked to save him the tree refused, but after three requests from the boy the tree said "Do what you like", and so the second boy was saved. Finally the tree came to rest on a mountain and the insects thanked them and left. The two boys were very hungry and found a house where an old woman lived with her daughter and a foster daughter. The flood killed everyone else and when the waters dropped back down to normal they began farming and the old woman decided to marry the two girls to the two boys. She thought her own daughter should go to the clever boy that saved them all on the tree. The Second boy wanting the real daughter told the old woman that the other boy could gather millet grain scattered on the sand. The woman tested the boy and though he despaired of the challenge, the ants did it for him and filled his grain bag in a few minutes. The other boy saw what happened so he told the woman that he hadn't done it by himself so the woman still wavered in her decision as to which boy got which girl. So she decided to let chance make the decision for her, so she put the girls in two different rooms and let the boys choose which room to go to in the same dark conditions. A mosquito told the tree's son which room the woman's daughter was in so he ended up marrying her, with the other boy marrying the adopted girl. The human race is descended from these two couples. [Internet based on Zong, pp. 16-18]

A fairy and a tree have a boy? What weirdness is this? Though this legend does talk of a flood that wipes out all life in the world, how did the old woman and her two daughters survive? How such quirky legends can get off the ground and be told down the ages mystifies me.

NORTH AMERICA

Many of the North America Native legends are full of allegorical animals such as raven, beaver, eagles, crows, blue jays, spiders, moles, falcons and coyotes that caused, rescued, or survived a flood; and later created man and lands, with mud or by planting feathers, rocks, or puma whiskers to make people out of. I get clogging of the synapses just reading so many of these allegorical legends. These legends clearly speak of vast floods, but little more can be deciphered without intimate knowledge of the symbolism, and I'm not sure even then one can really make sense of them. Here's an example of one from the **Queen Charlotte Islands or Haida Gwai** as it's now called.

There was a flood a long time ago that killed all the creatures except a raven named Nekilstlas. The raven was a person who could wear or remove his feathers when he wanted to, as he had been born of an unmarried woman. When the flood was over he looked but could find no mate and became lonely, so he married a cockle (a shelled mollusc) he found on the beach, but still longed for a companion. After a long while he heard a faint cry like that of a newly born child coming from out of the cockle shell. It grew louder and finally a small baby girl appeared. She grew and grew and when fully grown she married the raven and from these two came all the Indians. [Internet based on Frazer, p. 319] Not sure what kind of conversation a crow could have with a cockle; Cockle-doodle-doo?

TIMAGAMI OJIBWAY (CANADA)

A son of the sun and a mortal woman named Nenebuc happened by a lake and saw some lions in it in the distance. He disguised himself as a birch tree trunk and waited for the lions to come back to shore. When the lions returned they noticed the new stump and sent a snake to check it out. The snake coiled around it but nothing could be determined this way as Nenebuc held firm. Then when the lions came over to the stump Nenebuc wounded the chief lioness with an arrow and she retreated to her home in the cave. Then Nenebuc disguised himself as a medicine woman by wearing the skin of a toad and went into the lioness and jammed the arrow in further killing her. As soon as he did this water poured out of the cave, and the lake began to rise, so Nenebuc built a raft which he finished just in time as the flood got to him. While riding out the flood he saved several animals and pulled them onto the raft with him. When the flood appeared to be over he tied a rope to the beaver's tail and told him to dive to see if he could find the bottom, but he could not and returned to the surface. A week later he let a muskrat try and it stayed down a long time and drowned but returned to the surface with a little bit of dirt in its claws. Nenebuc dried this dirt and used it to make some land but it wasn't quite enough so it became the swampy areas of the world we have today. [Internet based on Frazer, pp. 307-308]

Well yeah, it's a flood legend. We might be able to say the water coming out of the cave is like the water coming from the fountains of the deep, and the raft with some animals is the ark, and animals sent to find land similar to Noah sending out birds to find land. But what is this killing a lion business, or disguising himself like a tree trunk, and wearing...a toad skin? I can only ponder so many of these quirky flood legends before my brain goes all mushy, (probably from scratching too deep) and my eyes glaze over. So now let's concentrate on legends that make some sense but appear to be a jumbled confusion or merging of more than one flood or catastrophe in the same legend. If you want more of the kinds of legends we just escaped from, follow the sources...oh, and wear a helmet.

THE INDISTINCT FLOOD LEGENDS (TYPE 2B): BLENDED OR JUMBLED.

I found that often some flood legends have elements of both a global flood and local flood combined in the same legend, but as mentioned they are simply all lumped together as just 'flood legends' by the masses. As we will see with a multitude of disasters occurring worldwide, sometimes flood legends got mixed, confused and even garbled. So I repeat this quote to keep in mind the state of the people that created some of these legends....

"For instance, Philo of Alexandria (20B.C. - A.D. 54) wrote: By reason of the constant and repeated destructions by water and fire, the later generations did not receive from the former the memory of the order and sequence of events." Some generations likes ours for example.

Some flood legends are more obvious than others that both kinds have been merged into a single legend, but some are only discernable as such after reading them over and over to pick out the details of each. This one had me scratching my head a few times.

Chaldean: Apparently a province of Babylon but located far south near the Persian Gulf (48°E, 32°N)

The god Chronos (equals Jupiter?) warned the tenth king of Babylon Xisuthrus in a vision about a flood coming on the fifteenth of the month Daesius. Chronos also told him to write a history and bury it in a place called Sippara, then build and supply a ship 5 stadia long and 2 stadia wide for himself, his friends family, and all sorts of animals. Xisuthrus asked where should he set his course for and Chronos replied "to the gods, but first pray for all good things to men." Xisuthrus built the ship which was five furlongs long and two furlongs wide and filled it up as ordered. After the flood was over and the water had receded to some extent, he sent out a few birds to see if they would find land but they returned. He tried this again after a while, and the birds returned again but with mud on their feet. When he did this a third time the birds never came back so he knew the land had finally appeared above the waters and started taking apart the safety closures of his ship, saw land and headed his ship onto the Corcyraean (Gordyaeans) mountains in Armenia. He, his wife, daughter, and pilot and everyone else got off the ship, and offered sacrifices to the gods. The four mentioned were converted so as to be able to live with the gods. The others that were on the ship grieved when they couldn't find the four they had sailed with so long, but when they heard Xisuthrus' voice in the air telling them to be virtuous and seek his writings at Sippara they were contented. Part of the ship remains to this day, and some people make charms from its bitumen. [Based on Frazer, pp. 108-110; G. Smith, pp. 42-43]

Though there are clearly global flood points in this version, there are also some striking similarities to the Epic of Gilgamesh version of the flood here which I determined must be a local flood (see chapter 4) so it appears there is some mixing of a local flood legend and world flood legend together here, though distinguishing one from the other appears to be only in the added details such as reference to the gods, and some of the family living with the gods. The gods were known by name only after they descended in Ur and helped the Sumerians build their civilization. Thus the four who left (half the family) to live with the gods could only have done so after the flood, but in the epic of Gilgamesh they did so after a local flood. For the flood to occur during the reign of the tenth king of Babylon's places this flood long after the flood of Noah, so some mixing up of times must have occurred here. Yet as noted there are also enough similarities to the global flood legend.

The detail of the birds sent out and the ark landing on the Corcyraean mountains in Armenia is basically the same as the biblical version of Noah's birds and the ark landing on the mountains of Ararat, so Corcyraean might be the area where the mountains of Ararat are as indeed the Armenians lived there for thousands of years up until the early 20th century and they claimed to be descendants of one of the sons of Noah and remained in the area of the ark all this time. On the other hand the flood is said to be forewarned on for the fifteenth day of the month of Daesius, meaning less than a year from the time the warning was given. Adding the detail about wondering where to sail is also quirky suggesting a very different kind of boat compared to the ark of Noah. The biblical version adds that God waited patiently for Noah to finish the ark and held back the flood until he finished.

The measurements of the ark are somewhat confusing and extreme. Furlongs being 220 yards long, Stadia being between 600 to over 700 feet long, could be the same unit of measurement so why use both terms? Be that as it may the boat would thus be about 3,500 feet long by 1,300 feet wide! This measurement is just ludicrous and to expect to have had it built in less than a year, yet not all the naval yards working together in North America could build such a vessel from start to finish in such short notice, so something is clearly amiss here. Consider Chronos telling Xisuthrus sail "to the gods, but first pray for all good things to men." This prayer for 'good things to men' strongly suggests other men somewhere else that won't be in this flood that Xisuthrus is being saved from, as why would you pray such for men that are doomed to be killed in a flood? Though I suppose it could be directed to the remaining people on the boat. One final curious bit; one wonders where in Sippara this history might be buried. Sippara apparently equals Sepharvaim which was apparently southeast of Bagdad near the Euphrates. (The Sepharvites of Sepharvaim are also mentioned in the bible in II Kings 17:31.) So buried probably in a safe container somewhere around there must be a history of some kind. Though many tablets have been found there as long ago as 1881, I don't know of a sealed container with a history encapsulated therein being found. Should one be found, the depth of the find would of course tell which flood it was buried in.

This next legend I initially thought of as a type 2a flood legend, but as I worked with it and reread it a few times I realized it had some elements of both world and local flood legends in it, so I moved it here.

Shan (Burma) (22°N, 97°E)

There were many worlds and during the middle world there was a time when there was no race of kings. During this time the bamboos broke open and animals came out and went to live in the forests. Down from heaven descended Hpi-pok and Hpi-mot to the Cambodia River place of Möng-hi and would become the ancestors of the kings. There came a time when the gods were forgotten and no sacrifices were made to them so the storm god Ling-Pawn sent large cranes to eat the people but there were too many people for them to eat. Snakes were sent to kill the people but instead they were killed by the people they were sent to kill. Drought was sent and many people died from lack of water and of famine. Ling-Pawn gathered a council of the gods and they decided to destroy mankind. Hkang-Hkak, the god of streams, ponds, alligators and water animals was sent to visit a righteous man Lip-Long, who had already seen omens, to tell him what was going to happen so Lip-Long was not surprised. This god told him to build a raft for himself and his cow, and keep the reason for this task a secret. His family mocked him while he did this seemingly futile task, yet he still warned no one, not even his closest family members. When he finished the raft, a few days later the violent flood came. Lip-long survived with his cow and he grieved when he found his dead family. This was how the race of kings died. While the spirits of heaven celebrated by eating cold crab, the rotting corpses from the flood smelled up the world. This bothered Ling-Lawn the storm god so he sent serpents to eat them, but there were too many so the god tried to destroy the snakes for not eating them all, but they escaped by going into a cave. He sent nearly a million tigers but they couldn't complete the task either and they escaped his deadly lightning into the cave. So he sent fire gods to burn the earth and Lip-long saw the fire coming so he killed the cow and hid inside. When the fire was gone he emerged from the cow with a gourd seed he found inside the cow and with advice from Hkang-Hkak planted it on level ground. The gourd vines grew in several directions, up mountains where it was scorched, down to the water where it rotted, and into the trees and bushes where it survived and multiplied greatly. When the world dried Ling-lawn cracked open a gourd that had grown with a lightning bolt and out of it came people to till the land. Another gourd was opened and out of it came kings which were sent to rule the lands, and more gourds were opened and released animals, rivers and plants.

In another version the survivors were the most righteous seven men and seven women, which crawled into a dry giant gourd shell and escaped the flood by floating in it. They emerged to replenish the drowned earth. [Based on legend as told by internet source quoting Frazer, pp. 203-204]

Often allegorical stories seem more popular with people than plain language. This might have something to do with why Christ so often used parables to teach the secrets of the kingdom of heaven with, such as the parable of the sower, which is similar to the gourd vine spreading and being scorched, rotted and growing in the bushes, almost as if he was saying you chose parables to teach with but you do not really understand them, as not even his disciples understood them and they had to have them explained to them. So I probably don't understand this allegorical legend, but let me make a stab at it just for fun.

This appears to be a combination of a global flood legend combined with vast catastrophic periods such as much fire or volcanic heat up on the mountains. The legend makes it apparent that this world was one of many ancient worlds and there were more worlds that had passed away or were destroyed. With this flood legend being called the middle world, this would normally be a clue that this was a later flood like those multiple worlds or suns as mentioned in other local flood legends.

Philo of Alexandria wrote: "By reason of the constant and repeated destructions by water and fire, the later generations did not receive from the former the memory of the order and sequence of events." This Burmese legend appears to be a prime example of this. And like children void of letters they know little of what happened in ancient times.

Gourds are a popular crop of Burma and they have multiple usages such as food, crafts and containers and so the gourd must have been seen as valuable focal point to the people and thus useful as a point of allegorical teaching. Bamboo is also a valuable crop and one world ended in which animals came out of bamboo. But for this legend they chose gourds, a very floatable live giving / saving item. The gourd here obviously equals the Ark, as I doubt even the largest gourd could hold and float 14 people. The raft and the giant gourd variations appear to be the same legend as the gourd was also linked with the cow, or a special animal in which all the people and animals and trees were saved inside from the flood. The death of the cow probably equates with clean animals that Noah sacrificed after the flood. Once again like the biblical version we see the people were far away from God so presumably their actions were not directed by godly influences. There are more gods that had bit parts in the legend which I ignored, including Kaw-hpa, Hseng-kio, Lao-hki, Tai-long, Bak-long, and Ya-hseng-hpa: these were the council members that decided mankind must die, indicating this catastrophe was a planned event, and not a natural one. This is very similar to the Epic of Gilgamesh where the gods counselled to destroy mankind, and suggests some of this or another world catastrophe was brought about by the gods...deliberately. This legend seems to be quite a cross section then of several catastrophes conveniently told as a single one. The escape into underground caves, the world devoured by fire, a dead crab in heaven, and giant 'cranes', which in fact could be pterodactyls as these are known to kill and feed on dead people. That's right; I said pterodactyls, which are quite similar to cranes in appearance. (See my first work) Here we also see the man Lip-Long was ridiculed, just as some have deduced Noah was ridiculed in his building of the ark. So there are a lot of clues to indicate this is a very similar global flood legend to the bible. It seems certain it is a legend intertwined with other legends of world catastrophes. Other cultures managed to separate the catastrophes a bit more and we will see them as we go on.

I think one of the most irksome things I've realized since starting this book is that there are indications that some of the gods conspired to kill mankind with at least one of these catastrophes. Not to be confused with God himself who allowed mankind to fall prey to his own folly, spawned from the excess "evil" or destruction taking place in the solar system. I had deduced in my previous work man had very advanced technology at his disposal and some of these items caused massive destruction on earth and in the heavens, but I had figured most of these incidences were accidents or unforeseen consequences, but I'm finding clues that suggest this may not have been the case. Again we see a clue in this legend of the gods descending down from heaven, as occurred soon after the global flood. And they become the ancestors of the kings indicating at least this part of the flood legend indicates that last global catastrophe after the gods left: So this legend is all over the map.

KIKUYU (KENYA): AN AFRICAN BEER FLOOD LEGEND.

A beautiful but mysterious woman agreed to marry a man on the condition that he never asked her about her family. He agreed, and they lived happily together until it was time for their oldest son's circumcision. The woman's family would not attend the ceremony so the man asked her why her family couldn't attend. Naughty, naughty! With that question from the husband, the wife bounced into the air and when she landed, made a hole seven miles deep. She called up her ancestors, who came as spirits from Mt. Kenya. The spirits raised a thunder and hailstorm as they came. They brought food, goats, cattle, and beer with them and, while the people took shelter in caves, they flooded the countryside with beer, turning it into a lake. When the spirits left, they took the couple and their children with them into Mt. Kenya.

This does have some interesting world flood similarities to some of the deductions I deduced for the cause of the global flood. The woman making a 7 mile hole is similar to an asteroid smashing into the earth bringing the ensuing rain as the asteroid smashed and collapsed the water canopy. It then seems to mirror or blends in more of a local flood type legend, such as people taking shelter in caves indicates, but a flood of beer? Could these references to goats and cattle be Noah's animals and then the beer a reference to Noah's wine from his vineyard? The reference to a circumcision, which as far as I know was never done until Abraham was told to do so, also suggests a post flood legend.

The latter part of this flood legend reminds me of the "Great Molasses Flood" of 1919, written about in August 1955 Readers Digest. At the time molasses took the place of the more expensive sugar to make rum, so molasses was often stored in large amounts. There was in Boston a huge molasses tank 50 feet high and 282 feet wide filled with 14,000 tons, not gallons, tons of molasses that burst open on January 15th and the molasses, oozing outwards at a speed of 35 miles an hour, faster than a man can run, and tore down an elevated railway, demolished several buildings and drowned 21 people. With people tracking through it, it spread every which way so that even when you rode a bus 44 miles away in Worcester, you were sticking to the seats. At the time of the article 36 years later you could still smell the 'sickly sweetish aroma' around some of the older buildings in Boston's north end. I wonder if in Boston this is still considered a 'local flood' legend?

EFIK-IBIBIO (NIGERIA):

The Sun and Moon are man and wife, and their best friend was Flood, whom they often visited. They often invited Flood to visit them, but he demurred, saying their house was too small. Sun and Moon built a much larger house, and Flood could no longer refuse their invitation. He arrived and asked, "Shall I come in?" and was invited in. When Flood was knee-deep in the house, he asked if he should continue coming and was again invited to do so. Then Flood brought many relatives, including fish and sea beasts. Soon he rose to the ceiling of the house, and then Sun and Moon went onto the roof. Flood kept rising, submerging the house entirely, and so Sun and Moon made a new home in the sky.

It's quite possible this is a world flood legend in mythological language. Here's the way I decipher this one: When just the earth was inhabited the flood never occurred. Man could see the moon and the sun through the water shell surrounding the earth, but the water never fell on man. Eventually man's abilities grew so that he could pass through the water canopy into space and thus appearing to invite a flood if not careful when passing though the water shell. But as man made his house larger by colonising the planets he spread his living space throughout the solar system. Wanton destruction in space caused the water canopy to break and cause the flood to come inside the house. When the house was flooded the sky changed consequently changing the appearance of the sun and the moon.

PERSIAN:

Early in the history of the earth it was full of harmful creatures created by the evil Ahriman. (Same as Angra Manyu of the Hindu gods)

The angel Tistar (the star Sirius) came to earth three times, appearing like a man, horse, and bull respectively, causing ten days of rain every visit. Each rain drop was as big as a bowl, flooding the whole earth to the height of a man. The first flood drowned the creatures, except the noxious creatures which escaped into holes in the earth. The second time Tistar came he took the form of a white horse to battle the demon Apaosha, who appeared as a black horse. Ormuzd (same as Ahura-Mazda) annoyed Apaosha with lightning, causing him to cry which is the sound we still hear in thunderstorms. Tistar won this battle causing rivers to gush. This ensuing flood washed all the poison from the land sending it into the oceans and making the oceans salty. The water around the earth was driven by a great wind and finally rested to become the sea Vourukasha. [Internet referring to Carnoy, p. 270; Vitaliano, pp. 161-162; H. Miller, p. 288]

Remember what the Egyptian Priest said "You remember one deluge only, whereas there were many of them...."

This legend clearly speaks of three floods, though it apparently only describes two. The first could be the world flood where the all creatures of earth (giants, and men) became harmful after an evil leader named Ahriman (man of renown, equal to the biblical version "men of renown"). The deductions in my first book showed that the flood was cause by war in heaven in which a manmade planet destroyed the 5th planet between Mars and Jupiter. Eventually an asteroid from that planet was missed by those protecting this earth from them, which consequently plunged onto the earth, through the crust and into earth's interior, causing the world flood. It's interesting that this manmade planet or "star" is called the star Sirius. The Dogons spoke of some very accurate knowledge of this star in the 19th century before their information was confirmed in the 20th. The manmade planet coming from the direction of Sirius to descend close to earth could link the two in legends, particularly if the people on the ship preferred us to believe this. Other legends are pretty clear that there is more than one of these manmade moons in existence as one such legend spoken of in the Drona Parva, speaks of three moons in the sky. Raymond Drake quoting the Drona Parva says "formerly the Valiant Asuras had in heaven three cities. Each of these cities was excellent and large. ...When the three cities came together in the firmament [they] were pierced [(with a] terrible shaft ...consisting of three knots. [The people] were unable to gaze at that shaft inspired with the yuga fire..." (book 34 pg 46)

Velikovsky notes that planets that come close to earth, such as Mars did, draw atmosphere from earth or distort their own atmosphere to look like a creature such as a wolf or a sword. Lightning discharges would also occur between the planets. If this legend speaks of two of these moons coming to earth ("Tistar, in the form of a white horse, battled the demon Apaosha, who took the form of a black horse.") this could account for the appearance, and the blasting of lightning from one globe to another from an electrical discharge when two large charged bodies come close to each other. Before the great flood it never rained, and lightning soon after the flood might have been rare, nonexistent, or not seen before due to the denser atmosphere of the early post flood era. So linking subsequent lightning to this event spoken of in the legend would appear logical. Before, during and after the first (global) flood, the ocean waters might actually have been drinkable with little or no impurities due to erosion before the flood, and all the fresh water descending from the canopy in the flood and little after. Any subsequent floods would have caused much runoff and erosion making ocean water salty and full of impurities. There are now thousands of feet of silt on the ocean floor that was at one time all part of terra firma. The last part of this legend with the wind driving the waters around the earth, seem to allude to massive tsunamis and shifting continents or the earth reeling from some impact as the massive winds that would accompany such an event (causing things like instantly frozen mammoths). The waters were driven one way or another across the land, and if the land was moving during the event, such as the earth tumbling, new seas would have formed. With the Americas moving away from Europe and Africa, the water rushing into the new Atlantic Ocean from across North America creating a 'wide gulf', between the continents could be what this or a similar event that this legend describes.

WESTERN AUSTRALIA

This flood legend was discovered by Anthropologists among an Aboriginal tribe in a remote area of Western Australia before any missionaries made it to the region. Naturally it is assumed to be their version of the Biblical flood, but there are key differences that indicate it is an amalgamated legend.

Very early on children tormented a winking owl named Dumbi which grieved the Supreme One whom the Aborigines call Ngadja. So Ngadja talked to Gajara telling him if he wanted to live, then he was to take his wife and sons and their wives onto a double raft filled with long lasting foods. He told him that because of the treatment of Dumbi the owl, he intended to drown everyone by rain and a flood.

So Gajara stored foods and gathered all sorts of birds including the cuckoo, mistletoe eater, finches, the helmeted friar bird, and the rainbow bird, along with a female kangaroo.

Then Ngadja sent rainclouds down on the people. The sea-flood came in from the North-Northwest and all the people were encompassed by the salt-water flood and the tidal waves from the sea. The flood waters whirled and the earth opened up drowning and flattening all the people. The people on the raft were swept by the current all the way to Dulugun, and then the waters eventually pulled them back. Gajara sent out the cuckoo to look for land but it found none and returned. When the waters went down some more, he sent them out again the next day and the land was already drying up and the creatures found a home and some food. When they landed they killed the kangaroo and cooked it in an oven along with other foods. The smoke from the cooking reached the sky and the smell pleased the Supreme one. Ngadja put the rainbow in the sky to protect us from the rain fall water rising too high. The rainbow is our sign that we know there will not be any abnormally heavy rain.

Though this obviously has strong parallels to the biblical flood legend, I place it here because the people weren't killed by rising water and no mention of it covering the mountains is suggested. The flood appears to be of a shorter duration, and key is the people were all killed by monstrous tidal waves that came from the sea and from a very specific direction, and not from above. We also see that the earth opened up and the sea went into the opening, and not the water coming out of the ground like the biblical and other legends specify. This legend speaks of a massive tidal wave and an earthquake so intense it opened the earth and swallowed up the sea along with the people. Even the double raft appears to have been swept away by the tsunami then pulled back close to its starting position, similar to a tidal wave. So this legend is clearly combining the global flood with a flood caused by massive earth disturbances and ruptures causing a mega tsunami. It would be easy to confuse the global flood with the latter mega tsunami after the fact by assuming the first flood was like the second after the second was experienced by the people, so it's understandable the two legends could have merged into one over time.

PAPAGO (ARIZONA)

When the earth was closer to the sun, Coyote chewed down a tree, climbed inside and sealed it when he anticipated a coming flood. Montezuma noticed what Coyote had done and made a dugout canoe for himself on top of Mount Rosa. He and his family were the only ones to survive a flood that covered all the land. The coyote and Montezuma met again at Mount Rosa which rose out of the flood waters. To see how much dry land there was, the man sent the Coyote out to explore, and the coyote came back and told him there was sea to the east, south and west, but there was seemingly endless land as far as the eye could see to the north. The Great Spirit, with Montezuma's help, refilled the earth with people and animals and Montezuma and Coyote taught and led the people.

Over time Montezuma became filled with pride and rebelled against the Great Mystery causing evil to come into the world, so the Great Mystery raised the sun to its present height with an earthquake that destroyed a tower Montezuma was building to reach the heavens. This disturbance caused the languages of the peoples to change so that people could no longer understand each other or the animals. [Based on Erdoes & Ortiz, p. 487-489; and Gaster, pp. 114-115]

This legend also notes that Montezuma was the first man, so this name appears to be a synonym for mankind. Once again we have a legend that links the size and distance of the sun from the Earth, with a catastrophe. Though this legend doesn't specifically say the mountains were covered by the flood, it seems to be implied. Later on an earthquake moves the sun further away. So this legend encompasses at least two global catastrophic changes, one that involves a flood directly and a second that would involve a flood in other parts of the world as the earth moved further from the sun, caused by an earthquake. This quake would obviously be of tremendous proportions, no doubt from an asteroid shoving the earth into an orbit further from the sun. Interestingly this legend also includes the tower of Babel incident.

HO (SOUTH-WESTERN BENGAL):

When people began to ignore God and became incestuous and unmindful of their betters, the creator destroyed all the folks except for sixteen people. Some say the creator destroyed them with water, some say by fire. [Based on Gaster, p. 96].

Though this is a very short legend the cause of the destruction is uncertain to the people because both a flood and a massive fire are recalled. Later we will see that some legends speak of the world being on fire so even though the south Bengals have not actually mixed up the legends together, they are confused as to the reason because both flood and fire causes are remembered and retold.

TOLTEC (MEXICO):

One of the sons of the twofold god made himself into the sun and created the earth and the humans, showing up his brothers. The other gods annoyed by this showmanship got Quetzalcoatl to destroy the sun and the earth by a flood and turned the people into fish. This ended the first age. The second, third and fourth suns ended by the heavens crumbling, in a rain of fire and lastly by overwhelming winds. [Based on Leon-Portilla, p. 450]

Though short it covers the four ages very concisely. It of course shows the first age ended with a flood and the description notes that the sun and the earth changed because of it. The sun visible through the water shell of the preflood world would no longer exist with that appearance so it's said to be destroyed and a new sun appears, or put another way the appearance of the sun changes. This legend quickly goes through the next three ages and how they end. The sky crumbling is an interesting way of saying Martian rocks pummelled the earth. We see a quick reference to an event filled with fire ending an age, and the ferocious winds ending the fourth age. These ages become more described as we go, so we'll leave it at that for now. Of note: we now begin to see the trend where the concept of the creator and 'the other gods' are blurred and put on an even footing as seen in this legend, something common in current books like Von Daniken's Chariots of the gods series. This has been going on now down through the ages. The bonus section tells us how this comes about.

GUANCA AND CHIQUITO (PERU):

Before the time of the Incas, the land was very populated. All at once the ocean burst out of its boundaries and onto the land covering it and killing all the people. Some say a few survived in caves on the highest mountains and other say that only six people survived on a float. [Based on Frazer, pp. 271-272]

Here again we see two very similar disasters which have confused the people that came afterwards. Two flood legends have been muddled up, but this one should clearly illustrate to you now that there was more than one flood and the 'order of things' has been confused. The flood of Noah had the people saved in a "float", and the tsunami type flood (where the "ocean burst out of its boundaries") only allowed people in caves in the mountains to survive. But because they both seem simply like 'the flood legend' to the tellers, some confusion has surfaced in the people's history. Fact is both sets of people's tales that think the people saved were in a boat or the mountains are correct, but they have simply mixed up the understanding of the flood to be a single flood, when there were at least two catastrophic floods in this location.

HOPI

The Hopi appear to have confused the order of the world ages.

The first world went underground to live with the ant people and when they were safe the world was destroyed by fire. The people underground lived in rooms where they stored food, and they saw by a light emitted by bits of crystal that absorbed light from the sun. (This could speak of technology similar to Light Emitting Diodes drawing power from solar energy explained by the Hopi as their concept of the equipment) With food running short the ant people ate less so the people had more. When the world cooled off and they emerged from underground, much of the land and water had switched places.

In the second world the animals became wild and lived separated from the people. Greed started in the second world even though people had all they needed but they wanted more and neglected songs to the creator in the search for more goods and began to fight with each other. The few who still sung were laughed at, so once again the world was destroyed after the people that were not greedy were saved underground. The time this age ended was when the twins abandoned the poles so that the world rolled over, went off balance and spun crazily. Mountains plunged into the seas and the seas and lakes sloshed over the land. The world spun through cold lifeless space and it froze into solid ice. The twins were ordered back to the poles and order returned. When the ice began to melt and the world became safe to live on again the people emerged from underground once again.

The third world ended this way. The people began to become occupied with their earthly plans, and used reproductive powers in wicked ways, and they began using creative powers in evil and destructive ways. Shields were made that flew through the air and cities were attacked using them, and then when they returned no one knew where they came from. After a while more cities figured out how to make the flying shields and more cities were attacked. To stop the few people who sang to God from being corrupted and killed off too, it was decided to destroy the world with water. The good people were told to hide in the hollow stems of tall plants and they were all sealed up together by Spider woman. The waters were loosed onto the world and waves higher than the mountains rolled onto the land. The continents broke up and sank beneath the waves and soon the people in the reeds could tell they were floating. The reed tops were removed and they could see the tops of one of the highest mountains. They floated on and on as the flood continued and it became plain that all the mountains were now sunk under the water. After a while they sent birds out to find land but they all returned tired, from not sighting any land to rest on. They drifted for a long time and were instructed to build paddles. After much paddling and a few short stops here and there they finally reached the fourth world as it slowly emerged from the sea. The people landed and migrated over the world. (Quick synopsis of Book 70 pgs 15-28)

It's easy now to see that somehow the order of the worlds here has been jumbled, with the global flood being said to have happened *after* two previous worlds were destroyed. This is the only time I've seen the ages put in an order, with the global flood occurring last. It simply has to be a flawed order and then repaired to make it seem like the correct order when narrated by the tellers. It clearly talks of the same features of the global flood: mountains over topped by water, a few people saved in a floatation apparatus, and after a long time finally coming to land. The abandoning of the poles causing havoc on the earth clearly describes the events on the world after the flood such as freezing solid great expanses of the world, and water sloshing over the land, and land and sea changing places. Consider this: if the lands were plunging into the sea before the great flood and the shifting in the continents then created the mountains, they would be higher than the water and couldn't possibly submerge the mountains if the global flood was the last disaster. It would in essence be saying the world as we see it today was covered by water over the tallest mountain; this is just not possible as there would be way too much water to account for. The land *before* the world flood was low profile making it possible for the mountains to become completely submerged. This clearly means the order is mixed up, though how it happened can only be caused by confusion that crept in at some later period.

INCA (PERU):

I've quoted this legend as found as it's so quirky I just don't know how to say it in my own words and not lose any meaning or obscure the irregularities.

"The creator god Viracocha made the earth and sky, and he created stone giants to live in it. After a while the giants became lazy and quarrelsome, and Viracocha decided to destroy them. Some of them he turned back to stone, and these stone statues still exist at Tiahuanaco and Pucara. He destroyed the rest with a great flood. When the flood subsided, it left the lakes Titicaca and Poopo, and it left seashells on the Altiplano at elevations of 3660 m. Viracocha saved two stone giants from the flood and with their help created people his own size. He reached down into Lake Titicaca and drew out the Sun and Moon to provide light so he could admire his new creation. In those days, the Moon was even brighter than the Sun, but the Sun grew jealous and threw ashes onto the Moon's face." [Internet quoting Gifford, p. 54]

This legend mixes up and confuses all sorts of events: it does however mentions giants destroyed in the flood like the bible and other legends do. But it confuses Viracocha who we know was one of the gods with the creator. And this legend speaks of the ability of turning people into stone which is possible only with unified field technology by causing people to merge with earth. (See explanation in my first work). It mixes up the floods that occurred when the continents moved west causing the water to swell above the Andes turning the port city Tiahuanaco (and the nearby Lake Titicaca) into high altitude locations with the flood that destroyed mankind and the original giants. The gods are said to have descended in a sun or a gleaming egg on Lake Titicaca, so bright flying machines and the sun are also mixed up. Consider: the disk of Ra is thought to mean the sun, yet at one time this disk of Ra was actually measured. It is seven cubits and the 'pupil' is three cubits...or about 16.58 feet and the pupil being about 6 1/4 feet. (Book 61 pg 305-306) So they are in fact measuring a flying disc and not the sun. Yet Ra and the sun are mixed up even today, even though the Book of the dead describes the actual measuring the eye of Ra. Interestingly it speaks of the moon being blasted by impact craters and it says the moon was brighter than the sun. This might not be possible as the moon only reflects light, but it accurately notes that a lumpier broken terrain would not shine and reflect as brightly as a smooth surfaced moon. The moon would have been considerably brighter and if it was closer to the earth as some point it could seem brighter than the sun, and could even be considered by some as a different moon, as some legends described it. There are of course the remains of sea creatures in the Andes, and specifically at Lake Titicaca and Tiahuanaco.

In trying to separate the flood legends into the defined categories of global, mixed and coming next, the local legends, you may have noticed this sorting process is not as easy as it sounds. For example when I worked on just the global flood legends and placed them in the first chapter, it soon became apparent that some of these legends even had elements of other catastrophes mingled in. A few times I placed legends in one category then had to move them when I analyzed them further. We now get to the crux of the matter, the local flood legends. Some preview glimpses have been seen up to now, but be prepared for a wild and woolly ride through these legends as they speak of an unbelievable series of periods of earth history that has been overlooked or deliberately hidden from you by standard geology, textbooks, archaeology and even palaeontology. When you piece it together and visualize it, it even becomes a little frightening. One might understand why this has been smoothed over by uniformitarianism beliefs, because it might scare the school children if they knew. So buckle up and get ready for a rough ride; this one makes roller coasters seem tame.

Chapter 4

Local Flood Legends (Type 3)

Preamble...or is that Pre-ramble?

Before some guy named Charles Lyell came along trying to discredit the bible by assigning arbitrary and ridiculously old dates to various layers and strata, and a chap fell into his web by the name of Charles Darwin, the founder of vertebrate palaeontology named Georges Cuvier (1769-1832) was highly impacted by the picture the geologic layers of the earth presented to him. He deduced that great catastrophes had repeatedly taken place on the earth. He could clearly see that sea beds had changed into continents and continents had changed into sea beds; which by the way is exactly like legends such as the Hopi mentioned. Part of what drove him to these conclusions was seeing a variety of animal remains inside various layers of earth, often at oblique angles. He concluded that catastrophes over vast areas annihilated all life in these areas suddenly. His reasoning for apparently new species now seen in these areas, but not originally present in the same localities, was they must have migrated from areas not affected by the cataclysms evident into these areas displaying upheavals. Though the evidence clearly indicated cataclysmic events, it really bothered him that he couldn't determine the origin or cause of those events. Strata which often appear at crazy angles are completely overturned or in a massive jumble. Hoards of animals of various species looked as though they've been herded literally in between a rock and a hard place and then pulverized as the land pressed in on them as though the land moved and pressed in so fast on them that they could not escape.

OBLIVIOUS IGNORATIONS

Charles Lyell ignored Cuvier's conclusions based on real evidence and deliberately set out to discredit the creation story by assigning huge arbitrary dates to various strata and invented the "Geologic Column" and then assigned dates to each layer of the column. Though there are apparently dozens of 'dated' layers in the column, there are few places on the earth where even three of the layers appear in the "correct order". But this didn't bother Lyell and he assigned the dates regardless. Now these dates, though modified upward in age since the 1840's, are set in stone. Now rocks are dated by the fossils in the layer and fossils are dated by the rocks in the layer. This illogical method of dating fossils led Charles Darwin astray helping him to conclude that some sort of progression of the species had to have taken place over time to account for the 'new' species seen in these areas. This was how he assumed species not seen in an area before certain stratification layers must have appeared as though through some evolutionary boost, and not like the logical migration theory that Cuvier figured out.

But Darwin had a hard time when he came across various strata beds with countless fossils jumbled together like a log jam and he thought it would be easy to conclude the creatures had been caught up in an upheaval that shook the very framework of the globe; which was exactly what Cuvier concluded. Somehow this obvious conclusion based on the plain evidence visible around the globe has slipped through or been shoved in between the cracks. Thus the theory of uniformitarianism has taken over geologic science despite the glaring contradictions seen in strata layers around the world.

This theory supposes that the mountains are what are left of plateaus eroded by a very slow process from wind and water. Sedimentary rock is supposedly the result of igneous rock gradually worn away by rain and making its way to the sea, then slowly re-deposited on dry land. Fossils were supposedly made from creatures that happened to be walking on this re-deposited sediment which we call sand, and just happened to die while walking on it and then like magic were suddenly covered by sediments before they rotted. All these theories are hokum and have been disproven but instead of evolutionary geologists crying uncle, they ignore the issue. Mountains have been shown to have been created in sudden surges; otherwise they would have eroded as fast as they rose. Sedimentary rocks are created from irruptions of the sea onto land then subsiding while the cementing agents quickly solidify. Without accepting these facts, how then could they hope to explain the reality that sedimentary rock is found in the Himalayans along with Seashells and sea critters? Not to mention the odds of a bird happily walking along the beach then suddenly dying are slim to none to begin with, as such a creature would have to be in good health to go out walking, but then suddenly die in the midst of a merry walk on the beach, then to have the additional fluke of the rare bird with the heart attack on a beach suddenly getting buried, which might mean one fossil in 10,000 years if that many. While trying to figure out how fast whale bones disintegrate on land by checking on line, I found this quote about fossil formation:

Some bones do manage to achieve true immortality, and you've probably seen dozens of them over the course of your life – most likely in museums! *Fossils are bones that were so rapidly encased in sediment that air was completely shut out*, making it impossible for any decomposition to occur. This is the case in volcanic eruptions, and other catastrophic events that displace large amounts of sediment on the earth. (Scienceabc.com) Emphasis mine... the *Italics* part.

And fossilization doesn't just happen with birds having heart attacks on the beach, or liver malfunctions, assuming it ever did. Fossils are found in the billions along the western coast of America all clustered together: Billions of fish, molluscs, and, uh... fish...did I say fish?... all along the California coast, and that's a lot of heart attacks, and kidney malfunctions: or did I say liver?! I always get those two confused. Having a kidney disease isn't helping me remember which is which much either. I mean do fish even have heart attacks? And why would fish be walking along the beach anyway? Oh I forgot; it's evolutionists that came up with that idea. I suppose if a fish were walking on the beach that would give the bird a heart attack if he saw one...not sure about the kidney failure though...or did I say liver? Evolutionists clearly think we don't have any brains to figure out the obvious. "Even authors of textbooks confess their ignorance. "Why have sea floors of remote periods become lofty highlands of today? What generates the enormous forces that bend, break, and mash the rocks in mountain zones? These questions still await satisfactory answers." (Book 14 quoting *A Textbook of Geology* by Longwell, Knopf and Flint)

The problem is further complicated when rock-solid igneous rock is found *on top* of sedimentary rock. So to fix the logistics problem, millions of years are just added to the timeline to somehow cure the contradictions. More contradictions are found where remains of man and dinosaurs are found together in layers that are supposed to be older than both of them. These problems are so upsetting that they simply say such sites that are found are a hoax or they ignore the finds altogether simply because they don't fit in their 'simple' version of world geologic history. To top it all off, the ice ages weren't something they deduced occurred by evidence, but the theory of the ice ages was something invented to somehow explain how clay, sand and gravel could be found sitting on top of igneous rock. (Book 14 pg 37) Though its true large masses of ice did cover vast stretches of land in the past, it does not work as an agent of depositing vast fields of sediment such as clay sand and gravel over these vast areas. At best it could explain only small areas of these loose materials at the edges of the glaciers when and where they ceased their slow movements; when they ran out of momentum and ice. What's almost pitiful is no satisfactory explanation for the origin of ices ages (whether they existed or not) is even known. Cooling of the earth doesn't work as is evidenced by Siberia which has never had a glacier or an ice age, neither is heating and cooling of the earth via a variable sun capable of producing an ice age, nor has a slow change in the earth's axis been proven capable of creating an ice age. Even establishing a time period for the retreat of glaciers is sheer guess work and the age of 12,000 years is simply a figure arrived at through consensus and not evidence. Ice ages further baffle geologist when they realized that the glaciers of the past moved from the equatorial region toward the poles and not the other way around.

Back to Cuvier who wrote "Repeated irruptions and retreats of the sea have neither all been slow nor gradual; on the contrary, most of the catastrophes which occasioned them have been sudden; and this is especially easy to be proved with regard to the last of these catastrophes, that which by a twofold motion, has inundated, and afterwards laid dry, our present continents, or at least part of the land which forms them at the present day. In the northern regions it has left the carcasses of large quadrupeds which have become enveloped in the ice, and have thus been preserved even to our own times, with their skin, hair, and flesh. If they had not been frozen as soon as killed, they would have decomposed to putrefaction. And, on the other hand, this eternal frost could not previously have occupied the places in which they have been seized by it, for they could not have lived in that temperature. It was therefore, at one and the same moment that these animals were destroyed and the country which they inhabited became covered with ice. This event has been sudden, instantaneous, without any gradation,..." Book 14 pg 41-42 quoting Cuvier's *Essay on the Theory of the Earth*) Note also that he said that the part of the land that forms our continents was overrun suddenly by irruptions of the sea. That is another way of saying the entire land mass above water was subjected to huge tsunamis that crossed the entire continents: excluding the continental shelves: Think about that.

Furthermore the plant life consumed by the creatures killed by these events does not grow in these regions anymore and the suddenness of the shift from temperate zone to deep frozen arctic is made vivid when you realize actual ocean waves were frozen suddenly in the very act of breaking. There is nothing slow or gradual about it.

Some overturning of this the theory of uniformitarianism has occurred with a new theory of called "Punctured equilibrium" where sudden upheavals might have occurred but then long time frames between events is assumed, to continue on with the myth of an old earth based on the geologic column, even though the layers between geologic eras show no erosion that would have taken place over these supposed millions of years they sat there. Indeed it's quite clear the geologic layers were laid down in quick succession, possibly in the very same event that laid down the previous layers. We will see first by the legends that these multi layered strata's of the earth were created in historic times, and then later we will see the evidence that should have proven Cuvier's conclusions long ago.

To set the stage for understanding the underlying events happening on the earth that started the following local flood legends to come into play, it will help to have a brief synopsis of the events occurring on the earth after the global flood was over to see how the local floods came into play. The synopsis you are about to read might seem completely fantastic but bear with me. We will slowly see that all the pieces fit this scenario as you work through it one piece at a time. It will also help you see why I interpret some of the legends as I do. Though the interpretations might at first sound off the wall, eventually the big picture will start to form in your minds, and it will start to fill in and make sense of what were formerly ancient "mysteries": The synopsis...

After the global flood was over the environment of the earth had changed. There was no longer the protective water sphere surrounding the globe so far more solar radiation was coming to the surface, and people's life spans rapidly diminished. Noah born 600 years before the flood lived to 950, Shem, born 100 years before the flood only lived to 600, and one of his descendants, Peleg born just 101 years after the flood, lived to just 239. Man's life expectancy was rapidly deteriorating as the atmosphere rapidly left earth to the point it found equilibrium of pressure a few hundred years after the flood. Radioactive Carbon 14 started to form in the atmosphere right after the flood with whatever detrimental effects it might have on life, and harmful radiation from the sun was poisoning the earth and the plants and animals to further reduce life spans and the strength of living creatures. After the flood, every aspect of mankind was devolving; his stamina, size, intelligence, capabilities and capacities along with genetic soundness were all deteriorating in the now degraded environment of the earth mankind now found he was living in. At first we were very slow to rebuild after the flood but something happened that ramped up mans efforts exponentially. We'll get to that in a sec.

While researching this new work, I found an interesting tidbit about the rainbow and related items that further demonstrates global deterioration. Before the flood there was no rainbow, meaning there was apparently no refraction of light in mists. There may have been some ultra or infra light waves visible in artificial detectors, but they were not visible to man. If they could determine 0.33750 parts of a second as post flood peoples were able to do, and include in data the wobble of the moon on some chronometer (Book 11 pg 54, 63), they probably had spectrometers before the flood. After the flood Gods gives the rainbow as a sign. We assume this is the rainbow we all see today, but it appears a large portion of the rays were still being filtered out at sea level (or even as high as mount Ararat levels) by the still denser atmosphere of the earth still extant following the flood. How so? Alan Lansburg in his book *In Search of Ancient Mysteries* clues into a very interesting observation that he assumes it is evidence of man still evolving. He notes that none of the "prehistoric" cave painters used any green or blue. However Lansburg hypothesises this was because the painters were partly colour blind. He uses as support for this idea the fact that just 2000 years ago or so, Xenophanes c.570 B.C.-c475 B.C. (one of those Greek philosophers, theologians and poets you never hear about, being overshadowed by Plato and the rest.) describes the rainbow as having just three colours; purple, red and yellow. Similarly Aristotle spoke of a three coloured rainbow too...(colours not mentioned). I think it's safe to say if it was common for people of the time to see all the colours in them we see today, Aristotle and Xenophanes would have realized there was a personal deficiency, so this existence of a 3 coloured rainbow had to be common to all men. Lansburg further adds that Homer thought the ocean was the colour of wine, [red or white not stated] and "primitive" Indo-European speech has no words for all the colours [that we do today]. He assumes this proves that we are still evolving where we see more colours today. (Book 8 pg 184) However I strongly suspect this means that as more and more atmosphere leaves the earth, less sunlight is filtered out, and more of the refracted spectrum becomes visible to our eyes. Thus this would appear to be another evidence for the steady deterioration of the earth's environment.

As an interesting side note, there is a rare 'condition' called tetrachromancy that some women have where they see four primary colours instead of three. What we see as dull grey pebbles on the beach, they would see them in technicolour. Also rare is the condition known as synaesthesia that lets people see the sounds they hear in colour and they can taste colours or words or music, and even smell the sounds they hear. What would the rainbow look like to them? I imagine that these were normal abilities that at one time all people had which have since gone dormant in the genetic pool and only rarely surfaces now in the population: I'm confident that before the flood everyone had these capabilities and far more. What else has gone by the wayside in genetic decline or "devolution"? One can only imagine a glimpse of what heaven, or just what earth was like to the people of preflood times when our genetics were so sound there were no mutations, and you could safely marry a sibling with no negative genetic repercussions. OK, on with the post flood synopsis...

THE ELUDIUM 637K SPACE MODULATOR.

Well once the flood was over, the people that were in space at the time of the flood came back to earth soon after, and though they stated their origin to the descendants of Noah, their undiminished physical capacity now vastly superior to the people born after the flood became painfully obvious, and as such they were now looked up to as gods. Their return to earth initiated what is now called the Age of the gods. Though the gods helped man to quickly build up civilization and helped with scientific, technical, domestication of animals and botanical aid, earthbound man quickly mastered the state of the arts. But deficiencies in man were becoming apparent; with a more warlike and destructive disposition they soon tried to become as the gods but with a far more volatile disposition. They started to build a tower to enable them to achieve space travel the way the gods did. However knowing the danger this put the human race in, God himself halted construction of the tower by confusing the language of the people, and apparently instructed the gods to disperse the people around the world after this event. Thus the people of similar tongues were taken to various places around the globe and set up in new civilizations with the aid of the gods. This would explain why the Eskimo's say they were flown to where they are in big birds. Similar to the Eskimo, Montezuma told Hernan Cortéz that their ancestors were not natives of the land, but that a lord brought their people to this land then returned to his own land. (Book 23 pg 132)

While all the gods were building cities around the globe using an antigravity system common to all, the overuse of the system disrupted the global magnetic field and ripped apart the continents and changed the face of the globe. The gods were forced to abandon all the building projects and focussed on civilizing the people. Some of the gods left and returned to their manmade moons and returned to space, while some of the gods remained. But all mankind, and the remaining gods were deteriorating to a more devolved, aggressive and warlike behaviour. The gods that remained realizing they too were diminishing fast in physiological soundness decided they had to leave the surface of the planet and tried to go back to the artificial moons with the other gods, but their deteriorated gene pool made their admittance impossible. There was a war in heaven but eventually they were forced back to the earth and went underground and underwater away from the destructive rays of the sun. At some point the gods realizing a direct hit was coming from space to wreak havoc upon the earth, so they warned mankind and built underground tunnels and living spaces to house the population that believed their report. The people that went underground to escape the coming cataclysms were spared but when they re-emerged to the surface they entered a strange and changed new world with a new sun and moon: that is the atmospheric differences would have made the sun and moon appear different as described in some legends which we will get to at length. If this synopsis is way too much to take in all at once, we will see in these following legends some of this summary played out in the tales and myths of peoples and these local flood legends. Now it's time to sort through the local flood legends, but to start, let's see what we are up against.

Here is a general description of deluge or flood legends found in Funk and Wagnall's 1950 *Dictionary of Folklore, Mythology and Legend*...as quoted on the internet.

"A world cataclysm during which the earth was inundated or submerged by water: a concept found in almost every mythology in the world. The exceptions are Egypt and Japan ..." general descriptions of these flood legends are given. "The gods (or a god) decide to send a deluge on the world, usually as punishment for some act, broken tabu, the killing of an animal, etc., but sometimes no reason is given. Certain human beings are warned, or it comes without warning. If warned, the people construct some kind of vessel (raft, ark, ship, big canoe, or the like), or find other means of escape (climbing a mountain, tree, growing tree, floating island, calabash, coconut shell, a turtle's back, or crab's cave, etc.). Sometimes they also save certain things essential to a way of life, such as food, [but] *rarely domestic animals*. The deluge comes (rain, **huge wave**, a container broken or opened, a monster's belly punctured, etc.). Bird or rodent scouts are often sent out, but this is *not universal*. When the deluge is over the survivors find themselves on a mountain or an island; sometimes they offer a sacrifice (*not universal*), and then repeople the earth, recreate animals, etc., by some miraculous means." (*Italics* and **Bold** my emphasis)

A close analysis of this barebones description of the flood legends in general shows clearly some legends would be perceptible as of a global nature and some local, but here again we see the concept of ancient flood legends are simply all lumped together in this general description as merely 'flood legends'. Many legends speak of the mountains covered or submerged thus a universal flood, whereas some legends of floods that speak of being saved by climbing a tree or a mountain or going underground clearly can't be the same flood legend. Also some flood legends say it was caused by rain, and some floods were caused by huge waves such as this general description above mentions. We've covered the global types of flood and as you are aware we stumbled across a few of these other types of floods when we showed some legends had been blended together. Now we will look at the local flood types which are often described as 'huge waves' which are more of a tsunami type of local flood, caused by massive upheavals, and these are the flood legends in general I will be concentrating on.

Now the causes of the local floods that occurred well after the global floods are several. Once again a quick recap of my deductions in my first book.

A global antigravity system that was used before the flood wasn't a problem, but with the earth's crust cracked into many fractures by the meteor that caused the global flood, and with the former preflood antigravity system being placed into service again by the gods after the flood, its use pulled the fractures zones apart causing the continents to come into being, with massive tsunamis worldwide.

It has been realized that the pyramids around the world follow a fairly regular path at the 30th N Parallel, and is often referred to as the Pyramid Belt. (Book 6 pg 121) The pyramids were at one time capped with manmade crystal, but almost all have had the crystal tops removed and destroyed to prevent the same thing from happening again. Some ancient legends say that man himself caused catastrophes with his science. The pyramids were part of that science.

"Traditions hint that millennia ago Black Magicians developed sidereal weapons more potent than the hydrogen bomb, whose explosions shattered civilization, displaced the magnetic poles and modified the protective radiation belts, causing intensified cosmic rays to mutate species and change climates, convulsing Earth in immense disaster." (Book 23 pg 114 quoting Jacques Bergier La Nouvelle aube des alchemists Planete 39 M/A 1968) Often in days gone by, technology was described by people that didn't understand the science, referred to it as a form of magic. Though I never came across this Bergier book or a translation of it, I came to similar conclusions in my first work. "Later generations condemned all science as black magic and persecuted those who practiced the secret arts, periodically burning their books, secretly dreading perhaps that scientists would again cause cataclysms." (Ibid)

We all know the dread of nuclear war, and other potential disasters caused by our technology: Here's one you might not be aware of; use of the Large Hadron Collider has apparently created upheavals in the neighbourhood the collider was built in. Buildings, bridges and roads alignment have been shifted out of true. Rivers and water-ways have also been skewed. Many cases of dementia and Alzheimer's disease and depression have occurred in the neighbourhood of the collider as well. The conclusion was that the collider had warped the physical reality of the area. Einstein's equations show that the Hadron Collider could in theory open up very small black holes. (Atlantis rising #82 and 86)

Here's another one: areas with large dams and where water has been extensively pumped from underground experience higher than average incidences of earthquakes. Nineteen dams were studied and a correlation between water depth and earthquake magnitudes and frequencies was established. (Book 19 pg 118) The Three Gorges Dam in China when it was completed and filled actually caused a wobble in the earth.

Bella Karish discovered that an array of human activity caused geological disturbances resulting in earthquakes. Because of this interface between man and his environment, earthquake frequencies and magnitudes will continue to escalate. Water depletion, nuclear tests, and the like increased the earth's wobble which in turn will cause minor land shifts and energize continental drift...which in turn would bring more earthquakes and more wobble, and this would continue back and forth until the earth tumbled or flipped its axis about 90 degrees. Thus she linked man's activity to earthquakes, wobble, plate movements and pole shifts. (Book 19 pg 165)

The earth itself has energy belts, also called ley lines and dragon paths. I had deduced that the pyramids belt linked all the pyramids together similar to an electric eye where each pyramid is part of the others and they can be used to tap into earth magnetic belts for antigravity. Although I try to stick with historical material, but because I had deduced this before reading something Edgar Cayce said in one of his 'sleeping' states, I thought it worth mentioning. He said that during the 'Golden Age' they had achieved the neutralization of gravity by the harnessing of the sun's energy through crystals. Misuse of these crystals caused two of the cataclysms that eventually destroyed Atlantis. (Book 64 pg 152) What's amazing is that I had indeed stated that the pyramids (capped with crystals) had likely caused two events in the separating of the continents, not one; the initial breaking up Pangaea into continents and then the later larger lurch that flung the continents away from each other. Note that Cayce said "eventually". With the continents now set in motion from the pyramid use, later interaction between Earth, and Mars, Venus and large asteroid impacts continued the drift which eventually destroyed Atlantis many centuries later.

Though the ancients had nuclear war, I've not been able to ascertain that these wars were linked to floods by any legends I've found so far, though we do know that nuclear tests have cause multiple tornadoes. (Book 62 Pg 222) So it's possible some of the ancient atomic wars did cause massive flooding, but legendary? An item I overlooked in my first book I found in this current research I include here: The Drona parvan speaks of "Brahma's weapon": "the son of Drona hurled the weapon and the great winds arose; the waters rushed upon the earth. The soldiers were defeated by peals of thunder, the earth shook, the waters rose up, [and] the mountains split asunder." (Book 21 pg 83) So mans technology of the era apparently is responsible for more than one type and period of flood legends. These wars would have occurred near the end of the age of the gods.

Further floods caused by a continued separation of the continents ensued over the centuries by more asteroid hits, and interaction between Earth and Mars (gone to in length in my first book) and as I've come to realize in this present research; between the Earth and Venus. The Earth, Mars and Venus had been knocked out of their regular orbits by the solar system under siege by the multitude of asteroids from the exploded planet, and possibly by the moon of Saturn.

Velikovsky made several predictions about the physical attributes of Mars and Venus based on his deductions of ancient histories from around the world telling their close proximity to earth causing upheavals. From his interpretations he predicted that Venus would be about 800 degrees and have a retrograde rotation, while Argon and Neon would be found on Mars and that it would be pockmarked and cratered. I don't know how remarkable some of these predictions are, but when it became possible to ascertain these things, people had to take a step back when he was proven correct.

There is a Greek legend called the Fall of Phaëthon. Phaëthon was the son of Helios, and had "...yoked the steeds in his father's chariot, because he was not able to drive them in the path of his father, burnt all there was upon the earth, and was himself destroyed by a thunderbolt." (Book 6 pg. 25) An Egyptian Priest explained to Solon the interpretation of this myth: "Now this has the form of a myth but really signifies a deviation from their courses of the bodies moving around the earth and in the heavens, and a great conflagration of things upon the earth recurring at long intervals of time" (Book 11 Pg 57) It's a flowery way of saying exactly the same thing...The planets were out of their proper orbits and somehow interacted with the Earth causing destruction down here. We'll go into more legends concerning Venus soon enough. Is your mind messed up yet? There's more.

TOP IS BOTTOM

Andrew Tomas in his book "We Are Not The First" after revealing page after page of clues that ancient man had technology and even space travel far beyond what we have today, he furthermore assembled a few clues suggesting that there were many major disasters in ancient times causing advanced civilization to crumble. Consequently near the end of his book he asks the questions "Did the ancients receive a scientific legacy from the survivors of an older civilization destroyed by tidal waves and the fires of submarine volcanoes in a geological upheaval? Or was primordial science and culture brought to this world by space visitors who had aeons ago reached the level of evolution on which we are standing now?" (Book 11 pg 173) Though he evidently saw these extreme conclusions as worthy of the questions, the questions should be asked in reverse; in the order these things occurred. Man before the global flood developed unbelievable technologies and at least one (and possible 3 or more) massive manmade moons were in space at the time of the flood. The people on these 'moons' came back to earth after the flood and were looked up to as the gods. They helped the descendants of Noah that survived the flood with technology and possibly started new civilizations, or helped with the dispersal of humanity after the tower of Babel incident, as we mentioned. Then they helped language groups afterwards to build their individual civilizations boosting civilization standards around the globe. Their technology accidently ripped the earth into continents and then with the earth's now more hostile environment forced their return to their man made moon and some gods genetically deteriorated from the now hostile earth environment (compared to pre flood conditions) became earth bound, and went underground or under water and where they are to this day. (OK I got to the same point by two different paths, so I repeated myself a bit there ...sorry.)

Man's civilizations had, as many a confused archaeologists has discovered, started with virtually all knowledge such as the Sumerians and the earliest Egyptians without any apparent progression from inferior to superior abilities, but from the very start knew all they needed to know to create their civilizations and vastly superior structures we still cannot duplicate today. "But a peculiar feature of ancient scientific knowledge is that the further it goes back in time, the more extensive it seems to be" and "A curious contradiction became apparent-the mathematical and astronomical knowledge of the Greeks seemed to be developed from a much earlier source" (book 6 pg 131-132)

Though not well known and probably hidden from the general populace on purpose because it doesn't fit the evolution model, this grasp of the older civilizations being more advanced than the later versions has been understood for quite some time. Ignatius Donnelly in his 1882 book *Atlantis* quotes a few contemporary scholars in this regard. I use one quote of an Ernest Renan from page 132 here "Egypt at the beginning appears mature, old, and entirely without mythical and heroic ages, as if the country had never known youth. Its civilization has no infancy, and art no archaic period. The civilization of the Old Monarchy did not begin with infancy. It was already mature." Another quote from a different scholar on page 360... "Instead of exhibiting the rise and progress of any branches of knowledge, they tend to prove that nothing had any rise or progress, but that everything is referable to the very earliest dates. The experiences of the Egyptologist must teach him to reverse the observation of Topsy, and to 'spect that nothing growed,' but that as soon as men were planted on the banks of the Nile, they were *already the cleverest men that ever lived, endowed with more knowledge and more power than their successors for centuries and centuries could attain to*. Their system of writing, also, is found to have been complete from the very first..." (Atlantis pg. 360-361. Italics in original)

Egypt's devolving has archaeologists and such stumped and grasping at straws for answers. "Certain scholars have assembled evidence that Egypt somehow inherited its culture from an advanced prehistoric nation. It has long puzzled orthodox archaeologist and anthropologist how Egypt's civilization could start at its peak and run down for 5000 years" and the author suggests that Egypt was the first major colony of Atlantis.(Book 35 pg 18) Suggesting Atlantis is a "Prehistoric" nation is a misnomer as there is history associated with Atlantis. We'll deal with Atlantis in a chapter dedicated to it at some point. It has also been observed that the Mayans started at the peak. "...at the outset of their cultural development, their script had already reached perfection." (Book 21 pg 177) "Oddly enough, the peoples further back in time had greater scientific knowledge that the nations of later historical periods" (Book 11 pg 5)

This decline of Egypt has stumped many a conventional scholar because they look at ancient history through the veil of the theory of evolution, thus they can't understand how any sort of advanced civilization could start at the peak and decline from there. This is explained two ways: by the devolution of mankind over time and by the destructive global upheavals that demolished civilizations which were subsequently rebuilt with inferior versions. But such explanations are rejected out of hand by archaeologists. Ancient history is full of anachronisms to the way archaeologists think. One tiny corroded lump found on a sunken galley near Greece caused Professor Derek de Solla Price to write in Scientific American (issue not noted c 1959) "It's rather frightening", because this lump turned out to be a highly sophisticated geared planetarium device that could calculate planetary positions and has since been realized that it could even account for the "lunar anomaly". Jacques Bergier concludes that this device "...forces us to admit that the ancient Greeks were advanced technicians, which is completely contrary, philosophically, to their abstract mentality, and to their contempt for machines; or to recognise that before the ancient Greeks there must have existed a technology, lost today, but equal to ours, especially in the manufacture of special bronzes and in gear calculation." (Book 5 pg 61) Since this was written it's been realized this piece had to be built even before the period of the boat it was found on and was likely and old computer when it was being used by the Greeks on the galley. Often when faced with anachronistic finds, the people creating the items are singled out as a highly advanced in this particular field such as "the manufacture of special bronzes and in gear calculation", or beyond us in working with stone. But this geared device speaks of an entirely built up civilization, as does the stone work they did. Many of the works of stone are obviously worked with machinery, but the blinding light of Evolution theory does not allow archaeologists to see this, or admit it. In fact is, the geared object is so sophisticated that no one seems to know what era to place the device in. Furthermore there has been found on some of the gears writing that measures eight-hundredths of an inch in size, "- far too small to have been etched with any type of ordinary metal tool." Analysts deduced that this writing must have been etched with a laser! (See Atlantis Rising # 76)

The Ancients had perpetual lights that burned for hundreds or thousands of years, lifted quarried stones weighing more than 2000 tons, telescopes, and flying machines that could go from "globe to globe", successful brain surgery evident in skulls found showing regrowth of skull bone in cut-out holes, and on and on, stuff that stupefies some of the researchers.

YE OLDE CAVE MEN

But archaeologists just ignore these bizarrely complex finds which amaze so many of us laymen with offhand superficial explanations if they deal with them at all, and force any evidence of "cave men" and early 'primitive' man into the time frame *before* civilization and suppose such fellows advanced over the millenniums to somehow create civilization even though their very own evidence shows civilization started at the peak. The fact is these so called primitive men or cave men came *after* the fall of civilization due to catastrophic intervention. And in fact some of the ancients said this very thing. I quote a paragraph from *We Are Not The First* by Andrew Tomas.

"In the Timaeus, Plato (427-347 B.C.) recorded the words of an Egyptian priest: "there have been and there will be again many destructions of mankind." When civilization is destroyed by natural calamities then "...when the stream from heaven, descends like a pestilence and leaves only those of you who are destitute of letters and education...you have to begin all over again as children and know nothing about what happened in ancient times, either among us or among yourselves." said the high priest of Solon." (Book 11 pg 162, book 6 pg 19) After the constant disasters caused by technology and the natural disasters, man slipped into various states of childish simplicity or barbarism and civilization was often reduced to ashes, or was overrun by waves, buried by moving mountains, or submerged by land and water changing places, or made suddenly uninhabitable by being thrust into unliveable altitudes or hurled into inhospitable climactic regions, thus those who survived these cataclysms had little incentive to rebuild, causing ongoing decline of civilizations around the globe.

Orthodox sciences suggests that the first European cave dwellers known as Neanderthals came into existence about 200,000 years ago, yet this contrasted sharply with 500 stone figures found on the banks of the Elbe near Hamburg which German archaeologist Walter Matthes coincidentally dated at 200,000 years old and called them the oldest ancient works of their kind in the world. The features of the human faces on the stone figures were clearly that of Homo sapiens. If that paradox wasn't enough, the author Peter Kolosimo notes that this contrasted sharply against human remains buried *under* the bones of a Toxodon, a Megatherium, and "the dinosaur" found in the Brazilian state of Minas Gerais all presumably extinct millions of years ago. Why? He further notes that million year old 'trogolodytes' evidence found in the Brazilian Santa Maria highlands indicated they used stone clubs, flint arrows, bred livestock, embalmed their dead and buried them in sarcophaguses made of Jute (a plant with linen burlap type of fibres). Kolosimo noting the contrasting dates of the European and American counterparts asks "how is it that the American primitives, who seemed to have advanced quite a way toward civilization, did not develop any further in the course of a million years?[to match the development or surpass that seen in Europe evident by Neanderthal and Cro-Magnon remains] He felt that there was only one explanation: "that the earth must have passed through more than one "prehistoric" period-that in some nameless, distant past mankind must have ascended a long way up the ladder of civilization, only to relapse into chaos and barbarism." (Book 21 pgs 5-10) Though the dates assigned to these finds will be seen as utterly without foundation, the conclusion is well merited. Kolosimo starts the next chapter with a nearly faultless observation "What force can it have been that wiped out flourishing civilizations at a single blow, decimating the population of the globe and condemning the survivors to take refuge in caves out of which their ancestors had painfully struggled thousands of years before? Clearly the cause must have been some fearful cataclysm affecting the whole of our planet." (Book 21 pg 11) The only misconception he has is that they spent thousands of years climbing to the heights of civilization; they actually started there, and the remains found were subsequent to the collapse, because as we've seen civilization started at the peak with no progressive steps or learning curves. That came later. But key is he grasped that cataclysms caused mankind's advanced civilizations to collapse and cause cave man to come into existence *after* periods of advancement, not leading up to it.

Some legends indicate that after some cataclysms the people even renounced any return to science, because they say that it was science that caused the earth's destruction. This is not just my guess or deduction. Charles Berlitz noted that students of "Atlantean concept of prehistory", felt that "This would account for the curious legendary descriptions, handed down through time, that man himself caused the destruction and desolation of large settled areas of the earth, accompanied by explosions, floods, and darkness." (Book 6 pg 211) Repudiation of science almost forces man to become cavemen with primitive tools as if to promote and advance prolonged global preservation. This could even be conceived of as their version of advancement, by learning from their mistakes.

The very concept of "cave men" suggests to us grunting savages with no form of civilization skills that would just as soon hit you with a club and eat you than say 'How do you do'. But this is what anthropologists would have us believe. Caves exist in many places where people obviously lived for long periods of time and these dwelling places show anything but evidence of being uncivilized. To make their surroundings more comfortable they often painted on the walls. The artistic talent of the paintings in caves varies from artist to artist, some are simple, maybe even drawn by kids, to where some are not only sophisticated, they reflect what can only be civilizations that the residents remember. Some are so sophisticated that investigators are stumped as to how they did the tricks or even how they created the pigments. John Brown in 1952-53 found cave art in the Mountains of Fire in central Africa's dessert areas. This cave art was anything but primitive, or reflective of how we perceive "cave-men". "The central figure was a pretty white woman, young, graceful, with her hair bobbed in the style of Ancient Egypt. She wore a beaded head-dress, a garment that resembled a modern jersey blouse, shorts, gloves, girdle, and shoes similar to those worn in modern Mediterranean countries." (Book 35 pg 71) Similarly "Cro-Magnon" ivory sewing needles have been found that are far superior to needles even up to the Renaissance, and not even the Romans had needles of this quality. (Book 8 pg 167-167)

Now admittedly many cave finds do exhibit what appear to be more simplistic or barbarous dwellers had stayed there. It's quite likely they only stayed for a short time while they rebuilt at least a more comfortable home outside nearby. One cave contained many smashed monkey skulls showing the dwellers just ate them. However, what the anthropologists initially told us about this cave was that two types of cave men dwelt together, or at different times in this same cave, or fought there. They didn't bother to mention that one of the 'hominids' was in fact these monkey with all their heads bashed in. Someone else had to re-examine the evidence to point it out.

Consider, if cave dwellers had just been made homeless by waves or earthquakes, and turned their backs on 'science', or were of a group of formerly civilized man that today we might equate with "upper class" or "couch potatoes", it stands to reason that some cave dwellers would display refinement and some barbarism, depending on the personalities and former backgrounds of the cave inhabitants, similar to today where some of us have might have afternoon biscuits and tea served at 2:30 pm precisely and some of us might slap together a baloney sandwich when we feel a bit peckish to tide us over 'till our supper of roast beast.

VISUALIZING THE NUTSHELL AND THE PROBLEM IN IT

Thus as we will see subsequent "local floods" (currently mixed in with and up with the legends of the global flood) played an active part in changing the course of mankind over the intervening centuries from the time of the world flood to around 687 B.C. when things globally finally calmed down. The point is ancient history constantly indicates something happened to degrade civilization suddenly or over time, but no one seems to have put their finger on what it was, because of the predominance of the Charles Lyell's principals of geology that introduced uniformitarianism, and Darwin's evolution theory. (Velikovsky and a few maverick researchers excluded) Catastrophism has been verboten, particularly when it comes to civilized times and recorded history.

People used ancient formulas to predict eclipses, formulas which were not to be messed with and have been traced back to the Sumerians. Maps of vastly superior accuracy were retraced down through the ages, but when renaissance explorers started to map the new world they made new maps or placed their crude maps on top of the older accurate maps with the result that maps got worse as more of the new world was explored. Knowledge of the correct view of astronomy were replaced by the more ignorant flat earth beliefs as the old correct astronomical models were replaced with incorrect ones. Building techniques constantly diminished over time, for example ancient buildings that go through earthquakes still stand when newer ones crumble and get rebuilt over and over again.

And with all the flood legends lumped together as one type of legend told in varying ways, the clues to the cause of ancient man's decline has been obscured by the 'misfiling' of these local flood legends so to speak. But now that we will look closely and separate the local flood legends from the global flood legends, we will suddenly see the cause of mans decline staring us in the face as bold as brass. But the story that these local floods tell is one of ongoing catastrophism which once again flies in the face of accepted evolution, geological and archaeological history. Consider this quote from *Worlds in Collision* by Immanuel Velikovsky....

"Traditions about upheavals and catastrophes, found among all peoples, are generally discredited because of the shortsighted belief that no forces could have shaped the world in the past that are not at work also in the present time, a belief that is the very foundation of modern geology and of the theory of evolution.

"Present continuity implies the improbability of the past catastrophism and violence of change, either in the lifeless or in the living world; moreover, we seek to interpret the changes and laws of the past time through those which we observe at the present time. This was Darwin's secret, learned from Lyell"[*] It has been shown in this book, however, that forces which at present do not act on the earth, did so act in historical times, and that these forces are of purely physical character. Scientific principals do not warrant maintaining that the force which does not act now, could not have acted previously. Or must we be in permanent collision with planets and comets to believe in such catastrophes?" [*H.F. Osborn, The Origin and evolution of life (1918) p.24] (Book 14 pg 308)

Keep in mind this quote I repeat. "For instance, Philo of Alexandria (20B.C. - A.D. 54) wrote: By reason of the constant and repeated destructions by water and fire, the later generations did not receive from the former the memory of the order and sequence of events." (Book 11 Pg 162) This could even include our geologists, and evolutionists. Thus many flood legends are garbled or a blending of both global and local flood legends in the same tales. But now, with the realization that this happened, we have a clue of what to look for and can keep our eyes peeled for what previously might have gone undetected or overlooked.

IT'S NOT ALL ATLANTIS'S FAULT.

One of the traps many researchers fall into is blaming 'the flood' for the demise of just Atlantis. For example Ignatius Donnelly continually interpreted all flood legends in the light of Atlantis' destruction. Part of the reason so many people do this is because Plato put Atlantis' demise at 9000 years prior to his day (c. 400B.C.). Thus people who believe the ice ages occurred 12,000 years ago assume Atlantis's destruction and the ice ages coincided. Although this may in fact be the case, the dates attributed to these events were much more recent. Indeed many geologists have realized that mountain building, volcanic eruptions and the ice ages are intimately linked together as virtually cause and effect events. And again, though this is true, the dates assigned to the mountain building, ice ages and accompanying volcanic action is vastly over estimated. For instance, some of the glaciers that existed during the "ice age" were actually included on old maps. Velikovsky and other authors recognized through careful measurements that the ice ages occurred during recorded history. Velikovsky also noted Plato's date was probably 900 and not 9000 years, thus timing the demise of Atlantis during a period "when the earth twice suffered great catastrophes as a result of "the shifting of the heavenly bodies."" (Book 14 pg 158)

Another slip-up many people make is the assumption that the melting of the glaciers from the ice age raised the global water levels between 300 and 600 feet, thus being a more natural and uniformitarianism cause of the flooding, but this too is a mistake. The ice ages only had a maximum increase of just 6% more ice on the earth at any given time, but because these glaciers covered so much area not covered by glaciers today, we assume all that extra ice was the cause of the increased water levels. But basically the area covered by glaciers simply swapped places so as some glaciers melted, others grew due to a sudden change on earth relocating where glaciers formed. This accompanied the fact that so many volcanic eruptions occurred simultaneously around the globe, that the soot and massive evaporation caused cloud coverage so substantial that the clouds filled the entire volume of the atmosphere and reached down to the ground. This caused world temperatures to plummet because the solar insolation could not reach the earth's surface, causing global "nuclear winter". These events were caused by the earth tumbling, poles switching and continents suddenly shifting. It's the cause of the relocation of glaciers then that is the key, not their mass.

Furthermore we will see that the assumption of Atlantis's demise at 9000 years before Plato is impossible for a couple of reasons. First the flood of Noah happened much more recently, and all subsequent floods occurred sometime after the big flood. For example someone is said to have visited Atlantis in 2350 B.C., a post flood date. (Book 22 pg 119) Secondly there's a further clue as to the correct time slot for the destruction of Atlantis that as far as I know everyone has missed. The key to knowing when the destruction of Atlantis occurred was that it occurred during the reign of the gods. Plato writes that the people of Atlantis "...began to appear base...", and "...were filled with unrighteous avarice and power." So Zeus called together the gods and felt punishment had to be inflicted upon them. Other Gods lived during the time of Atlantis such as Poseidon, so clearly the destruction of Atlantis occurred before or when the gods left the earth. (Book 6 pg 24, & 42) Though I can't go back and find out how Plato got the wrong date for the destruction of Atlantis, I agreed initially with Velikovsky that the 9000 should be 900 (or possibly 1900) and thus placing the final destruction of Atlantis during the time of the Israelites exodus when many earth upheavals were occurring around the globe. This made sense, as the cause of all these upheavals on a global basis could very well have finished off what was left of Atlantis or whatever islands remained in the Atlantic Ocean to this point in time.

Egyptian time lines show the reign of the gods occurred before their first dynasty which began around 3100 BC, which I had also determined appeared to be about the time when the gods left. It is decipherable to conclude they had left because they had caused some sort of destruction on earth that either made further residing on earth unsafe due to the further deterioration of the Earth's environment, or they felt bad because their powers kept destroying earth and killing vast numbers of the people they supposedly came to help, or both. Though the approximate date deduced for the departing of the gods from earth was around 3100 B.C., some possible variables exist which could have placed the departure of the gods at an even more recent date due to some other factors I won't repeat here. So my guess is there's some mistranslation from Egyptian to Greek that caused Plato to say 9000 years rather than whatever the correct time frame was. Though I can't go back and determine ancient Greek and ancient Egyptian to figure out what that translation error might be, I can offer an English similar potential error to give an idea of what I mean. If you say out loud 90 centuries and then you say 19 centuries, they sound extremely similar and some such error could be the mix-up that caused Plato's obvious error. Almost as an exclamation point to this, recently, after I wrote this, I offered $90 dollars to someone for five items and he thought I said 19 (each) thus thinking I was offering $95. I've also learned that when I go to the bank and ask for $15 or $50 dollars I have to be careful how I say these figures.

And of course another reason so many prefer to assume the destruction of Atlantis occurred 9000 years before Plato is it makes geologists, if they believe Atlantis ever existed at all, feel more comfortable with a longer timeframe in place and so they can call Atlantis "prehistoric" if they call it anything at all.

Consider this quote "It is just this question of land "disappearing" that has become the mainstay of critics of the Atlantis theory. Although an increasing number of scientists are tending to admit the possibility of important Earth changes during the existence of "modern" man on earth, by far the majority stand fast in their opinion that there have been no important world catastrophes (except for volcanic explosions and disappearances of a few islands) for several million years." (Sorry I've mislaid where this quote came from.)

No one seems even remotely comfortable suggesting that major earth upheavals might have occurred during the time of advanced civilized man. So they come up with extremely dumb sounding theories for places like Tiahuanaco, or other manmade structures buried under massive amounts of dirt. For example archaeologists and geologists have for some unknown reason determined that 18 feet of dirt over top of an ancient civilization equates to about 6000 years of elapsed time; even though they know that there is only 1/8 of an inch of dust on the moon and thus the same amount of space dust would land on the earth in the same time frame. They never bother to explain where all that extra dirt might have come from to cover all these old civilizations up. Why is it no one seems to see this elephant in the room? The evidence of massive earth upheavals during civilised times are all around us if we are willing to 'see' them. On top of that, the legends keep shouting that huge floods and upheavals occurred, lands swam, and mountains formed and fell during their days of terror on the earth. This is where that extra dirt came from; this is what these other flood legends refer to...a time of upheavals on the earth that changed the face of the globe speedily either in a moment or in some cases between 25 and a 50 year period.

The Egyptian priests explained the chances of survival after destructions based on previous occurrences. "...a great conflagration of things upon the earth, recurring at long intervals of time: when this happens, those who live upon the mountains and in dry and lofty places are more liable to destruction than those who dwell by rivers or on the sea shore....When, on the other hand, the gods purge the Earth with a deluge of water, among you herdsmen and shepherds on the mountains are the survivors, whereas those of you who live in cities are carried by the rivers into the sea." (Book 6 pg 19-20) When you keep this in mind you can understand why some flood legends show differing survival stories from the flood of Noah. And we will see there were different kinds of catastrophes that man had to overcome.

Well after writing *Worlds in Collision* many of Velikovsky's deductions were established as sound. In his new preface he wrote, "Signs of recent violence, disruption and fragmentation have been observed on earth and elsewhere in the solar system: a submarine gigantic canyon that runs almost twice around the globe- a sign of a global twist; a layer of ash of extraterrestrial origin underlying all the oceans; paleomagnetic evidence that the magnetic poles were suddenly and repeatedly reversed..." (Book 14 page 5-6) However these physical evidences have subsequently been said to have occurred millions of years ago by uniformitarianists, even though many of the geologic evidences were predicted by his work and the legends that helped him come to these conclusions clearly indicate they occurred during recorded history.

Furthermore these global upheavals most certainly happened during recorded history because the ancient legends are often verified by identical or corresponding legends told by people of different regions or even by people on the other side of the globe; often the same story is told time after time by many different peoples by the common threads in their legends. Though Velikovsky's main focus was on showing that cataclysmic upheavals occurred in recorded history, and their cause, my focus will be to show how these events are tied in with local flood legends. So though I will be using a lot of the legends he dug up, I'll be specifically linking the histories of upheavals with the flood legends to make the local flood aspect of the legends clearer...I hope.

Scientists have deduced by geologic evidence that there appears to have been two catastrophes. (Book 21 pg 143) We will see that the ancients speak of between 4 and 6 depending on location. Geologists might not be cluing into all of them because the upheavals of one could mingle and disguise a previous one. Nineteenth century geologists were mystified by what appeared to be many floods, when they were only aware of the one flood spoken of in the bible. It never occurred to them there were more than one type of flood legend.

Quite often it seems the flood parts of people's legends are often isolated and told separately as though they were a complete legend that supposedly reflects a global flood. In fact many incidences occurred before and after these floods indicated in ancient world histories that specifically clues us into what type of flood legend it is. Sometimes I've not even found a flood legend per se, but the story clearly indicates a flood had to have occurred because of the upheavals they describe, even if not experienced by the people to whom the legend belongs.

I've collected as many additional bits to try and reassemble the legends of the floods with the missing descriptions that caused the floods and the aftermaths. There are usually said to have been four previous world ages, though sometimes there are said to be as many as 7 to 9 periods of cataclysmic upheavals in various places around the globe, so it's not yet been completely determined the correct order and dates that some of these events occurred. With four or more world ages to sift through its quite possible one legend could mistakenly be linked with a different flood or time period. But suffice it to say, the legends when read one after the other should make it abundantly clear that these events caused massive floods and disturbances around the globe, and that these events happened in recorded history and explain the terrain we see surrounding us today in virtually every place we go. Afterwards we will look at the physical evidence that completely confirms the legends and we'll see it was staring at us all along. Individually virtually all of these legends have been discounted by many, but when read one after another, each becomes a piece of the puzzle supporting the picture that each of the other legends depicts. Occasionally you might feel like you're in the forest and might seem lost, but keep plugging at it, because every once in a while I bring you to a clearing or a mountain top and suddenly you can see the big picture. Alright I've beaten around the bushes long enough.

The Legends

First, before I go at it, understand it's going to come at you fast and furious and you are going to be swamped with weird and what seems like unbelievable material. I'm not quite sure how to break it to you gently or even how to put some of this into in any kind of logical order so that understanding slowly dawns on you. So like an unwelcome wave of debris from an unexpected tsunami descending on you, you may feel like you're sinking in a pile of rubbish for a while. However I'm confident you will eventually see the pieces actually create the big picture I've described for you, and will describe for you again: So get your snorkel ready.

SUMERIAN: THE EPIC OF GILGAMESH (48°E 30°N),

This text is quite long so I've boiled it down from a couple sources to the essentials.

Utanapishtim meets Gilgamesh who is shocked to see him where he is so Utanapishtim tells him how he happens to stand in the assembly of the gods. He says the city Shurappak on the banks of the Euphrates, where some of the gods lived, were encouraged by the great gods to hold a council in Shurappak and voted on the destruction of mankind. (The gods named in the epic include Anu, Adad, Atrahasis, Enlil, Ennugi, Erragal (Ereshkigal?) Ninurta, (Shullat and Hanish?), Ea, La, and Ishtar [Which gods were where is unclear to me]) But the god Enki/Ea in secret decided to warn Ziusudra, (or the more well known Akkadian name of Utanapishtim), to tear down his house and build a ship (presumably from the wood from the house), abandon wealth and save life. He is also told to bring seed of all kinds of living things. Utanapishtim asked Enki what should he say to explain the building of a vessel and the abandoning of all possessions? He was told to say Enlil had become hostile to him and rejected him, and he can't reside in the city or set foot in Enlil's territory anymore, so he will go down to the Apsu to live with Ea. (Apsu: is translated two ways: 1) who exists from the beginning: i.e. the sun or the space between the sun and Tiamat (Maiden of life) located between Mars and Jupiter the missing planet, and 2 Abyss, deep dark dangerous waters which one can sink into and disappear (Book 17). (Thus Apsu could be interpreted as the depths of space or the underworld)

Utanapishtim also added that if he left, Enlil would rain down an abundance of fowl, fish, increase harvests, loaves would fall in the morning and wheat in the evening. (Instead of the drought [or famine] they apparently had been experiencing.) This made sense to the people and some of them chipped in and helped build the boat, including a carpenter with his hatchet, a reed worker, and children carrying pitch. The boat had to be square with all four sides the same length with 6 decks of 9 compartments each. After 7 days the ship was finished. Utanapishtim says he loaded the seeds of all living things and brought onto the ship his whole family and kinfolk, and "whatever I had of all the living creatures" as well as "the animals of the field, the wild beasts of the field", and all the craftsmen (who helped him build the ship). The boat had to be launched, a difficult task, by running poles from the front to the back until 2/3rds was in the water. Utanapishtim was to board last and seal the entrance. Then a rain of eruption started to shower down caused by the gods. Adad rumbled inside a black cloud, Erragal pulled out the mooring poles (?), Ninurta made the dikes overflow and The Anunnaki (the gods of heaven) lifted up the torches, setting the land ablaze with their flare. All day the South wind (Sitchin's version used said "south storm swept the land") blew overwhelming the people and submerging the mountain. The gods were frightened by the flood [which] ascended [back up] to heaven of Anu.

For six days and nights the wind raged, the flood and cyclones devastated the land, then on the seventh day the battle against the elements was over and the sea became calm, the cyclones died away and the flood ceased. All mankind and the olden days had turned to clay, and the ground was flat like a roof. The gods were shocked by the intensity of the flood they had unleashed and wept at the results. Ishtar screamed "how could I say evil things in the assembly of the gods ordering catastrophe to destroy my people!? The gods wept with her.

After the flood was over Utanapishtim opened the window to receive light and the ship rested on the mountain Nisir or Nimush which held the ship so it couldn't move (wedged in). This mountain was not covered by the flood. On the 7th day Utanapishtim let loose a dove which came back. Then he sent out a swallow which came back, so later on he sent out a raven but it didn't come back. He offered incense and poured reeds, cedar and myrtle. The gods (except Enlil: not told because he caused the disaster) come to the offering. Then Enlil arrives and find the survivors and is enraged at the gods. Ninurta says it was Ea's doing. La spoke to Enlil asking him how you could bring the flood without consideration? You should have been compassionate and used lions, wolves, famine, and/or pestilence. Only a dream warned alerted Atrahasis (exceedingly wise) who thus somehow alerted Utanapishtim. So Enlil made Utanapishtim and his wife become like him as the gods and after being prepared he goes to a city, and Gilgamesh ends up in Uruk.

After I deduced that the epic had to be referring to a local flood I found that Immanuel Velikovsky also indicates that the epic is speaking of a local flood by dating it to the same period as a post flood event in Peru with similar incidences: that of a cataclysmic period where the sun did not appear for five days and during this time the earth changed its profile and the seas fell upon the land. He also notes the Epic speaks of land being shrivelled by heat of flames, accompanied by desolation where a brother could not distinguish his brother. (book 14 pg 77) You will see these sort of events will be a recurring theme time and time again as you read through the various legends of the earth that either directly or indirectly speak of a local flood. I also realize this epic speaks of ferocious winds which we will see is a common event for one of the world ages, suggesting this epic may even be an amalgamation of more than one catastrophes, though if it is, the demarcation lines are not obvious.

When the Epic of Gilgamesh was found and translated it was hailed as the Babylonian version of 'the flood' and Noah was assumed to be Utanapishtim. Though there are some similarities between the two legends, there are some irreconcilable differences and when other clues are compared we will see this was in fact a very vast local flood, which is the same one as the second flood mentioned in the bible which Abram came from across.

Interestingly even Zecharia Sitchin's deductions can only be taken to mean that the Epic is a record of a local flood when he says "The references to the "south storm", "south wind" clearly indicate the direction from which the deluge arrived,..." Well the global flood of Noah came from two directions, above and below, where the Epic's flood can only be indicating a storm accompanying a massive Tsunami, accompanied by winds, which is a short temporal though cataclysmic event.

Key differences include the time it took to build the boat, one week compared to Noah's 80 or so years. The shape square as opposed to Noah's very rectangular six times as long as it was wide. The gods are named and each had their part in how the flood occurred. Mythology clearly determines that the gods from the age of the gods were men of extraordinary abilities, and they were referred to as the people that knew everything, with extremely advanced sciences. The Bible refers to God who alone allowed the flood. Ishtar is a well known post global flood person, therefore placing the event after the flood of Noah. The gods came down after the flood at Ur (the place of descending) and taught and helped the Sumerians build, placing the event post Noah flood as these people who were flooded were Sumerians, and the abyss (if it refers to the underground) as a place to live was not known till after the flood of Noah when the gods referred to the place or places as a dwelling place or a place to move to. Utanapishtim uses a lie of the promise of abundance to deceive the people of the city and have people help him build the boat. It's assumed by most that Noah warned the people and Methuselah's name was a prophecy that meant 'when he died it will come'. Utanapishtim only took animals on the boat he owned or were nearby, God directed the animals to come to Noah. Utanapishtim's boat had to be launched by a complicated rollers system, whereas just God closed the door of Noah's ark and the flood bore up the ark from where it was. The gods had to do a series of tasks to get the flood to occur. Though from the description of their tasks I can't exactly know what it is they were doing, but my suspicion is what they caused the continents to move a bit causing the Tsunami. What evidence do I have? Well, instead of digging out all the evidence, as it happens, I wrote a letter to Atlantis Rising magazine (A.R.) for some reason about Lemuria which was published in 2009 in issue #73. I didn't even know it had been published for over five years, but this act of the gods to cause this flood in the Epic of Gilgamesh reminded me of that letter. I never used much of this stuff from the letter in my first book, but contents are applicable here. Though the letter is entitled "Atlantis in Antarctica", I stated clearly in the letter I was talking about Lemuria. Here is the letter. ...

"Antarctica could in fact be... Lemuria. Here's some evidence.

"An ancient Polynesian legend* spoken of in Peter Kolosimo's book Timeless Earth, concerning Lemuria says "...two 'great islands' of immense antiquity, inhabited respectively by Black and Yellow men who were continually fighting with each other. [Note added presently: Antarctica was originally pressed against what was to become Africa where the Black race of men are predominant and India was originally pressed against Antarctica which eventually moved towards Asia. It's not inconceivable that the "great island" beside India was the dwelling place of the yellow people which could have partially migrated towards India and on towards what was to become the Himalayan Mountains which were no more than hills at the time. Then, after the collision of India with Asia, the yellow men continued the migration onwards to China. So this deduction of this letter happens to fit well with the anthropology as well.] *The gods, it is said, tried to make peace between them, but finally decided that, as they were incurably quarrelsome, the only thing to do was to drown both islands beneath the waves.* (*book 21 pg 48)

"Antarctica was drawn as two great islands as far back as 1754 in the Bauche map. Furthermore I understand that in the International Geophysical year they actually confirmed that Antarctica was indeed two large land masses (Though I've yet to see new maps drawing Antarctica this way). We know that Antarctica was not covered by ice relatively recently- Recently enough to be mapped with correct topography as is shown by Charles Hapgood in his Maps of the Ancient sea Kings. This is further substantiated by coal deposits (from trees) found there and silt from river runoff found there as well.

"To say the two great islands were drowned beneath the waves does not mean the two islands sunk. Evidence suggests many of the continents around the earth were drowned by waves creating universal sandstone and fossils found in them, but they didn't sink [either].

"Based on my research I maintain that the gods did move the continents as recently as 3309 B.C. and possibly a little later than that. This is also confirmed by other ancient legends of the continents 'swimming' and such...obviously meaning the continents moved during recorded history...probably during the Exodus and possibly even as late as 687 B.C.

"I'm guessing that is similar to how we find artifacts in coal on these continents [and] we will also find some in Antarctic's coal, should it ever be mined, confirming that Antarctica was inhabited in ancient times, likely before the continent moved and was overrun by waves as it got to its present location."

Another legend found in the Tibetan Stanzas of Dzyan mentioned in *The Secret Doctrine*, appears to reflect this Polynesian legend. This following is expressed as though it referred to Atlantis, but it appears to be talking of the Yellow and Black races which would match up with my deductions above related by the Polynesian legend.

"...the great king of the dazzling face' the chief of all the yellow-faced, was sad, seeing the sins of the black faced....He sent his Vimanas (air vehicles) to all brother chiefs with the pious men within, Prepare, Arise ye men of the good law, and cross the land while dry.

"The Lords of the storm are approaching. Their chariots are nearing the land. One night and two days only shall the lords of the Dark Face live on this patient land. She is doomed, and they have to second with her. The nether lords of the Dark eye are preparing their magic Agneyastra.(?) But the lords of the Dark Eye are stronger than they and they are slaves of the mighty ones. They are versed in Ashtar (Vidya, the highest magical knowledge [science / technology]). Come and use yours.

"Let every Lord of the Dazzling Face cause the Vimana of every lord of the dark Face to come into his hands, lest any should by its means escape from the waters, avoid the rest of the Four (gods) and save his wicked (followers or people).

"Then the great King fell upon the dazzling face and wept. When the kings assembled, the waters had already moved beyond the water mark. The Kings had reached them in their vimanas, and led them on to the lands of fire and metal (East [India before it reached Asia?] and North [Africa?]) Stars showered on the lands of the Black Faces but they slept. The speaking beasts kept quiet. The Nether-Lords waited for orders but they came not, their masters slept. The waters arose and covered the valleys from one end of the Earth to the other. High lands remained; the bottom of the Earth remained dry. There dwelt those who escaped, the men of the Yellow faces and of the straight eye. When the Lords of the Dark Faces awoke and bethought themselves of their vimanas in order to escape from the rising waters they found them gone." (Book 23 Pg 76-77)

Based on Churchward's deduction that Mu was in the Pacific Ocean region, (Lemuria and Mu are considered by some to be the same continent) so maybe Antarctica *wasn't* Lemuria but an unknown name or a known name thought to be a mythical place because it is no longer known as something that would be associated with Antarctica. However a zoologist Phillip L. Sclater suggested that lemurs and dog faced monkeys found in lands bordering the Indian Ocean may have come from a vanished homeland somewhere between India and Antarctica which is now just a sunken ridge between the two land masses, a place he referred to as Lemuria: presumably the origin of the name lemurs. (book 23 pg 50)

There are other clues to indicate this epic does not refer to the same flood as Noah's, but a more local tsunami type of flood. The following is mainly the contents of another letter I wrote to A.R. (now published in number 131), but merges with the present work....

I found this interesting tidbit in the Glacial Melting story of Atlantis Rising magazine #129.

"...from "the heart of the Lion", the constellation Leo, near the star Regulus. Accompanied by loud thundering in the sky, a rain of burning stones shattered Egypt in "the first minute of Cancer." The Great Flood followed immediately."

This description even sounds a bit similar to the god's tasks in the Epic of Gilgamesh. When I saw this line in A.R. 129, I knew I had a missing piece of the puzzle staring right at me. And as chance would have it while doing some research for this book I stumbled on what has to be the exact same event that caused a flood spoken of by Zechariah Sitchin.

Many of the ancient legends refer to a 'great flood' and we automatically assume they speak of the biblical flood of Noah, and then such stories make us scratch our head and say this sounds like a local flood. Zechariah Sitchin as you'll see wrote of this exact same widespread event in his book the 12th planet. (Pg 403-404) He notes from the Epic of Gilgamesh, that Utanapishtim is riding out this flood in an 'ark', (Utanapishtim, as mentioned, is usually assumed to be the same person as Noah, but we'll see he is not) and as we've seen the Epic of Gilgamesh speaks of a deluge where an 'ark' was used to save people from a flood that Sitchen deduces came from the south, a flood where the moon disappeared, the sun could not be seen, the rains roared in the clouds, and submerged the mountains, blew six days and nights and then subsided. (More details mentioned by Sitchin from another version of the epic not included above) Sitchin states this storm moved up from the Antarctic into the Indian Ocean over hill and plain, to reach Arabia and Mesopotamia. Dams and dykes were torn out. He immediately tries to tie this in further with the biblical Noah flood but by white-washing over differences, by suggesting the biblical terminology "fountains of the great deep" equals water coming from the Antarctic or "great deep" and on up through the Indian Ocean. (Whereas legends and scripture clearly indicate the great deep refers to the water that came shooting up out of the ground as an effect from some cause (explained in my 1st book). So it is clearly not of the same sort flood as Noah's and thus not the same flood. Velikovsky notes that this great six days of wind and hurricane was created by the battle between the planet-god Marduk and Tiamat as this flood is also related in Babylonian Talmud, confirming this Gilgamesh flood as a local flood legend and not the great world flood. This also indicated the fierce winds and hurricanes came from a planet nearby. (Book 14 pg 83)

The bible speaks of Abraham coming from the other side of the flood and on the surface it could be assumed to be talking about the Great Flood, but root word search shows the two words "flood" in the bible are specific words describing different types of floods. In the case of the flood of Noah, the word 'mabbûwl' is used and means "in the sense of flowing; a deluge". The water from the canopy smashed through by the asteroid, creating a huge window in heaven, would have cause the water sphere to flow rapidly down to the surface of the earth. The New Testament Greek word for this flood uses a word that means 'inundation'. In the case where Abraham came from the other side of the flood the word used is Nâhâr and could mean a flood like the Nile but means more exactly a sea stream. The Greek reference to this event enhances the meaning quite a bit by using a word that means a flood tide which of course would include a tsunami. Close analysis shows Abram came from Ur and traversed a distanced to get across where a flood had been, and this can only be the exact same flood Sitchin and the Epic speaks of here as it's in exactly the same place.

Now consider this; any massive tsunami type flooding coming from the south that comes up from Antarctica through the Indian Ocean into the Arabian Sea into the Persian Gulf to inundate and overflow

Arabia and Mesopotamia is also going to come up through the Red Sea and inundate Egypt and the famous sites of the Pyramids and the Sphinx as well. (Amos 8:8 "Shall not the land tremble for this, and everyone mourn that dwelleth therein? And it shall rise up wholly as a flood, and it shall be cast out and drowned, as by the flood of Egypt". This verse appears to be referring to this flood too. What's very interesting and applicable here is the next verse indicates what sort of goings on caused such a flood by prophesying about a future event. 8:9 "And it shall come to pass in that day, saith the Lord God, that I will cause the sun to go down at noon, and I will darken the earth in the clear day" [Remember this bit because we will see very similar language concerning some of the things that happened in the past linked with flood legends.] Thus this would be the "great flood" mentioned in the article that hit Egypt quoted above, which was not a raining sort of flood, but a massive tsunami sort and must be the same flood Sitchin notes as the one in the epic of Gilgamesh. This is probably referred to as the 'great flood' because of how high the sea was when it came in. The water erosion marks on the pyramids are very high up, nearly at the top. The erosion on the sphinx is complete, so complete in fact that people have used this water wear visible on the sphinx to assume it safe to add several thousand years to the age of the civilization of Egypt, or at least the erecting of the sphinx itself.

This horizontal monstrous tsunami type of flood that scarred the pyramids and eroded the Sphinx would have been the same one that Utanapishtim rode out on his square houseboat that he and his friends and family managed to build in a week; the same flood that covered the Euphrates valley flat with a thick layer of clay to make it look like a roof, and the same one that Abraham eventually crossed over from his leaving Ur. Actually though Sitchin assumes the flood coming from the deep south refers to coming from Antarctica, but as one can see by studying Pangaea's movements, that this flood probably came from the Island of India as it started it's migration towards Asia.

Any similarities between the Epic of Gilgamesh and the account of the flood of Noah such as the use of birds to see if the land was dry could be simply confusion of the writers of the epic of the details of Noah's flood and Utanapishtim's flood, thus strengthening the conclusion in some people's minds that the two stories are of the same flood. But as we'll slowly see, the two types of flood legends often got smushed together to appear to be one legend as the later generations didn't realize there was more than one flood.

In a couple versions of the epic, overpopulation is blamed as the reason for the flood which was remedied by plagues and famines. After the flood Enki established barren women and stillbirth to avoid the problem in the future.

This additional information also suggests this part of the legend indicates a post global flood, flood legend. Earth before the global flood, was a very lush environment. (Geologists know a time existed on the earth where this was true, but they do not assume this environment known to have existed at one time on the earth was actually before the flood. They don't know what has changed on earth to change earth's environment, they only know it has changed) Thus famine likely wasn't a problem before the global flood. This local flood, as I've deduced being caused by the continents shifting, would have caused massive violent earthbound wind weather that would have forced more of earth's atmosphere into space, thinning the remaining atmosphere, and allowing genetic faults in humans. The first thing to be affected by extra radiation entering earth's atmosphere is the reproductive capacities of mankind.

ANOTHER BABYLONIAN FLOOD LEGEND

Three times (supposedly occurring every 1200 years), the gods become troubled by overpopulation on the earth. The gods dealt with this problem previously by plagues, and famine. Enki counselled men to bribe the god causing the problem. The third time the earth became too crowded, Enlil recommend that the gods should destroy all mankind with a flood. Enki had Atrahasis (called a god in above version) build an ark for himself, his family, cattle, wild animals and birds and so escape. When the storm came, Atrahasis sealed the door with bitumen and cut the boat's rope. The god Adad started the storm, turning the day black. But after a week had passed, the gods began to regret their action. When Atrahasis made an offering, Enki made it so that some women were barren and had stillbirths to avoid the problem in the future. [Dalley, pp. 23-

35] This gives clues that man's genetics were disintegrating noticeably after the flood. But it also suggests that the gods caused some of the destruction here on earth, whether deliberately or accidently and it hints that there were three occasions when they caused some of these troubled times or cataclysmic events. This version may be just a global flood legend, but with its relation to the previous version I placed it here.

BABYLON

The Euphrates Babylonians often refer to a time "the rain of fire" happened. (Book 14 pg 71) This doesn't sound like a flood legend to you right now, but it's another witness to a strange time in other legends referring to a time of fire raining down during catastrophes: in other locations vast floods *were* occurring.

The Babylonian Talmud uses the concept of a "cosmic wind" as though something from the stars was causing a fierce blowing. It also tells of a great disturbance in the movement of the sun at the time of the Exodus. (Book 14 pg 83 footnote, pg 128)

In the Babylonian seven tablets of Creation, tablet 4 speaks of the battle of the planet god Marduk with Tiamat. The description sounds like Mars and Typhon and indeed Velikovsky felt it also sounds like Zeus and Typhon. Marduk created an evil wind, tempest, hurricane, the fourfold wind, the seven fold wind, the whirlwind and the wind which had no equal. (Book 14 pg. 83) Each wind mentioned is stronger than the preceding one. With Mars close to earth the wind must have been unbelievable as some of our atmosphere was pulled to Mars. If the chill of space and the shifting of the globe occurred at the same time, these very winds described were blowing all around the earth, thus they could be the same ones blowing on another part of the earth that froze the woolly mammoths on the spot.

SYRIA

A 'poem' found in Ugarit was dedicated to a planet goddess named Anat which decimated the population of Levant and exchanged the two dawns and the position of the stars.

If we look at this 'poem' alone we probably ignore it as flight of fancy, but in light of the legends to come further on, we can't let this one slide. It speaks of a planet coming close to the earth and devastating a town near to the closest approach, and flipping the earth so dawn and sunset reverse the direction from which they occur, and of course the stars would appear to reverse as well, as the poem mentions. That may sound crazy right now, but keep reading and you will see the trend. It's quite probable that Levant wasn't actually on the closest point of approach as this event would have devastated the entire globe.

PERSIA (IRAN)

The Iranian book of Anugita tells of a day lasting three times as long followed by an equally long night, and another Iranian book called the Bundahis talks of the world being dark at midday as though it was the darkest of nights, so it can't be talking of just an eclipse. In fact it says the effect was caused by a war between the stars and the planets. It also relates that noxious and venomous creatures such as snakes, scorpions, frogs, and lizard appeared in such numbers that "not so much as the point of a needle remained free from noxious creatures" because of this event. (Book 14 pg 77, 191) Note that this is very similar to the ten plagues of Egypt mentioned in the events leading up to the exodus.

The Persian text called the "Bahman Yast" (Zand ī Wahman yasn,) tells of a time in Eastern Iran or in India where the sun did not set for 10 days. (Book pg. 78) If the earth's rotation was somehow halted or slowed down from an asteroid hitting some place on the earth, or a large heavenly body coming close enough to earth to interfere with its normal diurnal motion, the amount of time any place on earth would see night or day would alter depending on their location of the globe. It could indicate a twist or tumble of the earth where the lengths of days or night would have varying lengths depending on region until the earth overcame the effects of a hit or gravitational interference.

The Bahman Yast says a revelation to Zarathustra occurred which describes a tree with four branches, of gold, silver, steel, and "mixed" iron, symbolizing four periods (or ages) to come after the millennium of Zarathustra. Chapter 3 talks about a tree with seven branches, of gold, silver, copper, bronze, tin, and "mixed" iron, (very similar to Nebuchadnezzar's dream of the statue). As many ancient legends talk about their having been four ages after which a new sun, sky and moon were seen, this seemed worth noting here.

The Indo-Iranian Bundahis says "The planets ran against the sky and created confusion in the entire cosmos." (Book 14 pg 263) What does "ran against the sky" mean? Wait for it.

The seas boiled, all the shores of the oceans boiled, all the middle of it boiled." (Book 14 pg 106 quoting *Iranian Mythology* by Carnoy)

The Zend Avesta says that the sea boiled, including all the shores and the middle of the ocean boiled and it was the star Tistrya that caused it to boil. (Book 14 pg 105-06, 208-09) Looking up Tistrya I found it is supposedly the brightest Star Sirius, but Velikovsky based on legends of Tistrya equates it with Venus. Obviously the Star Sirius is never going to come close to the earth, so it appears to simply indicate the brightest star which would normally be Sirius, but with Venus coming close to the earth, taking water from the earth, evaporating it on its new world to become steamy clouds of Venus, thus ramping up the albedo or brightness of the planet Venus to make *it* the brightest star, could account for Venus high-jacking the term or name Tistrya: More on Venus later.

In the 1820's Sir William Ousley of the Court of Teheran translated a stone circle in Darab. It was in relation to a legend of a rain of fire stones which was followed by a great flood, and of the people who would crowd into this circle to pray to their god for mercy. (Book 31 pg 82) Mars came close to the earth and a large portion of the crust of Mars in one area is missing, and evidence shows a literal hailstorm of unearthly stones descended and amassed on the earth at some point, as this next legend indicates.

INDIA

Ancient religious, Sanscrit and Vedas legends of India tell of nine crisis of the world. (Book 7 pg 233)

The Vedas talk about the stones that Maruts hurls, and Maruts are comets coming from Martis or Mars, as Martis and Marut both have the same origin of meaning (Book 14 pg 286-292). This would be similar to how we think of to snow, sleet ice and hail. Maruts would thus be pieces of Martis being hurled at Earth. The Vedic hymns talk about the darkness, shaking, fire and misery these Maruts caused on the earth and in the sky. We'll get back to this shortly.

The Buddhist book Visuddhi-Maga makes a reference to the great flood: After the flood "when now a long period has elapsed from the cessation of the rains, a second sun appeared. When the second sun appears, there is no distinction of day and night," but "an incessant heat that beats upon the world".

After the flood the sun changed its appearance to people on the earth. But it's quite odd that this legend states there was no distinction between night and day spoken of here, and I'm not certain what this means. The bible speaks of a time to come when the sun will be seven times as bright and the moon seven times as bright and men will burn in the sun. The full moon is exactly one seventh as bright as the sun, thus the prophecy means the night will be as bright as the day would normally be, and the day will not only be 7 times as bright but proportionally so hot that you can't escape the heat, even in the night as it wouldn't cool enough during the night to offer any relief. This legend could suggest there was a time in the past when something on the sun was occurring that was particularly nasty, which might have been caused by excessive sunspots activity, possibly brought on by some of the asteroids pummelling the sun. It could also mean that a planet was close enough to reflect the sun enough to make the night as bright as the day, but that's just a guess. The full moon at night is bright enough to read by, if Venus or Mars was close to the earth, it in tandem with the moon, could possibly cause extra heat and reflect enough sunlight to make the nights as bright as the day.

A lot of local flood legends refer to the collapsing or lowering sky...this occurred as the atmosphere filled up with vapour and soot from en mass volcanic action with ash darkening the sky, from probably every volcano on the planet going off at the same time, vaporizing hundreds or even thousands of cubic miles of ocean. We'll see why this was occurring as we read on. So since the Buddhist book reference to the second sun should be read to mean how the sun appeared after the global flood, we might glean this interesting bit from it. However I can't figure why this would be the second sun, unless they are mixing up the sun that followed the global flood with a sun that followed a local flood caused by catastrophic events, or perhaps, shortly after the flood something like described in the prophecy above occurred. Since Mars came close to the earth after the flood and is responsible for taking enough of the water from the earth to lower the water level around the globe, and it could account for this legend.

I've concluded that there was virtually the entire volume of the atmosphere still on the earth just after the flood, as not much had escaped into space or been jettisoned into space by catastrophes or stolen by Mars and Venus yet. Thus this still allowed people to live to 600 after the flood, but other than that, it seemed to me not much more different than today's sky, except in volume.

"...when a world cycle comes to an end with the world destroyed and the oceans dried up, there is no distinction of day and night and the heavenly ambrosia serves as food." (Ambrosia here is the same as Manna, Book 14 pg 147 quoting *Buddhism* by Warren)

But it's possible that the more complete atmosphere existing immediately following the flood still allowed the sun to illuminate and heat the 'night' side of the globe via filtering its light through the much thicker, more humid atmosphere well into the night side of the globe. Could the earth have been far warmer for sometime after the flood due to the voluminous atmosphere now heated directly by the sun which retained heat due to an effect known as the Greenhouse effect, similar to how people today think the earth is heating up from CO_2 build-up? Then this effect diminished over time and after later global catastrophes transpired reducing the total of earth's atmosphere.

THE MULTIPLE AGES START TO APPEAR IN THE LEGENDS

The Hindu book Bhagavata Purana tells of four ages (called "Yuga's" or Kalpas) that passed which all ended in cataclysms that included conflagration, flood, and hurricanes, that almost destroyed mankind. Two other Hindu books also say there were four ages and only the time elapsed between each are different in them all. They see the present era as the fifth world age. Another Hindu book the Visuddhi-Magga says there were three world ages destroyed by water, fire and wind, but it also stipulates that there were seven ages separated from each by massive cataclysms. (Book 14 pg 47-48)

This matching number of world ages for the Hindus and other histories around the world are very important, not just for comparison of legends by similarities in details. (Most legends state there were four ages plus the current one, but from about Israel to China and India the number of earth ages is occasionally said to be seven. A close examination of scriptures also indicates there were locally about 7 catastrophes). The number of ages spoken of also helps calibrate sequencing and times spans for these events. It also has the added value of putting the kybosh on some of the ridiculous times spans some peoples histories attribute to the lengths of time between the ages and the age of the earth in general. If a global catastrophic event happens, the world affected on one side of the globe mirrors the same event and age on the other side; you aren't going to escape the catastrophic events, and legends will echo each other and thus timelines are forced to match up, regardless of what one legend might misconstrue as to how long these events took or the intervals between: time wise.

For example there are people who buy into these ramped up time spans the ancient give for the earth and their civilizations, and rationalize their faith in those dates by believing ages attributed to out of place artefacts which are also dated illogically old by unreliable dating methods. Items such as human artifacts or "modern" human bones found underground often dated as old as 400 million years old. Things found inside the earth such as ships found inside mountains or bells, bullfrogs and nails found in solid rock quarried from hundreds of feet below ground level, or people's footprints being found on squished trilobites or closely associated with dinosaur tracks. Instead of trying to figure out how these things got there, they assume old dates given to the items and the dating methods are correct, instead of trying to verify or disprove them. Yes the dating methods are unreliable; for example a known specimen of lava from a volcano that erupted in 1801 was dated by the uranium method at 200 million years old. Hard to believe? Recently Mt. Saint Helens ash was dated at 2.8 million years old and of course it's eruption happened in 1981. The outlandish dates attributed by some ancients to their civilizations are also disprovable. Consider.

Like the Hindu's, the Greeks, among others, also say the world has gone through four ages terminated by cataclysmic events and this age we are currently living in as being the fifth. But the Greeks unpretentiously date the events: they note that the appearance of a disc shaped comet which caused great upheavals on the earth coincided with the Exodus of the Israelites, and this event they say happened "in the year of the world 2453": that is 2453 years after creation (or 797 years after the flood) which Velikovsky places in 1495 B.C. (Book 14 pg 97)

Some of the ancients were trying to impress other civilizations with how old they were, as a few researchers have clued into. For example the Egyptians pride themselves on being the most ancient people in the world, (Book 14 pg 119), yet they admit there was an age of the gods before them. The age of the gods is dateable to ending around 3100 BC which can be determined by comparing ancient calendars of various civilizations; which has the added embarrassment of showing other civilizations are just as old...or young.

People who believe that civilizations are many millions of years old, because artifacts are many millions of years old, is in fact circular reasoning. How so? If for example the Hindus say their civilization had intervals of so many Kalpas (4.32 million years) between events, and they trust these dates because their forefathers wrote them and validate this faith because dating methods also date things as old or older; this is circular reasoning. Why?

Dates attributed to artifacts by dating methods are unreliable, and comparison of dates to other civilizations quickly shows which dates attributed to civilizations are trustworthy, and which dates are 'enhanced'. Just as evolutionists and palaeontologists use circular reasoning to date rocks and fossils*, so is the assumption that a civilization is really millions of years old because artifacts are said to be that old. (* How evolutionists date fossils and rocks is in reality somewhat self delusional. Rocks can't be dated so they rely on the fossils found with the rocks to date the rocks. But fossils can't be dated properly either, so they rely on the rocks they are found with to date the fossils. This is thus called circular reasoning and this is the same thing that people are doing when they believe old dates attributed to old civilizations and back their belief up with items dated by unreliable dating methods. It, as we can see, is truly a vicious circle.)

As you read on you will also see how some of these out of place artifacts could wind up inside solid rock hundreds of feet, and possibly even thousands of feet below ground level, and we'll explore how some civilizations happened to come up with some of these bizarre ages for the earth and world ages in the bonus book section.

By the way, Velikovsky dates the Exodus in at 1495 B.C. But he didn't translate that into the "year of the world" working forward from creation because he was an evolutionist)

Working with biblical dates I placed the Exodus on my chart occurring from the "year of the world" from between 2668 and 2708, or starting 1012 after the flood. This is not terribly far out from the Greek date for the same event they place at 2453, a difference of just 215 years. Though that difference is glaring to me, it's nothing compared to millions of years.

SOME BRIEF RECAPS

We saw earlier that the Hindu's have a world flood legend; well, the Visuddhi-Magga makes another reference to the great world flood. "There are three destructions: the destruction by water (the worldwide flood or a local flood), the destruction by fire [and] the destruction by wind." They say after the flood "when now a long period has elapsed from the cessation of the rains, a second sun appeared." {How the sun looks from the earth after the global flood...} "When the second sun appears, there is no distinction of day and night," but "an incessant heat that beats upon the world" yes, we read that earlier, but it continues. 'When the fifth sun appeared, the ocean gradually dried up', when the sixth sun appeared, "the whole world became filled with smoke." "After the lapse of another long period, a seventh sun appears, and the whole world breaks into flames." (Book 14 pg 51-52) (Looking at these extra ages again these may have occurred over a short period which are continuations of the same event; explaining it might go like this: volcanic action dries and evaporates the ocean, the sky becomes filled with smoke, soot and steam, a rain of rocks or volcanic action pushes flammable material into the sky and it ignites. The exodus was a span of about 50 years where the world was in constant upheaval. Viewed from India and China this might have had brief intervals of calm with the sun appearing slightly different in each interval: floods might have been evident elsewhere during these events but not in this neighbourhood) Anyway, back to my thread...

This seems like a good place to include a brief recap of how a lot of Martian rock has found its way to Earth. You'll see why in a sec. I first read about a piece of Martian rock being found in Antarctica and thought, this had to be a mistake, it had to be misidentified. But clues kept piling up...literally. Velikovsky assert by various evidences of past legends that Mars was close enough to the earth in the past for us to see Mars' moons, and close enough to shift Mars' atmosphere to look like a sword or various animals from earth. Its proximity also caused many earthquakes here and it hurled stones at us. Mars was pushed out of its circular orbit, by at least one huge asteroid from the exploded planet, in towards earth's orbit. But we need to go over some key bits briefly again as this action caused many local floods around the globe down here on earth.

Mars has been studied and there has been found "The crust of the entire northern hemisphere [of Mars], 3-4 kilometres in thickness was ripped off." (Atlantis Rising magazine #72) Susan B. Martinez noted in Atlantis Rising #104, that at one time in our past meteors, dust and stones "assailed the earth" and "fell in such quantities that it can be compared to snowstorms, piling up on earth in places to a depth of many feet, and in drifts up to hundreds of feet". Consider this as evidence of Mars coming close to earth. For a full proof of all this, see my first book and as a complimentary work I recommend *Worlds in Collision* by Velikovsky. (If you don't want my first book and you email me for the updates, they are free and that Martian proof is included in the updated version) By the way Velikovsy noted that the fiery "hail" that fell on the Egyptians during the plagues was not hail of the snow type, but hails of the burning rocks or small meteorites falling type. Now keep your eyes peeled for Earth legends that match up with this Martian hailing of rocks onto the earth: I start you off with this one.

The Hindu / Buddhist text Visuddhi-Magga says "When a world cycle is destroyed by wind...there arises in the beginning a cycle-destroying great cloud....There arises a wind to destroy the world cycle, and first it raises a fine dust, and then coarse dust and then fine sand, and then coarse sand, then grit, stones up to boulders as large ... as mighty trees on the hill tops." The wind "turns the ground upside down, and throws it into the sky." Large areas "one hundred (to five hundred) leagues in extent crack and are thrown upward by the force of the wind" and do not fall again but are "blown to powder in the sky and annihilated" "and the wind throws up also into the sky the mountains which encircle the earth...they are ground to powder and destroyed", "all the mansions on the earth" are destroyed in a catastrophe when "worlds clash with worlds". (Book 14 pg 68, 85) This apparent nonsense or allegorical meaning is only possible if a source of gravity is close enough to the earth to not only pull the ground into the air as it described the wind doing, but for actual mountains to be vaporised by the wind it can only mean a planet was pulling the ground upwards, like the moon pulls the water upwards in a tide, but only amplified beyond imagination. On top of that, this legend clearly links the clash or worlds with the Hurricane sun.

When the moon is directly overhead the tide rises, the ocean forms a hill, that follows the moon, and indeed the very ground underneath it rises a little as it passes over it. This legend is easily deciphered as when Mars came close to the earth and the two planets ripped each other's surfaces up. Nothing else could possibly account for such an incredible legend. If you missed it, read it again with this in mind. Velikovsky uses this in a footnote: One French Scientist Cf. J. Lalande, in a 1795 book *Abrégé d'astronomie* notes that if a planet the size of earth was just four diameters away from the earth, this would create a tide 2 ½ miles high(book 14 pg 85). Could Mars have been closer than this? As we just noted above, The Indo-Iranian

Bundahis says "The planets ran against the sky and created confusion in the entire cosmos." Earth has a much stronger gravity than Mars too, so if Mars was pulling our ground and water upward like this in its close encounter, earth would easily have pulled rocks from Mars, and account for the massive amounts of Martian rock and dust found on our planet, and explain why Mars had an ocean the size of our Arctic ocean at one time and why it disappeared into the subsurface of Mars to the bewilderment of Martian scientists... er...cosmologists...from earth...who are still here, and not on Mars. One wonders if any humans got sucked up into the void. If so, I hope they were packing a parachute!

Velikovsky notes that in such an event, if the earth had slowed or stopped rotating temporarily from the external force of a nearby planet, the water level, normally swollen at the equator from centrifugal forces of earth's rotating speed of 1000 MPH at the equator, would then drift towards the poles, and that if a planet were nearby, it would draw the water towards itself. (Book 14 pg. 85) This is as close as Velikovsky ever got: He never stated that our water left the planet by this force nor did he equate this action with that of Typhon. Even though he had the clues where he noted French Scientist Cf. J. Lalande above, and another legend which stated the planets ran against the sky) If this happened it's conceivable that the equatorial regions of the oceans could completely dry up for a short while. One commentary on the first five books of the bible states that the waters didn't just divide in the red sea "The waters of all oceans and seas was divided" (Book 14 pg 87 quoting *Rashi's Commentary to the Pentateuch*) The bible mentions when the Israelites crossed the Jordan, the waters piled up in a heap. I would also add that water would continue to surge in the direction the earth would normally be spinning, causing incredible waves, literally mountain high, just as the legends indicate it did. Only twisting of the earth in the same event would deflect the waves to any degree reducing their potential impact, which appears to have been the case. And again legends and ancient star maps indicate the earth changed its position in relation to the stars and even flipped making north become the south, and east switched places with the west, with the sun rising where it used to set, just like the legend say happened. If I haven't quoted these legends yet, they'll be here somewhere.

Hindu legends tell of a cosmic catastrophe that occurred at the end of a world age, that of the sixth sun: "The whole world breaks into flames... All the peaks of the mount Sineru, even those which are hundreds of leagues in height, crumble and disappear into the sky. The flames of fire rise up and envelope the heaven."(Book 14 pg. 110 quoting Warren)

On the **Andaman Islands** (between India and Thailand) the natives are afraid of a natural catastrophe that will cause the world to turn over. (Book 14 pg 132)

TIBET

Tibetan history says there have been four ages that have expired and the current one is the fifth. Their history says that the highlands of Tibet were once flooded in a great cataclysm, and that terrifying comets caused great upheavals. (Book 14 pg. 116)

Before a great cataclysm caused by an errant meteor struck the earth, changing the landscape, Tibetans hid in caves and underground safe places. When they emerged the world had changed; lands became seas and seas became land, a red sun loomed overhead (from excessive suspended particles still in the air), some seas had vaporised, the Celestial Island which was their home, had been elevated to a lofty plateau high in the clouds, surrounded by new peaks. Before the Himalayas had appeared, the land of the Tibetans was flat, fertile and surrounded by the sea. (Book 23 pg 68 relating Blavatsky *The Secret Doctrine* and Dr. T. Lobsang Rampa *The Cave of the Ancients*)

How could the Tibetans have had a system of tunnels ready to avoid a sudden flood? A Tibetan legends supplies part of the answer. At some point some blonde giants were listening to a warning a "psyco-scientist" named Yellus whose face showed unusual concern. Yellus was explaining that astronomers on Saturn had detected a celestial body approaching the solar system and the earth was in for a big hit. (Book 34 pg 67) This explains how the earth could have had sufficient warning to start building the tunnels, which other legends indicate the gods built. They probably had a few months to maybe even a year or more to build the tunnels and warn people. This also places this particular event before the leaving of the gods, and before the raising of the Himalayas. How's that snorkel holding up?

CHINA: ANCIENT CHINESE

Early on Jesuit scholars gained access to a 4,320-volume Chinese 'book of all knowledge' from ancient times. This collection told of the consequences of mankind's rebellion against the gods: "At the beginning of the second heaven, the earth was shaken to its foundation. The sky sank lower towards the north. The sun, moon, and stars changed their motions. The Earth fell to pieces and the waters in its bosom uprushed with violence and overflowed it [the Earth]...The system of the universe was all disordered. The planets altered their course, and the great harmony of the universe and nature was disrupted...The sky sank lower in the north..."(Book 31 Pg 14, and Internet used to piece it together) This is interesting in that it notes this was the second heaven and that it was at the beginning of it. Peleg happened just 101 years after the flood so it is quite possibly speaking of the same event, that being the initial breakup of the continents.

The Chinese say there were ten ages or "kis'" from the beginning of the earth to the age of Confucius (551-479 BC). The time span between world convulsions is called a 'Great year" in which the sea is carried out of its bed, mountains spring up out of the ground, rivers change their course, while humans and everything they made is ruined and the traces of the ancient civilizations are erased. (Book 14 pg 48)

During the reign of Emperor Yahou, figured to have existed during the same time frame as that of the Israeli Exodus, a great catastrophe brought the world age to a close. For ten days the sun did not set (the same length of time The Bahman Yast says the day lasted somewhere in eastern Iran or India. India is closer to China so it stands to reason it speaks of this location.) During these ten days the forests were ignited, and a multitude of abominable vermin were brought forth, and the entire land was flooded. (Book 14 pg 114) The water was heaped up and cast upon the continent of Asia; a great tidal wave swept over the mountains and broke in the middle of the Chinese empire. The waters *"Over-topped the great heights, threatening the heavens with their floods". The water was caught in the valleys between the mountains and the land was flooded for decades. "An immense wave "that reached the sky" fell down on the land of China. "The water was well up on the high mountains, and the foothills could not be seen at all", "Destructive in their overflow are the waters of the inundation ...In their vast extent they embrace the hills and overtop the great heights, threatening the heaven with their floods"* (Book 14 pg 86, 114-115 quoting *The Sun King, The Canon of Yao*)

Some time ago while researching my first book and while looking for pyramids in the Himalayas and in China with Google earth, I stumbled across a vast and obvious landmark in the midst of the Himalayan Mountains. I had previously thought the Himalayans were a continuous series of mountains from India all the way to China. This is not the case. Clearly this was a rippled plain and not a series of mountains. Even the terrain was fairly uniform in height above sea level and varied only by the sand waves themselves. Although the vastness of this area is as large as the Caspian Sea, the details of the terrain soon made me realize they were sand waves caused by water, but these features had to be maybe hundreds of miles in length and several miles in width. This feature verifies this legend. The emperor ordered that all efforts be made to drain the valley in between the mountains and this effort went on for years with no success. One person named Khwan was sentenced to death for failure to do this after nine years. Finally Kwuan's son Yu accomplished deed and was eventually made Emperor.

The Chinese refer to the collapsing of the sky that happened when the mountains fell. This led to the myth that the mountains supported the sky. (Book 14 pg 103)

Quick sidetrack: As another example of people confusing all floods with that of Noah's flood and then calling it a local flood, is recently (2018) evidence of an ancient flood was discovered and confirmed in China. Though the flood evidence found described one that engulfed two rivers raising the water level substantially, this was thought to confirm Noah's flood legend. NO!...this evidence clearly indicates it was a local flood! The containment area was obviously limited to just one vast area in China. It doesn't even match the descriptions of the legendary local floods in China's history. People keep trying to 'confirm' the flood of Noah with local floods around the world, thus diminishing the credibility of the biblical story and thus the bible as a whole. Keep your eyes peeled for this trend; it happens all the time. People keep trying to substitute the marvels in the bible with cheap imitations to make the people who wrote the bible look like con artists trying to pass off normal events as some exaggerated fairy-tale because they just can't believe the accounts as written. Yet people who honestly try and discredit the bible with serious genuine investigative techniques always come away as believers in the bible they tried to disprove. Ok I'll climb off my soapbox...

After the flood during Yahou's time, the astronomers were needed to study the stars and rebuild the calendar because the orbit of the moon, the suns movements, the season and the earth's axis had changed. (Book 14 pg 116)

After the age of Chaos (when the sky had lowered) the heaven and earth finally separated (or when the mass of cloud finally lifted due to prolonged and colossal precipitations) it was then that the heavens finally showed its face. (Book 14 pg. 131)

The Texts of Taoism mirrors this: "The breath of heaven is out of harmony . . . The four seasons do not observe their proper times". To corroborate this The Emperor Yahou ordered the astronomers "to investigate and to inform the people of the order of the seasons." And to observe the new movements of the sun and moon, and afterwards he introduced new calendars. (Book 14 pg 133)

"The Chinese say that it is only since a new order of things has come about that the stars move from east to west" "The signs of the Chinese zodiac have a strange peculiarity of proceeding in a retrograde direction, that is, against the course of the sun.' (Book 14 pg 125 quoting Moons, Myths, and Man by Bellamy)

In China around 2000 B.C. an emperor put to death his two chief astronomers for not predicting an eclipse. (Book 34 pg 78) Does this seem a bit extreme? Today who would care, so why was this a punishable offence? Many ancients watched the skies constantly and religiously in every aspect and regard. Why the fixation? Well they remembered how the stars, comets and meteors had caused cataclysmic earthquakes, floods and winds in the past and any astronomer worth his salt should be able to predict an eclipse. If they couldn't do that, they had no business being astronomers as the lives of all the people the king ruled were in their hands. If they missed an eclipse, they'ld fail to notice a meteor. The king had to have real astronomers, not wanna-be's in this position to warn people in time to take action that could save the people. Missing an eclipse to them was unforgivable.

About 700 years later another eclipse was miscalculated in 1311 BC. It was predicted to occur on the 15th day of the 12th moon of the year in the 29th year of King Wu-Ting, but it happened the next day! This heart stopping miscalculation caused the Chou ruler to order a sacrifice because the eclipse didn't happen on the right day. (Book 34 pg 79) Clearly the fear of missing a key astronomical event still loomed big nearly a millennium later.

Taoist texts also say "When the sky, hostile to living things, wish to destroy them, it burns them; the sun and the moon lose their form and are eclipsed; the five planets leave their paths; the four seasons encroach one upon the another; daylight is obscured; glowing mountains collapse; rivers are dried up; it thunders then in winter, hoarfrost falls in summer; the atmosphere is thick and human beings are choked; the state perishes; the aspect and the order of the sky are altered; the customs of the age are disturbed..." The Taoist author also speaks of the sun and the earth leaving their paths and that if the five planets "err on their routes", the state and the provinces are overcome by a flood. (Book 14 pg 261) This is important as it links local floods with a variety of weird occurrences in nature. Not all legends quote all the occurrences or even the mention of a flood, but we have to consider floods in the material, if not in the place where the legend originates, then somewhere else as a very real probability.

The Bamboo books note that in the tenth year of the Emperor Kwai, the 18th monarch since Yahou, "The five planets went out of their courses. In the night, stars fell like rain. The earth Shook." (Book 14 pg 260) This matches what we mentioned earlier where Susan B. Martinez noted in Atlantis Rising #104, that at one time in our past meteors, dust and stones "assailed the earth" and "fell in such quantities that it can be compared to snowstorms, piling up on earth in places to a depth of many feet, and in drifts up to hundreds of feet". Want some Martian rocks?... maybe do a little rock hounding in China.

HEBREW LEGENDS AND BIBLICAL CLUES.

Jewish historians convey that the earth had seven ages by saying there were several worlds before the one we live in and they were all destroyed and replaced with newly created ones. Six times the earth has been remoulded with new conditions existing after each catastrophe. Seven earths and seven heavens were created. This indicates not only did the sky change colour and whatever else might distinguish one sky or firmament from another, the land also changed...seven times. Great catastrophes changed the face of the earth. Some of these earths perished by water (indicating more than one flood) and some perished by conflagrations; and often these changes included a collapsing of the firmament or lowering of the sky. The names given to the seven worlds, with possible translations found for a few in brackets, are Eretz, (country), Adamah, Arka (back:Turkish), Harabah(Much), Yabbashah, Tevel (World) and currently Heled (the boy). (Book 14 pg. 49-50 referring to Louis Ginzburg *Legend of the Jews* and the Jewish philosopher Philo's works)

Philo also says "The mountain [Sinai] burned with fire and the earth shook and the hills were removed, and the mountains overthrown; The depths boiled, and all the inhabitable places were shaken." "...winds and tempest made a roaring: the stars were gathered together", The Lord "impeded the course of the stars" "Some perished by deluge, others were consumed by conflagration" (Book 14 pg 50, 109 quoting Philo)

Ginzberg *Legends* says that: The pillar of fire heated the mire to the boiling point and that it, and the pillar of smoke or cloud also levelled mountains.

Hebrew historical records (the Midrashim) note that at one time the sun and the moon did not proceed on its course but stood still for 36 itim, or about 18 hours, meaning the entire daylight time lasted about 30 hours (Book 14 pg. 61-62, 129) They also state that "naphtha, along with hot stones poured down on Egypt." (Book 14 pg 71) Velikovsky also asserts that when the bible says it 'Hailed on the Egyptians', this is a hail of stones and not of ice. (Book 14 pg 67) Though I could not confirm that with Strong's concordance, it appears the Midrashim does. The Midrashim also notes that four times the sun was forced out of its course in the few weeks between the Exodus and the day of Lawgiving. (Book 14 pg 128)

The bible also reiterates some of these events and gives strong clues to the occurrence of other catastrophes in the world by casually mentioning some interesting events that most people seem to find hard to swallow. Many of them have been thought mythical or figurative, but when we look at and compare the rest of the worlds legends of world ages, catastrophes, and irruptions of the sea onto land, suddenly the things spoken of in the bible start to fit in with the rest of the worlds legends, and are often confirmed by them.

Jewish history books Talmud and Midrashim both describe the mountain of lawgiving as quaking so greatly that it appeared to be lifted up and shaken above the people's heads, and that the people themselves felt as if they were no longer standing securely on the ground, but were held up by some invisible force. (Book 14 pg 108) The Midrashim also notes "The sky and the earth resounded... mountains and hills were moved".

The Midrashim notes an odd observation: during the entire wandering in the dessert, of 40 + years, the Israelites did not see the face of the sun because of the clouds, and were unable to orient themselves (tell north from south) on their march. It also states that in the time of Moses the course of the heavenly bodies became confounded. (I guess they figured that out before they left Egypt, or soon after entering the Promised Land...?) During the course of time the length of the year lengthened from 360 days to 365 ¼, due to hits by asteroids and such. Interestingly the Midrashim also points out that the time the planets took to get around the sun changed when it states "the greater length of time taken by some planets." (Book 14 pg 131, 135, 137) This statement immediately brings to mind Venus and Mars altering their orbits as these two are the planets said to have come close to the earth.

Josephus reiterates about the time when the great darkness fell on Egypt (which appears to have been a global event) with a more detailed description; the darkness caused blindness and choking problems! This would be from huge amounts of volcanic ash in the air and darkening the clouds around the globe reducing solar insulation and light to, apparently zero for 9 days.

The Talmud says that "seven days before the deluge, the holy one changed the primeval order and the sun rose in the west and set in the east". Another Hebrew authority named Hai Gaon in a work called *Responses* also refers to a time when the sun rose in the west and set in the east. (Book 14 pg 126)

BIBLICAL CLUES TO CATASTROPHES.

Velikovsky suggests that the fire that consumed the Israelites on the outskirts of the camp, after they kept complaining, was this same fire that fell from the heavens in other legends * and even in their own non biblical histories as we've just read. (*Book 14 pg 72)

Joshua 10: 11-13 "And it came to pass, as they fled from before Israel, *and* were in the going down to Bethhoron, that the LORD cast down great stones from heaven upon them unto Azekah, and they died: *they were* more which died with hailstones than *they* whom the children of Israel slew with the sword. 12 Then spake Joshua to the LORD in the day when the Lord delivered up the Amorites before the children of Israel, and he said in the sight of Israel, Sun, stand thou still upon Gibeon; and thou, moon, in the valley of Ajalon, 13 And the sun stood still, and the moon stayed, until the people had avenged themselves upon their enemies. *Is* not this written in the book of Jasher? So the sun stood still in the midst of Heaven, and hasted not to go down about a whole day." A rain of stones from the sky could stall the earth's rotary motion and speaks of a catastrophe somewhere on earth, but would Joshua or the recorder of this event know the stilling of the sun and moon would aid in the destruction of their enemies, or that they would even stop if he asked them to?

Have you ever had the urge to call someone and you did and the person you called said 'I was just thinking of you!' Or you've heard of people knowing someone is alive when others think them dead and they've been rescued because of their urging to keep looking for them, or in reverse they know someone has died even though they are across the ocean? We have spiritual links with each which is stronger when the ties that bind us are stronger. Similarly for those who are close to God, have spiritual links with him and his spirit. The writer of Joshua probably had no inclination to think the falling of stones could slow down or stop the world from spinning for a short time, yet the two incidents would be intimately linked. Though the stones that fell in the area would not have been sufficient to stop the rotation of the earth, they would be indications that either a much bigger one hit the planet somewhere else, or this might have been the time when the planet Mars was close enough to the earth that layers of Mars were ripped up by the gravity of the earth and hurled towards the earth; and when the ground in the earth shifted enough through this or a similar interaction so as to interfere with its diurnal progression.

Joshua probably would not have automatically linked the hailstones with such an event. However with his close ties to God and his spirit, I think the spirit urged him to tell the sun and moon to stand still, because the spirit knew it was going to happen, and God needed Israel to look up to Joshua as God's man with authority, and that they might fear God and follow Joshua's spiritual example. Interesting things like this happen time and time again. If you are not a church going person, I dare you to pop in to a bible believing church one day. Why? Because you just might get the same treatment from God's spirit. Many a person has popped into a church seemingly on a whim and heard the preacher say stuff they thought was one of their personal skeletons from their closet, and thought their wives, husbands or friends had spilled personal information to the preacher about them, and the preacher had used this information in their sermons. I remember sitting in church and thinking similar things; that someone or some friend had said something to the preacher and they used it in a sermon. I went up to the preacher afterwards and confronted him, and he said that it was the spirit talking through him to me. Well at first I didn't buy this, but eventually I got it. Man, I tell you if you are not prepared for this, it can be eerie! Now it might not happen all the time or if you're fiddling with your hand held device, you are going to miss it. But if you are listening to the services and not sleeping, you'll be surprised how often it happens in one way or another, either for conviction or confirmation, or just knowing that God is there confirming his presence, it's really quite neat. If you're bored one Sunday morning and actually out of bed, give it a try. But if you like to sleep in Sundays, don't worry, some churches have evening services.

But things like this happen in interesting ways too. I tend to wear things to death and then some. My jeans were holey and in style long before they were in style. I once thought "you know I need some shoes, these are all done for" and within a day I had found a box filled with second hand shoes, maybe 8 pairs, and they all fit me perfectly. Another time I wanted to make my coffee table a double decker to put stuff and the books I wanted to read on the first deck, but didn't really know where to get a second deck. Within a day or two I went out to recycle some stuff and wondered what was behind the bins, took a closer look, and it was another coffee table top exactly the size I wanted! We might conclude, and rightly so, that what we need sometimes God puts in the hearts of others to place in places he knows we will go. But sometimes it gets even weirder. Two soldiers were stuck on an island about to be overrun by the Japanese's in WWII and they were really in for it. Their truck had tires that were useless and the tires were a very unusual type. And there were no such tires on the island, and the Japanese were closing in. Suddenly they looked over and saw a perfect set of tires they needed for their truck right out there as plain as day. Perfect fit, yet no stock pile had ever been placed on the Island and the Japanese never used any similar tires. They fixed them onto the truck and they were off and running. Where'd the tires come from? Stuff like this happens all the time, and no one seems to know how these things happen.

Perhaps one of the strangest thing like this to happen to me involves a giant beetle. I come home from school and as I walk to the front door I saw an incredible huge white beetle just sitting on the landing. It was about 3 inches long, an inch and a quarter wide and an inch and a half tall. It had little greyish brown spots on it. It was so big I was afraid to touch it, in case it bit or was poisonous or who knows what, I mean I'd never seen such a big bug before, so I went in the house and grabbed something I could pick it up safely with to show it to people. When I got back out to the front step it was gone. I was about 14 at the time and I never saw another one before or after. When I was about 40 for some reason that beetle came back to mind and I thought it odd I never saw another one or even heard anyone else ever talk about seeing giant beetles in our neck of the woods. I supposed that maybe it was a fluke sighting of some beetle from some far away land that got lost in our neighbourhood and I just happened upon it that one time. Still I thought it would be neat to see another one, just to get a closer look at it. The next day I was walking to the store and by the side of the road there was a giant white beetle. I looked close and it was the same type, with the same spots. This time I picked it up by the sides and it made the strangest buzzing and vibrating noise that I quickly put it down. I stood there marvelling that just the day before I had wanted to see something I hadn't seen in over 25 years and just thought about it and there it was the very next day. I think Joshua's telling the moon and sun to stand still was something along these lines where he was just connected to God, his spirit and it all led him to by faith say this off the wall thing of telling the sun and moon to stand still. Though many think this sun and moon business just didn't happen, yet it's confirmed in legends around the world and those legends will be included in this work.

Velekovsky's thoughts on the mechanics of this event are also interesting: paraphrased here for brevity "The problem is one of mechanics. Points on the outer layer of the rotating globe (especially near the equator) move at a higher linear velocity that points on the inner layers, but at the same angular velocity. Consequently if the earth were suddenly stopped (or slowed down) in its rotation, the inner layers might come to rest (or slowed) while the outer layers would tend to still go on rotating."

(I think he got this backwards, the outer layers would stop or slow as the negative motion of comets / meteors hit, pushing the outer layer backwards, halting or slowing its forward momentum while the inner layers continued to move)

He continues... "This would cause friction between the various liquid or semi liquid layers, creating heat;

on the outermost periphery the solid layers would be torn apart, causing mountains and even continents to fall or rise."(Book 14 pg 60)

Though Velikovsky never suggests the continents shifted, moved or changed configurations in recorded history, possibly because the continental drift theory was still not confirmed when he wrote his *Worlds in Collision* in 1950, his words here clearly indicate this very possibility, particularly when he says "...on the outermost periphery the solid layers would be torn apart,..." Or at the very least this could describe the continent of Africa to a 'T', and indeed describes continental drift pretty good too.

BIBLICAL CATASTROPHES

Besided Joshua telling the sun to stand still, consider the following indications of catastrophes mentioned in the bible that few if any scholars would think refer to floods, yet many of these must have caused flooding somewhere if not in Israel. Some of these may be linked with Joshua's event and some certainly are linked with the Exodus, but not all.

Judges 5:4 "Lord, when thou wentest out of Seir, when thou marchedst out of the field of Edom, the earth trembled, the heavens dropped, the clouds also dropped water. 5: The mountains melted from before the Lord, even that Sinai from before the Lord God of Israel."

II kings 3:16 Elisha tells the Israelites to "Make this valley full of ditches. 17 For thus saith the LORD, Ye shall not see wind, neither shall ye see rain; Yet this valley shall be filled with water..." And in verse 20 "...behold, there came water by the way of Edom, and the country was filled with water." The thirsty Israelites after digging many trenches got water when it came from across the land, which came from the direction of Edom, meaning a sudden shift in the land must have made a lake spill over and travel across land to end up where the Israelite were.

Job chapter 9 Speaking about Gods abilities says in verse 5: Which removeth the mountains, and they know not: which overturneth them in his anger. 6: Which shaketh the earth out of her place, and the pillars therof tremble. 7: Which commandeth the sun, and it riseth not, and sealeth up the stars.

Psalm 104: 6...the waters stood above the mountains. Wild! It *stood* above the mountains, not overran. Though I suppose this could be a description of Typhon as seen from a distance too.

Psalm 18: 7 Then the earth shook and trembled; the foundations also of the hills moved and were shaken, because he was wroth. ...9: He bowed the heavens also, and came down: and darkness *was* under his feet. 13: The Lord also thundered in the heavens, and the highest gave his voice; hail *stones* and coals of fire. (II Samuel 22: 7-16 has the same bits along and a bunch more)

Psalm 29: 5 The voice of the Lord breaketh the cedars... of Lebanon 6: He maketh them to skip like a calf.

Psalm 46: 6 ...the kingdoms were moved: he uttered his voice, the earth melted.

Psalm 68: 8 The earth shook, the heavens also dropped at the presence of the God: *even* Sinai itself *was moved* at the presence of God, the God of Israel.

Psalm 82 is a prophesy for the gods, but it mentions the earth. 82: 5 They know not, neither will they understand; they walk on in darkness: all the foundations of the earth are out of course.

Psalm 97: 5 The hills melted like wax at the presence of the Lord of the whole earth.

Psalm 107: 25-26 For he commanded, and raiseth the stormy wind, which lifteth up the waves therof. 26: they mount up to the heaven,

Psalms 114: 4 The mountains skipped like rams, *and* the little hills like lambs 5: What *ailed* thee, O thou sea, that thou fleddest? Thou Jordan, *that* thou wast driven back? 6: Ye mountains, that ye skipped like rams; *and* ye little hills, like lambs? 7: Tremble, thou earth, at the presence of the Lord, at the presence of the God of Jacob; 8: Which turned the rock *into* a standing water, the flint into a fountain of waters.

II Kings 20: 8-11 Hezekiah was sick and Isaiah said at first he was to die from this sickness but after Hezekiah prays to God, Isaiah is told to return to Hezekiah and say he will live yet another 15 years. Hezekiah asks what sign he will see to know this is true. So Isaiah asks Hezekiah in verse 9 "...This sign shalt thou have of the Lord, that the Lord will do the thing that he hath spoken: Shall the shadow go forward ten degrees, or go back ten degrees. 10: And Hezekiah answered, it is a light thing for the shadow to go down ten degrees: nay, but let the shadow return backward ten degrees. 11: And Isaiah the prophet cried unto the Lord: and he brought the shadow ten degrees backward, but which it had gone down in the dial of Ahaz." And this episode is repeated by another chronicler in Isaiah 38: Verse 8" Behold, I will bring again the shadow of the degrees, which is gone down in the sun dial of Ahaz, ten degrees backward. So the sun returned ten degrees, by which it was gone down."

Habakkuk chapter 3 appears to be a review of some of the major instances of cataclysmic events from Peleg or the Exodus, but there appears to be a bonus episode. Two translations are used (I compare King James (KJV) with A New Translation (ANT) Moffatt 1924-25 as used in Book 14 pg 153) Remember we have to presume the scriptures are written from the perspective of Israel's location.

Verse 6 KJV: He stood and measured the earth: he beheld, and drove asunder the nations; and the everlasting mountains were scattered, the perpetual hills did bow; Verse 6 ANT: At his step the earth is shaken, at his look the nations are scattered, the ancient hills are shattered, mountains of old sink low.." This verse appears to speak of Peleg and the separation of the continents.

Verse 10 KJV: The Mountains saw thee, *and* they trembled: 10 ANT: The hills writhe at thy sight..,

Verse 11 KJV: The sun *and* moon stood still in their habitation: Verse 11 ANT: the sun forgets to rise, the moon to move. This verse can't be talking about the time of Joshua when the sun and moon stood still because in this case the sun hadn't risen! I suspect the original translators assumed it was speaking of Joshua's time, so they didn't use the term "forgets to rise".

Nahum 1: 4 He rebuketh the sea, and maketh it dry, and drieth up all the rivers, (causing Bashan and Lebanon to languish) 5: The mountains quake at him\, and the hills melt and the earth is burned at his presence, yea the world and all that dwell therin. 6: Who can stand before his indignation? And who can abide in the fierceness of his anger? His fury is poured out like fire, and the rocks are thrown down by him. (Other legends tell of the sea drying up too.)

The Earthquake during Uzziah's reign spoken of twice: Amos 1:1 "...in the days of Uzziah king of Judah... two years before the Earthquake..." and Zechariah 14: 4-5 "...and ye shall flee...as ye fled from before the earthquake in the days of Uzziah..." More on this later.

The Koran talks of two different east's and west's, and an Arab Philosopher Averrhoes sheds light on that by mentioning the eastward and westward motions of the sun. (Book 14 pg 126)

BIBLICAL PROPHESIES

Read without any background these sound extreme, but when you become aware of the legends of the past and the destruction they describe, suddenly these prophesies take on a whole new meaning.

Psalm 76 appears to be a prophetic scripture alluding to when Jesus said the meek shall inherit the earth. Verse 5: The stouthearted are spoiled, they have slept their sleep: and none of the men of might have found their hands. 6: At thy rebuke, O God of Jacob both the chariot and the horse are cast into a deep sleep. 8: Thou didst cause judgment to be heard from heaven; **the earth feared, and was still,** 9: When God arose to judgement, to save all the meek of the earth. Selah. 12: He shall cut off the spirit of the princes: *he is* terrible to the kings of the earth.

Ezekiel 38 19: For in my jealousy *and* in the fire of my wrath have I spoken, Surely in that day there shall be a great shaking in the land of Israel; 20: So that the fishes of the sea, and the fowls of the heaven, and the beasts of the field, and all creeping things that creep upon the earth, and all the men that are upon the face of the earth, shall shake at my presence, and **the mountains shall be thrown down, and the steep places shall fall, and every wall shall fall to the ground**.

Isaiah 13:10 For the stars of heaven and the constellations thereof shall not give their light: the sun shall be darkened in his going forth, and the moon shall not cause her light to shine.

Isaiah 13:13 Therefore I shall shake the heavens, and the earth shall remove from her place.

Isaiah 24:1 BEHOLD, the LORD maketh the earth empty, and maketh it waste, turneth it upside down, and scattereth abroad the inhabitants thereof.

Isaiah 24:18-20 .... for the windows from on high are open and the foundations of the earth do shake(19) The earth is utterly broken down, the earth is clean dissolved, the earth is moved exceedingly.(20) The earth shall reel to and fro like a drunkard, and shall be removed like a cottage.

Isaiah 40:4 Every valley shall be exalted, and every mountain shall be made low:...

Amos 8:9 "And it shall come to pass in that day, saith the Lord God, that I will cause the sun to go down at noon, and I will darken the earth in the clear day".

Revelation 6:14 "And the heaven departed as a scroll when it is rolled together; and every mountain and island moved out of their places...."

Revelation 16:18,20 18 "And there were voices, and thunders, and lightning's; and there was a great earthquake, such as was not since men were upon the earth, so mighty an earthquake, and so great" 20"And every island fled away, and the mountains were not found."

First Thessalonians 5: 3 "For when they shall say, Peace and safety; then sudden destruction cometh upon them,..."

Africa

The African Ovaherero tribesmen say that many years ago "the Greats of the sky" let the sky fall on the earth and that during this time nearly all people were killed, with only a few remaining alive. (Book 14 pg 104)

The tribes of Kanga and Loanga also say in times past the sky collapsed and fell during a time when most of the human race was annihilated. (Book 14 pg 104)

The "Wanyoro in Unyoro"(in or near Uganda) say that the sky fell on the earth in the ancient past and killed everybody when the god Kagra threw the firmament upon the earth to destroy mankind (Book 14 pg 104)

(I repeat a bit here for localization purposes) Diodorus of Sicily who wrote *The Library of History* around the time of Julius Caesar, had references to no longer existing texts, which told of a time when Africa's Lake Triton "disappeared from sight in the course of an earthquake, when those parts of it lay toward the ocean were torn asunder". (Book 14 pg 178) Indeed Africa has been almost ripped in half and geologists have actually confirmed this event took place, but have dated this event as having occurred millions of years ago. However as if to laugh at the dates assigned to earth changes, there are people groups all along the African rift zone that have histories recalling this event as well as the time when Africa nearly broke into two continents: Definitely not millions of years ago!

EGYPT

Though specific flood legends of Egyptian origin are rare due to chance destroying most of them, (probably most records were destroyed in the burning of the library of Alexandria), clearly what little remains shows they knew something very important that the people of back then and we today have missed. Consider: Plato's story of the Athenian Lawgiver Solon adds a very key piece; while visiting Egypt he was told by an Egyptian Priest "You remember one deluge only, whereas there were many of them...." (Book 7 pg 233-234)

The Papyrus Ipuwer talks about huge and pervading fires, which based on other legends, appears to be during the age of the 'Fire Sun'. "Gates, columns, and the walls are consumed by fire. The sky is in confusion." The ledger says that this fire almost "exterminated mankind". "Years of noise. There is no end to noise"..."Oh, that the earth would cease from noise, and tumult be no more." It also states that at one time "The Earth turned upside down." "the land turns round as does a potter's wheel" and the "Earth turns upside down", and talks about terrible destruction caused by upheavals in nature. It also says "The sun is veiled and shines not at the sight of men." "The sun, it hath come to pass that it riseth not." (Book 14 pg 71,120, 140)

Sudanese tribes (south of Egypt) refer to a time when the night wouldn't come to an end. Since they are geographically close to Israel, this obviously speaks of a different time than when Joshua told the sun and moon to stand still.

Egyptian priests told Herodotus about events during Egypt's history "They did say, however, that four times within this period the sun changed his usual position, twice rising where he normally sets, and twice setting where he normally rises. They assured me that Egypt was quite unaffected by this:..." (Herodotus book 2 section 142) Ten plagues of Egypt excepted, this is plausible. Israel was carefully led through the wilderness in the Exodus, while the earth was in incredible turmoil so it's likely God was literally leading them safely between rocks and hard places. Israel's homeland is not too far geographically from Egypt, and this might have been to their benefit as God chose the land of Canaan for Israel and appears to have protected or situated it in such a way that world catastrophes barely touched it while other places around the globe were wiped out by catastrophe after catastrophe. Almost like Israel and places nearby were in the eye of the storm. Careful study of the scriptures show catastrophic things had to have been happening around the globe. With Egypt close by, they too could have benefitted somewhat by this proximity to Israel.

Herodotus recorded that he did see seashells in the Egyptian desert and a high salt content in the sand, soil and rocks.

Pomponius Mela, writing some Egyptian history also tells about the differing sun sets but also adds that "...the course of the stars has changed direction four times..." (Book 14 Pg 119) "...and that the sun has set twice in the part of the sky where it rises today" (Book 19 pg 152)

Another papyrus named The *Magical papyrus Harris*, tells of a cosmic upheaval of fire and water during which "the south becomes north, and the Earth turns over." and "...the earth turned round upon itself" (book 14 pg 120, book 21 pg 16)

Yet another one called the *Ermitage Papyrus* held in Leningrad speaks of a catastrophe that turned the land upside down.

This legend is telling. "In the days before the flood, Thoth The First (I didn't know there was more than one) himself inscribed on the steles, in hieroglyphics and in the sacred language, the essence of all knowledge. After the flood, the second Thoth translated the inscriptions into the vulgar tongue." (Book 22 pg. 224-225) This is clearly speaking of a flood that occurred after the world flood. How can I be so sure? This is during the age of the gods and Thoth is one of the gods who taught the Egyptians to write. The sacred language would be the original tongue all people spoke in the world before the tower of Babel incident. The vulgar tongue would probably be the language the Egyptians were tagged with after the tower of Babel. Thus this is reference to the same flood or tsunami that is spoken of in the Epic of Gilgamesh that scarred the pyramids as we see them today.

Even texts found in the pyramids say the sun or 'luminary' ceased to live in the occident (west), and shines a new one, in the Orient." (Book 14 pg 120)

The *Papyrus Anastasi IV* complains about the gloom and absence of sun light and states "The Winter is come as summer, the months are reversed and the hours are disordered. (Book 14 pg 132-33)

According to G.A. Wainwright's *Journal of Egyptian Archaeology*, the Great bear constellation at one time never set and contained the pole star, but then suddenly the Great Bear "came bowing down". (Book 14 pg 318 quoting source) This is repeated in Spanish/Portuguese legends as we'll see.

LIBYA

Ovid has a line about Libya when the earth was scorched at the end of one of the ages: "Then also Libya became dessert, for the heat dried up her moisture...The Don's waters steam; Babylonian Euphrates burns; the Ganges, Phasis, Danube. Alpheus boil...The Nile fled in terror to the ends of the earth...the seven mouths lie empty filled with dust; seven broad channels, all without stream." (Book 14 pg 154-155) This is interesting in light of current theories for the African Dessert. Here we see recorded one of the events that caused the greatest desert in the world. Other places around the globe experienced this blistering heat too as we'll see.

LOWER CONGO

The sun once met the moon and threw mud at it, making it dimmer. There was a flood when this happened. Men put their milk stick behind them and were turned into monkeys. [Internet quoting Fauconnet, p. 481; Kelsen, p. 136]

Not much to go on... The moon getting dimmer could be caused on earth from excess evaporation and volcanic activity, or an effect from meteoric impact that hit the moon (coming apparently from the direction of the sun, with the earth getting hit as well in the same time frame to initiate the eruptions and excessive evaporation. The men turning into monkeys would mean after a catastrophe, man reverted to primitive behaviour, living in caves and trees, after the cataclysmic event which also caused a tsunami where few survived. This is a complimentary legend to Peru's where it stated "In those days, the Moon was even brighter than the Sun, but the Sun grew jealous and threw ashes onto the Moon's face." As I consider it a bit more, it sounds like this event happened right after or during an eclipse, or at least a new moon. This might be a clue to dating the event as astronomers can work backwards figuring out dates by eclipses. It would have to be an eclipse that both Peru and Libya (North Africa) would have been aware of.

YORUBA (SOUTHWEST NIGERIA)

A god, Ifa, tired of living on earth, went to dwell in the firmament with Obatala. Without his assistance, mankind couldn't interpret the desires of the gods, and one god, Olokun, in a fit of rage, destroyed nearly everybody in a great flood. (Internet quoting [Kelsen, p. 135])

This could coincide with the Tibetan warning from Saturn about an impending impact where the gods made underground safe places for the people then left and came back after. It appears as if the Yoruba weren't included in the program. This Olokun might have been disqualified from re-entry to the celestial city, and his anger coincided with the event...after all he was a god...it must have been his fault...right? But this is another legend where the gods or a god is blamed for causing a catastrophe on earth...deliberately. The serpent said "Ye shall be as gods, knowing good and evil". "...the thoughts of his heart were only evil continually."

Europe

BELGIUM

Almost like a child wishing on a star, when the peasants of Flanders see a comet, they say "The sky is going to fall, the earth is turning over". (Book 14 pg 132)

ROMAN:

Jupiter, angered at the evil ways of humanity, resolved to destroy them. He was about to set the earth to burning, but considered that it might set heaven itself afire, so he decided to flood the earth instead. With Neptune's help, he caused storm and earthquake to flood everything but the summit of Parnassus, where Deucalion and his wife Pyrrha came by boat and found refuge. Recognizing their piety, Jupiter let them live and withdrew the flood. Deucalion and Pyrrha, at the advice of an oracle, repopulated the world by throwing "your mother's bones" (stones) behind them; each stone became a person. Though this legend is very similar to some global flood legends, I've placed it in the local flood legends because it speaks of

Jupiter, one of the post flood gods from the age of the gods. As you will see some legends spoke of the sky being on fire so this legend may refer to a later catastrophe. With "storm and earthquake" as the cause of this flood, it appears to be in sync with the Mayan age or sun that ended with Hurricane. A Roman author of *Liber Memorialis* (c 200AD was a compilation of 50 chapters of knowledge collected in his travels) wrote "there were five suns" (book 14 pg 51). We'll see these five suns or seven suns is a constant theme of ancient legends around the globe. Once again we see the gods or a god presuming to be in the place of God and deliberately causing destruction on earth.

Caius Julius Solinus (c 190-250 A.D.) wrote that "following the deluge which is reported to have occurred in the days of Ogyges, a heavy night spread over the globe for 9 consecutive days" (Book 14 pg. 76) He also mentions that Egypt's history tells of the sun's changing direction. "The inhabitants of this country say that they have it from their ancestors that the sun now sets where it formerly rose" (Book 14 pg 124) Nine or Ten days of Darkness, close enough to be speaking of the same time, is a recurring period in legends and these would all be speaking of the same end of a specific age.

Italy (Ancient Etruria also called Tuscia by the Romans and Tyrrhennia or Tyrsenia by the Greeks: Harmsworth Encyclopaedia)

Varro records that this land recorded seven elapsed ages. The ages always ended with catastrophes and it's said that the gods notified mortals of the coming end of each age. (Book 14 pg 46) That's interesting. Just as some gods caused destruction on the earth, at least one other god was in the know and warned mankind. In my previous book I noted that some of the gods of the underworld were completely antagonistic towards surface men, and some were in our corner. And UFO occupants also seem to fall into one of these two categories. The gods looked upon us in two ways: a devolved vermin more destructive to our own environment, ourselves and each other and should be wiped out, and as people victims of the gods own folly from events they caused before the flood and not entirely responsible for our own plight or folly.

The Italian Sibylline books thought to be all burnt (according to my old Harmsworth encyclopaedia) appear to still exist according to my reference. I assume then this reference speaks of the Italian Sibyl, though there are many Sibyls in ancient history: Babylonian, Libyan, Delphian, Cimmerian, and others. So if this legend isn't of Italian origin I hope you'll understand my confusion. I quote the paragraph "The Sibylline books recite the ages in which the world underwent destruction and regeneration. "The Sibyl told as follows: 'The nine suns are nine ages....Now is the seventh sun' "the Sibyl told prophesies of two ages yet to come- that of the eighth and of the ninth sun." (Book 14 pg 52 quoting J. Schleifer "Die Erzahlung der Sibylle.)

Ovid (Publius Ovidius Naso 43 B.C.-17 A.D.) was a former president of judges until his exile by Augustus, and he was also a poet and writer of the mythologies. He wrote about Phaëthon while driving the chariot of the sun "No longer in the same course as before", The horses "break loose from their course" and "rush aimlessly, knocking against the stars set deep in the sky and snatching the chariot along through uncharted ways." Could any of the planets be the horses he refers to?

He wrote of a time wherein he described "the burning of the world" that occurred in Siberia, the Caucasus (between the Black and Caspian Sea) and in Arabia. And he seems to have information about catastrophes in many localities and rattles them off. "The earth burst into flames the highest parts first, and splits into deep cracks, and its moisture is all dried up. The meadows are burned...the trees are consumed... ripe grain furnishes fuel for its own destruction...conflagrations reduces whole nations to ashes...nor does chilling clime save Scythia (south east Europe) Libya became a desert... The Ganges (NE India), Phasis (42°E 42°N) by the Black Sea, Danube, Alpheus (Greece) boil; ...Even the sea shrinks up, and was but now a great watery expanse is a dry plain of sand.", and, "If we are to believe the report, one whole day went without sun. But the burning world gave light...Causing all things to shake with her mighty trembling, she sank back a little lower than her wonted place" (recording the change in the tilt of the earth's axis). (Book 14 pg 73, 154,155)

LATIN LEGEND: (OF ITALIC, GERMANIC CELTIC GREEK ORIGIN: TAKE YOUR PICK)

The Typhon comet (The comet that incurred or induced Typhon) is described by early Latin authors (Lydus, Servius, Hephaestion, Junctinus and Pliny) as an immense globe of fire lit up by the sun, but also described as a sickle which would be a planet seen in the day side of the earth only partially illuminated as visible from the earth. Indeed the description also says its movement was slow and its path was close to that of the sun. Its colour was of bloody redness (possibly due to impurities and smoke in our own atmosphere). It caused destruction in rising and setting and caused many plagues, evils and hunger. (Book 14 pg. 98) This also suggests that this globe could have been Mars and it stuck around for a while, however it could be Venus discoloured by looking though our own fouled atmosphere due to extensive volcanic reaction. Closer synchronization of legends would be needed to determine which planet.

Typhon "out topped all the mountains and his head often brushed the stars. One of his hands touched the east and one the west and from them projected a hundred dragon heads. He emitted a long loud hissing, fire flashed from his eyes he hurled kindling and rocks, Zeus pelted Typhon with thunderbolts and pursued him atop Mount Casius overhanging Syria. Typhon appears wounded but twined about him with his coils. Zeus recovering rode his chariot of winged horses and pelted Typhon all the way to Thrace and during the fight whole mountains heaved and while fighting over mount Haemus, streams of blood came out of the mountain. (This quite possibly does describe Mars, as its two steeds would be the moons, or "winged horses") He fled through the Sicilian Sea. Zeus cast Mount Etna in Sicily upon him from which blasted fire and bolts of lightning were thrown. The Syrians were terrified witnesses of the battle between Zeus and Typhon the dragon who when struck by thunderbolts fled in search of underground by cutting furrows in the earth forming the beds of rivers and descending underground made fountains break out of the ground hovering near the earth and the water of Typhon leaving the earth with a hundred streams up to Mars while electrostatic charges between Earth and Mars lit up the Stream of water (Typhon) leaving the earth. This appears to describe Mars slowly shifting in the heavens as Typhon followed, and this led to this description of the incident by the ancients. (Book 14 pg 93-94 Paraphrased quoting Strabo in *The Geography* 1925)

What is Zeus in this legendary battle? My initial thought was Venus or maybe Mars, but I started to doubt this as this doesn't fit with Zeus. The Greek god Jupiter is Zeus, but the planet Jupiter could not possibly be close to earth. Velikovsky thinks it is Venus because he thinks Venus came from Jupiter as a new planet, but I disproved this theory in my first book. Zeus is one of the chief gods but this battle between Typhon and Zeus resembles a planet coming close to the earth. So what Zeus might be here could be a man made planet (which is known to lurk near Jupiter) coming real close to the earth steered by this god Zeus to cause this destruction deliberately as we've seen other legends describe Zeus' actions.

THRACE (BULGARIA)

Mountains in Thrace, modern Bulgaria, received the name "Haemus" because at one time it gushed a stream of blood during the time Zeus fought with Typhon and Typhon was struck by a thunderbolt. (Book 14 pg 65) This blood by the way was caused by creatures being smashed as land shifted catching the creatures inside and causing their blood to run.

Greek: (Several writers and philosophers put their 2 cents worth in)

Zeus sent a flood to destroy the men of the Bronze Age. Prometheus advised his son Deucalion to build a chest. All other men perished except for a few who escaped to high mountains. The mountains in Thessaly were parted, and the entire world beyond the Isthmus and Peloponnese was overwhelmed. Deucalion and his wife Pyrrha (daughter of Epimetheus and Pandora), after floating in the chest for nine days and nights, landed on Parnassus. When the rains ceased, he sacrificed to Zeus, the God of Escape. At the bidding of Zeus, he threw stones over his head; they became men, and the stones which Pyrrha threw became women. That is why people are called laoi, from laas, "a stone." (Apollodorus Circa 140 BC)

Latin writer Censorinus said there is a period (called the "supreme year" by Aristotle) at the end of which the sun, moon and all the planets return to their original position (meaning *two* catastrophes in this period). This 'supreme year' has a great winter which the Greeks call "Kataklysmos" (where we get the word cataclysm) which means 'deluge', and a great summer called ekpyrosis or a combustion of the world. The world got drowned and burned during each of these epochs. (Book 14 pg 46)

Heraclitus (born from between 576 to 540 BC and died between 480-475 BC) stated that the world is destroyed by conflagrations every 10,800 years. Aristarchus said this alternating of destructions by combustion and deluge occurred only every 2,484 years. (Ibid) Hesiod or Hesiodus (circa 800-750+ BC) stated that there were four ages and four generation of men destroyed by the wrath of planetary gods. He said the third age (of Bronze) was destroyed by Zeus (placing this destruction simultaneous with the destruction of Atlantis). One of the ages he described as the earth collided, apparently with a celestial neighbour, and moved around burning, the land seethed. He also states that "The huge earth groaned, and a huge part of the huge earth was scorched by a terrible vapour and melted like tin by man or even as iron, the hardest of all things and is softened by glowing fire in the mountain glens. (Book 14 pg 106)

Plato mentions there was a time when the rising and setting of the sun and other heavenly bodies (stars, planets) changed. In times gone by they used to set where they now rise. Then he reiterates saying basically the same thing. At certain periods the universe has its present circular motion, and during other periods it revolves in a reverse direction..." He also indicates these alterations of the patterns of things were anything but peaceful events. "There is at that time great destruction of animals (now fossils) in general, and only a small part of the human race survives." (Book 14 pg. 122; Referring to Plato.)

Pythagoras offered proof of men once sailing in seas that are now dry land by the evidence of ship anchors found on mountain tops. (Book 23 pg 209)

Other Greeks before and after Plato also mention these events in world history. Sophocles: "Zeus... changed the course of the sun, causing it to rise in the east and not in the west". Euripides also notes that Zeus made the sun turn backward. And in his typical flowery language said "And the sun-car's winged speed from ghastly strife turned back, changing his westering track through the heavens unto where blush-burning dawn rose," (Book 14 pg 122-23) If Zeus, as I've suggested, caused the disaster of the end of the third age, the destruction of Atlantis and caused the earth to flip and thus the sun switch apparent direction, while in a manmade moon, how powerful is this moon? Others cluing into its existence, or at least the gods powers suggested that they moved moons around and returned or gave the earth another moon after one of the disasters (likely the original flood) with some of the clues they came up with.

Apollodorus in *Epitome*, states that at one time the sun went backwards and set in the east as promised by Zeus. (Book 23 pg 208) Zeus... uh... promised...or threatened? Either way, he did it on purpose?!

A book of Hermes describes Pyramids that were on the shore with sea shells at its base and the waves of the sea breaking at its foot. (Book 23 pg 145 referring to Blavatsky's *Isis Unveiled*) No pyramids that I know of today are sitting on the shore. The story apparently refers to Atlantis, or could there be Pyramids now underwater in the Mediterranean Sea?

Unlike legends from other places around the world that talk about different ages that ended by catastrophes ushering into the heavens new suns such as "water-sun", new moons and skies, the Greeks refer to these ages by various metals to reflect the glory of those ages. The first age is called the Golden age, the second the Silver age, then the Bronze, and the one we live in today they call the Iron Age. Some have tried to equate these ages with the metals they used, but they have to refer to the status of civilization before a sudden change caused by a cataclysmic event. They, like some American Indian legends, only refer to four ages and not five, so one may not be able to be positive to which suns they might be equated with, as Greek history is said to be younger than say that of Egypt, though that probably means they refer to later ages and would not count the earliest one. The civilization before the flood could be considered the golden age where man's technology was beyond compare and they reached and subdued the planets. But eliminating this, then of course the age of the gods might also be considered the Golden age until the time they left. The remaining ages would refer to the disintegration of civilizations after catastrophes and the amount of glory these civilizations attained before they too were wiped out, reducing the incentive to rebuild, thus lowering the standards of each successive age. The people of Athens drink or toast to the remembering the Flood of Deucalion, the flood that ended the Bronze Age. We spoke of this previously in the global flood legends as reading the legend gave me the impression that this was what it was. But this part of the legends speaking of it ending the Bronze Age clearly indicates it happened much later so the legend is probably the mixing of two floods in the same legend.

Plutarch in more poetical language recorded "The thickened air concealed the heaven from view, and the stars were confused with a disorderly huddle of fire and moisture and violent fluxions of winds. The sun was not fixed to an unwandering and certain course, so as to distinguish orient and occident (east and west), nor did he bring back the seasons in order." He attributes the changes of the "Destructive, diseased and disorderly" to Typhon that caused "Abnormal seasons and temperatures." (Book 14 pg 133)

During Plato's lifetime the Greek port city of Heliké on the Saronic Gulf, plunged so suddenly into the sea that twelve Spartan warships that were in the harbour at the time were pulled down with it. (Book 6 pg 20) However I've not been able to find any underwater pictures of the place so it may not have been found yet. The thought just struck me; we see this in ancient history and we tend to gloss over it. And though this is supposedly just one city, had this happened in our day, the world would have been aghast! Don't forget geologic history shows these incidences don't occur in isolation, but are often accompanied by simultaneous events occurring elsewhere on the planet as the entire lithosphere is interconnected. Now this might not be the result of a massive earthquake as this could be similar to say a sinkhole common in some places like Florida, where city blocks disappear in the night, but an entire city suggests there is no size limit in events like this.

FINLAND

A Finnish historical book called the Kalevala, tells of a time when hailstones of iron fell from the sky and the sun and moon disappeared and did not appear again, and in their place was a long period of darkness, after which a new sun and moon were "placed" in the sky.

(Some ancient histories tell of a time that existed before the moon was in the sky, and some astronomers and the like have hypothesized our moon is younger than the earth, [because it has so little dust], which they theorize signifies it was recently captured by the earth. More unconventional theorists have suggested the gods found a moon and brought it to earth to create the tides, and after reading the clues I suggested the possibility in my first book that it was lost due to being pummelled by asteroids and kicked out of its orbit around the earth, so the gods retrieved and returned it. Though all conceivable, it's also possible our forefathers just didn't think we had a moon because our sky was so filled with soot moisture and clouds that we couldn't see the moon or the sun for a long time, in one case as long as 25 years or more. So maybe it was captured, recaptured, or maybe we just couldn't see it. But that the ancient actually tell of a time when we had moon should make us ponder, particularly in the light of this material.)

Also told in the Kalevala is a time that the support of the sky gave away and then a spark of fire kindled a new sun and a new moon. It also says "The sun occasionally steps from his accustomed path". The Kalevala has a mournful ...poem(?) which states... "Even the birds grew sick and perished, / men and maidens, faint and famished, / perished in the cold and darkness, / from the absence of sunshine, / from the absence of moonlight.../ But the wise men of the Northland could not know the dawn of morning, / for the moon shines not in season nor appears the sun at midday, / from their stations in the sky-vault." (Book 14 pg 76, 103, 130, 143-44)

In the days of the cosmic upheaval, the world was sprinkled with red milk. (Possibly alluding to Martian dust mingled with rain colouring the oceans and land.) Another Finnish history tells of when "Blood turns the whole world red" which is followed by world upheavals. (Book 14 pg 66) Odd. When the world continents moved and trapped animals in large herds crushing them, the blood ran into streams and rivers, but this Finnish reverses the order, also suggesting the dust from Mars turned the world red too. Perhaps the order is mistakenly reversed and mistaking the redness of Martian dust colouring the waters with blood? Or more probably similar events occurring in different eras.

Dreaded shades enveloped the earth at one time and "the sun occasionally steps from his accustomed path", after which Ukko (equated with Jupiter) lit up a new sun and a new moon and a new world age began. (Book 14 pg 130)

LAPLAND (NORTHERN REGION OF FINLAND, SWEDEN AND NORWAY)

Lapland history says that the midmost part of the earth (apparently earth's interior) "trembled with terror so that the upper layers of the earth fell away and many of the people were hurled down into those caved-in places to perish. Jubmel the angry god spoke saying "I shall reverse the world. I shall bid the rivers flow upward; I shall cause the sea to gather together itself up into a huge towering wall which I shall hurl upon the wicked earth children...*" Jubmel touched the ocean waters "rising sky high came the sea wall, crushing all things...made the earth-lands all turn over; then, the world again he righted." (Book 14 pg 88) (*Interestingly this is an exact description of the water that parted in the Red Sea and then collapsed on the pursuing Egyptians; and water could flow uphill if a source of gravity was close enough to the earth to pull the water upwards towards itself, or the earth's normal motion was disturbed.) Victor Schauberger noticed water could acquire a magnetic influence that somehow aided fish propelling them upstream. Water does have some peculiar inexplicable properties. I've noticed when a hose running full blast which would normally push people holding the hose backward, (which is why it takes a few firemen to hold one) actually displays an opposite sucking property when placed at the bottom of a barrel filled with water: the bottom of the barrel actually pulls the running hose towards itself. What would two strong gravitational fields like two planets in close proximity to each other, do to the water down here?

One of the Lapland prayers is that the sky should not lose its support and fall down. (Book 14 referencing Ragnarok)

SPAIN

Spanish writer Mela (circa 1st century A.D.) had access to Egyptian records and he stated specifically these records noted the reversal in the movement of the stars. Some suggest he was copying Herodotus who noted that the sun had changed direction for the Egyptians, but this is considered unlikely because the movement of the stars and the change in the direction of the sun were not necessarily connected. (Book 14 pg 119)

Seneca (circa 61 B.C. to 30+ A.D.) noted that the constellations changed their positions. Key to the passages was that of the constellation of the "Wain" or what we know as the Great Bear which includes what we now know as the polar star: "And the Wain, which was never bathed in the sea, shall be plunged beneath the all-engulfing waves." Thus we can deduce that Spain had shifted southward in relation to these stars. (Book 14 pg 225) According to Seneca at one time the Great Bear had been the polar constellation, but after a 'cosmic upheaval' a star of the little bear (little dipper) became the polar star. (Book 14 pg 317)

Non continental

THE BRITISH ISLES

The British Isles also have legends related to floods, but the legends date around the Dark Ages. Avalon, the final destination of King Arthur is linked with the rising of the ocean, and the sinking of the continental shelf off of Brittany with a King Gradlon whose city of Ys was drowned by the ocean. (Book 6 pg 47)

Irish legends say that four previous world ages had existed, and then were subsequently destroyed. (Book 23 pg 108)

ICELAND

Icelandic legends believe that nine worlds went down in a succession of ages. (Book 14 pg. 49 referring to "The Poetic Edda: Völuspa translated from Icelandic by H.A. Bellows) The Edda goes further, "No Knowledge she [the sun] had where her home should be, the moon knew not what was his, the stars knew not where their stations were." (Book 14 pg 130) There was a world fire, followed by a Fimbul-winter at the end of the world, and only one human pair remained alive in the north who fed on morning dew (same as Manna, and Ambrosia). (Book 14 pg 146) Fimbul winter is a triple strength winter for those difficult to freeze Mammoths in your neighbourhood.

JAPAN

Japanese myths contain a memory of an event that included the noise and the tidal waves with the hurricane but adding the unnatural darkness which descended upon their land: "The source of light disappeared, and the whole world became dark" (Online quoting the Nihongi, The chronicle of Japan) "Of old, heaven and earth were not yet separated" (Book 14 pg 113) More from this record says "Then divine beings originated among them. Hence it is said that in the beginning of creation of the world the swimming about of the countries was comparable to the swimming of fish playing in the water." (Book 10 pg 104) This is one of the more distinct legends indicating that the continents shifted, 'drifted' or 'swam' during recorded history.

HAWAII

Though as we saw Hawaii has a flood legend almost identical to the Biblical flood account of Noah, it also has legends of different ages...9 of them, and in each age there was a different sky above the earth. (Book 14 pg 49) The sky before the flood being encompassed by water was probably a deep green sky, after the flood probably emerald, and after the ongoing global catastrophes, pushing more of earth's atmosphere into space or onto the planets Mars and Venus, the sky changed by various shades to today's pale blue.

POLYNESIA

They say at one time the earth was submerged in the ocean, but [the ocean] was drawn by Tefaafanau (or Taafanua... which is Typhon!). When I realized this had to be the Polynesian name for Typhon I had to check the legends behind Tefaafanau ...by cheating and looking...online. It was worth it!

The story of "Tefaafanau: Accompanying the hurricane was a piercing noise so terrifying and prolonged it is reminiscent of the testimony of "noise" recorded by the Egyptian scribe Ipuwer, and the Book of Exodus. The Polynesians talk of a deluge of water which was drawn away by the mighty pull of a hurricane called "Tefaafanau." To commemorate the event, the natives of this scenic paradise celebrate a feast of the same name in March -- the very time when the Exodus took place! (Williamson)"

Here we have a very good clue... an exact description as to what Typhon is and did. First we all know how much noise water makes in your taps while it's running. Tefaafanau is the drawing or tidal pulling of water from the ocean up into space by a 'star', which would be Mars, or Venus. Furthermore they also say that new islands were baited by a star, which indeed is the same cause and effect creating Typhon: the gravity of a celestial body coming close to the earth and pulling water and land upwards towards it by gravitational pull, creating a cyclonic stream of water leaving the earth and going to the planet or "star", with the islands being formed by the same action. This would indicate a permanent change took place to create the island. This also by association suggests that it pulled land such as continents towards it; thus this legend would also be a clue that during recorded history the continents shifted.

Though I used this Polynesian legend of Typhon in the global flood section as well as here, more definitively the Polynesians also say that, like Hawaii and India, the world went through nine ages, at the beginning of which a new sky was above the earth. India mythology is famous for saying these things happened hundreds of thousands or millions of years ago, but it has to be the same time frame as other places on the earth synchronised with their timelines, as they clearly are describing the same events. During this time "the sky was so close the earth that we could not walk and they blamed all the myriads of dragon flies for cutting the clouds away from heaven. (Book 14 pg 49,192)

One Polynesian legend talks about a chief named Tu-erui living in utter darkness in Avaiki who then decided to leave and try and find a place not covered in this eternal gloom and darkness. He paddled a canoe named "Weary of Darkness" for many years in hopes of finding a land of light. After years of wandering he saw the sky clear little by little and finally arrived in a region where they could see each other clearly. Avaiki is the Polynesian name for the underworld or an underground dwelling place. (Book 14 pg 143) Similarly Central American legends talk of a time of 25 years of gloom.

BORNEO

The people of North Borneo have always, even to date, said that at one time the sky was originally very low [before the current world age began] and that six suns have perished and the one in the sky today is the seventh, thus we are living under the seventh heaven.

SAMOA

The legends of the tribes of Samoa tell of a time during a great catastrophe when "in days of old the heavens fell down" and they were so low that the people could not stand erect without touching them. (Book 14 pg 103 quoting *Religious and Cosmic Beliefs of Central Polynesia* by Williamson) Once again we have mention of the sky falling caused by a great catastrophe. Though the catastrophe is not named, the sky falling in this region as well, indicates the wide spread influence of the catastrophe as this effect of a falling or lowering sky is mentioned around the globe.

NEW ZEALAND

The Maoris told a story of a time when an incredible catastrophe occurred, "the mighty winds, the fierce squalls, the clouds, dense, dark and fiery, drifted and burst wildly. They rushed on creation, and in their midst Tawhiri-ma-tea, the father of winds and storms, swept away giant forests and lashed the waters into billows whose crests rose high like mountains. The earth groaned terribly and the ocean fled. (Book 14 pg 83)

Pacific Island legend (which ones not noted) explain that their island groups were all that remained from the continent of Kalu'a, which was destroyed by explosions and tidal waves. (Book 6 pg 67) This sounds like a local name for Mu / Lemuria which sunk in the Pacific Ocean.

AMERICA: Central America

MEXICO: TOLTEC'S / AZTEC'S

The Toltec histories speak of just four ages, the first age was ended by floods and lightening, the second age was peopled by giants which disappeared at the end of this age when the world was devastated by earthquakes. Those that survived the second age were destroyed by men in the third age. The Toltec's recorded that a great flood engulfed the "middle creation". Some say they don't know what they mean by this, and suggest "middle kingdom" might be referring to Atlantis, but it appears to be talking of one of the ages that came to an end by another flood. (Book 21 pg 28, 182) Sometimes proponents of the former existence of Atlantis have a one track mind...blame it all on Atlantis.

I asked myself the question 'Did the end of an age wipe out the Toltec's so they could not record that a fifth age came to be?', so I did a little digging. The Toltec's history is a bit of a mystery and they seem to precede the age of the Aztecs. Then I found this statement on the net. "Michel Graulich (writer of Aztec and Middle American histories) argued that the Toltec era is best considered the fourth of the five Aztec mythical "Suns" or ages, the one immediately preceding the fifth sun of the Aztec people, presided over by Quetzalcoatl." But some conflict is clear about who the Toltec's are and when the Toltec's existed, as one mention of Tula, the capital of the Toltec's is thought to have fallen around 1150. If I had to guess I would say that date is wrong and the Toltec's were destroyed at the end of the fourth age, or like the Apaches, were sent underground to ride out the event in tunnels and followed them until they came out somewhere else as a new civilization.

We've seen previously the Aztecs had a global flood legend, and now we'll see their legends clearly indicate they recall at least one local flood and possible three of them that accompanied the conflagrations associated with the end of their four ages.

The Codices of Mexico are compilations of their history which say world catastrophes decimated humankind and changed the face of the earth. The Chronicles of the Mexican kingdom say "The ancients knew that before the present sky and earth were formed, man was already created and life had manifested itself four times" (Book 14 pg. 49). Thus this is the fifth creation or the fifth age.

The Nations of Mexico "believe according to their hieroglyphic paintings, that previous to the sun that now enlightens them and us, four had already been successively extinguished. These four suns are as many ages, in which our species has been annihilated by inundations, earthquakes, by a general conflagration, and by the effect of destroying tempests." And "five suns that are epochs" (Book 14 pg 51 re-quoting a Spanish writer of the Conquest of Mexico written in the 16th century by Gómara) Thus the names of each of the preceding suns are named after predominant elements of the disasters, that being deluge or water, hurricane, earthquake and fire. Apparently in a slightly different order than those of The Mayans, so some mix-up might have been penned in the original. This does not mean floods did not accompany the latter three of these ages, as these ages are named only for the principal contributing factors in each of the upheavals that initiated the world changes.

The Nahuas of Mexico in their annals of Cuanhitlan say that our present era is that of the fifth sun, which is in decline. All creatures suffer continual trials by the gods and if any species fails it is destroyed. (Book 23 pg 109) Many species were wiped out during each of the four previous worlds or ages ended, so the Nahuas speak from experience. Interestingly they note that these extinctions occurred during each of the four world ages. These wiped out species they refer to would be the fossilized evidence of extinct creatures palaeontologists insist became extinct millions of years ago to tens of thousands of years ago, during the more recent last ice age. So these people recall *all* the extinctions or what geologists and palaeontologists would refer to as the periods known as Cambrian-Permian (Palaeozoic), Triassic-Cretaceous (Mesozoic), and Eocene to Pleistocene (Cainozoic) periods.

A Mexican native historian Ixtilxochitl in his work called Historia Chichemeca only accounts for four ages, Water-sun, Earth-Sun; which ended in violent earthquakes when the Aztec Titans were destroyed. The third (Wind-sun) ended after incredible hurricanes decimated the population "reducing the few survivors to the level of monkeys". He says we are still living in the age of the fire sun destined to be destroyed by fire, a fate apparently prophesied by men from space. (Book 23 pg 109) Some legends refer to the Fire sun as having already passed when the heavens were set aflame due to the combustible gasses ejected into the atmosphere. Perhaps Ixtilxochitl's notes ended at the point before the fire-sun could be recorded by those who perished in that event? It's sort of curious, some refer to the sun as one that passed which was the cause of the destruction and new sun, but this one seems to suggest the present name for the sun is the cause of the future destruction. If so, one wonders how they know.

Archaeologists are starting to wonder if there isn't something to these five suns and world ages business as told by the ancients implying that four previous civilizations which flourished and fell might actually have been true, because some skulls and artifacts that have been unearthed are dated at millions of years old.

(Book 23 Pg 143) Well they need to get their head around the fact that these multi ages were all historical and that there is something that makes these skulls and fossils appear, to be older than they really are. These additional ages are all post flood, an event which is dateable. The earth in the recent past was in such geological upheaval that these disturbances have buried and reburied many creatures, civilizations and artefacts in the weirdest places. Manmade items and living creatures found inside rocks hundreds of feet below the surface clearly indicate it is these upheavals that put them there and not multi millions or even billions of years of slow sedimentation; otherwise these things would have disintegrated long ago. Only abrupt burial can make these things stop rotting and disintegrating, the very upheavals these legends talk about.

Mexican hieroglyphs indicate that four motions of the sun (or directional shifts in the apparent motion of the sun through the sky) refer "to four prehistoric suns" or "world ages". (Book 14 pg 125)

A Mexican pyramid at Xochicalco speaks of yet another disaster concerning a land in mid ocean whose people were killed and turned to dust. (Book 21 pg 145) Or perhaps fish food... A Pyramid is an odd place to put such a legend...did the pyramid have any connection with the event? The Mexican Pyramids Cholula, according to tradition were built to serve as a refuge from the next flood. (Book 6 pg 62)

The Aztecs legends states that long ago their ancestors, which they say were the first men, emerged from seven caverns at a place called Chicomoztec, north of Mexico. (Book 23 pg 145) Though this reference doesn't say why, based on similar legends of emerging from underground, they were probably down there escaping a flood from the end of one of the four ages. How they could have known in advance of a flood to descend below to escape it will be explained shortly.

Interestingly the Mexican Annals of Cuauhtitlan, written around 1570 relates how there have been seven sun epochs and that these "Seven Suns" designated as world cycles, acted out in a cosmic drama. This historical ledger also says during one of the catastrophes, the night did not end for a long time, one catastrophe was accompanied by a hail of stones, and one age ended in a rain of fire, which is the sun of the fire-rain. (Book 14 pg 51, 61, 68, 70) Thus this legend unwittingly endorses the Book of Joshua where the sun and moon stood still, and possibly confirms the hail of stones which would mean this was a worldwide event too.

Though five suns is fairly consistent, as we've seen some ancient cultures name as many as 7 different skies and ages, all of which appears to refer to shades of change in the heavens. Whereas the 5 suns appear to be more dramatic changes in the sky and appearance of the sun and moon: though 5 or 7 ages might have something to do with the location on earth too. This mention of seven suns in the Mexican Annals of Cuauhtitlan is an eye opening find for me. I had thought the new world only spoke of 5 world ages, but we see even here on the opposite side of the world to India and China and the biblical Israel which all speak of or allude to as many as 7 world changes is indeed a globally synchronise-able series of events.

Fernando de Alva Ixtlilxochitl wrote that just 52 years elapsed between two great catastrophes, each terminating a world age, and creating two new suns. (Book 14 pg 163; I see you instantly noticed two incredibly obvious very similar names which were spelled with just one letter different...it must have stuck out like a sore thumb. Methinks Ixtlilxochitl and Ixtilxochitl is one and the same person but different sources simply spelled it differently. Gosh you're the observant one...isn't this fun!? I bet you name your next kid after him.) Such a short age of just 52 years might signify a degree or shade of changes as opposed to an epoch. Immanuel Velikovsky determined that this 52 years epoch is synchronous with the time of the Israelites Exodus which started with the ten plagues in Egypt and ended about 50 years later in Israel when Joshua told the sun and moon to stand still, and shortly afterwards the stones fell from the sky, killing the Amalakites. Now this next bit is important: this short period between world catastrophes also has to be taken into account when looking at Lyle's so called "geologic columns" which supposedly took millions of years to form. These cataclysmic periods were all accompanied by massive irruptions of sea onto the land, overtopping the mountains and beyond, dragging debris such as sand and creatures and turning them into fossils, all within recorded history. There is an automatic belief that if they are fossils it must mean they are prehistoric bones, and thus they have gotta be zillion year old remains. This is clearly false but this is what evolutionists and old earth geologists want us to believe. Therefore pardon me while I repeat a bit from my first book here:

"This assumption however is somewhat diminished by the fact that Claude-Joseph Désiré Charnay found *fossilized* bones of swine, sheep, oxen and horses in the ruins of Tula in central America in 1870's. (Book 68 pg. 350) Tula was the capital of the Toltec's which we've seen appears to have existed up to or during in the fourth or the last age before the current one. This is fairly recently so clearly this indicates fossils can form far faster than one might assume is needed to fossilize dinosaur bones. I might add that dinosaur fossils when broken open have a rotten smelling interior clearly indicating they have not fossilized as much as we are led to believe. Since Mount St. Helens eruption in 1980 (I heard the blast) trees which were uprooted and cast into the lake nearby have already started to petrify! A cowboy boot with the leg still in it has been found and both the leg and the boot have petrified. A person found many jars of pickles in a house that had been abandoned since the 50's. But one had been opened and inside was a petrified pickle! The pickle could be no older than the thirties."

OK back at it...

Written Mexican history further stated that the world was deprived of light and the sun did not appear for a fourfold night. Sahagun's (1499?-1590) history of New Spain (Mexico) also found similar legends from the people, and wrote that at the time of one cosmic catastrophe the sun rose only a little way over the horizon and remained there without moving; the moon also stood still. (Book 14 pg 62) This history not only confirms the biblical reference of the sun standing still, it links world catastrophes to the event.

The Mexican Annals of Cuauhtitlan also talks about a cosmic catastrophe that was accompanied by a hail of stones falling from the sky. The Native population also have oral traditions that talk of some ancient time when the sky "rained, not water, but fire and red-hot stones" (Book 14 pg 69) Keep in mind, even with Mars close enough to throw rocks at us, they would literally be flaming meteorites as the heated up from entering our atmosphere.

The Aztec Codex Chimalpopoca chronicles "The sky drew near to the Earth and in the space of a day all was drowned. The mountains themselves were covered by water. It is said that the rocks we can see today rolled about all over the land dragged by waves of boiling lava and that there suddenly arose mountains the colour of fire."(Book 23 pg 157)

The ancient Mexicans mention a world age that came to an end when the sky collapsed and darkness enshrouded the world. (Book 14 pg 103) "A vast night reigned over all the American land, in a sense the sun no longer existed for this ruined world which was lit up at intervals only by frightful conflagrations, revealing the full horror of their situation to the small number of human beings that had escaped the calamities.

Following the cataclysm caused by the waters, the author of the Codex Chimalpopoca, in his history of the suns, shows us terrifying celestial phenomena, twice followed by darkness that covered the face of the earth, in one instance for a period of twenty-five years." (Book 14 pg 139 quoting Brasseur's *Sources de L'histoire Primitive du Mexique*) Gómara concurred when he wrote "After the destruction of the fourth sun, the world was plunged into darkness during the space of 25 years" (book 14 pg 139-40) If this 25 years of darkness wasn't during the 52 year period mentioned earlier, it could another series of events that caused more "geologic columns" to appear as more water and shifting of the continents occurred.

"Mexican sources", tell of how "at the closing hours of the age that was brought to an end by the rain of fire, mountains swelled under the pressure of molten masses and new [mountain] ridges rose; new volcanoes sprang out of the earth, and a stream of lava flowed out of the cleft earth" (Book 14 pg 105) There's a Mexican pyramid surrounded by lava and this would be the same event the Mexican histories tell about. They saw it happen. By the way, this lava surrounding this pyramid has been dated 6-8,000 years old, but the event that caused this pyramid to be surrounded by lava was obviously more recent than this.

The Aztecs tell of a time when "There had been no sun in existence for many years. The darkness was slowly turning to just gloom as the excessive vapour and dust settled back to earth. [The chiefs] began to peer in all directions for the visible direction where the light might come from indicating the sun. They even placed bets among themselves as to which direction the sun would rise from, but they were all wrong for none of them had expected or bet on it rising in the east. (Book 14 pg 130 quoting *Ragnarok* by Donnelly)

The cause of much of these events was from a 'smoking comet' which is what they call Venus. They say from this comet came all kinds of flies as guests from another planet. (Book 14 pg 194) Though high temperatures are a breeding ground for many insects, however, because of the link of Venus with flies around the globe some have seriously considered that Venus may be populated by vermin. There may be many dead ones there, as they could be pulled from off the earth simultaneously with water to their new home, but with no picnics or dogs to follow around there, they could not be sustained.

Mexican legends also include a mention of something that changed because of the flood. They tell of a world age that came to an end when the sky collapsed and darkness enshrouded the earth. (Book 14 pg. 103-104) At first I thought this was a legend referring to how the sky might have been a colour in the night-time sky rather than just black [before the flood and said so in my first book], but now, in light of the legends we are going over, it seems clear this is talking of the darkening lowered collapsed sky filled with ash in a subsequent flood, not the global flood. This legend could be talking about the collapsing sky which was filled with soot and steam from volcanic action going on around the globe. Actually this may not even be a flood legend per se as there is no mention of water in this source.

TLAXCALAN (CENTRAL MEXICO) (18° N, 97° 30'W)

There was a great flood and the men who survived turned into wild monkeys but as time went on they slowly came to their senses and began to speak and reason again. [Internet based on Gaster, p. 121] Just like the Lower Congo legend said they had turned into monkeys, here they specifically note it was psychologically speaking.

Solon couldn't have said it better when he said "there have been and there will be again many destructions of mankind"...then..." you have to begin all over again as children and know nothing about what happened in ancient times"

ZAPOTEC (OAXACA, SOUTHERN MEXICO):

The earth was dark and cold. The only inhabitants were giants, and God was angry with them for their idolatry. Some giants, feeling that a flood was coming, carved underground houses for themselves out of great slabs of rock. Some thus escaped destruction and may still be found hidden in certain caverns. Other giants hid in the forests and became monkeys. Curiously this legend suggests that some giants and underground dwellers still exist.

It said some tunnels stretch for hundreds of miles to southern parts of South America. By the way... giants have been spotted there as recently as the 1840's.

Mexican legends tell of times in the past when earthquakes, tidal waves, flaming volcanoes and cities were being swept into the sea when millions of people and animals died and the only survivors were people who fled underground into dark caves for months praying for the sun to return. (Book 23 pg. 157)

The legends about underground refuges seem widespread in the Americas. The Andes are said to be honeycombs with immense tunnels built by an ancient race of white men. An underground highway runs from Cuzco a distance of 380 miles to Lima, then turns and stretches for another 980 miles to Bolivia. The southernmost portion apparently ends somewhere in Northern Chile in the Atacama Desert (Book 23 pg 177)

The Chronicles of the Mexican kingdom say the ancients knew that before the present earth and sky, that man was already created and life had manifested itself four times. Clearly another way of saying there had been five ages. The Codices of Mexico, and the Indians which wrote the stories of their past, give much prominence in the legends to the world catastrophes that decimated humankind and changed the face of the earth. (Book 14 pg 49)

When scholars narrow their research focus to just one civilization they are often perplexed by some of the things they read in some of the legends and myths of those people. A German scholar, Seler who wrote in 1907 *Gesammelte Abhandlungen*, was confused about his discovery that the Mexicans have this legend of the sun going towards the east, and wrote "The traveling toward the east and the disappearance in the east...must be understood literally....However, one cannot imagine the sun as wandering eastward: the sun and the entire firmament of the fixed stars travel westward." (Book 14 pg 125) However I hope you the reader by reading several ancient "myths" from all over the world in succession, can see this is a common thread in all of them, which can only mean it must have happened, that is that the world tumbled sometime in recorded history. Not only that, but these events happened recently, just a few thousand years ago and these events were witnessed by hundreds of millions of people around the world and were survived by very few. These events did not happen in some "Prehistoric" Palaeolithic period of world prehistory, as geologists would love to have us believe so we don't get antsy reading the truth. The term "Prehistoric" is technically a misnomer that assumes evolution is true and the events happened before writing was invented. But clearly these events are remembered by these people's histories, meaning the events are not prehistoric. It seems that geologists are aware these brutal upheavals happened and that the continents moved speedily, but that these things have been deliberately censored from mainstream reading material. (Nexus V25#4 Pole Shift Hidden Evidence by David Montaigne)

Latin America

The Chronicle of Akakor says that on the day the gods left they told Ina to take the people to the underground dwelling place so that they would be protected from the coming catastrophe. They said they would return when they are threatened. Then Ina watched them sail over the mountains and up into heaven. When the survivors came out of their hiding places the earth had been transformed. (Book 10 Pg 114-15)

The Tatunca Nara describes the catastrophes: "What has happened on the earth? Who made them tremble with fear? Who made the stars dance? Who made the water gush out of the cliffs?...It was terribly cold and an icy wind swept over the earth. It was terribly hot and men burned up in its breath. Men and animals fled in panic-stricken fear. They ran hither and thither in desperation. They tried to climb trees, but the trees hurled them away. They tried to creep into caves and the caves collapsed on top of them. What was below was pushed up above. What was above sank into the depths...." (Book 10 pg 115)

People have not been able to determine what caused the ice ages, because they rely solely on things that would have made the earth cold. Velikovsky deduced it had to be an environment that had both extreme cold and extreme heat occurring simultaneously on the earth to vaporise oceans, and condense the vapour into snow in apocalyptic amounts. These legends often infer such was the case but this legend is great because it specifically notes the two weather conditions were concurrent.

MAYAN / YUCATAN

The Mayan history says there were new suns at the beginning of each new world age and they gave the suns names. As I alluded to earlier, they were called Water sun, Earthquake sun, Hurricane sun and Fire sun. (Book 14 pg 50) I presume we are living under the 5th sun, now. Naming them is actually quite useful to sorting out the order, not just historically and chronologically, but helps decipher the actual earth physical landscape for those who know how.

As I understand it, "Water sun" would be what the sun looked like through the water shell before the first flood of Noah. Clearly the end of the first age would have been the universal flood before the 'second creation'. The second "Earthquake Sun" the weather and atmosphere was going wild as the continents initially divided. Hurricane sun was caused by massive shifts in the continents as they were flung suddenly when one or more asteroids hit the earth, or the manmade antigravity inducer, violently extended the initial action of the first such continental breakup*. Legends also seem to link this hurricane aspect to a planet nearby wreaking havoc with the weather and causing a polar flip and / or shift. And Fire sun I thought was the sun we have today, just a hotter sun. But a further look shows a lot of flammable material was shot into the atmosphere that caught fire as it was accompanied by excessive volcanic activity, giving it the name Fire Sun, so this has to be the fifth sun age, though this source somehow mislaid that bit. Furthermore the Mayans say that during the days of a great cataclysm, the sun's motion was interrupted. (Book 19 pg 153, * see chapter 6 in my first book...too cumbersome to explain here)

Just as the Egyptian priest told how there were many floods, this legend speaks of four new ages or suns, preceded by huge upheavals, and cataclysms which would have included great but not universal floods. Unlike the universal flood, there are other things going on. These Mayan suns are clearly not universal flood legends, and as we go through legend after legend from around the globe it should become very clear that similar events happened as is accounted in other legends around the world, indicating several catastrophes, of which most or all were accompanied by major floods from the water irrupting from the sea onto land in massive tidal waves that swept over vast stretches of real-estate, and some even over topped mountains.

At least that's how I grasp the four ages up to now. In my first book I hadn't figured out even as much as that, and merely wrote: "Water sun (What the sun might have looked like through the water shell and this seems to refer to the time before the first flood of Noah) Earth sun (earth pre Peleg?) Wind sun (Ice age?) and Fire sun (a hotter sun?)" (Note: Some refer to this second age or sun as Earth sun, some Earthquake sun)

This tsunami action that over topped the mountains is no doubt a key reason why so many local flood legends are confused with the global flood legend, as the mountains were apparently submerged in both types of legends. However, the local flood legends give enough clues that the mountains were only overtopped by the sudden tsunamis, and were not actually submerged for long periods.

My good buddy Ixtlilxochitl (circa 1568-1648) who we met a few sections ago, was a native Indian scholar that explained the four world ages this way in his annals of the kings of Tezcuco: "The Water Sun was the first age, terminated by a deluge in which almost all creatures perished: The Earthquake Sun (or age) perished in a terrific earthquake when the Earth *broke in many places* and mountains fell. The world age of the Hurricane Sun came to its destruction in a cosmic Hurricane. The Fire Sun was when the world age that went down in a rain of Fire" (Book 14 pg 50-51). Now if I could just learn how to pronounce my buddies name... and the correct spelling would help, is it Ixtlilxochitl or Ixtilxochitl?

I'd passed over this legend the first time I read this source but it appears I was bang on for three of them. Water Sun obviously speaks of the flood of Noah. Earthquake Sun refers to the creation of the continents also spoken of in the Bible where it says in the days of Peleg the earth was divided (Genesis 10:25) Peleg means "Earthquake" {See chapter 6 *Earth, Man, & Devolution.*} But it was really great to find this confirmation not only of my deduction but because it's another source telling us of the breakup of the continents in recorded history. Hurricane and Fire Sun's will become evident by the descriptions found in legends.

Being on income assistance I can't just go out and buy any source material I would like to have, so I don't have the many histories I refer to here: and besides they can be hard to track down, so I'm dependent on piecing together from what is quoted in sources; however what I *have* found should prove ample to demonstrate the points. SO...the Descriptions of one or maybe of two of the suns catastrophes (probably Hurricane Sun and Fire Sun) that occurred on the earth is pieced together here from two sources and it seems like two translations are used, so some overlapping occurs, and I partly summarise for expediency....

The Mayan Popul Vuh appears to indicate a local flood: "It was ruin and destruction... the sea was piled up... Then were the waters agitated by the will of Hurakàn, and a great inundation came upon the heads of the creatures...people were drowned in a sticky substance raining from the sky/They were engulfed, and a resinous thickness descended from heaven...the face of the earth was obscured/ grew dark and the gloomy rain / a heavy darkening rain...endured for days and nights ... And there was a great din of fire above their heads/ there was heard a great noise above their heads as if produced by fire...men were seen running, pushing each other, filled with despair; they wished to climb their houses and the houses tumbled down, they tried to climb trees and the trees shook them off, they wanted to go in caves and the caves closed before they got in.' And then "water and fire contributed to the universal ruin at the time of the last great cataclysm which preceded the fourth creation." Velikovsky notes that 3 Mexican sacred book including the Popal Vuh speak of a closing of an age ""...all record how the mountains in every part of the western Hemisphere simultaneously gushed lava." And that the god "'rolled the mountains", and "removed the mountains" and Great and small mountains moved and shaked"' (book 14 pg 70, 105-06, book 6 pg 200)

This mirrors identically the Aztecs four world ages.

One Mayan fragment translated by O.M. Bolio reads this way "The disaster befell on the eleventh day of Ahau Katun...it rained fearfully, ashes fell from the sky and the waters of the sea engulfed the land in one great wave...the heavens collapsed, the earth subsided, and the Great Mother Seyda was amidst the records of the destruction of the world". Internet search on who the heck was "Great Mother Seyda" just shows a bunch of ladies, but based on context and other clues I'm guessing she was a queen of the engulfed land. (The source {book 21 pg 145} interprets this reference as speaking of Atlantis, but it is in a Mayan chronicles so I put it here) The same source says this quotes a pre Mayan history which states "In the year 6 of the Kan, terrible earth quakes began on the 11th of the month of Zac and continued till the 13th of Chuen. Mu, the country of the clay hills, was destroyed: it was raised twice into the air and then disappeared in one night, with earthquakes never ceasing. At many places near the sea, the land sank beneath the waters and rose up again more than once. Finally the whole land split up into many parts and was engulfed with its 64 million inhabitants." (Ibid) "the country of the clay hills"! It just dawned on me. After the great flood clay would have been forming as sediment settled onto land before it resurfaced. Mu is said to be the first land that submitted to the waves. If this is the case it would not have been subjected to continental shifts rearranging the land and soil to cover up the clay from the flood. Furthermore, What's very telling in this legend is the fact that the earth quaked, not for a few seconds, or minutes, it quaked for at least a month (assuming "Zac" and "Chuen", are just consecutive months) This can only be interpreted as the continents moving. Alaska has huge drops and uplifts that occurred in a few seconds of an earthquake in 1964. So how much physical earth changes do you think could occur in over a month of continuous earthquake? It spoke of the land sinking and rising in and out of the water a few times. These long earthquakes, which in essence all continue the continental drift, means the continents could have drifted a few hundred miles in this span of time.

It has been noted that 78% of all the worlds' active volcanoes are in the Pacific. This probably has something to do with the direction of flow of the continents. They spread from the mid Atlantic ridge spreading outward both ways pushing the Americas west and Eurasian and African continents east. This force would be like squeezing the pacific landmass (above or under the waves) upward and then downward to be sub-ducted like a conveyer belt under the crust, causing massive numbers of Volcanoes to come into existence. These volcanoes in such a destruction as described would all go off simultaneously shooting millions of tons of ash and soot into the air, vaporizing hundreds if not thousands of cubic miles of water and creating global dirty steam so vast on a global basis so as to block out 95% of all the sunlight reaching earth for years, creating a global "nuclear" or Fimbul winter as some Ancients referred to it. (Fimbul winter is the winter at the end of the world or a triple strength winter) There is a worldwide layer of whitish ash in all the seas that was determined to be of volcanic origin. (book 53 pg XX). Other ancient histories speak of ash being carried by the wind and covering the entire earth. (Book 6 pg 201)

There would have been so much steam in the atmosphere that the sky was saturated with it to the point the "sky fell" or as this particular history states "the heavens collapsed" as dense clouds were literally filling the volume of the sky right down to the ground level around the entire globe. With global temperatures dropping as a result of almost no sunlight reaching the lower levels of the atmosphere, snow would have fallen in unbelievable amounts, creating glaciers in some areas virtually on the spot, while other areas plagued by volcanic action from the crust of the earth shifting, would have kept the local areas really hot. It appears from this set of legends that there was blown into the sky, huge volumes of natural gas that burned as it was ignited by local volcanoes, or even just the radiant heat from them making the sky burn. Figuring out the global geological history makes me shake my head at the ridiculous concern people have now over CO2 build-up. It barely touches the levels that are known to have been in history. Many people treat CO2 as a pollutant, which is absurd, it is simply spent oxygen we breath out which enhances vegetation growth around the globe.

The Mayan manuscript Troano tells of a time when the ocean fell on the continent and a terrible brutal hurricane swept over the earth which carried away all towns and all forests. Volcanoes were going off, while tides swept over mountains, winds threatening the survival of man, and these events actually did eliminate several species of animals. The face of the earth changed, including collapsing mountains, new mountains growing, and other mountains grew and rose over the onrushing cataracts of water driven from oceanic spaces, and rivers lost their beds, accompanied by wild tornadoes, including one that moved through the debris descending from the sky. The end of the world (or Age) was brought about by Hurakan which brought darkness, blew away houses, trees, mounds of earth and rocks, and killed a major portion of the humans. (Book 14, pg. 82, book 19 pg 113)

Three ancient "New World" books, Popol-Vuh, Manuscriot Cakchiquel, and Troano all say that in the past volcanoes in every part of the land all burst with lava at the same time. (Book 14 pg 105) The Popol-Vuh also says that the god "rolled mountains", and "removed mountains" and they swelled with lava. "Great and small mountains moved and shaked." (Book 14 pg 107)

The Quiche Mayans say they escaped a cataclysm by being in refuges underground (book 23 pg 145) Interestingly they have roads that continue on into the ocean, making it obvious that their histories include a time when the ocean rose suddenly, as the Mayans also have a custom of abandoning some cities and building new ones further inland. (Book 6 pg 62) So they have two traditions concerning escaping floods, suggesting they have ongoing ingrained habits and legends that are reactions to at least two of the changes of the ages, a further indication they are more than just legends.

During a long persistent darkness the Mayans realizing the earth had changed and could not figure out from where the new sun would appear, (suggesting they had been through this before). They looked in all directions but couldn't determine where the sun would rise. Though some guessed it would appear in the south, or what *was* the south at one time, their guesses included all directions because it looked like dawn all around. Some guessed that the sun would appear in the Orient and it turned out that this opinion was correct because that was where the sun rose! (Book 14 pg 130)

A large portion of Stone inscriptions found in Yucatan refer to great catastrophes which are found in "Calendar stones". "The most ancient of these [Calendar stone] fragments refer, in general, to great catastrophes which occurred at intervals and repeatedly, convulsed the American continent, and of which all nations of this continent have preserved a more or less distinct memory" (Book 14 pg 49 quoting C. E. Brasseur)

This one is a stunner. When the Spaniards conquered Yucatan they heard some history that had them agog. They said "their forefathers were delivered from pursuit by some other people when the Lord opened up for them a way in the midst of the sea." The Spanish thought they had found a lost tribe of Israel or something. Though people have attempted to somehow link this people with the Hebrews, no avenues leading to a possible link between them have been found. It appears that the waters were divided around the globe for a short spell, and not just in the red sea. This is a most unexpected verification for the dividing of the Red sea as told in Exodus.

South AMERICA

PERU (INCAN)

A religious history of Peru written in 1548 called *The Discovery and Conquest of Peru*, by Augustin de Zarate states that the South American Indians believed that their ancestors were forewarned of a coming great flood and took refuge in great caves near mountain tops which were prepared in advance with a well stocked cupboard to sustain them for as long as would be needed. They filled up the openings so the water couldn't seep in. After a long while they sent out dogs which returned muddy so the people emerged into a changed world. (Book 23 pg 191)

The Peruvians tell of a time that a period equal to 5 days and nights the sun was not in the sky, and that the ocean then left the shore with a terrible noise and broke over the continent, and subsequently the entire surface of the earth was changed in this catastrophe. (Book 14 pg 86)

Since this legend appears to be a mixing of global flood and local flood legends I repeat it here.

The first race created by the gods before the flood was a race of giants. Two giants of renown were Atlan and Theitani (Titan). (Book 4 pg 34) Previously we noted that pictorial records of ancient Incan rulers showed that a flood rose above the highest mountains. All created things perished, except for a man and woman who floated in a box. When the flood subsided, the floating box was driven by the wind to Tiahuanacu, about 200 miles from Cuzco, where the Creator told them to dwell. The Creator moulded new people from clay at Tiahuanacu. On each figure, the Creator painted dress and hair style, and he gave each nation distinctive language, songs, and seeds to plant. When he had brought them to life, he ordered them into the earth to travel underground and emerge from caves, springs, tree trunks, etc. in their various homes. He then created the sun, moon, and stars. They went underground to escape a cataclysm they knew was coming. (Book 23 pg 145)

It appears the Incan's have used these tunnels again. It was estimated that when the Spaniards first arrived in the Americas the Incan population was around 10 million, yet when a census was taken in 1571, the Inca's numbered only around 1 million. Though the Spaniards massacred many of the Incas, no one would suggest they killed nine million of them. It's thought that at the time of this census many of the Inca's must have been hiding in the tunnels. (Book 5 pg 141-42)

The Foggaras of Adar somewhere in the Sahara are a series subterranean passages apparently built to collect water, and go as deep as 250 feet underground. They are looked after now by people trained for the job, but no one knows who built them. Naturally archaeologists assume they were built with "utterly inadequate tools" and apparently they are as much a titanic undertaking as the pyramids themselves. "Even today, with all the mechanical means we have at our disposal, the creation of such a system of tunnels under the dessert would present engineers with greater problems than would be the building of a similar system in one of our big cities..." (Book 22 pg 161, referring to a work by Canadian writer Michel Poirier)

Built for water collection like the Foggaras or for protection from sudden floods one wonders not only how they built them but how they could have built them fast enough to be ready for what is clearly a sudden flood or a massive tsunami type? We know of people caught in tsunamis in recent times had little or no time to get out of the way let alone build tunnels to escape. Yet clearly as these legends suggest some had a feeling that a flood was coming and some were forewarned. How could they possibly be warned far enough in advance to build the tunnels or build them so fast with apparently staggering feats of technology!? This was something that I wondered even though I had proven at least one of these legends to be true: that of the Hopi's. Though I covered the proof of the Hopi legend in my first book it bears repeating due to the nature of this book. But first the missing solution which I had initially overlooked the first time I read these sources.

A Tibetan legends (briefly mentioned before) supplies part of the answer: At some point some blond giants were listening to a warning a "psyco-scientist" named Yellus, whose face showed unusual concern was telling them. Yellus was explaining that astronomers on Saturn (I suspect these are some of the "watchers") had detected a celestial body approaching the solar system. Some listening to the story thought it must be an asteroid coming right for earth, and some thought it was a missile from Sirius. Obviously a missile coming from Sirius is a bit silly but the Gods had led many of the inhabitants on earth to believe that's where they came from, probably to veil their true origins. Some fell for this Sirius subterfuge but most knew who the gods really were or believed another story. But clearly the earth was in for a big hit. Whether it truly came from outside the solar system, or was an asteroid blown from the fifth planet into the outer reaches of the solar system and was returning on a collision course for earth, or if it was actually coming from Saturn itself as indeed one of the moons of Saturn it is said to have been destroyed to create the rings of Saturn; can't be stated for certain. Whatever the case, the bottom line was a huge stellar body was coming directly for earth. (Book 34 pg 67) This explains how the earth could have had sufficient warning to start building the tunnels. They probably had a few months to maybe even a year or more to build the tunnels and warn people. But with the technology we know of at our disposal could we really build any substantial underground safe havens sufficient to house feed and save 60,000 people in a single underground construction? And would we believe such stories and would the governments of the world even bother to warn us? Knowing the bureaucracy of our world today, would the projects even gotten off...er...into the ground? You and I both know the answer to that...we would have been blissfully unaware until it was too late, while the powers that be hastily saved themselves and their loved ones. It would be *Alternative 3* all over again. (Read that book, one of the most gripping ones I've ever read!)

However, this asteroid was going to happen during the age of the gods. The gods were looked up to and they would have quickly spread the word and they had the technology too, and legends tell of them warning us.

The Apache Indians have the other half of the solution to this riddle. They tell the stories of tunnels running between their lands all the way to Tiahuanaco and they say that their ancestors, fleeing from other tribes traveled for years, using these underground tunnels. But they also have in their legends the origins of the tunnels. The Indian chiefs say that the tunnels were "carved out by rays that destroy the living rock, and that their creators were beings that live near the stars". (Book 21 pg 67) We might doubt this is possible but the technology is at least comprehensible. First there is something recently discovered known as "John Hutchinson effect". This chap invented some weird technology that made porcelain cups melt at room temperature. He made metal melt at room temperature and ooze around wooden items without damaging or burning the wood. "Prehistoric man understood the power of vibration and used it as a means of carving flint" (book 21 pg 100) Hutchinson's devices apparently used vibration to achieve his results. This has to be the same or similar technology that the gods used to make some of the Cyclopean building sites of Sacsahuamàn and Ollantaytambo which were *not* built with precision stone cutting methods but they were using a form of technology that softened the rocks to make them fit like they do.

Obviously this is not how the tunnels were made. But consider the nature of the atom. It is virtually empty space held together and made visible simply by energy. Overcome this energy and the atom falls apart and collapse into virtually nothing. I'm betting that if the surfaces of some of these ancient tunnels was analysed there would be very peculiar substances sitting on the floors or possible all the walls, or possibly heavy atoms on the floor that would either have very high atomic numbers or be completely unknown to science. You may have heard of people being almost completely consumed in a phenomenon known as 'spontaneous combustion' where people suddenly burst into flames and virtually nothing is left of them, even less than what would normally be expected of any ashes of the remains. This concept was undoubtedly understood by the gods and they used the technology to create the tunnels. The Andes are said to be 'pierced with immense tunnels built by an ancient race of white men. As mentioned, a subterranean highway is said to run from Cusco to Bolivia and ends somewhere in the salt desserts of Chile. The Tibetan Lhasa Dalai Lama confirms the Apache Indians legend: When he was thought to have died in 1933 it was later found that he had made a long underground journey to the Andes where apparently the Lamaism religion began!

When questioned about the tunnels he said "Yes, they exist: they were made by giants who gave us the benefit of their knowledge when the world was young. (Book 21 pg 35) The Tibetans refer to the tunnels as 'citadels 'which continue to afford a refuge to the survivors of an immense cataclysm. These people now use an underground source of energy that replaces the sun giving off a green fluorescence, breeding plants and prolonging life. This Tibetan belief ties in with an American legend: an explorer in the Amazon jungle (name not mentioned; possibly Colonel Fawcett?) said he found his way into an underground labyrinth that was illuminated "as though by an emerald sun". He had to leave in a hurry to get away from a 'monstrous' spider but before leaving he saw at the end of a passage shadows of men. (Book 21 pg 66)

This would also explain the origin and purpose of some other mysterious underground 'cities' as no one seems to know why or even how they were built. I think this is the answer. There are some astounding underground refuges such as Derinkuyu and Kaymakli. Another series of tunnels and underground chambers exists on Malta whose purpose is unknown. These are known underground places, though not 'cities' per se, they are underground facilities of as many as 13 floors deep. Surprisingly the air is quite fresh in these places showing advanced ventilation. This underground system could hold 60,000 people. At least 14 underground 'cities' are known to exist in Turkey alone. Apparently as many as 1.2 million people were sustainable in these underground places for as long as a year. (Book 10 pg. 281, Book 21 pg 124)

But not everyone believed the warnings of the gods. The Lhasa tablets tell the rest of the story. "When the star Bal fell into the earth at the place where there is now nothing but sea, the seven cities with their temples and their golden gates were shaken; a great fire sprang up, and the streets filled with dense smoke. Men trembled with fear, and great crowds flocked to the temples and the king's palace. The king said to them: 'Did I not predict all this?' and the men and women in their precious garments and bracelets begged and implored him: 'Ra-Mu, save us'. But the king told them that they were all doomed to die with their slaves and children, and that a new race of mankind would rise from their ashes" (Book 21 pg 54)

"It is said that before they were engulfed by a "fiery cataclysm" the Hsing Nu were a highly civilized people and cultivated arts still known to the Tibetans, including "speech at a distance" and thought transmission through space." (radio transmission?) "However, the survivors of the catastrophe lapsed into barbarism and superstition." (Book 21 pg 70) And I might add that perhaps a few of them lived in caves, and became cave-men.

ORIGIN OF THE ANDES AND TIAHUANACO.

Peruvian traditions describe a time when the sun did not shine for five days. During this time the entire surface of the earth changed its profile, and the seas fell upon the land. (Book 14 pg 77, 86) Land changing its profile can only mean the land shifted, that is to say the continents moved...another history indicating this happened during historical times.

Coniraya-Viracocha, the Incan god is said to have raised mountains from flat plains, and flattened other mountains. (Book 14 pg 107) This of course would have wrought havoc with the ocean spilling onto land.

Spanish historian (Avila & Molina) recorded traditions of the Indians of the new world. They were told that there was a time when the sun did not appear for 5 days, a cosmic collision of stars happened before a cataclysm, and people and animals tried to escape to mountain caves. "Scarcely had they reached there when the sea, breaking out of bounds following a terrifying shock, began to rise on the Pacific coast. But as the sea rose, filling valleys and the plains around, the Mountains of Ancasmarca (in Peru just north of Cusco) rose too, like a ship on the waves. During the five days that the cataclysm lasted, the sun did not show its face and the earth remained in darkness." (Book 14 pg 76-77) This would have been the entire Andes mountain range coming into being, but witnessed from a single vantage point.

This is a great piece of legendary history that I've been looking for. Here we have clear indication that mountains in the new world rose during historical times and were witnessed by and fled from, by people who recount this legend in their histories, and this event was accompanied by a local flood. It's felt certain that Lake Titicaca and the ancient city of Tiahuanaco were at one time coastal cities. The description of events in this legend shows that both the mountains and the sea rose simultaneously. This had to be when the continents of the Americas were being pushed west by upheavals occurring from the expulsion of material under the sea in the mid Atlantic pushing the 'old world' and the 'new world' farther apart. Dr. Maurice Ewing explains this rift system and oceanic earthquake belts action this way "…The opposite effect of tension is compression, which results in a folding of the earth's surface. The mountain system of the continents, such as the Rockies and the Andes, were probably caused by such folding.", (Book 64 Pg. 104) Meaning push or pressure from the Atlantic Ridge shoved North and South America west, compressing the western coasts against resistance of the 'land' of the Pacific, folding the western edges to make the mountains. I might add this pressure from the Atlantic ridge would have affected Europe and Africa pushing all the way to the eastern edge of Asia and sub-ducting the Pacific Ocean floor down, and outward again like a global conveyer belt.

Velikovsky summarises the traditions of the new world: "the profile of the land changed in a catastrophe, new valleys were formed, mountain ridges were torn apart, new gulfs were cut out, ancient heights were overturned and new ones sprang up. The few survivors of the ruined world were enveloped in darkness, "the sun in some ways did not exist," and in intervals in the light of blazing fires they saw the silhouettes of new mountains." (Book 14 pg 106) Once again he came within an eyelash of saying the continents drifted in recorded history.

BRAZIL / PERU

An aborigine group from western Brazil called the Cashinaua'a have a frightful traditional history. "The lightning flashed and the thunders roared terribly, and all were afraid. Then the heavens burst and the fragments fell down and killed everything and everybody. Heaven and Earth changed places. Nothing that had life was left upon the earth." (Book 14 pg 104) I like the term "fragments" from heaven…interesting name for a piece of Mars.

American North

The Choctaw Indians of Oklahoma say that "The earth was plunged into darkness for a long time." Eventually a light seemed to appear in the north, "but it was mountain high waves, rapidly coming nearer." (Book 14 pg. 86)

The Quillayutes, or the Quileute, a Native American people of western Washington state, U.S.A. say at one time a wicked man stole the sun making the world dark. People shot arrows into the darkness and climbed to heaven on the arrow ladder and seized the sun and fixed it back into the heavens. The sky people (gods) often descended to Earth, depicted as a chief on a cloud, and one time when the sky was much nearer the earth, they became so angry at the constant strife among men that they moved mountains and caused earthquakes. (Book 23 pg 125-26) This appears to be another reference to the gods apparently using their technology to inflict catastrophic incidents on earth and mankind.

Another Washington tribe, the Sachomish complained that the creator had made the sky so low that tall people bumped into it and others climbed trees to enter the sky world.

The Navajos Indians call our present world, the fifth world. They also say at one time men traveled from world to world, indicating man at one time traveled in space and visited other planets. (Book 23 pg 109 quoting Burland's *North American Indian Mythology*) The Navajo say ancestors came from underground to teach them, and then returned, but they were driven underground in the first place by a flood. Legends of underground civilizations exist all around the earth.

The Pawnees taught that when the world ends (or the end of a world age) the moon would darken, the sun becomes dim, the north and south stars would dance in the sky. Earth would be destroyed in meteor showers. Then when the end of the world occurs the south star would come higher and the North Star would disappear from the sky, then the stars will again fall to the earth. (Ibid, Book 14 pg. 198)

British Columbia native histories say that "Great clouds appeared...such a great heat came, that finally the water boiled. People jumped into the stream and lakes to cool themselves, and died." (Book 14 pg 106 quoting *Journal of American Folklore* collected by J.A. Teit)

Other Pacific Northwest natives have a similar history. "It grew very hot...many animals jumped into the water to save themselves, but the water began to boil. (ibid quoting *Tales of the North American Indian* by S. Thompson) The southern Ute tribe of Colorado also say that the rivers boiled (Ibid: quoting another *Journal of American Folklore* by R.H. Lowie)

Quoting bits from *North American Mythology* by Alexander, in relation to Pacific coast Indians: "Could see nothing but waves of flames: rocks were burning, the ground was burning, everything was burning... roaring all over the earth, burning rocks, earth, trees, people, ...water rushed in...covered the earth, and put out the fire as it rolled on toward the south...water rose mountain high." (Another reference to mountain high water which no doubt caused mega tsunamis or "local" floods.) A celestial monster ...made a terrible noise...looked like an enormous bat with wings then spread and touched the sky on both sides." (book 14 pg 195)

A British Columbian Tribe called the Kaska note their legends talk of a time when the sun had stopped on its way across the sky then became small and has remained small ever since. When this happened the sky became very low and close to the earth. This clearly indicates that the earth shifted slightly further out on its orbit around the sun. Only a massive hit from an asteroid or interplay between planets could shift a planets orbit, which would cause massive volcanic outbreaks then the evaporated water causing the sky to fill with steam thus the very low sky. It's a theme repeated time and time again in legends around the earth. It's important you see that, so you don't think it's a few nutty dreamers making up stories, but the virtual universality of the legend means it happened.

PUEBLO INDIANS (ARIZONA)

Most Pueblo Indians refer to this current time period as the "fourth world." The prior three worlds were destroyed by fire, ice and flood with some versions also talking about winds and earthquakes, suggesting a fifth world they somehow lost track of. Before the world cleansed itself at the end of a particular world (or age) life is destroyed to start in the new succeeding world. The people (who are pure of heart {or I might infer, people who believed the warnings of impending disaster were true and followed survival orders}) were led underground to be cared for by the Creator during the cataclysms occurring above ground. The people that went underground were then cared for and protected by these people, in this underground sanctuary until Creator tells his subordinate gods that it is safe for the people to re-emerge and live on the surface world again.

The Oraibi say the firmament hung low and the world was dark, and no sun, no moon or stars were seen, and that the people murmured because of the dark and the cold. Then the planet Machito god appointed times and seasons, and the way for the heavenly bodies. (Sorry: reference lost)

ZUNI INDIANS

The Zuni's say they too were led underground by *kachinas* or star people to avoid a catastrophe. Here we have a direct link with the creation of the underground retreats, with the people on the artificial moons built before the world flood. They also appear to be the people or linked with the people who warned the earth as the 'watchers' who saw the asteroid coming. The Zuni Indians also mention an interesting detail not found in other accounts of people living in and emerging from the underground. It might be because they were forgotten about as they appear to have been underground for a long time, but not residing in places especially built for long term underground dwelling. In the Zuni version, as a result of being underground for many generations, the people were called the "raw people" which have become deformed and adjusted to pitch-darkness after living underground for generations. (There must have been a vast supply of foods and or some sort of edibles that could be grown in very dark environments) When they emerged up into the new world, they were poorly prepared for their new life above ground. Their deficiencies were corrected by the "star people" that helped them lose the webbing between their fingers and toes, their tails and slowly help them become re-adjusted to the light. When they had recovered, they were then divided back up into clans, and were sent on migrations to the four-directions. (Legend found on the internet).

The catastrophes shifted **the terrain suddenly, slamming the land on fleeing animals and caused many species to become extinct** or at least they vanished in some areas where they survived in others. The Zunis Indians also have "race-memories" of reptilian monsters. (Book 23 pg 111) Wow! Here we have a legend describing exactly what I had deduced in my first book and mentioned here earlier; that the land moved so fast animals couldn't get out of the way in time to escape thus they were crushed by the land itself. The continents shifted very suddenly due to forces acting on the globe that shoved land masses into each other (or buckled it as it moved) crushing hoards of animals trying to escape at breakneck speeds. Not to mention the Zunis remember the dinosaurs: how would *you* describe them? "Reptilian monsters" sounds good to me.

IROQUOIS

Eastern Woodland Iroquois inform us that a pregnant woman fell from the sky and had twins; one good (Tsanto) and one Eeeevill (Taweskare) and between them they shaped the earth. This is similar to the Hindu and Persian gods of Ahura-Mazda– chose to be good and the Angra Manyu (Ahriman) who chose to be evil.

The Iroquois, Huron and Wyandotte Indian legends taught that the first people (Not gods) lived in the sky before the great turtle created earth on the face of the waters. If we see that as a description of the time of the flood with Noah waiting for the dry land to appear and men in space not in the flood it fits pretty well. So we see that they too have the legend of people living in the sky, obviously in some sort of craft, planet or planetoid.

ARIKRA

This South Dakota prairie group tell of how men from a previous world [age] lived in a great civilization under the earth called Agharta, who were survivors of Atlantis. The sky spirit Mesaru had been sent to destroy the giants of earth with a flood. He created men from seeds underground and sent the Corn Mother to lead them to the sunlit surface. When she returned to the skies, men quarreled and she and Mesaru came back and taught men about the stars, and how to live in peace and cure disease. (Book 23 pg. 127)

This could be combining of a local flood legend, and a universal flood which also killed the giants, with a later flood, where some went underground to escape the flood, and were later led back to the surface. However some legends note that Atlantis (a post flood empire) had giants too, so it's more likely speaks of a latter flood, that of a catastrophic flood that destroyed Atlantis.

PAWNEE INDIANS (33°N, 97° W)

They tell of a time when giants were placed on the earth by "Tirawa Atius" (the Pawnee name for Creator), which grew proud and had to be destroyed in great floods (plural). They also recall Cannibal giants which matches up with Central American legends about Cannibal giants. (Book 23 pg 109)

AMERICAN + CHALDEAN

(I found this reference similar to something mentioned above) In Atlantis by Donnelly (page 431-432) he refers to Chaldean and American legends. The legends quoted appear to be speaking of a flood of the tsunami type when global catastrophes changed the earth. "The pillars of heaven were broken; the earth shook to its very foundations; the heavens sunk lower toward the north: the sun, the moon, and the stars changed their motions; the earth fell to pieces, and the waters enclosed within its bosom burst forth with violence and overflowed it. Man having rebelled against Heaven, the system of the universe was totally disordered. The sun was eclipsed, the planets altered their course, and the grand harmony of nature was disturbed." This flood does not appear to be of a down fall description but of something causing the oceans to overflow the land, and it's one of very few mentions I've found of the moon changing its motions. (Obviously the sun can't change its motion but the earth in relation to it changed, probably referring to a global reversal or crust shift.) The heavens sinking lower would place it in time as a post global flood and make it a local type, though apparently it was worldwide in effect, as both American and Chaldean felt it. Admittedly there are some similarities to the universal flood, though it depends on how you read "the waters enclosed within its bosom burst forth with violence and overflowed it ", it could describe the suddenness of a monstrous tsunami. However, if a second giant asteroid hit the earth after the flood of Noah, as clues suggest strongly one did, it too could cause water to come shooting out of the ground a second time. This could be difficult to be certain which flood the legends describe, but I lean strongly toward it being a local flood description, particularly because of the description of the planetary motions changing as other legends tie together with local floods..

MANDAN SIOUX: THEY CAME FROM UNDERGROUND

Lewis and Clark discovered a Mandan legend about the underworld. They say they came from an underground village which was near a subterranean lake. But the legend says some larger women when climbing the way to the surface broke the vine they climbed leaving some of them underground. (Book 68, pg. 114) here is a more complete version of the legend found online. (Sorry, reference lost)

Mandan Sioux

The earliest people lived under the ground near a beautiful lake. Once, a great grapevine grew above their home. A root from the grapevine poked down into the village of the underground people. A few of the most courageous then climbed the vine into the world above. When these explorers returned, they reported that the world above was more beautiful than anything they had imagined, teeming with fish and game, full of light and beautiful flowers. Soon large numbers of people began climbing the vine into the new world above. One day, however, an obese woman began to climb and the root broke, leaving half of the people underground, where they remain to this day. When we die, we rejoin our cousins under the earth. Boy does that sound like Jack and the beanstalk or what?

What really gets under my skin is how the theory of evolution has further clouded men's minds in their attempt to interpret what these myths mean. Consider this statement found online accompanying this myth. "What is the significance of such myths? Are they representative of successive stages of cultural development or consciousness? Are they evolutionary?"

No!... it's a relating of exactly what happened to the best of the memories of the people telling the tales! There was a flood which the peoples of the world were warned about in advance and the people went underground in prepared hiding places to wait out the catastrophes. When it was safe to return to the surface a new or changed world presented itself to the people that came out of the ground. Some people who knew better stayed underground to get away from the harmful effects of the sun which included premature aging and genetic decline. To explain why some people stayed underground, some imagination crept in to the legends if the real reason wasn't completely understood. So maybe they added the fat lady and the beanstalk business to keep the kids happy, or something. We will see that the emerging from underground is common to many Indians nations which also include The Navajo, and Mojave Apache's, and as this next section tells us...the Hopi.

PATHS TO UNDERWORLD DANGEROUS TO FIND.

The Hopi Indians are said to have gone underground to escape a coming tragedy and that their origin in this era is from the time when they emerged from underground or the underworld with a white brother named Bahana, who had supernatural wisdom. The Hopi Indians speak of underground civilizations and say an entrance to this place is near the junction of the Grand Canyon and the Little Colorado. Apparently

Bahana returned to the underworld, and, similar to Quetzacoatle, said he would return. Their ancestors, the Sipapu are said to have emerged from there. (A sipapu is a small opening found in the floors of the Kivas or below ground level pit houses common to the Pueblo Indians.) This Sipapu or small opening in their homes seems to be a constant reminder of their origins rather than where they actually emerged from. They hide the actual place from where they originally emerged from, as the sipapu is also described as some place in or near the Grand Canyon.

Hopi legends speak of mountains falling into the sea, lakes sloshing over the land and freezing solid, (apparently from the cold wind from space) and that only those that went or were already underground survived.

Most of my quotes about the Hopi in my first book were reliant on other people's quotes, but finally I was able to obtain and read the book of the Hopi for myself (bibliography book #70); I can quote a couple paragraphs here. Some of this is repeated from my first book.

"So again, as on the first world, Sotuknang called on the Ant People to open up their underground world for the chosen people. When they were safely underground, Sotuknang commanded the twins, Poqanghoya and Palongawhoya, to leave their posts at the north and south ends of the world's axis, where they were stationed to keep the earth properly rotating.

"The twins had hardly abandoned their stations when the world, with no one to control it, teetered off balance, spun around crazily, then rolled over twice. Mountains plunged into seas with a great splash, seas and lakes sloshed over the land; and as the world spun through cold and lifeless space it froze into solid ice. This was the end of Tokpa, the second world." (Book 70 page 20, Book 19 pg 154) Take note that this legend says "So again, as on the first world..." meaning this happened at least twice.

"So he loosed the waters upon the earth. Waves higher than the mountains rolled upon the land. Continents broke asunder and sank beneath the seas. And still the rains fell, the waters rolled in. (book 70. page 23)

(Side step: I'm sure it's abundantly obvious that this is a different type of flood from that of Noah's and the mechanics are all different. The legend also notes the continents broke and sank. This does not necessarily mean a continent broke *and* sank, it could mean continents did either; sink or break, and one continent necessarily doing both. Atlantis broke and sunk, but some just broke and moved. But however you want to interpret it, the key is that it clearly speaks of continental changes...during recorded history. We have been indoctrinated to believe that the earth has experienced a slow steady pace during the process of any world changes, so we don't look for any evidence of speedy continental shifts or motion, or we try and interpret obvious evidence in a tortuously illogical way that is not based on any real evidence. But once you free yourself from this conviction, and dare to look for evidence of the continents shifting in recorded history, you see it often in legends: statements like 'the landscape changed', 'they emerge to a new world', and other hints of shifts if not spoken of in plain language. O.K. back at it.)

Not only do the Hopi say there is an entrance to the underworld somewhere in or near the Grand Canyon, they apparently guard it. An underground passage was found by a Seth Tanner who it was said was half Hopi (though I initially missed the part that indicated that he was born in New York) so he may have been married to a Hopi or had some special relation to the people group. Anyway, as he was constantly in the company of the Hopi Indians and being in the neighbourhood of the Grand Canyon on an ongoing basis and possibly even hearing some of the legends and doing some casual inquiries, he eventually discovered a cave and explored it and found it to contain Hopi artefacts and religious treasures . But because he went into the place, and the Hopi found out, they blinded him with a potion thrown at his eyes, because no white man was allowed to see the place. He never spoke about the find after that, no doubt for fear of something worse happening to him or to the people he told these secrets to. It is said that normally other people are killed if they find the place, but because of his Hopi link, whatever it was, they didn't give him the full treatment.

David H. Childress stumbled on a very interesting newspaper clipping from the Phoenix Gazette from

April 5 1909. He makes some quotes from the old article in his more recent article and gives an online link to the old newspaper article which I followed for more of the information; which follows.

Apparently someone from the Smithsonian (G.E. Kinkaid) found this entrance but was fortunate enough not to be caught or found out by the Hopi so the story of this place got out. If he found the same site as someone in 1990 discovered, he would had to descend down a crevasse, I presume with *a lot* of rope. Just short of one mile down, a huge chamber was found which had scores of passages radiating out from the main chamber. Steel and copper weapons were found there. But the entrance is on Government property and there is a penalty if you're caught, but with him being part of an archaeological expedition they were protected by the Government. Many mummies were found sitting cross legged with lilies or lotus' in their hands. Artistic vases, urns, as well as cups of copper and gold were found. Granaries as well as several hundred rooms were also found! It was deduced that 50,000 people could live in this underground citadel, and they figured that the local people may have been descendants of the people of this underground site, and indeed the article mentions the legends of the Hopi in connection with the site. The entire complex was not fully explored as some places smelled awful and / or were so dark they just passed up the opportunities. Some passages were explored but not to the ends. So whether this place had a passage to the underworld of course was not determined. It's quite possible that any connection to the underworld may have been sealed deliberately off from below. This underground section found and explored may have been built specifically for local North American survivors, which of course in this location, means the Hopi. Apparently the Hopi were warned about a coming catastrophe, and led to the place. (See Atlantis Rising #75)

It's not certain in my mind if the place Seth Tanner and G.E. Kinkaid explored is the same place as Tanner referred to it as a cave, and Kinkaid had to descend a mile down to get to the place, though I suppose it could be a cave that led to this mile long descent. But as a semi local knowing the legend of it being in the underworld, perhaps Tanner was prepared for the long descent.

So where is it? Near the entrance to the underground site is an archaeological site of a town called Unkar where the Unkar stream meets the Colorado, so the general area *is* known...if you're the daring sort. Those who studied the artefacts in the underground haven, said they seemed to be similar to Egyptian according to the gazette, but were also described as "...doubtless they had their origin in the Orient." (Though the article equated the Orient as interchangeable with Egyptian: so take your pick)

It's interesting that the Hopi want this place's location kept a secret. My guess is because they plan on returning there one day. They state that the next cataclysm is coming soon and they have signs that they look for, so I'm guessing that when they think the time has come, the Hopi will just disappear from their homes one day. Apparently the Hopi feel the time for serious global destructions is once again upon us.

The finding of this place vindicates the Hopi legends of its existence and their local flood legends completely. It proves beyond any reasonable doubt that the Hopi were saved from a local flood just like their legend reports and it should make it clear that there are indeed two kinds of flood legends.

However the enormity of the "local floods" has to be grasped. Their legend clearly indicate the earth was experiencing a huge cataclysmic turmoil so by association if the part of the legend that says they came out of caves saved from the flood is true, the other part of the legend, as horrendous as it reads must also be true which means that the entire continent was indeed overrun by waves. The Hopi legend isn't the only one describing such devastation. By the mouths of two or more witnesses shall all things be established. Just as there is a multiplicity of universal flood legends confirming the biblical tale of Noah's flood for the hearts of the believers in the biblical narrative, so are there a multiple number of 'Local' flood legends that must also be taken into account to truly grasp the geological history of the earth. Exasperatingly all books proving the flood of Noah constantly used local flood evidence to prove the global flood. We now have to not only sort the flood legends, as I've done to some extent in this work; we also have to sort the flood evidence.

One ancient legend suggests that if we continue on with our wars 'they' may come to the surface world and make it a dessert. I guess the neighbors downstairs have complained before! Did they cause the Sahara to come into existence? They can turn dry land into ocean and caused mountains to disappear. (Book 43 pg. 230) We appear to have been aware of these legends of underground cities for a long time but we have ignored them, refused to believe them or thought them to be the same as, or allegorical, of death.

A Mayan book called the Chilam Balaam has another description of disruption in the heavens. Ah Mucencab (?) came and obscured the heavens and the earth began to awaken. No one knew what was to come. Suddenly subterranean fires erupted into the sky and fire rained down from above, ash descended, rocks and trees were thrown down, wood and stone smashed together. The heavens were seized and ripped apart. Then the skies were buffeted to and fro and thrown on its back, the people were all torn to pieces, and the hearts of those that lived failed them and many were buried in the sands and in the sea. Then in one huge sudden rush of water the great serpent (this is most likely another reference to Typhon) was ravished by the heavens. The sky fell and the earth sank when the four gods, the Bacabs, arose and brought about the destruction of the world. (Book 6 pg. 199-200 paraphrased) (The Bacabs were four brothers, Hobnil, Cantzicnal, Saccimi, and Hosanek, whom God, when he created the world, placed at the four points of the globe, holding up the sky so that it should not fall. They escaped when the world was destroyed by the deluge." As you can see, this mirrors the Hopi legend so much as to give one chills.)

ESKIMOS AKA INUIT

Greenland Eskimos are afraid that the support of the sky might fail and consequently the sky would fall and kill all human beings. They note that a darkening of the sun and the moon happens just before the sky falls. (Book 14 pg 104 quoting traditions of the Eskimos as told to P. Egede between 1734 and 1740)

They also say that in ancient times the earth turned over and the people who live then became 'antipodes', meaning the place they lived in would not have been facing the northern stars but the southern stars.(Book 14 pg 126) Or said another way; the poles switched or the earth turned over.

The Eskimo legends speak of a time when the land they lived in had no ice, suggesting their verbal legends go back to a time before the ice ages, drastic climate changes, or a rearranging of the continents occurred. Any one of these scenarios is hard for old earth evolutionists, anthropologists and geologists to swallow. They also speak of a time when fire fell from the sky frequently and snow could burn like fire [acidic?]. (Book 10 pg. 111) This sounds very similar to one of the plagues of Egypt. Instead of saying "Oh what nonsense, fire doesn't fall from the sky" we should ask ourselves what conditions on earth would account for fire falling from the sky: meteors, lava, burning particles?

Australia

AUSTRALIA GETS THE HAMMER.

I found this legend in a magazine I advertize my first book in while proofreading to this point, so it's a timely find to say the least.

Australian Aboriginal lore was banished or destroyed by people trying to replace this culture and enforce colonial culture and religion on the Australian native populace. Once again, legends that actually parallel biblical ones were unwittingly fought against. So in order to preserve the legends of the aborigines they were turned into art expressions to escape the purges. These art expressions took on the form of poems to survive. One poem is written in the Sept-Oct 2018 issue Nexus. I quote or summarise parts here.

Stella Wheildon states that at one time India and Australia were linked by land bridges connecting the two lands together. The poem says it like this: "From the beginning this land was one whole land from here to India." She states that India and Australians often went on excursions to war with each other. Then on one excursion to India, while the two nations fought, two wives that were beaten by their husbands to stop them from following them to the war, began to dig one way and the other. They kept digging until they met each other and water filled the gap between India and Australia. It states that the dirt they dug through gave way to the "roughest water in the world". When the aboriginals finished their war and were on the way back, they saw the way blocked by a vast expanse of water. The poem continues: "He made the mountains and islands rise out of the water. Then with their "borror", (the string that they pull out of their mouths), the clever-fellers took this cord and threw it from island to island. They crossed over this cord until they landed back in Australia." After they returned, they turned the two women into stone and the Aborigines after this time lost touch with the rest of the world and never went back fighting any more. This was said to be the beginning of the [present] world.

Naturally the author assumes that with the accepted geologic timing of continental drift set at about 15,000 years per mile, means this story is stupidly old, because if this snail's pace to the continents shifting were the case, the warriors wouldn't have had to go through all that trouble to get back to Australia, they could have hopped over the few inches of continental separation: that or the war lasted 30,000 years or so and these warring people lived for millions of years or some such nonsense. And as we've seen in other legends the land shifted suddenly and fast enough to crush animals as they tried to escape, and the distance in these shifts was often vast. The legend-poem, only gives a clue to the cataclysmic action by saying it was the "roughest water in the world". The apparent clincher is a mural of a map that exists in the Hierakonpolis tomb which depicts earth's landmasses from the west coast of Europe to Australia and also shows North America separated from Asia by a thin river, and Australia only slightly removed from South East Asia, not far from India. Basically it is a period map of Gondwanaland, or maybe even Pangaea. A map like this existing should rock the geologic world.

Now in looking up this map in its original state without place names added to it, it is not absolutely certain in my mind that this *is* a map of the world, but admittedly it is possible, and indeed other people besides the writer of the article felt it was a map of the world too. If indeed this is an ancient map of the world in its former Gondwanaland state, this is yet another strong piece of evidence that civilized man recorded and mapped the earth before the complete breakup of the continents. Now there are some of course that would say that if this was mapped 200 million years ago, it had to have been done by the gods or visiting spacemen and thus boost the panspermia belief. However this time that line of reasoning doesn't work. Some of the maps we've seen of Greenland showing no ice and the mountains in the right spots or maps of Antarctica which show no snow, also with mountains and other geological features in the correct places, might get some air with 'the Gods mapped them' line because the maps show high level of skill and the use of spherical geometry. But this Hierakonpolis tomb map is crude and archaic with simplistic figures drawn all over it. If the gods drew this map, they were on drugs when they did so. However the very fact that legends exist telling of a time when land masses were not separated adds weight to all we've covered to this point.

A LITTLE REALITY CHECK

If, as geologists would have us believe, this Gondwanaland state of the land masses of the earth that existed a supposed 200 million years ago, then no way on earth could legends such as the Australian one that predated the breakup of the same survive this long. One thing I've seen while working through many legends, is simplification, disintegration, blurring and merging, and as is the case with the previous Australian legend, conversion to poetry. Though as we've seen, there are many similarities between many legends, they speak of events that occurred just 4,000 to 6,000 years ago. And yet though they are describing the same events, they are already often so distinct from each other in odd ways, they are often looked upon by many historians as complete rubbish. Many of the legends that I read, as much as I tried to understand them, I felt were already incomprehensible. If legends have disintegrated to mumbo jumbo in a few thousand years, what do you think would have happened to them after 200,000,000 years?

Furthermore many attempts throughout history have been tried to destroy knowledge in any form in favour of other predominant religions or societies taking over. Many civilization on earth or buried under earth have been forgotten and no one knows any origins of them, and even what remains of their texts are completely undecipherable to us now, such as Indus script, Peruvian Quilpi's, Easter Island and Canary Island texts and on and on. Some libraries were purged by the Muslims, because they felt the books in the libraries were either ungodly or superfluous to the Quran. Whole libraries have been burned in the past. Whole civilizations have been wiped off the map. "Scholars" routinely ignore legends in favour of their own myopic theories and actively seek to stamp out opposing theories and opinions, and evidence suggests they even destroy evidence that counters their theories.

Similarly, domineering barbarians want complete control of whatever situation they come across and will do anything to force their dominance onto the people and the societies they subdue, and they don't care what they destroy in the process. Red China routinely destroyed whole affluent or western influenced households in the quest to make all people's lives reflect the new order of the communist world, which Chairman Mau inflicted on his people. We already know that what remains of ancient knowledge is an infinitesimal residue of what was once common knowledge in vast libraries. People's histories were recorded in the year of a king's reign and not a year of the world and by and large so it is virtually impossible to correlate events in history with each other.

Even the fiercely guarded scriptures have been translated and retranslated almost ad infinitum to match ongoing societal standards and trends and even politically correct agendas; changing its value and veracity and even its contents. Giants have been purged from some versions of the bible, Christ as God is purged from many others, God changed to non gender thrust on believers in other versions, and several books referred to in the scriptures are completely lost. Some religious sects have even deleted, added or changed parts of the book of Revelations, even though the book itself says they will have added to their lives the plagues the book speaks of if they do so, and the promises to believers will be deleted from their lives if they take stuff out: Yet they've changed the contents simply because they don't really believe the scriptures they are translating. Furthermore, the many different translation of the bible have eroded much of believers confidence in the bible (which one is best?) and created some divisions among believers, almost as if it was planned that way. Even the genealogies of the kings in the scriptures through the bible don't match up properly. As much as scripture believing people would like to believe the bible is guarded by God himself, it is guarded by our imperfect efforts to do his will, and we are a fallible people, slowly subject to the ongoing opposition and attack on the word and the very Christian's and their beliefs. It's also attacked from within by 'progressive' scholars and preachers belittling the fantastic stories in the bible as impossible and only meant to be allegorical and not literal. At one time people memorizing or quoting scripture quoted just one version and, though it was somewhat cut and dry, it maintained uniformity. Now few people quote or memorize the same version if they memorize at all, and it becomes little more than personal interpretation. Many legends have already succumbed to interpretation and generalities. Can disintegration or total collapse of all legends and scriptures be far behind?

I've discovered to my dismay that even the bible itself like all of mankind and creation is subject to disintegration and devolution over time, until the time of the end. Bible believers know there is a time coming when all of mankind will fall away from God and his values, and all bible believing Christians will be killed wholesale at the time of the end. Only Christ's return when Israel is surrounded by all her enemies closing in for the kill in the battle of Armageddon will his intervention end the madness. I say all this not to just show how biblical appreciation and accuracy is waning. I use this point of reference to show that if it's happening to this ancient book when it was so supremely looked up to for two thousand years or more, by millions, even billions of people, then it is happening in others cultures too. My point is if this disintegration is happening to the former rock of the western civilizations, (that being the bible) who knows what intervention, reinterpretation and tinkering and disintegration has happened to some of the other ancient legends of the world as well? No doubt people who live by other ancient legends have seen similar decline in value placed on their ancient legends and traditions and they are, or were as important to those people as the bible is and was to other people. I've often read in various sources that the younger generations in all the cultures around the world are less and less appreciative of their forefather's ways and legends, and would rather buy the latest video game or trendy shoes than attend a traditional event. Even in strict Muslim countries, cultural disintegration has become a bothersome burr in the religious political systems of these countries. Erosion of cultural ideologies through lack of appreciation of parental values is a global trend. Parenthood's supremacy has been exchanged for politically correct indoctrination promoted through consumerism and schools with complimentary agendas. Schools want children in school as early as possible to erase the teaching they've received from their parents and exchange it for the unisex one size fits all anti god rhetoric now virtually forced on the masses. With the moorings or parental guidance being pulled out from under the children's feet, sociologists wonder why this generation is so full of antisocial dissatisfied dishonest even criminal and murderous behaviour being perpetrated by the young. This is not a good environment for ancient traditions to be successfully handed down from generation to generation; it is a recipe for disaster and complete political and even religious domination by those who have engineered society this way.

If that's not enough, actual genetic disintegration of mankind as a species means man himself cannot possibly survive 200 million years let alone the survival of his mythologies. Before the great flood, less than 6,000 years ago, man was able to marry a sibling; now even marrying a cousin leads to genetic deformities and abnormalities. Genetic disintegration is rampant in the species...all species. Things like peanut allergies almost unheard of in the 1970's are rampant now, and so too has autism become far more common problem today than it was just 40 years ago. As more and more impurities leach into our food chain and medical practices, health problems multiply throughout the system. Sterility is an ongoing and encroaching plague on all of mankind as more and more radiation leaches into the earth environment through the thinning atmosphere and radiation leaks from manmade sources such as nuclear reactors into the environment. Yes, all reactors leak, even the most strictly maintained ones. Even things like pesticides used in Great Britain are being found in trace amounts in Antarctica's wildlife. Cab drivers in New York City are not allowed to give blood as there is so much carbon monoxide in their blood and Mothers milk across the board is laced with harmful impurities that we all absorb from our toxic highly technological society. Cancer occurrences have increased exponentially since 1900 in direct relation to expansion of technology and the chemicals that accompany the spread of the same. In 1900 12% of deaths were traced to environmental causes, in 1940 it increased to 38 % and in 1976 it stood at 59%. (Book 49 pg. 178-79) Cancers have been positively linked to environmental factors, and not *just* from radiation sources, yet the public has been deluded and tricked into thinking cancer is genetic or from some other cause, to milk us for as much money as they can to 'fight cancer', when in fact just moving to the country farm would reduce your chance of contracting cancer significantly.

Legends speak of vast catastrophes that wiped out people too, so that even if man left the remnants of ancient knowledge completely alone and legends remained in a perfect state of preservation, catastrophes would have wiped them out long ago: that is if 200 million years is the time frame we measure civilization by, as in fact some people do. Add a few nuclear reactors being destroyed by a global catastrophe and guess what happens. Indeed ancient legends speak of nuclear wars which way back then helped speed up genetic devolution. Today nations are rattling nuclear swords and terrorists are striving to gain hold of nuclear arms to deliberately speed up global demise. No way on earth is any legend or verbal traditions going to be handed down through the generations for 200 million years. At the rate civilization is becoming more and more lethal by various means, we'd be lucky to last 200 more years, let alone 200 million.

A HEART WITH FREE WILL CANNOT BE FORCED

One comment I think needs to be said. There are some Christian divisions or groups that assume that if you haven't believed in Christ or if you've never heard of him, then you have no hope of life after death and thus they assume whole nations for generations are thus lost, which is in fact patently silly. If an area of the globe didn't have missionaries there until say 1850, it's ridiculous to say everyone that lived in this area up to that date are all doomed. God sees the heart and if you are an honest person, God's ways are written in the hearts of men, regardless what you know or have been taught. But sadly some people forced these ways and religions onto people groups, actually diminishing the value of what they believed to those who they tried to "convert", creating an ongoing mistrust of their beliefs that lingers even to this day. It doesn't matter what the value of what you believe is, even if its acceptance guarantees perfect nirvana, if you force it on people, they are going to reject it, even if they give the appearance of accepting it to appease your wrath, like the Australians did. And the irony of it all is the gospel they tried to force on people was something that was always meant to be chosen by free will by hearers, not inflicted and forced upon them.

VENUS Wanders

It seemed easy for me to accept that Mars' orbit had become elliptical due to being slammed from the exploding planet between Mars and Jupiter. Mars is a smaller planet and more easily pushed by a blast, and the place where the blast occurred and the subsequent creation of Olympus Mons on the further side confirmed this deduction. I managed to finally explain how this happened more convincingly with much better evidence in my updated version of my first book. (If you bought an earlier version of my book feel free to contact me for the free updates that increased the book from about 250,000 words to 338,000, which also includes the illustrations and new cover) However I wasn't as convinced of Venus's wandering. Often when reading and something strikes you as interesting and it catches your attention, if you keep reading while thinking about what you just read, instead of stopping and thinking it over, you miss stuff. Rereading my material I found all kinds of stuff I missed and have been trying to be a bit more careful noting and keeping track of and quoting more exactly the evidence. While revisiting my sources, a key piece of the puzzle convinced me that Venus also had strayed from its circular orbit in the past too.

First consider, we know the moon and Earth were hit by many asteroids in the past, one of which caused the great flood and others flipped the earth and stalled the lithosphere to make the sun appear to stand still in the sky or go backwards as these many legends we've read clearly indicate. We've even seen the odd legend that noted the apparent size of the sun changed to make it appear smaller to us on earth which is also evidence of a consequential collision. So it is safe to deduce from these clues that the Earth at some point must have strayed from its normal circular orbit, and moved farther out from the sun. This would account for us coming closer to Mars to meet it as it came closer to us once every 16 years on the near edge of its elliptical orbit. We could also assume that if we had an elliptical orbit from being knocked around by asteroids, that our orbit would also bring us closer to the orbit of Venus in another part of our year / orbit. If then we could find evidence that Venus too had an elliptical orbit or an erratic orbit we could complete the chain and realize that on rare occasions Earth and Venus could also be close enough at one point in our orbits to cause some serious effects down here on earth.

We've seen how the Chinese were very meticulous and had high standards of celestial observation to the point a king had one astronomer killed for not predicting an eclipse. Indeed many ancient civilizations had extremely accurate calendars, star charts and were meticulous recorders of stars, comets and planets and their positions, probably because of how these stars and planets have affected the earth. That and the fact that some of the gods came from what appeared to be stars or moons. Some researchers have said, for example, that the Mayan calendar was more accurate than out own! Mars was known for causing earth quakes and throwing rocks at us. If then, the ancients were very careful in their observations of the planets, and in particular Venus, then if this premise is to have any weight, there must be some record of an errant Venus.

There is.

Velikovsky deduced that Venus was a new planet expelled from Jupiter which had come close to the earth around 700 B.C. I figured out the Jupiter connection with this planet that Velikovsky confused for Venus, was in fact the man made planet or moon built before the flood that returned to earth after the flood which is also associated with Jupiter because it usually stays there and has been spotted there even in recent times. This was an error on Velikovsky's part that partially discredited the Venus aspect of his theory and partially dissuaded me from accepting his Venus connection. Also some of the clues he deduced as being that of Venus were about a red planet that was causing the problems here on earth, meaning he appeared to be confusing Mars for Venus in at least some of his evidence. I then found evidence that conclusively proved that his date for Venus coming to the earth around 700 BC was impossible, which explains my reluctance to have accepted his conclusion that it was Venus that came close to the earth and not just Mars coming back for another visit. So he had three strikes, and though I still didn't count him out, I didn't rest any weight on the Venus connection. Before I show you what changed my mind, first I repeat my evidence for proving Venus could not have been wandering in our back yard around 700 BC from my first book.

"But there is evidence that proves he was wrong about Venus being a new planet. There is a diagram of the zodiac and the positions of the planets on a mummy case that is in the British museum indicating the time of the death of the occupant. The planet positions of the diagram were worked backwards to determine these positions indicated the autumnal equinox of 1722 B.C. They got a professor Mitchell and assistants to determine the position of the planets on that equinox of 1722 B.C. and the position of the planets the scientist came up with was exactly the same as those on the coffin. (Atlantis: Donnelly page 364-365) If Venus wasn't in the diagram it would have been noted as its absence would have stuck out like a sore thumb, meaning Venus was obviously in existence in 1722 BC [and in a predictable position], thus disproving Velikovsky's new Venus theory. Furthermore, Bode's laws which show planetary orbits follow natural predictable distances from the sun would clinch it. This however doesn't disprove that Venus came close to the earth as Velikovsky maintained; it just suggests he mixed up Venus [on one occasion] with another planet, but that's another story."

So we have to ask ourselves, what made Velikovsky so certain that Venus came near to us in 700 BC?

"The year-formula of an early king, Ammizaduga, was discovered on one of the tablets, and since then the tablets are usually ascribed to the first Babylonian dynasty; however a scholar has offered evidence to the effect that the year-formula of Ammizaduga was inserted by a scribe in the seventh century. (Book 14 pg 206) If the tablets originated from the beginning of the second millennium, they would only prove that Venus was an errant Comet at that time.

The date of this tablet and the contents (which I will get to shortly) convinced Velikovsky that these events with Venus happened around 700 BC. But as we've seen above that by 700 B.C. Venus had a very steady and predictable orbit, so predictable that worked backwards through time all the way back to 1722 B.C. by two separate studies came up with the exact same positions for Venus as each other and as that of the positions of the planets as indicated on the coffin. So it appears the tablets that Velikovsky dated to 700 BC, do indeed date from the 2nd millennium BC. However regardless of the date of the tablet, it doesn't change the contents of the tablet.

Before we get to the tablet, first let's grasp Venus as it is now. It is the brightest "star" in the sky, it's not hard to see, and in fact it's hard to miss. It is a planet on the inside of Earth's orbit so it comes from behind the sun then slowly gets higher in our night sky as it catches up to earth then it starts to get lower in the sky until it disappears in the glare of the sun and daylight. Then it crosses between the earth and the sun and starts to appear in the early morning and gets higher and visible earlier and earlier in the morning then it gets ahead of the earth and starts to go around the sun and disappear behind it. Then, because it goes around the sun faster than us, it once again emerges from behind the sun and we see it in the early twilight and it starts to rise again. It gets to approximately the same point /elevation above the horizon in the sky once every 225 days. It's the evening star for about 35% of the year, and the morning star about 35% of the time, and the rest of the time we can't see it due to glare or from it being behind the sun. It's clockwork.

One last thing before I get to the contents of the tablet. There was a legend I mentioned before that had me begin to think that maybe Venus *did* wander.

Ovid wrote about Phaëthon while driving the chariot of the sun "No longer in the same course as before", The horses "break loose from their course" and "rush aimlessly, knocking against the stars set deep in the sky and snatching the chariot along through uncharted ways." I wondered...could Venus be one of those horses?

Now the Tablet: Velikovsky gives five consecutive years of observations of Venus from the tablet. The first year Venus disappears from the west (night) sky for 9 months and 4 days till it was seen again in the east (morning sky), The second year Venus left the east (Morning) sky for 2 months and 6 days when it arrived in the west (evening sky), the third year it disappeared from the west (Evening sky) for 11 days then appeared in the east (Morning) sky, the fourth year she left the east (morning) sky and was gone for 5 months and 16 days to reappear in the western sky, and the fifth year she disappeared in the west (Night sky) and was gone for 7 days and reappeared in the east (morning sky), then went back around the sun and appeared in the western sky again just one month later. (Book 14 pg 206-07)

Any astronomer would look at that and say "That's Crazy! That can't be right!" Some scholars said these observations had to be inaccurate, others said the observations were defective. Well perhaps you might miss Venus for a couple days and see it a couple days later or cloud coverage might have obscured it, or see it a bit earlier by luck a couple days, but no way on earth are you going to miss it by months. These observations were done in strictly professional ledgers by astronomers of the day, and Venus is the easiest 'star' to see, it's brighter than anything else in the sky except for the sun and the moon! How could they miss it! One scholar wrote "The period between the heliacal setting of Venus and its rise is 72 days. But in the Babylonian-Assyrian astrological text, the period varies from one month to five months-too long and too short: The observations were defective." (Book 14 pg 207 quoting M.Jastrow's *Religious belief in Babylon and Assyria*) another quote "The invisibility of Venus at superior conjunction is given as 5 months 16 days instead of the correct difference of 2 months and 6 days," (Book 14 pg 207 Quoting Langdon-Fotheringham's *The Venus Tablets*) Another refers to the time as "impossible intervals". If you'll notice, one of those observations *was* 2 months and 6 days so they were clearly recording it right, so something happened to Venus. It had to be hit so hard by such a massive asteroid that it strayed by a difference of almost 9 months during what appears to be the inferior conjunction! (that is being in between the sun and Earth.) Venus is way out of its proper orbit here and such a drastic difference or orbital deviation easily puts it within reach of the earth, and possibly even behind us! And not just the Babylonians figured this out. Hindu record tables of the movements of Venus also befuddle scholars. "the details referring to Venus... are difficult to unriddle"

Not only did modern scholars scratch their head at reading these records, the ancient who recorded these were mystified, and concerned!

Babylonian prayers "Ishtar (Venus)... how long will thou tarry?" Iran "...Tistrya, the bright and glorious star,...looking forward for him and deceived in their hope: When shall we see him rise up, the bright and glorious star Tistrya?" The Septuagint (The earliest Greek translation of the old testament from 3rd century BC used by the Greek Jews) translates Job 38:33 "Knowest thou the changes of heaven."

The Mexican called Venus a 'star that smoked', and so they considered it a comet. It of course would have 'smoked' when it came close to a heavenly body and the mutual attraction would have disturbed the atmosphere and pulled it off the planet towards that source. The Vedas also say Venus looked like a fire with smoke. The Chaldeans said that Venus had a beard, and called it a "bright torch of heaven", "a diamond that illuminates like the sun" and compared its light to that of the sun. Venus would have to have been very close to the earth to have all these apparitions that are attributed to it. Chinese ancient astronomical texts from Soochow say there was a time when "Venus was visible in full daylight and, while moving across the sky rivaled the sun in brightness. The Egyptians say that Venus was "A circling star which scatters its flame in fire", and the Arabs and the Babylonians called Venus the one with hair. (Book 14 pg 173-74) The Babylonians note that Venus approached Mars and when it did so its horns grew longer: Venus has the appearance of horns, similar to when our moon is in its phases and this is a reference to this aspect of Venus (Book 14 pg 176)

Velikovsky states that Rabbinical sources (Jewish histories) note a comet, which he determined by its description was Venus, left its own orbit and followed Earths for a while, then during a pair of close encounters six days apart Venus changed the direction of its motion. During these close encounters, seas were torn apart, tidal waves rose to their highest points. The battle between the planets appeared like a snake attacking, with lightning being returned from the comets long tail as the atmosphere of Venus distended in various directions. It also looked like a brilliant globe and a dark column of smoke. Extensions of the planets were attracted to each other then repelled as though electrical magnetic forces were involved. The globes pulled away from each other, then, six weeks later they met for another battle in the heavens. (Book 14 pg 91-92)

Venus' orbit changed drastically, undoubtedly by a massive strike from an asteroid sending it reeling out of its normal orbit, and many legends talk about its presence close to the earth, and they indicate it created havoc down here as legend after legend states.

A very amazing correlation to the straying of Venus is found on a map of the stars discovered in a cave of the Himalayans foothills. This map was considered very accurate but apparently of a sky that had shifted giving it the appearance of where it might have been 13,000 years ago, probably indicating a shift of the earth. But more importantly it showed a line inscribed on it that connected Earth, and Venus! (Book 21 pg 57)

There are more indications mentioned by Velikovsky of Venus acting out of the ordinary in his book *Worlds in Collision* (book 14) See pages 180: Venus Changed course and appearance, Pg 185: Venus reverses position of Dawn, called serpent cloud, Pg 186: Causes the heavens to quake and earth to shake, fire fell from Venus, pg 188-190: Venus's horns' was the cause of the Cow being venerated in India, and was the cause of Ambrosia, / manna being created and falling to earth.

In the second century Roman Historian Suetonius said the ignorant thought blazing stars were to portend disasters to rulers. Very few people in the 17th century had a telescope so if you saw a comet it was big enough to see with the naked eye. If you were aware that all through ancient history the sighting of comets was often followed by huge calamities and then you saw a comet, what do you think your reaction would be? In January 1681 the town council of Baden Switzerland (or what Roman Historian Suetonius would call "Rulers") issued a proclamation when a "frightful comet" with a long tail appeared in the sky. They said "All are to attend Mass and Sermon every Sunday, abstain from playing and dancing, and evening drinking is to be on a modest scale." Andrew Tomas though this reaction by the people of Baden was "incredible by its stupidity". (Book 11 pg 68) Was it? I'm, not so sure.

As we can see Venus had a part to play, causing floods on the earth. Plato notes that "...the earth twice suffered great catastrophes as a result of "the shifting of the heavenly bodies."" (Book 14 pg 158) This would even link the timing of Atlantis destruction with other floods occurring around the globe.

MARS UPDATE

Recently a moon rock found in Africa made the news as part of an upcoming event telling that it was to be auctioned off. Naturally it was suggested the moon rock must have come to the earth "millions of years ago". Though I knew that Martian rock had been found in Antarctica and included that tidbit as evidence in my first book I don't recall hearing about Moon rock here on earth. Martian rock made it to earth as the close proximity of Mars and the gravity of the earth pulled that Martian rock towards us in rock blizzard events spoken of in many legends. How moon rock got here is probably a little more difficult to explain, but a guess would be Mars coming close enough to the moon during its travel towards earth pulled some of the moon's surface towards itself, some landing on Mars, and some temporarily becoming Martian satellites. As Mars came close to the earth, these were pulled down to the earth along with more of Mars itself.

Atlantis Rising issue #132 (page 11) brought something to my attention about Mars that I had completely overlooked. I had stated and offered sufficient proof in my first book that showed that Mars had taken a lot of the earth water bringing down the global water level after the flood and periodically after that. Evidence of a body of water on Mars the size of the Arctic Ocean was found on Mars as well as obvious signs of water streams that had since dried up. Naturally cosmologists want us to believe this water was on Mars billions of years ago. My book maintained that this water went to Mars from earth possibly as recently as the first millennium B.C. Well the article in Atlantis Rising gave a clue to show my deduction is absolutely correct.

We all know that Mars has a stormy season where winds blow there obscuring visibility of the surface for months at a time. The point A.R. made was winds as we know are a form of erosion, and if the water evidence on Mars truly was millions of years old, these storms would have erased the evidence of water on Mars long ago, by blowing the loose surface and erasing or burying the flow marks. With storms on Mars an annual event, I find it amazing that the evidence of water on Mars lasted even 2500 years or so! In fact this suggests that the water remained on the surface much longer than I would have imagined and only recently must have finished being absorbed into the Martian soil, to leave such obvious signs of water on the surface to this day. So this is more evidence that these cataclysmic events were occurring during the recorded history of mankind.

Chapter 5

Local flood Evidence

I've heard it said by supposedly informed sources including a pastor that would supposedly accept the biblical histories including the flood, disasters of the ten plagues of Egypt, and other global catastrophes alluded to in the scriptures, that certain things could not have happened in the past like huge asteroids smashing into the planet and the rotation of the earth stopping because if these things happened all life on the planet would be completely wiped out. On top of that, I recall a movie from the 1930's where a man (I think Charles Ruggles?) without him knowing it, is given at random all power by the gods. When he figures out that he has all power, it goes to his head and at some point he stops the world and all the earth is destroyed as people and buildings on the earth are hurled at 1000 miles an hour towards the east. I suppose if the earth did stop dead in its tracks, that might be a possible result, but scientists have figured out that this might not necessarily occur.

"The physical effects of retardation or reversal of the earth in its diurnal rotation are differently evaluated by various scientists. Some express the opinion that a total destruction of the earth and volatilization of its entire mass would follow such slowing down or stasis. They concede however, that destruction of such dimensions would not occur if the earth continued to rotate and only its axis where tilted out of its position. This could be caused by the earth's passing through a strong magnetic field at an angle to the earth's magnetic axis. A rotating steel top, when tilted, by a magnet, continues to rotate. Theoretically, the terrestrial axis could be tilted for a certain length of time, and at any angle, and also in such a fashion that it would lie in the plane of the ecliptic. In that case, one of the two hemispheres-the northern or the southern- would remain in prolonged day, the other in prolonged night." This would be similar to Uranus that is tilted at about 80 degrees.

"The tilting of the axis could produce the visual effect [for people on the earth] of a retrogressing or arresting of the sun; a greater tilting, a multiple day or night; and in the case of still greater tilting, a reversal of poles with east and west exchanging places; all this without substantial disruption in the mechanical momentum in the rotation or revolution of the earth."

"Other scientists maintain that a theoretical slowing down or even stoppage of the earth in its diurnal rotation would not by itself cause the destruction of the earth. All parts of the earth rotate with the same angular velocity, and if the theoretical stoppage or slowing down did not upset the equality of the angular velocity of various parts of the solid globe, the earth would survive the slowing down, or stasis, or even a reversal of rotation. However, the fluid parts- the air and the water of the oceans- would certainly have their angular velocity disrupted, and hurricanes and tidal waves would sweep the earth. Civilization would be destroyed, but not the globe."(Book 14 pg. 385-86) Exactly as described at the end of the "Hurricane sun".

Not mentioned or apparently not considered was that fact that the continents lie on liquid under carriages which would cause the land masses slide as well, minimizing the effect of the waves. The disruption of the atmosphere interacting with the near absolute zero temperature of space itself would freeze animals solid and waves in mid motion, exactly as has been found in the arctic where frozen waves have been found that looked ready to break on the shore, and mammoths have been seen which were thought to still be alive when in fact there were seen upright in a frozen state.

They estimate it takes 1000 years to create a one inch layer of diatoms which when on land are called diatomaceous earth. This fact alone shows what is now land was once under water, either via flood or uplifts turning former ocean floor into land. There is one spot with so many diatoms, that it supposedly took 50 million years to form the deposit. First, it's entirely likely they grew at a far greater rate before the flood accumulating faster, but more importantly, it's illogical to assume they all deposited in this one spot; it has to be a build up from some kind of horizontal hydraulic action. One report says an 80 foot whale fossil was found standing on its tale among such deposits. However the whale was actually parallel with the layers of the stratum which was on a 40-50 degree which had been uplifted by seismic folding to that angle. Creationists say this proves the flood, but it doesn't explain how so many diatoms would end up in one place. Clearly the deposits happened fast or the whale still would have rotted. It does prove a flood, but not the global flood with its different 'mechanics'.

This find illustrates two events happened to this area. One: something shovelled the layer of diatoms to create such a large deposit, something like a vast bulldozer bunching up the diatoms. The continents sideways motion bunched up the diatoms while the waters above spilled over the land. The whale fighting the force stayed in the water below the spilling, but was then caught in with the diatoms as were other creatures such as seals. Similar or even the same motion of land would have bunched together animals as far away as Wyoming where there is a log jam of fossils. Evolutionists often poke holes in Creationists flood evidence when Creationists assume all geologic evidence confirms just the global flood. For example Kent Hovind, though a great creation scientist, does not as I write this, believe the Continental drift happened. His reasoning is because there is dirt under the oceans connecting the entire globe to each other. So whenever he discounts continental drift, slow or fast, he creates holes in his flood evidence, if perchance some flood evidence is also altered by subsequent uplifts. He thinks all the uplifts were a result of the flood, but clearly many, if not all of them occurred after the flood, and he has not found a cause for the uplifts. His own material notes that the continents are about 30 miles thick before you get to liquid substrata, but the ocean floor is only 3-5 miles thick. This is like a layer of skin that forms on a glass of hot milk by comparison or an onion skin compared to the rest of the planet. This can easily be pushed aside by the Atlantic ridge when it was active, or when an asteroid hits the earth at an oblique angle, interfering with the earth's rotation, changing the momentum of the various layers of earth, and pushing the continents further apart.

SUNKEN, RAISED, BURIED AND CRUSHED LAND, ANIMALS AND CIVILIZATIONS.

Many legends speak of land getting submerged to become ocean and land rising out of the ocean to become new lands. These were not hypothetical musings or guesses as to what might have happened at some time in some place, these were eye witness accounts where few people survived the events, or observation by those who emerged from underground safe places. If these myths and legends are true we should be able to find land that has evidence of being underwater, and underwater sites that indicate they were above sea level at one time. But the legends also say cities and towns, people and animals were crushed by mountains rising or falling, or submerged into the sea. The legends on average talk about 4 ages with this being the fifth. Each age ended in cataclysmic upheavals, often describing the same or similar events occurring over and over again. If this is the case, we should be able to find evidence of Men, items he used, and animals not just buried, but hidden inside mountains, under great depths of earth, rock and sediment combined with evidence of the earth itself being in some sort of upheaval. The legends also talk of the earth stopping, flipping and twisting during these events, so there should be evidence of land masses shifting, turning, magnetic alterations, and land being overrun by massive waves as the legends also describe. Well we don't want to write a geology book text book here but we'll see there is ample evidence to show that what the ancient legends describe happened is exactly the evidence we see all around the globe.

Velikovsky said in an interview "There were civilizations like ours that were destroyed". "Civilizations at that time had risen to great heights, where events similar to those of today had previously occurred. These civilizations are now buried so deeply within the lower strata of the Earth that we simply do not have archaeological evidence of their existence. But we have abundant references in literature – even in rabbinical literature – that many times ... before this present earth age existed, in fact several times the same earth was created – then it was levelled and recreated; all civilizations were buried." (Book 30 pg. 39-40)

John Keel substantiated these statements with some of his own. "We now know that there is much archaeological evidence that our planet has sustained large civilizations in the distant past. These civilizations vanished abruptly or were destroyed by some great natural calamity..." "It is possible that many great civilizations rose and fell during the at least three billions years that the earth has existed." (Book 30 pg. 40) Well except for the "three billions years" idea he's right; sometimes these destructive calamities recurred less than a single lifetime apart. These incredibly old dates are used because archaeologists tend to assume if it's buried it must have taken millions of years to do so. (Astronomical and radiometric dating reasons were refuted in my first work) But we read of episodes in earth's geologic past that buried, crushed, submerged, burned, or possibly were even pulled off the earth in such abrupt fashion that these "millions of years" of supposed slow destruction occurred so fast, that even very fast animals could not escape these forces. Civilizations around the globe recorded the exact same occurrences in ways or language often so similar there can only be one conclusion: the survivors witnessed these events.

WHALE SKELETONS FOUND IN MINNESOTA.

We mentioned before why this might be evidence for a global flood, but an equally or even better case exists for these whales to have been washed "ashore" from the Pacific Ocean as waters were forced overland and rushed onto the continent before the mountains were pushed up in the same or subsequent catastrophic upheavals. Any sea life in the water being forced overland would have come with the water as the continents were shoved eastward, or the water's centrifugal motion carried it overland as the earth's axis tilted. A closer examination of the setting in which the whale bones were found would indicate whether this was of a deposit of whales based on the tsunami type of flood, or a global flood that trapped the whales in an inland sea that slowly dissipated.

AARON ANGLE

Once while chatting and spreading custard on Nanaimo bars at a "cakery" where I used to work, one of the chaps said with his British accent that it was possible for people living in Sidney to see Victoria, by looking down south "air an angle"(meaning to say "At an angle") . I keyed into it right away and repeated his words to which he got all flustered and I said "That's your new name...Aaron Angle", so here's to you Tony.

In some of the underwater limestone caves called the "Blue Holes" near the Bahamas have been found stalagmites and stalactites, which can only be formed above water as they are formed by dripping mineralized water. Some of these formations are "Aaron Angle", showing they didn't slowly submerge at the whim of the water levels but stalled in these angular positions as the land suddenly shifted then stopped. (Book 6 pg 175, book 8 pg 75) If these stalagmites and stalactites were formed only slowly over the millennia tipping over, they would have formed in a curved way, with the liquid always dripping straight down changing the angle of the bottom part. And there actually wouldn't be stalagmites *and* stalactites, because the dripping would migrate in the slow direction of the tipping. Thus this proves they were submerged and tipped very speedily.

In Kashmir (over 900 miles from the ocean) it was discovered that sedimentary deposits of an ancient sea bottom was elevated to 5000+ feet and tilted Aaron Angle of 40°, but to the diggers surprise they found the deposits contained Palaeolithic fossils. This meant that these mountain passes in the Himalayans "May have risen, in the age of man...however fantastic changes so extensive may seem to a modern geologist." (Book 53 pg 70 quoting Hein, & Gausser's book *The Throne of the Gods*) By the way, Kashmir flood plains are dated to 3000 B.C and are in all likelihood the same date as these elevated parts, and don't forget, the Tibetans tell of a time during their history when this area was flat. Evidence of Pleistocene era glaciations is rampant across the Himalayans and several studies have suggested they too rose during historic times. (Book 53 pg 70-72) In many of the Himalayan valleys there are unexplored ruins and even a pyramid was seen by pilots that flew over the "hump" during WWII to supply China with materials to fight the Japanese. With enough patience, these ruins can be seen in Google earth.

Though many a global flood proponent might use these evidences to prove the global flood, however they more properly indicate the continents shifted suddenly some time after that flood, during a time when the earth was experiencing the dawn of new ages, new suns and skies; where waters overran the mountains in waves that brought disaster to those creatures in their way and then ocean sediments to cover them up.

WHERE'D THOSE COME FROM?

In the Andes Mountains are ruins that befuddle and even jolt archaeologists. Listen to what some researchers say about the Andes and these ruins.

"The Andes themselves, geologically fairly recent, seem to have been thrust or forced upward, perhaps carrying with them such cities as Tiahuanaco,..." (Book 7 pg 161) "The surrounding area looks like the dour landscape of some dead planet" "why build a city in the clouds? The rarefied air makes breathing a precarious action. My lungs gasped for oxygen as I walked among the ruins" ..."nothing will grow. There is nothing edible up here. How did the dead ones work in this air?"" (Book 29 pg 105-06) Speaking of Tiahuanaco Berlitz writes "The technique and engineering ability implied in these constructions is out of historical sequence; in fact, with all our expertise, it would be almost impossible to accomplish today. It would certainly be considered impossible for prehistoric builders to have done so thousands of years ago were it not for the fact that the buildings are still there in the high Andes, a visible proof of their conquest of time." (Book 6 pg 161) [not] "a likely spot for the site of a great culture...(Pg 220) The stone used in the construction came from 50 miles away. (Book 35 pg 79)

This city is called the "greatest survival mystery" when Berlitz notes that the ruins of Tiahuanaco (and Bolivia) have on their stonework depicted a Toxodon, supposedly extinct for millions of years. Tiahuanaco, now 13,000 [13,500] feet above sea level, give indications of having been constructed at a time so long ago that the climate as well as the altitude has since changed. (This by the way is the same approximate height above sea level as the Ark of Noah on Mount Ararat. You may recall the difficulty many explorers had there.)"It appears to have been a port, because of stone docks and quays, but the only nearby water is lake Titicaca, several miles away [about 12] " "...must at one time supported a large population...but the area is too high and too barren to support such a culture" "Saltwater ocean fossils are found on the land, in the mountains, and under lake Titicaca." He goes on to say that it is probable the whole Andes chain has risen from sea level, and is visible as the most recent because of a great fault running through the entire chain. (Book 6 pg 192) "No one has been able to date Tiahuanaco" (Book 1 pg 40) Why? This is because of the paradoxical situation, no one wants to be ridiculed because civilization is supposedly 5000 years old, and this city's building techniques are identical with others around the world, meaning great mastery of building must have existed before these mountains rose, or the builders were idiots to make it a port city 2 miles up.

There are angled strandlines from 90 to 360 feet above Lake Titicaca that are very fresh and contain fossils of a "modern character". Chemical analysis of this lake and others on the plateau, establish that the lake was at one time at sea level and very recently, as the lakes still have a chemical composition similar to the ocean. Rain water and runoff still hasn't flushed the lakes enough to eliminate the obvious ocean origin of the water! At an even higher elevation there was a very large lake that has since dried up in which the water was almost drinkable, and *it* is full of common mollusks indicating it is "geologically speaking, of relatively modern origin." (Book 53 pg 77) Indeed there are several lakes in the area that are still completely salted such as the lakes Uyuni, Coipasa, Chiguana in Bolivia, Atacama, Punta Negra, Pedernales, in Chile, and Arizara, Pipanaco, and Hombre Muerto in Argentina; all telling the tale of very recent rising of the land to isolate these pockets of sea water turning them into interior lakes and not flushing them out as yet. (Book 21 Pg 152)

"According to Incan legends, Tiahuanaco was built by a race of giants, whose fatherland had been destroyed in a great deluge that lasted for two months" (Book 35 pg 76) The German archaeologists Arthur Posnansky "theorised that a terrible cataclysm in comparatively recent geological time might have caused this gigantic upheaval that had raised the entire area. Although these changes in the earth's crust did not swallow the city or destroy it, the changes in climate and altitude had made it a less desirable place to live and the inhabitants left it voluntarily" "The surgeons of Tiahuanaco were skilled in trepanning the brain, as were the Egyptians physicians" "The Tiahuanacans' copper trepanning instruments are identical to those used by the Egyptians" (Book 35 pg. 77-78) One wonders how many ancient cities *were* swallowed.

So not only were the building techniques of Tiahuanaco the same as around the world, so were their medical practices and even the instruments used, indicating the people that built Tiahuanaco are contemporary with the ancient people around the world. Only the bizarre altitude of the city has people afraid to date the place.

Ok get the picture? I now repeat this...

Peruvian traditions describe a time when the sun did not shine for five days. During this time the entire surface of the earth changed its profile, and the seas fell upon the land. (Book 14 pg 77, 86) Land changing its profile can only mean the land shifted, that is to say the continents moved. So this is yet another history indicating the change in the physical contours of the landscape happened during historical times.

Coniraya-Viracocha, the Incan god is said to have raised mountains from flat plains, and flattened other mountains. (Book 14 pg 107) This of course would have wrought havoc with the ocean overrunning onto land.

Spanish historian (Avila & Molina) recorded traditions of the new world Indians. They were told that there was a time when the sun did not appear for 5 days, a cosmic collision of stars happened before a cataclysm, and people and animals tried to escape to mountain caves. "Scarcely had they reached there when the sea, breaking out of bounds following a terrifying shock, began to rise on the Pacific coast. But as the sea rose, filling valleys and the plains around, **the Mountains of Ancasmarca** (in Peru just north of Cusco) rose, too, like a ship on the waves. (This would have been the same time that the **entire Andes mountain range** elevated but as witnessed from this one point) During the five days that the cataclysm lasted, the sun did not show its face and the earth remained in darkness." (Book 14 pg 76-77) Thus if you piece it together it looks like this: the mountains of Peru, that is the entire Andes range, are the same age as early Egyptian civilization. They rose in historical times and eyewitness legends exist to substantiate this claim. We also know the Andes rose suddenly because on them are found giant 11 ½ feet wide fossilized clams weighing 661 pounds and they are in the close position, meaning they were caught and buried suddenly as the sea level they came from rose up to the Andes mountains current elevation. And to top it off this event may have been caused by one of the gods. This legend confirms Arthur Posnansky deduction that the Andes rose recently, but the legend indicates it happened even more recently than anyone dares suggest or believe.

EXAMINERS OF THE EVIDENCE

Charles Darwin was impressed by the clear evidence of recent uplifts of the mountains of Chile 1300 feet up by finding undecayed shells on the surface. He also noted the mountains didn't rise gradually but in jumps as only a few intermediary surf lines were detected showing the land didn't rise little by little.

Alfred Wegener, a German polar researcher, geophysicist and meteorologist believed that the evidence pointed to a change in the earth's axis taking place quickly, indeed fast enough to cause extensive flooding throughout the earth's oceans [by] inundating the worlds equatorial lands. (Book 19 pg 147)

Forty years before Immanuel Velikovsky rocked the world with his *Worlds in Collision* and *Earth in Upheaval*, Comyns Beaumont after examining the evidence he studied concluded that the greater part of British Isles and Scandinavia had been submerged by earthquakes and volcanic activity caused by the fall of a tremendous heavenly body (IE an Asteroid). However he went further and concluded by artefacts of carved stones found in Scotland that the event occurred in dateable time period. (Time period not mentioned, but presumably he means during a historical period) (Book 31 pg 30-31)

WATER, WATER EVERYWHERE

On top of Herodotus' observation of there being sea shells and high salt content all over Egypt's desert, soil, and rocks, the remains of sea life has also been found at the foot of the pyramids; and layers of salt have been found in the "queen's chamber" inside the pyramid. (Book 6 pgs. 20, 146)

"New discoveries in geology show that there have been many violent changes in continents and seas, climate and cultures, apparently explained by a shifting of the Earth's axis, and displacement of the poles,..." "Whatever the precise date, it is obvious that more than once the whole American land-mass and its people suffered earthquakes, floods and changes of climate, which shattered all civilization and plunged the stricken survivors back to barbarism, from which they slowly emerged." (Book 23 pg 107)

FOSSIL CLUSTERS

Unfortunately, creationists in the 19th century didn't grasp the meaning of fossils and some said silly things like they were made at the same time with creation, even though the bible itself points to the very cause of the fossils. A close look at biblical texts in conjunction with ancient legends can unlock the world view wide open, as though seeing world history for the first time. Often Protestant and Catholic alike cast aside ancient legends and myths as pagan heathen psychobabble not worthy of their attention. I too fell into a similar category when I started researching my first book for a while, until I realized these legends were for the most part just historical memories. And the bonus about them was they served as many more eye witness accounts to the events which often are only barely inferred to in the bible. The legends and the bible often vindicated each other's accounts just as more than one witness can seal the case for the defense or the prosecution in a court.

In New Mexico there is a whole graveyard of dozens and dozens of dinosaur bones all intermingled with each other in one site. Even those that found them made the observation that they appeared to be overtaken in a catastrophe. Looking at a few pictures of mass fossil sites such as one seen in China defies description unless you assume the catastrophe card.

In Nebraska there are thousands of buried crushed rhinos, clawed horses, and giant swine, all violently destroyed. In Ohio and Michigan is block limestone packed with 'splendidly preserved fish." (Book 23 pg. 108)

In Alaska there are several miles worth of frozen silt which holds the fossils of MILLIONS of Mammoths, Mastodons, and other extinct animals. In some places islands or high points of refuge seem almost entirely made up of their bones. The site is a mix up of skin, hair, and flesh all entwined with uprooted trees. This parallels tusks of mammoths that have been found in such huge numbers in northeast Siberia that this has become the world's go to source of ivory for centuries. Occasionally whole islands appear to be made up of just bones.

Remember Cuvier's deductions? I'll repeat it here so you don't have to hunt for it... "Repeated irruptions and retreats of the sea have neither all been slow nor gradual; on the contrary, most of the catastrophes which occasioned them have been sudden; and this is especially easy to be proved with regard to the last of these catastrophes, that which by a twofold motion, has inundated, and afterwards laid dry, our present continents, or at least part of the land which forms them at the present day. In the northern regions it has left the carcasses of large quadrupeds which have become enveloped in the ice, and have thus been preserved even to our own times, with their skin, their hair, and their flesh. If they had not been frozen as soon as killed, they would have been decomposed to putrefaction. And, on the other hand, this eternal frost could not previously have occupied the places in which they have been seized by it, for they could not have lived in the temperature. It was therefore, at one and the same moment that these animals were destroyed and the country which they inhabited became covered with ice. This event has been sudden, instantaneous, without any gradation,…"

The entire top of the world including Northern Europe, Central Asia and China and indeed the entire northern hemisphere experienced a rapid climate change at the same time as these mass death scenes. The animals didn't die of starvation either, as their stomachs were full of grass and leaves, which are kinds of vegetation that are no longer native to Siberia. This also shows they died from a sudden cause and it's been established that the food found in their stomach and mouths do not, or no longer grow in the region where the animals died. "…the bodies of the animals were found not decomposed but well preserved in blocks of ice, the change in temperature must have followed their death very closely or even caused it" (Book 14 pg 43, Book 7 pg 162)

Keep in mind the mammoths were a thriving species when mysteriously they all died at once. Their extinction was not the result of the very last one being shot by overzealous hunters like the Dodo bird, but literally MILLIONS of them died at the exact same time on terrain that stretched from Alaska to Siberia in a single SUDDEN event, that occurred so fast they froze immediately on the spot to the point their meat, even in the innermost parts, was edible thousands of years later in a place where the climate and fauna also changed in the same instant. No conclusion other than a sudden catastrophic one fits this picture! Though writers refer to the one that was found with buttercups in it mouth and a full belly, mammoths are repeatedly found in this state. (Nexus V25#4 Pole Shift Hidden Evidence)

A polar shift and / or a magnetic reversal should it occur is thought would induce winds at the speed of up to 200 miles an hour. (Book 19 pg 161) That is virtually tornado force winds, but on a continent wide scope.

Velikovsky determined that for the mammoths to have been eating food in a climate where the food they ate would have grown, then the creatures to suddenly be frozen and preserved like they are while the geographic area they were in to be suddenly shifted to a northern extreme zone, the earth would have had to tilt, or the continents shift into the northern area in just a few hours. (Book 14 pg. 330) I might deduce, that would mean the shift in location probably happened faster than global movement occurs during the normal rotation of the earth.

Frank Hibben is quoted…"This death was catastrophic and all-inclusive. What caused the death of 40,000 animals? The "corpus delicti" in this mystery may be found almost anywhere. Their bones lie bleaching in the sands of Florida, and in the graveyards of New Jersey. They weather out on the dry terraces of Texas, and protrude from sticky ooze of the tar pits off Wilshire Boulevard in Los Angeles. The bodies of the victims are everywhere. We find literally thousands together …young and old, foal with dam, calf with cow…The muck pits of Alaska are filled with evidence of universal death…a picture of quick extinction. The argument as to the cause must apply to North America, Siberia, and Europe as well. Mammoth and bison were torn and twisted as though by a cosmic hand in godly rage. In many places the Alaskan mud blanket is packed with animal bones and debris in trainload lots…Mammoth, Mastodon…bison horses, wolves, bears, and lions…A faunal population…in the middle of some catastrophe…was suddenly frozen in a grim charade." (Book 19 pg. 107, book 6 pg. 198)

More than this occurred in North America. Charles Berlitz wrote "Fish died too in the sudden tectonic changes. Near Santa Barbara, California, the United States Geological survey has located a bed of now petrified fish on a former sea bottom where more than an estimated billion fish died suddenly within a four-mile area" (Book 6 pg. 199) He adds "The tracing of death pits of large and small animals in different areas throughout the world indicates that the phenomenon was not a local but a general one. Something very sudden and deadly happened at the end of the Pleistocene Era about 12,000 years ago. It changed the climate and the land and water distribution over large sections of the world. While the story of the great flood is common to almost all the world's peoples, many tribal legends connect the Flood with earthquakes, fires from the skies, and the sinking of inhabited lands into the sea."(Ibid) Only two errors in his deductions, 1) It's supposed that these things happened 12,000 years ago, when in fact they occurred in recorded history, and 2) equating all these with *the* Flood legend. He does however show that floods accompanied these earthquakes and incidences of fires from the skies, which illustrates my main emphasis that there were the great flood legends and local flood legends, which most people toss in the same basket as simply *the* "Flood Legends", when it is in fact several types of flood legends. But give Berlitz credit, he does note that "...violent seismic activity that occurred before **a** flood.", and that the Mayan Chilam Balaam describes (as mentioned before) where he says "*a* Flood", not *the* flood"

Similar mass death scenes also exist in South America. "...the deposits of piled-up mastodon bones found near Bogotá, Columbia, indicate that these animals existed in ancient South America and died simultaneously as a result of some great unusual occurrence. Colonel A. Bragine (*The Shadow of Atlantis*: 1940) suggests that the great herd was killed during seismic convulsion that caused an enormous upthrust of their grazing ground." (Book 6 pg. 197) This upthrust was witnessed and retold in a Peruvian legend mentioned before.

Huge elephant grave yards exist in the Columbian Andes and an enormous sea elephant graveyard exists off the coast of Georgia where these creatures met their sudden deaths in areas that are not their natural habits... any more. (Book 7 pg. 162)

Clusters of dinosaur bones are also found as though the same catastrophes that created the other fossil sites also herded the dinosaurs together and crushed them as the land shifted too fast for them to escape. If this is the case, then that would mean dinosaurs died in the same catastrophic events and are contemporary with man. This is very probable, despite constant indoctrination by text books, children's books and media to the contrary. Many of the Ica stones of Peru show man and dinosaurs together. Drawings of dinosaurs exist that were correctly drawn long before the way they walked was known. Stegosaurs are found on pottery, and dinosaur pictures have been found with circles on the sides of the creatures to the bewilderment of dinosaurologists, (if there is such a word...sounds good to me!) Then not too long ago intact dinosaur skin was found and it had circles on the sides. Surprise, surprise! Many clay figures of dinosaurs have been found also correctly depicted before science knew the proper way they stood or walked. Often dinosaurs have been depicted with humans in non confrontational ways as though they were pets or beasts of burden; similar to how some people use elephants today. China had an official position in the court called "Feeder of the dragons", dragons which Marco Polo recorded that he saw. Fact is dinosaurs such as Brontosaurus (Apatosaurus a.k.a. stopper of rivers), Pterodactyls, Plesiosaurs, possibly triceratops a.k.a. "Killer of Elephants"', and Giant snakes with 5 foot heads that have eaten soldiers and others still exist. I dealt with this in my first book.

"In 1901 a sensation was caused by the discovery of a complete mammoth carcase near the Berezovka River, as this animal seemed to have frozen to death during midsummer. The contents of its stomach were well preserved and included buttercups and flowering wild beans: this meant that they must have been swallowed about the end of July or the beginning of August. The creature had died so suddenly that it still held in its jaws a mouthful of grasses and flowers. It had clearly been caught up by a tremendous force and hurled several miles from its pasture-ground. The pelvis and one leg were fractured- the huge animal had been knocked to its knees and had been frozen to death at what is normally the hottest time of the year."(Book 21 ph 11-12) Woolley mammoths are often depicted as living in frozen snowy environments because of where their remains have been found, and because of their nice furry appearances. But research has determined that these creatures could not possibly have survived in such climates because where they are now found are places that can drop to 49 Celsius below zero (-56 Fahrenheit) and that they were accustomed to living in temperate zones like the horses, antelopes, bison and tigers that were also taken up and destroyed in the same catastrophic event. (Book 21 pg 12) Kolisimo is also forced to conclude "... the whole mammoth species was killed off in an instantaneous tragedy, ..." (Ibid) Conventional geology generally imposes on us the belief that Antarctica has been under ice for millions of years, but this too has been overturned, (though not generally told in academia), because muddy sediment found in Antarctica indicated rivers in comparatively recent times had been flowing there when it was ice free about 12,000 years ago. This is the same time frame attributed to the cataclysm that caused the death of the mammoths and changed the climates in Antarctica and Siberia. (Book 21 pg 13) But this 12,000 years time span can be knocked at least in half when you realize that maps of Antarctica have been found with the continent free of ice, and mountain ranges, and rivers drawn on the maps which recent studies have determined to be very accurate. Furthermore, some of the mountains plotted on the "Topkapu maps" gave the correct height of the mountain ranges, which were unknown until 1952. (Book 21 pg. 252: This map wasn't shown and I've not been able to find and example)

Quoting Charles Hapgood, Kolosimo writes "although complete carcases and skeletons are sometimes found, the remains usually look as if they had been torn about by some gigantic force. In some places there are heaps of bones as high as a small hill, the remains of mammoths being interspersed with those of horses, antelopes, bison, huge felines and other smaller animals."

Dr. N.D. Watkins and H.G. Goddell wrote in a 1967 issue of Science and stated "We must consider the possibility of a direct connection between geomagnetic polarity and faunal changes." "… the Correlation between reversals and extinction level is indeed striking." "…not only did these times of extinction affect a wide variety of animals but they were worldwide in extent," (Book 19 pg. 163)

Darwin couldn't understand or explain all these mass extinctions, especially the Mammoths which he deemed was an animal better developed and suited to survive than the elephant. The obvious answer to him was a catastrophe but it meant one that shook the *entire framework of the globe*, and this seemed inconceivable to him.

I want you to think, to imagine, what on earth could herd hundreds, thousands and in some cases tens of thousands of animals or more and then crush them all together. Animals in such clusters that made Darwin muse to the point he thought it would be easy to conclude the creatures had been caught up in a catastrophe that shook the very framework of the globe. How fast would the land have to move to catch creatures and kill them so they couldn't escape the movement of the land about to crush them? Not all fossil clusters are from water forcing them between a rock and the onrushing tidal waves; some fossil clusters were literally crushed by the land. They weren't all three toed sloths here, some were animals that can run 20, 30 40 miles an hour, so how fast did the land have to move to trap and crush them? They aren't going to sit there, they are going to run as fast as they possibly can to get out of the way and live, and yet, they were still caught and killed, and their blood ran and filled the rivers and ocean shores all around the globe as these mass fossil sites are literally a global phenomena.

Fossil clusters sites like those mentioned here exist all over the world! They are found in Patagonia South America, Bogata Columbia, and Peru Cordillera. Santa Barbara California is a site of about a billion fish fossils in a four square mile area in a place that was once under water. The list goes on…California, Mexico, Los Angeles, Fairbanks Alaska, Bering Strait, New Siberia, Llakov Island off Siberia is actually built of millions of skeletons, Harz Mountains in Germany, Switzerland, Italy(Monte Bolca near Verona,) Mediterranean islands, Gibraltar, France, England, Orkney Scotland, Nebraska, Ohio, Michigan, and Arizona, to name a few. Even whales have been found on the Himalayans. In Alaska animals are mingled with uprooted trees and at least four warped and distorted layers of volcanic ash, showing volcanic activity and earth upheaval was going on at the same time as the animals were literally being torn limb from limb.

THE CONTINENTAL DIVIDE

One thing that makes people think archaeologists have psoriasis from scratching their heads so much, is the mysterious fact that so many standing stones, mounds, dolmens, cairns, and stone circles are common to Europe as well as areas of the U.S. that include Rhode Island, New Hampshire, Maine, Massachusetts, Connecticut, New York and Vermont. (Book 13 pg 91) They can't figure out how "Prehistoric Neolithic Man" could conceivably spread his weird practices of these stone things from Europe to across the Atlantic Ocean on into America. Well first mistake is assuming the people that made these curious stone sites were some sort of grunty prehistoric barbarians. What was being built using "ley lines" or "Dragon paths" as guides, was probably a global orientation system based on the earth's natural dodecahedronal magnetic divisions, that have been proven to exist; which divide the earth into 12, 5 sided patches similar to a Soccer ball, and not some star gazing aids. (The intersections points of these 12 patches are known earth magnetic anomalies such as the Bermuda Triangle, Japans Devils Sea, and the poles) The stone sites are likely laid out quite similar to how the ancient Portalano maps were gridded with a 16 wind system on global circles to aid in mapping a sphere, which point to each of the other gridded circles; kind of like a mall map that shows you where you are and where the lingerie store is. If this deduction is correct, then the stone sites are indeed as high a form of technology as the portalano's which clearly indicate they had spherical trigonometry mapping aced. But the mystery is also solved when you allow the possibility of the continents dividing in historic times and not 200 million years ago. We know that the floor of the Atlantic Ocean is young: not the part of the floor that was once above the waves which we call Atlantis, but the composition of the base. At one time there was just one ocean, the Pacific before the continent of Pangaea split. The floor of the Pacific Ocean consists of sima, but the Atlantic Ocean is much younger and consists of stretched sial (an abbreviation of Silicon and aluminum, the predominant elements of terrestrial rocks.) This is the composition of the outer crust of the planet. Underneath the outer crust is sima which is an abbreviation of silicon and magnesium which contains a higher proportion of Magnesia, short for magnesium oxide. You could literally determine the original exact shape of Atlantis by mapping the sima and the sial of the Atlantic Ocean floor, then 'unwind' continental drift to get the shape of Atlantis...if that was important to you. Another indication that the Atlantic Ocean is young is the amount of sediment, which on the Atlantic floor is less than 100 feet thick, instead of the usual thousands of feet found in other oceans. (Book 53 pg 108-109)

It is supposed that at some time during the Devonian period (400 to 350 million years ago) a link between Europe and America existed because the fauna on both sides of the Atlantic preserved in the rocks are identical. (Book 53 pg 194) I find some strange anomalies in this whole ancient earth premise. They say it took 200 million years for the continents to divide and reach their current position, but they think there may have been a land bridge between North America and Europe 400 million years ago? Really? Anyone out there got a slide ruler!? Quite simply the reason both sides of the Atlantic have the same man made stone features is because after the flood about 5400 years ago Pangaea still existed, that is to say North America and Europe were still attached and people in this area were creating this system with stones when the dividing of the continents interrupted the work. Yep that's hard to swallow, because we've been spoon fed the Old earth theory and we've been told it took 200 million years to spread the continents from Siamese twins to what we have today. But clearly the legends and scriptures and fossil sites, and archaeological remains around the world show definitively that the land moved speedily during the four ages which so many ancient cultures have in common in their legends.

Horses vanishing from the American landscape at the end of the ice age for some mysterious reason when climate was so favourable, yet those few horses that escaped from the soldiers of Cortez grew into massive herds in America by the time America was settled a century later indicating it wasn't the highly favourable environment that killed the horse off the American plains. Why did American fossil hunters find fossilized horse bones in huge numbers and fossils imbedded in rock and in lava, the same horses as we have today? The woolly mammoth was widespread from all parts of America to Siberia and Europe and deemed to be evolutionarily advanced and their numbers were well into the millions. Beds of their bones are so numerous they virtually comprise complete islands. Yet something caused the extinction of all the mammoths worldwide at the same time. Evolution says survival of the fittest, and mammoths had better teeth than normal elephants and were considered a superior species evolved in the struggle for survival by adaptation to a degree which was considered perfect. (Book 53 pg 207) Thus no evolutionary model can possibly account for the mammoth suddenly going extinct all around the globe simultaneously. The mammoths themselves, speak plainly about a violent global incident when they are found frozen whole in blocks of ice or found flash frozen with stomachs full of undigested food, and food still in their mouths, with fractured hips and broken forelimbs. Climate change, disease, and hunters have been ruled out as the cause of these and other extinctions. Only cataclysmic events could account for this data. Star maps in one place which should be found 1900 miles away or maps of southern hemisphere stars where only northern stars are visible indicate shifting of continental masses and global tumbling to account for the evidence, and furthermore it all points to these events happening while civilization was more advanced than we are today. .

Jeffrey Goodman appears to grasp this likelihood when he wrote...

"For example, a good [deal] of geological evidence indicates that our planet has been through global catastrophe several times before, and such evidence correlates with the archaeological account in which the events of one such destructive period--at the close of the last ice age-- were actually recorded by ancient man. (Book 19)

Associated with the ice age is a "swarm" of meteoric impacts sites from Florida to New Jersey and the impacts sites have been found in Virginia, North and south Carolina, Georgia, Alabama, Kentucky and Tennessee. Some have even dated these impact sites as more recent. (Book 53 pg 91-92)

"There is even evidence that the earth periodically exceeds the equilibrium point of its diurnal wobble and tumbles over in space-- a sudden shift that would instantly rearrange the world's oceans, ice caps, and climates. Such an event, if viewed from space, would be stupendous to behold. Think of the earthquakes and volcanic eruptions, the rifts where the earth [IE continents] would split apart, the mountain chains that would thrust upward, the cyclonic winds, the mountainous tidal waves, and the electrical storms of inconceivable intensity." (Book 19 pg 6) I think he's been reading some of the legends! But he's also been looking at the physical evidence, which forced him to ask some telling questions like "Was the towering Mount Everest (29,028 feet) gradually pushed up just a few inches every century? Scientists of the nineteenth century were dismayed to find that the highest rocks of these massive peaks yielded skeletons of marine animals, ocean fishes, and shells and molluscs. How are we to explain the sea floor becoming the lofty highlands of today? Were the Himalayas born when the Indian subcontinent *slammed*, not pushed, into the Asian mainland? Were colossal upheavals and uplifts triggered? Did it take millions of years or just a few centuries to create the Himalayas?" (Book 19 pg. 96: his italics) I might add that not only is it probable that the Indian subcontinent *slammed*, into the Asian mainland, it did it in far less time than a "few centuries", as the Chinese legends clearly indicate. He adds several pages later the observation "On the other hand, pole shift could suddenly propel the continents forward. The slow continental drift observed today may be the residual momentum of a once great surge." (Book 19 pg 159) Legends speaking of four ages suggest it was 3 or 4 great surges.

Though Raymond Drake accepts the old earth theory and dates attributed to some events, if we read with the mind that these events were described in the legends and substitute his dates for historical ones his summary is fairly correct when he writes "Geophysicists at Cambridge have discovered that at intervals in the past the Earth's magnetic field has reversed, with North and South Magnetic Poles changing places. The last flip 700,000 years ago was accompanied by the extinctions of some species of small marine creatures and possibly by the sudden deaths of many humans and animals, leaving only a few men and women to start civilization again. It is speculated that a similar flip may have accounted for the dramatic and unexplained mass-extinction of giant reptiles some 65,000,000 years ago. A most extraordinary discovery has come from magnetic surveys of the ocean floors. Over huge areas the sea-floor rocks appear to be magnetized in alternate stripes of normal and reversed polarity, likened to a zebra by Sir Edward Bullard, Professor of Geophysics at Cambridge, in his 1967 Bakerian lecture at the Royal Society." (Book 23 pg 45) We just read legends that often spoke of only a few survivors after catastrophes, but these were telling of events just a few millennia ago, not 700,000 years. Thus the events Raymond Drake speaks of were historical ones, and not from millions of years ago.

"Examining of magnetism of some igneous rocks reveals that they are polarized oppositely from the prevailing present direction of the local magnetic field and many of the older rocks are less strongly magnetized than the more recent ones. On the assumption that the magnetization of the rocks occurred when the magma cooled and that the rocks have held their present position since that time, this would indicate that the polarity of the earth has been completely reversed within recent geological times." (Book 14 pg 127 quoting A. McNish in *Terrestrial Magnetism and Electricity*") What people don't read is that the magnetic poles were found to have shifted 6 degrees a day! (Nexus V25#4 Pole Shift Hidden Evidence) Keep in mind the legends we covered speak of the earth flipping and giant lizards and dragons existing during history, forcing the dates they use into far more recent time frames.

Francis Hitching notes that the Stonehenge, in its collapsed condition, has been thought to have occurred, by a number of people in an "unrecorded catastrophe". (Book 13 pg 270) Perhaps unrecorded nearby, but well recorded in adjacent global places.

GEOLOGIC INCIDENCES ARE LIKE THE BARKING DOGS SYNDROME

I remember when I had to come home once a week from air cadets and we had to walk about 2 miles from the bus stop to home, just the sound of our footsteps on the dark road got a dog barking near the road, which caused another dog to bark and then another and another until about 5 or 6 dogs were all barking at the same time, and they would continue barking while we walked for about a ¼ mile until we got out of foot step hearing distance. The reason so many ancient legends of catastrophes are so similar or identical to places on the other side of the globe is because when one place on the earth experiences a geologic event, other places on earth are similarly affected, because the liquid or molten stratum underneath the earth's crust somehow transmits energy from one location to another weak point in the crust almost like a geologic echo. It appears that global catastrophes (or would that be dogastrophes?) also transmit kinetic energy from one location to another, and indeed geologic science is figuring this out.

Here are a few examples of geologic incidences on one part of the globe affecting other parts.

It's believed that when an earthquake hit Alaska in 1964, it affected Yellowstone Park's Old Faithfull's geyser a short while later with increased frequency of eruptions for a short while.

Similarly when Alaska had an earthquake on Good Friday in 1966, the eastern seaboard rose and fell 2 inches. (Book 23 pg 217)

It's felt that occasionally world volcanic activity can be intensified because of the interconnectedness of all the volcanoes to a single underground system. These occasional volcanic surges would have "revolutionary effects on the development of life on land as well as in the sea." . (Book 19 pg. 121: quoting Physicist John S. Rinehart, and Oceanographer writer Peter Vogt.) Vogt deduced that surges of molten material from earth's plumes or hot spots seem to travel through channels in the floor of the lithosphere connecting a horizontal 'plumbing system' underlying the mid ocean ridges. He saw the global plates as all linked where incidences in one region affected all other regions. For example, Vogt found correlations between Iceland's molten surges and eruptions on Hawaii.

In 1976 a series of geological incidences were thought to have triggered each other over the year. An Indian earthquake accompanied by tidal waves was soon followed by disturbances in Japan, then Italy, the West Indies, and soon after the west coast of North America, then on August 17th Honshu Japan was hit with a moderate quake followed by one on the same day 50 miles north of Naples Italy. Then on August 21st the Volcano on Guadeloupe Island in the West Indies erupted. The next day a strong quake hit off the Kenai Peninsula in Alaska. Many hundreds of geologic incidences occurred in 1976 that also included floods droughts and hurricanes. (Book 19 pg. 84-85)

SAHARA DESERT

Every now and then geologists leave little holes in their dating methods that force the dates they attribute to things, downward to a reality which they refuse to accept. So...follow the thread...

The Sahara Desert is an intriguing part of the puzzle which also happens to provide one such hole. We are told that the ice age ended about 12,000 years ago, and that during this time a great lake (this can only be Lake Triton) that was in what is now the Sahara desert drained into the ocean.

Stokes, in *Essentials of Earth's History*, says the "the one invariable accompaniment of glaciations appears to be mountain-building." Furthermore "...it was noted that certain geologists believe that the Himalayas were driven up suddenly during the last ice age. (Book 19 page 158) Flint, another Geologist, wrote in *Glacial Geology and the Pleistocene Epoch* "Mountain uplifts amounting to many thousands of feet have occurred within the Pleistocene [Ice Age] epoch itself' This occurred with '...the Cordilleran mountain system in both North and South America, The Alps-Caucasus – central Asian system, and many others..."(book 53 pg 68 quoting source from its pgs. 9-10) As much as it bothers geologists they are forced to concede that Pole shifts, Mountain building and Ice ages are all interrelated and their occurrences are synchronised. Meaning they all happened in the same time frame as interrelated events. Thus dating one event such as magnetic reversals or mountain building at millions of years ago is simply impossible if they happened at the same time and are directly linked to the last ice age. One caused the other, at the *same time*. This bothers them because it makes the mountains geologically speaking very young. What is also really bothersome is the Ice ages have been shown to have occurred within the last 4000 years. But the picture for geologist is worse than they think.

Also "It has been ascertained that the Sahara was once part of the ocean, later diminishing to a lake, and then before becoming a desert, a verdant area suitable for human habitation." Indeed cave paintings in the Tassili Mountains of Algeria depict men and animals living in a land of trees, rivers and lakes. (Book 6 pg 68) People want to date cave paintings to the time of cave men period also around 12,000 years ago or around the ice age; though in reality such cave paintings do constitute a historical record. It turns out there are drawing in the Sahara desert that have been determined to be of Phoenician origin clearly placing pre desert conditions in the time frame of civilization, and other Sahara art sites have been determined to be of Egyptian origin. (Book 53 pg 87) (Whether it's these Tassili Mountain cave paintings or others I'm not sure). Cave paintings are not the only record. The King Jaime world map from 1502, shows the Sahara, not as a desert, but apparently as a "fertile land of rivers, woods, and lakes." (Book 6 pg 142) I'll add that the illustrations were drawn on a portalano map. Indeed The Sahara Desert has evidence of civilizations that once lived there, as well as a forest, and inland lakes. (finding a picture of the map, I do admit this map has contradictions in it. Being a portalano with some highly accurate areas, mostly central, yet India and Asia were distorted and the Americas are unfinished and appear to be way out of sync with each other in relation to Greenland.) Even if we take this map with a grain of salt, evidence still mounts.

Stories of Lake Triton's demise in Africa are found which occurred at the time of the birth of Athene as her name was given to her because of the event, just like Peleg (Earthquake) was named because "for in his days the earth was divided" Genesis 10: 25). Diodorus of Sicily who wrote *The Library of History* around the time of Julius Caesar, noted that Athena (Minerva) is named after Lake Triton and that during the days of Ogyges, this lake disappeared in a catastrophic earthquake that occurred in Africa wherein this lake broke into the ocean. Minerva is also "styled Tritonia". Thus Athene aka Minerva aka Tritonia and Ogyges and Lake Triton's demise are historically synchronised. Furthermore both Minerva and Ogyges lived during a time when a long night lasted 9 consecutive days, that occurred following a flood, an event that would also be associated with quakes and the loss of this lake. (Book 14 pg. 76, 178)

This huge lake in the Sahara disappeared after a large earthquake caused whatever was keeping the lake back from the sea to be destroyed, draining it right into the ocean. (Book 14 pg. 178) It's been realized that at one time the Sahara Desert supported a great population, but the demise of this lake would explain the almost complete lack of populace in this area today. So civilization is determined to have existed during the time when this lake existed. Local African legends often recount a time when mundane things like the climate and landscape changed, meaning the locals also have histories that recount the event! It seems to me everything the geologists and uniformitarianists say occurred millions of years ago during prehistoric times have historic legends concerning the same events.

Looking at the topography of Africa one can see it nearly broke into two pieces. During the time that the Sahara was a nice place to live they found fossils of dinosaurs that were living there associated with this same period. Is the Sahara Desert heat getting under your collar yet? Wait there's more.

So what this all spells out is this; it all happened during the time of a flood event associated with mountain building, continents shifting, ocean tsunami's flooding the continents creating dinosaur fossils, nearly ripping apart Africa and a lady being named after the event in which the giant lake Triton was lost as a result. All these events were recorded in part or in whole in historical records either by cave paintings, maps, legends, local histories and people that recorded the events, not millions of years ago, or 12,000 years ago, but at some point in time after the global flood, maybe around 2000 B.C.

By the way the Sahara Desert's growth rate has been tracked as spreading 90-100 KM from 1958-1975. I suppose if you were bored, using that growth rate, you could work it out to see how long it took to make the desert as large as it is and see roughly when it began to become a desert. I dare say you probably won't find yourself anywhere near 12,000 B.C. when you're done.

Checkmate!

J.W. Gregory an explorer of the African rift concluded the rift wasn't a local fracture but included about one sixth of the earth's circumference... which must have been from a worldwide cause. He noted it first came into being at an early point but saw signs of movement at a recent date. Some features were so bare and sharp they had to have happened during the human period. Not only that, but he also found that "All along the [fracture] line the natives have traditions of great changes in the structure of the country" (Book 53 page 84)

American Continental civilization wiped off the landscape.

One of the unforeseen conundrums of flood evidence is something anthropology insists never existed. The ruins, in Egypt, Roman, Greek, Babylonian, Persian, Indian, Aztec, Peruvian, and Mexican sites all speak of advanced civilizations all over the world, except, in North America. No civilization in what we call North America; that vast expanse of fertile land teeming with game...who would have wanted it!? No one? Really?

Similarly, if you believe the ages attributed to some of the human fossils or traces of human habitation found in Africa, Europe, Asia and South America you might find it odd that nothing of this age is said to have also existed in North America. This is particularly odd when you consider that the Mexican advanced civilization at the southern part of North America didn't somehow migrate north. Or even the strange belief that the phantom migrants that came from the Bering Strait ignored all of North America and passed it by to live down in South America. Though anthropology does suggest that the Eskimo's stayed in the north to wrestle with the harsh elements of the far north rather than migrate south, this too seems a bit counter intuitive. If they migrated that far, why not go further south where logic has to assume it would be warmer, and more suitable for habitation. The Eskimos have an answer to this obvious question that the anthropologists simply reject out of hand as absurd. The Eskimos insist they didn't come from Asia but say they were brought to the north in "great iron birds". They were brought <u>North</u>. From where?

As mentioned, the Eskimo legends speak of a time when the land they now live in had no ice, which would be when they arrived, and for however long before the cataclysmic periods that ended four world ages and changed the northern climate to the ice box of earth, and killed all them thar big cuddly wooly elephants. So it makes some sense that they didn't subsequently migrate south after these cataclysms when the cold hit, thinking it might be a global change and not just a regional change. But could the entire continent of North America with all the great land, rivers, lakes, game, trees, fish, minerals and whatever else encourage man to stay and 'set fer a spell', really not entice anyone in all of world history to stay and build here!? Really? Why? What's the logic of this assumption? There isn't any.

Could this anthropological axiom that monkeys first discovered pointy sticks in Africa and evolved to men then set out to explore the world, and somehow never made it to what is now America, yet they did make it to Alaska *and* Mexico which are north *and* south of America, really be true, or is something amiss here? Anthropologists rigorously deny and attack any suggestion that ancient man lived in North America. Every single time anything found here that could suggest man was here during the same time frame as anywhere else on the globe, conventional anthropology insists its fake, a hoax or misdated or it just can't be.

I'll grant based on the biblical flood of Noah that civilization would spread in all directions slowly, possibly reaching North America late, but at the time "North and South" America were still part of the giant continent called Pangaea. Or if you reject that theory, even conventional anthropology sort of follows the same approximate frame for expansion of civilization except they seem to think it came from the heart of Africa. Prints found in Africa have been dated 3.6 million years old, but lately older is better and pushing dates backwards through aeons of time seem to be the in thing to do. Now they are suggesting early man came from some bizarre ancient period of maybe 200 million years ago and then spread outwards from there. (200 million years ago, which by the way is the same time frame they suggest the continents began to split, so even then there is no real barrier to wandering in the direction of what would become North America, so they shoot themselves in the foot here too. So any way you slice it, it doesn't make any sense that North America would be overlooked as a suitable place for man to live and build a civilization. So why isn't there any evidence of his existence here...or is there?

Well if you believe conventional anthropology, then there isn't any and there's no point looking for it so stop reading, it's only going to get controversial, and we don't want that now do we. But if you're not afraid of whatever it is I'm going to mention as I casually thumb through my references, well keep reading... besides, this book probably wasn't free anyway!

First there is a possible reason why man didn't come here or doesn't appear to have come here, that is at least to the region of the Canadian Shield, which is a mere 2 million square miles, because the Canadian Shield is nice thick lava which is between 20,000 and 50,000 feet thick...probably not the best place to grow crops. As I deduced in my first book this was where the approximately 500 mile wide meteor slammed into the earth destroying the water canopy and causing the flood of Noah. So it stands to reason, any trace of North American civilization in the region of the Canadian Shield would have been wiped off the face of the planet, burned to a frazzle and buried under 5 to 9 miles of the earth's core as it oozed out onto the surface. So that could effectively be a stalemate...no civilization here because it was burnt, melted and buried deeper than any archaeological site on the planet, or because as anthropology insists, it was never here in the first place: but what about the rest of North America? However that was what caused the great worldwide flood. After it was over it could have been settled, right? Lake Huron would have been in the kill zone of the asteroid, so consider this little paragraph from my first book:

WHY WERE YOU FIRED?

Once institutions and theories are thoroughly entrenched in society they become virtually impossible to change. Take this case in point. In the 1950's Thomas Lee of the National Museum of Canada found incredibly advanced stone tools in glacial deposits at Sheguiandah, on Manitoulin Island in Lake Huron. These deposits were dated at 65-125,000 years old. The director of the museum was fired for not firing Thomas Lee, the discoverer of these artifacts and stone tools! Tons of these artifacts just disappeared into storage bins and the discovery was swept away. Why? Because "it would have forced the rewriting of almost every book in the business". Accuracy is NOT an option!

A fossilized shoe or sandal print was found near Delta in Utah...the same shoe that squashed a trilobite. This finding means all kinds of things to different people as presumably trilobites were extinct 400 million years ago. At face value that would mean that the person squashing the trilobite precedes all human civilization everywhere. Naturally evolutionists, anthropologists, geologists and dino-dudes, shout "say it isn't so Shoeless Joe!" I used it to show something wrong with dating methods in my first book, but here, we'll say man was here at least when Trilobites were somehow washed ashore long enough to get squished.

It's thought trilobites could be the same as Graptolites and they are still found alive in the South Pacific, so if that's the case this is no big deal, as it means man was here only long enough ago to fossilize a shoe print.

In the 1930's Geologist Dr. Wilbur Greely Burroughs found ten complete normal human tracks (Size 7 ½ EE[width]: the distance from heel to toe was 18 inches) along with several other partial tracks in "Carboniferous" sandstone from the Paleozoic Era, supposedly 250 million years old in the Kentucky hills near Louisville. They have been dubbed "Phenanthropus mirabilis which means "looks human; remarkable". Greely didn't want to completely commit to them being human and get railroaded out of his peer group's society now did he? They were however proven to be genuine foot prints by compression evidence. (Book 30 pg 15-16) These dates attributed to these finds equal or precede those found in Africa, and like some child saying my find is better than yours, African originists cry false with any find in America remotely contesting the title.

In Tucson Arizona was found a child's footprint in a slab of shale that had been buried under several layers of dirt, but had obviously been on the surface at one time. Inside the 6 inch long footprint was part of a fossil. To the finder Dr. Clifford Burdick, with 25 years experience under his belt, he declared that it was clearly a child's footprint, but when he showed it to another paleontologists, one of them tried to slough it off as something with no biological origin or as an impression from a broken fossil due to the partial fossil seen in the print. Obviously it couldn't be the print of a child, because it was …in America, right? Silly doctor. (Book 30 pg 20)

In 1817 in the Herculaneum Missouri quarry, there was found "humanlike" tracks. In 1822 on the west bank of the Mississippi, a 'number' of human footprints were found in a "crinoidal limestone slab". These had been seen much earlier too by French explorers who offhandedly mentioned the prints when they first arrived at what would become St. Louis. Those who fear American ancientness said the foot prints were "carvings". What… The Indians carved them to play tricks on the French explorers? To what end?

Footprints that were obviously human, were found in sandstone near Carson City Nevada in 1882, but they were called prints of a giant sloth by a dissenting "scientist" simply because it was impossible for them to be human tracks. Why was it deemed impossible? Because… the tracks were in America. (Book 30 pg. 21) OH my, the logic is impeccable…if you're a scientist, and have indoctrinated all the common sense out of your brain, and replaced it with a system of belief.

Way back in the 1930's a flood had revealed many footprints in solidified mud at Paluxy Texas. Giant human tracks were found in ancient layers of mud that had turned to stone. The discovery of these huge footprints were so closely associated with something amazing, that the people who came across this site, chiselled them out to sell. What was the big deal? They were amazed because the human tracks were in the same layer and in close association with dinosaur tracks. The supply of prints was eventually exhausted, but their existence was not forgotten. So in the 1970's the site was revisited, with camera men to record the event. While cameras were rolling, nearby dirt was excavated and more prints were found 100 feet down. That 100 feet of dirt had been bulldozed away right down to a limestone ledge which when all cleared away, along with another 3 inches of gravel, they found many more foot prints from the same layer. More tracks of man and dinosaur in the same layer and indeed some of the human tracks had stepped into the dinosaur tracks. (Book 30 pg 23) If man in America can't be older than man in other parts of the world as is assumed then these must be fakes. An evolutionist was at Paluxy during the event but he refused to look at the find, but instead, while keeping his back to the find made comments contradicting the find saying he saw nothing that disputed or contradicted evolution. How could he say that with a straight face: Because he refused to look. Do you really trust evolutionist that refuse to look at evidence that might contradict their theory? That's not very scientific now is it.

Similarly finds of ancient man in America are many, but apparently they are all fake, frauds, and lies, simply because they can't be true. This is based on first come first served contradictory theories that are assumed to be true, and nothing to do with actual evidence.

In Tulsa Oklahoma an engineer (Troy Johnson) removed many layers of dirt, roots, and stone from an outcropping revealing many prints underneath from various animals and human foot prints. He happened to be an amateur archaeologist with 13 years experience whose training told him the prints were found in what was at one time a sandy beach. He made plaster casts of the prints and every one he showed them too said "Impossible" and whispers of "hoax" permeated the air.

For some reason the fact that "there really are undisputed human footprints preserved in rock" is considered a riddle for modern science. Why is this? Because the rock with the prints was found in the carboniferous layer of the Geologic column: The geologic column that Charles Lyle just made up.

Because catastrophic events that occurred in civilized times that jumbled the earth, with oceans overrunning the land, creating bonding agents that mixed whatever dirt, mud or gravel which solidified after some people walked on the stuff apparently is just too hard for them to believe. Science Newsletter Oct. 29 1938 discussing this 'riddle' had no answer for such evidence, because it simply doesn't fit into their construct of human history. (Book 30 pg 27) There is an answer to that problem...maybe their construct is wrong, that might solve the "riddle". This riddle is admittedly potentially disastrous to established geologic and anthropologic theories. "If man or even his ape ancestor, or even that ape ancestor's early mammalian ancestor, existed as far back as in the carboniferous period in any shape, then the whole science of geology is so completely wrong that all the geologists will resign their jobs and take up truck driving". (Book 30 pg 29 quoting Scientific American January 1940 Issue) Perhaps some of these geologists should take up studying ancient legends to solve these "riddles", and leave the truck driving to professionals who know what they are doing. HEY! Someone's gotta stand up for our truck drivers!

DETERMINING THE PROCESS

Dr. Clifford Burdick with four others found hundreds of feet under the surface of the ground, an imprint of a shod foot along with a child's footprint preserved in rock. He stated "These tracks, with human appearance, were preserved in rock, hundreds of feet below the surface of the ground, as if at or near the beginning of some great catastrophic, earth-shaking event that buried many forms of life all together, some marine and some non marine. This mixing of fossil types is very common all over the world. This could well have happened at the time of the great flood, at the time of Noah, described in the book of Genesis." (Book 30 pg 30) Actually not all, this evidence agrees with the legends of subsequent ages after the flood spoken of by various legends all over the world and alluded to in later books of the bible. This is clear evidence of Tsunami's with sufficient force to carry huge amounts of debris over land to bury surface features hundreds of feet below, and / or accompanied by continental shifts forcing earth materials across land surfaces to bury the items as well or further and deeper. This is describing completely different mechanics than a flood caused by a collapsing water shell, accompanied by water bursting out of the ground due to impact from a huge asteroid. Such prints from before the great flood, might be covered by some sediment, clay and settling dirt a few feet down, but not hundreds of feet below ground level.

Dr. Clifford Burdick agrees with how devastating human prints in rocks is to geology as it stands. He said "If these [fossilized footprints] are verified as human tracks, the discovery...will practically collapse the geologic columns [which Charles Lyle, mind you, made up out of thin air], and the only plausible explanation to fit the evidence will be the Genesis explanation that the creator made the various forms of life during Creation Week. Since then some have become extinct, and others have through radically altered ecology varied by adaptive radiation within the limits of the kind." (Book 30 pg 29-30) Yes, every now and then you get the odd old earth scientist that gets completely exasperated with the evidence not fitting the predominating theories and realizing that maybe the bible is correct after all; it must be a hard fought fight within the confines of their minds. I'm not being factitious; it's very difficult to overturn long standing beliefs. I had a hard time in my first book digging into U.F.O.'s to determine their origins, and had to make concessions that changed long standing beliefs I had based on evidence I found. However once again he misinterprets the evidence to arrive at faulty conclusions. He assumes the radically altered ecology that buried these prints was caused by the great flood of Noah. Life spans were reduced and gradual diminishing of the size animals due to the collapsing of the water shell and the intensified solar influences would have been nominally apparent through slow variations in size over time. But it was the breaking up and the shifting continents that radically altered the ecology, and stepped up the huge disintegration of the size animals became. This is likely the cause of the demarcation line between fossils before the "Cambrian explosion", where animals sudden shrinking in size and migrations occurred.

Finding prints of any kind means they are either very recent or found before the weather made them dissipate erode and get grown over, or something suddenly occurred to preserve them. Brad Steiger gets it when he wrote about some human and dinosaur tracks found together on the same stratum in the Sierra's as written about by Dr. Emerson Hartman: "The question is, *how* did those tracks remain on that primordial beach long enough to become fossils? Why didn't other creatures stamp out the tracks? And surely the next good rain-or tide-would have washed them away.

"The majority of contemporary geologists subscribe to the theory called "uniformitarianism", which maintains that once the laws of Nature were set in motion, the aeons progressed in smooth, orderly fashion, without interruption. If the uniformitarianists are correct, it seems impossible that something would not have messed up those creatures' tracks in the hundreds of years it would have taken for them to turn to stone. In order for those tracks to have become fossilized, they had to be covered and protected in some way. A sudden catastrophe (and if you have ever observed the activity at the edge of an alligator pond, it would have to have been *very* sudden) would be as one of the most effective means of rapidly covering an impression of the ground." (Book 30 pg 34) This statement was contrasted by the acknowledgment of the millions of buffalo killed on the plains and prairies during 400 years of colonization of America, and yet NONE of these have been found to fossilize or are even found in any state of preservation that would look likely to become a recognizable fossil.

Velikovsky summarized: Their bone and teeth resist decaying for a while but finally they weather and crumble to powder, and this is the same with the prints of cows and buffalo, their prints aren't found from even one season previous, so how on earth did tracks get preserved from primordial times? Again only catastrophic action displacing earth, water, sand, volcanic ash flood and sudden sub zero temperatures can answer the riddle of the prints and creatures being instantly covered to create the conditions for them to become fossils and rock hard prints.

The Mammoths and multi species fossils sites are testimony to the suddenness of the actions that made fossils and tracks remain from the time of their impressions to our uncovering of them today. Indeed some finds include hundreds of tracks of varied species together, both predator and prey, running together at breakneck speed from the very cataclysm that covered the tracks they made. And the legends and histories from around the globe make it very clear these events happened just a few thousand years ago, and not millions of years as many would have us believe.

This is reiterated by Dr. Melvin Cook in *Prehistory and Earth Models*. "sudden burial has a higher probability of yielding fossils than any uniformitarianistic model, because it removes the specimen from exposure to weathering. Not only organic, but even the hard parts [bones, teeth, horns] of animals tend to disappear in a relatively short time when exposed at the surface. Under ordinary conditions decay and weathering processes proceed more rapidly than sedimentation, and fossilization is most unfavorable." [Whereas in the case of catastrophes] ...such upheavals increase the chances of burial and bring about favorable conditions such as "the increased possibility for burial under antiseptic conditions, hydrothermal activity, dehydrating conditions, mummifying conditions." In his judgment the existence of fossils is evidence for the occurrence of catastrophes. (Book 30 pg. 34-35, quoting the source) Many fossils are found in bunches as though something made them run together get trapped together and crushed together and the remains have been distorted and stretched which would only be possible if the skeletons were still new and ductile to permit these distortions and stretching. Meaning the land that caught the animals and killed them in massive clusters was still moving after they died and were still fresh.

Allow a slight digression...reflective of the four or more ages that many cultures histories recall that ended in catastrophic incidences, is an exploratory shaft dug in southern Iraq in 1947. As the spot was dug into, it first found Babylonian then Chaldean and then Sumerian relics with flood levels between each of the civilizations levels. Between the levels were layers of "clay that could only have been left by water". Below them it found village's levels, then a primitive faming cultural level, then below that a herdsman culture then at the bottom was a floor of fused glass, identical to that found in New Mexico that was created by an atomic blast. (Book 7 pg. 229-30, book 1 pg. 106-07, and book 6 pg. 216).

An Arab Historian named al-Masudi wrote that the great pyramid had been built by a pharaoh named Surid 300 years before the flood. It's assumed this is meant to be the great flood, but it is just as likely this was a local flood, the same one that funneled up the Persian Gulf. Any catastrophic tsunami type of flood channeling up the Persian Gulf on the eastern side of Saudi Arabia would also have channeled up the Red Sea hitting Egypt; I repeat this bit here. "There is evidence that the Great Pyramid has experienced one or more floods, since the shells and fossils from the sea have been found around its base, and indications of a salt deposit have been noted in the Queen's Chamber within the pyramid." The pyramids show an obvious high water mark that even Alan Lansburg noted was visible on the pyramid. (Book 1 pg 61) If the great flood covered the mountains it's not going to leave a "high water mark" on the pyramids, it had to been accomplished by a later flood, that is a local tsunami type of flood for it to have the abrasive qualities strong enough to create the scarring visible on the pyramids. And keep in mind, some human prints have been found HUNDREDS of feet below the surface. That is just exactly what happened!

DEAR ANTHROPOLOGIST...

Anthropologist Dr. George Hunt Williamson found more hieroglyphics on July 10th 1957 in unknown country on the Sinkibenia River Near Cusco now known as the "Rock of Writings".(Book 23 pg 179) This site is not in the North America, it's in Peru, so for some reason no one seems to question these. They constantly do if anything similar is found North of Mexico.

On the rocks of Klamath Falls in Oregon are thousands of petro glyphs that some call Hieroglyphics, which the Indians of the place never used or understood. Marine deposits indicate the place was under the ocean at one time. The writing is thought to be a remnant of the land of Mu, considered the oldest or first civilization to be submerged after the great flood, and thought to be written by survivors of Lemuria. (Book 23 pg 112) (I'm not sure why some people say MU and Lemuria are the same place and some refer to them as two different places. Near as I can figger, Mu was a Pacific Ocean continent, and Lemuria was an Indian Ocean land.) Anyway, the Modoc Indians from this region do have a legend attached to the place where these hieroglyphics are found: They say the ancients were men of great learning, and called this place 'Walla-Was-Skeeny' which apparently is very similar to the Greek meaning "Valley of Knowledge": It makes one wonder just what those writings say.

In the fall of 1868 (a misplaced source dates the event as occurring in December 1869), in Hammondsville Ohio, while miners starting to make an entry into a coal bank 100 feet below ground level, part of the bank fell forward falling into the shaft unveiling a wall on which several lines of hieroglyphics were inscribed. Though a crowd observed the writing, no one was able to decipher the script before it oxidised. (Book 5 pg 17)

A clay tablet bearing a cuneiform inscription was found by the Susquehanna River near Winfield, Pennsylvania. When deciphered it was determined to describe a short term loan of an Assyrian Merchant in Cappadocia from about 1900 B.C.

Around 1910 a boy playing in Flora Vesta New Mexico dug up two slabs of carved rock from old Indian ruins on the Animas River, containing symbols of an ancient language that has never been deciphered. Also depicted on the stones were two elephants. The existence of these items has never been satisfactorily explained. (Book 30 pg 72)

On June 27 1969 workmen in Oklahoma City uncovered a rock formation 3 feet below the surface that looked like a inlaid mosaic tile floor. The stones were set in perfect parallel lines that intersected to form a diamond shape. An archaeologist said it had to be a natural formation. Not likely as the smooth surface was found to cover several thousand square feet. A geologist named Delbert Smith said "There's no question about it. It has been laid there, but I have no idea by whom." (Book 30 pg 53-54)

Buried under Rockwell Texas is a walled city, in which some parts have bevelled edges, and mortared seams. Pulled from the wall were four large stones that appeared to be inscribed with some sort of writing. An archaeologists named Count Baron Kuhn de Porok came to Dallas in the 1920 and he felt the walls were very similar to those he had seen buried in North Africa and the Middle east. (Book 30 Pg 53)

COINS...

A Roman coin was found near Norfolk Virginia in 1833, in 1882 an Antiochus IV coin (reigned 175 to 164 BC) was found with a Greek inscription, and in 1913 another Roman coin was found in an Illinois mound. If you're going to explore the wilderness there isn't much use for coins, so why were the Romans here with coins?

...and stuff...made in America... copyrights expired.

Near Eureka, Nevada, a fossilized human tibia was found embedded in quartzite, and in 1889 at Nampa Idaho, a well was drilled down 300 feet, and from the dirt came out a tiny female doll about 1 ½ inches tall. (Book 23 pg. 117)

At American Falls, Idaho, a bullet hole was found in an extinct bison skull that had started to heal: presumably from about 43,000 B.C.: Guns in the Wild West, long before the Wild West.

Found in California was a piece of auriferous quarts which was brought to Illinois where it was accidently dropped on the floor and broke. Inside was a perfectly made nail. (Book 30 pg 44)

An iron fork was found in a "prehistoric" Indian site near Eddyville Kentucky. (Book 30 pg 71)

While plowing a field in Sullivan county Missouri, a farmer uncovered a mask made from silver and iron. It had no ties with any aborigines or even the mound builder, and is a mystery as to its origin. (Book 30 pg 44)

The July 1882 edition of Scientific American tells of something found between the Blue and Allegheny mountains. Found were incredible and unique sculpted household utensils and decorative items. The people decorated onto the crafted items were clothed in tight fitting garments, and were not in the likeness of Amerindians. They showed people sitting in armchairs, riding bears, hippos, rhinos, prairie dogs, birds and two humped camels. Scientific American hypothesised that the items were made from an earlier and more civilized race which may have been subjugated and destroyed by the Indians. (Book 30 pg 45 referring to the article)

On June 9th 1891 a lump of coal found in Morrisonville Illinois and about to be used for fuel which when broken was found to contain a gold chain which still held pieces of the coal attached to it. (Book 30 pg 46)

1912 in Oklahoma a large piece of coal that came from the Wilburton, Oklahoma mines was broken open and revealed a large iron pot inside. (Book 30 pg 46)

While digging in a south Boston cellar to plug a leak, a ten pound sculpted stone head was dug up. It was determined not to be the work of Native Americans. (Book 30 pg 47-48)

Sometimes we dig and find things, and sometimes we dig and find nothing...not even dirt. An estimated 2 million pounds of copper was mined on Isle Royale in Michigan, but not by any Americans or any known miners, but the copper is gone...where?... when?

Sometimes we dig and find things, and sometimes we dig and find nothing...not even dirt. An estimated 2 million pounds of copper was mined on Isle Royale in Michigan, but not by any Americans or any known miners, But the copper is gone...where? when?

Stone ruins adorned over one hundred hills when settlers arrived in Ohio between 1790 and 1810. Some of these ruins still exist on Fort Hill, Spruce Hill and Glenford Hill. Some additional ruins can be found on Hill Fort Georgia and Manchester Tennessee. Late in 1885 a massive stone wall was revealed in a quarry a mile away from Lexington Kentucky. The wall was completely encased in limestone which had formed since the wall was built. (Book 30 pg 51)

Coal miners in Wattis, Utah broke into a network of tunnels apparently of a far earlier coal mine that was so old the coal was weathered and useless. No entrance to that old coal mine was discovered; which had either been covered up in some tectonic action or just eroded away over time. (Book 30 pg 52)

Rock collectors south of Olancha, California gathered stones and geodes 340 feet above a dry Owens Lake bed at the 4300 foot elevation. One geode was encrusted with fossil shells and fragments on it. When they cut it open the next day, they found the geode wasn't hollow like most. However inside was a bright shaft of metal. When the geode was x-rayed the item inside turned out to be some sort of two part cylindrical device (part of which was hexagonal) held together with a metal stem and what looks like a spring on the end. Analysts think the thing most resembles a spark plug. I'd like to see the car THAT thing came out of! It was suggested that it had to be less than a hundred years old, but a trained geologists examined the fossils attached to it and felt it had to be about 500,000 years old. (Book 30 pg. 12, 67 and photo section) Thus it must have come from a highly advanced pre-American civilization before ours that was destroyed in some event that could encapsulate a highly technical item in a liquid that would soon form into rock.

No one has ever explained the clearly man-made spheres found in Cannonball North Dakota, which range in size from children's marble size to six feet in diameter. If there was no advanced civilization in America, how were they made?

In Guthrie Oklahoma, Mrs. Alleyne, while having a well dug, pulled out of the excavated dirt a bit of red clay that caught her attention. Inside was found a carved robed figure with a beard made out of wood that was harder than ebony, a tree type that has been extinct for centuries. Years later two Chinese students saw the figure and identified the figure as Shou Hsing, the Chinese god of longevity who was esteemed as such several centuries B.C. (Book 30 pg 73)

If there are many people called not real archaeologist because they believe in stupid theories, like the idea that man had an advanced civilizations in North America at one time, and simply because they find lame things like the lousy evidence I was idiotic enough to refer to here, then what could possibly have happened to this so called fictitious advanced civilization we non archaeologists insist once existed here?

The waves that came over the shores of North America overtopped the mountains as they proceeded eastward and buried all the evidence. We saw some things proving man was here but buried and found 400 feet below the surface. That's a lot of dirt that no conventionally archaeological or geological explanation can account for unless you allow for catastrophic occurrences. Some are going to say that's just too extreme.

James Churchward concluded "We have positive proofs that the whole of Western North America was peopled by highly civilized races during the latter part of the Tertiary era and before the geological Glacial Period." He determined they came from the country of Mu. (Book 23 pg 118 quoting Book 16. I didn't feel like reading the entire book again to find the paragraph.) So why don't archaeologists refer to his material?

Archaeologists want us to believe that North America was not inhabited by any advanced civilization because no old structures exist here for them to play with. Well maybe there is, if these archaeologists would like to take up scuba diving.

Just off the coast of the northern part of Manhattan Island (72°38'W to 72°41 W and 41°12N to 41°14N) is a stunning complex of seven, eight or maybe nine step pyramids laid out very similarly to a pyramid complex in Mexico and Peru which appear to be on submerged land that had circles incised into it like it was a combination of ancient Incan architecture and a stone circle. Any archaeologist that would see this would be forced to admit there had to have been a vast advanced civilization here at least on a par with the Inca's of Peru. This small sampling may be the tip of the iceberg, or it may serve as the last remaining example simply because it managed to get out of the way of the waves harkening to the cry of "Go East" and managed to submerge as the continent shifted. This seemed worthy of a picture so I drew the sight as found on the internet. (**See image 1**)

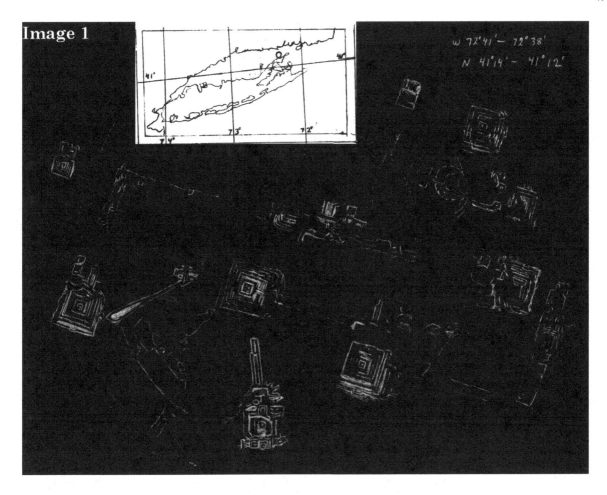

Image 1

w 72°41' – 72°38'
N 41°14' – 41°12'

No doubt this would be a great National park if the site was surrounded by a structure that allowed the site to be drained of water, to allow tourists visits, assuming the archaeologists didn't somehow block the process.

"Land Ho…uh oh…splat!"

I remember once looking at a large iron ring attached to the rocks by the inner harbour of my home town of Victoria B.C. Someone with me said the ring was the oldest part of Victoria as it was the mooring rings used to secure the ships that arrived here in 1843 when the city was founded. Though at first I doubted his story, I found out years later it was true, and I went back to that ring and looked at it again with my mind's eye cast back to that first day of colonization…a relic of Fort Victoria, or at least it's initial conceptions still existed.

Near Chambéry, France were found huge brass (mooring) rings fixed solidly into the rocks. The local peasants assure inquirers that the rings go back to the time when a great deluge covered the land. (Book 31 pg 18) By the way, Chambéry is about 170 miles from the shore of the Mediterranean Sea.

In the Alps there is apparently evidence of ships finding anchorage on high cliffs, though what the actual evidence was not noted in the source. Could these be the ships anchors found on mountain tops referred to by Pythagoras? In the 16th century the remains of timber ships were found "in a lake on the summit of a high mountain known as the "Stella", in Portugal. In 1730 Strahienberg reported about his examination of the whole lower hull of an ancient ship with keel at Barabinsk (Russia) about 730 miles from the nearest ocean access. (Book 31 Pg 18)

In 1460 miners working deep underground in the mountains of Berne Switzerland came across a nicely styled "Bronze age" European wooden ship complete with an anchor of iron and the bones and skulls of 40 men: Men, not Australopithecus, not Neanderthals, the bones of Men. (Book 31 pg 18) This is clear evidence of a sea going vessel caught between Italy and Switzerland as they collided during a continental shift during the Bronze age of civilized times. I imagine the accompanying flood...might even be connected with the same or similar evidence noted above in Chambéry France.

After a huge earthquake that occurred in the 16th century in Naples or Napoli Italy, there was found inside a mountain that had cracked open a large ancient ship. (Book 6 pg 155)

Eusebius Newcombergus in his fifth book of natural history wrote about a goldmine near the port of Lima Peru where workers inside the mine came across an "Ocean going vessel of exotic design" on which were [written?] many characters very different from "ours". (Book 23 pg 203, book 6 pg 155)

GEE I HAVEN'T SEEN THOSE ONES BEFORE.

The ancient's legends around the world consistently spoke of new world ages, usually 4, but occasionally more, depending on the position on the globe, and the extent of the local phenomena. They spoke directly about the sun standing still, moving backwards, the sun getting smaller, the night or day lasting as long as 9 or 10 days, constellations setting that never set before, and the world tumbling. These are no small assertions and if all the people in these locations weren't drunk, or stoned and the few people that could write or tell a good story weren't making these things up, then there should be some physical and puzzling evidence that could be explained perfectly by these legends. We've seen much and there's much more.

Australian astronomer George Dodwell studied solstice shadows recorded by the ancients such as Eudoxus, Amen-Ra, and Stonehenge and concluded that these places in fact record a tilt of the earth. Graphing this tilt he discovered the wavy line on the graph that was a match of the wavy line a spinning top makes when it is struck by an object. He deduced that the earth had been struck by a large object 4350 years ago. Well that's one, and obviously it had to have been a significant hit to still be noticeable today. Smaller asteroids might not have had as much an impact and only slowed, temporarily halted or slightly shifted the crust.

In 1966 the ocean floor, termed the "fossilized compass", had been studied and they discovered that at some point the poles had been completely inverted, and that the strength of the earth magnetic field was diminishing now to the point where it would not exist in as little as 2000 years. (Book 22 pg 144)

As mentioned before a discovery was made while surveying the magnetic fields of the ocean floors. Huge areas of the sea-floor rocks appear to be magnetized in alternate stripes of normal and reversed polarity, almost like a zebra as Sir Edward Bullard said in an1967 Bakerian lecture at the Royal Society." (Book 23 pg 45) The alternate polarities are said to have happened, geologically speaking relatively close together, based on the way they like to date such things. But the fact is the stripes of alternate polarity are steady and continuous, meaning the earth magnetic polarity was spinning rapidly or the earth itself was tumbling. Velikovsky suggested a third possibility, that two planets in close proximity could flip each other's magnetic poles. For all we can tell, all three things could have been happening at the same time. Don't forget, there's a 25 year span where the sun was not even seen; who knows what the earth was doing in that time if the people couldn't see the heavenly bodied as a point of reference.

A panel on the ceiling of the tomb that Senmut built for Queen Hatshepsut shows the celestial sphere with signs of the zodiac reversed from the vantage point of the southern sky. (Book 14 pg 121) That doesn't make any sense unless you accept the legends that indicate the earth flipped over during recorded history making north south and south north, and the Egyptians determining that the sun rose where it used to set and visa verse. This tomb has been dated from some time after the Exodus but before the days of Amos and Isaiah. (Book 14 pg 316) This tomb shows the sky in two different epochs, the one mentioned and the one during the life time of Senmut. This could indicate the time frame in which the earth flipped over changing the north and south poles.

YEAR CHANGES LENGTH

In 1937 3 experts analyzed a calendar found in Tiahuanaco and determined it indicated the year to be only 290 days but each day was 30.2 hours long, making the year 8,758 hours long. Another scientist determined that in "Tertiary" time the year was 298 days long with each day lasting 29.4 hours long for a total of 8,761 hours for a year. Then subsequently they suggest a "Tertiary" moon entered the picture slowing the earth's rotation down so that it now appeared to be a year of 365 days long. (Book 23 pg 172-73)

"It is thought that before the last great cataclysm the Earth revolved around the Sun in 360 days. Perhaps the collision of some cosmic body hurled our planet further into space or retarded its solar circumnavigation. Afterwards the survivors were startled to find the year had lengthened to 365 days. These five extra days were an annual reminder to the Aztecs of the catastrophes past and the catastrophes to come; their superstitious souls thought these days 'unlucky'. During the last five 'empty days' of each year fires were extinguished, sexual intercourse ceased, business stood still, no one worked, all waited anxiously, wondering if the world would end." (Book 23 pg 158-59)

Texts of the Hindu Veda speak of a 360 day long year. "All Veda texts speak uniformly and exclusively of a year of 360 days." "It is striking that the Vedas nowhere mention an intercalary period (days inserted into the calendar), and while repeatedly stating that the year consists of 360 days, nowhere refer to the five days or six days that actually are part of the solar year." (Book 14 pg 333 referring to Thibaut's *Astronomie, Astrologie und Mathamatik* from 1899.) Why do you think this is the case? Because the year was only 360 days long, or is that too extreme and overconfident a statement for me to make? Ok listen to these folks.

The Indian Aryabhatiya says the year has 12 months and each month has 30 days. (360 total) The ancient Persian year was also 360 days long consisting of 12 months each 30 days long. The Old Babylonian year was also 360 days long. The Assyrian year was 360 days long and they also mention that ten years equalled 3,600 days, indicating a very stable year with no leap years. The Ancient Romans also asserted that the year was 360 days long. The Mayans year was also 360 days, but later on they had to add 5 more days, and every 4th year they had to add yet another day...thus leap year was introduced. Back when I was a 5 year old and 1964 was a leap year I asked what a leap year was. I was told every February they added a day to the month. I thought they meant at one time February was a new month with one day in it and wondered when February started, and was looking forward to when it would be the longest month. Well now I know when it *really* started: Thank you Mayans. China too had a calendar in the ancient days that was only 360 days long also with 12 months of 30 days each. Scholars have now realize that before some event changed the length of the year, every ancient text that mentions the year's length specifies it was 360 days long, which include Egyptians, Chaldeans, Hebrews, Greeks as well as the ones mentioned. (Book 14 pg 334-43)

Thus something huge must have happened to lengthen the year abruptly. Tablets of Nineveh indicate a change. One tablet says the equinox occurs "On the 6th of the month of Nisan, the day and night are equal." And another tablet notes that the days are equal on the 15th of Nisan...9 days later, something scholars can't explain. Noteworthy is the tablets of Nineveh also have three different schedules for the movement of the planets, as though they too had experienced orbitus interuptus. Other Nineveh tablets note that the perihelion and aphelion, that is when the earth was nearest and furthest from the sun, doesn't match the current schedule. The moon too altered its course. Chaldean records show that from new moon to new moon the difference is on average 3° 14' too great, far too much a difference to be an error. The Nineveh tablets indicate that the astronomical world order had changed repeatedly in a single century. (Book 14 pg 350-51) This matches up with some legends that say there were two new ages and suns just 52 years apart.... not millions, like geologists would have you believe.

As noted it appears that the area that contained the frozen woolly mammoths had to have suddenly shifted north as determined by the food they were eating in a place that doesn't grow the stuff anymore. They are often depicted as living in frozen habitats, but this is all hokum as they are known to have had a diet consisting of 500 pound of vegetation every day, something not seen on snow drifts. (Nexus V25#4 Pole Shift Hidden Evidence)

In 1778 missionaries in India found some local star maps, which they brought back to France for study. These maps were many thousands of years old. They determined from the astronomical tables that they appeared to contain mistakes, because many of the stars visible on the maps are not visible from the place of origin in India where the maps were found. They determined these stars would be visible in the region of Mongolia and the Gobi

Desert somewhere near the 49 Latitude north where they would be correct, indicating a north south shift of the earth of about 1800 miles. Other documents and some "Tables of Tirvalour' were brought by other missionaries to this same group of specialists from the East Indies, and they concluded "...there must have been a very highly developed antediluvian civilization which has been 'obliterated as a result of natural and political upheavals." (Book 21 pg 58, Book 22 pg 137: These two references regarding what appears to be the same material seem to be equating/ interchanging India and East Indies... or this is a confirmation of both?)

THE ERRATICS

One of the more fascinating finds that proves horrendous tsunamis, are the boulders, and large rocks strewn around the planet by some mysterious force. Upon their discovery the origins of their presence in their alien surroundings was quickly and correctly deduced as being caused by massive waves. However the people that deduced this as the cause, couldn't explain the origin of the waves. Then, subsequent analysis by uniformitarianists put their origin in question and they came up with an alternative explanation. Since the geologic establishment has wholeheartedly rejected catastrophism, uniformitarian explanations have been endorsed to deliberately discredit the catastrophic model, so in spite of the evidence, uniformitarianists' concepts have forced illogical explanations for the origins of the erratics. However, now that geologists have become somewhat resigned to the insurmountable evidence of sudden changes in geology, uniformitarian beliefs have been somewhat disrupted by what is now termed as 'punctured equilibrium'. What this concession amounts to, is pretty much exactly what the evidence presented in this book puts forth, but with the exception of the time factor. Punctured equilibrium, suggested there were brief periods of upheaval followed by millions and millions and MILLIONS of years of uniformitarianism. But the legends strongly suggests these upheavals happened during recorded history, history which states on average that there were four such episodes of "Punctured Equilibrium" followed by some years or a few centuries of geologic calm. The ancients in a sense agree with the theory, only they say No no no no! Not millions of years, we saw it!... that is they saw the "Punctured equilibrium" and recorded the times and incidences as you have read. And the legends and records match up exactly with the geologic evidence.

So what are erratics? Rocks have very identifiable characteristics that can positively pinpoint their place of origin, so when a rock doesn't match its surroundings, the origin of how it got there is in question. Here's an example: "Immense erratic blocks of granite torn from Canada and Labrador, weighing thousands of tons [each], were piled high on mountains in New Hampshire, Massachusetts, Wisconsin and Connecticut." (Book 23 pg 107) That means somehow vast numbers of thousands of ton boulders managed, through natural means, to travel around 7 or 800 miles across land and in many cases climb up mountains. Geologists want us to believe glaciers pushed or icebergs lifted these massive stones and deposited them all over the place. But a look at specific erratics in this example compared with known glacier moraines clearly suggests different origins for the erratics than geologists are promoting. At the head of advancing glaciers or when glaciers retreat they leave behind what looks like a gravel yard with the odd small boulders strewn about. The Kolka Glacier of North Caucasus is good example showing an accumulation of rocky debris at its head...and yet not a single big boulder is in sight; just little more than piles of sand.

But often erratics are single huge boulders out in the middle of nowhere, with no accompanying gravel yards, so clearly different forces are involved in placing those boulders there than we are led to believe. Take the Madison Wisconsin boulder estimated between 4,662 and 10,000 tons, or the 13,500 ton monstrosity in Warren county Ohio; No glacier could move these, the glacier would just ooze around them. Yet geologists want us to believe that erratics spread out across New Hampshire, Massachusetts Wisconsin and Connecticut came all the way from Canada and Labrador because a glacier pushed them there. No way! (Book 23 pg. 107, 157)

Similarly what the uniformitarianists want us to believe is that icebergs dropped giant rocks all over the ocean floor, then the land slowly emerged leaving the rocks high and dry, and as we've mentioned, glaciers pushed giant rocks hundreds of miles from their original starting point. There's a very real problem with this theory. Icebergs barely float because they are just frozen water which is only slightly less dense than water. Anyone seeing an ice cube in their drink knows they have just about 2% of the volume above the surface, so any sizable rock embedded in an iceberg would simply sink the iceberg and it wouldn't go anywhere. Besides, icebergs freeze the surface of standing water, and it rarely freezes down to the earth or ocean floor: and if it did, the ice would be stuck and wouldn't move. Only when the ice was free of the earth could it move so it wouldn't even carry a boulder, and at best would grab a few loose pebbles which would soon drop as the glacier moved to warmer climes.

One of the problems with the glacier theory is that the direction of glacier migration is obvious and the erratics seldom come from the same direction the glaciers came from. Even if the directions lined up, all the erratic rocks would be in the same general area where the glacier stopped its migration and began to recede as it melted. These sites are obvious as to their origin as there would be waves of small rocky debris as we mentioned, all of which would be together in the same general area and would demarcate the line of the glaciers edge.

Also as a rule glaciers tend to slide downhill, so how would they push an erratic boulder, weighing thousands of tons up the side of a mountain? Erratics are mysterious, and are often giant rocks strewn higgely-piggely all over "Gods half acre" with no definable edge, but the glacier theory has been high jacked to explain them as well, hoping the uninitiated won't notice. Have you ever noticed how lessons are taught to school students? They ramble on like everything they say is positively proven fact to give the impressions all is known. If you say things with enough confidence you can fool just about anybody. I recall in school specifically questioning the iceberg theory as the explanation for erratic and being told that land does emerge. (from beneath the waves where the rocks would have been deposited to appear on what was now above water). I still thought something was wrong with this explanation but I just couldn't put my finger on it. On other occasions I doubted my questions before I even asked because of I thought, "Ahh... you are probably missing something obvious and if you ask a question you'll just look like an idiot." Einstein said we should never stop asking questions.

The problem with the iceberg dropping rock bombs theory is that most, if not all of the erratics in question are on land, and continental drift by and large doesn't make new land appear from the depths, it only changes its location. The iceberg theory is dependent on sea floor turning into land. Now true, some land / water areas have changed, but I've not heard of any erratics in these places, but I suppose if they exist, I could have missed them, and they could have been rolled there sometime after the land rose. Another problem is that icebergs break off of places like Greenland and Antarctica and any rocks that might have been caught by the iceberg in the process, which by the way would be very few as icebergs usually break off of massive giant ice walls and not from shorelines strewn with boulders. The land where the iceberg originated would have already acted like a glacier pushing rocks into the sea before they ever attached themselves to a chunk of ice when it turned into an iceberg. Fact of the matter is I've never seen a single picture of an iceberg with rocks attached to them, on top or under the surface of the water. For this theory to have any validity at all, rocks attached to icebergs would have to be the norm, not the rare exception as erratic boulders are all over the place. Erratics in Germany came from Scandinavia and the Harz Mountains in Germany have erratics that came from at least 400 miles away in Norway! Finland erratic stones have been found to have overrun Latvia and Poland and ended up over 800 miles away in the Carpathian Mountains! And gullible us are told by the really reeeely smart geologists that glaciers and icebergs did all this. Seriously? It is not only improbable, it is not even possible! Not convinced that water from the direction of Finland deposited these rocks in the Harz Mountains? W. Buckland who wrote *Geology and Mineralogy* in 1837 discovered in the Harz Mountains vast deposits of fossilized fishes that had been deposited there in some immense surge that buried them in contorted poses, so quickly that they never even started the rotting process as the same influx of bituminous mud that brought them there, caused their destruction and buried them. (Book 53 pg 19 referring to this work) I will add that the same influx of water that brought the fish and the mud also brought the erratics into the Harz Mountain region.

The only solution is the original one, that giant waves pushed these massive stones hundreds of miles as the continents were overrun by massive tsunamis. And the only thing that could create such a wave would be the continents shifting or moving, or a meteor splashing down in the sea.

In 1883 Krakatoa went off. That one single volcano put so much dust into the atmosphere that it reduced the sunlight coming to the entire earth by 10 to 15 percent for years! Farmers around the globe for three years or more had reduced crop yields. After it erupted, half the island disappeared under the waves and the tsunami created by the blast was a 120 feet high! The wave diminished somewhat to just 70 feet by the time it reached Sumatra an hour later. Coral blocks weighing as much as 600 tons were thrown ashore! That was the result of just one volcanic eruption. The ancient speak of a time when virtually all the volcanoes on the planet were disrupted by displacement of the earth's crust causing virtually all of them to blow their tops simultaneously. Legends speak of the endless noise of them going off continually, and the recorders of the legends wondering when it would stop. That would easily explain the universal layer of sandstone created by waves overrunning the continents, the fossils, mass extinctions, and erratics. And it wasn't just volcanic action pushing the blocks around the world that would come to be known as 'erratics', but the shifting of the continents that forced not just waves but half the ocean onto land. (Book 21 pg 14, book 14 pg 110, 138, book 19 pg 80-81)

Recently the ash from the eruption of an Iceland volcano interrupted flight from Europe to North America. Similarly in 1783 an Iceland volcano named Skaptar-Jökull blowing its top darkened the world for months. One unnamed German contemporary likened the gloomy world of the day to the Egyptian plague of Darkness. (Book 14 pg 138)

Dr. W. J. Humphrey of the U.S. Weather Bureau studied weather patterns of three centuries and found that cool rainy summers followed periods of major volcanic activity. For example when the Sumbawa Island volcano Tomboro erupted in 1815, USA experienced the "The Year without a Summer" in 1816. A series of major Chilean volcanism in 1932 was followed by an unusually cold and rainy winter. By the way it has been established that nuclear tests have also affected the weather adversely. In 1953 a few atomic tests were done in Nevada and by the end of May there had been 130 tornadoes, the worst year on record. (Book 62 pg 221)

We've seen that these irruptions of the sea onto land moved massive amounts of dirt, pebbles, fish, and trees and whatever to cover vast expanses, while destroying and covering civilizations up with foreign debris leaving them buried deep underground. This catastrophic action often covers these places up with what ends up being fossils, confusing the picture for archaeologists that pop by a few thousand years later.

I can think of a few places that indicate where some of that dirt coverage came from. First consider this small example: Foot prints or animal tracks compress the soil underneath them, which sometimes harden over time. If later on, a moderate surge of water comes by, the soft dirt is washed away leaving the foot prints behind which are elevated above the surface as they resisted erosion from their being compacted. Have you ever wonder how chimney and 'flower pot rocks could form? Or wondered how the badlands of Alberta, the Grand Canyon and Needles district and canyon lands of Chesler Park in California and nearby states came into being? I drew a few examples of such places to pretty up the book a bit. (**See image 2-7**). These features are the result of rushing tidal wave water coming across the continents, scouring the landscape leaving these peculiar landscapes behind. Image 2: the Nebraska Courthouse rocks, Image 3: The delicate arch as seen on Utah's licence plates, Image 4: the famous flowerpot rock of Bruce Peninsula Ontario (My mom grew up not far from this site), Image 5: after drawing this I could not find a picture of this location again but the name on the file I saved suggests this is somewhere in Algeria, Image 6 is of the Drumheller Hoodoos in Albert which are part of a vast landscape similar to the Grand Canyon, and image 7 is of the famous Chimney Rock in Nebraska which is also depicted on their state licence plates. Look at these drawing and imagine the ocean suddenly rushing across this landscape, drawing away all the loose soil with it and leaving solid rock pillars behind, and then depositing that rocky pebbly soil somewhere else. Originally these chimney features would have been completely underground, but the rushing water wore the dirt away revealing these curious (formerly) underground features. That's how these landscape features came into being. And that's how all those whales' skeletons were deposited and later found in Vermont, Montreal and Minnesota.

Image 2: Nebraska's Courthouse Rock

Image 3 Utah's Delicate arch

**Image 4: Flowerpot Rock
Bruce Peninsula, Ontario**

Image 5: Algeria Rocks

Image 6: Drumheller Hoodoos Alberta

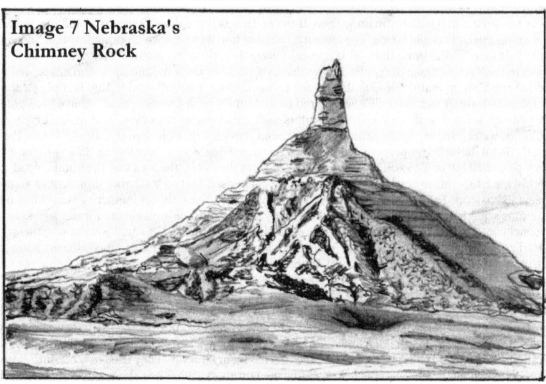

Image 7 Nebraska's Chimney Rock

Trying to figure out how such features might have formed underground; my guess is at one time percolating magma rose through soft soil then cooled and hardened before it reached the surface. But also had the water continued rushing much longer some of these features would also have succumbed to the waves as well. Only sudden stopping of the water left these sites standing before they too were turned to silt and rubble and carried away.

ICE AGES

We are told that from about a million years ago to about 12,000 B.C. during what's been dubbed the Pleistocene age, the earth was enjoying a nice series of about 3 cold spells where a large extent of the globe was engaged with Jack Frost's ice sheets covering much of the land masses, and these periods have been termed "Ice Ages". We will see that these so called "ice ages" were far more recent, and do not clarify what they were dreamed up to explain. What you might not know is the ice ages were invented to try to account, or more properly, to discount or discredit catastrophic explanations of events. The clue to these huge events was the abundance of large boulders, found mostly in the north which were carried, pushed or transported by some immense force over great distances from their point of origin. These are known as the erratics as we've just briefly discussed. For example sometimes a huge granite boulder can be found sitting on a high ridge of dolerite, clearly incongruous, and geologists have to try and explain these inconsistencies. Some of these erratics boulders weigh as much as ten thousand tons. I might add that though the geologists have made these "ice ages" a geological axiom, the causes of the ice ages has never been satisfactorily explained. Though many theories from position of the sun and earth, variety of space temperatures, the sun being a variable star, an altered gulf stream, continents altitude changing, and on and on, yet no satisfactory origin of the ice ages has been accepted. Velikovsky presented a theory of the cause of the ice ages that explains them handily but it is rejected out of hand because it relies on a catastrophic model. (Book 53) I'm confident his premise is correct and I continue to advance it too.

Heat has to be a major factor in an ice age. If the earth was just cold, the oceans would just freeze and not end up on the land as glacial ice. The ancients spoke of horrible heat which came from the blowing off of all the volcanoes at the same time. This constant volcanic activity evaporated the oceans, which is also spoken of in the legends. Once the continents settled to their new positions, and the volcanoes cooled off, so too did the earth's temperature drop and snow fell in 'nuclear' or "Fimbul" winter, that is triple strength or end of the world winter as some cultures referred to it. Actually both events appear to have been going on simultaneously, volcanic activity and brutal winters with unbelievable snowfalls. The atmosphere reached saturation of water vapour, accompanied by suspended particles that blocked out all light from the sun, making the inhabitants live in perpetual gloom with the "Lowering sky" or "sky falling" falling to the ground level as a perpetual fog or gloom. The sun was blocked from the sky by the soot and the humid clouds, then the worldwide temperature crashed and the moisture condensed first as torrential rain then as snow that never seemed to stop. The sun wasn't seen for years on end. All these things happened simultaneously as "...numerous scientists who conducted their field study in various areas outside the former ice cover came to the conclusion that those areas had experienced periods of torrential rains that were simultaneous with the glacial periods in higher latitudes (Not 'altitudes'). Meanwhile water levels dropped globally at least 300 feet during this period. (Book 53 pg. 119,123) There is an example of conditions on the earth that could have spawned one of the ice ages.

As we mentioned before in the Latin American myths: "That is the news of the downfall of man. What happened on the earth? Who made them tremble with fear? Who made the stars to dance? Who made the water gush out of the cliffs? ...It was terribly cold and an icy wind swept over the earth. It was terribly hot and men burned up in its breath. Men and animals fled in panic stricken fear. They ran hither and thither in desperation. They tried to climb trees, but the trees hurled them far away. They tried to creep into caves and the caves collapsed on them. What was below was pushed up above. What was above sank into the depths..."

(Repeating Book 10 pg 115) One can see that there was at least one time on earth spoken of in legends when we experienced intense heat and intense cold on the earth which was accompanied by a complete state of catastrophism.

Looking at the evidence around them, the scholars of the early 19th century deduced that these erratic rocks were moved to various places, sometimes thousands of miles distant, by tides and giant waves that swept these boulders across the continent. But the conundrum came when they realized that though some of these waves would have had to cross the continents, they could not account for existence of such huge waves in the first place; waves that would have had enough force to actually cross the continents because such giant waves have never been observed in today's world. They had the physical evidence of the event, but they couldn't account for the cause of the event. This is what comes from scientists restricting their focus to one science. Had they been aware of the ancient legends, perhaps this explanation for the erratics would have stood the test of time right to this day. But uniformitarianism was taking over science and this catastrophic explanation of the erratics had to go; thus was invented the theory of the ice ages. Make no mistake, the ice age hypothesis does have some basis in fact, but they have overblown their effect on the planet. They could not accept the 'giant waves' theory because unfortunately for this explanation or theory, "...it violated right from the very outset the first principal of science, by assuming the former existence of a cause of which there was little in nature known to warrant." It was further stated that "...spasmodic rushes of the sea across a whole country had fortunately never been experienced within the memory of man." (Book 14 pg 90 quoting J. Geikie's book *The Great Ice Ages and its relation to the Antiquity of Man* from 1894) That's just saying that nothing in that past could do this because nothing today is doing this, is the basis for the belief in uniformitarianism. Giant waves can't be the solution because it's not happening today so it couldn't have happened in the past. This belief in uniformitarianism is a huge limiting factor in solving any geologic puzzles, because you have to force all explanations based on current geological experiences, and not the evidence which might suggest something different occurred in the past that is not occurring today.

So what has been thrust on the masses, is an invented theory of the ice ages that has no plausible explanation for how they occurred and doesn't actually work to explain what it was invented to explain anyway, but was simply dreamed up to discredit a very plausible theory of cataclysmic mega tsunamis to account for the same evidence of huge erratic rocks strewn about the landscape. Curiously the one theory that does work to explain Ice ages has been rejected because it relies on a cataclysmic model, and the one theory that explains the erratics has also been rejected because it too relies on a cataclysmic model. Cataclysms are therefore rejected out of hand then, simply because they don't fit with the theory of Evolution or Uniformitarianism. Neither of these theories has any basis in fact nor evidence to back either of the theories up, and so the geologists and evolutionists have been forced to accept "punctured equilibrium" because uniformitarianism doesn't explain the evidence. And yet 'punctured equilibrium' is really just another way of saying 'catastrophism'. So in essence they validate the original theory they tried to discredit, by using different terminology, making it seem like their theories eliminated the theory that actually explained the dilemma in the first place by using the same solution but with a different name.

However an example in Palermo Sicily clearly refutes the uniformitarianistic model. They found so many bones of animals in fissures of the rocks from old to foetus, that they quickly exhumed over twenty tons of bones which were so fresh that they were sent to Marseilles to be used as animal charcoal for use in sugar factories. Joseph Prestwich professor of Geology at Oxford (1874-1888) stated about this site that it was "impossible to account for the specific geological phenomena ...by any agency of which our time has offered us experience." Whatever swarmed all these animals together, the event or "agency, whatever it was, must have acted with sufficient violence to smash the bones." Looking at evidence found at the Rock of Gibraltar, France, England and as far away as Sicily it's clear that a catastrophe of truly continental dimensions hurled stones onto land, shattering mastiffs, rushed water into fissures, and broke, crushed, and smashed every animal in the way. Prestwich felt the cause had to be the sudden sinking and subsequent elevation of land which was sudden and had to have happened during the Bronze Age. (Book 53 pg 49-51)

Thus this find has been dated to the 'Bronze Age' and 'Neolithic Stone Age' period, ridiculous numbers of thousands of years old, even though the bones were FRESH! This dating attributed to this event is Horseman-Oor." How do I know? A land bridge between Sicily and Italy that submerged into the Mediterranean was an event that was recorded in ancient documents.

Furthermore, volcanic eruptions had destroyed cities, great floods had occurred, and islands had sunk and often had not risen again." (Book 6 pg 20) Unfortunately Berlitz did not note in this case which ancient documents commented on this cataclysm. But it was clearly not a Bronze Age or Neolithic period occurrence, but occurred during recorded history.

I'll toss in continental shifts would do these things too. The La Brea Tar pits are also evidence of a sudden calamity trapping a multitude of animals. We are told the tar pits caught stragglers which, like quicksand, sucked them down to preserve them to this day. But contrary to this theory, whole connected skeletons are not common at this site. The bones are splendidly preserved yes, but they are broken, smashed and contorted and mixed in a "most heterogeneous mass", in fact so much so, that their demise "...could never have been the result of chance trapping and burial of a few stragglers."(Book 53 pg 61)

Yet the theory of uniformitarianism persists? As you are no doubt very cognisant of now, you have just been reading over the past however many pages that we *did* experience geological catastrophes, and told stories of these waves, and what caused them, but these geologists either never read the legends or discounted the stories as those of primitive nutcases. Instead they want us to accept that glaciers pushed these massive boulders literally thousands of miles. But there is another problem. Ice is pliable and bends around or slides over objects large enough that it can't push. A thousand ton block would more likely stand its ground while the softer glacier oozed its way around the massive roadblock, especially if the rock was going downhill toward the glacier. The glacier could not push a huge rock uphill. True it would push some smaller rocks until the glacier looses steam. But glaciers like water don't go up hill or upstream, they flow...downhill. When glaciers retreat they do show what could be dubbed erratics, but they are all in massive pebble sites and all concentrated at the glacier head. And there is no way a glacier is going to push a boulder uphill anyway, so this theory still doesn't explain at least half if not all of the erratics. Geologists, glaciologists...or whatever branch of science this unworkable theory belongs to, just wants you to think this theory holds water and they hide the spurious erratics behind their backs. Even if a glacier did somehow push the heavier rocks uphill, the rocks wouldn't be pushed with it but they would sink gradually into the ice. (Book 14 pg 90)

An example that refutes the glacier model as the cause of erratics is found in northern China. Here as in Northern Siberia where no glacial conditions and no formations known to be caused by glacial coverage exists, were found strewn about the country erratic blocks and striated boulders situated in the valleys and on the hills. (Book 53 pg 57) It's even been determined that the mountains in western China have been elevated *since* the glacial age, so a hydraulic cause of the erratics is more likely, as the cause of the uplift is no doubt the cause of the erratics found there as well.

Erratics are found where continental ice could not possibly have played a part in their placement. Charles Darwin noted that erratics are found on the Azores, separated from any ice fields by plenty of ocean to rule out glaciers as a cause. The Isle of Man also has erratics and only waves could have put them there. In Labrador boulders are seen slammed against hill slopes which could only have been put there by waves. In India blocks and flotsam are found that did not come from higher altitudes, but came from lower altitudes, the opposite of what glacial action could accomplish.

They now know that ice ages, mountain building and polar shifts occur in direct relation to each other, that is they are simultaneous geologic events, and thus we can gather that these events are the result of the continents actually shifting, as no other cause could initiate all these effects at the same time. It was these events that caused the giant waves that moved the erratics. Thus we can now see the original explanation for the erratics *was* correct.

SHIFTED COVER, NOT EXPANDED.

Though we think of ice ages as covering the whole top half of the North American continent, this is an exaggeration. Geologists know that we know the north of Canada is an ice box: and some people not well versed in geography or geology think that everything above the 49th parallel is pure snow and igloos. However the north of Canada is not a glacier, yet the ice age is depicted as a glacier covering most of North America and receding northward. Not so and in fact this also contradicts the evidence of many of the erratics that came east from the Pacific Ocean's direction or southwest from the direction of Labrador to New Hampshire, Massachusetts, Wisconsin and Connecticut; the erratics were not pushed southward from the Polar Regions.

As we've mentioned the Ice Ages never covered more than an additional 6% of the earth's land masses than is now covered by glaciers today. Geologists want us to imagine all these vast regions formerly covered by ice at one time slowly melted and receded from these vast areas that were at one time covered by ice, to the little that is left covered up by ice today. But this is not correct. If all the area that was covered up by glacial ice at one time or another were added to what is covered up by ice now, the total would far exceed that 6% added to the ice on the earth today. What happened was global ice placement altered when mountains were being built, and the poles were shifting because the earth was experiencing continental readjustments due to exterior forces. Thus completely different areas of the planet were covered with ice than what are covered by ice today. Areas such as the equator: and the glaciers didn't recede back to the south, they receded towards the equator, not from it. If as we've seen, the Polar Regions were a temperate zone that supported millions of woolly mammoths, and the parts of the equator supported glaciers, we can only surmise that the two regions switched places and also switched climates to a large degree in the past. The switch was sudden and therefore a catastrophic event, or a series of up to four events.

As a side note, this is why I scratch my head at people bending over backwards trying to prove the pyramids line up with this star or that cardinal point, because as we've seen and will see further, that these geographical switches occurred in recorded history. We've already seen that Egypt has star maps that infer the globe flipped over, and India has star maps that infer that the globe shifted about 1800 miles, all happening during the times frames we were making detailed star maps, so why would we even bother trying to figure any lining up of the stars and cardinal points with a place like the pyramids and stone circles, as all these alignments had to have changed since these things were built, if they were ever lined up with any of these things in the first place.

We now grasp by the legends how the ice ages occurred; but a quick recap. Meteors bashed into the earth and / or planets came so close to the earth that they caused magnetic polar switches which tipped or knocked the earth. This action shifted the continents causing myriads of volcanic eruptions all going off simultaneously around the globe, shooting ash into the sky blocking out the sun, dropping world temperature for years on end. Furthermore, the volcanoes in the ocean evaporated large volumes of the oceans to the point some parts of the ocean literally dried right up, filling the atmosphere with so much steam turned into clouds which not only filled the sky but crammed the entire volume of the atmosphere to the point the 'sky fell', as so many legends and even the bible records. With hyper saturated atmosphere filled with steam, ash and soot blocking out the light and heat of the sun, global temperature dropped causing massive snowfalls that lasted year after year, snowing in some places during the winter and the summer, creating vast regions of land to be covered by snow which would then become glaciers; and there is the origin of your ice ages. And this origin of the ice ages is recorded in historical writings and legends and did not happen a million years ago or even 12,000 years ago for that matter as we'll see.

ICE AGE A RECENT EVENT.

Even if some legends didn't specifically mention the growing ice fields around the world, the legends clearly place the ice ages into historical periods. We've seen that many world legends speak of the passing of 4 world ages, with this being the fifth. The first age, ended by the global flood, likely would not have created an "ice age", but the subsequent world ages would all have caused an ice age. This means legends tell of, or at least infer, that there were three or four ice ages depending on location on the earth caused by the events they experienced. Some locations spoke of as many as seven ages, though not all would be accompanied by an 'ice age'. Coincidentally, geology, generally speaking, speaks of Four (Quaternary) ice ages. This lines up with the number of world ages. Why do you think that might be? Because the ices ages were caused by the destructions on earth that ended the four world ages the ancient spoke of! Now these ages did not cover all the land, so dividing them into four specific ages may actually be overlapping some areas calling one, two. But I'm no expert. I think it's significant that all three / four ice ages are historical events, and not some 'Pleistocene' event that happened a million years ago for the earliest ice age.

In fact the evidence that forces the conclusion that the ice ages occurred during historical times and not between 1,000,000 B.C. and 10,000-12,000 B.C. is so conclusive that I can only conclude there is some ulterior motive for keeping the truth out of the general public's knowledge. So let's look at the evidence.

Chapter ten of Immanuel Velikovsky's book *Earth in Upheaval* is so filled with evidence of a recent ice age and his books were so controversial that evolutionists and the geologist must know this evidence exists. It's so filled with information that I'd love to just quote the whole chapter verbatim, but no doubt that would be plagiarism, and my book deal limits quotes to 300 words at a time anyway. So I will simply summarise concisely the points of the chapter here. This section is based on Chapter X from pages 140-156 of his work. (Book 53).

You no doubt are aware that by measuring things like mud, salt, silt, salinity, build-up or erosion and by knowing how much occurs in a certain amount of time, and if we account for known variables that we can get a fair estimation of how long things took to occur from start to finish, or to the present. It's like that with glaciers, lakes and rivers: melt rates, creeping speeds and such can determine how long those glaciers have been there.

Using these methods and assuming that ice ages in one area like Sweden didn't necessarily mean they happened in another area like North America at the same time, thus it was concluded originally that the ice ages ended between 25,000 and 40,000 years ago. But as we've seen the events that caused the ice ages were happening simultaneously around the globe, as the similarity between the legends around the world clearly indicates. Later on, radio carbon dating shocked the geologic world when this dating method determined that the glaciers were still advancing as recently as 10,000 years ago and not retreating as far back as 30,000 years ago like was previously supposed. However radio carbon dating assumes many things must be constant over time, like the amount of radiation reaching earth, and the quantity of water in the oceans remained the same. These points are apparently *very* important to get an accurate reading. If these things had fluctuations the readings then are not correct. But variation in ocean depth vary as much as 600 feet, and we've seen that radioactive Carbon 14 build-up and decay are not at equilibrium, so there could not possibly have been the same amount in the radioactive C14 in the atmosphere 5000 years ago as there is today. The assumption that the amount of radioactive Carbon 14 in the atmosphere today is the same as it was 12,000 years ago would greatly increase ages arrived at by this dating method. Even so, these unjustifiably high dates were considered a shockingly *low* figure! So when radio carbon dating method gave young readings they were assumed to be just flaws in the dating methods that were puzzling exceptions to the experts. For example wood associated with the Late

Wisconsin (most recent) glaciations dated at only 3,300 hundred years old (+ or − 200 years). Other findings reduced that to just 3000 years, and not 10-12000 years old insisted by the standard. Meaning these ice age events happened even more recently than the apparently ultra low figures of 12,000 years indicated! So the geologists compromised so that at least the ices ages appeared to be older than what was deemed to be the limits of written history, even if it was younger than their preferred 25.000-40,000 years they initially assumed.

As we know at one time the ice age covered a lot of North America and when that ice melted it created a huge lake known as Lake Agassiz, which encompassed Lake Winnipeg, Lake Manitoba and many other Canadian lakes and spread down into the states with a total area that was larger than the combined area of the five Great Lakes we have today. A study of the sediments from this lake indicated the lake and the ice that melted to create the lake existed for less than a 1000 years, which shocked the geologists. It's not known what made this vast ice sheet across most of Canada and into the northern part of the States start to melt. (Book 7 Pg 160) The only thing that could have made the ice and lake melt and dissipate so quickly had to have been some sort of catastrophic condition that at the very least had to involve a lot of heat. But it gets worse. Because of the erosion evidence on what were the shores of Lake Agassiz, it was determined that this lake and ice disappeared recently. Furthermore the shoreline of the lake was not horizontal indicating it tipped recently too. Based on the lack of weathering of exposed rocks and the preservation of the glacial striation in an area of known for its extreme climate, this indicated the lake could not have disappeared any longer that a few thousand years ago…"at the most"! This discovery placed the existence of the lake within the period of human history. Thus the cartoon geologists Snidely Whiplash said "curses, foiled again".

STUPID LOCAL YOKELS.

Our fiend, er, friend, Charles Lyle who made up the geologic column nonsense, apparently couldn't take anyone's word for anything. He was told that the Niagara Falls recedes about 3 feet a year by the locals when he visited the area, so he automatically assumed the people were exaggerating. Subsequently he reduced that figure to one foot per year and came up with 35,000 years for the falls to cut from Lake Ontario to the then current position towards Lake Erie. It turned out the locals were *underestimating* the rate of erosion and the falls were receding at the rate of five feet per year, as determined by a known starting point in 1764 to when Velikovsky published *Earth in Upheaval,* or a total duration of 7000 year for the entire distance covered. This 7,000 years would be a maximum too, because this time frame is reduced during the initial stages as the water would have scoured its way down the path much faster because of the swollen stream from glacial melt. If the glacial Lake Agassiz was responsible for some of this wear, it could vastly reduce the time it took for the distance covered. We've already seen the Lake Agassiz disappeared very fast apparently due to some catastrophic conditions melting the glacier far faster than would have been occurring in today's conditions. No doubt the great lakes and these falls were eroding under the same conditions, rapidly eroding the path, and so it's felt that 5,000 years would have been ample time for the distance to be covered by the falls. But, facts be damned, Lyle's estimates of 35,000 years are still being used in text books.

An excavation for a railroad bridge in 1920 discovered some glacial boulder clay, indicating it had been re-excavated by the falls and it meant that the post glacial period was vastly shorter than was generally assumed, which changed the picture of the falls rate of erosion considerably. Now I admit I can't seem to translate the written description into a visualization, so I don't quite understand the reasoning of it all as it seems kind of complicated, but the bottom line is that it reduced the time frame to between 2,500 and 3,500 years, meaning the Niagara Falls actually started their erosive ways somewhere between 1500 and 500 B.C. What this means, is the topography of the area, in all likelihood had to have changed at that point, to start the process in the first place! Indeed we just talked about a change of topography concerning Lake Agassiz…no doubt the same event.

Existing glaciers in Switzerland were measured from their maximum size at the height of the ice age to their current size by comparing the rates of movement on similar large glaciers which moved at the rate of 54 centimetres a day and by measuring their stone and detritus accumulations. Thus it was determined that the Swiss glacier took between 2475 and 2400 years to travel the distance from the beginning point. This flew in the face of accepted wild guesses of one million years from the height of the ice age to present, because even though the math was not was not questioned; the date was bothersome because it didn't fit with the evolutionary model. Nor did it accommodate the presumed changes in nature and animals the theory insists must have taken a million years to accomplish *"if no catastrophes intervened"*. However based on "quantitative analysis", these figures have been determined to be "approximately correct". Thus the Rhone's glacier and other Alps glaciers maximums fall well within the bounds of human history, and *none* of the glaciers in the Alps (which were formed by the ice ages) were over 4000 years old. Keep in mind glaciers are the remnants of the Ice ages.

THE DELTA DAWNS.

With all that ice age ice melting away around the great lakes and Agassiz Lake, it's felt a lot of if it was diverted and drained through the Mississippi river, and possibly a lot more than one might expect: if the St. Lawrence river was blocked by ice. But even without this massive amount of drainage added to calculations, the sediments added to the delta at the end of the Mississippi River was calculated out to have taken just 5,000 years to accumulate. If one did include glacial drain in the age of the delta, this estimated age of 5000 years would be considerably reduced. So one way or the other, the Mississippi delta ages out to the end of the global flood, or the end of the ice ages which came after the flood. Either way, the time it took to accumulate this delta is a frustratingly short period for those who want to attribute vast ages to any North American sites.

Lake Champlain and the north eastern states were studied and the conclusion was reached that the area endured floods of unimaginable magnitude that accompanied the melting of the ice age ice. The lower part of the Connecticut River indicated that the flow at one point was 200 feet above the present high-water mark: this is a staggering amount of drainage occurring. This vast flood melt was probably occurring in the Mississippi and the drain areas of Lake Agassiz at the same time. These unexpected findings prompted a study of the delta of Bear River supplied by a still existing glacier that drains into the Portland Canal on the Alaska, British Columbia border. It was done as a sort of double check on the low ages indicated by the other sites. Three accurate surveys had already existed of this delta from 1909, 1927, and 1934, so a fairly accurate dating of the glaciers age via sedimentation was in the offing. Unfortunately for old world promoters, the date of the delta was established as being only 3600 years old. Meaning the ice age glacier that feeds the Bear River only started doing so around 1650 B.C.

ICE AGE IN RELATION TO ARCHAEOLOGICAL EVIDENCE

Human remains were found on the Atlantic coast of Florida, intimately associated with animals that went extinct or disappeared from North America during the period of the Ice Age, such as saber-toothed tigers and camels. And not just human remains were found but they were in association with hand crafted bone implements, worked stone, along with pottery identifiable as the same type used by the Vero Indian tribes of Florida. So similar were they, that they were compared with known pottery of Indian origin found in Florida earth mounds and there were no significant differences noted. In fact they were deemed to be "identical", and thus were determined to be Vero Indian relics. Because the human evidence was of an advanced nature, an anthropologist could not accept them being associated with the ice age animals. However a palaeontologist (E.H. Sellards) also examined the site and he concluded the mineralization [that is fossilization] of the human bones and the animal bones was identical and confirmed that the human and animal remains were contemporaneous, and thus proved that man reached America at an early date, in contradiction of accepted archaeological theories.

This wasn't the only site like this found: in Melbourne Florida, 33 miles north of the other Florida site, more human remains in association with tons of extinct Ice Age animals were disinterred. A different qualified examiner (J.W. Gidley of the United States National Museum) scrutinized the bones of both humans and animals along with the human artefacts and determined they were from the same stratum, period, and had the same degree of fossilization. The artefacts included awls, pins and "projectile points" (presumably arrow heads) and they were the same workmanship as those of the early Vero Indian sites. The conclusions arrived at skirted about the obvious: it proved that the Vero and Melbourne people existed in North America as early as 2000 B.C. and possibly as late as "zero A.D.". (I've always wondered what the year "Zero" might be called.) But all these experts couldn't bring themselves to 'solve' the riddle of the close association of the human remains with the Ice age animals at the site. The only way out of the problem was to simply admit that these animals lived during this period in time and that previous dating attributed to the ice age animals was incorrect. The only conclusion possible based on the evidence was that they lived to a later period than was formerly assumed, and that the Ice Age was a more recent phenomenon than formerly promoted or believed.

Sometimes glacial lakes have no outlets and they can be dated in similar ways. For example, there are Lake Abert and Lake Summer in Oregon: and the saline content of these two lakes based, on a series of measurements, determined that the post glacial lakes are no more than 4,000 years old. I might add there's a reason they could even be younger; we've seen that the ocean waves crashing over the mountains in a cataclysmic event, which could have filled these lakes at some point, and could increase the salinity and make the lake appear older if such an incident was not accounted for, which these tests and the author did not consider. Owens Lake in California also with no outlet was shown to be 4200 or 3500 years old, depending on chlorine or sodium content respectively. Again there was no consideration to tidal waves making the lake appear older as well, and no accounting for freshening of the lake by torrential rains was considered in the dating of the lake either: they were dated based on a closed system analysis.

Lakes Lahontan, Pyramid and Winnemucca in Nevada, all part of the same glacial build-up of the area, at one point were shown to be only 3881 or 2447 years old depending on chlorine or sodium build-up since the glacial maximum. It's worth noting that the lake deposits contained evidence of human habitation, as well as ice age mammals such as horses, elephants, camels and some now extinct animals such as Felix atrox, all of which could not be older than the lake. Analyst J. Claude Jones concluded that extinct animals lived in America into historical times.

American Indian traditions speak of a time of the elephants, and archaeology has proven Indians hunted elephants. (Book 53 pg 187) If that is the case, is it really a stretch to link the time they were with elephants to also infer that they were there during the same time as the other extinct species such as saber-toothed tigers from the same period? Further tests of these lakes since those results have never given the age of the lakes as greater than 3000 years, again placing all the ice ages and the mammals associated with the ice ages as all ending well within human history. (Reference for this section: Book 53 pgs 140-157)

Originally when the ice age premise got a foothold on geology, deducing it's time frame came from analyzing the physical evidence fairly, which led to the conclusion that the ice ages occurred during the same period that the civilization of Egypt, Babylon and western Turkistan had achieved a high degree of development. (Book 53 pg 189) Only geologists and evolutionist with incentive to make the world appear older and discredit creation science pushed up the supposed age of the ice ages to occurring a million years ago. It would seem the original estimated time frames for the ice age periods were correct all along.

LAND SHIFTS MAPPED

We've already seen that the near splitting of Africa in two and the formation of the Sahara Desert did not occur sometime in a mythical Pleistocene age 12,000 plus years ago, it had to have happened more recently, because records have survived mentioning the existence of a giant lake Triton and of its disappearance into the sea. On top of that, the memory of the events by the people living all along the fracture zone seal the fact that lake Triton emptied into the sea during civilized times. In addition, these occurrences had to have happened more recently for the reason that cave paintings exist in the midst of what is now the desert, back when it still supported forests and lakes, which by the way, a King Jamie map exists depicting Africa with this region as a lush area. Thus this vastly reduces the time frame for the events linked with the Pleistocene and even back to at least the Triassic era where things like, new mountains, pole shifts, reversed magnetic lines in magma, sinking of lands, new lands rising out of the ocean, mass extinctions of animals, continental shifts and of course continent inundating tsunamis, among other things associated with these time periods and firmly places them into historical time frames. Fact is all the geologic ages can be accounted for even back to the earliest Pre-Cambrian age from the results of the cataclysmic events on the earth, recorded by the ancient legends along with verbal and written histories. But we'll start simple and see that the ice ages were recorded during historical times too.

What few people realize is the ice ages were recorded in a completely unexpected way; areas that were covered with ice age glaciers were mapped while that period's ice was still on site and places that have had ice for a supposed 100,000 or 200,000 years were mapped accurately without any ice coverage at all.

The Oronteus Finaeus world map of 1532 (One source calls it the Cronteus Finaeus map of 1531) has Antarctica drawn on it larger than life though correctly, but rotated by 20 degrees. (**See image 8**)

Image 8:
Oronteus
Finaeus
Map of 1531

The Antarctic Circle and the 80th parallel were confused somewhere along the line, and this error was repeated on most of the period maps depicting Antarctica. Captain Cook using these ancient maps proved Antarctica didn't exist in the 1770's, because with Antarctica being drawn too large, all he found was floating ice where he thought there should have been land. If the maps were right he should have been about 700 miles inland, so he concluded Antarctica didn't exist. After his failure to find it, Antarctica was taken off all maps from that point forward until it was rediscovered again in 1818. So why was Antarctica depicted correctly on maps before 1818?

The weirdness gets stranger. The frozen continent, has supposedly been covered with ice for 10's of thousands of years, yet it is depicted with little or no ice coverage, with mountains drawn on it that have since proven to match up with seismic portraits. Meaning Antarctica had to have moved to this spot on the globe, either by continental shifting or global tumbling, shortly before it was mapped, but before it turned 20 degrees to its current orientation. In the South Pacific (south 57, 120-140 west) is the Eltanin fracture zone and it is a twist of 20 degrees, which means this twist occurred *after* the continent was mapped. So this twisting event would have caused massive flooding when it occurred, possibly causing the flood spoken of in the Epic of Gilgamesh and the flood of Egypt that scarred the pyramids and deposited ocean debris and salt in and around the pyramids, but more probably causing, or in conjunction with a later event.

But think about this, if Antarctica wasn't discovered until 1818, then maps that exist of this continent from before this time, accurate or not confront us right between 1`11111111112 the eyes (or as my cat just typed... 'between the 1's...not sure what she meant with the '2' there...), we have to ask the question: what the heck are maps of Antarctica doing, even existing in the 1500's!?

If the stunning maps of Antarctica that exist aren't enough, the Zeno map of 1380 is far too accurate for the known cartography of the period, and oddly as it sounds it is probably recopied from an even older ancient map. I've found this map exists in at least four states from different eras and it seems to get simpler with reduced grids and less skilled copying in each state. I've included three of them here. (**See image 9-11**)

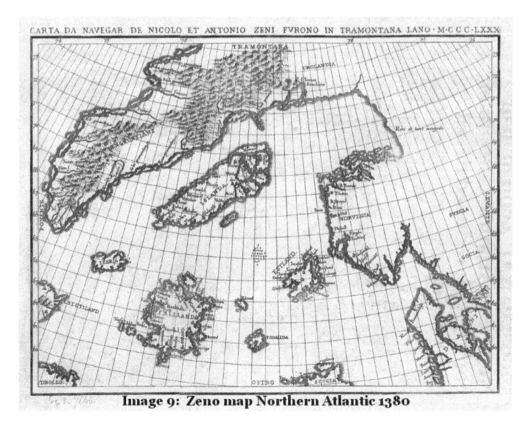

Image 9: Zeno map Northern Atlantic 1380

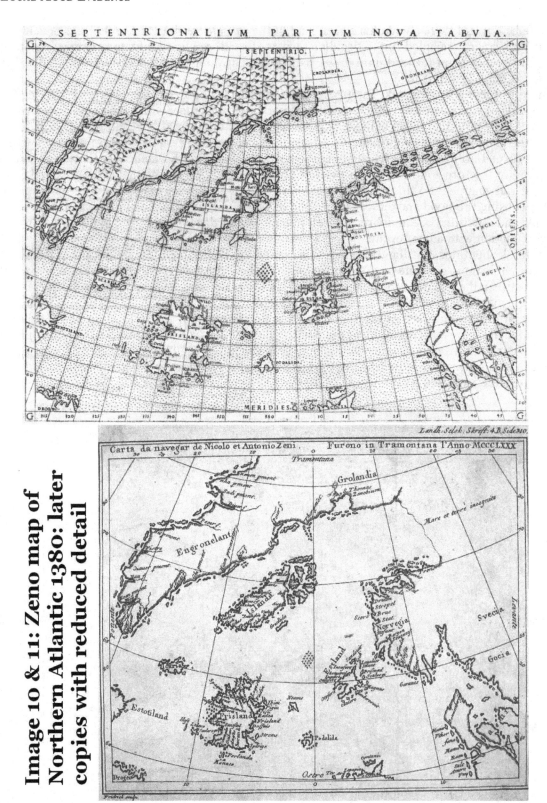

Image 10 & 11: Zeno map of Northern Atlantic 1380: later copies with reduced detail

Assuming Greenland is in the same position as it is today; the grid system on the map is not understood and thought to be distorted. The map however does indicate the earth was known to be a sphere long before Columbus proved this was the case. The map includes some very interesting features. The northern half of Norway and Sweden do not appear to have fully finished its North West portions, or even raised them from off the ocean floor or however they got there. But that's my unprofessional opinion based on the research in my books and my unprofessional eye looking at this map. The angle of the western coast might just be angled strange due to the unusual projection. On some versions of the Zeno map the top area of Norway / Sweden isn't even there but a channel with Guardus Insvia: (which seems to mean 'Guard Inspire'?) or "Mare et Terre Incognita" being written there, meaning 'Sea and land unknown'. One version also appears to show the northern half of what should be Norway / Sweden attached to Greenland by glaciers continuing out to sea as ice pack. But this may just be another way of depicting 'Sea and land unknown'. Though these glaciers did not exist in 1380, they are known to have existed about 10,000 years ago, or so conventional geological time frames would suggest. (Book 5 pg 56) This map also appears to indicate the ice pack of the northern circle is shifted away from the northern part of Greenland towards what is now the northernmost section of Russia, as if the North Pole were shifted from today's orientation several hundred miles. My thought was it might be about 1000 miles which could be depicting the same global polar shift as indicated by the India star maps. However this may not be correct as the northern area of Norway/Sweden not really depicted makes this deduction uncertain. However something is definitely odd about this map, that I've not seen anyone clue into or mention.

The southernmost tip of Greenland is sitting at 65 ½ degrees north. But in today's world the same tip is sitting at about 60 degrees north. That means this oddly accurate map has placed Greenland nearly 400 miles north of its current position. Iceland is drawn about half that distance north of its current position. This by the way would mesh somewhat with the fact that North America was covered with ice further south during the ice age. If North America along with Greenland were further north at one point; that is the pole was shifted south towards Canada's north, the ice coverage would have reached further south as indicated by the last ice age. (Obviously this map is a little confusing to me because on one hand the ice concentration appears to be shifted towards Russia suggesting a pole shift towards the same, whereas North America and Greenland appear to be shifted north by today's' standard suggesting Canada is further north, or the opposite to the location of the ice concentration.) If that isn't confusing enough, the reason we know the map is accurate, is that it depicts Greenland without ice on at least the southern 90% of the island, with many mountains showing, and certain inland parts of Greenland sporting place names. What's interesting is the northern most part of Greenland has never been glaciated*, so the map goes back to a time when there was no glaciated ice on the island! (* Book 53 pg 39) So if I had to guess the period this map was originally drawn, it would be sometimes between world ages (Which I can't guess) before the glaciations of North America set in, and before the world tipped making the north star change from somewhere in the great bear or Big dipper constellation to the current location in the little dipper.

Back to how do we know is accurate: the existence of the mountains shown on the Greenland part of the map have been verified to exists in these locations by probes done by the French Polar expedition of Paul-Emile Victor back in 1947-1949. (Book 11 pg. 90) This is staggering news too, because the ice on Greenland like Antarctica is also supposed to be 10's of thousands to 100's of thousands of years old too; and some insist Greenland's ice is as old as 200,000 years! Clearly this is not the case! Legends indicate lands were changing their profiles and if one place on earth has continents shifting, all places on the earth are probably experiencing shifting or readjustments as well. Thus the horrendous catastrophic times mentioned simultaneously in all the legends concerning the ends of ages which were so filled with cataclysmic events is supported by this map as well as the maps of Antarctica that exist. Needless to say the expert geologists won't refer you to these maps unless they want to ridicule them in some way, possibly because of the extra islands on the Zeno map...we'll get to those in a sec. But most spectacularly this means Greenland had to be virtually ice free during historic times, just as this map indicates. What's really interesting is this map of Greenland has a building or town on it named "S Tomas Zenobium" in what should be near the northern most part of the east part of the island. Has anyone looked for or found this ancient civilization? I've not been able to find any information on these places.

This map as mentioned indicates that Greenland and Iceland have shifted significantly south since this map was originally drawn: that or the world tipped. Since the grid system is not understood, this shift is probably the reason why. We can't blame it on poor cartography because it would seem impossible to place the southern tip of Greenland as much as 400 miles north of its true position. Why? Because although longitude was nearly impossible for medieval mapmakers to do accurately due to the fact the mathematical formulas were not invented yet to compute longitude; latitude was easy by just sighting the stars. So a 400 mile shift north south has to be evidence of a shift, and although it doesn't account for *all* of the shift noted in the India Sky map, it does account for part of it, but if my deduction is right, it appears to be in the opposite direction, so it might have something to do with a rotation or twist of the continental masses somehow being depicted here as well. We can conclude though, that this map appears to originally have been drawn sometime before the start of the current world age.

Iceland isn't depicted with the current features, suggesting some readjustment of that island took place when the other islands sunk and it moved south. With Iceland's penchant for continuous volcanic activity it's not surprising its features on this map don't match those of today. It would seem that when Greenland and Iceland were relocated southward this event also sunk several of the remaining islands that were once part of Atlantis.

Legends tell of Atlantis sinking and leaving many surviving islands behind and these are probably some of those islands which sunk sometime after this map was originally drawn. But since Atlantis had many islands under its dominion, this map, in theory could have been drawn before Atlantis actually sank; but it doesn't extend south far enough to have included the landmass of the fabled land on it, so this may only be conjecture. However...

It would seem this map is drawn before the Atlantic Ocean had reached its present width. It shows Iceland just 5 degrees west of Norway when today this distance has been extended to 19 degrees. What is shown on the Zeno map as a single island named Estland appears to have been split into two islands to become what is now the Faeroes and Zetland islands. And the island named Frisland shown separated 3 degrees from Scotland may now be just the submerged Rockall Bank 6 or 7 degrees to the west of Scotland. A map entitled "EVROPA recens deferipta á Guilielmo Blacuw" from 1644 **(See images 12)** places Frislanda a little further north than Icaria in the 1380 Zeno map. (Was Icaria renamed Frislanda, after Frislanda sunk?)

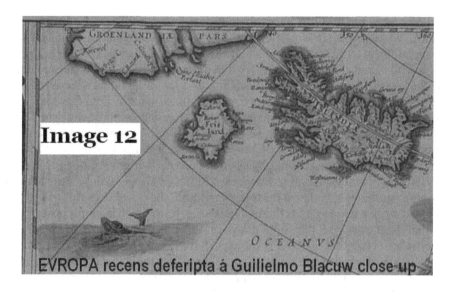

EVROPA recens deferipta á Guilielmo Blacuw close up

Another map from 1570 of this area of the globe has stacked the words or letters titled "SEP / TEN / TRI / ONA / LIVM RE / GIONVM / DESCRIP" (**See image 13**). One thing interesting on this map is it now shows two cities on Greenland, one of which is not on the Zeno map called "Alba" about 4° or 5° south of "St. Thome cenobium"(Zenobium) that is shown opposite an island which on the Zeno map appears to still be part of an ice covered mass. This map has Frisland on it as well below Islant Thule (Iceland) and it also has the island Drogeo fully delineated. It has Estoliland more fully drawn making clear it is not an island but part of "AMERICAE", probably the north east part of Labrador, suggesting it was closer to Greenland at some point as even The Zeno map places Estotiland just 2° directly south of Greenland. Did part of what is now Labrador extend out to below Greenland at one time only to have it submerge when Greenland was pushed further south and or the pole shifted north?

Image 13: North Atlantic 1570

This map no longer has Estland but has it divided into two islands now called Farre (Fearoes) and Scetlant Isl. (Zetland). These maps show islands in the Atlantic Ocean that are no longer there. Some have suggested these were put there to fill in space; which by the way is the most ridiculous theory you can imagine. Columbus had maps with islands on them that he tried to find to provision his boats from and almost starved looking for them. The last thing any cartographer is going to do is put fictional islands on maps.

Some will no doubt suggest I'm a complete idiot to suggest these maps indicate the land masses of the globe shifted after the locations depicted on these maps were drawn. They will say these were simply drawn by people who did not have the cartographical expertises we have today. Perhaps, but there are problems these maps present that ineptitude just doesn't account for. Not to mention the legends that indicate the world land masses changed in historical time. We can't automatically assume poor cartography or distortion on several ancient maps, because they have clues to suggest extreme antiquity during a time when the continents shifted and before islands disappeared into the depths, and new lands emerged from the ocean, exactly as the ancients described. Consider. As mentioned some have suggested these islands were drawn to fill in empty spots, but you don't make maps with islands that don't exist, so if they were drawn on there they had to have been there at some point in time. And it appears at least one of these island is known to have existed exactly where it was mapped.

It's very much worth noting that from the 1550's to the 1660's people from Greenland and Europe traded with the people of the well populated island of Frisland's*. Then in the late 17th century Frisland just disappeared from maps and apparently from the face of the waters. Indeed all of the islands west of Estland (or the Fearoes and Zetland) and at least 4 islands shown east of Great Britain, all just disappear from maps. (*. Though sources say this is true, I've not been able to independently find any historical records of trade with this island)

This disappearance of the well established Frisland (as well as all these other islands) should serve as a form of proof that a huge land can just disappear beneath the waves. Since this map accurately depicts Greenland and other details of this part of the globe, I'll safely assume the part of the map showing Frisland is accurate too. The map shows single degrees of longitude and latitude, so assuming these are accurate I estimate this island to have been around 35,000 square miles of real estate drastically losing value overnight. Countries that are smaller than Frisland: Austria, Belgium, Denmark, Ireland, Netherlands, Switzerland, Ceylon (now called Sri Lanka), and Panama, among others. Furthermore, it was about the same size as Portugal or Hungary. The loss of this huge island happened just around 250 years ago, but if this land had disappeared today, it would have made world headlines and gone down in history as one of the greatest losses in the age of the earth. Surely this has to add credibility to the legend of Atlantis which this island had to have been a part of at one time.

THE FINAL NAIL: ICE AGE AND ICE READJUSTMENT MAPPED.

The Andrea Benincasa map of 1508 appears to be showing "ice age" glaciations. This map is a portalano that is known to exist in at least three states, all of which are far too accurate for the period. It shows a glacier that spans from around the base of Denmark cutting it off from the Netherlands, to the northern coast of Germany (though Denmark is clear of ice) spanning eastward to the northern boundary of the Black Sea, then proceeding northeast from the sea of Azov, then arches back to the Baltic Sea. I've not bothered to show this map as it wouldn't reproduce well.

However, another portalano map that most convincingly depicts this area as glaciated, though delineated slightly differently from the Andrea Benincasa, is a portalano map showing incredibly accurate details of the Mediterranean, and is a striking example of a known ice age glacier that no longer exists being mapped. It's entitled "Joan · martines · en · mellina Añy 1567". (See Image 14)

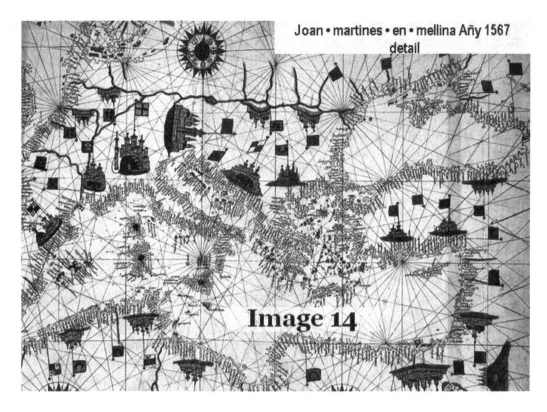

Joan • martines • en • mellina Añy 1567
detail

Image 14

It shows an obvious and massive glaciated demarcation line from around the southern boundary of a large inlet in Netherlands to the northern coast of Germany, though Denmark is clear of ice, spanning eastward to the northern boundary of the Black Sea, and then proceeding northeast from the Sea of Azov to the edge of the map.

It has been suggested that several maps depicting the Mediterranean islands show them much larger than today indicating they were drawn either before erosion whittled them down to size, or a different ocean level existed at the time they were drawn. (Book 5 pg 58) I'm not sure I buy the erosion explanation, though it could be a factor, but the ocean level change is plausible as many authors and geologists have conceded that the ocean levels have changed, possibly even in historic times. And indeed the legends mention oceans evaporating from the constant volcanic activity, so that explanation does fit and *do* place the change in ocean levels into historic times.

But if Greenland was accurately mapped showing the mountains with no ice isn't enough to convince you something is rotten in the science books you've been bombarded with, then maps of Antarctica free of ice existing in a few startling projections should be the final nail. Some ancient maps of Antarctica show it as two islands which the international geophysical year (and a half) in the late 1950's proved to be the case. And as mentioned other maps exist of Antarctica which show it not only drawn properly, if too big, but also with no ice with accurate topography such as mountains shown. Furthermore, Professor Charles Hapgood with his students determined that the Piri Reis map, also depicting Antarctica, was determined to be a compilation of several accurate local map slices spliced together at some point in the past. This indicated to him and experts that he consulted with, that at some point in the past an advanced society existed that had apparently mastered flight and which mapped Antarctica accurately while it was still free of ice. Furthermore there is enough physical evidence to indicate Antarctica was free of ice just 6,000 years ago or less, not hundreds of thousands of years ago. (Book 35 pg 45-47)

The evidence we've seen so far indicates the globe tumbled and shifted in recent times to have taken

Antarctica from a more temperate zone in the recent past to its present location, while North America was possibly part of the polar region covered in a massive ice pack or the victim of the fallout of the "nuclear winter" caused by all the cataclysmic weather brought about by the global catastrophes talked about by the ancient legends.

These maps and these conclusions exist and should not be ignored, but the evidence has been shoved under the carpet by people who want us to believe we have been advancing through evolution from monkeys and ignorant savage cave dwellers to our wonderful state we exist in today, when in fact the opposite is true. We were a society of advanced physiological and physical beings with scientific capabilities we still marvel at when peered at through the centuries.

We have yet to rediscover the secrets of their technology which, through many cataclysms in the past, have been deteriorating the evidence, both physical and recorded, due to environmental and social degradations. But this deterioration is also slowly eating away at our genetic viability, physical and mental attributes and our environmental habitats. Meanwhile the knowledge of the technology that slipped from our understanding over the centuries is hardly grasped by a few 'maverick crackpots' that insist the ancients had vast technological knowledge which our archaeologists refuse to accept or believe. Some would like to escape the obvious by saying the maps and the buildings around the globe that are more advanced than we can build today, but were built by spacemen or the gods and not by us miserable monkeys who would someday become what we are today by the help of these same gods or spacemen. We shall see the spacemen in fact are us, in a former state.

Well if you were paying attention you saw the name "Atlantis" written here a few times. What's worse I said Atlantis like it was a real place. Yup, I've gone and done it...and even mentioned sunken islands in relation to Atlantis. So now as far as archaeology is concerned, I'm just a stew-pid fringe maverick crackpot. Maybe I am, maybe I'm not, so let's have it out and see if Atlantis is fictional or real, and see if some of the stories about Atlantis relate to any flood legends.

DARK AGES

Not all the confusion of legends and historical catastrophism happened before the age of Plato or Before Christ. There appears to have been about a millennium of calm when there suddenly appears to have been some dramatic goings on during the years 536-545 AD, as the trees from this era were highly affected from some factor which appears to be the cause of the Dark Ages. (Atlantis Rising #99) Other correlated events around the planet such as a "John of Asia" (554 AD) describing "the world shaking like a tree before a wind for 10 days" indicate this period that apparently initiated the Dark Ages lasted about 20 years. If this span of about 20 years of comparatively mild worldwide catastrophic activity from a relatively recent period between 535 and 554 AD could plunge the world into the dark ages, then we can see how the events spoken of before Christ could seem so incomprehensible, unintelligible, and mythical to historians and archaeologists. Indeed the historical records from the period of Dark ages are often steeped in allegory and larger than life events. With that in mind, let's delve into what conventionally geology and archaeology would have us believe is sheer fiction....the existence of Atlantis.

Chapter 6

Atlantis linked to flood legends

Though many have heard of Atlantis, and it is written about in a smattering of ancient documents; mainstream archaeologists, geologists, evolutionists and anthropologists, and who knows else, refuse to accept the possibility that Atlantis ever existed, except in the overactive imaginations of ancient story tellers. Indeed for centuries scholars regarded Plato's description of Atlantis as fictional literature, even though "...its terse informative prose contrasts starkly with the persuasive rhetoric of his philosophical works" (Book 23 pg 82) Plato suddenly switches gears from "aery disquisitions" to "recount factual history with a wealth of detail worthy of Herodotus." Yet scholars simply won't buy it. Anyone even remotely appearing to believe in Atlantis is put into the same category as people believing in tooth fairies, goblins, Easter bunnies, demons, and ancient spacemen and even spirits or God, and are classed as nutcases from the lunatic fringe or childish ignorant simpletons. But one has to wonder why the established resistance to the former existence of Atlantis exists at all, because one 19th century scholar who *did* take the existence of Atlantis seriously, Egerton Sykes, noted that by that time there were already over 150 classical references to Atlantis known! (Book 23 pg 84 referring to *Atlantis* by Donnelly) We'll get to some of them soon enough. Think of it, 150 ancient references to Atlantis, and not JUST Plato's, yet standard archaeology and geology refuse to accept its former existence. Why; are they hydrophobic?

Standard geological history does not want to concede the prior existence of Atlantis. Why...? Because it would mean an apparently vast and influential civilization on a continent that some suggest was as large as Greenland or even as big as Australia, could just vanished underwater due to geological upheavals during the recorded history of mankind. This is too unsettling to many. If this is the case it would mean these same geological disasters happened as they are spoken of in ancient legends all around the globe in the same time frame, and these legends are too extreme for current geological history to accept either. You've read some of them...they can be a little disconcerting. Professor Marcel Homet an authority on ancient man, said something worth repeating, though his comment is regarding Roman swords found in Peru, his comments is equally justifiably used in relation to evidence found proving Atlantis, so I use it here. [These finds] "should have had a sensational effect, and yet they remain unnoticed in the haze of everyday life and the prejudice of fixed opinions. So they wait, forgotten and covered with dust in the corners of museums, as patiently as they waited when they were still buried. They will continue to do so until, one day they are exhibited as illuminating pieces of evidence." (Book 21 pg 250) When one considers this find concerning Roman swords found in Peru, you can see putting his quote here is justified.

A seasoned, but anonymous diver (to protect his find from other divers), found some pottery and ceramic figurines buried beside an underwater building, with an identical floor plan to a building in Yucatán, which was just one of 14 buildings found in this area, off Andros Island. He took photographs of the pottery and sent copies to many archaeology experts around the world for two years to see if anyone could identify them, as he couldn't even guess what civilization made them. None of the people he sent them to had seen similar pots. Furthermore no one would even risk categorizing them for fear of ridicule from other experts. (Book 8 pg 71-73)

Hopefully I can arrange the evidence for Atlantis in such a way as to appear that its former existence is obvious to an unbiased reader. By and large most legends and myths are ignored as stories of a less evolved civilization told by simple minded primitive societies to try and explain the world around them. Thus alternative incongruent theories are substituted for what the legends account for. For example we are told the Eskimos migrated maybe 12,000 years ago from Asia on what was once a land bridge between Russia and Alaska and they ignore how the Eskimo's say they got there. Eskimos speak of the first men, who were much bigger, and could fly in their magic houses, (book 56 pg. 231) and Eskimos say they were brought to the north in "great iron birds!" (Book 11 pg 111) Well such 'fairy tales' and myths just won't cut it with anthropologists, so these apparently childish myths are ignored and replaced by more acceptable dogma that says these primitive people migrated back when the bridge was supposedly still above water. That's a much more comforting thought to these bastions of education because it doesn't suggest man is declining from an advanced civilization...can't have that...that makes us look inferior to our ancestors and suggests that the theory ...er "science" of evolution and some people's mentor, Darwin, was wrong.

Well if you haven't thrown away this book in disgust, good for you for being willing to consider evidence that might cause you to alter opinions you may have held dear for years. If scientific research was *really* willing to overturn pet theories based on actual evidence, there really would be a need for students to buy new textbooks every year.

Some who have dared to entertain the possibility of Atlantis' existence as having been a real place that sank because of some cataclysm, often tend to place the timing of the occurrence around 12,000 years ago when the event apparently matches up with Plato's -9000 year date for the calamity, and the era when glaciers formed, because one event would initiate the other. People seem to put the time frame for the existence of Atlantis way back in time because it sooths our fearful natures with a comforting belief that these upheavals were in the long distant past and our planet is a nice safe place to live now. Never mind that it doesn't match up with historical period of Atlantis' existence in a much more recent time frame. But since you're still reading maybe I can have you consider a slightly more uncomfortable possibility.

Though J.W. Spencer, barely makes reference to Atlantis in his book *Limbo of the Lost*, his evaluation of Atlantean history illustrates the point where he makes a common mistake often made by those who are willing to acknowledge Atlantis' former existence, by attributing the world flood as the cause of Atlantis' demise or more specifically, it is assumed that the story of the flood only refers to Atlantis.

Brad Steiger also notes "Many Atlantean theorists see the universal flood story as being directly related to Atlantis's sinking beneath the sea." (Book 35 pg 15) Case in point: "Antediluvian history means the history of Atlantis" (Book 22 Pg 140)

"Suddenly an upheaval of nature overwhelmed the country by an onrushing sea, causing the entire island-continent to sink beneath the waves. This is supposed to be the origin of the Flood story, which is curiously and inexplicably universal" (book 26 pg 126) Indeed if this were the origin of the universal remembrance of a world flood it would be 'curiously inexplicable' indeed. Was Atlantis supposed to be the only antediluvian civilization in the world before the flood? If so, why do none of the other preflood civilizations filter into our memories or histories? All the other legends of the universal flood just have scant traces of preflood life. Yet mention Atlantis and a wealth of information of life in Atlantis exists, what's going on here? It's because Atlantis came into being and existed *after* the universal flood. It was later floods and upheavals that destroyed it while other civilizations were spared and lived on to remember them, and tell to their story.

Though many flood legends are tied to and geologically associated with the destruction of Atlantis, the universal flood is *not* one of them. It is only the assumption that all flood legends are equal, and the linking of some local flood legends with the sinking of Atlantis, that the association of the universal flood legends is linked with the destruction of Atlantis.

We'll see that Atlantis not only existed, it is actually tied to a specific era in time, and intimately linked to history. But first we need to get our feet wet. Once we see a historical and geological trend we should be able to make the leap to the middle of the Atlantic.

WASHED OUT SAND CASTLES CONSIDERED ACCEPTABLE: OUR FEET GET WET.

Atlantis isn't the only place that has sunk beneath the waters due to great upheavals. There are several ancient civilizations that have been submerged over time. The point of searching out these other sunken lands here is to show a trend, or part of a bigger picture.

The Temple of Serapis at Pozzuoli on the Adriatic Sea's Gulf of Venice (46°N 13°E) had to have been built when the site was above water as is the case with the site now. But at one time it was actually below sea level by at least 20 feet as evidence of boring clams which can be seen at 15 to 20 feet above the present sea level in the vicinity. Naturally the date for the submersion is placed way back in time around 12-19,000 years ago, even though it's obviously a site built by an advanced civilization on a par with ancient Egypt. Though the site is around 46°N, it's deduced that it was at one time at 40°N due to the earth doing a 'roll around', assumed to be caused by an eccentric rotating mass of ice at the North Pole. (Book 35 pg 16: Brad Steiger, quoting an article by Hugh Auchincloss Brown from Jan 1969 issue of Fate Magazine) Well whether or not orthodox geology accepts the relocation of the place from 40°N to 46°N for reasons said, it's hard to escape the evidence of the sinking and rising of the place that occurred during civilized times because of those miserable clams.

Right in front of Marseille (5°E, 43°N) underwater there is a series of mine shafts and smelting facilities that no one seems to know any history about. The period for the site is presumed to date back to "cave man" periods. (Book 6 pg. 220) Smelting facilities linked to cave man? Yeah sure! I guess it *must* be prehistoric, dating back to when cave men were still attaching their stone arrow heads to forged irons shafts. Ahh... these archaeologists...what a bunch of cut-ups.

A diving archaeologist, (which may be a contradiction of terms in some archaeologist's dictionaries) named Jim Thorne diving **off the Aegean Sea island of Melos** (Milos?) found that when he stood on the bottom, that it in fact wasn't the bottom, but the top of an ancient Acropolis and from the center of it roads led out farther down into the blackness. Even Jacques Cousteau found a road on the bottom of the Mediterranean Sea which he followed until his air ran low. (location not noted) No rainbow or sunken city was found, but maybe if someone else follows it who knows...if it's ever found again.

While climbing the highest mountain and swimming the deepest sea, in search of the missing comforting arms of Venus de Milo, (the rest of her wasn't good enough for him), an archaeologist at a depth of 400 feet, (OK, not quite the deepest sea), found the ruins of a city which had roads extending outward to even deeper depths...can I say that? Deeper depths? (Book 64 pg 157)

Off the **east coast of India near Madras** were found the remains of a sunken city. (N°13, E°81) (Book 64 pg 156)

BAIAE (40°42'N, 1°10'E)

This is a sunken piece of Roman real-estate on the West side of Italy, a little west Naples in the gulf of Pozzuoli. It is a sunken town or perhaps neighbourhood as I saw no buildings in the pictures of this place. It had beautiful and masterfully carved statues, and inlaid tile walks. Many of the statues have been overgrown with sea stuff, but nothing a few toothbrushes, and a little Vim couldn't help clean up to make these statues as good as new. One or two of the statues are still immaculate and truly on a par with Michelangelo.

NEAPOLIS

Not much I could see in the water here, but it is another Roman settlement that was found off the coast of Tunisia in the southern Mediterranean.

THE CITY OF YS (APROX 49°N, 5°W)

There is a legend about the city of Ys somewhere fairly close to the coast of Brittany, the extreme western part of France, which existed as much as 2000 years before the account of its demise. Whether or not the legend of this particular city is true, there were known to be settlements off the coast of France which have been covered by the sea. The city of Ys was something of a technological marvel built up to withstand the encroachment of the sea as the sea level rose over time closing in on the city. Thus the city was surrounded by a wall already built up by the time king Gradlon began his reign. To keep the city from the sea there was a gate which was only opened by a key to let ships in at low tide. The king's held the key for safekeeping to prevent the city from being flooded. Legends differ as to the details that caused the gate to be opened at high tide, but apparently the key was in the hands of Dahut the daughter of the king who opened the gate by mistake flooding the city. I'm not sure this really would have destroyed the city, as you could just drain the city when the tide went out again.

Once during an extremely low tide, (1950's?) there could be seen off the coast of Brittany what appeared to be piles of rocks that looked like part of a construction, but they were covered up by the incoming ocean before anyone could reach them for a closer look. Was it the ruins of Ys? (Book 64 pg 156, plus internet)

DOGGERLAND: MEGA OR MIRACLE TSUNAMI. (4°E, 56°N)

Mastodon and human bones, along with "prehistoric" weapons have been found on the bottom of the North Sea. (Book 7 pg 165, pg 197) I'm not aware of any lost islands in this area, but it doesn't mean it's not possible or that I've missed them. At least one ancient map might indicate an island or two in the vicinity but the accuracy and resolution of the map is far from definitive. The entire North Sea is quite shallow so perhaps at some point it was temporarily dry ground during volcanic evaporation. It's also known that the British Isles were washed over by massive waves that reached as far as France and probably Denmark. Perhaps some of these artifacts and remains were carried away in the waves to end up on the ocean bottom.

But after a little digging I did find there is some sort of history linked to this location, and I *did* miss something in my initial research. It's conceded that there was probably at one time, a land bridge connecting eastern England to areas on the west coast of Denmark called Doggerland. This area is thought to have been low lying land consisting of beaches, marshes and mudflats with great fishing, fowling and hunting, along with a local human population. It is hypothesised that this land submerged due to a mega "70 foot" tsunami that is supposedly known to have occurred in this general area caused by an underwater landslide off the coast of Norway around 6100 B.C. If it was '6100 years ago how do they know it was 70 feet high? This Tsunami left significant 2 foot deposits on the Shetland Islands (just north of Scotland, and Scotland itself along with Bergen Island and what was Doggerland supposedly submitted to the tidal wave. Another theory of the disappearance of Doggerland is after the glacial ice covering in this area melted, "Isostatic adjustment" tilted the land.

I gather then, that with this Isostatic adjustment theory, the weight of the ice lost from the land would rebound the land upward, but the melted glacial ice raised the water levels submerged it. So in this theory, then Doggerland could never have existed as a place of habitation, because it was first covered by the Ice, making it uninhabitable, then submerged by the melted ice making it... not land but submerged. HUH? So when was it ever land in this theory?

I'm not sure I buy this as the cause of the 70 foot tsunami explanation leaving 2 foot deposits either. If part of the Bonin Trench could rise 6000 feet in May 1973, that's over a MILE and no Tsunamis was caused by this sudden uplift, how could an underwater slide submerge Doggerland and bury half of Scotland and the Shetlands? Admittedly if caused by a large earthquake it could of course cause a tsunami, but one big enough to wipe out a land bridge? I usually connect subsidence with the disappearance of land, not destruction by waves. But subsidence suggests cataclysmic action....no good, can't have that.

Another hypothesis as to the cause of disappearance of Doggerland is that when Lake Agassiz (in Canada: we chatted about it earlier) burst, it flowed into the sea and rose water levels around the earth and submerged Doggerland. Seriously!? People make up ridiculous theories and hope we'll swallow them? Let's look at how ridiculous this theory is. A large lake, let's generously say is maybe 125,000 square miles (I calculate Manitoba is about 254,000 square miles, so it's about half the size of one measly little province). Now, this admittedly large lake, is what...going to raise the water levels around the world enough to submerge Doggerland? (You can place the square mileage of the oceans of the world here--à(....... And see how many times the area in square miles of this lake Agassiz goes into it), because I'm not figuring out this ridiculous equation) How deep does the theorist think Lake Agissiz was; 50 miles? Not even that would sink your kid's toy boat on the shores of Sidney Spit! (Come to Vancouver Island and find out where this neat place is) Not convinced? Look at a world map; compare how much ocean there is to how big a lake would be half the size of Manitoba and imagine it spread out, every last drop of it onto the oceans of the world. How much do you think it would raise world oceans? The amount of margarine you put on your toast is deeper than this! OK Ok Ok, so some of you use butter, so what... I can't afford butter, I'm on income assistance, but if you are one of those well-to-do folks that uses the stuff on your toast, or if you can't use margarine because it has too much of this or that ingredient in it which is not healthy for you, just substitute butter here for margarine...but I bet you don't use as much butter as I use margarine... especially with Peanut butter...Hmmmm yum.

Where was I...

Oddly enough "Doggerland", as we'll see, may have a connection with Atlantis. Could these theories have been invented to obscure an Atlantis connection? By the way massive Woolly mammoth skulls with huge black tusks have been found in this general area. So obviously "Doggerland" wasn't just a sand bar.

I can tell you categorically that the tsunami that buried Doggerland was no measly 70 foot midget caused by some puny underwater landslide off the coast of Norway; this did not and could not cause the evidence that a Tsunami of biblical proportions left on Scotland and the Shetlands. The evidence is vastly understated in the theories presented that buried Scotland, the Shetlands and submerged Doggerland in this supposed 2 feet of material. Once again evidence of cataclysm in the past has been soft peddled by uniformitarianists. How so?

Back in the late 1830's Hugh Miller did a special investigation and study of the red sandstone in Scotland, a study which soon spread to the surrounding areas when he discovered something disturbing. He found that over an expanse of about ten thousand square miles [of land surface or about 45,000 square miles in total area affected] which included the northern half of Scotland, the Orkney Islands and beyond (which would include the Shetlands: the Hebrides not mentioned) had vast deposits or "stratum" of water-rolled pebbles of every description such as "porphyries of vitreous fracture that cut glass as readily as flint" to quartz which were all ground down "into bullet-like forms" and 'of almost every variety of ancient rock' covering this entire region to a depth of "fifteens stories' height in thickness". The action that created these deposits was instant and sudden as can be determined by the fossilized fish found in contorted poses buried alive so rapidly soft parts were undecayed and sign of skin colour remained. He wondered "...what could suddenly destroy... ten thousand square miles at once with instantaneous suddenness" (Book 53 pg. 17-20) On average the height of each floor of a building is about nine or ten feet. This means the deposits left by the tsunami were at least 135 feet deep! Or as Miller alternately stated "...varying in depth from a hundred feet to a hundred yards (300 feet). Do the math: do you think a little itty bitty 70 foot wave could leave deposits four times its own height onto land in an area 10,000 square miles, PLUS on the Orkneys and the Shetlands: an overall area 45,000 square miles or more? HECK NO! Don't forget when we started out, the British Isles were washed over by massive waves that reached as far as France and probably Denmark. Thus the total area was exceedingly greater than my conservative 45,000 square miles estimate. But for fun let's do the math. If a 70 foot wave could deposit 2 feet of material, how high would a the wave have to be to deposit a minimum of 100 feet of material, that is fifty times the 2 foot deposits stipulated by the uniformitarians lame theories mentioned above? 50 x 70 feet = a 3500 foot wave was needed to deposit the minimum 100 foot depth of pebbles covering this vast area; and don't forget some areas were covered by as much as 300 feet of deposits. Does such a huge wave sound unbelievable? It sounds small to me, because many legends talk about waves that overtopped the mountains. 3500 feet was probably one of the small ones; bigger ones hit North America.

THAT NEW LAND

In 1966 during an oceanographic research in the Milne-Edward Deep depression (part of the Peru-Chile Trench near Lima Peru: (12°S, 77°W) Dr. Robert Menzies discovered at the 6000 foot depth the remains of carved stone columns with a kind of writing on them. (Book 7 pg. 18, Book 35 pg. 16-17, Book 64 pg. 157) Naturally he assumes these would be many thousands of years older than the Incan ruins on the nearby coast of Callao in the port of Lima. Why this assumption? Simply because they are under over a mile of water therefore they must be much older. It's not comfortable thinking of these occurrences happening during historical civilized times. I contend they would be the same age as the ruins nearby and the same event turned both sites into ruins...as well as the sites that follow. You read earlier the very legend that would have included the submersion of this site which is the same one that caused the lifting of Tiahuanaco and the raising of the Andes themselves to their current elevation. I refresh your memory by quoting a bit from earlier on.

"Spanish historian (Avila & Molina) recorded traditions of the Indians of the new world. They were told that there was a time when the sun did not appear for 5 days, a cosmic collision of stars happened before a cataclysm, and people and animals tried to escape to mountain caves. "Scarcely had they reached there when the sea, breaking out of bounds following a terrifying shock, began to rise on the Pacific coast. But as the sea rose, filling valleys and the plains around, the Mountains of Ancasmarca (in Peru just north of Cuzco) rose too, like a ship on the waves. During the five days that the cataclysm lasted, the sun did not show its face and the earth remained in darkness." This rising or lifting the land "like a ship on the waves" would have been the entire Andes mountain range but witnessed from a single vantage point."

It would have been this event related in this legend that also sunk whatever civilization it was that this 6,000 foot deep carved columns belonged to.

You might be asking yourself, 'how could the same event sink one site 6000 feet underwater, and lift upwards another site a few miles away 2 miles above sea level'? As the continent of South America moved west, it bunched up the land near the western coast forcing the land upward, while at the same time any land on the actual coast got climbed on by the land as it moved westward, pushing the shore and any civilizations unlucky enough to be in the way underwater. It's entirely probable. That were you to dig down through 3 miles of dirt around Tiahuanaco, you would come to remnants of a buried civilization as the land would have steam-rolled over itself like a conveyer belt.

Not too far away there are more submerged ruins 95 feet underwater in Lake Titicaca. (16°S, 69°W) What's peculiar, is in the area there are "Massive" docks that have been cut out of solid stone. (Book 35 pg 17) The reason this is peculiar is because this site is around 13,500 feet above sea level.

Twelve miles away from Lake Titicaca, is the ancient city of Tiahuanaco full of disturbing archaeological ruins. Dating for the city is guesswork and ranges from 600-900 A.D. to 2,500 to 15,000, even 20,000 years ago because of the startling altitudes the city sits at. Even 250,000 years has been suggested as the age of the city in the nosebleed section of the Andes. On the stonework are images of Toxodon; an animal similar to a hippopotamus considered to be extinct for "millions of years". I might add that Sacsahuamàn is another ancient fortress city in the Andes, which sits at the 12,000 foot level, and Cuzco sits at 11,444 feet. These places were probably built and pushed upwards at the same time as Tiahuanaco and the Andes. They had to have originally have been built at a lower altitude, because people even at Cuzco get altitude sickness without special care just from being inactive from the thin air. Like Tiahuanaco, building this city would have been physically impossible, even with a slightly denser air at this altitude 5300 years ago when they were built during the age of the gods. Furthermore, no way enough crops grow at this altitude to support any kind of civilization. In addition virtually nothing edible grows and no game lives at this elevation, certainly not enough to have supported the presumed 100,000 people it is thought would have been needed to build the place. And something of a clincher is totally unexpected...there are tales that no white women has ever given birth at this altitude; presumably similar difficulties for other races? (Book 8 pg 25) No births? No population.

On top of that, Tiahuanaco appears to have been a port city originally too, because it has stone docks, wharfs and a breakwater indicating it was a port city, which means it was at lea level at one time after it was built. Further evidence is found in a deep lake nearby which has ocean fauna, and saltwater ocean fossils are found on the land, in the mountains, and in Lake Titicaca. Additionally the remains of some ocean life are found on what would be below water level on the 'docks'. This huge city had to have been built before it rose to its present altitude of 13,500 feet because it is so obviously intended for ocean traffic. The mountains are dated to 30,000 years old but even this generously young date defies the evidence of the city situated in the same mountains, which was obviously built by a similar or identical civilization as other megalithic building sites around the globe before the land and surrounding peaks reached this elevation. The existence of these civilizations can also be dated and narrowed down to existing around 3300BC. The city is not an Incan one because when the Inca's found it, apparently around 200 A.D., it was deserted. This city, as we'll soon see, may in fact have an Apache link. Some of the stones were linked together with others by huge silver bolts, weighing between a half ton and 3 tons each. These silver bolts were inserted into extremely smooth holes, and as soon as they were discovered were plundered by visitors from the old world. Egyptian building stones and cornices have also been found with extremely smooth holes in them indicating a similar or identical technology was used in both locations during the same period. Even though tons of stone was pilfered from this site for construction in Laz Paz, it is clear the city was never finished but construction suddenly stopped.(book 1 pg 40, book 6 pg 161,192, Book 7 161, 220, book 8 pg 44ish, 55, book 29 pg 105-106,book 35 pg 76-79, Book 64 pg 104)

UNDERWATER RUINS

In the Gulf of Mexico near Cozumel there are underwater buildings (N°21, W°87) (Book 64 pg 156)

Off the Continental shelf near the Bahamas, a French submersible named Archimède kept bumping against stone steps at a depth of 1,400 feet. (Book 6 pg 174) Presumably these steps were located off the shallower side of the Bahamas, where over 50 archaeological sites, packed with the remains of stone buildings have been found. These submerged structures are way beyond the building capabilities of the cannibal Carib Indians that were found on the nearby island by the first explorers. (Book 6 Pg 175)

Roads continue out to sea from the shores and beyond from Yucatan and Belize (Book 6 pg 175), and I've seen on Google earth what look like very long maybe 100 mile long roads underwater off the east coast of Cuba, (74°W, 21°N) but last time I checked they disappeared. Air brushed out?

Though not underwater ruins per se, there was found in a cave system of Yucatan some statues very different from Mayan and more reminiscent of ancient Middle East. But even more striking was …"Evidence of water marks within the caves, now several hundred feet above sea level, had been under water after the strange stone figures were carved." This means these statues, obviously carved by man, were submerged in a cataclysm, then in a subsequent cataclysm resurfaced. (Book 37 page 151-152)

LAKE ATITLAN – SAMBAJ & CHIUTINAMIT (92°W, 14°30"N)

This lake in Central America in the Sierra Madre Mountains in southwestern Guatemala feeds two nearby rivers and is shaped by deep surrounding escarpments in a basin of volcanic origin. This formation is said to have been formed by an eruption 84,000 years ago. (If lava erupted in 1801 was uranium dated at over 100 million years, you know what I think about this "84,000 years ago" nonsense) Around the lake are many villages where Mayan culture is still customary and traditional clothing is used. I guess it would be like walking back in time.

More than a few Mayan archaeological sites have been found at the lake, and one, Sambaj, was found to be about 55 feet underwater, and appears to be from the pre-classic period or earlier. Found there are several groups of buildings, and one large group of greater sized buildings is assumed to be a city hub.

DWARKA: ATLANTIS OF THE EAST. (68°E, 22°20"N)

In their determination to prove the existence of Dwarka, Amish Shah Joshua and Aderhold Drew Martinez in their documentary movie: *Atlantis of the East*, pursued information about this lost city described in the Mahabharata in which it is said that it was built by Krishna and succumbed to the sea around 3067 B.C. This city Dwarka was a city twice the size of Manhattan / New York and was proven to exist off of the current city by the same name, lending credibility to the ancient text. With much digging and the runaround by people involved in the original archaeological work, they found out that evidence discovered in it showed advanced ancient technology indicating the ancient's texts that said they had advanced technology is true. However what this evidence is was never stated. In fact excavations in the city were suddenly stopped by the government with no explanations, and all documentation has been made inaccessible. Not only that, even though all along the shores are found ancient relics, the documentary indicated further access to the underwater site is denied anyone, and not even casual divers are allowed to dive in the area. What did they find!? Has the world's archaeological dogma's of no advanced technology existing in ancient times now infected India as well? If so, did you know that Indian scholars have long been studying the ancient Indian texts to see if they can decipher the technology they spoke of about their "vimana's, or flying machines, they used to conquer space? Did you also know that a skeleton was found in India which was 50 times more radioactive then the surrounding soil? And did you know that in Mohenjo-daro India and Harappa Pakistan, there were found a number of skeletons at street level which seemed, by their scattered positions, that the people were attempting to escape something and all the skeletons were highly radioactive? Nothing is known about these cities except they ended their existence abruptly. (Book 7 pg 228-230, book 6 pg 216, book 22 pg 160)

If these startling finds *are* known about, just what *did* they find in the underwater Dwarka that caused them to suddenly slam the door shut on further underwater archaeology and furthermore forbid anyone else from diving in the area? Did they find something like a sponge diver found near a Greek island that killed him the next day? I repeat a little bit from my first book...

> In 1919 off the south end of a tiny uninhabited Greek Island a sponge fisher named Zalakhos came across a sponge that burned his hand because of the sand they grew in. His partner Gabriel went and got some of the sponges (I guess without touching them) and found a piece of iridescent metal described as neither metal nor glass. Apparently there are several jars of this stuff down there. Shortly after Zalakhos was feeling terrible and his body was burning up even with them pouring water on him to cool him, and he died that afternoon. Later that night they decided to bury him and found him glowing with a phosphorescent golden light...they decided to bury him at sea as soon as possible. Gabriel did not completely escape either. The hand that touched the 'metal' got bad, slowly swollen up and twisted. Doctors commented that it must have been in contact with something stronger than radium. Other divers have also died in this area.

Though I did find some pictures of this underwater Dwarka on line, one has to wonder; did they take important relics, and cover up and disguise what remained, then shut down further exploration? What does history say happened to Dwarka? There was a war and Krishna counteracted with an arrow like weapon that roared like thunder and shone like rays of the sun. Though it didn't say if the weapon caused the destruction and sinking of the city, Mahabharata history does say that Dwarka sank in one day and night.

HERACLEION OR THONIS (30°E, 31°30"N)

This was an ancient Egyptian city situated about 32 km northeast of Alexandria near the western outlet of the Nile, 2 ½ kilometres off the coast, which sank either during the 2nd or 3rd century A.D., or around the 8th century B.C. (depending on whose guess you read) apparently due to earthquakes that caused liquefaction of the silts it was built on. Not built on a rock but sand and great was the fall thereof. This city only has two known classical references to it and it appears to have fallen off the radar and so wasn't rediscovered until 1999 by accident under just 30 feet of water. No one was even looking for the place. The Greeks historians mentioned it once around 12th century B.C.

When the city was found, divers discovered that it sank along with 64 ships, as well as 700 anchors, gold and lots of amazing statues.

Though I don't know the origin of this explanation of the demise of Heracleion, as I only found two references to it on the internet because its discovery is pretty recent, I dare say that here again we see minimization of the cause of the disappearance of a sunken city. This would have had to have been an incredible earthquake to sink not only the city, but 64 vessels along with it! You see, vessels... are boats... and boats float...usually, so this city would have had to have sunk suddenly and fast to sink all these boats... er..."vessels". (And not "wessels" either, nuclear or otherwise)

If this happened in the 8th century B.C., could the demise of this city have been synchronized with the loss of the land bridge connection of Sicily to Italy and the demise of the animals slammed into the fissures at Palermo Sicily and the sinking of than mine and smelter off the coast of Marseille, and other catastrophic occurrences around the Mediterranean and possibly the globe?

PAVLOPETRI. (23°E, 36° 30"N)

An ancient submerged archaeological site determined to be Pavlopetri, was discovered while swimming from an island back to the southernmost part of the mainland of Greece, that being Laconia in Peloponnese. At first the ruins were thought to dated to around 1600–1100 B.C. but they were later determined to be much older, circa 2800 B.C. Around 1000 B.C. the region went through three large earthquakes which are believed to have caused the loss of this town causing it to sink, which is obviously impossible as this explanation would mean it sank 1800 years before the cause. But you get the picture; no one really knows how to date these places.

Technical stuff like computer 3D surveying and sonar mapping exposed at least 15 buildings sunken in 10 to 14 feet of water which includes a layout of the town plan. Found on the site was pottery and textiles, suggesting Pavlopetri was a trading harbor.

ATLIT YAM (35°E, 32°40"N)

Atlit-Yam may be the oldest evidence of an "agro-pastoral-marine" life arrangement ever found and it's off the coast of Israel. The site, under between 25 to 40 feet of the Mediterranean Sea in the Bay of Atlit, presumably near Atlit Israel, has been carbon-dated to around 6900 to 6300 B.C. (I remind you that carbon dating tends to overestimate dates, exponentially as things get older and closer to the time of the flood. Also underwater items do not get exposed to additional radioactive C14 in the atmosphere which would likely make the place appear older still by this dating method) It's assumed the site belongs to a "Pre-Pottery Neolithic B" period.

This former inhabited piece of now drastically devalued piece of unreal estate, covers an area of about 10 acres. Divers have unearthed rectangular houses, fireplaces, a stone semicircle, as well as a well, and a burial site.

In Russia there is a sunken city in the **Bay of Baku**. Masonry blocks with carved animals are found there. (40°N, 50°E) (Book 64 pg 156)

WRONG LOCATION

Yonaguni-Jima. Near the Ryukyu Islands. 120 Kilometres east of Taiwan, and 70 feet below the surface at approximately (123°E, 24°N) is a fabulous underwater sight known as the "Japanese Atlantis". At this location is what is called an underwater pyramid, but to me it looks more like it was at one time a quarry they cut massive squared blocks out of; though it looks like a quarried stone hill it's not really pyramid shaped. But whatever it is, the obviously squared edges and straight plains and walls clearly means it is an human formed site. Pictures of this place can be found online.

Around 1960 a tidal wave **ten miles south of Baku**, on the shores of the Caspian Sea exposed the remains of a city. Right away someone called it the remains of Poseidonus, AKA Atlantis. (Book 22 pg. 127) Source doesn't mention if it was explored or if its real identity was determined.

A diver named Beetle discovered some huge red and white stone blocks 27 feet below the surface of the **North Sea, just off Heligoland**. This would be south of, though in the same general area as "Doggerland". A pastor Jürgen Spanuth had no doubt this was Atlantis. (Book 22 pg. 127) No Comment... we'll get back to this place later.

A massive volcanic blast destroyed **Thera** around 1500 B.C. causing the island to have a crescent shape since then with the lost part of the island becoming part of the Aegean Sea. (Book 6 pg. 57-59, book 27 pg. 88) Some have suggested this is Atlantis, but it's only suggested to be the location by those who completely discount the belief that a vast island continent could sink in historic times. However it is possible that Thera's demise occurred at the same time as Atlantis because of the interconnectedness of the Earth's plate system, or what I've dubbed the 'Barking Dog' syndrome.

HELIKÉ

During Plato's lifetime the city of Heliké on the Saronic Gulf (37°, 30"N, 23° 30"E), fell into the sea with all the buildings and population so quickly that a dozen Spartan warships that were in the harbour also were pulled under the surface. Sounds just like Heracleion or Thonis that sunk along with its 64 ships.

NORTH OF VENEZUELA 100 MILE UNDERWATER ROAD

I could not find this sunken under water road, but I mention it to add to the pile of sunken places that had evidence of civilization associated with them.

NOTE THE TREND

The Atlantic Ocean is probably the most geologically active spot on the globe. It stands to reason that if some land happened to be situated on this massive fault zone it would be subjected to extreme disturbances. Of all these other sunken places I've referred to, few if any are situated on active fault lines, yet they sunk. If these places could sink, then it stands to reason a large land mass situated on an extremely active fault line would be staring down the barrel of a gun. It is entirely probable, that the events that caused the sinking of these other lands around the globe mentioned above, whether they happened at the same time, or spread out over centuries, would due to the nature of the "Barking Dog" syndrome, cause Atlantis, because of its placement on a huge active fault line, to have experienced all the quakes that sunk the other places. Indeed, through time islands in the Atlantic have, disappeared, reappeared then sunk shortly after when little of any consequence was happening elsewhere around the globe, almost like the Atlantic ridge was the first and sometimes the only dog to bark.

It is said the Tectonic plates that make up the Pacific Rim: Ring of Fire, is the most active and potentially dangerous tectonic area in the globe: Maybe. Though the universal flood legends have been demonstrated to be truly universal, most of the sunken sites that I was able to find out about were linked with known historical cataclysms that were caused from the later four world ages. These places are mostly east or west of the central Atlantic Ocean: that is in the Mediterranean Sea or the immediate vicinity, or on the opposite side in the Caribbean, Gulf of Mexico, or West Indies area. Furthermore as we shall see, there are many places in the Atlantic Ocean located on a very active fault line where traces of former land life have been found under various depths of water.

The sunken cities that *are* acknowledged to exist simply because archaeologists can't ignore the obvious, are as a rule, explained away in some bland dreamed up, long time-consuming, uniformitarian scenario which we see on the earth every day. Such lame explanations like, glacial ice melts filling the ocean, isostatic adjustment, or tsunamis that somehow drown all these cities could even be considered a conspiracy against catastrophism by scientists, of which would include geologists, evolutionists, archaeologists, and palaeontologists, and we could probably include astrophysicist, too. On top of that they never question how an ancient city could become buried under many feet of dirt and blandly insist that so many feet equals so many years of burial, never once questioning where the dirt came from. If their uniformitarianistic principals they hold to were in fact true, then the amount of water on the planet should either be constant or continually diminishing as it turns into vapour which in turn is expelled into space during periods of excess solar activity expanding the atmosphere and forcing it off our world. Never ever do they dare lean on cataclysmic explanations for sunken or buried cities, they insist they all submitted to the elements slowly over time.

Yet this is completely contrary to the historical records either directly or by association to the true cause of the destruction of all or most of these places. All the Mediterranean linked sunken cities such as Temple of Serapis, Heracleion, Atlit Yam, the offshore smelting facilities of Marseille, and Pavlopetri, have legitimate links to cataclysmic explanations as to the causes for their demise. We saw that the whole of the Mediterranean Sea was exposed to violent upheavals during historical times which destroyed the land bridge from Sicily to Italy. We saw that the loss of Lake Triton in Africa was recorded and began the destruction of the fertile African climate paving the way for the Sahara Desert to take over, an event that nearly split Africa in two. This event occurred so close to the Mediterranean Sea that it had to have a huge impact on the entire sea and surrounding area. Surly these results must qualify as a cataclysmic cause for the adjustments and changes of these places from civilizations where you can ride your chariots to, to places where you now have to dive to, to visit.

We saw a legend of a cataclysm that caused the sea and the land rising together which would explain the stone columns near the Peru-Chile Trench. Legends exist that talk about land submerging in Central America caused by cataclysmic action which would include the underwater buildings in the Gulf of Mexico we mentioned. Legends of the sinking of Mu, and or Lemuria could have some connection to the sinking of Yonaguni-Jima known as the "Japanese Atlantis". And Dwarka appears to have been destroyed in an ancient war which caused a cataclysmic subsidence. With the possible exception of the city of Y's, it seems every last city, sunken or buried, has a connection to historical cataclysms as the cause of their destruction. Yet in not one case do any of these 'experts' dare blame cataclysmic events outside the uniformitarian ideals as the cause of their demise. And then there's Doggerland. On the surface of it, it seems this place appears to be "prehistoric" or Neolithic, as no actual history appears to be known about this place, or is there? We'll get back to that...I promise.

Central to the point of all this talk of sunken cities, is my intent to show that not only have cataclysmic events been linked to the destruction of them; many of them are in turn linked directly with the demise of what is supposedly the mythical Atlantis. It's important not to forget that if Atlantis was real, and historically it was on the doorstep of the Mediterranean Sea, where a lot of chronicled seismic activity occurred, thus linking the two series of events closely geographically, a perfect scenario for the barking dog syndrome: the Mediterranean dogs barked after it heard Atlantis. Similarly, if the continents shifted and moved in historical times, this would also place Atlantis at some point in the past, considerably closer to the Caribbean where so many other sunken sites have been found. These too have also been shown to have cataclysmic events linked to their demise.

If then, legends and historical records say plainly that to the East and West of what is now the Mid-

Atlantic-Ridge the Caribbean (west), and the Mediterranean waters to the east, was subjected to catastrophic cataclysmic upheavals in recorded history, does it not stand to reason that something in between the two general areas, where all this cataclysmic action took place, would also be subjected to like or even greater upheavals?

And what would that be that lay between the Caribbean and the Mediterranean waters? The Mid Atlantic ridge, or formerly known as Atlantis! So the point is, If there is a sound historical background of cataclysmic happenings to left and right of Atlantis, could not this 'fabled' land situated right in the center of all this known historical seismic cataclysmic activity, also have been subjected to identical or even more intense seismic activity? Of course it could! Indeed submarine surveys have proven this very area to have been an extremely volatile area, and *far more* so than those areas to the east or west where all these historical locations are known about. If then this is the case, does it not stand to reason that any islands or land mass that might have been in this general area would have experience a similar fate? And what was the fate we spoke about with all of all those sunken cities? THEY SUNK!

I hope that made some sort of sense and was written at least moderately properly: I never was too good at French. So let this reality then lend credibility for what we are about to receive. Eat hearty and drink it in.

One thing that also needs to be made clear is that we've sampled just a few of the known ancient civilization centers that sank, got buried or were stumbled upon long after they were forgotten. And of course we don' know about the ones we don't know about. The Mediterranean Sea is literally surrounded by sunken civilizations around the rim, north, south and east. Furthermore it will be clear or evident that more civilization centers were lost and presumed destroyed in some catastrophic events in which they were either sunken or buried. The point is these lost civilization centers that we know about are quite literally the 'tip of the iceberg' in almost identical ratios to ice seen above water, to that invisible below the surface: because today, urban centers take up just 3% of the land, and it's a safe bet that urban centers in ancient history took up considerably smaller proportion of the entire land mass than this, maybe as little as one half of a percent or less. Cities such as we see today just didn't exist in the past as most people lived in homesteads, growing their own crops and making their own goods. Cities were often little more than forts for the people to go to in times of invasion or market places for the people's excess goods to sell or trade. There were of course places like the sunken Dwarka and the still above water city of Nineveh, which were vast civilization hubs, but these were probably rare exceptions. This means at least 33 to as much as 200 or more times the amount of land of the cities known to have sunk was also subjected to like forces and sunk, or was buried besides these known civilization hubs. So if an ancient city took up 10 square miles of real estate, then at least 330 square miles of land to as much as 5000 square miles of land for each city that sunk also submitted to the waves as well. And who knows how many cities were buried on the land by waves that carried flotsam and jetsam with them to obliterate and bury them; or were crushed and scattered by mountains that were shoved across vast stretches as the continents folded and were crumpled by the forces they were subjected to. Virtually all of North American civilization was obliterated from these forces: with a destructive force that was so great, that archaeologists today refuse to believe there was ever any established civilization on this continent.

So the bottom line is, whether all these obliterated cities were destroyed in an ongoing series of small local catastrophes, or were all destroyed in a series of global catastrophes, or were all crushed to powder in just one gigantic global catastrophic event, any one of these scenarios validates the concept of a sinking continent in the middle of the Atlantic ocean, that being Atlantis. So the sinking of a place like Atlantis in the middle of the ocean *is* geologically plausible.

ATLANTIS LINKED TO REAL HISTORY: EVIDENCE

People have either called Atlantis a prehistoric civilization or have tried to prove it never existed at all. A cataclysmic end to a continent buried under the sea goes against current accepted geology based on evolution and uniformitarianism. Consider what Archaeologist Dr. Valentine speaking of scientists of the anthropological and biological disciplines, stated: "despite overwhelming evidence to the contrary, they are still reluctant to relinquish the century old theories of Darwin and Lyell who flatly contended that only slow, gradual changes in evolution and geology were possible." "Thus was born the school of 'Uniformitarianism' in direct contrast to the more objective views of those earth scientists who have come to recognise the principals of periodic stress build-up in the planet's magnetic field, with consequent, swift environmental changes at the breaking point. The concept of a subcontinental island in mid Atlantic ('Atlantis') lost through catastrophic assault, is by no means alien to the latter philosophy." Based on geologic evidence Dr. Valentines states that there can be no reasonable doubt that a "...highly evolved, precataclysmic civilization did exist."(Book 35 pg. 209-10)

Plato states in his history of Atlantis that the 10 kings of Atlantis subjected or ruled over the whole island along with other Atlantic islands, and the Columns of Hercules (Strait of Gibraltar) to as far as Egypt on the African side and as far as Tyrrhenia of Italy on the European side of the Mediterranean Sea. They also had a great number of elephants. (Book 24 pg 87-88)

If there were so many elephants in Atlantis, maybe some remains of them could be found at the bottom of the Atlantic Ocean to verify this statement. In 1967 an issue of Science magazine reported a "...discovery of elephant teeth from the Atlantic Continental shelf between 200 and 300 miles off the Portuguese coast **at more than 40 different dredge site locations** from the depths of 360 feet. The teeth were recovered from submerged shorelines, peat deposits, sand banks caused by surface waves crashing against a beach, and depressions that formerly contained freshwater lagoons." By the way the article places the sinking of Atlantis coinciding with a series major natural catastrophes that happened at the same time, such as a huge eruption of the volcanic island Thera-Santorini in the Aegean sea and a "nuclear-like equivalent" simultaneously happening in New Zealand, which scholars have dated at 1628 B.C. (Atlantis Rising Magazine #71) We mentioned Thera earlier as one of the dogs that barked. Correct me if I'm wrong, but I've not heard of elephants being found swimming 300 miles from shore, so it stands to reason that elephant remains found here were not remnants of elephants that sunk.

The Aztecs insist they originated from a lost land called Aztlan in the eastern sea that had a great mountain on it. This confirms Plato's story that on Atlantis there was a huge plain surrounded by mountains that were celebrated for their size. The Mayans also say they came from a land that was in the eastern sea (Atlantic Ocean) that was called Atlan. When they arrived in central America they maintained the same political system of Atlan(tis), by continuing the tradition of ten kings, another confirmation of Plato's Atlantis narrative.

The Toltec's add another piece of the puzzle: they came from an island in the eastern sea called Tlapallan (Possibly the name of a key island of Atlantis series of islands) that was the home of the civilizing gods. This by the way is a major piece of the puzzle. We know who the civilizing gods were that came to central America to help the civilizations to become established and pulled people out of the mire of savagery and barbarian status: there was Quetzal-Cohuatl (Quetzalcoatl) for the Aztecs, The great white stranger Kukulcan for the Mayans, Gucumatz for the Quichés, Viracocha for the Peruvians, and Bochicha for the Columbians. (Book 24 Pg 90-91, Book 23 pg 142) This Toltec calling Tlapallan the home of the gods confirms Plato's reference to some of the other known gods of the island such as Atlas, Hercules, and Poseidon, which places the date of Atlantis' period of influence once again during the age of the gods. These gods of Atlantis are the same ones of Greek mythology that battled in a war in heaven against Zeus, linking them not just to the age of the gods, but the same gods around the world of which so many ancient legends refer to. This is not a fictional time period and even the Egyptians, ancient Indians and Sumerians note that there was such a time when the gods taught and ruled people around the world. It's a safe bet the Toltec's and the Aztecs weren't reading Plato to help them make up their history, so these confirmations add tremendous credibility to Plato's and others stories of the existence of Atlantis.

Plato mentions fresh water springs in Atlantis surrounded by planted trees, roofed over, used as baths, some of which were set aside for horses, and some were diverted to a grove, while some others were diverted through aqueducts, suggesting they were pretty major springs. Though the Azores were deserted when they were rediscovered in 1431, clearly people had at one time lived on the island in ancient times as there was found a statue on the island of Corvo. Though all the people of the Azores must have perished in the cataclysm that destroyed Atlantis, the Azores must have been at the very least part of the westernmost region of the kingdoms, as much of the physical evidence of Atlantis will show. When the islands were colonized by Isabella of Burgundy in 1466 they found many mineral springs on the island, and the fishermen discovered springs in the sea issuing with such a quantity of fresh water that they can literally dip their buckets in the sea above where the springs issue from and have them filled with fresh water. (Book 6 pg. 33)

Some European peoples have very compelling historic links to Atlantis. The Basques of the western end of the Pyrenees' by the Bay of Biscay say they came from a sunken island in the Atlantic called Atalaintika. The Berbers of North Africa claim that they were invaded by people from the direction of Northwest Africa that came from an island in the Atlantic called Atlantioi. This confirms Plato's story that they influenced this part of Africa. The Arabians tell of a land that existed west of the Mediterranean Sea before the flood called Ad. This flood could be a reference to the one that hit on both side of Saudi Arabia, and up the Persian Gulf to flood the plains of Ur and Bagdad as mentioned in the Epic of Gilgamesh and in the bible as the flood which Abraham crossed over. And the same flood, that raced up the Red Sea to Flood Egypt, scarring the pyramids, eroding the Sphinx, and may be linked to the reason the gods left.

A writer named Aelien or Ælianus Claudius (circa 250 A.D.) in a work called De Animalium Natura that was about the peculiarities of animals, mentioned that he interviewed descendants of the survivors of Poseidon: (another name for Atlantis). These survivors at the time inhabited the ocean shores (probably along the cost of Portugal or southern Spain), and told him they used to wear on their foreheads, as a symbol of power, headbands of the male 'rams of the sea', and their wives used to wear headbands of the female rams. The 'rams of the sea' were the survivors' names for seals, which, as it turns out still exist around the Azores. The male seals have around their foreheads a white band! This offhand information is a very interesting tidbit. People that survived the cataclysm that destroyed Atlantis referred to something Ælianus could not possibly have verified but has since been proven true, which becomes a strange and subtle confirmation of the former existence of Atlantis. (Book 6 pg. 189)

Plato mentions that a great city of Atlantis had palaces that shone with massive stones of red, white and black. This has been seemingly confirmed. Once in 1953 during some diving excursions in the North Sea near Heligoland or Helgoland, was found at a depth of 45 feet parallel rock walls which were coloured with black, white and red rocks. (Book 6 pg. 60-61) By the way, this is the same general area as Doggerland, and yes, we will get to this link very soon. Though not in the Atlantic it's being sunken with a connection to a sunken Atlantis can't completely be overlooked; indeed because of this find (along with the Mastodon bones found in the area) one chap we'll mention later decided this *was* Atlantis. (Book 22 pg. 127) Much more importantly because of this being in the right place, the prevailing colours of the rocks on the Azores are white, black and red too. (Book 6 pg. 31) This adds much more weight to Plato's story in that the same formations were found on the apparent wrong side of the British Isles. If nothing else, writing this book, like the stamp clubs I'm in, is teaching me my geography.

When the Canary Islands were rediscovered in 1334, the inhabitants called themselves Guanche's and their name for the islands is Atalaya. They said they were the only survivors of a worldwide cataclysm...or at least they thought they were. Though their land was vastly reduced in size by the cataclysm, they, like the Mayans, maintained the same political system of ten kings to rule over what was left of the kingdom; more confirmation of Plato.

They had become a mixture of civilized culture and Stone Age barbarians and clearly their civilization had declined after some cataclysm that they never recovered from completely, as was plain, because they had writings on stone all around them that they could no longer read. They had the physical attributes of the Cro-Magnon, showing us this so called prehistoric type was in fact contemporary with other races of humans on this planet and not some inferior link to apes. Very significantly, though they no longer maintained the grand structures around them, they built their houses with tightly fitting stones which were coloured red, white and black! (Book 6 pg. 26, 47-48, and book 64 pg. 189) They claimed they were descendants of the first ruler of Atlantis King Uranus (one of the god's names), giving us another clue and link of Atlantis with the age of the gods, and of course another connecting dot to the former existence of Atlantis. (Book 22 pg. 124)

COOKED AND READY TO SERVE

In 1882 Cap David Armory Robson while sailing the *Jesmond* from Sicily to New Orleans, spotted at sea (200 miles SW from Madeira: 31° 25' N, 28° 40' W) muddy waters littered with cooked dead fish which were killed by the millions, and some of the species of fish were unknown. While sailing through all these dead fish, he saw smoke on the horizon that he thought must be from another ship. Though the charts indicated the water he was in should be several thousand fathoms, his anchor hit bottom at just seven fathoms while he was using it to look for unseen reefs. The next day he spotted an uncharted island that had mountains in the distance. The island was rocky and steaming as though it was newly emerged from the sea. The distant mountains now appeared to be where the smoke appeared to be originating from, and not from a ship as he had originally thought. He and some crew landed and among the usual basalt cliffs covered with marine growth, they found flint arrowheads, and small knives which encouraged them to dig in the area. The next day they found an apparently ancient tomb containing spearheads, axe heads and a sword, along with figures of birds, and animals made of stone or pottery. They also found two large urns containing bone fragments and part of a human skull. Nearby, was a 6 ft statue made from a solid block of stone that they took aboard the ship. Some pottery was also found there that had what appeared to be writing similar to Egyptian or Hebrew. (Admittedly these two types of writing are so different I don't know how they could be confused.) When they returned, the statue disappeared somewhere on route to the British museum and to make matters worse, the island soon afterwards sank. The Atlantis statue is probably in someone's back yard, and its significance not known. Another ship came across the unknown island at the co-ordinates of 25°30'N, 24°W, indicating the island was about 20 by 30 miles and the dead fish were seen there as well, indicating they covered an area of about 7500 square miles, or put another way, about a half million tons of fish were killed by this event. (Book 23 page 65, Book 6 pgs 78-79)

MUDDY WATERS

Plato notes that before Atlantis sank, the Atlantic was navigable from an island that existed to the west of the Straits (also known as the Pillars or Columns of Hercules. book 11 pg. 85).... and beyond so that you could reach the other islands to the west and further on to the continent beyond them...(you know, the *continent* that some guy with three boats discovered and was supposedly the only person to ever find out about it up until that time in 1492...*that* continent. Plato's writings are not the only one that refers to the continent of America. The Greek Varia Historia refers to an enormous continent, larger than Asia (Turkey), Europe and Libya put together. (Book 22 pg. 119)

A lot of authors key in on this obvious reference to America being known about in Plato's time and seem to pass over this next bit. What he's saying is the area between the Straits of Gibraltar and the now sunken mainland of Atlantis was *not* navigable at that time. This is something few if anyone seem to have keyed in on. What this means, is that he places the continent of Atlantis very close to the outer mouth of the Strait of Gibraltar, and he's saying that at the time of his telling of the story, you could *not* get out of the Mediterranean Sea by normal shipping methods. The Phoenicians also stated the same thing that you couldn't get out of the Mediterranean Sea that way by boat. People have suggested the Phoenicians were hiding something about their trade routes, but Plato confirms their story. This means the continents of Africa and Europe were very close to Atlantis, which also means the continents of Africa and Europe were easily accessible to the Atlanteans for the purpose of influence. But this also means Europe and Africa were close enough to escape to in ships when Atlantis sunk before the waters became impossible to sail. When volcanic ash lands on the sea it forms into a hard floating crust which can't be sailed through. In the 1870's the Challenger confirmed Plato's Atlantis story by finding volcanic deposits where Plato said it would be.

We've just read, based on the evidence of elephant teeth found underwater between 2 and 3 hundred miles from shore, that not only does this confirm Plato's account of Atlantis having lots of elephants, It also substantiates that Atlantis could have been no further than 200 miles from Portugal and probably considerably closer when it sank because of all the lava and or mud making navigation impossible. Furthermore Plato says nothing about volcanic ash as the cause of the inaccessibility to the Atlantic, but that the impassable barrier was one of mud. This again speaks of the close proximity of Atlantis to the mouth of the Mediterranean. Furthermore the Challenger found that "...the entire ridge of Atlantis covered with volcanic deposits; these are the subsided mud which, as Plato tells us, rendered the sea impassable after the destruction of the island." (Book 64 pg 71) Ridge of Atlantis? Did they mean the Atlantic ridge?

If you are wondering why evidence of Atlantis is found in the middle of the Atlantic Ocean, when the ancients describe it location as formerly being very close to the Pillars of Hercules, continental drift explains this.

LINKED LEGENDS (AKA OTHER PEOPLES HISTORIES RELATING TO ATLANTIS)

Robert Charroux mentions that the story of Atlantis is not only mentioned by Plato but by Homer, Hesiod, Euripides, Strabo, Diodorus / Siculus, Pliny and Tertllian as well as others. (Book 22 pg 114) I decided to check these specific leads on the net. The first time I had information on most of them, then the library computer turned itself off on me and I hadn't saved my work. That is frustrating to the max, and knowing I had to start from scratch when I restarted the computer I didn't find the exact same searches. OK I'm whining. I hate doing things twice, so if my second attempt isn't as thorough as it should be forgive me. Here's what I found. (By the way, I'm sorry, normally I rely on written work (AKA hard copies, formerly known as "books") but I didn't feel like finding all these ancient records and buying them then waiting weeks for them to arrive in the mail, then having to read through countless pages just to find one tiny reference to Atlantis, or something that might have been interpreted or construed as Atlantis. After all I already had enough evidence through the old tried and true method of reading books and confirming material by cross referencing with others who said the same things, such that I felt I could take the easy way out here. It was a little interesting what I found, and it was a smidge quicker too. So I hope you'll forgive my short-cut used here.)

First, there is a lot of negative press about Atlantis on the net. Right off the top of the searches Wikipedia states right out of the gate, regardless of which place I typed in, that Atlantis is a fictional place. So you have to somehow navigate between the net mines that want to blow Atlantis out of the water. The net, despite what you think, has a biased agenda and anything that contradicts established biases is a little harder to track down, as search engines strategically place them lower down in priority, so I'm not surprised my searches weren't automatically duplicated...especially since I was still fuming about my lost work and couldn't type straight. OK enough stalling...

Homer only mentions an island in the ocean which cannot be the Mediterranean. Some suggest he meant the North Sea. I suppose that is possible as the ancient Egyptian walls referred to the Atlanteans coming from there at one point (more on that later) so it could be an island or politically tied place to Atlantis that was situated in the North Sea. Though predominant thought is he refers to the Atlantic Ocean outside the Mediterranean.

Hesiod does use the name Atlantis in his Theogony centuries before Plato and Solon. He talks about the Hesperide or fortunate islands which some refer to as Atlantis, that sunk beyond the pillars. I think I recall another search saying something like 'the blessed islands', but we all know what happened to *those* notes... they weren't played on a Stradivarius, I can tell you that.

Strabo quotes someone called Strato which I had to read twice to see it wasn't some sort of typo. Strato talks about a cataclysm that ruined a dam between the Atlantic and the Mediterranean. Were the pillars dammed at one time? (This is reminiscent of the non navigable waters Plato spoke of beyond the pillars) Strabo made his only mention of Atlantis, discussing the lost work of Posidonius, in a passage discussing earthquakes. In my previous search and notes I found someone I thought was saying that Atlantis was called Posidonius which made sense to me as Poseidon is another name for Atlantis. But I lost those notes, or did I already say that? Anyway this "Posidonius" stated Atlantis might not be fiction but a real place and that Solon's story about it that he got from the Egyptians was about an island almost as large as a continent that did exist and has since disappeared.

Diodorus Siculus, that's apparently one person...not two, was a contemporary of Augustus and Julius Caesar. My circa 1906 encyclopaedia says this writer of *The Library of History*, was "entirely wanting in the critical faculty, and combines legend, history, and fiction." I wonder why? Because he took Atlantis at face value?...because he bothered to include the legends? Anyway he tells us that the Phoenicians discovered "a large island in the Atlantic Ocean beyond the Pillars of Hercules several days sail from the coast of Africa. Yep sounds like fiction to me! This so called "Historian" adds more silliness by talking about the climate and residents of this fantasy island that Ricardo and Tattoo welcomed people to. He says the climate of the island is very mild and the island grows a great variety of fruits that for the most part of the year, at least some sort of fruit was always in season. This apparently fortuitous happenstance is the reason that the people that lived there were in fact a race of gods and not just ordinary men. Yep, a completely absurd historian, except for the fact so many other ancient historians also say that the gods lived on this island. Thus we can only conclude that either this was the case, or every ancient historian has been nipping a bit too much out of the wine cabinet. I guess it was a problem with historians back then. History was just too dull...full of stupid cave men, worthless boats, useless arrowheads, and infantile buildings made out of Lego, that they just had to colour history up a bit. Yes sir them ancient historians were just a bunch of dreamers.

Well let's see what Pliny says about Atlantis shall we? Hey why not,.. He's the last one on the list Charroux gave us: You can stand another ridiculous uncritical historian, right?

Pliny states there was an island off the mount of atlas called Atlantis off the west coast of Africa. I mean imagine that, how could he just dream up a place like that, and what a coincidence that he dreamed up the exact same place that a bunch of other drunken ancient historians dreamed up. Maybe it was a really popular wine that all these ancient historians drank, maybe it was called something like *Atlántico Spirited* on the label...I mean that could explain it! Apparently because some errors are conceded to exist in Pliny's work, many later version of Pliny's writings have had the name Atlantis actually removed from the text. Seriously!!! Has archaeology sunk so low that they can't leave the ancient texts as found but have to 'correct' them? Well why not; they've been doing it to the bible for a couple hundred years too. This is literally rewriting history to suit the archaeologists! They should be fired...or...do they actually get paid for digging in the dirt? Maybe when no one's looking they bring out their toy dump trucks. This is a fact I've found out about slime that change ancient written history to aid in forcing their slanted unsubstantiated opinion of ancient history on ignorant masses that really steams me. Where was I before my rage blinded me...?

OH yeah, my mistake, there was another person on Charroux's list: Tertullian. This guy apparently doesn't count; he lived after Christ and thus long after Atlantis sunk beneath the waves. He equated the loss of Atlantis as a place that sank in Noah's flood. Sound familiar? However here's the point, he understood the place did exist at one time; he didn't discount its former existence at all. But then what do you expect when you read history written by a bunch of drunken dreamers. Aren't you glad we now have such informed historians living in our day to help shield us from the ancient historians that were 'entirely wanting in the critical faculty, that combined legend, history, and fiction'? and can replace it with their own version of history as they see fit, even though they weren't there!

Facetiousness aside, there are now people on the net deliberately calling the ancient historians liars. That's right, if you think Atlantis really existed you are said to believe lies. How far away can the time be when they put you in the funny farm for accepting ancient historians at their word? Russia puts Christians in mental institutes because they think they are sick because they believe the bible. (By the way the bible *is* one of the ancient histories) Yet what do we see in Hollywood movies: almost nothing but ridiculous fantasy. The TV show Myth Busters is constantly showing that the stunts or tricks they pull off in Hollywood movies are completely impossible. People actually die trying the things done in movies because they thought the things were possible...or safe. Kids, when you see the warning on TV that says "Don't try this at home", don't try it at home!

(II Timothy 4:3-4). 3: "For the time will come when they will not endure sound doctrine; but after their own lusts they shall heap to themselves teachers having itching ears; 4: And they shall turn away their ears from the truth, and shall be turned to fables".

Some people think that politicians that ignore "climate change" because they do not believe the fairy tale that bogus science propagated by those with vested financial interest in selling "green" technology, should be put in jail. Jail because they disagree with something that has no basis in reality. Jail because they care about the taxpayers money being wasted on unproven, unsubstantiated theories. So just for your itching ears I'll include some of these fairy tales that so many people believe these days, at the end of the book...you know...just for laughs. (And for fun I'll actually have some fairy tails of my own to share. That should be fun...yup; I cut the tails right off the fairies myself.)

Well >hic< back to the hints of Atlantis' former existence in the ancient legends...>hic<

The Okanagan Indians of British Columbia say they came from a piece of a White Man's Island that was broken off by Queen Scomalt who was of the supernatural beings (or gods), when the giants kept fighting. Before the land sank the last remaining pair built a canoe and paddled to America which was smaller than it is now. (Book 23 pg 121) If this is an Atlantis story it appears to be a pre sinking story before North America moved far enough west to merge with the remains of what some geologists call "Pacifica" which would probably be Mu.

Pacific Island people have legends they tell about their ancestors that used to dwell in a great and wonderful continent which sank long ago below the sea.(Book 23 pg 121) Whether this is an Atlantis legend or more plausibly a Mu or Lemuria, that it exists to substantiate the reality of a sinking continent is worth mentioning.

THE APACHE CONNECTIONS

There are a couple links associated with the Apache's to the ancient world that are eye opening and they place the era of Atlantis' existence and the time when Tiahuanaco's was built, to the period of the age of the gods.

The Mescalero Apaches have a dance they term the 'lost land of the sunrise sea', where they use the symbol of the trident aka Neptune's or Poseidon's trident, which as we know is closely associated with Atlantis. As they enter from the east to begin the dance and then turn around to face the east, they utter the statement "I remember the old red land of my forefathers, and how it sank beneath the sea", then while still facing the east they turn the prongs of the trident down. (Book 35 pg 53) For those of you who like to take up the causes of Natives realize these phony historians are also calling the natives stupid for believing this stuff, thus are ignoring their histories and marginalizing them too. I hope that gets *your* dander up if the historians changing ancient historians text like Pliny doesn't.

Anyway, we've determined Atlantis' existence was during the age of the gods. Once during a time when an ethnologist, Lucille Taylor Hansen, was watching ritual dances of the Arizona Apaches, she saw something that made her want to show the natives pictures of Egyptian carvings to see if they meant anything to them. She was apparently on the right track, because they recognised one of the pictures as depicting the 'god of light and fire', which was known to the Egyptians as Ammon-Ra. So their traditional memories traced back to the periods of the gods there too. So she dug a little further. She mentioned Tiahuanaco, and the Apaches knew the place, and without ever having been there, described the statue of the "bearded white man" that stood there holding upright a sword in both hands. The swords and the head together form the shape of... a trident, which is their secret sign of recognition. The place where the statue stands they say is the ancient home of their tribe. (Book 21 pg 213) So what they were saying was that they, the Apaches, were the original dwellers of Tiahuanaco. Two connections to Atlantis and the gods, and two for Tiahuanaco the city of unknown origins directly linked with the Apaches!

Apache Indians appear to have another connection to the age of the gods that we already mentioned. We already indicated the city was built during the same period as the Egyptians and during the age of the gods as were the tunnels that lead from there. You may recall earlier how they fled from enemies in Tiahuanaco through the tunnels and dwelling in them for years before coming out into their (new) land. And of course they even described the origin of the tunnels as "carved out by rays that destroy the living rock, and that their creators were beings that live near the stars". All in all, the Apache legends pieced together like this are staggering in their implications. It would appear Apache legends point to the gods who came from the stars, lived in Atlantis, built Tiahuanaco, and the tunnels, and were on earth just before the Egyptian's first dynasty in the era known as the "Age of the Gods". The picture of the puzzle becomes clearer. The destruction of Atlantis simultaneously shoved America westward to merge with Mu to become a bigger continent, while pushing South America and Tiahuanaco up, and simultaneously causing massive worldwide floods. Other clues signify this probably initiated the departure of the gods, where some went down into the interior of the earth, and some returned to the stars, or more likely the man made moon known as Elysia. Another link of Atlantis to the period when the gods were making building sites around the globe like Tiahuanaco and Baalbek with huge quarried stones is underwater near Morocco. There is another underwater wall which was discovered by divers spearfishing off the coast of Morocco which extends several miles out to sea. The stones used in this wall are comparable in size to those used at Baalbek ..."the largest building stones known to have been quarried in ancient times." (Book 6 pg. 94)

ATLANTIS CROPPING UP IN HISTORICAL RECORDS AND ATLANTIS LINKED TO REAL HISTORY: EVIDENCE.

The Egyptians told Solon that the story of the demise of Atlantis was inscribed on some of their pillars. In 310 B.C., A Greek Philosopher named Crantor said or wrote that he had seen these pillars. Today these pillars are not known to exist or are buried somewhere in the sands of Egypt. (Book 23 pg. 82) (Or maybe no one has translated them?)

Diodorus Siculus, a contemporary of Julius and Augustus Caesar, and author of *The Library of History* written in Greek containing history of the world from mythical times down to Caesars' invasion of Gaul, mentions the Amazons, led by Queen Myrina during the time when she and her people still lived in Libya (North Africa). He recorded that they defeated the Atlanteans then migrated to South America. (Book 23 pg 185)

Critias notes that when Atlantis sunk the whole of Greece's army was also swallowed up into the earth at the same time. This clearly shows that cataclysmic events on one part of the earth have a ripple effect to a wide extent around the globe, if indeed the entire globe doesn't feel the effects. Clearly Atlantis' demise coincided with much destruction in the Mediterranean. This Greek destruction appears to mirror the same destruction that occurred in Heracleion which sunk and pulled 64 ships under with it. In an attempt to try and match up a few events for confirmation sake, if it wasn't for the fact that as I mentioned during Plato's lifetime the Greek port city of Heliké on the Saronic Gulf plunged so suddenly into the sea that twelve Spartan warships that were in the harbour at the time, were also pulled down with it; that I might consider this confirmation of Critias narrative. But clearly Atlantis' and this army's demise was a much earlier incident, indicating violent cataclysms occurred in the Mediterranean more than once, and more than likely coincide with ends of world ages which may even help date the events.

This event could have been a continuance and linked to the same geologic strata, meaning it could be linked to what destroyed the remaining islands that are seen in Zeno's map of 1380. Though hypothetical maps of Atlantis exist, I know of no genuine period maps showing this land. The theosophical Map of Ruta and Daitya (not shown) are supposedly ancient maps of Atlantis and Lemuria, but the volume of land belonging to Atlantis or Lemuria proposed on these maps is so extensive to the extreme that I can't possibly take these maps seriously. Taking continental drift into account, Atlantis on the map is shown to have almost filled the northern half of the Atlantic, yet Africa and South America fit so exactly, that if the drift is reversed there is no way there could have been such a huge land mass in the northern half of what is now the Atlantic Ocean. Though Atlantis is termed a "continent", and it may be have been by ancient world standards, its main land mass was probably smaller in area than Greenland.

ASSOCIATIONS

Constant Basir wrote that Melpomene (spoken of by Herodotus) mentioned someone he knew visited the land and maritime parts of Atlantis in 2350 B.C. (Book 22 pg. 119) This piece of history justifies some researchers deduction that Atlantis wasn't sunk 9000 years before Plato, but more likely 900 years prior, and was somehow mistranslated or botched with an extra zero. I know...it's still a "he said she said" or "I knew a guy who knew a guy"..., But it's yet another classic reference to the existence of Atlantis, and assuming this date is remotely correct, this also helps confirm for us an approximate era and time frame for the age of the gods; as Atlantis and this age of the gods are clearly intimately linked.

Interestingly giants are also associated with Atlantis. "All traditions agree that the Atlanteans were giants." (Book 22 pg 120: I haven't read all the accounts, I don't even know where to find all of them and if I had them all I wouldn't even know I did. However I haven't noticed absolutely everyone mentioning giants associated with Atlantis, but I have seen it mentioned quite a few times, so I assume this statement is a fair though possibly exaggerated assessment or he hasn't read them all either). This connection of Giants with Atlantis has the unfortunate consequence of people assuming Atlantis' demise and the flood spoken of in the bible or the world flood, is one and the same flood that destroyed the giants or Nephalim of the preflood or antediluvian period. But people forget that giants also existed after Noah's flood, such as those that were in the land of Canaan when Joshua destroyed that group. Their origin is not exactly the same as those of the pre-flood era, though there is a link. I covered this in my first book, but I'll summarise this reintroduction of giants to the earth in the bonus section.

LINKS

A Pastor Jürgen Spanuth suggested that the North Sea may have been the location of Atlantis based on some finds in that area, such as the red, white and black rocks, of which the island of Heligoland or Helgoland also has, just as Plato's description of Atlantis mentioned, suggesting to Spanuth that Heligoland may be a remnant of the fabled isle. This seems to go against the directions of Atlantis being beyond the Pillars of Hercules, but this doesn't mean Heligoland couldn't have been an outpost or satellite, or even one of the islands belonging to Atlantis. Many of the islands of what were parts of Atlantis spoken of by Plato extended to the northern parts of the Atlantic as seen in the Zeno map of 1380. The North Sea is within reach and may have been a good place to launch a surreptitious attack on Europe by the Atlanteans. OH... really? Yes.

BACK DOOR ENTRY.

The Medinet Habû is a very interesting Egyptian structure that gets overlooked from being in the shadow of the Pyramids, the Sphinx and other well known Egyptian building sites. On the walls of this building are inscribed the history of a major expedition undertaken by the Atlanteans where they came southwards and occupied all of Greece except Athens and Attica. How could the Atlanteans have come southwards to occupy Greece? Atlantis was far to the west of Greece, not the North. However Helgoland would be a good spot to start a campaign against Greece if you want to completely surprise the enemy, and it's about 800 miles closer to Greece; so, if they started in Helgoland they would have to come southwards to get to Greece. One might pick The Baltic Sea as a starting point today, but this area as we've seen was likely still covered in glaciers at the time, making access from there somewhat impractical or impossible. Actually the Netherlands in that map was covered by ice too so one can only guess that changes in the glaciations had occurred or the glaciations depicted on that map actually came after the expedition. This makes sense as the destruction of Atlantis would have set off another end to a world age accompanied by the weather that started one of the ice ages. Actually now that I think of it, this is obviously the case because the Atlanteans were in existence during the age of the gods, meaning these ice ages and catastrophes happened after they were gone, or at the very least the second or third world age and first ice age was ushered in with their island's demise.

Also remember, the history of Atlantis shows they ruled the north of Africa, all the way to Egypt, and they ruled Europe all the way to Greece who had stopped them cold. (Book 27 pg 88) So they had incentive to try and see if they could beat both Greece and Egypt, no matter how difficult the task. So trekking across Europe to sneak up behind the Greeks must have made the Atlantean army giggle as they marched. After sacking Greece, they proceeded to Crete and Cyprus and from there continued their attack, with additional Libyan allies, on into Egypt by land and by sea, but were finally defeated, thus the reason for this history to be inscribed on the walls of the Medinet Habû. (Book 21 pg. 139)

Similar to the Egyptians writing some history about Atlantis on their walls, the Mexicans wrote on their pyramid at Xochicalco. The walls of this structure say a land situated in the mid-ocean was destroyed and the people were killed and turned to dust.

ALTER EGO

The Greeks substantiate this Atlantean history written on Egypt's Medinet Habû walls with a parallel history of their own where they tell of being invaded by the Hyperboreans that came from the North Sea which allied themselves with the Tyrrhenian's of Italy. The Tyrrhenian's were known allies of the Atlanteans, so the Hyperboreans were probably Atlanteans, possibly disguised at first not to tip off the Grecians. Egyptians state the starting point of the Atlantean attack are given by clues such as their 17 hour day, pointing to where these people came from, which would place them at 54° north which again could point to Helgoland. The clincher is the description of the island they came from: "High as if shorn with a knife, rising direct from the sea, with red white and black rocks..." Helgoland is apparently the only island in the world (above sea level) that fits this description. Thus these two histories build another link with Italy and the Tyrrhenians and of course a solid link of Atlantis to ancient history. So who are the Hyperboreans? Herodotus links the period of the Hyperboreans with Apollo thus to the age of the gods, (Herodotus book 4 C 35) and he notes that the Hyperborean's didn't just live beyond the North wind but also to the South wind, suggesting Hyperborea extended south to what again is probably Atlantis; and Egypt equates the Hyperborean with the Atlanteans as well. If then Hyperborea is Helgoland and continues south, this could place Doggerland above sea level as a continuation of Helgoland, and connected to Atlantis if not physically, at least politically, so that you just round the northern part of Scotland and go south, fitting with the historical description, and thus placing Doggerland into a historical context. And of course the Greeks refer to Hyperborea as a fabulous nation beyond the North wind, in a land of perpetual sunshine and of perfect happiness, also suggesting Doggerland was above sea level. Why? Perpetual sunshine indicates somewhere beyond the Arctic Circle, but this is a strange way to describe the nation that sacked your country. However we've shown that the globe shifted which could place Doggerland / Hyperborea this far north, or more properly the Arctic Circle shifted further south. (Even though the sun might set in Doggerland for example, at the right latitude, it would still be daylight 24 hours a day, and of course it appears Atlantis still had positions further north so this description might not necessarily describe Doggerland but some part of Atlantis further north previously visited by some Egyptians.) Hyperborea to the Greeks supposedly was a place where the sun always shone presumably because Apollo says this. Indeed Apollo liked to visit Hyperborea but only 6 months of the year, obviously when it was summer and the sun shone all day during his visits. Thus it can only be a place north of the Arctic Circle. But since during his visits it seems Hyperborea was more of a warmer paradise, this would place his visits before any cataclysmic events changed the climate drastically. (Book 23 pg 48-49)

What's interesting in this whole affair is the reason the Hyperboreans or Atlanteans ransacked Greece and Egypt. It came about because of a great famine which followed a disaster that afflicted the whole of Europe and other parts of the world. This is described as "the most fearful catastrophe in the last 4000 years of human history" and is thought to have occurred about 1225 B.C., or about 725 years before Plato. Could Atlantis destruction 900 years previous to Plato's' day and this 1225 B.C. or 725 years before Plato be a subsequent event soon after, but just slightly misdated? It would fit if the survivors of the destruction by not being on the main continent of Atlantis (which caused havoc and famine in Europe and beyond) were still living on the remaining islands such as Helgoland during the time of Plato. They, through desperation, plundered Europe from Helgoland, down through Germany, then linking up with the Italian Tyrrhenians and others, and continued on and sacked Greece. But their success going to their heads and their ongoing desire to wipe out Egypt too made them overextend themselves thus causing them to fade from history after this time. (Book 21 pgs 137-139)

SEARCH FOR THE MISSING

One more connection to *written* history belongs to Atlantis. Heinrich Schliemann ...the guy who read about Troy, and was then foolish enough to believe the report to the point the upstart went and dug Troy up making all the other archaeologists blush....Yeah *that guy*...: he was in the Hermintage museum in St Petersburg around the mid 19th century looking for whatever clues he could find to anything else he could dig up. Well during his searching he didn't find Hermin, or Waldo, but he did find two Egyptian Papyri which he had the audacity to read. He read in one of the papyri that the Egyptians, once they knew about the demise of Atlantis, sent an expedition to the west, dispatched by the Pharaoh, to see if anything remained of Atlantis. They spent 5 years searching but none of those in the expedition found any trace of the extinct civilization. (Book 6 pg 45) Now Consider: leaders of countries don't spend valuable resources chasing rainbows. Atlantis by all accounts was a vastly rich country, and even if everyone died from whatever caused its destruction, if by chance ...say...a tidal wave killed most or all the inhabitants, but left some nice juicy buildings lying around with all that gold, silver and orichalcum, still stuck to the walls, the trip would have paid for itself many times over. The expedition I presume was large enough so that even if they did find some bedraggled Atlanteans still alive, they could easily handle them and take what they wanted. Their expedition only proved that the demise of Atlantis was complete.

Also, consider: there was no love lost between Egypt and Atlantis, as their history clearly indicated they were prone to conquering and taking spoils of wars, so I'm sure the Pharaoh no doubt thought, turn about was fair play. During the Egyptians hunt for the remains of Atlantis, they quite possibly came across the Canary Islands, and it may have been part of the backdrop behind what Solon the Egyptian high priest said about survivors of large tragic events "...when the stream from heaven, descends like a pestilence and leaves only those of you who are *destitute of letters and education*...you have to begin all over again as children and know nothing about what happened in ancient times, either among us or among yourselves.". When the Canary Islands were rediscovered the disintegration of the culture was obvious. They had ancient stone houses which they no longer took the time to repair, and they had no boats, and tellingly, there were stone inscriptions all about which they could no longer read. (Book 6 pg. 48) Their story of being the only survivors of a worldwide cataclysm which we understand as being the sinking of Atlantis was confirmed by Spanish scuba divers in 1981. They found at a depth of 50 feet stone slabs which were fitted together over a 900 square foot area and from this place some steps led downward. Some of the stone slabs had letters or characters carved in them that were the same as those on the island. (Book 6 pg 93) Point here is the Egyptian knew full well Atlantis existed and they went to see what was left of it. You don't do that if you're looking for Oz; you go to bed and dream about it.

THE REMNANTS

After Atlantis was destroyed and some survivors managed to get to land, what would you do? Your home and your country are gone and you have nothing but what you might have managed to grab and toss in a boat. Assuming the first land you manage to get to is sparsely populated you, being exhausted and depressed, would just set up home near where you landed, or you'd force your way to colonize something nearby because you've had a bad day and you're not going to let someone make it worse if you can help it. You squat and people knowing the story of the destruction of your home would give way, if there were even any survivors after the tsunamis hit. Where you landed no homes would likely be built that could accommodate you if there were any, so you'd take shelter where you could, such as in caves, or build makeshift lodgings until something more permanent was made. Charles Berlitz showed a very interesting map on pg. 165 of his book *Atlantis the Eighth Continent*. It shows the western edge of Europe from Portugal to as far as Italy and it plotted where "prehistoric" cave paintings and artifacts are most concentrated. The picture it paints clearly indicates there was some sort of mass exodus from the Atlantic Ocean to the western most parts of Europe and Morocco. The ocean edges of Morocco, south-western Spain and Portugal have so many dots that the western quarter of the Iberian Peninsula and the same amount of Morocco is almost black. And most of Ireland is covered with dots, as is the south western portion of Norway. The western coast of France isn't because it was farther, to travel to, and knowing their geography they would head for the closest landfall. The picture it paints absolutely verifies Plato's locating Atlantis beyond the Pillars of Hercules as this is exactly where the concentration of Atlantean immigrants would have landed. But he notes there were other Atlantean owned islands which were probably larger but whittled down and this would explain western Norway's influx.

Interestingly, considering what we just talked about concerning Heligoland, the western edge of Denmark and the west coast of Netherlands are also heavily dotted with ancient artifact sites as though there was a part of Atlantis in the North Sea, or at least a populated island that underwent the same experience as Atlantis: this area would be none other than the "prehistoric" Doggerland.

There is evidence of a vanished south-western Spanish civilization called the Tartessos originally thought to be an outpost of an Eastern civilization. But there have been clues and investigations based on the premise that they came from the direction of the western sea. (Book 6 pg. 219) If Atlantis could be seen in the distance from a point near the opening to the Mediterranean Sea, then landing on Spanish soil within sight after a cataclysm fits perfectly, and would also help explain all those cave paintings and artifacts in the area. If they *were* Atlanteans, then they might well have vanished after being paid back for their conquering ways by troops only too happy to join in together to pick them off and rob their carcasses of any goodies, leaving the remains with little more than rudimentary utensils that no one back then valued. This would result in giving us the impression they were a Stone Age society. This might even hold true for all the areas seen with cave paintings perpetuating the concepts this was a prehistoric civilization archaeologists seem so sure fits for all of the sites.

RANTING THE ARCHAEOLOGICAL BLUES.

Anthropologists want us to believe this massive cluster of cave paintings and artifacts spanning from the coast of Morocco to Norway have nothing to do with history, and are all examples of 'prehistoric' numbskull cave men paintings from 20, 40, or 50,000 years ago. "Prehistoric" is supposed to mean before man conceived of writing to create historical records. So if I paint a picture and don't add any words to it, does that mean I'm prehistoric? I put forth in my last book that man was so advanced and physiologically superior to us in the past they didn't even need to create writing as they knew everything: writing was beneath them. The Egyptians balked at having their children taught writing as they should be expected to learn and remember. Indeed many legends were never written down and relied solely on the memorisation of verbal legends. Are these legends 'prehistoric' then? No explanation as to how the paintings were preserved for so long when a little air deteriorates them in less than 50 years. Is this a tangible clue of atmospheric changes over time? Are not paintings a form of record? Indeed many civilizations use pictograms to tell a story. I'm willing to bet the Egyptians used pictogram writing because it at least employed some skill beyond an alphabet; not because they were too stupid to make up letters. And pictograms can have nuances that just letters can't have.

No explanation why such clusters of human evidence all along the western shores of Europe and Africa even exists. We are told to believe human history started in the heart of Africa, yet no such cluster of ancient artifacts exists there. It almost looks like civilization started on the western extremities of Europe / Morocco and not the heart of Africa. No explanation for the density of these sites has been offered. They just say they are old and treat us like idiots for even considering the Atlantis solution. They treat us like blithering idiots if we dare to consider an alternative explanation their theories can't possibly explain. Except for the coast of France it almost looks like a nuclear blast hit all along the coast of Africa and Europe...only the blast was of people rushing towards land. One thing most anthropologists conveniently forget to mention is not all of this so called primitive cave man art concentrated along the west coast of Spain, Africa, and Ireland is "primitive". Many of the paintings not shown the man on the street, or in the museum, or in the class, or on the couch, depict people clean shaven and wearing stitched garments. (Book 6 pg. 156-57) Indeed some of the needles found in the caves were far better than needles the Romans used. Clean shaven? Well they must be shaving with those arrow heads they were so fond of making. When archaeologists find high tech devices or even evidence of high technology with any ancient civilization remains, they don't advertise these; they bury them in the basements of museums.

Sometimes with such obvious evidence I wonder what motivates anthropologists or whoever makes up these farcical theories to deny the former existence of Atlantis and an ancient history filled with stories of cataclysmic events. And if that's not enough, the evidence of Atlantis former existence isn't anywhere near finished with here. Are archaeologists in denial? I seem to recall being referred to as a denier of certain theories being forced onto the earth's population of late. I may just add some 'denier' literature at the end of this to make these people think I'm a freaking basket case. Sometimes the evidence is so obvious the only deniers around here are those who turn a blind eye to any theory but their own and ridicule those who don't swallow their Swiss cheese theories.

In some places, such as under water or in other buried ancient civilizations, have been found a geared device capable of computing location of users on the earth with adjustments like one that could account for the wobble of the moon, with writing on it etched so tiny it had to have been done with a laser. Obsidian blades have been found sharper than the scalpel we use today in the operating room; screwed threaded devices have been found as good as items in your hardware store, and a spark plug imbedded in a geode, and even perfectly ground optical lenses have been found. Who knows what high tech evidence has been found in these caves we've not been told about. Needless to say people who refuse to accept the truth that man was more advanced in the past and know about these and other items, either hide, ignore, destroy the items, or come up with theories like earth was colonized by people from the stars. When civilization is destroyed by natural calamities then "...when the stream from heaven, descends like a pestilence and leaves only those of you who are destitute of letters and education...you have to begin all over again as children and know nothing about what happened in ancient times, either among us or among yourselves." The "stars" bit is will be explained later.

Atlantis: Physical Evidence of remains

If Plato's and other peoples' story of Atlantis was a bunch of balderdash and made up hooey, there wouldn't actually be any physical evidence of the place, now deep below that Atlantic waves...would there. So then why is there?

Some examples: a Russian group working north of the Azores (around the late '60's or early 70's) dredged up rocks from the ocean floor 600 feet down which were determined to have formed under atmospheric pressure. A project of the University of Halifax concerning geothermal energy done in the school year of 1973-74 revealed that when they drilled near and around the Azores, cores to the depth of over 2500 feet deep that they brought up from the ocean floor indicated they had to have been formed above sea level in the open air. (Book 6 pg 171, Book 7 pg 163)

An 1898 dredging operation that occurred while repairing a break in the transatlantic cable in the vicinity of the Azores brought up a piece of tachylyte or tachylite, a type of lava that only forms above water under normal atmospheric pressure. According to Pierre Termier, it dissolves in sea water after 15,000 years so it had to be considerably younger than this.

More clues discovered during the same event: the 1898 the cable-ship working in the Atlantic 500 miles north of The Azores, pulled some vitreous lava from a depth of 10,000 feet which had the chemical composition of basalt. This was a strange find because this only occurs with lava under normal atmospheric pressure. Lava, if spewed out under water turns into pillow lava as seen on say Mount Ararat (which by the way puts that mountain under water at one time) The lava pulled from the sea could only have been formed on land when that part of the ocean floor was still above sea level. (Book 22 pg 118) Professor Ewing, who we quoted before concerning continental drift, also found lava at the ocean bottom that gave him problems. Though antagonistic towards the Atlantis concept, he said "Either the land must have sunk two or three miles or the ocean must once have been two or three miles lower than now. Either conclusion is startling. .. If the sea was once two miles lower, where could all the extra water have gone" " (Book 6 pg 24, Nat Geo. Nov 1949) This was what Dr. Maurice Ewing Professor of Geology stated in November 1949 National Geographic when they discovered beach sand in the mid Atlantic Ridge 1200 miles from any land.

In 1956 some fresh water diatoms were brought up in a sample core from a depth 12,000 feet near the Atlantic Ridge. They were determined to have been from a fresh water lake that had to have been on the surface at one time but at some point had sunk to the ocean floor. (Book 6 pg 184)

A Swedish ship named Albatross took core samples near St. Peter and St. Paul rocks from a depth of two miles and pulled up shallow water microorganisms preserved in bottom mud along with twigs, plants and tree bark. The conclusion: this site had to have submerged rapidly into the depths. (Book 6 pg 185)

Beach sand is formed at beaches...not at the bottom of the ocean, yet what were once sandy beaches were discovered on underwater plateaus near the Azores. (Book 7 pg 164) National Geographic Nov. 1949 issue reports this sand exists in two layers which Dr. / Professor Ewing acknowledged had to have been formed "at or near the surface of the sea". The sand around the Azores was found at depths of 5,000 feet. (Naturally they gave ridiculous ages dates attributed to both layers of the sand) (Book 30 pg 55, Book 6 pg 24)

In 1968 an underwater wall or road a quarter of a mile long which displayed regular patterns, with some near square blocks, perfect rectangles, and linear formations, clearly indicated this was a manmade structure. This was discovered off the Bimini Islands and is similar to Ancient structures in Malta, Yucatán and other new world places with long names I don't feel like spelling out right now. (Book 7 pg 168, book 6 pg 96-102)

The ocean shelf around the Bahamas when calm and flown over by a plane reveals all kinds of underwater construction in the shapes of squares, rectangles, crosses, parallel lines, right angles, triangles, concentric circles and hexagons seen bare on the ocean floor, or traced out by sea grasses; all of them clearly indicate they were human made designs of buildings which are now underwater. (Book 7 pg 172)

Soon after a seismic rise in part of the Bahama Banks, new formations were seen where none were seen before. A 100 foot long underwater formation likened to an arrow was found between north and south Cat cays. A group of divers when they found a Spanish anchor accidently scratched the ocean floor surface and stumbled on a sunken mosaic floor or terrace. (Book 7 pg 173)

A magnetic survey of the Atlantic floor showed that the rocks there had stripes of normal and reversed polarity, indicating the globe was subjected to whatever geologic actions would accompany such a series of continual reversals. This could of double as evidence for Atlantis which of course was in the middle of the action that would be linked with these reversals.

St. Brendan's Isle known to exist was sought vainly during the middle ages. Why? Because it appeared on ancient maps. But it was never found and eventually it was taken off the maps and its existence was assumed to just be a legend or mythical island. It's location was thought to be about 600 miles west of the Canaries and a little more south of the Azores. Then suddenly on April 26 1967 it rose out of the sea, and then sunk back in a short time later. (Book 22 pg 25) Now taken out of the myth category what is real interesting is that it is clearly visible in some satellite photographs, and has an identical shape to some ancient maps delineation of it. (It was drawn correctly)

ATLANTIS? EVIDENCE

It's been admitted by Alfred Wegener that if Atlantis ever existed, the continental drift would have caused and accounted for its destruction. (Book 22 pg 118) Exactly as I'm saying here, except the continental drift occurred in historic times, which the known destruction of Atlantis in historical times and the other legends we've already covered testifies to.

You may or may not consider this evidence of the former existence of Atlantis, but for what it's worth, the Azores have lots of mainland birds like crows, hawks, doves and a lot of rabbits. No one can explain why these islands that are a thousand miles from the nearest continental mainland have all these types of birds and animals on them. (Book 6 pg 188)

Based on several sites found on the eastern shores of Central America, John Baldwin in his 1871 book *Ancient America* concluded that the continent of America at one time extended far into the Atlantic Ocean. The hundreds of underwater archaeological sites found there confirms this deduction and it situates the event into recorded history. This was substantiated another way when the 1969 Duke University expedition did extensive underwater dredging from off the coast of Venezuela and on out to the Virgin Islands. They found granite rocks on the ocean floor which geologists believe are supposed to be confined to the continents.

There has been spotted from the air, starting at the Bimini Chain and going to Orange Key "rectilinear arrangements", squares, rectangles, pathways, roadways and straight lines which were all underwater. So these have been investigated by divers and one building found underwater was <u>identical</u> in design and dimensions to the "Temple of the Turtles" at Uxmal in Yucatan. It measured 60 by 100 feet and just like the one at Uxmal, the east side is partitioned off. (Book 30 pg. 57)

Another building that is 240 feet long and 80 feet wide, has been found off of Andros Island, and it too is the same as another building in Yucatan known as the Temple of the Dwarfs. It was made with perfectly fitted together limestone blocks, on a par with the construction of the walls seen in Peru. (Book 8 pg 73) Along with other sites around the globe, it's considered a mystery why the sophisticated and advanced civilization at Yucatan came to an end. (Book 11 pg 96) Well if you ask me, any event that can submerge about 2 million square miles of land to become what is now the Gulf of Mexico and beyond, sounds like a pretty good explanation as to what made the civilization of Yucatan disappear to me. But don't take my word for it. I repeat A Mayan fragment ""The disaster befell on the eleventh day of Ahau Katun...it rained fearfully, ashes fell from the sky and *the waters of the sea engulfed the land in one great wave...*the heavens collapsed, *the earth subsided*, and the Great Mother Seyda was amidst the records of the destruction of the world ". This Mayan record speaks of a frightful ring side seat to this event.

"Many Atlantean theorists see the universal flood story as being directly related to Atlantis' sinking beneath the sea." (Book 35 pg 15) This is because A) the cause of the sinking of Atlantis was a spreading of the continents further apart caused by, as Plato suggests, "the shifting of the heavenly bodies" which triggered many floods. We've seen Venus coming close to the earth which caused many floods. But the actual sinking of Atlantis exacerbated and caused further floods by the very act of its submersion. B) So many local floods occurring around the globe as a result of the sinking of Atlantis that this fact has given these Atlantean theorists the impression that all these floods linked with Atlantis must mean this is the universal flood; an understandable error. Atlantis' demise occurred simultaneously with all these local floods, as well as fast destructive upheaval in Europe and into the Mediterranean, and in the Caribbean. If you can date any of these floods, and link them to other events you could date all the four world ages. Tree ring dating would be a great aid in doing this, and atmospheric conditions changed immensely around the globe when these local floods occurred, and tree rings give exact dates. Matching the ring anomalies up around the world would help clear up the picture virtually perfectly.

It stands to reason that since the geologists have already deciphered that many floods occurred and that they were vast in scope, we can assume this also meant some sort of catastrophe is linked with the floods. So we have a sort of double confirmation. The floods indicate some sort of disaster must be linked to have caused the floods, and the disaster known as the sinking of Atlantis is linked with many floods. Thus the two have to be part and parcel of same event. With events linked to this occasion such as the complete destruction of the Grecian army, and the loss of the land bridge between Italy and Sicily causing massive destruction of animals on Sicily, this also was happening around the globe in many other mass fossil destruction zones, apparently occurring at the same time, indicate just how vast an area these floods affected. And like the legends tell, few people survived, which is yet another similarity to the global flood causing still more confusion.

The event that sunk the Sicilian land bridge probably also sunk the series of mine shafts and smelting facilities by Marseille, the sunken ancient Acropolis Jim Thorne found near the island of Melos, and the road that Jacques Cousteau found and followed. Clearly the sinking of Atlantis had to have massive global repercussions and caused massive flooding or more subsidence of land worldwide; while in other places land emerged from the murky depths, almost certainly causing catastrophic tsunamis. This event probably caused the earthquake the Hebrews ran from during the reign of Uzziah. The Earthquake during Uzziah's reign is one of the few cataclysms actually mentioned more than once in the bible. Amos 1:1 speaks of an event that occurred in the reigns of Uzziah (Judah) and Jeroboam (Israel) two years before the earthquake. It would have to be a major earthquake to be singled out as *the* earthquake". The verses of Zechariah 14: 4-5 informing the people about a prophesy of Christ's returns, also mentions this quake: Verse. 4: And in that day His feet will stand on the Mount of Olives which faces Jerusalem on the east and the Mount of Olives shall split in two, from east to west making a very large valley; half of the mountain shall move to the north and half toward the south. Verse 5 goes on to say "And ye shall flee *to* the Valley of the mountains; for the valley of the mountains shall reach unto Azal: yea, ye shall flee as ye fled from before the earthquake in the days of Uzziah King of Judah".

This valley that is to reach all the way to Azal, is a name that is strikingly similar to other names of Atlantis, though I can't be certain this is what is spoken of and I assumed it was just a lost Israeli place name nearby. However checking into this name I could find no knowledge exists as to what this place Azal is or was. Following east west would actually get you to where Atlantis was... Azal is very reminiscent of the Aztec name of Aztlan the Aztecs call their destroyed homeland. To be fair, there is a sunken civilization off the coast of Israel near Atlit-Yam. Could this verse be referring to this place after it sunk? However it is considerably north of the east west split of the mount while Atlantis is almost directly east of this mount. Indeed older Portalano maps actually place what would be where Atlantis was directly east of Jerusalem which is very near to the Mount of Olives. Could Azal be a biblical reference to Atlantis?

The sinking of Atlantis could also have sunk the Bimini wall as well as other Bahamian, Bermudan and Gulf of Mexico sites. Of course as we've seen the ancients spoke of four previous world ages, three of which are post flood so I can't say definitively which age sunk or raised what land. But they probably all involved Atlantis in some way with it being right in the middle of all the action, and even Plato notes that two cataclysms hit Atlantis.

Still the sinking of Atlantis is linked with the flood of Noah but it should be linked with a global series of floods and not the global one. But it is understandable how some Atlanteanologists, or whatever they call themselves, can make the mistake of confusing flood legends here.

As mentioned an anonymous diver found some pottery and ceramic figurines buried beside an underwater building (identical to one in Yucatán) off Andros Island. Photographs of find sent to many experts around the world yielded no identification. None of the people he sent them to had seen similar pots, and no one would even risk categorizing, fearing ridicule from other experts. (Book 8 pg 73) However any pottery fired can be approximately dated, so the pots were tested and they were dated to between 5000, and 3000 BC. Nearby some underwater caverns are studded with stalactites and stalagmites. (Book 8 pg 75) These formations, by reason of close proximity, indicate this whole area was above water around the same period, which happens to be the same era as the age of the gods.

ATLANTIS LOCATIONS

The continent of Atlantis in theory has a limited potential original size based on what matches up from the eastern and western part of the Atlantic land masses before continental drift commenced. Looking at a current political map of the world placed on a map of Pangaea I come up with some possible examples of match-ups. The most obvious matchup being the easternmost part of Brazil fitting into Cameroon. So if geologic rock compositions along with the vegetation of eastern Brazil matched the south western part of Cameroon perfectly, and fitted like a glove in the place, then no remnant of Atlantis could be in between these two points after the split of Africa and South America occurred, which would of course be the initial cause of the creation of Atlantis. Well, that's the theory, and thus some say because the east and west continents fit so well together there really is not enough remaining vacant or missing land to substantiate the existence of a continent that some say would be about half the size of Australia. There are two possible loop holes in this argument. It's possible that the action that pushed the land masses apart also pushed up new land from under what is now the ocean floor. Indeed the entire Atlantic Ridge could be such a new land mass that emerged then subsequently submerged as the western and eastern continents migrated further apart over the centuries.

Another possibility is that even though, as some suggest, there is no space left for such a continent to fit, perhaps not all places supposed to be fitting west and east are accounted for. Motion of continents is going to deform the land shapes and contours. We can't assume for instance that the western coast of the Central America moved smoothly westward without changes in the shape of the land as it moved. The ridges and fracture zones are not dead straight; several sites on the earth indicate continents twisted and turned as they moved, such as the 20 degree rotation of Antarctica; I mean after all, the world is a sphere. Take the western part of South America, some of it must have subducted under Peru and neighbouring countries meaning some land mass that once existed is probably underneath some coastal mountains as the land folded in on itself like a conveyer belt. That sort of action could slow the continents movement in some parts and offer no resistance in others. Only positive matches of eastern and western shores can eliminate the possibility of extra land masses in between. One obvious case is Africa and South America. When Africa and South America are placed beside each other, though there is a pretty good fit, and the subterranean deposits also match up very well, it's clear some land has gone missing. Yet some maps of Pangaea place Africa and South America tightly together when this is not actually the case; they fit loosely at best...something is missing. A dramatic possible example is in the famous White cliffs of Dover as this is clearly a dividing partition break up point of land masses...a matching piece has to be somewhere. If say the cliffs were on the western part of the British Isles, and if there was no Atlantean matching or missing land in between, then we could also expect to find the corresponding white cliffs of Greenland or Iceland existing where the break-up would have occurred. If nothing could be found to match then we could assume that matching part is now underwater somewhere in between and thus is part of the missing land mass.

Surprisingly, though many maps of what the continent of Pangaea looked like before the break-up exist, and they all have the same basic pieces in the same spots, they don't all match each other exactly. There appears to be some discrepancy as to what exactly it looked like or how tightly to fit the pieces. So there is the possibility that such a continent, if not too large...maybe more properly a long island could have existed. One of the originators of the continental drift theory, Alfred Wegener, felt that the land masses of the earth fit perfectly together like a jigsaw puzzle, except for a vacant area in the southern part of the North Atlantic which, which as it happens, is exactly where Plato said Atlantis used to be. (Book 6 pg 179) This should be considered a further substantiation of Plato's assertions.

Only a definitive geological survey matching grove for tongue; from east to west could either eliminate or delineate the existence of such a land mass or define its former exact location and former existence. The floor of the Atlantic Ocean does have some aid in this matter, as there are definitive areas of old and new ocean flood bottom. Plot these accurately and you get an exact determination of lost land. I'm not the guy for that survey. But for fun I've plotted as many suspicious underwater findings that suggest or positively identify underwater archaeological sites on a map of the Atlantic. Now they may not all have been part of Atlantis, as it appears some parts of Central America have succumbed to the waves. And it's quite possible some parts of Atlantis are still above water where we don't expect. For example one map of Pangaea suggests Nova Scotia was originally connected to Atlantis and then further on connected to Morocco, thus part of Nova Scotia could actually be a remnant of Atlantis, or at least delineate part of its western coast. Well anyway, for what it's worth and for the fun of it and curiosity's sake, here are the points I've plotted on the map of the Atlantic, some of them mentioned in text. (**See Image 15 and following details**)

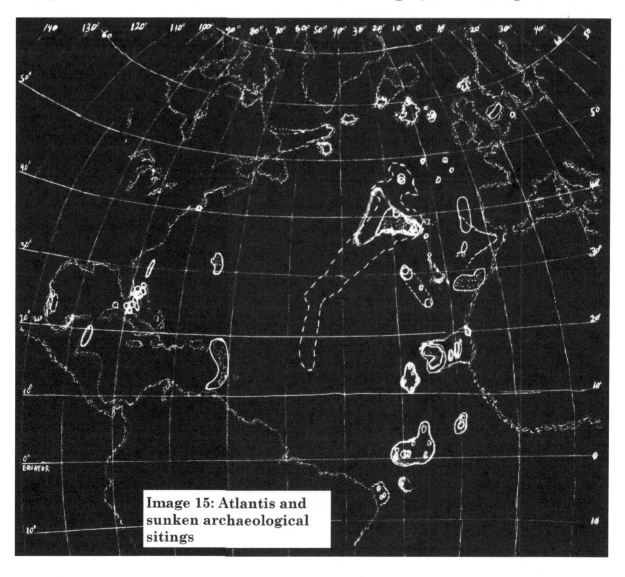

Image 15: Atlantis and sunken archaeological sitings

SUNKEN ATLANTIC LANDS PLOTTED ON A MAP OF THE ATLANTIC OCEAN AS IT APPEARS TODAY.

Extra Island and partial islands, probably remnant islands of Atlantis seen on Zeno map of 1380, named Estland, Icaria, Estotiland(western half only), Drogeo (Northeast part only), Frisland and a few smaller ones now no longer there, are plotted on the map. What is shown as Frisland separated 3 degrees from Scotland may now be just the submerged Rockall Bank 6 or 7 degrees to the west of Scotland. It's very much worth noting that from the 1550's to the 1660's people from Greenland and Europe traded with this well populated island of Frisland's people.

I've also included some of the now missing islands seen on the map titled "SEPTENTRE / ONA / LIVM RE / GIONVM / DESCRIP" which has a lot in common with the Zeno map, but covers more area.

The Book of Adela's followers apparently in the know of ancient Atlantean geographic history indicates that the eastern boundary of Atlantis was closer to England than the width of the North Sea and extended northward toward the coast of Denmark and Norway. (Book 31 pg 20-21 referring to this book) So the Estland Island* by Norway on the Zeno map of 1380 also appears to have been part of Atlantis or one of its islands. Furthermore it states that there was only a narrow straight between Atlantis and Greenland. (Ibid) Though not really plottable, it does lend further credibility to the additional lost islands plotted on the map. This suggests that the islands, Iceland, Icaria*, Estotiland* and possibly Drogeo* were all connected and very close to the northern part of Atlantis or even connected. (* All islands named on the Zeno map of 1380) Indeed the Reykjanes Ridge, connected to the Iceland shelf, is twisted away from the Mid Atlantic Ridge. This ridge is parallel to Greenland and likely contains the remains of these islands. Also Heligoland near the southern most part of the North Sea, may have been closer to Atlantis' northern most regions than would normally be thought if Estland is also included as part of Atlantis, and if you add Doggerland into the picture. These may not have been physically attached to Atlantis but within their political sphere. Plato said "Now in the island of Atlantis there was a great and wonderful empire, which had rule over the whole island and several others." And note he doesn't call Atlantis a continent here, her calls it an Island, though probably the largest.

Solon's story of Atlantis indicated that Atlantis was fairly close to the Pillars of Hercules compared to the far side of Atlantis and beyond which was a real ocean. Indeed he stated that Atlantis was "in front" of the pillars as thought it might have actually been visible from the coasts of Portugal, the southern part of Spain and Morocco. This would account for the straight being impossible to navigate at the time, on account of the massive build-up of mud / lava on the water from the destruction of the land so close by, and why such a concentration of ancient artifacts and cave paintings exists on the coast of Portugal and Morocco because these lands were pretty close and not too difficult to reach. It would also account for Atlantis ongoing invasions of Europe and Africa; they were in striking distance and their homeland was never far from the 'front'. Also, if the Mid Atlantic ridge is part of the former continent, it suggests that the Americas drifted further and faster away from Europe and Africa, rather than both sides moving equally away from the ridge. They would have been pushed by some agent causing the Atlantic fault expansion, such as a meteor, the pyramids, or a close encounter with a planet, causing a magnetic displacement that subsequently shifted the continents, and this movement was possibly aided by the very rotation of the earth itself.

THE PLOTTING THICKENS

Here are the underwater sites of interest plotted on the map.

A possible pyramid 23°27'N - 24°10'N and 079°25'W – 080°35'W 23°26'N, 79°43'W (book 6 pg 106)

Cay Bank Sal (Near Bahamas Just north of the previous site; book 6 pg 105).

45 Miles north east of Miami huge building spotted underwater from a plane (Book 6 pg 107)

Diver finds Pyramid by Berry Islands (Book 6 pg. 108-09,)

Between Florida and Bahamas spotted from chartered flights stepped terraces, walls, and pyramid like structures (book 6 pg. 80)

Bahamas fifty underwater Archaeological sites, plus stalactites and stalagmites. (Book 6 pg. 175)

Roads continue out to sea from the shores and beyond from Yucatan and Belize (Book 6 pg. 175)

North of Venezuela 100 mile underwater road. (Book 6 pg 175)I plotted this only by guesswork. I couldn't see any trace of it on Google Earth, and the long road I had seen on the east coast of Cuba that extended about 100 miles into the Caribbean had disappeared...Erased?

Ampere Seamount north of Madeira [Walls pavements and steps] (Book 6 pg 176)

Southwest of Azores near Sao Miguel and Santa Maria towers and pyramid as suggested by bathymetric profile (Book 6 pg. 181/184)

About 500 miles north of the Azores (at the location of the 1898 Atlantic cable break was found tachylite, above ground open air formation of lava: Now known as Telegraph Bank. (Book 6 pg 171)

North of Azores rocks found formed at atmospheric pressure, found in same general area as Telegraph Bank (Book 6 pg. 171)

A "...discovery of elephant teeth from the Atlantic Continental shelf between 200 and 300 miles off the Portuguese coast at more than 40 different dredge site locations from the depths of 360 feet." (Atlantis Rising magazine #71) With over 40 spots yielding sites from this area we have a very large plotted lozenge off the coast of Portugal.

Solon told Plato that Atlantis was in front of the Pillars; language that suggests it was quite near the Strait of Gibraltar. Solon indicated this, first by saying mud blocked passage out from the Pillars of Hercules and by stating Atlantis was "in front" of the pillars which suggests Atlantis may even have been visible from the European shore. (Book 14 pg 157) So how far can you see across water before land disappears beneath the horizon? So we need to check how far one could see to a point on the horizon and then land beyond the horizon. Atlantis is said to have had some major mountains. If they were close to the eastern coast of Atlantis, they would have been visible beyond the ocean horizon. The Rock of Gibraltar though 426 meters or 1398 feet high cannot see out to the Atlantic as its view is blocked. So picking a point on the Spanish coast I chose Andalusia which is 3300 feet or 1006 meters high and has an unobstructed view of the Atlantic. This means the horizon would be visible from this point to about 77 miles; the greatest distance you could spot an incoming invasion force on water. If we assume Atlantis was at least this high near the coast, it could have been visible as far as 154 miles away. If the large mountains said to have existed on Atlantis were visible and obviously much higher, Atlantis could have been seen from much further. But we'll assume Atlantis was visible 150 miles as a minimum distance from an elevation of 3300 feet. I've plotted the shape of the Azores Plateau in this region on the map. If it was visible from the "Pillars", Atlantis was considerably closer than this.

Between Venezuela and Virgin Islands continental granite and basaltic rock (Book 6 pg. 171)

Coral (which grows around islands in shallow water) found near Great Meteor Seamount Approx. 30°N, 28° W (Book 6 pg. 183)

Volcanic ash and insects found in many places along Mid-Atlantic ridge (book 6 pg. 183)

Freshwater Diatoms and plants found in Mid-Atlantic ridge. (Book 6 pg. 184)Could not find any location attributed to this find

Cores brought up by Swedish ship Albatross with shallow water organisms and twigs plants, and tree bark near St. Peter and St. Paul Rocks 29°W 1°N(Book 6 pg. 185)

Captain David Robson on *Jesmond* finds dead fish and a new island with walls, ruins, swords, carvings and other artifacts. 31°25'N, 28°40W (Book 6 pg. 77)

Captain James Newdick of Westbourne finds more dead fish and new island at 25° 30'N, 24°W. (Book 6 pg. 79: Joined by dotted line on the map to above site.)

Another island known to have existed at one time is called St. Brendan's (Brandan, or Borondon) Island

(28°N, 7°W,) directly east of the canaries and straight south of the Azores) is on some ancient maps and has since been eliminated. It lies right between the two sightings just mentioned.

Planes spot clusters of buildings near St. Peter and St. Paul Rocks at 1°N, 30°W. (Book 6 pg. 80)

Stone and possibly marble ruins spotted off northern coast of Cuba. (Book 6 pg. 80)

Underwater stone work photographed on Bahama Banks. (Book 6 pg. 81)

Underwater stone work photographed off East coast of Mexico. (Book 6 pg. 81)

So many sightings of underwater ruins near the Bahamas have been reported that the Bermudan Government has set up a museum to house artifacts from the underwater finds to preserve them from being exploited and lost to posterity. Firm proof has established these underwater ruins as definitely man made and not natural formations or 'intrusive', that is to say not dropped by ships. Because this has now been established, increased investigation has found more buildings at increasingly deeper levels. (Book 24 pg. 99) So the entire Bermuda Island has been encircled on the map.

The Buache map of 1737 shows the Canary Islands but it includes the outline of the plateau they rest on as well. (Book 6 pg. 142) Finding this Philippe-Buache-map it appears this writer has confused the Cape Verdes Islands with the Canaries which are not on this map but further north. The Cape Verdes have the islands connected at least by a surrounding shoal and three more islands between them and Africa along with shore lines or shoals continuing from the Cape Verde Islands back to Africa. But what is interesting is there is a large island to the west of them slightly westward of the central part of the Atlantic between South America and Africa. The southern most part is on and south of the equator. And there are other islands making the area between Africa and South America filled with large stepping stones of islands that are no longer there. Interestingly the map I used to plot the St. Brendan Island also shows a shallow island (or sand bar?) well off of Africa towards the Cape Verde which now delineates the continental shelf: all these are gone now.

The 1489 Portalano map of Albino de Canepa has several islands in the north south orientation depicted as a 'string of pearls', or islands that are no longer there. Amaziningly, satellite images show sunken islands in these same areas.

"Ruins have been sighted near the Canary and Azore Islands, off the coast of North Africa and Spain, the North coast of Cuba [already plotted] ...and giant walls off the coast of Yucatán and Venezuela." (Book 24 pg. 98) With what has been said to this point about the Canary Islands I think it's safe to encircle the entire islands with one large plot.

Five miles north of Heligoland in North Sea (book 35 pg 21) Has Atlantis links so it too is placed on the map.

I've also placed Doggerland on this map.

Though location not noted a Dr. Valentine found manmade sloping walls off the Bahamian islands. But this confirms other sightings in same Islands if not the same one.

Off northern tip of Andros Island, Robert Brush spotted from an airplane a square structure in shallow water. (Book 35 pg 206-207) This claim is backed up by a diver who discovered 14 buildings somewhere off the Coast of Andros Island. Some had limestone walls 4 feet thick. The biggest building was 80 feet wide and 240 feet long. Relics found near these underwater buildings were dated to be between 3000 and 5000 B.C. (book 8 pg 71-73) Divers don't like to tell where their secret dive finds are, but since there are so many sightings of buildings underwater in this general area, they serves as confirming witness in a class action suit trial of Truth versus the school textbooks and the conspiracy of the established sciences. I can't even plot this sighting as the map already has too many spots plotted in this general area.

In the Grand Bahama Bank west of Andros Island there was spotted man made rectangular constructions. (Book 35 pg. 207)

Lava spread over parts of the Mid Atlantic Ridge indicates some of, or this entire ridge, was at one time above the surface. (Book 6 pg. 183) Plotted as a dotted line.

The Challenger stated the entire ridge of Atlantis was covered with a volcanic deposit, which is subsided mud and volcanic fallout. (Book 64 pg 71) If they meant the Atlantic ridge, it would mean the entire Atlantic ridge was at one time above water because the previous plot description notes that the entire ridge was above water. This sort of surprised me. Why you say when here I am trying to prove Atlantis existed? Looking at maps of the world underwater ridges, I've always assumed the shape of ridges, and the Atlantic ridge in particular, was due to the forces within the planet that pushed the Atlantic Ocean floor bottom sideways and caused the continents to part company. But it suggests this scarring is a result of what was once land being deformed to make it appear this way, similar to what the St. Andreas fault line looks like on land. It then dawns on me that most Maps of Pangaea press the outlines of the continents together assuming these form the edges of the puzzle pieces, when in fact they should be using the continental shelves as the edges of the pieces. Key in all this would be the continental shelf around Newfoundland. This apparently is the section that came from the area of the Pillars of Hercules. This is a difference of as much as 600 miles added to in between the continental jigsaw not accounted for, which in turn adds more space between the continents which allows more land to have existed before the breakup of the continents and thus more space to squeeze a small continent or large island in, making the former existence Atlantis that much more feasible. HOWEVER, on the other hand if the volcanic ash and mud landed on dry ground then the destruction of Atlantis occurred forcing the mid Atlantic ridge to spread the continents apart, this could make Atlantis appear larger than it really was by spreading the former surface ash farther apart as the ridge expanded. It's kind of like a balloon. When you buy them they are about 2 inches wide, but when you blow them up they can be as big as a foot. So if Atlantis was originally 2 measurements wide, the spreading of the Atlantic ridge spreads out the remains of Atlantis to make it look like it was 12 measurements wide. Thus accurate deciphering of all these facts such as continental shelves and ridge and ocean floor expansion would need to be done to get a truly accurate picture of what Atlantis looked like. Many people suggest part or all of the Gulf of Mexico may have been part of Atlantis, but based on the mapping of the continental drift, this section was attached to the northern parts of South America. It was therefore just part of Central America, and not part of Atlantis, so its ties are more associated with the Mayan, Yucatan, whereas only that which is found east of Florida, such as the Bahamas, and around to the Antilles could have Atlantis association. Still, in the big picture, plotting the points in the gulf which have archaeological evidence is still important.

Enough finds have been found near the Azores that I feel it safe to surround these islands in one large encirclement plot.

A paved road containing magnesium oxide was discovered by the deep diving submarine *Aluminaut* in January 1967 that lay off the coast of Florida and extended up past Georgia and along to South Carolina at the 3000 foot depth.(Book 35 pg 100) (plotted as the long thin oval in this area)

Step pyramid complex just off north tip of Manhattan Island.

INVASIONS...YARRR!

Though probably not plottable, "Irish legends tell of invasions by the equally mysterious Firborgs, also from the Atlantic, and ruins of Irish stone forts, thousands of years old, show evidence of calcinations from extreme heat. The Atlantic coasts of Spain and France as well as the islands of the Mediterranean also retain legends and ruins traced to invasions from west at a point far back in time." (Book 6 pg 22) Berlitz is relying on his knowledge of legends here to show they back up what Plato's story of Atlantis relates, without quoting specific legends. So based on just this blurb I don't know how Mediterranean evidence can be ascertained to be of Atlantic origins; but the Spanish, French and Irish legends speak volumes.

A strong civilization had to have lived close enough to the western coast of Europe to make it worth their while to invade multiple times. No one would dare suggest the North American Natives or Inuit Eskimos canoed all the way from America to invade these lands let alone do it several times over a broad expanse of the coast. The invasion had to have come from somewhere closer to Europe, but where? Only the history of Atlantis can explain this.

Correspondingly the Atlanteans are said to have been highly advanced technologically. What else could explain the calcined forts of Ireland? All other attempts to explain the partially melted forts fall short of logic, such as the enemy piling massive piles of combustible material on the walls of the fort and setting them on fire to weaken the walls; as if they would not get shot at by arrows from the wall while doing this at the same time as tossing water on the fire, or how it could accomplish the calcification of the entire fort. Some have suggested the sun went berserk and got so hot as to melt rock here on earth. I find this explanation clutching at straws to ignore the legends such as the Chinese histories that tell of aerial craft scorching fortifications. No one wants to suggest high technological weapons such as near nuclear capacity bombs could have accomplished this, or something more exotic like lasers or who knows what. Vast technology was known and mastered by the ancients, which I go into more detail in my first book. But don't take my word for it, several other explorers of ancient legends, mysteries and archaeological evidences have also concluded that ancient man had nuclear capabilities and used them. Point is, these attacks came from close enough and strong enough enemies to rule out a North American origin, but from some land much closer. No 'close enough' place exists today to explain these invasions unless the place these invasions came from has since vanished beneath the waves: Ergo Atlantis. To add weight to this, the Irish legends also speak of a Tirnannoge which has to do with a great city that sunk beneath the waters. Celtic legends also refer to a 'City of the Golden Gates" that also had extensive use of gold in the capital city also under the Atlantic waves, and quite similar to Plato's story of Atlantis. (Book 6 pg 46)

ATLANTIS OTHER ISLAND BEHIND

As mentioned Plato stated that before Atlantis sank, the Atlantic was sailable from this island onward to the west and beyond so that you could reach the other islands further on, then clear of them to the continent past them. Islands don't just litter the oceans so you can make a lucky guess; there are plenty of areas in the world oceans where there are no islands over vast stretches of water. But there are islands a-plenty directly west of where evidence clearly indicates some great land existed at one time, exactly where Plato indicated it was: and this can only be Atlantis. In addition, there is similar evidence to indicate that much of the floor of the Caribbean, Gulf of Mexico, and West Indies were also above water during historical times. There are so many underwater ruins in these areas that these islands also had to have experienced the same destructive force Atlantis was subjected to, and at the same time and with similar results.

DESTRUCTION LEGEND

A very interesting story comes from an antelope skin found in Guatemala which tells of the destruction of an island with clues, which I won't go into, that lead people to believe it speaks of Atlantis. This island split open in a burst of flame and an enormous serpent coming through the ocean from the east swallowed up the giants that inhabited the island along with their treasures and even some gates.

This 'serpent' almost certainly has to be Typhon, which we've established is linked with the close approach to the earth by a planet, and this ever-present Typhon legend suggests this water spout took not just water, but giant people and even relics to Mars or Venus. The Serpent king of the island escaped into a tunnel leading to his other realm. (Book 22 pg. 156) This mention of the serpent or Typhon links the destruction of Atlantis with the same destructions that were going on around the world and thus at the same time. Charroux's realizes this too. "These civilizations were destroyed by the cataclysm, and it goes without saying that the continent of Atlantis did not sink without occasioning world-wide tidal disturbances that caused destruction and disaster in all nations." (Book 22 pg 117) One Greek legend speaks of Typhon traveling all across Greece and the surrounding area. The wandering nature of Typhon would be because of turbulence between the planets, and as the world turns, Typhon's general direction of travel would be in whatever direction the world turned in conjunction with the position of Venus or Mars at the time. And indeed many ancient legends from around the world from the Pacific Ocean to the new and ancient world and Asia spoke of this phenomenon. A battle between Zeus and Typhon is also described as ranging over a wide area on the earth and in the skies, also indicating that as the planet Venus moved around, and the trail or Typhon water 'snake' followed the motion. (Book 17 pg 54) And of course Zeus is intimately connected to Atlantis.

Look! Up there! *A bird? A plane?* No...Evidence!

Nope, you're not looking high enough...see that round thing in the sky...yeah the moon, there's your evidence.

How can the moon be evidence confirming the ancient flood legends? Well, consider...the moon is littered by impact craters or scars from asteroids and these scars are ubiquitous. (Get your dictionary out) There is a crater on the far side or the 'dark side of the moon' that is positively monstrous and frighteningly hideous. Look at Mercury...no, not that neat old car parked next door...the planet. It too is loaded with impact craters with not a stone on the entire planet left unturned by their crashing force.

Uranus is orbiting the sun on its side with its pole facing the sun and it is thought this tilt occurred as a consequence of a huge asteroid tipping the planet over onto its side. Mimas one of Saturn's moons was almost blown apart by one huge asteroid which makes the moon look like the death star of *Star Wars* fame. Miranda, one of Uranus' moons, is theorized likely *was*, or nearly was, blown apart and just the gravity of the pieces caused the moon to pull itself back together. The rings of Saturn are composed of a crumbled moon that apparently lost its battle with the asteroids. Mars' moons are considered to just be captured asteroids. What all these examples say, is the solar system was under siege by the destruction of the planet that *was* between Mars and Jupiter. Yeah I know, cosmologists want us to believe these events happened millions of years ago. Ignore them; they are full of champagne from toasting your gullibility, and getting their ridiculous theories used in text books while young earth Creationists are _made_ to look like idiots by an all too agreeable media and an evolution **_THEORY_** infected society. Man in the preflood era blasted that planet and it caused havoc in the solar system; and the fun is not over yet. So now ask yourself, why do Mars and the Earth not have the same number of craters as seen on Mercury, and many moons of the solar system?

The answer is water. Mars stole vast quantities of our water washing out the evidences of the craters like a child's chalk board, and us, we have seven oceans of water, so when these asteroids hit the earth, the water got busy like scrubbing bubbles and cleaned craters off the face of the earth to the point few are visible today. But some evidence still exists that they hit us is still there if you look closely for it...or them.

Besides the obvious craters still existing like the one in Arizona, which babysitting cosmologists want us to think happened 50,000 years ago so we won't wet our pants worrying about the next one. We also have the Canadian Curswell, Deep Bay, and Chub crater 3.22 km across hidden in the northern section of Quebec. Manicouagan crater is 66 kilometres across. We have to assume there are thousands of impact craters on the planet. The Hudson's bay is probably one as it's in the center of the Canadian Shield; which by the ways is 2 million square miles of lava between 20,000 and 50,000 feet thick: This is the one I think that caused the first flood...you know the flood with the big boat filled with critters and the family of eight.

There are multiple scars on the eastern half of USA that can be seen from satellite pictures as washed out impact craters. There's a 65 mile long chunk of something buried under Greenland. In 1964 Otto Muck (a German Rocket engineer) discovered two 'twin' deep sea holes in the ocean floor (exact location not mentioned) that were caused by an asteroid that had split in two before contact. They "...set off a chain reaction of geologic violence along the mid Atlantic ridge". (Atlantis Rising Magazine 35) One giant crater was spotted by the Landsat satellite in 1975 in the Turtle Mountains between North Dakota and Manitoba that is 125 kilometers across. The Reis Kessel Crater in Central Europe was hard to spot because it's filled with vegetation, woods, fields, and some towns. Apparently it's kinda big so not easy to spot. The Vredefort Dome in South Africa is so huge it took a long time to be recognized as an asteroid impact crater. (Book 6 pg 202, 203) How many craters haven't we found yet; say in the backwoods of Brazil, or destroyed as the continents shifted forcing the water overland to erase the evidence, or that just landed in the sea making instant tsunamis? THIS was why the ancients were scared stiff of comets; because there were so damned many of them and virtually all of them spelled d-i-s-a-s-t-e-r! Historians checking ancient records often note there were far more comets visible in the skies then now. Why is this? Because like a marble collection being tossed at your brother, you eventually run out of marbles and you are more careful with your shots. (I assume brothers do this to each other...*My* marble collection was picked up from the wrong end and they all fell out of the sock...unfortunately everyone in the park saw this mistake. Needless to say the marble collection suffered a huge decrease in size that day...no one threw them at me...though a few friends did give me some of the ones they picked up....yes I had friends!)

The asteroids came from that blown up planet, and there was a time when there were thousands of them up there causing havoc in the solar system. But, as they landed on the planets, the moons and the sun, the total asteroid / meteor count dwindled and they came to earth less often to the point where we are today. Now we only see them occasionally and only when someone on the news mentions them and you happen to know someone with a telescope to spot the tiny things. The Russian Astronomer S.K. Vsehsviatsky observed "The rapid decrease in luminosity of periodical comets points to some unusual activity in the sky in the geologically recent past and felt this unusual activity took place in historical times, only a few thousand years ago" (Book 53 pg 139) Thus historical observations of comets has diminished over the millennia.

Take for instance the historical records show that there were many more comets in the sky in Roman times. Sometimes two or three comets were visible at a time to the naked eye. Some were even visible during the day. Often events were linked to the sightings of comets. Diogenes (5th century BC) wrote that things in the sky *frequently* fall to earth. Because it rarely happens now, modern historians at first ridiculed these stories. Now we know better, but Joe average citizen isn't told about these. It wasn't until recently it was admitted that an asteroid the size of a house hits the earth on average once a month.

So, this is why we only see a small fraction of all the impact craters, because they were wiped out by tsunamis of apocalyptic proportions caused by the impacts. All this activity is what helped supply the ancients with all the material for their legends of new suns, and a hand full of world ages. All these impacts punctuated their lives with no equilibrium whatsoever.

INTERCONNECTEDNESS OF GLOBAL MOVES WERE SIMULTANEOUS

Archaeologists have become a little more cynical since Heinrich Schliemann dug up Troy. Evidence of Atlantis has emerged or been dug up countless times, and yet these so called archaeologist refuse to believe the evidence no matter what is found. Lost civilizations they thought were mythical they immediately accept if a single coin confirming its existence is found, yet over 150 classical references to Atlantis exists and countless physical traces have since been unearthed (...or would that be "unwatered"?) Even a perfectly formed pyramid found smack dab in the middle of the Atlantic has failed to convince the elite and the denial of Atlantis's existence is still deafening. Well we here are not trying to prove that Atlantis existed, we're going beyond that. I've assumed that for those of you crazy enough to have kept reading this 'trash' to this point (as I'm sure some...no ...most of the established sciences would ridicule you for reading, not to mention a few English teachers might give the odd thumbs down for my grammar and such) that you have probably accepted Atlantis' prior existences as unassailable. I've only scratched the surface of classical references to Atlantis as I just wanted enough evidence to at least make its existence plausible, as this isn't a book about Atlantis, but of floods. So we are going beyond the proof of Atlantis here, because you no doubt are convinced beyond a reasonable doubt that Atlantis existed...I hope. So more tangibly we are trying to see how the demise of Atlantis fits in with the rest of the world cataclysms you read about.

If the remains, and ancient historically mapped placements of lost lands that we have today of lost Atlantic Ocean lands, as plotted on the map, have been spread east and west by continental drift speeded up by cataclysmic forces in the past such as we've read about so far, then this fairly large mass of land called Atlantis was probably about the total area of Greenland, (if you include the extra islands that were politically linked with the main island) This ancient land appears to have been spread out a bit across the Atlantic, but mostly with a north south orientation. There would indeed seem to have been a long major island which would have been the main Island of Atlantis as delineated by the higher portions of the Mid Atlantic ridge. It would also appear, based on plotting, that the finds in the Caribbean area clustered around Florida and Cuba were not part of Atlantis, but more closely associated with local lands based on archaeological finds, and possibly with the advanced ancient civilizations of North America as found near Manhattan Island. No doubt this map of plottings is far from complete, indeed Plato spoke of several islands beyond Atlantis or on the western side of the island which I've at present found no points to plot, although they may be found on the western half of the mid Atlantic ridge in subsequent searches. The only possible island fitting the description would be Bermuda and the plateau it lies on; surely there must have been more.

However it's a reasonable assumption that the Atlantic abyssal plains are new ocean floor and not part of the masses of land on either side of the Atlantis or any islands that were once there. So they could be considered limiting factors to island extensions. These abyssal plains range from about 12,000 feet to over 19,000 feet deep. We might even use the Atlantic Basins as the farthest reach of the island. But I admit that is just my uneducated guess.

The conclusion I have to come to, is the entire distance between the America's and the Euro-African continents was created between 3309 BC and about 670 B.C. If, as Plato stated, Atlantis had two major cataclysms over its duration, or even if we take the four past world ages spoken of in so many ancient legends, all of which would have been associated with the spread of the continents, then we could see that a huge amount of continental drift would be associated with each cataclysm or world age. If we use Atlantic Ocean floor maps and the abyssal plains as our borders, the continents would have drifted east-west about 400 miles during the close of each world age. Even if we use the basins as our guide, the spread is still over 300 miles per world age. Or if we assume the continental spread is associated with just the width of the Atlantic ridges as mapped on ocean floor maps divided by two (half being the spread, and half being what was land) that is still about 800 miles of additional distance between the Americas and the Euro-African landmass, after the initial dividing of the land around 100 years after the flood of Noah. This still translates to about 270 miles of continental divide for each of the subsequent three world ages: not counting the flood of Noah when there was no divide. Now of course some cultures such as India, Asian and even the biblical clues suggest there may have been as many as 7 to 9 world ages or cataclysmic incidences major enough to initiate global structural and continental changes. This might suggest these continental drifts were divided into smaller portions, but it's still a spread of about 100 miles each time the world experienced these upheavals.

WHY DID WE SURVIVE?

No doubt the spreads were uneven, but even so, such huge upheavals and massive, fast continental drifts would suggest we should all be dead. Why did anyone survive? The first and possibly the biggest divide or continental drift creating the continents in the first place would have spread the land masses away from civilization pushing water over the farthest reaches of land where few if any people lived to be overrun by the waves. The new Atlantic Ocean created in the first drift would have been full of active volcanoes evaporating the inrushing seas as the divided area spread and the waters came in from around Africa and South America and from the polar region. Assuming Mount Ararat was at the center of the spread of civilization, few people if anyone would have been affected. This initial drift would have created the islands of the Atlantic including Atlantis. With the Gods causing this initial drift, it might have been the inspiration for moving their center of operations to the newly created island in the new ocean. After all they 'created' it; why not flaunt the fact by moving there. And indeed it appears many of the gods were associated with this island, as both sides of the Atlantic have legends of the gods coming from or living in this place.

But there were more continental drifts that caused the break up and eventually the demise of Atlantis along with the spreading of the continents further apart: why did we survive these? Well as we saw some people were warned by the gods and they built underground passage, tunnels and cities to live in and they led the surface people down there to be safe from the waves. Again all ancient legends speak of underground civilizations and tunnels and to be sure we've even found some of these tunnels to verify the legends. But that still only accounts for three of the world ages. Also once again it seems the spread of the continents was away from the former center of civilization so the more populous civilized areas would only have been affected by massive tsunamis and not continental ones as experiences by North America and a large part of eastern Asia. In addition, polar shifts and continental twists deflected water directions and the hurricane force winds. Some tornado force winds originated from space itself and actually froze some of the waves in mid crest, some of which are still frozen to this day! Furthermore, global volcanic action served to evaporate a large share of water, in some cases actually drying up ocean beds, leaving little water to cause much damage. Also with Mars and Venus coming for a visit, apparently during three of these events, they pulled much of the water upward towards them in the sky restraining the water's destructive potential. Clearly the legends of people on the outer rims of continental land masses spoke of few people surviving, but these restraints seemed to limit the destruction to a survivable series of catastrophes.

WHOSE BREAK IS IT?

In a group pool game that's the question you ask if you're not sure who broke last. To understand how a cataclysm event could be experienced globally we need to understand that what happens in one part of the globe, can affect places in other parts of the globe, depending on the severity of the event.

In a game of pool 15 snooker or billiard balls are racked up in tight equilateral triangle formation and left to be struck with the cue ball by the shooter whose break it is. When you hit the front part of the triangle of balls, the balls in the back of the triangle scatter through kinetic energy transferred through all the balls. The kinetic energy of the hit shatters and scatters the pool balls. A similar phenomenon occurs in the earth when one area is affected by a seismic event.

Nikola Tesla understood that the power of resonated harmonic vibration, when tuned to the right frequency, could in fact destroy the earth. He made a link of the finest steel which was capable of bearing 100 tons. Crowbars and sledgehammers couldn't touch it, but with an adjustable device attached to it and then started up with a tuned timed rhythmic tapping on the steel link ...tapping that wouldn't harm a baby, he had the link starting to contract and dilate within minutes like a "beating heart" and finally break. His experiments showed the earth has a periodicity of 1 hour and 49 minutes and that a similar power could destroy the earth. He figured this could be done with dynamite set off at this specific interval of 109 minutes and within a few weeks the crust of the earth would be heaving hundreds of feet in the air. What appears to have been a larger version of a pocket resonator he made was attached to a pole in his apartment on Houston Street (NYC) and set tapping. Soon the police station 14 blocks away on Mulberry Street began to shake with plaster falling off the ceiling and chairs moving around. Interestingly, the police knew where to go and when they got to Tesla's place they found him smashing the device, as turning it off would have not been quick enough! Yup, it happened on Mulberry Street. (Book 52 pg. 102-103)

Places on the earth are thought to be linked with other areas geologically and when something happens in one place, like sound traveling underwater, or like those pool balls breaking, the effect is felt in other places setting off further incidences there. Geyser activity in Yellowstone Park altered significantly after the major earthquake that struck Alaska in 1964. (Book 19 pg 121) Another earthquake that struck Alaska on Good Friday 1966 caused most of the eastern seaboard to rise then fall two inches. (Book 23 pg. 217) Molten surges in Iceland have been linked with similar ones occurring in Hawaii. (Book 19 pg 121) On September 10 1978 25,000 Iranians lost their lives in a quake considered to have been caused by an underground nuclear test 36 hours earlier 1500 miles away. A U.S. Geological Survey determined that a quake on August 13 1978 in Santa Barbara was caused by activities at an exploratory oil well off shore four days earlier. Reports of a lithium bomb exploded by the Soviets in 1953 on the neck of the Kamchatka peninsula caused a major earthquake, that "dented" the earth and a seismic shock wave traveled several times around the globe. (Book 47 pg 183) As mentioned before, the Three Gorges Dam built in China is the world's largest dam by 50%. While the dam was filling up, the earth experienced a measurable wobble. And it's acknowledged that the dam and reservoir can induce seismicity, that is, earthquakes. That was caused by just displacement of water sitting on land! Just the weight of the water put pressure on the land underneath causing an earthquake. Engineers that were consulting on the Three Gorges project realized the magnitude of the potential disasters plausible with this dam, and begged off the project not wanting to be associated with any possible failure of the dam. Were this dam to fail, or be damaged by an earthquake, millions of lives would be lost.

If these somewhat tame events can trigger seismic activity far from the initial source, what on earth could have happened in the past?

Robert Charroux deduced that the event that destroyed Atlantis also would have caused worldwide tidal disturbances and disaster to all nations. Well that is pretty minimal, and I think his guess falls way short of what happened.

Geologists in some ways have clued in. They have determined violent earthquakes that occurred around 1500 B.C. destroyed part of the world and caused colossal tidal waves that changed much of the geography of the earth. (Book 22 pg 117, 128) Well that's a little better. Indeed that's a hair breadth away from admitting the continents shifted in recorded history. Why? Would a mere tidal wave or tsunami really change the delineation of continental land masses? Not likely. Only continental shifting could do so outside of small areas suddenly submerging, such as a giant sinkhole under a coastal region, like we've seen happened to some Mediterranean locales.

Seismologists fear that a major quake along the San Andreas fault-zone could actually shatter the continent. (Book 23 pg 217) Better still. Indeed some psychics and prognostications feel this fault will cause massive global upheavals in the near future. One book's research felt this might happen before the end of the 1990's (Book 19). Some sources continue this probability and say as early as 2019. (Nexus Magazine) Studies of the northern section of the globe suggest the entire northern hemisphere appeared to have experienced a sudden, rapid unexplained climate change across the entire area at the same time. (Book 7 pg. 162) A correlation between pole reversals and animal extinctions, sudden climate changes and a maximum of volcanic activity has been determined to have occurred around the entire planet simultaneously, extinguishing marine and land animals alike. Yes animals we've seen before and animals that are now extinct as a result...such as flash frozen woolly mammoths...and yes...dinosaurs. (Book 19 pg. 163-64) And these events did not happen 65 million years ago, but are clearly described as events occurring during the changes of the world ages.

Alfred Wegener concluded that it was continental drift that accounted for the destruction of Atlantis (Book 22 pg. 118.) Now someone has clued in! Yes that's exactly what happened; the two events were part and parcel of each other...the same event. And it was in all likelihood linked with the same event just mentioned...the one with the wooly mammoths...and >cough<...dinosaurs. AND ...drum roll please... Charles Berlitz found evidence that brought about the conclusion that the rising of the Andes was propelled by the same event that sunk Atlantis. (Book 6 pg. 193) Is the picture clearing up for you now?

Discovery of Ancient American civilizations and Atlantean proof isn't entirely due to hostile opinion of archaeologists towards the idea, though it appears to be the bulk. Atlantis has resisted discovery and full disclosure partly because Spanish gold sunken in the new world waters was more attractive to seekers than looking for something archaeologists, geologists and historians said didn't exist, combined with the problem of...where do you look!? Physical evidence of Atlantis, other than classical references, has almost completely, simply been a series of chance discoveries to this point. The Atlantic is a large place, so only these chance discoveries have slowly dotted the waterscape. A marked rising of the Grand Bahama Bank since 1968 has added to the mix, by now revealing things in new pictures that were not visible before, such as a 100 foot long rock arrow pointing southeast found between North and South Cat cays, Bimini and South Caicos. Other sites previously found have been cleared of sediments from tidal actions not previously happening due to the rise. Atlantean research has accelerated since 1968 and at some point will reach a watershed and the floodgates will open forcing Archaeologists to finally admit its existence. This is a hard fought battle because doing so means admitting violent cataclysmic catastrophism occurred on earth during historical times. However not even that is not assured, as many seekers of the lost continent consider Atlantis 'prehistoric', although this is a contradiction of terms because it is in fact classical history that revealed it existence to us in the first place, therefore Atlantis is "Historic" and not "Prehistoric"

Even when conventional archaeology does finally admit Atlantis existed they will stick with Plato's 9,000 year version and place its existence at the end of the ice age, and blame ocean rise on its sunken nature and justify this by new dating forced dates attributed to the Sphinx and other ancient civilizations with the phony exaggerated dating methods going on. Civilization as we know it started after the flood of Noah and this had a date, depending on deductions, of between 2400 and 3300 BC. Civilization spread after the flood and therefore all global civilization can be no older than this unless preflood relics are unearthed. These will date incredibly old owing to the fact that little or no radiation entered earth's atmosphere before the flood, as most dating methods rely on radiometric decay measurements. Thus if no radiation existed on earth at the time, relics will appear to date incredibly old because the water sphere before the flood filtered out all that radiation. This near zero radiation count in earth's atmosphere even affects early post flood relics which absorbed very little C14 due to there being so little of it around after the flood. This explains why some post-flood sites appear to be so old because they were dated by relying on Carbon 14 method dating wood from just after the flood (and not relying on tree ring matches). For example Gobekli Tepe was dated 12,000 B.C. by relying on Carbon 14 to date wood found on the site. Sphinx was dated around the same period due to apparent rain water wear, which by the way was dominant on one side of the statue. But this little detail was assumed to be from predominant windy weather and rain hitting that side of the structure. But water wear affecting only one side could happen if one side of the statue was worn by a tsunami, thus wearing away one side faster than the other. Since this explanation was not considered, it made the Sphinx appear much older. Since the dating of Gobekli Tepe was considered reasonable because the Sphinx was now dated from this same period, consequently it appeared to confirm and add weight to the Gobekli Tepe date attributed to it. So what has happened in archeology is that circular reasoning has now gotten a firm foothold in dating ancient sites. They date something older, which makes people free to assume their item is older too. If that is this old then this must be that old too. It is the same way they date fossils: by the rocks they are found with, and the rocks are dated by the fossils found with them. No one wants to rely dating based on ancient history, with the possible exception of Indian dates, because they all place these events in finite date windows, the windows that everyone seems to be jumping out of to get the restraints of history off of their backs. And this is probably a contributing factor to archaeologists, geologists and paleontologists ignoring the legends. I mean if paleontologists say dinosaurs existed 65,000,000 years ago, yet Indians say they remember hunting monstrous lizards, then not wanting to look like idiots, the Paleontologists are going to say the legends are ridiculous.

Admitting Atlantis existed might even tip the scales violently in the same direction. I mean people are dating manmade things found underwater in the millions of years. Maybe shoe and foot prints found in rock will allow archaeologists to promote civilization as being millions of years old, maybe even started by spacemen... anything to get away from the biblical and historical dating that lends credibility to the Bible and ancient peoples legends and their version of history.

Modern science resists this eventuality like the plague, and so will continue to dream up ridiculous theories to divert our attention from a God that cares how we are, what we do, and our eternal destinies. Even the ancient legends point to God as existing, though you have to be a bit more careful with them because they often confused God with the gods. So like Von Daniken and others who have followed in his footsteps, they will equate the God of the bible to be just another one of the gods, just like India has done. They will justify this by saying the gods of India said they were millions of years old so therefore civilization must be this old also, thumbing their nose up at the biblical and other historical ages of the earth as ridiculous.

Close analysis of the gods of India would however match up and identify them as the same people as other gods of ancient history such as Zeus, Atlas, and Poseidon and so on; meaning they are not millions of years old but from the same age and period as the age of the gods. (that or the events they tell of would match up with events elsewhere) Such a match-up of the gods would show their stories to be full of exaggeration. The gods appear to have made our ancestors ogle in suspense and hang on their every word and gotten us to serve them, build with them and even mourn their departure. It even appears some of the gods promised immortality to humans if they served them and preserved their bodies after death so they could be cloned, as they did with Osiris. But as we'll see, the gods were not adverse to stretching the truth or even lying to men to serve some malignant or selfish purpose, or just because it was fun to lead the comparative idiots astray. Some of the gods were truly benevolent doing their level best to help and aid man to prosper and become civilized and overcoming the effects of cataclysms and the harmful environment that was dulling our brains turning us into savages. And some were just using us for their own purposes and some apparently were just plain belligerent to our very existence as a vastly devolved version of themselves that probably should have been wiped out. They may even have attempted to do so.

Chapter 7

Adding it all up

A QUICK RECAP

The epic of Gilgamesh tells of the destruction of Shurappak caused by a massive wave from the south; legends tell of the time of decimation of the Syrian population of Levant when the position of the stars changed and dawn began from a different place.

An Iranian legend of a day lasting three times as long followed by an equally long night, and their history that speaks of another time when the sun did not set for 10 days.

The Hindu story of four Kalpas or ages that passed when all these ages ended in cataclysms including conflagration, flood, and hurricanes all of which almost destroyed mankind.

The Tibetan history of four ages that expired when the highlands were flooded in a great cataclysm, by reason of comets that cause great upheavals that changed the landscape from flat to mountainous, and also when lands became seas and seas became land, during a time when a red sun loomed overhead.

Chinese history about the earth shaken to its foundation, when the sun, moon, and stars changed their motions, the Earth fell to pieces and the waters in its bosom up rushed with violence and overflowed the Earth and the planets altered their course.

The Jewish histories that speak of a time the mountains burned with fire and the earth shook so bad that the hills were removed, and the mountains overthrown.

The Egyptian Priest telling us that there was not just one but there were many floods, and their own histories telling us of a time when the sky was in confusion, and fire almost exterminated mankind along with years of noise when the Earth turned upside down the sun altered where it rose four times and once when the sun didn't rise.

Then there's the Roman history when after a deluge occurred, a heavy night spread over the globe for 9 consecutive days.

Of course there's the Greek history telling of a time when the rising and setting of the sun and other heavenly bodies (stars, planets) changed their usual movement.

Then there's the Finnish story of a time when hailstones of iron fell from the sky, the sun and moon disappeared causing a long period of darkness, after which a new sun and moon appeared in the sky.

And the Spanish history about reversal in the movement of the stars, the constellations changing their positions including the Great Bear that never bathed in the sea before, suddenly plunged beneath the all-engulfing waves after a 'cosmic upheaval when a star of the little bear became the new polar star.

Then there's the Icelandic legends referring to the sun as having no knowledge where her home should be, and the moon not knowing his place, and the stars not knowing where their stations were.

The Japanese myths of an event when tidal waves with hurricane wind accompanied by unnatural darkness in their land happened when the source of light disappeared, and the whole world became dark, and when the countries were swimming about.

And of course there's the Polynesian legend of utter darkness that just wouldn't end.

We can't forget Mexican history about world catastrophes decimating humankind that changed the face of the earth and causing the four times the sun changed direction, while earthquakes, tidal waves, and flaming volcanoes caused cities to be swept into the sea killing millions of people along with animals where the only survivors were people who fled underground into dark caves for months praying for the sun to return.

And then there's the Aztecs story of when there had been no sun in existence for many years and the world lived in endless gloom.

The Latin American legend of land that was pushed up above from below, and what was above sinking into the depths.

And then who can forget our friend Ixtlilxochitl telling us about four world ages which were named Water Sun which ended with a deluge and almost all creatures perished; Earthquake Sun when the Earth broke in many places and mountains fell, and a couple more catastrophic suns he liked to give us nightmares about.

There is of course the Peruvian legend of a time equal to 5 days and nights when the sun was not in the sky, and the ocean left the shore with a terrible noise and broke over the continent, causing the entire surface of the earth to be changed.

Up in North America there's the Oklahoma Indians recalling mountain high waves, and the Pacific Northwest natives also tell us of a time when the water rose mountain high. British Columbian Kaska natives tell us of a time when the sun had stopped on its way across the sky then became small.

Of course we can't forget those silly Inuit Eskimos who tell us they were flown north in big birds back when the north land had no snow and how now they still worry that the sky will one day fall again like it did before when the sun and the moon were darkened just before the sky fell and such misery followed this event.

The bible which has become fashionable to ignore and ridicule also says this happened in Psalm 68 8: "… the heavens also dropped…" and many other ancient legends tell of the time when the heavens fell to the earth.

These are just a few of the legends we covered and they all clearly indicate the earth experienced incredibly frightful cataclysmic upheavals during recorded history that transpired on the earth. And if you were to bother to plot the position of these peoples on the map you would see there wasn't a safe place on earth you could escape from these events…except underground, and curiously as it happens, many of the legends of these peoples told of going underground to do just that.

Here's a few of the ancient civilizations that went in underground caves or tunnels to escape cataclysms, which were most likely continent traversing waves: Mexicans, Aztecs, Apaches, Hopi, Quiche Mayans, Moroccans, Tibetans, Polynesian, Peruvians, Turkey, Maltese, Pueblo Indian, Zuni Indians, Arikra, Mandan Sioux, and others.

If only one of these peoples spoke such legends like this, such a legend would be easy to discount as a fairy tale. But no! This small sampling is of over twenty peoples from all around the earth describing identical events. I don't know about you, but I think the ancient histories about all these events are exactly that: history; not fables, or myths.

ANCIENT NORTH AMERICAN RELIC'S REMAINS EVOKE VISIONS OF CATACLYSMIC DESTRUCTION.

A metal bell was found in an "immense mass of rock" when it was blasted on Meeting House Hill in Dorchester (Boston)(Similar or same bell also described as being found in dynamited solid rock that had been supposedly millions of years old. This metallic bell was displayed in a circuit of museums then just disappeared. (book 5 pg 24 referring Scientific American Magazine June 1951). A piece of quartz from California was dropped on the floor and when it broke open, a manmade nail was found inside. A silver and iron mask was found when plowing a field in Sullivan County Missouri, and precisely carved figures were found near Mount Pisgah North Carolina. Coal from Pennsylvania was found with a gold chain imbedded inside, an iron pot was found inside a large chunk of coal from Oklahoma, and an ancient stone head was found while digging in a cellar in North Boston.

Excavations found 15 distinct archaeological horizons or levels of dirt in the same place in the Illinois River Valley which *all* bore traces of human habitation. Two million pounds of copper were pulled from Isle Royale Michigan long before any settlement reached this area, and at least 100 abandoned stone fortifications were found on the hills of Ohio, as well as bog-iron smelting furnaces with things like 42 pound iron bars found in them when the settlers arrived in 1790.

Hieroglyphics were discovered on wood turned to coal deep under the ground level of Hammondsville Ohio, and well dressed stone walls were found buried in limestone in Lexington Kentucky. Ancient coal mines were discovered in Utah that were excavated so long ago, that the coal was useless, and a city was found buried under Rockwell Texas in which some of the stones in the walls were inscribed with writing, and an inlaid mosaic floor was found in Oklahoma city Oklahoma, and on and on and on.

These examples of ancient human habitation that have been found spread right across America were levelled and buried or laid waste by cataclysmic events. Billions of fossils found along the west coast of America as the continent suddenly shifted west, trapping and burying them all together, and log jams of "prehistoric" beasts shoved violently against rock faces from massive waves plowing them against the cliff walls with such force they were crushed and mutilated by the accompanying debris.

I mention these American sites, simply because no archaeologists or anthropologists want to credit North America with advanced civilization any time before America was colonized. But similar ghastly destruction can be found in various amounts on every continent around the globe. All these remains of buried civilizations and mass fossil sites all point to catastrophic tsunami type flood events that annihilated these locations. Massive clusters of fossil are found around in sites like this which exist all over the world! They are found in Patagonia South America, Bogata Columbia, and Peru Cordillera. Santa Barbara California is a site of about a billion fish fossils in a four square mile area in a place that was once under water. Billions of fossils found all along the western coast of California showing the land shifted west so fast as to herd the sea creatures into slurry tombs. The list goes on as similar events that played out all over the world creating fossils in appalling bunches on literally every continent of the world. California, Mexico, Los Angeles, Fairbanks Alaska, Bering Strait, New Siberia, Llakov Island off Siberia is actually built of millions of skeletons, Harz Mountains in Germany, Switzerland, Italy (Monte Bolca near Verona) Mediterranean islands, Gibraltar, France, England, Orkney Scotland, Nebraska, Ohio, Michigan, and Arizona, to name a few. The land moving and crumpling so fast, that even the fast animals were unable to get out of the way of the land as it surrounded them and they, along with people were crushed by the land itself. Some were otherwise buried under the continent tsunamis with accompanying debris to be found as fossils by us just a few thousand years later.

Whales remains have been found on the Himalayans and in the plains of the Minnesota, Vermont and Montreal, and in Alaska animals are mingled with uprooted trees and at least four warped and distorted layers of volcanic ash, showing volcanic activity and earth upheaval was going on at the same time as the animals were literally being torn limb from limb. Weather so intense it froze woolly mammoths with food in their mouths, and froze waves in mid crest, simultaneously shifting the land from a temperate zone to the north to maintain these ghastly marvels in this condition to this day.

ERRATICS

The Codex Chimalpopoca relates: "the sky drew near to the Earth and in the space of a day all was drowned, and even the mountains themselves were covered by water. It is said that the rocks we can see today rolled about all over the land dragged by waves of boiling lava and that there suddenly arose mountains the colour of fire." I don't know of any theories that suggest erratics were placed there by lava, though that would be possible for some erratics placed where lava is predominant. I've seen tsunamis footage and the waves are often so filled with debris one wonders if they confused such waves with lava. I do know waves of water with sufficient force can move massive blocks of stone. As pointed out, when Krakatoa erupted, it shoved coral blocks weighing up to 600 tons onto land a distance of maybe a hundred miles away onto Sumatra when the waves had diminished to just 70 feet high. We don't know the upper limit to the size of rocks water can push. We found probable evidence of 3500 foot waves overrunning Scotland...what kind of rocks could these waves move? Once a rock starts to tumble and roll on land, just like an avalanche, very little additional force is needed to keep up its momentum. If a continent sweeping wave is the cause, then once a boulder gets moving, like a rolling stone, there is little to stop it from taking a trip of hundreds of miles with the wave, like a groupie hanging out with an irresistible icon. If, as I suggest, chimney rocks left high above the surrounding landscape are the result of massive waves scouring away the rest of the land, certainly any boulders found on the ground would have been carried away with the rest of the dirt and soil. In July 1991 Mount Pinatubo erupted causing flash floods which hit a 16 foot wall that had been built quite some time prior to the eruption to contain floods. However, the flash flood overtopped that wall and soon scoured its way underneath and the onrushing flood quickly scoured away until it got to a depth of 60 feet! The retaining wall was left high up in the air as though it was not a wall at all, but an arch built to cross over a gorge; and this all occurred as the result of just one volcano! (National Geographic Dec 1992) This volcano demonstrated on a micro scale what these continent traversing waves did to the landscape: they left this gorge 60 feet deeper than it was originally, leaving the sides standing 60 feet high above the surrounding landscape, similar to leaving a chimney rock high above the surrounding area, and it carried the soil and rocks miles away. If this is what just one little itty bitty volcano can do, imagine what a continent crossing superwave consisting of a large portion of the ocean's water would do. The land would change it appearance completely, and if you were lucky enough to survive and you came out of a cave, you wouldn't recognise anything.

Earlier I explained how erratics could only be carried by waves across vast stretches of land, in contrast to geologists telling us 10,000 ton rocks were shoved or carried great distances by glaciers or icebergs. Geologists want us to believe that glaciers often supposedly pushed these huge erratics on a different bearing than the glaciers direction of movement; which of course is illogical. The Ototoks erratic near Calgary is a prime example of the absurdity of this theory. The question is how did an 18,000 ton erratic boulder, called the Ototoks Erratic, move 500 kilometres from the Rocky Mountains to the Ototoks Farm Field near Calgary Alberta. The geologists want us to believe a glacier moving North-South shoved this huge rock 500 kilometres (311 miles) east west from the Rocky Mountains. Does that seem like a sound theory? NO! This is just impossible! If you're asking 'what about considering the iceberg idea on this one', this is an even worse waste of time. It had to be another force that put this rock there, and the only solution is the cataclysmic one: the North America continent moved westward forcing a huge volume of the pacific ocean over the land while mountain high waves were forced over the Rockies, I might add in the correct direction of ...east west... and the wave was immense enough to move this rock and deposit it 311 miles away from the mountains where it came from. With the land moving in the opposite direction of this rocks travel, this continental shifting motion also aided the rock's momentum. I will also add that this moving of the continents that created the massive tsunamis, also created the Rockies.

What about Icebergs? For fun I did an experiment. I found some pebbles and placed them in ice cubes of about 35 CC's in volume and worked with progressively larger pebbles and froze them into the cubes. I then placed them in a nice big clear container to see if they would sink. I must admit I was surprised in the first attempt as all the ice cubes with pebbles in them stayed afloat. The largest roundish pebble in the first attempt was only about 13 x 9 x 5 millimetres. However it is important to note that all four pebbles dropped within 2 minutes of being placed in the cold tap water! No erratic could be dropped hundreds of miles away, if they fell out of the cube 2 minutes later! And don't forget I froze the pebbles inside the ice. In the real world the ice would have frozen on top of the boulders, dropping them even sooner. Anyway, I did the test again with 5 more pebbles progressively larger than the first 4. The largest of the five had a volume of 1 CC or about 1/35th of the volume of the entire cube. I dropped the ice cubes with these pebbles in the water one by one and the three smallest pebbles (all larger than the first four of course) still stayed afloat; however they visibly lowered the ice cube in the water. Again all the cubes dropped their pebbles within two minutes. I then clued into something that was happening with the cubes that should be happening with Icebergs, but is not. Can you guess? I'll get back to this in a minute.

The third and second largest pebbles pulled most of the ice cube underwater, but it still floated and then they too dropped the pebble within two minutes. Here's what I clued into with these cubes. Once the pebble dropped, the ice cube lurched upward. Think about that. Finally I put in the water the cube with the largest 1CC pebble in it and it too was pulled downward, but only floated for about 2 minutes as the ice slowly melted. Then the rock won and pulled the ice cube to the bottom of the container and stayed there for about 2 more minutes while the ice slowly melted. (The shape of this particular pebble was erratic so it was housed better in the cube allowing the cube to hold it for twice as long) Then when the ice melted enough and the rock fell out, the ice cube soared to the surface and breached beautifully creating a wave. Now think about this. Were this a full sized iceberg and if the theory that icebergs carried all these erratics boulders hundreds of miles away, then this would be happening today too. We would often see icebergs suddenly lurch higher above sea level when they dropped massive rocks to the ocean floor beneath. We don't ever see this. We do see icebergs roll over when they become top-heavy, and these are extremely dangerous to be near. But when icebergs roll over we don't' see cavities where a boulder might have been housed, only a smooth icy surface. Furthermore if icebergs were pulled completely underwater by a rock too large for the iceberg to remain afloat, this would be a ticking time bomb and no one could safely sail the northern or southern seas because suddenly without warning icebergs would drop their rocks, and surge upwards and literally jump out of the sea, either swamping vessels or hitting them and we would see boats with broken hulls sitting on top of icebergs. None of these things are known to ever happen. Yet if the theory of the erratics was true, then based on the number of erratics that are known, this would be a fairly common occurrence. Boats would be forbidden to sail in arctic seas in peak iceberg seasons to prevent disaster. Iceberg patrols have been in existence since soon after the sinking of the Titanic in 1912, yet nothing like these events have ever been witnessed. Some countries in Europe, have hundreds and hundreds of huge erratic boulders lying all around the countryside. The theory that icebergs carry 10,000 or 18,000 ton boulders hundreds of miles is demonstrably impossible and this theory was created simply to discredit the cataclysmic wave solution. The erratics were placed where they are found by huge ocean waves that overran the continents; no other solution to this occurrence is feasible.

Now as a confirmation of this deduction, remember some erratics were found in New Hampshire, Massachusetts, Wisconsin and Connecticut that came from Canada and Labrador (which is of course part of Canada) and remember that a huge number of whale skeletons were found in Minnesota, Vermont and Montreal. I'm willing to be that the waves that pushed the huge erratics also carried with them all these whales, as geographically they are in pretty much the same area. So I guess my previous deduction that the whales came from the Pacific Ocean doesn't hold as much water as this theory. Fact is I didn't even realize that both these whales and these erratics were in the same area until my second proof read. (Obviously I don't know the positions of the States very well)

WHAT'S THE POINT OF CONTINUING?

Some of the ancient building sites are truly mind boggling, such as the Ajanta Caves of India. This is a semicircular wall of a rock face, presumably a natural site, though based on the work done there and the capabilities of the ancients, it wouldn't surprise me if this site was formed this way by the incredibly advanced technology of the ancients. These 'caves' are carved with artistry on at least the scale of Angkor Wat but done on the interior of the solid rock face, now called 'caves', with all the waste stone excavated leaving amazing structural design work behind. There is no way this was done with ordinary stone tools and whatever else archaeologists will tell you they were created with. This was created with lazar light saber rock cutting technology of some kind like we would cut butter with a hot knife. And it appears similar technology was used on a lot of the unfinished sites around the globe as well. Though this one may have been completed, I'm not sure. But for some reason other similarly highly advanced construction sites around the globe all stopped construction work suddenly and it would seem at the same time. Here are some examples.

The lonely Arabian castles in Saudia Arabia that stand in the middle of the Arabian dessert are also carved in similar ways to Petra and the Ajanta Caves. The huge but isolated rocks they are carved into appear to be worn by water and wind before they were carved. Though these appear to be finished, this might help place their creation after the Age that ended with Hurricane or Wind sun. Another example of colossal carving is in Bamian, a small half ruined town in central Asia that lies between Cabul and Balkh. In front of partially artificial caves there are 5 huge statues, of which the largest is 173 feet high. By comparison, the statue of liberty is 103 feet high. (Book 12 pg. 21) Though the statue is part of the mountain and not actually a lifted block, the statue and area it is cut out of is staggering. I only mention these to highlight the fascinating skill of the ancients when it came to creating monolithic structures on a scale we just are not able, or barely able to duplicate.

The super massive, 16,300 ton Stele of Yangshan China as well as the perfectly straight nearby wall cut off of the rock face is staggering. The size of this semi quarried or carved stone, boggles the mind yet this site was just left unfinished. Why? What happened? The Yangshan quarry also boggles the mind with the scope of whatever capabilities they had to cut this quarry so cleanly in such vast proportions.

All three of these and other sites around the world have huge carved rock faces with smooth, level flat vertical surfaces of enviable precision. Archaeologists just assume these were painstakingly chiseled, by stone masons that didn't have anything better to do with their lives and must have lived hundreds of years and passed this work on down to their great grandchildren. The scope of these works is beyond comprehension and there is just no way that these sites, as well as others, were painstakingly quarried in this manner. The work is just too perfect on too large a scale to have been done by just hand tooled craftsmanship. You have got to see these sites to grasp the immensity of the work. I only stumbled upon the Ajanta Caves of India while looking for other ancient examples and was just blown away by this site. I don't recall any of the authors of my reference material referring to this place; how did they miss it?! If you doubt my conclusions look up this and these other sites. These quarry sites had to have been created with a technology we simply do not have at our disposal today, and we would be hard pressed to duplicate anything like Petra. Even if we could do it, the futility and tediousness of the jobs would mean we wouldn't even attempt them. And yet archaeologists just assume the ancients just loved to waste their years away cutting and polishing stone and completely forgot economic realities. This is just unrealistic; people are going to want to finish building projects in a reasonable amount of time. I'm sure we've all had people at some point in our lives tell us not to get too picky about some job or task we've taken on, (Except maybe for military people and some nurses making beds). We strike a balance between craftsmanship, and economical efficiency. There is no way these places were done "efficiently" if they were done in ways archaeologists tell us they were. They clearly had to have had advanced technology to make these jobs far, far easier, and economical.

The Baalbek site has some of, if not the largest, unfinished and finished quarried stones; as well as utilized stones known in the world. During the work on one or two massive stones partially or completely detached from the quarry, the work stopped cold. No technology of today could touch these huge quarried stones, if it could the builders would continued the work. They didn't...something happened. Now archaeologist, if they are brave enough to tackle the logistic of these sites, will assume 200,000 slaves were forced to push, pull, drag and sweat over these huge stones, but this is just plain impractical and a waste of resources. It would have been far more efficient to use smaller stones and cement along with fewer people to transport them. So whoever did create these stones, to them this *was* the efficient way, which again means they had extremely advanced technology at their disposal. I managed to find a couple old picture of one of these blocks to draw. Some people and or camels are also in the picture to illustrate scale. It measures 21.5m by 4m by 4.5m: (70.55 feet x 13 1/8th feet x 14.77 feet inches) (**see Image 16**) Nearby these quarried stones are the buildings they were used in and the picture has a person standing nearby go give a sense of scale here too. (**See image 17**). A site with equally sized, dressed, and used megalithic blocks has also been found off the coast of Morocco...under water.

Image 16: Baalbek stone c1898 before site 'cleaned' up

Image 17a: Baalbek circa 1898 showing giant stones as used

Image 17b: 1880 Baalbek wall drawing

Both Ollantaytambo and Sacsahuamàn in Peru and some Chulpas in Titicaca, high in the Andes were constructed with identical advanced building technology. The large rocks were laid together, and then with an electro vibration tool or process, were partially liquefied to allow the blocks to ooze into place to fit so tightly together that not even razor blades can be squeezed in between the joints: some of the rocks clearly oozed into horizontal crevasse in the stonework. **(See image 18a to 20b)** The technology used in all

Image 18a: wall of Ollantaytambo

Image 18c: wall close-up Ollantaytambo

Image 19: Chulpa at Titicaca

Image 18a:
Ollantaytambo Doorway

Image 18b:
Ollantaytambo Doorway

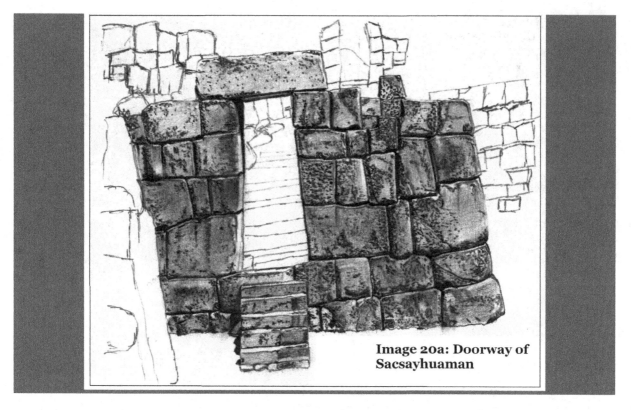

Image 20a: Doorway of Sacsayhuaman

Image 20b: Sacsayhuaman wall section

three places is so similar one might not know which place you were in if you just looked at the wall construction. So similar in fact that when I looked at two different pictures of door construction I thought I was looking two different pictures of the same door from both sides, before I realized they were two different doors: one from Ollantaytambo and one from Sacsahuamàn. The work on the Titicaca Chulpas is also of the same type of construction.

This technology used at Ollantaytambo and Sacsahuamàn loosened the stone at a molecular level, allowing the rocks to flow a bit like cookie dough. The technology used in these sites is similar to something invented by John Hutchinson; while using his tool, a porcelain cup upstairs above his apartment soften and oozed, giving the appearance it had melted; but at room temperature. He also did this with metal that cold melted around wood without burning it. The rocks at these ancient sites are clearly not carved or created with normal masonry skills, but they evidently settled into position using vibratory technology that liquefies the rock: often the surface of the rock has identical patterns to water that is subjected to sound or vibration, and just as often the rocks appear to have bulged from the weight pressing outward during the process. And it does not appear they even use roughly shaped stones to build all the 'bricks". Each site represented here (Ollantaytambo, Sacsahuamàn and Titicaca) have what look like random rocks placed in what would be the next spot to be built upon. It's been suggested that the natives initially attempted to add to the construction, but this just doesn't fit as the exact same thing was done at all three sites and only minimally that is not in any way extensively that suggests the buildings were being extended. But even if this were true, this would point out that two very different techniques were used in the construction, advanced and primitive, effectively having the archaeologists figuratively shoot themselves in the foot. These small piles of rocks rather suggests that the builders used these smaller rocks with the vibratory technology to meld them into single form fitted rocks, meaning some of the stones were not cut to fit but cold melted together to create larger rocks, which then oozed into place. They could do this with the scrap rock from quarries so that there was no waste and zero to negative entropy in the building process. The position on the rocks of the Peru sites where the machines were connected often left an extrusion point where their technological device was disengaged from the rock faces.

Archaeologists would say this is absurd to suggest the ancient had such advanced technology at their disposal, particularly when we don't even possess it ourselves today. But there is no way these blocks were carved, as they would be impossible to carve so accurately, and it would have been impractical in the way they built. By our way of thinking it would be much simpler to just use identical square blocks, rather than form fitted. The 'blocks in no way match each other and it's safe to say, no two blocks are the same shape, something that would be completely economically impossible in our day. Today we optimize the building process by the exact opposite building methods by making the blocks identical. If we carved the way archaeologists say they did, too many mistakes would be made and there would be unfathomable piles of waste which just don't exist. Furthermore, the assumption of inferior or even conventional building practices being used by the ancients by archaeologists is based on the assumption evolution is true. But even a cursory look at the ancient sites soon dismisses the possibility they were using anywhere near normal building equipment. Only the closed mind that assumes the ancients could not possibly have been more advanced than us prevents preconceived ideas from being overturned. This construction of fantastically advanced highly expert practice stopped in its tracks and none of these places were finished, leaving no sign of the builders behind. Why? What stopped construction so suddenly?

Tiahuanaco when seen from the air clearly has a masterful and precisely laid out 'floor plan'. Unfinished megalithic stones used in the construction of the 'city', or neighbourhood, though laid out and partially built, clearly indicate work was interrupted in a cataclysmic way. Massive stone structures were fractured and broken and finely created stonework is strewn about the site like children's toys on their bedroom floor.

Puma Punka, probably a part of, or a suburb of Tiahuanaco, also exhibits vastly superior machined blocks in an incredibly advanced city project, which was also clearly left unfinished. When it was found by the conquistadors, the site was mostly buried in red mud. In 1833 the place was drawn and the drawing indisputably depicts a highly technical and precise building site that was never finished which was clearly overcome by a cataclysm, with extremely accurately incised stone lying about as if they had been thrown about by Godzilla. (**See Image 21**) Sadly much of the stone from this site has been pilfered by the locals for building material in nearby locations. Recently nearby a huge pyramid was discovered that was also buried in this mud.

Image 21 as drawn in 1833

There is an Obelisk sitting in a quarry in Egypt that is completely cut out inside the quarry except underneath where it is still attached. Pictures of it from above show people walking on it and it is about six people wide standing side by side in the upper portions of it, and it is about 50% wider at the base which is about one tenth of the length. It is easily the size of the finished block pulled out of the Baalbek illustrated above. So it gives some kind of clue as to the process and intent of the workers as to their expectations. Somehow the creators of this work intended to undercut this and pull it straight up out of the quarry in one piece. In theory an abrasive wire could be used to saw its way underneath with a guide to keep it straight. But the scale of this obelisk is so huge, that no amount of pondering seems to solve how they intended to cut out and extract this huge block in one piece, which was clearly their intent and obviously within their ability to accomplish. Regardless of how they intended to do this, the work, like so many other monolithic sites around the earth, was stopped dead in its tracks.

The curious yet clearly unfinished cut stone of the Inca period chulpa towers of Cutimboperu and Sillustani Peru, presumed to be for burial, though this doesn't explain why they needed to be built with an accompanying so called "construction ramp". Their purpose in my mind is unclear; I could not find confirmation that these were indeed burial sites, but if I missed it; forgive the oversight.

The Elamite Ziggurat of Tchogha Zambil, in the province of Khuzestan Iran, is a massive structure similar to a ziggurat on steroids which was also never finished.

The statue of Osiris still lying in an unfinished state in the southern granite quarries of Aswan Egypt, lies waiting for the crew that will never return, and the surface appears to appears to worn away by water full of abrasive materials.

These sites are all around the world and most, if not all, were left unfinished. All of the construction on these building sites was halted in mid work, and usually it appears as though a cataclysm halted the work. The conclusion that I came to in my first work, was that it was the work itself that caused the cataclysms that suddenly ended the work. I won't go into re-explaining that paradox here. Obviously the cataclysm that stopped these works had to have been the cataclysms spoken of by the ancients, thus these unfinished sites become silent confirmation of the legends.

Dr. M.K. Jessup is thought by some to have been killed because he hit a nerve with his UFO research, also researched some ancient mysteries. He concluded that spaceships of vast proportions brought colonists to various part of the earth and supplied this heavy lifting power for erecting the great stone works before it was suddenly destroyed or taken away. (Book 35 pg 84)

He is not alone. Joseph Goodavage deduced that the ancients appear to have conquered some elemental force which enabled them to construct the buildings they were working on. He deduced the power used had to have been levitation, and the people who held this power had to be extra-terrestrial in origin, who they stayed for a while, either because they were unable or unwilling to leave and when they did leave, they left their work unfinished. (Book 35 pg 84)

Whether the conclusions of these researchers sound eccentric or not, the point is they too saw the technology was A: incredible to have come up with a UFO answer and B: that is was suddenly stopped for some unknown reason, all around the globe.

QUIET ON THE SET!

We've rambled our way through a bunch of ancient clues, and it might be a lot to take in and really see the big picture. So let's rifle through the material. In a literary sense what we've done so far is like drawing a whole lot of pictures closely linked to each other and then seen them one at a time. Now we are going to flip through them to see it like a movie speeded up really fast. It might help grasp the big picture and it will also serve as a concise encapsulation of the catastrophic local floods of the world. We won't go over the global flood again, just the clues or descriptions on the cataclysmic local floods. Ok fasten your seat belts...

Several legends exist such as the Mexican one telling how lava flowed all across the western hemisphere, and caused the sea to boil. Though lava naturally flows to the ocean and boils the sea nearest the land; the fact that vast stretches of North and South America flowed lava at the same time and the sea as far as could be seen boiled, indicates this was no small event such as can be witnessed on Hawaii. New valleys were formed and mountain ridges were torn apart, and the silhouettes of new mountains were seen through the gloom. The Mayans say God (or possibly a god) rolled the mountains, and removed more of them. Mountains rose out of flat plains, while other mountains were flattened....and they saw it happen. Israel when leaving Egypt saw mountains "skip like rams", mountains removed, overturned, and the sun not rising when it should. In conjunction with these events, and not just tsunamis but oceans fell on the continents, tornado force hurricanes blew away towns and the forests, and eliminating many species of animals. Like the Mayans, the Maoris also tell of giant waves sweeping away forests, and Buddhist texts tell of actual mountains being blown into the sky. Samoan legends speak of land that sank into the sea, and new earth rose out of the abyss. Finnish legends say the sun and moon disappeared from the sky, and birds grew sick. This speaks of the vastness of the event which eventually filled the skies with so much vapour the sky filled with steam, smoke and debris that the sky became dark, gloomy and fell to the earth like other legends say.

The Hopi say the earth was destroyed three times before, once by volcanic eruption and fire, once by earth quakes and the world axis changing, and the third by aerial warfare. Evidence of nuclear blasts are found in places no known modern nukes were tested, suggesting nuclear war would be far more destructive than just the radiation involved and indeed it is known nukes have caused earthquakes far from the test sites.

OK Scotty... warp speed...

The sky collapsed on the Mexicans, Egyptians, Chinese, The Hebrews, The Finnish, Samoans, Eskimo's, several African tribes of such as the Kanga, Wanyoro and Loanga, Brazilian natives, North American natives, Indonesians, Japanese, Aztecs, Belgian, Lapland, Borneo, Samoan, Mayan, Sachomish, Kaska, Oraibi, Chaldean and others.

The bible mentions this same event in Judges 5:4 "Lord, when thou wentest out of Seir, when thou marchedst out of the field of Edom, the earth trembled, the heavens dropped,

The drying up of the oceans filled the sky with steam and vapour causing the 'sky to fall'.

Endless gloom was usually stated as a result of this falling sky by the Mayan, Aztec, Indian, Hebrews, Egyptian, Finland, Polynesian, Choctaw, Quillayutes, Oraibi and others.

Mountain high waves that reached the sky or collapsed on the continent were seen in British Columbia, China, The west coast of South America, Britain, Scotland, Israelites, Lapland, and by the Toltecs, Hopi, Maoris, Aztecs, Mayans, Peruvians, Choctaw and others. Geologists have even realized that Mexico was overrun by the Pacific Ocean at least twice, though they don't seem to be aware that the Mexicans saw it happen.

Like the Hopi telling of the axis of the earth being altered, so too do the Egyptian papyrus', Eskimo, Syrian, and Andaman Islands legends, which say the earth turned upside down; as do other legends give clues in this regard.

Hindu, Hebrew, Mayans, Mexican, Romans, Persians, Peruvians, Polynesians, Sudanese, Iranians, Chinese, Oklahoma natives, Japanese, Greeks, Hawaiian, tell of very long nights or the sun stopping its motion across the sky that lasted for periods varying from five, six, seven, nine, and ten, times as long as normal.

The world ages ended in devastating cataclysms 3, 4, 7 even 9 and 10 times, for the Aztecs, India, Hindu, the Mayans, Mexican, Buddhists, Greeks, Roman, Egyptian, Finland, people around the Bengal Sea, British North Borneo, Scandinavians, Irish, Navajos, Iceland, Hawaiian, Tibetans, Navajos Indians, the Pueblo Indian, and the seasons changed their order.

Each age that ended in catastrophic events was followed by a new or different looking sun, moon, and sky, where the motion of moon, stars, and planets, and rising of the sun, changed as specified by the Eskimos, Romans, Egyptians, Tibetans, Mayans, Arabs, Syrians, Indians, Greeks, Spanish, The Hopi, Chinese, Mexicans, Babylonian, Hebrews, Spanish, Icelandic, Hawaiian, Pawnees, Kaska, Chaldean and others.

Physical evidence and written records of the Egyptians, Hindu, Babylonian, Chinese, Arabian, Brahman charts, Roman, and others show that the earth tilted suddenly at some point during their history.

Length of the year changed abruptly for the Greeks, Peruvians, Chinese, Incas, Mayans, Persians, The Brahmans, Indians, Hindus, Babylonians, Assyrians, Israelites, Egyptians and others.

The month changed its length for the Greeks, Hindus, Persians, Babylonians, Egyptians, Chinese, Rumania, Lithuania, Sardinia, The Celts, Mongols, and West African tribes as well as other peoples around the globe. Often the year was divided into ten months but later the year was divided into 12 months as the months suddenly became shorter in duration, so something speeded up the moon on its path around the earth.

Typhon: the gravity of Venus and / or Mars caused earth's waters to be pulled towards them and ascend high into the sky in a form that resembled a multi headed snake in Greece, Ethiopia, Egypt, India, Babylon, German, Bulgaria (Thrace), Polynesian, China and more places, sucking water into space and onto these planets. With the water were also pulled a giant crab, dirt, rocks, mountains and people, which would be found drifting in space or possibly mummified or as fossils on these planets if they didn't rot.

The mountains moved, collapsed, and were created, while the land moved or changed its appearance in front of witness's such as the Mexicans, Greeks, Hebrews, Mayans, Tibetans, Hopi, Japanese, Chinese, Latin America, Mayan, Peruvians, Zuni Indians....and others.

Maps showing a narrower Atlantis Ocean and an Antarctica before it experienced its last 20 degree twist indicate huge earth shifts happened during or after a technologically advanced period where spherical geometry was known by the map makers. Maps also show 'ice age' coverage.

We could continue on and on with accounts of stones that fell like hail on Egypt, Iran, India, China, Israel's enemies, Finland, Toltec, Aztecs, Mexicans and Italy, drastic communal deterioration, often into barbarism or "cave man" status of the people in the Congo, Mexico, France, Morocco, the Sahara, Algeria, Norway as well as the Tlaxcalans, Zapotecs, Burmese, Norwegians and the Egyptians to name a few. Legends tell of Venus and Mars coming far too close to the earth, extinctions of many species were witnessed, prolonged intense heat experienced around the globe, and the fear of comets and asteroid impacts is instilled in all of mankind. That reminds me...

THEN THERE'S THE METEOR FACTOR

We noted that the earth would have experienced as many meteoric impacts as the moon and planets, and that monstrous waves wiped them out. As recently as the time of Christ it wasn't uncommon to see two or three comets in the sky at the same time, and often they were visible during the daylight! So how many more impacts did they have back during these cataclysmic times and changing world ages compared to today? The ocean floor gives a good clue; it contains an incredible amount of red dust that contains nickel, a key clue to the presences of meteorites in the past. If you think all this blaming stuff on meteors and Mars is clutching at straws; there is so much of this red dust on the ocean floors that on average, 10,000 tons of meteorites must have fallen a day; this is 1000 times the rate that we experience today. By the way, we have a lot more meteoric activity on earth then are generally known. Recently it was admitted that on average every month a meteor the size of a house hits the earth! So what was it like back then with that happening a 1000 times a month, and obviously with even bigger ones hitting the earth? These impacts, spoken of in legends are directly linked with floods and landscape changes.

WHAT DID THE 'MOVIE' SHOW TO YOU?

Ok you saw the clues go by really fast... How do you interpret it? You probably know what my solution is, and are scratching your head to figure out a different one, because you say it just CAN'T be the continents moving...well maybe a little bit. The ancients gave us all the clues...there is no other solution. Ask yourself, what causes tsunamis today...answer: earthquakes. Yes I mentioned volcanoes, but volcanoes cause earthquakes too. When Alaska had huge Earthquakes in 1964, it was the biggest on record in North America; we got tsunami damage in Zeballos and other places on Vancouver Island. I just wanted to include Zeballos as my aunt lived there a few years after but near enough to the event that it was well remembered.

Recently people around the Indian Ocean and especially Indonesia experienced a horrible tsunami after an earthquake killing thousands. But these were ripples in a pond compared to the earthquakes that forced the ocean to become the mountain topping waves the ancients tell us about. Earthquakes are usually caused by the plates of the earth slipping a little bit. Sometimes like in the Alaska quake the land altered a bit; like Fourth Avenue in Anchorage suddenly had huge fractures down the middle of the street and a part of it dropped 11 feet. Some areas 200 miles southwest of Kodiak Alaska permanently rose 30 feet. This is just an inkling of the cataclysms experienced by the ancients. They talked of lands swimming and mountains being destroyed and new ones appearing, and land sinking into the ocean while land was also rising out of the depths. So we can understand then that the land shifted far more than we've experienced today in our worst quakes. I guess it becomes a matter of degrees. If an Anchorage street level dropped 11 feet, how much of a shift in the continental plates would be needed to create a new mountain? A TON! And the Hebrews said the mountain skipped like rams, The Peruvians indicated the Andes **range** rose because of those events and the Tibetans said the *mountain range* came into existence because of the events that transpired. To the Tibetans the sea appeared to have been vaporized and their island was suddenly a very cold plateau in the clouds surrounded by great mountain peaks. (Book 34 pg. 68) You might have been distracted or not concentrating and ask 'What mountains were the Tibetans talking about'? THE HIMALAYANS! The tallest mountain range in the world was built overnight! What sea were they talking about? Whatever it was, it has disappeared as it was forced out of the way by the Indian subcontinent as it shoved this seaway out of the way on top of itself and rammed into the land forcing the terrain upwards. We have been told that some geologists have finally admitted that these Himalayans rose as recently as the ice age, and they were a result of the Indian sub plate pressing into the Chinese land, forcing the mountains upward. Jeffrey Goodman bravely asked if it could have been as fast as a few centuries and clues like clams and whales in these mountains suggest it might have been quicker than that. But the Tibetans said they had them rise all around them overnight; there was nothing gradual about the process! Can you visualize it? The continental plates shifted hundreds of miles in one go! This is what was causing mountain climbing, and continent spanning erosive tidal waves, and the accompanying details such as heat, the erratics, atmosphere filled with steam, tornado force hurricanes, burying of many civilizations, sinking of continents, ice ages, and on and on. It was no picnic.

They give us clues as to what caused the motion to occur so quickly...they talk of planets coming near the earth; both Mars and Venus. Well this makes perfect sense! We saw that the gravitational pull of Earth, pulled the crust off the Mars and hurled it at us on the earth. But this same interaction between the planets would also pull the land plates of the earth towards the wayfaring planet, be it Mars or Venus. Now obviously Venus didn't just stay in one place in the sky; we saw Typhon, caused by the gravitational pull on the waters towards itself, moving all over the Mediterranean areas as it followed the path of Venus. So too would our home planet's continental plates shift accordingly, as they were pulled and steered towards the visitor. In response, the waves washed over the land, some of which froze in mid crest as the hurricane force freezing temperatures caused from bringing down the chill of space to the surface here in tornado force winds, which occasionally froze some of the water in its tracks, making it possible in some places not to be overrun by waves, where in others the continents were scoured hundreds of feet deep or more. In such conditions, these mysterious erratic 18,000 ton boulders would have rolled around like pebbles! This scoured away so much dirt, and piled it up in places like the Ukraine where they have so much top soil; Hitler was shipping it in box cars to Germany. In the Midwest people have dug through over 200 feet of topsoil to get to water. And this will maybe, just maybe, explain to you why so many civilizations and artifacts got buried hundreds of feet underground or got covered by mountains, and ships found their way into the interior of mountains, and why so many of these human evidences appear to age so old, either by inferring that depth of burial equals age, or because radiometric dating was so skewed. And Mars, like Venus was seen close by and as the world turned it sent rocky hail to everyone around the globe. There was so much rock from Mars thrown on the earth, that you've probably seen Martian rocks and don't even know it.

Oddly enough geologists don't know what caused the plates of the earth to form and initiate the continental drift. The plates most likely came into existence when the 500 odd mile asteroid that caused the great flood of Noah, crashed into earth creating the Hudson's Bay and the 2 million square mile area of lava that's between 20,000 and 50,000 feet thick, which we now call the Canadian Shield. This impact also forced water out of the ground all around the globe and fractured all the earth into plate zones. Simple. I suppose it is possible for the planets Mars and Venus to have put such pressure on the earth's crust it could have cracked the earth and created the plates, but physicists, mathematicians and geologists would probably have to work together to figure that one out. So, what caused the plates to start to move. Since Mars started taking the water right after the flood it might have destabilized the plates...sure that would solve it handily. I could cheat and say I just told you what caused the earth's continental plates to move, you know, blame it on Mars...and Venus and this could have been the end of the book. Except, it appears that something or someone else got the continental plates moving: it seems the gods themselves actually started the drift. Yes those pesky gods that keep mucking up ancient history and infiltrating all those crazy legends.

WHOSE FAULT IS IT?

Though much of these incidents in history were caused later by meteoric impacts, the first clue as to what exactly happened on the earth to cause these 'local' floods of continent sweeping waves occurred soon after the flood of Noah. In the days of Peleg the earth was divided. Peleg was named after the event and 'Peleg' means 'earthquake'. This was just 101 years after the flood.

One of the ancient gods we have to include in the big picture of the continents coming into existence during recorded history of mankind is that of Janus. He is called the god of gods, Father of the gods, or the "god man" and is symbolized by a two faced head with each face looking in opposite directions, east and west: sometimes one face is old and one is young. His other symbol is the club which symbolizes the breaking in pieces of the earth, and this symbol is the same as the hammer of Vulcan; and it was this 'hammer', or 'club' that is the cause that cut the earth asunder and was broken by it. And Vulcan was also the forger of Thunderbolts (Book 41 pg 26-28, 229, 272, 273,)

Hislop tries to make the case that this god is the cause of the diversion of languages of the tower of Babel fame, through a convoluted series of matching him up with Cush and Nimrod which I don't think is convincing; nor is his struggle to say the breaking or cutting of the earth is the same as the diversity of languages. This appears more to indicate that he is the cause of the breaking up of the continents. The saying that Vulcan was the forger or creator of thunderbolts also fits with this. Before the flood it never rained, and lightening would have been a new phenomenon first occurring sometime after the flood as well. The atmosphere immediately after the flood was still mostly adhering to the earth and probably quite tranquil, but when the continents broke, the weather would have gone crazy, causing a new phenomenon: lightning mixed with thunder. Thus is makes sense that the same god who is linked with the breaking up of the land into continents is also linked with the formation of thunderbolts: the two events would have been intimately linked. The two faces of Janus, young and old, might also be interpreted as the old world and the new and looking both ways, possibly from the position of Atlantis to see the parted continents he caused to come into being by looking east and west. Indeed the month of January is named after this god as the start of the New Year or the new world in which we now live.

Bonus section

THE AGE OF THE GODS

ometimes people will grasp at straws to avoid a hard reality they do not want to accept. In the nineteenth century, once an old earth concept was thrust to the forefront by Charles Lyell, along with the evolution theory put forth by Darwin, learned people started to swim in the primordial soup. Once these concepts got a foot in the bastion doors of academia and within the vicinity of scientific conceptualization, the theory of how life could have started on earth took uncharacteristic and alien inclinations. The Swedish chemist Svante Arrhenius suggested that spores could have been blown to earth from another planet in the solar system. Lord Calvin went a little further out into space and proposed life could have arrived on a meteorite. In 1907 Arrhenius took these theories a little further in a book he wrote called *Worlds in the Making* in which he portrayed a universe in which life had always existed in spore form, which drifted chaotically through interstellar space, propelled by the solar winds, and occasionally landing on planets starting life there; a process he called panspermia. This theory did take hold of the imaginations of academia for a while, until it was realized a meteorite could never escape another solar system and come to ours, and destructive solar forces such as radiation, x-rays, ultraviolet even the earth's van Allen belts would destroy any such spore, no matter how well they were shielded.

Francis Crick and Dr. Leslie Orgel (Nobel Prize winners for discovering the structure of DNA) co-authored a paper published in a periodical devoted to studies on the solar system called Icarus. Realizing the impossibility of the panspermia theory as put forth by Arrhenius, they took a more hypothetical approach for "our own amusement". They had perceived that since molybdenum was a very rare element that was a vital part of biochemical reactions, they reasoned that something that life is dependent on should be somewhat more common if life was to spontaneously initiate in some form from the environment it sprang from. It seemed to them that the uniformity of life on earth, that is, the basic molecular structure and the singularity of the genetic code, would suggest life started in a more molybdenum rich environment than exists on earth. Since molybdenum is so rare here, to dispel their boredom, they wondered if life didn't start somewhere else in the universe and might have been brought here on rockets by advanced aliens through something they termed Directed Panspermia. (Book 8 pg. 2-4)

Even though this article was written more as an intellectual exercise, once again people have seized on this concept to allow people's hearts and reason to escape from the creation model. Erich Von Daniken may be the most well known proponent of this position, particularly when in researching ancient history he discovered evidence in many ancient legends of gods coming down to the earth from space. This discovery cemented his conviction that life did not originate on the earth but was brought here by these gods, seemingly exactly as Crick and Orgel hypothesised. He even equated the God of the bible and other world religions as just another one of the gods. This, of course, does not sit well with some branches of theology. However, despite what would be no doubt some strident opposition to this apocryphal idea, it has taken a hold of many people's imaginations and they have become convinced this is the case. I know of one well distributed magazine whose publisher puts forth this belief as a certainty and is one of the pillars that underpins the articles published in the publication.

When I started researching for curiosities sake, and then eventually for the purpose of writing my first book, I eventually came face to face with the same evidence Von Daniken came across. However, though Von Daniken never pointed out or even figured out who the gods were, or he never believed it, I did figure out the origins and the identity of the gods. Though some of the gods deliberately attempted to divert mans attention from the truth, by saying things like they came from Sirius, or Venus or a few other places, it was fairly simple to decipher where they came from, if you weren't led astray by your biases, or Crick and Orgel's hypothetical paper they did for amusement.

Though I explained the origin of the gods and who they were in my first work, I felt it was necessary to recap some of it here as they are historically linked with the cause of at least a couple of the floods. We can't just assume the gods did it as a good enough explanation or rationalization; you need something concrete to persuade you, as did I. So I present a bonus section about the age of the gods.

Now I'm not going to go into deciphering for you which god in India is the same god of the Greeks, Romans, Egyptians and whoever else. I'm not qualified for that, heck even some of the source material I read made me realize that some of those researchers got some of it wrong. And I'm not going to go into all the details of the gods written about in the classics either, I'm no good at that either and some of those ancient writings are just too difficult to figure out what the heck they are talking about; you read some of those flood legends in chapter two so you have an idea what I'm talking about. Man those will give anyone a headache. However I was able to find and decipher enough clear cut evidence in my research to make the case as to who exactly the gods were...and are, as they are still around, just not overtly participating in the affairs of man.

All I'm just going to do is give enough key information to see the picture clear enough to realize that this is indeed the origin and true identity of the gods along with a brief synopsis of their activities here.

Before the reign of the gods

Masudi, (c. 900-957 A.D.) a traveling Arabian historian found evidence that made it clear to him the pyramids were built before the flood, during the reign of the gods, for the purpose of safeguarding ancient knowledge. (Book 6 pg. 146) But which flood? The evidence on and in the pyramids is of tsunami type of wear and of a salt water intrusion into the interior of the edifice. The global flood would have been a far less salinated event, as it is global erosion caused by the mega tsunamis that has ramped up the salt content of the oceans over the ages. This would indicate the flood he talked about was a local flood and not the global one. Of course one could say the pyramids went through both the global flood and the local flood, but as we move forward it will become clear the ages of the gods occurred just after the great flood, and indeed that might already be clear in your mind now as I've deposited several of these clues throughout this work. But another piece of evidence that might not be clear is, before the flood we had all knowledge, something that dissipated from our grasps after the flood, as the sun and entropy had their way with our genetics and our cognitive faculties. Masudi also indicated the pyramids were not a tomb at all but a book in stone that could be read when generations in the future garnered enough scientific knowledge to understand what it meant. In my first book I'm fairly confident I figured out what the pyramids original use was, and I also concluded that Nikola Tesla almost stumbled on the original purpose of the pyramids, as some of the things he did and some of the earth science mysteries he was unravelling parallel what I feel the pyramids were used for. But I spent 50,000 words getting to that point in chapter 6 my first book, so I'm not going to summarise it here. Suffice it to say the pyramids here are linked with the age of the gods.

One of the moons of Mars, Phobos, has some peculiar characteristics that have garnered some strange conclusions as to what it actually is. For example this moon, only 10 miles across, has been analysed by our instruments and found to be just one thousandth the weight of the same volume of water. Meaning; it would appear this moon is hollow. If this is the case, the reasoning arrived at by Dr. I.S. Shlovskii, a soviet mathematician, is that this is an artificial satellite, disguised as an asymmetrical moon and placed in the orbit of Mars by space explorers. He even has an origin for those space explorers. He surmises that there is a very quirky moon orbiting Jupiter as well. This innermost moon's orbit is completely unpredictable and has the odd habit of disappearing and reappearing at irregular intervals. (Book 8 pg. 18)

In the March 1945 issue of *Amazing Stories*, a Sci-fi magazine, Richard Shaver had a story of his published. Though it came across as science fiction, Richard Shaver insisted this was a factual account he was reporting. Based on other research I did, I am convinced this story is true, as it ties in perfectly with my conclusions based on other far more ancient evidence I found that was completely unrelated to this story. Shaver insists that somehow he found his way deep underground and stumbled upon a vast civilization deep inside the earth. He found out the origin of this subterranean civilization and it was this account that was reported in *Amazing Stories*.

He asserts that early in our solar system's history, a race of cosmic super beings came to the earth. Though Shaver was told they came from another solar system, this as I've discovered is an ongoing deception often perpetuated by some of these people. These super beings or "Elder Race" as Shaver called them, live incredibly long lives and have mastered such magnificent technology that they were regarded as gods, and were also called the Titans by the people they came in contact with on the earth. They could scan great distances, produced new foods, and cure diseases. They also destroyed and killed when they felt it was necessary. After some time of being on the earth with the humans they realized that the once beneficent sun now contained detrimental rays which were shortening their life spans. To escape the harmful rays of the sun they descended into underground caverns and started to carve out their subterranean kingdom. They also built an artificial sun that still had the healthy rays of the sun we have, but eliminated the detrimental radioactive rays. They say that we were unaware of these rays or lacked the technical knowledge to escape them, and consequently we were puzzled by the withdrawal of the gods from our presence. The Elder Race admitted that not all of their kind was this advanced and some of them varied in morality and intelligence. Humans were deemed their cousins and they would pull the strings behind the scenes for their favourites. The more humane of the gods did their best to assist their favourite tribes and warriors to develop a more functional culture and technology. Shaver stated that the ancient myths about the gods that have been handed down through the generations were our unsophisticated surface dwellers versions of the activities of the Elder Race. Supposedly some of the Elders returned to their homeland, but some were unable to take all their machines so they hid them underground and left. (Book 35 pg. 139-41)

The gods left to go back into space, and are underground, so they did both, they stayed and they left. The ancient legends also said they did both; there was a power struggle or war in the heavens and the clues indicated that the more infected or deteriorated of the gods were forced underground, and the least impacted or devolved left Earth altogether. We read legends where the people underground warned us on the surface that a huge impact was coming and they got many people around the globe to go underground to escape the catastrophes that would result from the impact. They got this news from people near Saturn. Something is fishy here. Who was out there warning us, and why would they care? There are telling contradictions in this that give clues as to their real identity.

Raymond Drake summarises some of the ancient legends he found. "...down the ages tantalizing echoes tell us of that Golden Age when the sky gods winged to Earth and taught their wisdom to men. After many millennia the glorious civilization dissolved in wars, then cataclysms devastated countries, changing entire climates, and the Celestials returned to the stars leaving the survivors to rebuild their shattered world." (Book 23 pg. 1) In 1968 Drake's published assessment is that The Sumerians, ancient Indians, Japanese,

Egyptians and Greeks believed in a golden age when the earth was ruled by gods. He notes that "When the gods walked upon the earth", the Indian, Tibetan Chinese, Japanese, Egyptian and Babylonians all tell of the gods or supermen descending from the skies and ruling the earth in divine dynasties. (Book 34, pg 178, 223, book 23 pg. 180)

The conclusions or a deduction of Drake's is published about the same time frame that Erich Von Daniken published a similar conclusion. Drake's deduction doesn't change six years later when he notes that the Greeks, Sumerians, Egyptians, Hindus, Japanese, Egyptians, Babylonians, Pacific Islanders and the Mayans all spoke of a golden age when the earth was ruled by the gods. Babylonians state that several wondrous beings civilized them. (Book 23 pg. 58, 209, book 34 pg. 186) Peter Kolosimo discovered that the Tibetans infer the gods were giants as they were also the ones that built the tunnels around the world and taught the benefits of their knowledge to the people when the world was young. (Book 21 pg. 35) The Greeks were a bit more puzzling and said these gods came from inside a machine. But he goes on to interpret that these gods returned on occasion to coach certain people of their choice to inspire them and advance the evolution of mankind. And then when they were done with their task, they would return to the skies once again. This was Drake's conclusions of the legends he read too: so Kolosimo also found the evidence that Daniken stumbled across. So did the gods really go back to some distant solar system or Sirius, or did they remain closer to the earth than they wanted us to believe? Did they leave or didn't they? And why would they return just to coach some random individuals; what do they care, or do they have some more intimate connection to us they didn't want to admit?

Brad Steiger also came to a similar conclusion. He noted that in the ancient times there were highly cultured and technologically advanced civilizations that were almost completely wiped out by disasters of some kind. Coupled with the evidence that pointed to these advanced civilization in ancient times, was the universal legend that at one time gods walked the earth "in direct intercourse with man" until a dramatic fall or series of events separated man from the communication he had with the gods. After these events, either connected with an earthly paradise from which man was expelled or an advanced civilization from which the gods withdrew, he determined that there was a link to huge disasters. He found that great floods and natural catastrophes that destroyed civilizations around the world were linked with these times. Though he also assumed the great flood was linked with the destruction of Atlantis, he reminded us that Atlantis is also said to have been an abode of the gods. (Book 35 pg. 15) So, by and large Stieger also found this evidence. He notes that there was a universal series of legends around the globe that spoke of an age of the gods, which was permanently interrupted by global cataclysms; thus these cataclysms must have been global if the legends were universal.

I speak of these other researchers coming to the same conclusion and, in a small way, validate this section to some extent as I'm the new guy, and I don't want you to assume this new guy who admits he doesn't read Sanskrit and hasn't been past a pile of books or the library computer or whatever, is some out of touch whacko. The researchers, no matter who dared take the legends at their word, continually arrived at the same conclusion: that there was a period of time when the gods descended to earth and ruled and taught and brought mankind out of backward savagery which came about as a result of a science and technology induced disaster that wiped out most of the earth's peoples which also destroyed their desires to re-attain some mastery over the simple civilized behaviours. So the gods came to the earth to help the remnants of mankind all over the earth revive their wills and civilizations: Or as the archaeologists and palaeontologists might word it, to stop being cave men.

MOON LADDERS

It is also important to realize that the Chinese and the Indians histories also agree that there was a reign of the gods. The Chinese believe there was a time or an age of Magic followed by a heroic age.

Tibetan history claims they were ruled by seven heavenly thrones similar to the divine dynasties of Vietnam, India, China, Japan, Egypt and Greece. (Book 34 pg. 69) China was ruled by divine kings, supposedly for 18,000 years. Like other legends, China too states that communication between heaven and earth existed, but because of a rebellion Emperor Yao got a descendant of Tchang to quell the disorder and he did so by breaking the communication between the heaven and the earth.

India's earliest legends tell of India's first dynasty ruled by divine kings which was a race of the sun and a second race of the moon. (Book 34 pg. 64) Many legends around the globe tell of a race of ruling people that emerged from an object as bright as the sun descending to the people to rule and teach civilization. On top of that, many legends speak of a series of beings coming from the moon or a moon that descended, such as that spoken of in the Tibetan book of Dzyan which says their lunar ancestors descended to earth from the moon. (Book 34 pg. 27) Meaning they apparently lived on our moon but as other legends imply, it could mean they descended to the earth on a ship shaped like the moon.

The Egyptian Menes may be the origin of the Moon's name, and Menes being a Thinite whose origin is a mythical place in heaven, and the land Menes ruled from called Khemennu means land of the moon. Meness is the Latvian Moon god and the Cretan King Minos means moon being or moon creature. (Atlantis Rising Magazine #96) "Divinities in the sun and moon were worshipped as part of the state religion..." (Book 34 pg. 81) And there was Sin, the Moon god which was revered at Ur. (Book 34 pg. 202)

In 1686, Cassini, the guy who first spotted the red spot on Jupiter and the division in the ring of Saturn, now named the Cassini division after him, spotted a satellite of Venus which was also seen many times in the 18th century as well. (Book 23 pg. 11) The Venusian moon also showed phases, and it was quite large at a size of about ¼ that of Venus. He also noted that it was orbiting very close to Venus at a distance of just 60% of the planet's diameter away. (Book 11 pg. 80)

Astronomer James Short on October 23 1740, also saw a moon of Venus which he estimated at 1/3 the diameter of Venus. (Book 11 pg. 81)

But, in case you don't know, Venus *has* no moon, so what is this that was seen orbiting Venus over such an extended period of time? We've seen that some 'spacemen' say they came from Venus, (Book 47 pg. 30) but that doesn't mean they live on the inhospitable surface of the planet; it could mean that they came from the vicinity, which then of course would not really be a lie.

The Tibetan books of Dzyan state that the first men were offspring of celestial men who descended to the earth from the moon. (Book 34 pg. 27)

Brahmin traditions say that lunar patriarchs descended from the moon. (Book 11 pg. 62)

Another anomalous planet was seen on March 26 1859, inside the orbit of Mercury transiting the sun whose size was 1/17th the mass of Mercury. This small planet was given the name of Vulcan. Then it disappeared, and years later turned up again in 1878 with a companion. All these inexplicable temporary planetary sightings prompted Andrew Tomas to ask the question "Was the Venusian moon a huge space city cruising the galaxy?" (Book 11 pg. 82-83) We could include Vulcan in this question too. If these estimates of the size of these erratic moons or planets are accurate, then we have two completely different sized erratic or wandering moons in our solar system. If one is only 1/17th the mass of Mercury, that is far smaller than the one that is a ¼ or 1/3 the size of Venus, as Mercury sitting at a diameter 3100 miles is far smaller than Venus weighing in at 7519 miles diameter; the near twin of Earth, so these sightings couldn't be of the same planetoid.

The coming of the gods

Watchers are people of history thought to be of divine origin or extraterrestrial gods that ruled or enslaved the human race in ancient times. Some say watchers were the angels that married the women before the flood. Some think they became unclean spirits or shape changing watchers when the giants were killed in the flood. One of the advanced ancient technologies spoken of by the Jewish, Rosicrucian and Islamic traditions were lamps that burned or functioned indefinitely without consuming any type of fuel. These were not to be touched as an explosion that could destroy an entire town was a possible result. These lamps were said to come from the Watchers of the sky and such lamps have been found in tombs still burning after a thousand years or more.

The book of Enoch speaks of these watchers too: Enoch was to talk to the Watcher of Heaven who had left the high heavens, and the abodes up there to be with women down here, to their own hurt and ruin and who bore children that became giants. Though it is assumed these are the preflood giants, we realize that giants also existed after the great flood and are spoken of in the bible such as sons of Anak which were in the land of milk and honey, along with Goliath and his brothers. And were the same that came to the Sumerians and to the people of Ur to rule as gods there. Abraham lived in Ur, and he and his father's served the gods, so the Anu and the watchers may be either or both the gods and some of the giants (explained shortly).

An American association known as the Sons of Jared (Jared was a son of Enoch the father of Methuselah) claim that Darius and his son Xerxes were watcher kings. Looking up these "Sons of Jared indicated their existence is so obscure, some say no evidence of the existence of the Sons of Jared currently exists. (Book, 34 pg. 209, Book 23 pg. 75, book 10 pg 164, 165, book 5 pg 97, Internet)

We saw that people by Saturn watched space and warned the gods and the people of earth to prepare for an impact. Watchers are mentioned in the bible in Daniel 4:13, 17 and 23: where a watcher and a holy one come down to chop the tree, that is Nebuchadnezzar life and rule. So this clearly shows watchers are *not* angels. So whatever a Watcher is they don't seem to be fixed as to their identity or their character, and it's possible some of them could have been considered as some of the gods, as their place of origin seems to be from above, be it heaven or space. Point is, they are part of legends and scriptures and they came down to earth, from somewhere, so they could be some of the gods the legends refer to when they talk about the gods coming down from the heavens. But 'Watchers' and 'gods' almost seem to be an interchangeable term, and may only differ in roles played or a name given to them after the gods divided the realms; where watchers obtained the realm of space in our solar system.

The Hopi Indians believe their ancestors came from Mars and Maldek before the planet Maldek was destroyed by its evil inhabitants. Navajos and Zuni speak of blond sky gods of other worlds that came to earth from which their tribes are descended. (Book 23 pg. 122) A quick peek into a can of worms I just realized was there: "Maldek was destroyed by its evil inhabitants"? I'd always assumed the fifth planet was destroyed by a war where an artificial moon got the best of the dwellers of Maldec...similar to the Star Wars movie concept. But it appears from this brief note by the Hopi's that they destroyed themselves similar to how mankind sits on the precipice and how in the ancient past a weapon was spoken of that could destroy the world. Ok back at it...

Von Däniken found out that Assyrian cylinder seals and written tablets had names for people that when translated included such titles as The "Heavenly ones", the "pilots", "space travelers", "earthbound" and / or "earthmen", clearly suggesting some off world capabilities in the hands of the ancients, during those times. (Book 10 pg. 101)

The Navajos Indians call our present world, the fifth world. They also say at one time men traveled from world to world, indicating man at one time traveled in space and visited other planets.

The Japanese people of Hokkaido tell of the Ainu god who descended from the skies and landed in Haiopira in Hokkaido. The Pre-Ainu language (?) uses the term 'Chip-san' which means "the place where the Sun came down.' He taught the people a righteous way of life, and destroyed an evil god. This is an intriguing link between the Japanese, the Sumerians and the bible. Ainu or Anak appeared to the Sumerians first, but his name was translated Anu. Anu descended from the heavens, so the Sumerian Anu, the Hebrew Anak and the Japanese Ainu must all be the same gods, as the description of each and their coming to earth are all the same.

The Indian Book Samaranagana Sutradhara quoted by Tomas states that in the distant past men flew in the air in skyships and Heavenly beings came down from the sky. And the Rig Veda states that the "Gods came to the earth often times" and some men were privileged to visit the immortals in heaven. (Book 11 pg 116-117)

Japanese history recorded in the Nihongi, speaks of their "heavenly ancestors" that opened a barrier of heaven, clearing a cloud path, descending in a heavenly rock-boat, and coming to rest during a time of widespread desolation and governing the western border; and / or ruling the isles of Nippon. What the Japanese history is saying is basically that after some sort of catastrophe they were ruled by gods who descended from the heavens in a flying craft, shaped like a heavenly rock: which is just another way of saying this event ushered in the age of the reign the gods. Though the time stated from the present back to when this happened was said to be 1,792,470 years. (Book 34 pg. 91, 97, 202, book 23 pg. 38)

We have to take the dates attributed to when the gods came and ruled earth with a grain of salt. It doesn't take much to realize they were on the earth with every civilization on the earth at the same time. This is only logical, but a point of proof is the fact they came and ruled as a result of catastrophes that affected the whole globe, and they are almost always said to have come from the north and / or lived in the middle of the Atlantic. It's also clear the gods around the globe built the tunnels, and warned the people to go underground to escape coming disasters. All the clues mean they were on the entire earth during the same time period known as the age of the Gods. There could only have been one age of the gods. The point I don't want to escape your attention is if they were here and there and everywhere during the same time frame, then the dates attributed to their presence are also speaking of the same time regardless of what date any civilization in particular appears to attach to the age of the gods. So if the Babylonians say they were here about 240,000 years ago, and the Chinese say they were here millions of years ago and the Egyptians say they were here 25,000 years ago and the Indians say millions or billions of years ago, and the Japanese say 1,792,470 years ago, clearly indicates someone is adding a few years to reality to appear to be the oldest civilization on the earth. But it's all obvious baloney. The true time frame we are likely talking about for the age of the gods is somewhere closer to the Greeks, Hebrews and Mayans calendars that have a much more realistic time frame. Indeed other people's calendars give away the millions or whatever number of yearss game by their calendars starting points or important events they attribute dates to. So no matter what age they say the gods arrived, they give away the years game somewhere else, either unintentionally or by design.

ERA OF THE AGE OF THE GODS DEFINED

The Greeks say the year of the world 2453 (or 797 years after the flood) was a finale catastrophe, this narrows the period of the age of the gods to a very small window of time as they came after the global flood and left around the final catastrophe. The Hebrew history of the last catastrophes appear to date at 1012 years after the flood and Velikovsky dates the Exodus around 1495 B.C. which is either the last or second to last global catastrophe. (Though it might be during Uziah's reign when an earthquake happened that people ran away from which could possibly be as recently as 687 BC) Mayans appear to place the date around 5000 years ago or 3114 BC, or 3111 BC. The Egyptians, when push comes to shove, place the date of the first dynasty around 3100 BC. (Book 13 pg. 54) The Egyptian historian Manetho states that before the Egyptian dynasties there was a period of rule called the Reign of the gods. (Book 6 pgs. 19-20) This effectively shows the Egyptian suggestion the era of the gods was 25,000 years ago is twaddle, and indeed actually closely resembles the Greek, Hebrew and Mayan placement of the age of the gods in history, and further goes to show the gods were here during a small time window.

India's Calendar starts 3113 B.C.; Krishna's time ends 3101 BC. Mesopotamian civilization starts around 3100 BC. (Atlantis Rising Mag, #76) Near as I can figure, China's Calendar starts 3366 BC which might be when the gods arrived. But there appears to be another Chinese calendar which seems to start at 2700 BC which might be when the gods left China. Indeed Tibet seems to be the last place they left before they went underground, or sporadically visited.

These many calendars or important dates to so many civilizations are all very close to the same point in time and are all floating around the date of 3100 B.C. which no doubt is a reliable clue to the time frame for the end of the age of the gods, as they all seem to indicate the time the gods left, with the probable exception of China's older calendar which may indicate when they arrived, meaning the age of the gods was probably at most 265 years in duration, or roughly from about 50 years after the flood to about 300 years after the flood...give or take, with the age of the gods ending around 3100 B.C. Unless we assume the younger Chinese calendar is when they left China.

Constant Basir wrote that Melpomene (spoken of by Herodotus) mentioned someone he knew had visited the land and maritime parts of Atlantis in 2350 B.C. This may have been the remnant of Atlantis before the remaining islands sunk. (However based on a variable or Ushers' calendar this could be about 50 years after the flood)

THE EAGLE EGG HAS LANDED

Latin America Amerindians were originally like animals with no reason or knowledge or laws, wore nothing and roamed with one or two others like them. Suddenly gleaming gold ships appeared and illuminated the heavens causing the earth to quake; then from the gold ship came the gods who brought their knowledge to the world. They claimed they came from a distant world in the depths of the universe. They implied that they came every 6000 years, suggesting they would return. They said that 130 Families were sent to earth. (Book 10 pg. 111-114)

Where are they coming from...130 families? This almost sounds more like an invasion.

The Egyptians told Solon that the gods divided the whole earth among themselves.

Sumer moon. In the legends of Etana it's noted that after the flood, kingship was lowered again from heaven in Kish, and consolidated all countries. (Book 34 pg. 179) Here we have another clue that the gods work in all the countries at the same time. Sumerian texts say after kingship descended from heaven several kings reigned for a total of 241,200 years, and then the flood came. (That would be the flood of Epic of Gilgamesh: book 1 pg 112, book 23 pg 38) That's obviously a silly date, but if we divided that figure by 100 and we might have a reign of the gods that lasted 241 years and 2 ½ months, which is close to the previous guestimate for the duration of the age of the gods of 265 years, though I suppose 241,200 years could be an accumulative total for all the gods on the earth added together.

Though I've not been able to retrace my steps completely to see exactly how I came to this conclusion, in researching my first book I found that Ur of the Chaldees, is a place of the descended in the region of light. It's felt by some that this was in a place where there is a temple known to be dedicated to the moon. (What I deduced from all the clues I had was that a moon descended in or near Ur which soon after became a region of light and the gods actually helped and built building there. Now "region of light" suggests to me it could be seen from a distance at night because the whole place was lit up enough to make the horizon and the sky glow: Though I suppose it could refer to the 'light' of knowledge.

The Roman Virgil wrote a prophecy (?) about a new race descending from the celestial realms. (Book 11 pg. 67) and they also associated Zeus and the gods with Jupiter.

The Mexican codex Vindobonensis portrays Quetzalcoatl descending from the sky. (Book 11 pg. 121) And some say he came from the east (Book 21 pg. 162) It's quite possible he did both: descended first when he came and taught laws, how to make corn crops excel, and grow cotton in various colours, then lived with the gods on the eastern continent (Atlantis) or under the sea as an earthbound god that returned as promised.

In 1553 a mixed marriage between a Spaniard and an Incan princess allowed this origin of the advancement of the Incas to be shared. It was told that the Incan father the sun, seeing humans having descended to baser natures and living like beasts, sent down to earth a Man and Woman to instruct the people. After their work was done they returned to heaven in a vehicle that shone like a "resplendent sun" which rose from an island in Lake Titicaca. (Book 8 pg. 36)

The Babylonian's priest and historians also includes how people lived like beasts in the field with no order or rule and Oannes a fish-man came out of the water to teach them letters, science and arts, how to build houses and temples, make laws, geometry, distinguishing seeds, and how to collect fruit, and in general taught them civilization during the day, and then he returned to the ocean at night. He had feet similar to a man (book 35 pgs. 96, 179-80, book 34 pg. 185)

The Eskimos tell how their ancestors were flown to the polar region by gods inside beings with metallic wings. The Mayans tell of a gigantic metallic eagle that came from the heavens roaring like a lion, and landed. Then the 'beak' of the 'eagle' opened up and four creatures who did not breathe our air came out of the eagle's beak. Peruvian legends tell of gold, silver and bronze eggs that came down from the heavens and the people of the area were born from these eggs. (Book 35 pg. 180, Book 23, pg. 191)

The Egyptians say that Osirus and Isis descended from the sky in a sun ship, and brought wheat, and the arts of civilization with them, (Book 23 pg. 90)

The Tibetan book of Dzyan states that divine kings descended and taught men sciences and art. (Book 23 pg. 49)

The stanzas of Dzyan say that people descended to earth from Venus in a huge spaceship to guide and civilize man who had become primitive. They also descended to inspire the people of Lemuria. It goes on to say lords of the moon also descended to the earth, and indeed some of the ancients such as the Sumerians also venerated Celestials on the Moon. (Book 23 pgs. 50, 62, 64)

The Gobi desert was once a great sea in which there was an island in the middle. Chinese legends tell of a time when that island was inhabited by white men with fair hair and blue eyes who had descended there from heaven, then taught the people the art of civilization. (Book 21 pg. 57)

North American Indians never climbed above the snow line of mountains lest they anger the gods. Greeks wouldn't climb mount Olympus to meet Zeus. Japanese felt that the demons danced on the hills. Drake continues and states that in every country of the world the mountains were sacred and the abode of the gods. And he asks the question: "Were they landing-places for space ships?" (Book 23 pg. 123) That might sound like a crazy question, but I'm not so sure. The pyramids, and mountains have some sort of energy that seems to be centered at the tips, and indeed clues suggest that the gods landed on the tops of ziggurats. I've noticed on old movies that the high points of objects seen in the film have bright areas above each of the objects in the film. Some people cannot even be photographed because the energy they exude is so strong they overexpose the film in the area where their faces are. Moses was on one occasion glowing so brightly he had to wear a veil. The God of the bible descended to the top of Mount Zion to talk to Moses and the Israelites were scared to death to get near the mountain, and they were warned not to. If I recall right they were not supposed to even eat on mountains and the naughty people of Israel were constantly making idols or some sort of thing to burn incense on *high places*. Ancient structures and hills have been found to have rounded cones on top such as seen on the coin of Byblos had depicted on the roof and the Stelle of Naram Sin which had a sun like object landing on the tip. Were the ancient gods aware of some phenomenon and able to utilize it somehow to aid their craft when they descended?

The Chippewa, Osages, and the Cree all believe that in the past star people came to the earth and taught men civilization, or occasionally behaved like demons and brought destruction. The Noctkaus tell of a time long ago when a hero came and later sailed away in a copper canoe to a celestial land in the skies. (Book 23 pg. 128) Another Chippewa legend is of a man who saw a strange circle of grass worn down with no path leading in or out of the circle. Wondering what made this ...crop circle... he hid beside it in the long grass. Soon a flying speck in the distance came towards him with a melodious sound, which was a carriage that held twelve maidens. They danced in the circle and he fell in love with the youngest. He chased her but she escaped into the car, but returned the next day and they married. Missing her home she returned to the sky with her son. Missing them he spent all his time by the circle, and one day she returned and took him back to the star country. (Book 23 pg. 130) This might be a way to meet girls, if you can convince the farmers to let you stay on their farms where crop circles appear without creeping them out. But which crop circle and on which farm do you wait by? It would be like Linus waiting for the great pumpkin...

The Hopi believe their ancestors came from Maldec and its moon: Maldek is the exploded planet between Mars and Jupiter. (Book 23 pg. 151) The lost moon of Maldec may be Ceres, the only spherical "asteroid" in the belt.

Though we dealt with flood legends earlier, so much of this one speaks of the age of the gods that I'm using this one here...

NISQUALLY (WASHINGTON)

The world became so overcrowded the all the fish and game were eaten and they started to eat each other so Dokibatl the Changer decided to flood the earth. The only creatures that survived this flood were a woman and a dog because they were on top of Tacobud (Mount Rainier). From these two all the next race were born, and they walked on all fours and lived and acted like animals. A huge bear came from the south which could paralyze with its look anything it wanted to eat and the people were all in danger of being eaten. This prompted the Changer to send a Spirit Man from the east to teach them civilization, by using bows, canoes, clothing, fire and whatever else would help them flourish. They also taught them about the spirits and the potlatch custom. Spirit Man killed the bear with seven arrows and he also put all the ills of the world in a large building, however years later a curious daughter peeked in the building and let them out. [Clark, pp. 136-138]

The natives of Honduras tell of a woman named Comizaguel skilled in magic that descended from the skies to teach the people civilization. (Book 23 pg. 165)

The Machiguenga Indians of Eastern Peru speak of people of the heavens who came to earth on a shining road in the sky, and of the days when their forefathers communicated with the celestials of the sky. (Book 23 pg. 177, 179)

The Incas say Manco Capac and his wife came down from the sun to teach men civilization. (Book 23 pg. 194)

Furthermore, the Incas tell how in the past the royal family descended to the Island of the Sun in Lake Titicaca in a craft as bright as the sun and they later left from this same island in the same way they came. While they were here a man and woman taught them so they would stop behaving like beasts. (Book 8 pgs. 35-36)

Mayan legends tell of white gods with fair skin and blue eyes that came from the east in great ships with swan wings. (Book 21 pg. 180) And the Mayan record Codex Vindobonensis shows Quetzalcoatl descending from a hole in the sky. (Book 11 pg. 121, 166)

Traditions near Tiahuanaco tell of Orejona who came from Venus in a flying machine more dazzling than the sun to become the mother of the human race. (Book 22 pg. 42)

The Greeks say that Ouranos, (Greek for "sky" but probably means the god Uranus) ruled over the whole world. (Book 23 pg. 209-10)

The Scythians near the Black sea believe that the gods threw down from heaven tools, the plow (or plough), the axe, the cup and basic tools to facilitate civilization. (Book 23 pg. 213)

Polynesians have a history that speaks of winged women that came down from the skies to give them aid then flew back. (Book 34 pg. 224)

Native's texts of the Caroline Isles tell of beings of wonder that descended to earth in flying discs and taught their ancestors. (Book 34 pg. 224)

African Bushmen tell of the gods from the skies and a people from heaven which sent messengers down to earth, as do the Vietnamese legends which say their first kings came from heaven. (Book 10 pg. 85, Book 34 pg. 225)

The Congo Bantu people say that a man and two women came down from heaven with seeds and things to start fire with, and taught them how to use things. (Book 10 pg. 90)

Lake Victoria Ja-Luo people say a god named Apodho came down from heaven with grain, cattle and taught them how to farm. (Book 10 pg. 90)

Mugulu came down to the Jagga people of Tanzania bringing banana, potatoes, beans, but forgot corn so he had to go back to heaven but never returned because he died. (Book 10 pg. 90-91)

African Dogon tells of a time the eight Nihongi descended down from heaven amidst great noise and smoke when they came, and were just as spectacular when they left (Book 10 pg. 106)

Nihongi sounds very reminiscent of Japan. A Japanese ancient history book *Koyiki* states that the sun queen Amaterasu sent her grandson Ninigi to the earth. He landed on a mountain in Kyushu and brought a metal mirror of some kind, a sword and a string of jewels. These items still exist but are wrapped up and sealed. Ninigi stayed, apparently married an earth woman, and his grandson, Jimmu Tenno, became the first Monarch, indeed the title of Japanese Monarch means heavenly monarch and the dynasty traces it's hereditary back to Amaterasu, thus the line is descendant from the gods. (Book 10 pg. 107)

The Indian Samaranagana Sutradhara tells how in the past heavenly beings came down from the sky. (Book 11 pg. 116)

MORE JACOB'S LADDERS

As mentioned before in a flood legend of the eastern Taiwan Ami people, Kakumodan's house was flooded and he and his wife escaped. However in this case they escaped, by climbing a ladder to the sky. This is particularly interesting. Most people in either the global flood or the local floods either were drowned, survived by floating in a boat of some kind, climbed trees or escaped underground. As mentioned some were already in space when the flood occurred so they were never actually in the flood. But here we have a couple that were rescued out of a "local" flood by what could only be through some sort of flight with a rescue rope ladder let down to them, similar to how we rescue people from floods or pull them out of some sort of disaster like falling off a ledge or a forest fire or what have you. Only as a rule we don't fly the rescued off into space somewhere, and legends don't appear to made of these events. It appears one or more of the gods stayed, or returned and rescued some people from certain demise.

African Madi-Morui legend states that the first men lived in heaven then came down here, and while they were here a lively traffic existed up and down to the earth and back to cloudland until the bluebird pecked the ladder to heaven to pieces ending this state of affairs. The tribe of Kuluwe say the first human came from heaven with gifts such as the axe, seeds, rakes a pair of bellows and other things to help civilization progress. These gods also brought some animals down from heaven. African tribes like the Masai mention that some of the gods were red, blue, white and black and came down from cloudland to teach civilization and yet they all seemed to have different opinions as to how to accomplish their mission. They often destroyed what each of the others had built up. The gods were quarrelsome amongst themselves. Some of the gods were forgetful, forgetting to bring promised presents from above, or they died before they returned. (Book 10 pg. 86)

The Ashanti say that seven men descended to the earth on a chain, produced some men here then returned to their heavenly home.

The Queets of the Washington tribe remembers how two girls of the prairies watching the stars were stolen by two men and taken up into Skyland. The chief led his tribe up a ladder of arrows from earth to Heaven and defeated the sky people and returned with them back to earth. On the surface this seems impossible, but it speaks of a war or a struggle in heaven with man having the technological knowhow to get into space and be on a par with the gods. Maybe not beat them, but reason with them enough to have the two girls returned. (Book 23 pg. 126)

Tibetan folk tales tell of a boy with a deformed head that married the daughter of a king of heaven after she descended to the earth. She stayed on the earth for nine years, and then out of the blue returned to the sky. Sad at the loss of his wife he roamed to many places in search of the woman. One day he saved a Gryphon from a dragon and as a reward he was flown to the skies where he was reunited with his wife. The gods were so moved by their love for each other she was permitted to return to the earth with him. (Book 34 pg. 72) Tibetan documents state that the first seven kings came from the stars, and were able to walk in the sky, and climbed down to the earth on the ladder of heaven. While they were here they brought writings in an unknown language which no one could understand, and these were only partially taught to one pupil who was allowed to translate *some* of them. The rest were hidden in caves for the day when someone could translate the part of what remained that the pupil did not translate. After this the gods returned when their work on earth was done. (Book 11 pg. 117, book 10 pg. 125-26)

A Puyallup myth tells of two sisters that were taken in their sleep to star land where they were married to star men. But being unhappy with the situation they found themselves in, they managed to dig a hole and climb down a rope back to the earth. Later on the older of the two had a baby that was of the star people. The Blackfeet tell a similar tale but when the girl returned to earth by a web like thread, she decided later she wanted to return to her husband in the sky, but was forbidden and died of a broken heart. (Book 23 pg. 125, 129)

The North American Indians are adamant that sky people in the past used to descend to the earth. They picture the lord of the sky as a chief on a cloud. (Book 23 pg. 126)

The Iroquois say a pregnant woman fell from the sky and bore twins, one good and one evil. And another god came from the heaven in a magic boat named Tarenyawoga and brought civilization to them. (Book 23 pg. 127, Book 22 pg. 95)

The Objibwa-Algonquins say a handsome youth descended from the sky and brought or turned into corn. (Book 23 pg. 127)

TOLTEC (MEXICO):

I repeat this legend: One of the sons of the twofold god made himself into the sun and created the earth and the humans, showing up his brothers. The other gods annoyed by this showmanship got Quetzalcoatl to destroy the sun and the earth by a flood and turned the people into fish. This ended the first age. The second, third and fourth suns ended by the heavens crumbling, a rain of fire and lastly by overwhelming winds.

Of note: the creeping in of the concept where the creator and the other gods are blurred and put on an even footing as seen in this legend, something common in current books like Von Daniken's Chariots of the gods series. Eat the fruit and ye shall be as gods. People after the flood saw these people return from the skies with their abilities and they equated them with gods and the confusion has continued on down through the ages. This is also interesting because it states that one of the gods purposely created a catastrophe here.

The Dakotas were also mindful of the Spirits of the sky which often in times past used to descend to the earth in human form to direct man and the animals, inspire the warriors, control storms, and alter the path of migrating buffaloes. (Book 23 pg. 126) And here we see the gods had control of the weather. Of late it has been suspected that some of the world governments have acquired the ability to control weather surreptitiously so that people might not realize they are under attack. The gods and to some extent the world we live in today has acquired sciences that mimic the powers of God. We saw Jesus stop the storm, but the gods appear to have captured this ability to use for their own purposes, and it seems some leaks and investigations suggest some governments today have secret advanced technology capable of similar activities. The serpent said ye shall be as gods. Many of the things the gods did were so similar to what we expect God is capable like creating different types of foods, peoples, animals, storms and catastrophes and this got mankind serving them and after the gods left missing them and trying ways or prayers to get them to come back. But the way the gods acted sometimes was often all too human.

FROM THE NORTH?

The Moon was said to be very close to the earth at Hyperborea...in the north. Hyperborea is often assumed to be Iceland but it could be Doggerland as we've discussed earlier, or possibly further north in the now sunken Frisland or the broken in two Estland. (Book 22 pg. 141) However at this point I know of no other legend from this general area that speaks of the moon as being so large due to close proximity to the earth. This may in fact be a clue. If Norway, Denmark and Great Britain have no legend of the moon being so close then it could well be a smaller artificial moon hovering above these, now lost or sunken islands which of course appear to have been part of Atlantis and as such this moon would not be visible from too far away.

Chinese thought the gods lived in the celestial North Pole. (Book 34 pg. 82) The Egyptians believed the "Seven Shining Ones" and the "Holy Ones" dwelt in the Northern sky. (Book 34 pg. 135) Tibetans also believed there were seven heavenly thrones. (Book 34 pg. 69) Sumerian Anu, father of the gods dwelt in the North Constellation of the Great Bear. (Book 34 pg 201-202) The Babylonian god Ea, dwelt near the North Pole (Book 34 pg. 202) I'm betting there is a connection between these legends and the concept of Santa Claus living at the North Pole.

Authors ask questions like "Was Apollo an extra-terrestrial being [Robert Charroux Book 22 pg. 141]. Eric Norman quoting Gunther Rosenberg who believed that "...Grecian and Roman gods were actually spacemen; their supernatural powers were nothing more than an advanced technology in a primitive world." (Book 29 pg. 56) Andrew Tomas seems to fall prey to one of the ruses of the gods when saying "This monster, which could have been a cosmic visitor in a spacesuit after "splashdown"..., referring to Oannes as a 'fishlike god.' (Book 11 pg. 166) Raymond Drake assumes "a few extra-terrestrials descended in their ships of light to teach man civilization." Based on a battle between the Lhas and goat, dog headed and fish bodied men, he assumes that Oannes was one as well. (Book 34 pg. 68). But then who could blame him. However; Oannes was not an alien. Sitchen note some texts (Sumerian and Berosus relating legends) that, though Oannes looked like a fish, he had a human head under the fishes' head and had feet like a man's under the fish's tail. "His voice too and language were articulate and Human". (Book 17 pg. 287) Some ancient wall carvings show Oannes as simply a man wearing a fish type garb. (**See image 22**) This disguising of the gods reminds me of an Unidentified Object sighting of June 7 1971 in Rosedale Alberta...

Image 22

Oannes as carved by the ancients

A woman realized something unusual was taking place outside and took a look. She saw a lit box like capsule with two inhabitants, one apparently deliberately hiding a control panel with his body and arm. A third person was a few feet from the capsule. They all had sort of claw like hands covered by gloves. But their adeptness with the claws was pitiful as though the claw like hands were a disguise to hide normal hands. The inhabitants appeared like normal humans otherwise. (Book 46 pgs. 65-67)

Though often it's stated that the gods dwelt in Atlantis, and some say they came from a northern location such as Doggerland, the Greeks Plutarch refers to places in the western sea called Ogygia, Venus, Calypso and another one furthest west called Cronos which appear to be names for some islands beyond Atlantis in the 'western sea'. He then notes that some fierce warriors came from the great mainland 5000 stadia beyond Cronos that was originally inhabited by 13 descendants of Hercules' companions. Picking an average distance of 650 feet for a stadia, that works out to about 615 miles beyond Cronos is the mainland. I get the sense here that at this point in time the Atlantic Ocean was not as wide as it is now. At some point Chronos, the person the island is named after, is held prisoner by Zeus on either an island beyond Ogygia or the mainland where "...for thirty days on end, the sun sets for little more than an hour, and for several months the night is faintly illuminated by the western twilight." (Book 21 pg. 251) Could this be another description of Hyperborea? No, because Hyperborea for part of the year was in eternal sunshine, indicating a place north of the Arctic Circle. But it reinforces the legends that speak of the gods living in the northern regions. This piece of history also suggests that the gods didn't come from the *planet* Venus, but from an island of the same name. Tricky: the gods could say with a straight face they came from Venus, and let the people assume what they want. Indeed this line of thought even works today. Some UFO's people have said they came from Venus: UFO's are often spotted coming out of the sea in the "Bermuda Triangle" region and based on the description of the location of this island named Venus, it could be a sunken island that was once associated with Atlantis in this same area. Could this be what these UFO pilots mean when they say they came from Venus?

SIMILARITIES BETWEEN GODS / TITLES OF GODS
NAMES OF GODS OF DIFFERENT PLACES

It is pretty certain the gods were all on the earth at the same time with the same mission in what is known as the age of the gods. All around the world these gods, which for the most part had the best of intentions, descended to earth to pull mankind out of his deteriorated state to an advanced civilized condition which was considered the normal standard to the gods, but apparently beyond the ability of men on earth to attain…or re-attain after some cataclysmic events.

Though I initially thought that every god from a given legend and place could be identified as the same god of another legend in another place: but I'm no longer even remotely sure this is the case. Many people who have studied the gods appear to assume the same thing IE Uranus = Cronus = Saturn= Zeus = Jupiter… and so on. How could one god be in Egypt, China, Peru, Rome and Greece and wherever else he or she was supposed to have been on earth at the same time? Now it's true perhaps one God who was the leader of the gods might be the same god in many nations but with a different name or translation of the meaning of his name, such as our example. But this is probably not the case for the vast majority of the other gods. Some might suggest that because they lived so long they just went from one place to another over vast stretches of time. That might work except for a couple problems. Some of the gods died, some of the gods left with tears, and the conclusion to the affair is usually the same in all the legends: Wars in heaven that usually destroyed the earth in some way and caused cataclysmic repercussions; so why would they return to another location on earth years later and start the process all over again? Wouldn't they learn from their mistakes? It seems more plausible that all the 130 families of gods as the legend states came to all the peoples of the earth, at some point in time, apparently after the tower of Babel incident, and even relocated some of these peoples around the globe as some legends imply. Once they were settled in their new place they left. Then after some disaster, they looked in on their people, saw their miserable state and stayed and taught the people, and establishing their civilizations. They also came and left in different ways and in different methods and vehicles. Vehicles used were described as rocks, eggs, eagles, flying discs and the like.

Then with the men learning and wanting to be like the gods, conflicts arose, technology was stolen or re-engineered, and turned on the gods or others causing huge destructions and further worldwide cataclysms. The end being the gods left the service of men to return to their habitations which the legends state were three fold; either back to space, underground or into the sea after a dividing up of the realms between them. The gods even warred among themselves and they had to determine where their future dwelling places were; space, underground or the sea, as the surface world had been determined to be detrimental to their longevity due to the deteriorated nature of the environment and the sun's radiation, resulting in reduced life spans and genetic decline. And I surmise that some genetic entropy had occurred in some of the gods so they could no longer mingle with the original gods to degrade their gene pool and reduce life spans, thus the need for separate realms depending on the degree of decline or lack thereof.

Here are just a few examples of parallels or gods of one people thought to be the same gods of another. Some of these may be wrong; I only repeat other researchers' conclusions here. This is by no means a complete list; this is just a sampling of what I've come across in a cursory rereading of my source materials while looking for other stuff.

SOCIAL REGISTRAR; WHO'S WHO.

Drake noted similarities of the gods described in the Ramayana and the Iliad, where husbands hunt for captured raped wives who in retaliation start wars that set the world aflame, and the gods intervening in human's affairs. (Book 34 pg. 39) Thus suggesting some of the gods of the Iliad are the same gods of the Ramayana.

Hesiod (860 BC) in his *Theogony* and other Greek legends tell of wars between men and gods (book 34 pg. 42) Furthermore he notes Sumerian Anu' being dethroned by Enlil, in turn overthrown by Merodach, parallels the succession of "Uranus-Cronus (Saturn) – Zeus (Jupiter) ruling in the Golden, then Silver and Iron ages. Merodachis is therefore Marduk and is identified with the War god Asshur. (War god also said to be Nergal, and another War god (Assyrian) is called Ninlil. Oannes the fish man of the Sumerians is equated as Dagon and thought to have fathered Semiramis. He even equated Jehovah, one of the names of the God of the bible with Shamash, a Babylonian god. (Book 34 pg 202-203) This confusing the God of the bible with other gods or just any god is done by a few authors usually because the gods did similar things to the god of the bible like teaching rules to people for civilization. But close inspection shows The God of the bible stated categorically he was the only God, he knew no other and we were to worship no other. The other gods didn't expect worship and were flesh and blood, living here and ruling teaching and marrying. But many authors appear to be confused because of the similarities of the missions and the purpose. If they were people, as many legends insist they were, then don't forget the serpent's words: "ye shall be as gods".

Kolosimo also states that Chronos is Saturn, and Zeus is Jupiter. (Book 21 pg. 251)

Ahriman is same as Angra Mainyu, Ukko = Jupiter, Ea = Oannes (Book 34 pg 202)

Charroux insists that Osirus is the same as Asari and Asar, an Aryan or an "Asianic" god. And says Isis was the mother goddess Da, Koridwen, Cybele and Demeter all later worshipped as the Queen of Heaven which with Constantine's "conversion", was later pressed into service by the Catholic Church as the Virgin Mary. (Book 22 pg. 225)

Xlotal was the Aztec god of death and resurrection (book 1 pg. 23) Often Quetzalcoatl (who descended from the sky) and Viraccocha are assumed to be the same god. The Greek God Imouthes is felt to be Imhotep of the Egyptians. (Book 8 pg. 49, 91, book 11 pg. 121)

To Tomas, the Babylonian god Anu equals Zeus equals Jupiter (book 11 pg. 113, 120) And, Thoth is equated as Hermes and Mercury and Thoth = Hermes, = Mercury according to Andrew Thomas (Book 11 pg 166)

Though not stating specifically at this point that the Greek's god Zeus, Icelandic's god Odin, the Finnish god Ukko, the Russian god Perun, the Germans god Wotun, the god Mazda of the Persians, Marduk of the Babylonians and Shiva of the Hindus are the same god, Velikovsky does state they all discharged interplanetary force such as lightning bolts that overwhelmed the world with water and fire. (Book 14 pg. 101) He does later state that Athena, daughter of Zeus, equals Ishtar, Astarte and the planet Venus, Minerva of the Romans and Isis of the Egyptians. Then he says Venus and Lucifer are one and the same. Saturn is Phaenon, and Chronos. (Book 14 pg. 178, 179, 185)

Ammon = Jupiter (Book 21 pg 198)

Isis = Greek Selene, the Moon goddess is Hera or Juno wife of Zeus, or Jupiter. (Book 34 pg. 125)

Costa Rica's Tamagastad = Quetzalcoatl (book 21 pg. 182)

Set has been equated with Greek god Typhon (book 34 pg. 125). But Typhon though depicted as a snake with many heads, wasn't actually a god, it was a phenomena.

There are of course many other equating, but that's hardly my focus.

However if, as one reference states and others suggest, that 130 families were sent to the earth's surface, then all these gods supposedly equated with each other might actually be just different members of this group of 130 families which were all sent at the same time with the exact same mission.

Many authors of the material I researched spoke of similarities of the god of one place with the gods of other places. Many have stated that one god from one place IS the same god as talked about in another place. I have not and cannot read all the ancient legends to compare the gods and categorically state that this god of say, Egypt is the same god as this one in Rome or China or the Incas. Some historians are certain that some of the gods of Egypt, Rome and Greece are the same gods with different names, and they may be. I am not qualified to agree or disagree with any certainty. But it seems to me if the gods sent 130 families to the earth to teach and rule the children of men who had disintegrated to savages, then these similar gods thought to be the same may in fact be all different people or gods, but with identical missions. The identical mission therefore creates the parallels and similarities between the gods. Like I said I'm no expert, but I have on occasion found errors of identification where two different authors identified one god as someone that was completely impossible compared to another's deduction. Velikovsky found many misidentifications, and these conclusions rocked the scholastic world to its foundations and he was the target of criticisms from seemingly every branch of academia. So if the experts get it wrong, then I almost certainly would too, and any attempt would quickly find me out for the complete novice I am, so I'm not even going to try. Not because I'm not up for the task, but because I suspect it's entirely possible that almost none of the gods of one place are the same gods of another. (With a notable exception of the Queen of Heaven whose husband was killed cut into several pieces then cloned, placed inside her and she had him as a son, which started the world wide belief in reincarnation.) This exception could indeed prove that some of the gods known in one place were the gods of another. Why? Because if all the people lived in one place at one time before the tower of Babel incident that caused the dispersal of people around the globe, any stories these people repeated would be the same stories with different languages around the globe with a common origin and any people in those stories would be the same persons. But it appears that it was the gods that helped facilitate the dispersal. So we have a conundrum. Some of the people in one language will be the same in another, leading people to assume all the people in ones people's histories are the people of another people's history. For example some of the Sumerian gods could be spoken of in many places because they came before the dispersal. So the exceptions would be any of the gods that came to earth before the tower of Babel incident when all mankind was still in the same region speaking the same language. The gods of the Sumerians would fit this bill. Thus as we saw Anu of the Babylonians probably equals the sons of Anak of the Hebrews and Ainu of the Japanese.

Reign of the gods

As mentioned, the Egyptian historian Manetho stated that before the Egyptian dynasties there was a period of rule called the Reign of the gods. (Book 6 pg. 19) There was a time when the rulers of Egypt were the "gods, who dwelt among mankind", the last being Orus son of Osiris. The first pharaoh was said to be the son of Horus that descended from Ra the sun god. His capabilities were the ability to make Egypt green and fertile and preserved the people's lives. (Book 34 pgs. 117,121)

The Egyptians made a very key observation about the gods. They stated that there was a single God creator of all, and there were the gods, completely different from God. Landsburg summarising the Egyptian book of the dead, states that this "colony of lesser gods who raced around the known world displaying behaviours, both productive and destructive, [like that] of any ordinary mortal." But the one thing that separated them from us was their ability to seemingly live forever. (Book 1 pg. 91) The Incan Viracocha said their stay was a "life without death". (Book 8 pg. 52) To people living maybe 175 years old a couple generations after the flood, a god living 7-950 years would appear somewhat eternal. But as we've seen a couple of the gods were known to have perished in their abode in the sky, so they were not immortal, only they had a very prolonged existence, not unlike the people from before the flood who lived on average about 900 years or so.

Plato notes that the gods lived in and or ruled from Atlantis, and that their behaviour was becoming very unbecoming; they were succumbing to avarice, and lust for power to the point where this honourable race was in a wretched state. So Zeus summoned them all to the 'center of the world' for reproving and punishment. (Book 6 pg. 42)As to what happened is unknown as Plato's narrative ends there.

The Toltec says that an Island in the Eastern Sea, that is the Atlantic, was the home of the civilized gods. (Book 24 pg. 91)

The Tibetan histories in the Dzyan says the Great kings of the dazzling faces, used air vehicles to rescue chosen Atlanteans and took them away, apparently to Venus; which once again links Atlantis with the age of the gods. (Book 34 pg. 28)

Tibetan tales describe a city of the gods in the sky 2500 yojanas wide and broad. A hundred yojanas is said to be 5-900 miles. (Book 14 pg. 316-318) So 2500 Yojanas would be between 12,500 to 22,500 miles; (For some reason I calculated that at 1,250,000 miles previously, two too many zero's, which is a ridiculous figure, though still 12,500 miles is still too large for the artificial planets because it is bigger than the earth. Though it's closer to feasible than I originally thought, it's far too large to be the one that has been spotted around Venus, or near the sun. I'm betting a translation of Yojanas is either incorrect or an exaggeration is in place, which wasn't beyond the Ancient Indians to use. After conquering the world a king went up to the city of the gods and shared the throne and eventually tried to take over. During his time there the city was attacked by other gods in their war chariots but they were repelled and sent back to their own fortress far in space. Once again indicating there is more than one artificial moon or 'city' in space. Sometime after this the usurping king was cast back down to earth and died. (Book 34 pg. 72, 73)

The gods sometimes took such as King Etan on trips in flying machines shaped like a shield to the moon, Mars and Venus. These pilots were described as blond with dark complexions, dressed in white and as handsome as the gods. (Book 34 pg. 180) This bit indicates than some men or possibly partially deteriorated gods, had access or grasp of the technology of the gods.

Giants have been filtered from modern versions of the bible because some translators have swallowed the evolutionists poison. John Battle says that in order to read about the giants in the bible, you have to read the King James or related versions. I suspect one reason giants might bother some creationists, is because they don't fit the evolutionist's so called "scientific" model and if not that, then because they existed *after* the flood. The bible explains how they came to be before the flood, but if they all died in the flood, how could they exist after the flood if they weren't of Noah's family? In the bible there doesn't appear to be any mention of the angels returning to the earth to make more giants with more willing women; so the doubting Christian has to ask 'where did they come from?' Where did the sons of Anak (giants) come from, or Og or Goliath? The existence of Goliath for some reason doesn't bother creationists too much...maybe because he's such an intrinsic part of key Jewish kingship lineage that they can't escape him. But these sons of Anak are a real problem because the word for giants here is the same as the word for giants used before the flood...Nephalim. How do giants appear after the flood? This is a question no creationists seem to have tackled or answered.

Another key clue and something I missed that Drake draws our attention to, is a curious fact of something written in the bible. He quotes the New English Bible that has a footnote explaining a verse that refers to the giants, saying that the probable Hebrew reading of Genesis Chapter 6 verse 4 reads "in those days and also afterwards," (book 23 pg. 211) This appears to clue us into them coming back somehow. Indeed the King James Version full verse states in Genesis 6:4: "There were giants in the earth in those days; and also after that, when the sons of God came in unto the daughters of men, and they bore children unto them, the same became mighty men which were of old, men of renown." No explanation appears to exist as to why there were giants after the flood: could this verse explain it? Could it be a key verse that alludes to the coming of the gods? Other parts of the bible do refer to the gods but little or no background about them is given: the original writers just assume the readers are aware of them. Perhaps even as an assurance to the people, Psalm 82 appears to prophesy for the gods in that he will judge among them too.

It's often assumed that all the giants from before the flood died in the flood, so it doesn't explain why they appear after the flood: particularly the sons of Anak in the Promised Land that Joshua led the Israelites to take over. "Numbers 13:33 "And there we saw the Giants, the sons of Anak, which come of the Giants: and we were in our own sight as grasshoppers, and so we were in their sight". This is actually another clue when you read it straightforwardly. It's plainly stating that the giant sons of Anak came from the giants! Interesting! This is saying some giants still existed for them to have come from them, or at the very least, it's saying these were descendants of the giants. How is this possible if they all died in the flood!? The only way is that some of them *didn't* die in the flood! So how is *this* possible if all the flesh on dry land died? Because they descended down to the Sumerians...from space, meaning they were in space during the flood. No other answer fits! Keep in mind the giant that existed after the floods were the sons of Anak, which were those that came to the Sumerians and to the people of Ur to rule as gods there. And Ur means "a place of the descended". There is no escaping it: some of the giants were in space during the flood.

Perhaps we could deduce that before the flood, people were using genetics to make clones, giants and different coloured races, suggesting giants may be caused by breeding or genetics, or both. But like the bible, the book of Enoch as quoted in Book 12 page 135 says "...the Grigori broke through their vows on the shoulder of the hill, Ermon, and saw the daughters of men how good they are, and took to themselves wives, and befouled the earth with their deeds, who in all times of their age made lawlessness and mixing, and the giants were born and marvellous big men of great hostility." I don't know this for sure but I throw it out there just so it's said: It's assumed this book of Enoch is a preflood document because of the preflood patriarch Enoch. Couldn't there be another person with this name after the flood? If the people before the flood were so smart they didn't need to write, then why would a preflood document even exist? And couldn't this section be referring to a post flood event, or a post flood document recalling preflood events? This mirrors the preflood biblical reference to them and seems more clearly to state they were the result of intermarriage. Did it happen again but not with angels but with the gods that came down?

Note: these would not be a recurrence of the angels marrying women again after the flood and these would not the children of angels but their descendants' children.

As pointed out in a previous work, several verses in the bible indicate the gods were known about and their location is indicated as being below us, the hosts of heaven, or in the water. I heard this psalm partly quoted in church one day from a different more modern version of the NIV...Could this psalm be another biblical reference to the gods that I've missed?

Psalm 89: 5 Let the heavens praise your wonders, O LORD, your faithfulness in the assembly of the holy ones! 6 For who in the skies can be compared to the LORD? Who among the heavenly beings is like the LORD, 7 a God greatly to be feared in the council of the holy ones, and awesome above all who are around him? 8 O LORD God of hosts, who is mighty as you are, O LORD, with your faithfulness all around you?

The work of the gods

BUILDING

Similarity and commonality of the arts, sciences, customs, habits, legends, and buildings in many ancient cities on both sides of the Atlantic and around the world suggests a far reaching culture in which all these places find a common thread. (Book 35 pg. 20) Historically, through legends and biblically speaking, one could assume such parallels are a natural extension of the family from the flood expanding with common roots as traces of this are found everywhere, and indeed much of ancient history and legends can be linked to this common point of origin. But the legends also point to gods infiltrating them with their own standardised teachings to pull many of the peoples out of a primitive lifestyle as a result of cataclysms they experienced. And this is what some of this commonality points to as well, such as in building techniques, civilization forms and common tales of the gods.

Baalbek platforms have erected on them 54 pillars 8 feet wide 90 feet tall that support stone slabs between 1200 and 1500 tons each (Book 29 pgs. 114-15) Levitation was almost certainly used in ancient times for lifting massive weights. Legends of the Chaldea or Babylonian, Arabian, Syrian, Taoist, Buddhist, Indian, Abyssinia, and other ancient cultures and histories all talk of levitation or antigravity existing in one form or another in the past. Thus it is probable that huge stones such as those in Baalbek Lebanon, Egypt, Babylon, Hierapolis in Syria, Brazil, China, Sacsayhuaman Cusco Peru, Ollantytambo, Mexican, Lions Gate

Greece, Hattusa Turkey, Ellora and other carved sites in India were built using anti gravity technology, almost universally credited to the gods. (Book 11 pg. 99-106, Book 12 pgs. 149-150, Book 21 pgs. 32, 101, Book 23 pg. 164,)

Dr. Morris K. Jessup, researcher and writer of four books on UFO's and thought by some to have been killed because he hit a nerve with his UFO research, also researched some ancient mysteries. He concluded that spaceships of vast proportions brought colonists to various part of the earth and supplied this heavy lifting power for erecting the great stone works before the capability was suddenly destroyed or taken away. (Book 35 pg. 84)

He is not alone. Joseph Goodavage deduced that the ancients appear to have conquered some elemental force which enabled them to construct the buildings they were working on. He deduced the power used had to have been levitation, but assumed the people who held this power had to be extra-terrestrial in origin, which stayed for a while, either because they were unable or unwilling to leave, or when they did leave for whatever reason, left their work unfinished. (Book 35 pg. 84)

Whether the conclusions of these researchers sound eccentric or not, the point is they too saw the technology was A: incredible to the point they have come up with a UFO answer, and B: that is was suddenly stopped for some unknown reason, all around the globe.

Nevertheless we can't just automatically assume the gods did all this heavy lifting; we somewhere have to balance what the gods did with how man afterwards somehow managed, to some extent, repeat some of their feats. Consider.

Josephus mentions that some stone blocks used by King Agrippa in refurbishing Jerusalem were 20 cubits long and ten cubits broad. The third measurement though not given immediately, he does mention the wall was 10 cubits wide, in the next sentence: so the stone may have had this third measurement. But then he suggests the wall wasn't this high at the time (War of the Jews IV 2) I supposed the stones used might have been 20 X 10 X 10 and the rest of the wall not this high. For ease of calculation we'll assume 1 cubit equals 1 ½ feet (which by the way would be the minimum measurements). This would mean these stones used were (6750 Cubic feet) or (based on 600 cubic feet equalling 50 tons) were about 562 tons. Shortly after this he mentions some other stones that were in the wall but not necessarily placed there by Agrippa were 45 x 5 x 6 (Cubits) = 67 ½ X 7 ½ X 9 (Feet) or 4556 cubic feet weighing about 380 tons

In the next section (4) he mentions the wall had some white marble stones and using all three dimensions states that were 20 X 10 X 5 cubits. Marble is heavier than stone so this block weighed about 315 tons

If my math is right, the heaviest stones were placed in Jerusalem's wall in a comparatively modern period that weighed over 550 tons: (Note: In 1960 or so 200 tons was barely within the ability of man's technology to move.)

Many people suggest that the ancients were using antigravity and alien technology to move some of the dressed stone around. Granted some of them were 4 or 5 times as heavy and lifted to 90 feet in the air. Even so, how did King Agrippa and the Romans move these stones which we today would still have difficulty accomplishing? Not to discredit the antigravity theory, but at what point does a stone become too heavy to lift with any sort of conventional method? No explanation of how the Romans moved these great stones exists on the internet, and no ancient mysteries writers seems to mention them, maybe because they throw a monkey wrench in the works. It's entirely possible that antigravity and good old grunt and sweat work moved similar sized stones in the past. Perhaps the Romans not wanting to be out done by stones they've seen used on other ancient structures determined they could do it too. They were very organized and I might add they built the Aqueduct of Nimes which is 16 stories high and amazingly it is still standing after 2000 years in a place where high winds would normally knock down something a third the height. So they were clearly no slouches in the architecture department.

I'm not sure where to put this head scratcher, but the ancients across the board refer to the gods as flying various machines. No record of the production of these craft on earth appears to exist; at best there are only attempts of technical descriptions. (Book 10 pg. 150) So where were they made…or when?

MEDICAL HELP

One skull was found with four surgical holes, all of which showed significant regrowth, meaning the patient survived all four operations. (Book 1 pg. 12)

Evidence of successful thoracic or heart surgery exists, where patients lived an average of 3-5 years after operation. (Book 1 pg. 48)

Evidence that gynaecology was practiced with equal, faultless and even superior medical instruments have been found when compared to modern instruments (Book 21 pg240, book 30 pg. 64)

Egyptian civilization didn't progress, it just happened, advanced understanding of anatomy, metabolism, genetics anaesthetics, brain operations, heredity, nervous system and circulation were all known and understood or performed by the Egyptians, and 700 medicines were used. . Imhotep was the 'god' of medicine & architecture. Imhotep means "he comes in Peace" No tomb of Imhotep has been found… did he just leave? Greeks called him Imouthes and he equalled their god of medicine Aesculapius. And then like so many other civilizations around the globe, their civilization and grasp of their sciences declined from an advanced state to little more than mumbo jumbo. (Book 11 pg. 48, book 8 pg. 90-97)

GENETIC MANIPULATION

"Mythology" speaks of many odd creatures such as Lion Man (origin of the Sphinx) men with hoofs, women with fish posteriors, and the creation of unusually tame animals such as dogs not possible through breeding. Cheetahs are all genetically the same, which in today's world only occurs with lab rats and mice that have been genetically altered. Cheetahs never attack man and are easily tamed. The Sumerians stated that domesticated plants and animals were the creation of the gods. Many plants such as corn, bananas, cotton, wheat, barley, spelt, millet, & rye, are all mysteries as to how they came about. Not only were the ancient taught how to grow, the soil actually became richer, not poorer, with use.

Egyptians tell of smart monkeys that took care of children and did chores around the house. (book 5 pg. 152, book 11 pg. 73, 136, Book 17, Atlantis Rising Mag.#92) The Sumerian 'god' Ea is said to have wanted new workers and imprinted an aspect of the 'gods' on a creature that already existed. (Book 17 pg. 344) Ancient Aryan writers say at one time apes spoke. Egyptians said that apes could understand everything being said. (Book 22 pgs. 205, 207) Ancient Indian writings speak of apes that could write. Egyptian drawings show baboons taking care of children and picking fruit.

It didn't stop at plants and animals. The gods cloned people, which started the nearly universal belief in re-incarnation and the fanatical preservation of the body through mummification to preserve tissues to facilitate cloning at some future time. The Egyptian book of the dead speaks of the flesh germinating like a plant (book 1 pg. 91-92) Before the flood cloning also took place as is evident when Adam had a son in his own likeness and image. (See Genesis 5:3, Book 0 chapter 3)

Eric Norman notes this tendency for the gods to mate with us. He quotes Gunther Rosenberg:"There was frequent mention of union between earth women and the gods" (Book 29 pg. 56) However Rosenberg incorrectly assumes these unions were the reason there were creatures such as Minotaur's (Half bull and Half man) Pan, (Half Man half goat)and assumes these were results of failed unions. There were other creatures such as Centaurs, Sasquatch, chimera, a female fire breathing monster with a lion's head, a goat's body, and serpent's tail. The list of such creatures goes on and I list here a good cross section: Cyclops, Lion Man (the bible also mentions these people in 2nd Sam 23: 20, and Chronicles 11:22, and 1st Chronicles. 12:8) half man half goat…which is traced to the Sumerians, mermaids (1/2 women half fish are well known and people still insist these have been sighted in modern times), men with horse feet, bulls with the heads of men. If these were really the resulting offspring of the gods, the gods would have looked like horrible monsters and the only way they would have mated with mankind was under extreme duress and force.

No remote suggestion exists that the gods were anything but people or beyond that they are termed as demigods. None of these so called mythical creatures would have been the result of breeding but could only have come through the process of genetic manipulation.

Consider just how many strange creatures the ancient refer to. Centaurs and Anggittays were half men or women and horse, Onocentaur; Half man and half donkey, Ipotane top human bottom horse, Satyr's part man part goat like Pan, and a Glaistig was the female version. And there's Harpy's, Kinnaras, Sirens and Lilitus which were half birds and half girls or half human, Inmyeonjo or birds with human faces, Ichthyocentaur or Torso of human legs of a horse and the rest like a fish. Half snake and part human are told of in various degrees, like just the head of a woman, four arms, or more commonly upper portion female and lower portion snake tail with names like Echidna, Fu Xi, Lamia, Ketu, Naga and Nure-Onna. More such creatures existed in ancient legends like Kurm: half human half tortoise, Scorpion man, Selkie: half human half seal, men faces on winged horses, Cows with human heads and tails of peacocks (Kamadhenu), Meduza which were female faces with striped bodies. And there are tales of a dragon with the mouth of a snake and the feet of an elephant. Penghou was part dog part man, and on and on and on, most are part human with other parts being bear, pig, cat, stag, bull, frog, falcon, crow, moth, spider, and others.

But there were also creatures that were mixtures of various creatures other than human, like horse deer cat and lions with wings, donkey camel mix, cockatrice which was chicken reptile mix, dog and reptile mix, eagle lion mix called a griffin, horse fish, dragon horse that flew, half bull half serpent, half leopard half snake. Yet there were more still; some that were parts of three, four or more animals like the jackalope which was part rabbit, pheasant and pronghorn, or a creature that was fox eagle lion and wolf called an Enfield. Other genetically created creatures are also mentioned in the past such as horses with dog heads, horse fronts and fish rears and a creature with the front and head of an eagle and the back is that of a lion which also had wings. A Baku was part elephant, rhino, tiger, bear, and ox all schmushed together. This little list just scratched the surface of the creatures that are spoken of in ancient legends around the globe. Can this speak of anything else but genetic tinkering?

Curiously queer creatures have been turning up in relatively modern times as well, when we still had not mastered genetic manipulation to any degree. For example in the 1700's legends of a Loup-garou (wolf man) persist. In 1883 in Australia, a headless pig like creature surfaced that had an appendage similar to a lobster tail. In 1878 an incredibly frightening creature was obtained and led through London. It was about 2 feet long, two feet high, described as a "living cube". It had hair like wire, it had a head and a tail like a boar, but its eyes were said to be "satanic". It had no abdomen, and its hind feet were unusually close to its front feet. It was so disturbing it caused a panic and accidents and the owner was told to get rid of it in no uncertain terms! It had been originally found in the Pyrenees in southern France.

In 1951 in Ramesgate Kent, a hedgehog like creature was found which had the tail of a rat, and the head of a cat.

In 1954 A reverend Joseph Overs found a 2 1/2 foot long creature that looked like a fish with 'staring eyes" and a big mouth. What made the creature even weirder was that it had "two perfect feet each with 5 pink toes" (Book 47 Pg. 96)

The New Jersey Devil is a horse headed creature that flies and has a devil-like tail. Has someone been doing genetic tinkering still? If so, who could it be? The ancients say some of the gods went back to their cities or moons in the sky but some went under the sea and underground and are still here. Have they been letting loose some of their experiments into the surface world?

The god Anubis unlike Lion man, doesn't appear to be linked in appearance to any individual with dog features but is linked to jackals that characteristically dig up graves, and he is the person who taught the art of embalming for the purpose of preservation.

With conventional archaeology unwilling to allow cloning into the technological sphere of the ancient history of Egypt, or any culture for that matter, Anubis is therefore only linked with preservation of Osiris but not of his cloning. The date of Anubis existence in Egypt has been dated at 3100 B.C. around the end of the age of the gods. But Osiris was cloned: Isis gathered the parts of Osiris after he was cut into pieces before burying them. And "...she managed to extract from the body of Osiris it's "essence," and self-impregnated herself with his seed, thus conceiving and giving birth to the boy Horus." (Book 42 page 42) This can only be relating to either planting an egg or cloning. Why? Osiris' reproductive parts were never found, and the offspring was identical to the father, thus eliminating planting an egg by artificial insemination, leaving only cloning.

The gods are no doubt even the creators of the different races. Myths also speak of red, grey, green and blue people existing at some time in the past; this would also suggest that the amount of atmosphere was considerably more than today to filter the effects of the sun to allow people to remain these colours.

OTHER STUFF

It would appear that the gods must have accurately mapped the planet as Antarctica was mapped using spherical trigonometry and flight, long before spherical trigonometry was mastered, or the continent was discovered and not covered in ice. (Book 5 pg. 50-51)

There is a mountain in Havea which has a 3000 foot smooth vertical face with 10 foot tall characters on it. It is a complete mystery as to how this was accomplished. (Book 21 pg. 36)

Thoth taught writing because normal children were becoming unable to learn by memorization as before. The Monarchs protested the use of writing because he or they felt it would reduce reliance on memory and cease to have children apply themselves. (Book 8 pg. 98)

They appear to have had guns of some kind as many fossils and even long extinct animal skulls have been found with bullet holes in them, like an extinct buffalo found in Yakuzia Russia, and a "Neanderthal" found in 1968 in a block of ice in the Bering sea who had died of a bullet wound. (Book 23 pg. 118)

Inca of Peru regarding the god Viracocha: say he has been equated with the creator in some ways because something he did changed the earth and sky, and he created stone giants to live in it. After a while the giants became lazy and quarrelsome, and Viracocha decided to destroy them. Some he turned back to stone, and these stone statues still exist at Tiahuanaco and Pucara. He destroyed the rest with a great flood. When the flood subsided, it left the lakes Titicaca and Poopo, and it left seashells on the Altiplano at elevations of 3660 meters. (Obviously speaking of a later "local" flood) Viracocha saved two stone giants from the flood and with their help created people his own size. He reached down into Lake Titicaca and drew out the Sun and Moon to provide light so he could admire his new creation.

Similarly, The North American natives state that once when the sky was much nearer the earth the lord of the sky became so angry because of the constant strife of amongst the men that he moved mountains, and caused earthquakes. (Book 23 pg. 126)

CHARIOTS OF THE GODS

M.K.Jessup refers to an anomalous "dark spot" that astronomers occasionally observed moving across the face of Jupiter. The annotated version of this book states this dark spot was "The Great Ark", apparently referring to an artificial moon that prevented the dwellers from experiencing the Great flood of Noah. (Book 30 pg. 165)

Ancient Indian Texts speak about Rama and Sita flying in an enormous beautifully painted two storied aerial car that emitted a melodious sound when heard from the ground. (Book 34 pg. 38) Interestingly this term "melodious sound" has also been used to describe the sound of some modern sightings of UFO's. The La Paz Indians say that thousands of years ago their ancestors traveled on great golden discs which were kept airborne by means of sound vibrations at a certain pitch, which was created by a continuous "hammer blows". (Book 21 pg. 206)

The bible refers to chariots of fire, such as the one that picked up Elijah separating him permanently from Elisha. I've seen paintings of this event depicting horses drawing a flaming chariot such as you might see in Ben Hur. However no mention of horses exists during this event. Other people refer to "chariots" of the gods too and they do not fit the standard description of chariots. Indian Sanskrit tells of a time when many suitors vied for the hand of Princess Panchala and even "...the gods in cloud-borne chariots came to view the scene so fair" It also mentions "Maruts in the moving car" (Book 34 pg. 42)

An Indian Asura Maya was said to have a golden car 12,000 cubits around, (5730 feet in diameter or more than a mile across) with four strong wheels and weapons that could fly. (Book 34 pg. 51) These chariots shone like the sun, had "padmaraga" stones (a pinkish orange sapphire) set in them and they move in all directions lighting up the city and looked like moonbeams. And it too moved through the air with a melodious sound. (Siva Purana)

The Tibetan Lama, Lobsang Rampa, one of the people whose names my dad often mentioned, stated that flying saucers have visited Tibet for thousands of years, and that he had personally seen them in the sky and on the ground and was even given a ride in one; no, not my dad, the Tibetan Lama. (Book 34 pg. 74)

It's possible the Egyptians even "carved" (with some sort of advanced moulding system used on the stone) the vehicles the gods used. In the temple of Osirion are fascinating depictions of what look like a helicopter, a hover car like that seen in Star Wars and a UFO. (**See image 23**)

Image 23: Temple of Osirion wall relief

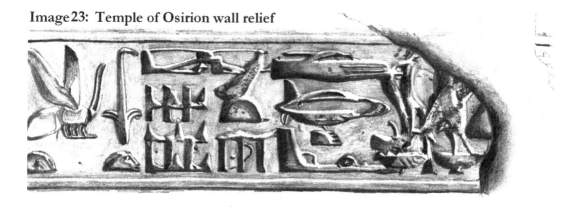

AN OLD MEANING TO BEING "GREEN"

The date is sometime in the 12th century, and two green children, a boy and a girl, walk out of a cave. OK that's not the starting line of a joke, and no, they don't walk up to the bar. The place is Suffolk England and the kids are wearing unfathomable clothing. Eventually they learn the language and say they came from a place with no sun that is in eternal twilight called St. Martin's land (thought to be Merlin's land which is a subterranean world). While feeding their flocks there, they hear bell like sounds, and were caught up and suddenly find themselves in a cave and wander out where they are found. (Book 47 pg 97-98)

The scene is repeated about 700 years later at Banjos Spain in 1887 when a green boy and girl walk out of a cave. Though people from the period assumed Mars was inhabited and that these two children must have come from there, they told a different story. Soon after their discovery, the boy died and when the girl learned the language she said they came from a country with no sun. (Mars doesn't fit this description.) After a whirlwind and a terrible noise the two were lifted up and found themselves in a cave. They weren't in Kansas anymore, and were probably never on Mars either. (Book 5 pg. 143, Book 50 pg. 120-122) Speaking of Green, the Eskimo's of Greenland say the immortals live in a subterranean paradise where it warm and there is plenty of food, some of which might be green. (Book 22 pg. 95)

Hattiesburg Mississippi 1943 Mrs. Virden screams and tells the children running to her 'his face was green'. A Finnish forestry worker (no date) came across a little green man in a space suit escaping into a UFO. (Book 32 pg. 135-36, 148)

One again we see possible connection between UFO's and the underworld.

GODS WERE MORTAL

The gods, though living very long lives, were not immortal and died like us too.

The Jagga of Tanzania tell of two of the gods dying: one man sent to heaven died before returning as did a woman who forgot something went back up to get it also died. (Book 10 pg. 87)How the tribe knew they died as opposed to just not bothering to come back, was not mentioned; presumably another god down here or another that descended to tell them the news. The scene appears to have been repeated for another African people, the Tussi, of Ruanda (now Berundi). A heavenly prince Named Mugulu brought banana, potato, a bean, a corncob and a hen with him but had forgotten corn for the hen and had to go back to heaven to get some for it and never returned. Their heavenly lady named Unyoro also returned to heaven to get seeds of some kind of grass that she had forgotten but never returned because she died up there before returning. (Book 10 pgs. 90-91) The stories of both the Jagga and the Tussi are so similar it is probably about the same two gods helping to civilize the people of the general area, as these two locals group are from neighbouring areas. This then in a sense adds weight to the veracity of the story by it being witnessed and retold by two peoples. It also indicates some gods were assigned to regions and not the entire globe and being the same god but with different names.

The gods of India were also stated to have grown old and senile and suffered similar aging problems we do. And they too mention couplings between the gods and the people of earth and their offspring inheriting the knowledge and weapons of their fathers. These weapons were used and are said to have been the origin of some deserts. (Book 10 pg. 142)

Gods fib Horseman Ooor

Parsee scriptures suggest the first rule of the gods lasted 1,879,740,000,000,000,000,000,000 years. Do we think there might be just a *little* exaggeration here? Just a smidge perhaps? This bizarrely large time span was worked out from Zoroastrian Parsee writings of 7th century Persia comparing Saturn's year (29.5 years) to a day and other astronomical factors and Persian words and some math. (Book 10 pg. 140) It sounds like hocus-pocus to me.

Von Daniken brings this point up: Einstein showed that there was such a thing as time dilation. (Book 10 pg. 229) This theory was proven by two identical and synchronized atomic clocks, one which was on a supersonic plane (or maybe it was a Boeing jet, I forget which) and one which was stationary on good ol' terra firma. I'm recalling this from memory but if I remember correctly, the clock in the airplane slowed down, lost time or whatever compared to the stationary one. The gods would easily have understood time dilation and probably explained it to the ancients, possibly with various motives depending on who explained what to who. If the ancients had to be taught civilization, farming, and other skills to be brought out of barbarism, how well do you think they took to Algebra, or calculating Gravitational physics? I'm guessing they thought "food good...math bad". No doubt some tried to comprehend it all and master the skill. But get one factor wrong, or misunderstand the significance, or accidently mix ounces for pounds, or as some evolutionists have done deliberately by switching measuring scales mid sentence such as switching from grams of DNA to number of DNA links*, or be spoofed just a little bit by the gods for their amusement and some screwball numbers are going to be handed down through the ages. (*Book 0 2017 Pg 13-14)

The Egyptian priest Manetho states the gods were the first to rule the Egyptians but places this era to about 30,000 years ago. Berosus places the reign of the gods of Babylon 432,000 years before the flood; well let's just say *a* flood. The Sumerians put this reign's start at 241,000 years before the flood. (Book 23 pg. 38) But if 130 families were sent to the earth at the same time to teach and rule mankind, it seems to me some; let's call them math problems, (23333333333333333333256 ←...The cat just typed that for me... looks like a math problem all by itself. Now I can say the cat helped me with my book) have crept into the calculations here.

The Cree claim a trickster named Wisagatcak sometimes aided the sky father and taught civilization and sometimes acted like a demon causing wilful destruction. (Book 23 pg. 128: his name reminds me of Wisecrack or Wiseacre) Could such a god be trusted implicitly to always tell the truth and not sometimes lead the people astray with one form of bologna or another, and could the people be certain they could always know when he was telling the truth or spinning a yarn?

In my first book I took the time to prove that the UFO's of today trace themselves back to ancient times and were the gods of old. (Book 0 chapter 9) If this is the case, consider this snippet from a recent UFO story. During one UFO incident where it swooped low over the field, eerie lights danced around the field. Then invisible entities snatched the keys in the house and started jingling them and terrifying the children. Then a mattress on which two were sleeping was lifted up. They had been visited by strange people interrogating them and they were afraid of strangers. (Book 30 pg. 212) Does that sound like responsible adult UFO pilots with our best interest at heart then?

Contrariwise, based on some of the conversations with the pilots of an airship that was seen across America in 1897 (when no airships are known to have existed) means this might have been a UFO shaped to look like a slightly advanced flying zeppelin balloon type apparatus to set at ease any observers of the craft. It showed up in Rockland Texas and may be a disguised version of the oft sighted cigar shaped UFO seen since 1947. People from this craft chatted with a farmer there borrowing things like bluestone (a kind of acid) and lubricating oil, telling them they couldn't show them the secret craft right then but promised to return to give them a ride in appreciation for their help, after they went to Greece, came back from Mars and had placed the ship on exhibition. (Book 32 pg. 16-17) Of course the ship never returned and I don't think it showed up in Greece either. What must have been the same ship appeared two miles east of Houston Texas and the pilots were found drinking from a well in the middle of the night. Approached, the farmer was shown the craft telling him they had constructed it out of newly discovered material that had the property of "Self-sustenance in the air", which had been built in Iowa, and would soon been given to the public after a stock company was formed and this machine would be in general use within a year. (Book 32 pg. 17) Some think this craft may have actually been a contemporary secret invention being tested that at some point crashed and whose existence was covered up and cleaned up. But if this was a UFO, then both stories of these diverse UFO pilots demonstrated conflicting attitudes toward people: some nasty and frightening and some friendly, but both, for whatever reason, clearly lied to the people that chatted with them. To keep their identity secret they seem to disguise themselves as inventors, scientists, or even aliens depending on the technology of the time frame they are seen and what people seem to expect them to be. Indeed it's been observed that the garb of the notorious Men in black that frequently visit UFO observers seems to reflect the time periods popularized dress code.

Some UFO occupants are nice and some border on hostile. Thus this pattern of the gods uncertain ambivalent behaviour to men continues on down through the ages, as well as their penchant for stretching the truth or even complete deception.

The Persian Zoroaster when he was at home conversed with "Archangels" and he was also conversant with whoever was in control of the chariots of Zeus. Zoroaster at some point is said to have ascended to heaven to get instruction from God or more likely a god. Zoroaster went on a mountain retreat and got a revelation about Ahura-Mazda (Ormuzd, whose symbol is Winged disc) – and the Angra Manyu (Ahriman). (Angra means ("destructive", "chaotic", "disorderly", "inhibitive", and "malign") Manyu means evil; also thought to be "deceiver" deceitful and the Angra Manyu are also equated with daevas.) Zoroaster stated that the daevas are "wrong gods" or "false gods" {not demons} that are to be rejected. Curiously the daevas that deceive humankind are also said that they deceive themselves.

A branch of these legends say the two are twin brothers, almost as though part of a plan, in which they each chose an opposite character trait. Ahura-Mazda chose to be good and the other, (AngraMainyu) chose to be evil. AngraMainyu states "It is not that I cannot create anything good, but that I will not." And to prove this, he created the peacock. What a strange way to prove this! Though nothing to do with this research, what astounded me was about 1 hour before I read this legend for the first time, I had just cut out of a newspaper a dazzling picture of a peacock! The peacock is considered one of the most treasured birds on earth, and furthermore this legend suggests the peacock is a genetically engineered bird. If this is what occurred one can see how normal men could be led astray by fibs perpetrated by the gods, and this should be disturbing to people who look up to the ancient gods, even to this day. Ahura-Mazda with his 7 heavenly hosts fought Angra Manyu and his gang apparently in a war in heaven: more on this later. Zoroaster's teachings were written down (in the Avesta) and spread as far as India. (Book 34 pg. 210-11, and internet sources)

"Eyes of the first men were covered and they could only see what was close" so that "the "wisdom and all knowledge of the first men were destroyed." (Book 29 pg. 52, Book 11 pg.162) Brad Steiger summarises his findings this way "The "sky people knew the secrets of the universe, and when the tribesmen became determined to steal these secrets, the visitors fogged the earthmen's minds." (Book 35 pg. 181) "The gods took council and clouded the sight of men, destroying their wisdom and knowledge"' (book 23 pg. 110 quoting Popul Vuh). It seems to me if the gods were playing mind games with this 'good god bad god' business and trying to restrain man's technological advancements, it doesn't seem a stretch to say they did a little fibbing to man to throw him off in other ways too.

Kashmir North India You'll recall, even if I have to remind you, that while Manu was meditating *thousands and thousands of year* passed and after all this time Brahma showed himself to Manu and told him to ask for something. To which Manu said he wanted to save the world from any coming global catastrophe. Anyway this Kashmir flood legend is a great example of how some legends add ridiculous numbers of years to events when other legends experiencing the exact same event date the events more realistically. Or do some people really believe Manu meditated for many thousands of years, and lived proportionally longer during the non meditative parts of his life? Seems like a bit of a stretch to me.

YORUBA SOUTHWEST NIGERIA

We mentioned earlier about a god named Ifa, of the Yoruba in southwest Nigeria, who grew tired of living on earth so he left earth and went to dwell in the firmament with Obatala. Without his assistance, mankind couldn't interpret the desires of the gods, and one god, Olokun, in a fit of rage, destroyed nearly everybody in a great flood. This is another legend where the gods or a god is blamed for causing a catastrophe on earth...deliberately. But just as importantly, if one of the gods could be so callous to us, do you think we were always going to be told enduring truths by these gods, if they don't care if we live or die?

WARS IN HEAVEN / OF THE GODS

One of Drake's conclusions of his research, which like many writers he starts his book off with, was that Worldwide legends agree that in ancient times there was a war waged on earth and in the sky with Nuclear weapons, aerial craft, and laser death rays which shriveled cities and blasted mountains, and the effects of which are still seen and found in our day. He even realized that later on one (or more) comets continued the destruction on the earth destroying what was left of civilization and changing the earth climate which killed off any communication between the planets and earth, and the few survivors descended into barbarism. (Book 34 pg. 2)

The ancient gods had nuclear weapons and they, or the people who clamored after the gods technology used them, and their effects are described in ancient texts as well. A skeleton was found in India which was 50 times more radioactive then the surrounding soil. (Book 22 pg. 160) And in Mohenjo-Daro India and Harappa Pakistan, there were found a number of skeletons at street level which seemed, by their scattered positions, to be attempting to escape something, and all the skeletons were highly radioactive. Nothing is known about these cities except they ended their existence abruptly. (Book 6 pg. 216, Book 7 pgs. 228-230, and Book 34 pg. 46)

In my conclusions I include the deduction that the continents shifted from all these causes which affected the world climate and sunk many cities and islands around the globe. These events also destroyed, changed and created new mountain ranges, with continents swimming and crashing into each other, catching animals and people where the land masses met which consequently formed all the vast fossil clusters around the globe, causing rivers and oceans to turn red with their blood. Drake mentions Greek legends including Hesiod's tales of celestial wars between gods and men. Some interpret the conflicts that the Mahabharata speaks of, as a war between the drivers of the sun and the moon; which would be the craft that landed on the earth that gave the observers the impressions that these were like the moon or as brilliant as the sun. The Indian Sanscrit speaks of "...the gods in cloud-borne chariots" which "...rested on the turrets high", and "bright celestial cars [that] sailed upon a cloudless sky", "Bright immortals robed in sunlight sailed across the liquid sky"(book 34 pgs. 42-43) I must have missed that key bit before, but "turrets" can be defined as angular towers or, as we know them, Pyramids or Ziggurats. I had always suspected and concluded that gods had for whatever reason landed on top of these things, but here it was actually stated in the ancient Sanskrit.

The ancient Chinese histories tell of aerial craft flying into the sea and sky, scaring the people, *scorching fortifications,* kidnapping people and landing divine strangers that inspired mankind. This story about ancient flying craft scorching forts is an interesting note. I've read a few mentions of these mysterious forts all across the British Isles like Tap o' North and others across Scotland and Saint Suzanne France, which mystify researchers. They try and explain scorching and partial vitrification of them away by assuming that during sieges the invader piled wood up on the walls to burn. But this explanation for the vitrification of the rock and stone work are woefully inadequate. These scorched forts appear to be actual physical evidence of ancient flying crafts and the technology they housed.

The records also show that their Golden Age, led by a gold coloured heavenly man and Divine Emperors symbolized by the dragon, was soon reduced to an era of wars, and calamities that deteriorated their world to a state of barbarism. Only after a long period did it slowly ascend to any state of civilization that was far inferior to that golden culture of the past.

Mandhotar Earlier we mentioned there was a king, who by the way was named Mandhotar, which had conquered the world then ascended to the celestial city and shared the throne up there. But like any good prohibition gangster, a piece of the action was never good enough for long, he wanted the whole ball of wax. So Mandhotar was attacked by the Asuras or war chariots of the gods, and clashed in the sky and in the celestial city in the sky apparently visible to all on the earth, and cast Mandhotar back to the earth where he died. (Book 34 pgs. 72-73)

The Drona Parva tells about Three Cities in the sky (moons?) which were destroyed (Book 34 pg. 46) We've seen two still exist, so there seems to have been at least five of these.

Hindu mythology an incomplete legend found online has some key passages that give the gist to a war in heaven which I have to fill in between the lines based my ongoing deductions:

Ahura Mazda is said to have created 16 lands [on earth] which I suggest refers to him and his pals creating the ancient cyclopean cities seen around the earth and /or civilizing 16 peoples after the tower of Babel incident. Angra Manyu is said to have created of sixteen scourges such as winter, sickness, and vice; suggesting that he is somehow responsible for the cataclysms that affect and alter the earth. Later on in what appears to be an event in the war in heaven, a line reads "serpent recoils at the sight of Mithra's (Hundred Knotted) mace (?)" The serpent (presumably the snake Ananta) is apparently another reference to Typhon as a following line "Angra Mainyu's (Angra Manyu) plans to dry up the earth" completing the link. As we've seen the serpent Ananta or Typhon is the stream of water and air leaving the earth in a pillar towards a source of gravity which in this case is possibly a man made moon under Angra Manyu leadership. Though such a moon couldn't take all of the water on earth, the people recording the incident could think it to be so. Angra Mainyu's loses the war in Heaven, is vanquished and subsequently is assigned to the nether world, a world of darkness. This of course would be the underworld. Other statement from the same source have him dwelling in the region of the daevas, which is asserted to be in the north, suggesting the way to his location is a passage underground located in the north. (Book 23 pg. 17)

Others peoples copy of the Mahabharata note that nuclear war existed in the past during the age of the gods. (Book 23 pg. 38) Could the wars of the gods having polluted the atmosphere with so much radiation that they left have been a contributing factor as to why after the flood, man's life expectancy suddenly dropped?

Unfinished sites & Sudden destruction

Stone ruins of Bolivia and Peru such as Sacsahuamàn and Tiahuanaco have legends of the gods intricately woven in their lore. They say the gods caused enormous rocks weighing hundreds of tons to fly into position apparently after traversing mountain ranges, deep valleys and across rivers. The mysterious construction of Tiahuanaco is so disturbing to archaeologists that many are willing to entertain the thought of them being built before the mountains that they exist in were raised, which in fact is true, as we've discussed. It's admitted that not only the technologies with which they were built is out of conventional historical sequence, but they are virtually impossible to build with the technology at our disposal today. If not for the fact these building exist, archaeologists would say these were impossible to build knowing what they allow into their theories about the ancients. (Book 6 pg. 161) These sites really mess with the minds of archaeologists as a whole, because of the inability to place these buildings in any historical context, thus no one seems able to date them because it is impossible to date stone, and there's nothing to compare them with.

Actually there is: they match the building techniques of the ancients all around the globe and they are tied to the period when the age of the gods existed on the earth, and their destruction is tied to the catastrophes the ancients talk about in their histories and legends, the ones the archaeologists and the geologists simply discount because they are 'impossible'. One thing that really messes with the minds of the conventional scientists and those that would date Tiahuanaco is the fact that an easily recognisable image of toxodon is found there. This creature, conventional palaeontology insists became extinct millions of years ago. (Book 6 pg. 192, book 7 pg. 220) Thus scientists who believe in "prehistory" tie their brains behind their backs when they insist extinct animals didn't exist during civilized times frames, despite the fact that various 'extinct' animals are carved on walls around the globe, such as stegosaurus in Angkor Wat, and people riding pterodactyls in Ica Peru, and dinosaurs depicted in American ravines and sightings of brontosaurus in the Congo, and Pterodactyls in Indonesia, on and on. Refusing to allow recalibration of history based on new, albeit controversial, evidence is hampering the sciences of archaeology, geology and palaeontology attempts at accuracy around the world. Not allowing catastrophism, 'extinct' creatures and advanced technology during ancient civilised times is making archaeologists and company appear further and further separated from the reality that the evidence points to.

Beriltz notes the evidence of a historical catastrophic past is evidenced in "racial memory", and is witnessed in "...vast risings, sinkings, and buckling of the land and the sea bottoms, such as sandy beaches under thousands of feet of water, around the Azores, and coastline beaches thrust hundreds of feet upward along many coasts, especially in Greenland, Northern California, and Peru (where human artifacts are found near the bottom of ancient geological striations resulting from the upthrust)." (Book 7 pg 161) Just his observations alone call all of archaeology, as taught to students, into question.

Alan Landsburg asks the enigmatic question about Tiahuanaco "But was it ever really a city?" (Book 8 pg. 44)Why does he ask this: because it was never finished and lies in ruins. A catastrophic event had to have stopped construction of the city suddenly. You know something really ridiculous just occurred to me about conventional history and archaeology. Here we have several vastly superior ancient building sites all across the Americas, and yet historians seem completely unwilling to admit anyone before Columbus ever came to the Americas, even though some of these ancient sites were still occupied when he arrived! Talk about ridiculous!!! Do you really want to assume these historians know it all?

Something kind of creepy exists in ancient legends about Viracocha connected to Tiahuanaco. Apparently Viracocha long after Adam and the flood, made clay figures of people and somehow gave life to these creations, very similar to how God created Adam out of red clay and breathed life into him. Viracocha was going to duplicate this process over and over again and he sculpted in stone resemblances of all the nations he intended to create. (Book 8 pgs. 54-55) Why is this creepy? It appears this capability, likely either through genetic engineering or something even more bizarre that can make a sculpted figure come to life through advanced technology is something the false prophet in Revelations does: he makes an image of the Beast then brings it to life causing all people to worship the person and image of the beast. Man and the gods it seems all want to be like the most high and will use any form of trickery, magic or technology to deceive the masses. The ancient gods may have had the well being and best interests of the people they taught as their motivation, and they may even have had megalomania complexes that went to their heads. Indeed some of the gods fought each other for superiority until it all came crashing down on them when global catastrophic events put the kybosh on all their activities.

There is a great temple-pyramid above Tiahuanaco which was originally thought to be damaged from cataclysmic action, but it has since been realized that it, like the rest of Tiahuanaco, was never finished but the construction was interrupted as well. German archaeologists figure the last stone was placed about the same time as the destruction of Atlantis, supposedly around 9000 BC. (Book 21 pg. 152) Smooth holes are to be found in this city, and no one can explain how they were made. It's believed that it was from these holes that Pizarro and his men pulled out the huge silver bolts. Clearly advanced machinery was used in this city. (Book 29 pg. 106) Tiahuanaco according to legend was built by a race of giants whose homeland was destroyed in a two month long flood. It's been deduced by a German archaeologist named Posnansky that the city experienced a recent gigantic upheaval that didn't swallow the city but changed the climate and the altitude so drastically, it caused the builders to leave the city voluntarily. Others archaeologists have by and large fallen in line with this reasoning. He determined the architecture in many ways was very similar to structures found in Egypt. The Temple of Karnak's design and construction techniques match those found in Tiahuanaco to a 'T'. He also noted that the Egyptians method of brain surgery was the same as that found in Tiahuanaco. Even the instruments used in the surgery were identical. (Book 35 pg. 76-77)

Easter Island, famous for the huge stylized Moai head statues, holds an enigma as to how the statues were moved and set into place. The island has had three successive cultural levels of civilization in the past, and the earliest was the most advanced. (Book 37 pg. 128) Relying solely on some tablets it's assumed the Easter Islanders are of recent Polynesian origin, and so some scholars have decided the statues were raised as recently as 1350A.D. (Book 21 pg. 42) I guess this is based on the assumption the Easter islanders didn't know their own history...just like anthropologists insist the Eskimos don't know theirs and insist they came from across the Bering strait, when the Eskimo's maintain they were flown there from the south in giant birds.

When Jacob Roggeveen, the first explorer to reach the Island of Te Pito o Te Henua (translated: Navel of the world) on Easter day of 1722 (subsequently renaming the island Easter Island) he documented two races of people on the island, referred to as long ears and short ears. These long ears were an average of 12 feet high! The tallest members of Roggeveen's expedition could walk under their legs without bending their heads. (Atlantis Rising #90 Pg. 71) You don't hear this fact paraded in the history books...we can't have giants living in modern times...or anytime for that matter, it upsets the evolutionists.

Just as the Egyptians were supposedly moving stones by rollers created from trees to build the pyramids, trees have been suggested as a method of moving the stones of Easter Island, yet in both cases, no evidence of forests exists in either place. On Easter Island there are several unfinished statues, including one that when finished would be 164 feet tall. (Book 21 pg. 41-43) This would appear to dwarf the giant stone of Baalbek which is just 70 feet long. And even dwarfs the statue of liberty at 103 feet tall. That would be considerably longer and possibly heavier than the Baalbek monstrosity. Also on...or in, or under the island are huge tunnels that have no apparent purpose. (Book 21 pg. 45)

It would seem like the statues of heads, these tunnels were unfinished too, yet it's assumed the islanders made these curiosities, yet no explanation as to why they never finished was put forth. However Easter Island history say "bird men" in their prehistory built them: those long ear people were apparently descendants of magical builder gods and they made the stone heads walk through the air. Walk through the air? If that doesn't speak of antigravity, nothing does! By the way the statues have long ears on them too.

However they were built, Easter Island statues stopped construction suddenly. During the construction of the Easter Island statues something happened. The ruins show traces of sudden interruption. Scores of the Easter Island statues were being worked on when something caused the carvers to drop their tools. Dressed stone blocks were stacked awaiting shipment, and at Nan Madol some of the cyclopean walls under construction were never completed." (Book 37 pgs. 126-127) So we see that the Easter Island tunnels, walls and statues all halted through some interruption all at the same time.

I don't know if the ancient megalithic ruins on Malta with the vast inexplicable underground tunnels were unfinished or just in ruins from catastrophic occurrences, but their similarity to the other ancient ruins built by the gods are a pretty fair case. (Book 21 pg. 124)

Leaving of the gods

According to Incan traditions handed down through the ages, the people had become brute beasts without houses, towns, government or religion, so the father sun sent down a son and a daughter to instruct them, so when they came they landed on an island in Titicaca in a sun like object. When they had finished their task they returned to the island and rose into the sky in a brilliant sun like objects or "resplendent sun" never to return. (Book 8 pg. 36)

The Amerindian Tatunca Nara from near where the Amazon begins, state they wrote their history known as the "Book of the Jaguar" when the gods left so as to remember their history. They came from heaven in gleaming gold ships that illuminated the heavens, shook the earth when men and everything was in chaos. Men bowed awed by them. While they were here they lived in pyramids and underground dwelling places, rode in ships that flew faster than birds, and saw things in stones that happened at a distance. When their work was done but before they left, they made sure the people were led underground to escape a coming catastrophe. Then they sailed up into heaven beyond the mountains in their ships amidst fire and thunder and never returned. The time they left has since been marked as "zero hour". Thus 'time', or their calendar, starts from this point onward. It is said they will return after a third great catastrophe has annihilated mankind, similar to two previous catastrophes that changed the climate and flooded the land as mentioned before. It would appear that the two previous catastrophes were what caused the decline of the people to act like the beasts without houses and such in the first place. (Book 10 pg. 112-15)

Tibetans tell of seven heavenly kings, or gods of the light, that descended to earth on a" little chest" and taught, then returned when their work on earth was done. A teacher brought unreadable texts and taught one person to translate *some* of them, and assured that the rest would be translated in the future when someone figured out how. The teacher then left into the sky on a horse of gold and silver that was in a cloud that came down to pick him up. He was gone for good and today there are still Tibetan books in a language no one can read. (Book 10 pgs. 125-126) Tibetans note that the Hsing Nu, were once a highly civilized people that knew things like speech at a distance, thought transmission through space; but the survivors of a catastrophe lapsed into barbarism and superstition. Here we find the existence of an important historic link between men when he was reduce to barbarism and before when he was like the gods in his knowledge.

These same people are somehow connected with a three storied pyramid with a strange history attached to it. The Tibetan histories have, what might appear to be an enigma, if you don't get it. If the teachers or gods of light left never to return to the earth, how do you interpret their explanation of a three storied Hsing Nu pyramid where the bottom level means "The Ancient land when men rose up to the stars; the middle land [story of the middle section means] when men came down from the stars; and the new land, the world of distant stars". It is another clue to who the gods were. (Book 21 pgs. 69-70) We'll get back to this.

A Tibetan book known as the *Records of the thirty-five Buddhas* says that the kings of light have departed in wrath. The sins of men had become so black that the earth quivered in agony. This led to the azure seats being empty and no one being found to occupy these seats of knowledge and mercy and the blessed anymore. (Book 34 pg. 135)

The Indian Mahabharata continues on "When the guardians of the world had gone..."(book 10 pg. 128) Since I don't have the Mahabharata with all the Brahmin bits still included I can't determine the context here, so I can't say for certain the gods and the guardians were one and the same people, but clearly the Guardians were here for a span of time and then left. And their name is reminiscent of "Watchers" too.

We know the gods divided the regions of their domain after they left into three regions: outer space, the sea and under the earth. My guess, based on what we've learned, is the Guardians are those gods that took over the domain of space.

Chinese legends from the book *Shi Ching* say that when the divine Emperor saw crime and vice increasing on the world he commanded communication be cut off from between the earth and the sky; and since then, there has been no more descending and ascending. (Book 11 pg. 116)

Another ancient history of China, the Shoo-King, says virtually the same thing: The Lord Chang-ty, a king of the divine dynasty saw that the people had lost the last vestiges of virtue, so he commanded two people named Tchang and Lhy to cut away every communication between heaven and earth. And since that time there has been no going up and coming down from that realm. Then Drake refers to another source which speaks of the same two people: in which Tchang lifted heaven up, and Lhy pressed earth down. (Book 34 pg. 76) Drake states that students of mythology see the pattern repeated in many ancient myths where gods from space ruled the earth during a golden age. Then, mankind rebelled, catastrophes raged and ravaged across the planet, the gods returned to the stars breaking off communication and leaving man to rebuild civilization.

Seemingly confirming earlier deductions that the ancients created the maps using advanced math and aerial technology, the Guatemalan *Popul Vuh* states the first men examined the four corners [of the earth: like a map], the four points of the arch of the sky and the round faces of the earth. They could also see the large and the small in the sky and the earth (microscopes, and telescopes and Binoculars) (book 11 pg. 162) But all this knowledge was lost when the gods asked "Must they also be gods?" So they covered the eyes of the first men so that they could only see what was close. This then instigated action that destroyed all wisdom and knowledge of the first men. Thus this legend indicates that the "first men" here were near equals of the gods, and we too had the technology until the gods messed with our minds somehow. (Book 11 pg. 162) "These beings were upset because men were learning the secrets of the universe, so they fogged man's memory so he was not capable of knowing everything. So man's knowledge of certain universal secrets was reduced."(Book 29 pg. 52)

In the vernacular of the period Andrew Tomas sums up the Gods of Egypt in this regard. Thoth "civilized the dwellers of Egypt by giving them [writing] symbols to record sounds and ideas, the harp to play upon, charts of the stars, numbers to count with, names and herbs, and remedies with which to cure sicknesses. Then the benefactors bid adieu to the people of Egypt and ascended into the sky." (Book 11 pg. 166) The celestials originally had come from the "thigh in the northern sky", which was an Egyptian name for the constellation of the Great bear...in the north. (Book 34 pg. 135)

The Finnish legend in Kalevala speaks of the time when a god named Väinämöinen left them in a copper boat which sailed off into the sky. It doesn't say if he came to them in the same fashion, but it does say that a people called the Noctkaus tell of a god that came to *them* in a copper canoe. (Not sure who these Noctkaus people are as it's the only reference to them I can find, and none exists on the internet) The Ojibwas history speaks of Hiawatha who killed a giant, then after accomplishing his mission soared toward the sunset in a magic canoe that moved with a melodious sound. (Book 23 pg. 128)

Both the Chippewa's and the Hindu have legends about beautiful girls descending to the earth, being successfully wooed and married to men of the earth, then being home sick, leaving their earth men and returning to the skies. The Chippewa's has her coming back and then both leaving to the starry abode, the Hindu one never returned. Similar legends exist in Tibet and Scandinavia too. (Book 23 pg. 130)

On the Keweenaw Peninsula and Isle Royale of Michigan about 2 million pounds of copper were mined. Apparently the mines still contained copper because archaeologists ask who mined this copper and why did they suddenly abandon the mine and it vast operation. (Book 35 pg. 52) Whoever worked this mine just stopped and left.

Quiche Mayan documents also notes that the four leaders stated that their mission was accomplished and they were returning home which was east beyond the sea. (Book 22 pg. 94)

The Yoruba (southwest Nigeria): A god, Ifa, tired of living on earth went to dwell in the firmament with Obatala. Without his assistance, mankind couldn't interpret the desires of the gods, and one god, Olokun, in a fit of rage, destroyed nearly everybody in a great flood.

The Aztecs told Cortés that they were brought there by a Lord then that Lord returned to where he came from.

The message is the same time and time again, the gods descend to earth from space, disaster, the gods teach, save many from another disaster, the gods leave. Maybe not all legends have all the elements as some elements the peoples forgot, got blurred or got mixed up through time but the pattern is repeated everywhere.

SOME OF THE GODS WENT UNDERGROUND.

Brad Steiger reaches a conclusion that in ancient times (assumed to be millions of years ago) there was an immensely intelligent and scientifically advanced race known as the "Old Ones", presumably because they lived so long, that retreated underground to escape natural catastrophes and the hidden death that exists in the rays of the sun. He states that their history "crosses the path" of the Atlanteans that survived the great cataclysm and learned to perpetuate themselves in underground caverns also to escape the deadly radiation on the surface of the earth, after their island was destroyed as a result of their super science. The Navajo legends states that the ancient ones were driven from their underworld caverns by a flood and stayed to pass along great knowledge to them before returning underground. (Odd it says "driven from", not 'driven to'...I wonder if he got it backwards, as this is the first I recall it said this way. Unless it means they came out to save those on the surface and bring them down to safety?) The Pueblo Indians say that the dwelling place of the gods is now in the inner world connected to the surface world by a hole in the north. (Book 35 pgs. 136-38)

It's worth noting that Philippians 2:10, Revelations 5:3 and 5:13 all refer to people under the earth.

GODS RETURN

Another of the books of the Amerindian near the source of the Amazon is the Chronicles of Akakor: it notes that after the gods left, just prior to a great cataclysm, the survivors were the that people went underground. This is presumably the same place that some of the gods dwelt before the event. They escaped the flood type cataclysm and came back above ground. When they emerged the gods returned in golden metal clay rolls which were about 12 feet around without sail or rudder, would fly faster than an eagle, and they stood on seven bendable legs when they landed. The order of the story is written piece meal so I'm a little confused but there were earlier gods that never came back but after the second catastrophe later (?) gods came back whom the survivors met with gifts to lay at their feet. (Book 10 pg. 112-116) The point grasped from the story is the gods knew about a catastrophe coming so they left after they made provision for men here to escape underground. After the flood, they came back up, and met some gods coming back. Apparently as a clarification Von Daniken later on pg. 132 states "The oldest gods responsible for creation always come from space and return there once their work is done. (Only the later gods come out of caves, the depths of the earth or water.)" This was my deduction based on the material I've seen too. Once they lead the survivors back to the surface, they return underground. (Book 10 pg. 132)

But there were at least three cataclysms mentioned by Tatunca Nara in the series of legends of his people. Their stories were not spelled out meticulously in this source so you'll pardon my confusion. I don't have the Chronicles of Akakor, or the Book of the Jaguar that he takes excerpts from, (or the Book of the Eagle that he bypasses).

TUNNELS

Incan tunnels are known to exist from Lima to Cuzco, which then turn to the Bolivian border. Ancient and inexplicable tunnels are also known to exist in California, Virginia, Hawaii, Sweden, Czechoslovakia, Balearics, Malta, Oceania, Spain to Morocco. Tunnels are said to span under the Pacific through Oceania, under Mongolia, and of course Tibet and an Ecuadorian one is suspected since a Tibetan Lama was seen there after apparently walking from Tibet through the tunnel. (Book 21 pg 35, 39) They are also known on the Island of Samos and Easter Island. Sahara desert has some underground structures that are technologically so superior, that they are baffling to archaeologists. Egypt has them and they, like the others, have no evidence of smoke on the walls indicating artificial lighting was used in them. Egyptians in days gone by claimed they could get to the underworld by a guarded way that only initiates were allowed to access. Tunnels in Greece and Rome have smoke in them but this was probably a result of people hiding in them, long after they were built to escape persecution. Legends do speak of some of the tunnels in Greece being lit by "cold lights" at one time, which is the same description of lights that lit Atlantis (Book 23 pg. 179). Tunnels through coal in Utah may or may not count as tunnels as we don't know if the ancients used coal or not. However coal miners in Utah broke through some coal in a new extension and found a series of tunnels with no history attached to them.

They also exist under Azerbaijan on to Georgia, and throughout the Caucasus and have the same construction as those in Central America. And of course they are under the mysterious unfinished city of Tiahuanaco stretching to the lands of the Apache. (Book 21 pgs. 65, 67) In 1770 a labourer in Staffordshire England while digging a tunnel came across a large stone and behind it he heard the sounds of heavy machinery. He followed the sound down a tunnel on a stone stairway and came to a large room but was chased out by a man with a club in his hand running towards him. In 1138 a dwarf escaped into the floor of a German monastery. The Hindu god Mithra is said to have come out of a cave.

UNDERWORLD

Peruvian legend speaks of their founder Manco Capac who came out of the "splendid opening" that leads to the nether world into the depths of the earth. There are three of these openings said to exist in the region but due to the terror of being turned to stone as legends say Manco Capac was, no one looks for them even though they know there is supposed to be one in a hill called Tampu-Tocco near Cuzco. (Book 5 pg. 33) Being turned to stone may sound like a ridiculous superstition but it is scientifically plausible if a person is near an intense electromagnetic field such as is often noted near UFO's. The body, ships and airplanes begin to phase through matter such as the air, water or the earth itself when they are near such a field, and if they happen to have phased through earth when the field is disrupted or ceases, they merge with the matter around them, which would give them the appearance of a stone statue. One could undo the problem by simply submitting the 'statue' to the same force and the extraneous material would simply vacate the body, leaving the person unharmed. (Book 0 Chapter 9)

Indian Sanskrit texts say the Nagas or serpent gods live in underground places lit by gems in the stronghold of the Himalayas where no sickness, sun, moon or stars are, and they live a very long life and no physical deformity exists. (Book 11 pg. 117, book 34 pg. 54-55) This incidentally is a very similar description to the place the green children describe.

In 1956 workmen of the Head Well and Pump company were drilling a 145 foot hole on the property of Mr. And Mrs. Earl Meeks near Douglas Georgia when they suddenly stopped work. They had to listen to noises coming out of the hole which sound like an underground railroad. These noises became so loud and distracting that the Meeks had to cover up the hole at night so they could sleep. (Book 35 pg 149)

I gather that sometimes legends of underground refuges go missing if all the people die without handing down the traditions of the elders through the generations. Such is the case with the underground 'cities' of Derinkuyu and Kaymakli in Turkey. (Book 10 pg. 281) The reason no legends are associated with these cities may be the same reason no legends exist for Gobekli Tepe in the Taurus Mountains of Turkey. Yet archaeologists automatically assume if there is no history these places could be older than anything else in the world, and indeed the lack of history is an excuse to do so; that or they can attribute any theory they like to the archaeological remains. With the lack of legends attached to any site, archaeologists have a free hand assigning their logic to such places. For instance they suggest these cities in Turkey were dug out of desperation by the Christians attempting to escape persecution. Even though the ventilation is technologically way beyond the ability of the 1st century civilizations to create, and even though no obvious signs of it being excavated exist in the neighbourhood of the cities on the surface, this doesn't seem to matter, as long as Archaeologists can do away with the concept of advanced technology in the hands of the ancients. These cities 'diggings' go down at least 13 stories and at least 52 ventilating airshafts have been discovered so far. This excavation is something today's engineers would be *very* hard pressed to accomplish. The dwelling capacity of these underground dwellings is estimated to be around 1.2 million people! We haven't even built any above ground complexes capable of housing that many people, let alone building one underground. So burrowing Christians acting like badgers is hardly an adequate explanation for the existence of these underground cities. I'm willing to bet the same event that buried Gobekli Tepe is the same event that wiped out any legends of the underground cities and remaining surface evidence in the same region. But archaeological licence has dated one event (the underground cities) circa 1st century A.D. and the other (Gobekli Tepe) 12,000 B.C. with clearly flawed methods for each site. (I addressed the flaws of Gobekli Tepe dating in my first work)

North America has copper and coal mines, ruins buried, ruins above ground, and even sunken cities with no history attached to them, yet in reality, by association they do: The Hopi speak of a vast flood, and Plato speaks of a catastrophe that wiped out Atlantis, and the physical evidence fits this explanation, and yet no archaeologists or other ancient civilization specialists accepts it because it's an unconventional "catastrophe" solution. Other places around the globe have underground tunnel systems and underground dwelling places in legends that are thousands of years old and all of them are linked to the gods. If Derinkuyu and Kaymakli have no history attached to them, and the mines and ruins of North America, nevertheless by association they do: because it stands to reason that the origin for these underground cities is the same as other underground cities and tunnels around the globe. Indeed the Hopi legends have been confirmed by the finding of their underground tunnel/city spoken of in their legends. It's a safe bet Derinkuyu and Kaymakli have a similar story, only the tellers have all been wiped out just like the people who made the mines and the now ruined remains of North America.

After they left

In 1491 some very noble looking...shall we call them gods with red skin, showed up and visited Facius Cardan and stated they lived about three centuries and they appeared to possess great knowledge. Asked why they wouldn't share their knowledge, he was told there was a law to restrain them from doing so and stiff penalties were imposed if ignored. (Book 5 pg. 86-87) The Surya Siddhanta states "this mystery of the gods is not to be imparted indiscriminately". (Book 11 pg. 60)

Other 'messengers' with "garments of light" visited rabbis during the middle ages and stated curiously that they were not the guardians of the sky, but they knew them. (Book 5 pg. 92) We mentioned the Guardians once before from Indian Mahabharata: "When the guardians of the world had gone..." which comes from an ancient story about Arjuna's journey to Indra's Heaven. (Book 10 pg. 128) The Name of Sumer aka Sumerians meant "land of the guardians". So these men chatting with the Rabbis knew the gods who of course were in the heavens or space. Thus the Guardians ...of the sky...must be the ones that warned us, that is, the ancients, of the coming asteroid as seen from Saturn...AKA..."the gods".

"On the day the gods left the earth" they said their work was done and that they would return when we were threatened. They said this before the people of the book of the Jaguar, the book of the Eagle and the Chronicle of Akakor went underground to escape an imminent catastrophe. (Book 10 pgs. 112-115) Does this mean they will return and warn us before the next big one hits us? These gods left the earth, they didn't go underground. Were they some of the Guardians?

The Kachinas, the name of the gods for the Hopi were "high spiritual beings" who "were equipped with space attributes", also promised to return. (Book 10 pg. 129)

Raymond Drake realizes the Mayans, the magi of Babylon, Druids, Etruscans as well as many other ancients had and have an ongoing practice for centuries of vigilant star watching and asks "Did the ancients fear invaders from space, the return of the sky gods?" (Book 23 pg. 215) Or perhaps they maintain a constant vigil to see when the gods return?

The clues Admiral Richard E. Byrd gathered suggested to him that the legends found in Mongolia, Tibet and eastern central Asia about an underworld with such named as Arghati, and Shangri-La was where the demigods and men occasionally come up out of. (Book 24 pg. 148) In some of his flights over the poles he saw grass and animals and detected warm temperate blankets over some areas, which doesn't fit with what appears to be solid ice and snow as seen from satellite pictures. Do technicians white out these areas to keep them secret, or did Byrd see visions of the past such as some people see for brief periods while walking where they suddenly appear to be in a different neighbourhood and time, then some trigger pulls them back to the present?

Eric Norman in his book *Gods, Demons and Space Chariots* grasps that there were UFO's in the ancient past recorded about by the ancients and makes the connection between the UFO's as vehicles of the gods, but he assumed they came from distant galaxies to the earth to teach men. Then for some reason they decided go underground as hidden 'kings of the world' such as they are believed to be by such people groups as the Tibetans. (Book 29 pg. 85) However other legends clearly show they went underground to get away from the deadly radiation aspects of the sun that reduced the lifespan mankind lived to, including themselves. We on the other hand assume this is how the sun has always been. Yet even we have figured out that the amount of radiation from the sun is increasing, and sterility is becoming more of a problem in general. We haven't seemed to make the connection that the giant lizards of the past, got that big because they lived so long and that many of these lizards are still with us today but simply do not grow as big because they don't live as long: Reptiles, unlike regular mammals, grow all their lives.

In the annotated copy of *The Case for the UFO* by Jessup, the writers of the notes indicate that Jessup is right about there being two types of beings that observe us and that they live here under the sea (and elsewhere) where the short people of Mu can easily catch and scare people on boats.(book 30 pg. 164)

There appear to be a few races of people living inside the earth. They range in attitude toward surface man from friendly to virtual enemies. It is stated that there is a dark order in the underworld that is bent on the total destruction of surface men (book 12 pg. 117)

SYNOPSIS

This may be not completely correct yet, but this appears to be the approximate order of events

After the flood, the gods come back to earth and live with and aid in reinstating civilization with the Sumerians. The Sumerians advance, technology thrives and man trying to become like the gods cause some havoc with separating of the continents. Determined to be like the gods they build the tower and the language becomes many. The gods return, apparently by direction from some great authority, possibly God himself directs them to disperse mankind around the globe. They do so and go back to where they live or some decide to live in the newly created Atlantis. Further destruction occurs, either from the overextended use of the pyramids dividing the continents exponentially, and possible more asteroid hit, prompting the gods to leave. But they return when they realize man has become depressed not wanting to advance as science has destroyed the earth and continue to do so, so they lapse into uncivilized beings. The gods return and aid the various people groups back to ordered and civilized living, even living with them long term and in some cases creating families. It soon becomes apparent that the gods are devolving due to earth's compromised ecology and they leave to safeguard themselves from reduced lifespan. Then when they try to return to their space moons, they are rejected and sent back to earth and they divide the underworld realms among themselves. More cataclysms are expected so they build the underground safe places for the surface people and direct them down. Then when the all clear is given, the people are returned to the surface world, the gods return underground and are not seen again except occasionally as they visit the surface world in their protective flying craft.

GODS SEEM AWFULLY HUMAN

Landsburg finds that the lesser gods, not to be confused with the one God, in the ancient past were written about as people that "raced around the known world displaying behaviours, both productive and destructive, [like that] of any ordinary mortal." (Book 1 pg. 91)

Drake quoting his work *God or Spacemen?* :"The reported landings from flying saucers show the planets are inhabited not by monsters made of silicon but by passionate, wise and sensitive humans like ourselves."(Book 23 pg. 10) When these "sensitive humans like ourselves" are spotted during cold weather they have been seen quite obviously breathing our air by the condensation of their breath.

Norman finds deductions that the ancient Roman and Greek gods were spacemen and their supernatural powers were just advanced technology that was at their disposal in a more primitive society. He also noted that there were many unions between the spacemen or gods and people of the earth. But some people that make these deductions assumed the unions created the abnormal creatures we've mentioned and not the technology of the gods. Though Norman does suggest the possibility of genetic experiments, he assumes these creatures were failures. (Book 29 pg. 56) These creatures may not have been failures as such but created just out of curiosity...most likely at the expense of the creature's wellbeing.

Norman further notes that other researchers have concluded that the gods descended from above in many civilizations such as the Greeks, and North American Indians; and subsequently came and lived with people here and also had, shall we say, bedroom adventures, with the people of earth. These gods were of exceptional stature, had the appearance of marvellous beauty, and transcendent wisdom. (Book 29 pg. 167) I'm just supposing, out on a limb of course; but that's probably not how we would describe creepy ugly smelly dangerous aliens. Not much alienisms here. Though I suppose they might describe us like that. Heck, some of us describe each other like that.

In Northern Tibet there is a 3-story pyramid built by "star worshippers" called Hsing Nu. Nearby is a palace with thrones surrounded by images of the sun and moon. In 1952 some information about this pyramid was discovered. The lowest story of the pyramid meant "the ancient land when men rose up to the stars", the middle floor meant "the middle land when men came down from the stars" and the top floor means "the new land, the world of distant stars". (Book 21 pg. 69-70) It seems to me that this is a clue as to who the gods were: I interpret it something like this: Before the flood when men ascended to the stars, after the flood when they came down from the stars, and after the war in heaven when they lived among the stars.

SOME CLUES TO THE ORIGIN OF THE GODS.

Like the Eskimo's being brought to their land by great birds (or aircraft) The Aztec Montezuma told Hernan Cortés that their ancestors were not natives of the land, but that a lord brought their people to this land then returned to his own land. (Book 23 pg. 132) Whoever brought the Aztecs to their land didn't go off into space but stayed here on earth, as Montezuma was certain that this lord had sent Cortés from where this lord returned to. The Aztecs say they originally came from Aztlan or Atlantis. (Book 6 pg. 10)

Since the Aztecs say their lord returned to where the Aztecs came from, it is safe to say this was Aztlan or Atlantis, which was a land known as a dwelling place of the gods, thus this lord left the Aztecs there before it's destruction and thus *during* the ages of the gods.

The Aztec god Quetzalcoatl was in every regard human and came from the east. (Book 21 pg. 162, book 8 pg. 49) Quiche Mayans note that some of their numbers were <u>descended</u> from the god person called Naxit. Who is this Naxit? (Stupid moi, I don't even know where I got this name "Naxit" from! Obviously my notes aren't perfect) Anyway I looked him up on the internet. I quote the last part of a sentence: "according to this description, it appears that Qocaib went toward Yucatán, where lord Naxit —that is Quetzalcoatl— lived". (Wikipedia) Apparently another fuller name for Quetzalcoatl is Viracocha Tachyachachic. Me? I'm beginning to suspect there may be more than one god here, but with virtually identical missions causing people to assume they were the same person. Some other authors weren't completely certain the two were the same person either.

The Aztecs legends states that long ago their ancestors, which they say were the first men, emerged from seven caverns at a place called Chicomoztec, north of Mexico. (Book 23 pg. 145) They had to have been down there escaping a flood from the end of one of the four ages. Aztec legends say Quetzalcoatl went to Mictlan, the name of the Aztec underworld, via the route of the sea to get away from the harmful elements of the earth, like direct sunlight and elevated radiation now permeating planet earth. (See Atlantis Rising mag. #101 Creatures of the Underworld)

I hope you were paying attention just now. Though, as you may have perceived, my notes aren't always meticulous, this section is something that can happen when you take *some* notes and manage to match them up: you find what appear to be conflicting legends, such as in this case. What we're seeing here are *two* origins of the Aztecs, one from a distant land where someone from Atlantis brings them to the new world, and one where they emerge from underground. This second origin of coming from underground could only be right if it occurred after a great cataclysm. So what we have here is a more complete picture. Initially the gods brought them there; later on a cataclysm occurs from which they, the Atlanteans, and many other civilizations around the globe go underground to escape and survive, such as the Hopi, those unidentified people in Turkey, the Tibetans and whoever else we covered to escape this cataclysm. Then when it's safe they return to the surface, usually led there by the gods, and then the gods return underground. By the way, the catastrophes that these peoples and the gods were escaping from would be the same global catastrophe that people today say killed off the dinosaurs 65,000,000 years ago when an asteroid hit the earth. I hope you clued into that. It would also be the same asteroid that the watchers warned us about and why they created the underworld tunnels and caverns for us to escape into. This would be the same event that shifted the continents and created so many fossil sites around the globe. Now true, I haven't found any legends of the dinosaurs being taken down to the underworld, but I don't think they could write, and they may not have been invited down there anyway, as some of them can be kinda nasty, eating people's pets, and chomping on people and causing general mayhem; not really what you want to escape to. And besides, some of them were probably too big to get into the entrances anyway. During this event, Atlantis is destroyed, and many cities around the globe sunk, including islands in the Mediterranean, and this may have been the same time that the earthquake in Israel occurred that the people during Uzziah's reign ran from as mentioned in the bible....twice. The land shifted, Mountains crushed civilizations. If you've heard of ancient civilizations that are thought to be myth, these would likely be the civilizations that were destroyed, Mu, Lemuria, and Atlantis. I repeat a paragraph from my first book here:

What were thought to be mythical tales of Minos turned out to be true when Knossos was excavated. Gold coins were found under Cochin China's coast bearing the likeness of Oc-Eo, a person who was previously thought to be mythical emperor. In fact most ancient legends handed down through time appear to have at least some basis in fact. As to how the owners of these legends ever obtained such knowledge is a mystery to many unless one assumes a time existed when man knew a lot more then we give them credit for.

Here's the case where a single coin confirms for archaeologists the existence of a "Mythical king, and yet 150 + classical references to Atlantis are not good enough to convince archaeologists of its existence? Archaeologists don't seem to like the unknown or the unconfirmed, it has to be seen to be believed, and they definitely don't like catastrophism: gives them nightmares. I wonder how many people, kings, and civilizations we don't know about, or are "Mythical" that were simply buried by waves, mountains, the sea or were subducted under the earth, like a tree that was found 14,000 feet below the surface of ocean flood under the Gulf of Mexico. How would an archaeologist or a geologist explain that?

Egypt credits "lion gods" as living in the underworld. Lion men appear to be one of the more successful genetic and enduring genetic merges between men and animals, as this group is mentioned in the bible and in Egypt and a great statue known as the sphinx was created to celebrate the genetic merge between lion and men, or some god that was like this. It's quite possible this statue was erected to remember such a pharaoh or reigning god during the age of the gods in Egypt. Interestingly kings are likened unto lions in Proverbs, and the king of Israel is to emerge out of the tribe of Judah, and he is known as the Lion of Judah. This is the title of the Christ, and this commonality of lion like kings between Egyptian and Israeli histories may be one of the reasons Egyptians and Israeli's have peace in the end times between each other, when no other nation will be Israel's friend. But I'm going by memory on some prophesies and interpretations of them so I might be out on a limb here.

Eskimo legends about underworld kingdoms exist. (Book 56 pgs. 226-229)

Ishtar seeks a banished loved one in the underworld. (Book 17. pg. 123)

Osirus is said to have ruled the world and Akert (A name of the underworld) (Book 61 pg. 19, 20) Also "...and An looked beautiful in countenance in Ta-tchesert" Another name for the underworld.

A Greek legend infers that after an interplanetary war, a stellar race retreated underground. Tunnels to these places were lit with cold lights. (Book 23 pg. 178-179)

And again, after a war in heaven or a battle for supremacy Zeus won the control of the skies or space, and the earth was divided up into territories. The underworld was divided between groups, Poseidon went under water, Hades was given the domain "far below". (Book 17 pg. 54) The surface world was left for us. Interestingly the beast of revelation infamy is said to emerge from the water.

ARE THE GODS HUMAN?

The colour of the god's skin is often anything but common today: Plato and the Egyptians mentioned or painted the gods skin in their art such as Ammon as blue. The Egyptians paint Thoth between light blue and green, and sometimes Thoth and Osiris were painted olive green. Atlanteans are often stated as having blue skin, and indeed the Picts and other painted themselves blue to resemble the sons of Atlas. The legends of Peru, Bolivia, Columbia and Mexico also have legends of blue men in their past. (Book 21 pgs. 198-200) (Anubis has also been painted blue.) Yet even these different coloured people married earth people and had children. So why don't we have blue or green or red people today? Consider the green children; when they were exposed to the sun for a while, the green pigment faded and they began to appear more like a normal Caucasian. (Book 5 pg. 144) Perhaps the reverse might be true, if we went underground for several years our skin would lose the tones we have and resemble the gods.

Pardon this repeat of a repeat: The Navajos Indians call our present world, the fifth world. They also say at one time men traveled from world to world, indicating man at one time traveled in space and visited other planets. The word 'gods' is not in that sentence...the key word here is "men".

A thirteenth century Norse book called the *King's Mirror* has a report of a flying craft's anchor getting stuck on a church. The people in the church heard the commotion and went out and saw men in the flying ship, one of which was climbing down the rope to attempt to dislodge the anchor. He was caught, but upon the Bishops entreaties they let the man go, and right away he clamoured up the rope, they cut the rope and flew off. (Book 32 pg. 14) No description of these people describes them as anything other than men.

There's a rumour going around that some guy named Albert, (though people now seem to refer to him by just his last name, that being "Einstein") believed something that some people would consider a little... how shall I say...out of this world. This so-called smarty pants believed that more worlds were inhabited than just earth. He figured that the navigators of the flying saucers are humans who left earth 20,000 years ago and have returned to see how their descendants are doing. (Book 21 pg. 194) What a guy...apparently kids liked him too. Einstein wouldn't have said something like this unless he had some sound reasoning behind the deduction. Except for the 20,000 years business, his deduction just might be right on target.

Raymond Drake found in his research about the gods that the so called "Venusians" are said to resemble earthmen and therefore any drawings of them would include something extra to make them appear as gods such as wings, which they may not actually have had, just to discern them in the drawings. (Book 34 pg. 205)

CHILDREN OF THE GODS

Like the Aztecs, it looks like the first gods and rulers of Egypt also came from Atlantis. Fr. Pierre Perroud determined that a Pharaoh from the second dynasty had sent an expedition to look for the remnants of Atlantis from where the ancestors of the Egyptians had come. Furthermore in a book written by Drioton and Vandier, they found that the teacher (Horus) who taught the Egyptians came from the western sea, stayed and ruled over them, then moved on towards the east. (Book 22 pgs. 154-55) Once again historical records point to the prior existence of Atlantis and it being the earthly source and apparently the headquarters of many of the gods. The Egyptians of course mention that before the first dynasty they were ruled by the gods, but this refers to Atlantis as the place of origin of at least one of them. With the gods leaving the earth at some point, one wonders if the destruction of Atlantis *wasn't* something that caught the gods unawares, but rather had been planned by them, and only caught the normal populace of the island by surprise. Remember, Plato stated that Zeus called together the gods, to Atlantis, and felt punishment had to be inflicted upon them. But we don't know what happened as Plato's narrative ends here.

Brad Steiger during his research on UFO's, had many letters sent to him about sightings. In 1969 and 1970 a series of odd coincidences occurred: he found that he was getting a lot of reports from young women that were born in March, April and May of 1948 that claimed they were being sexually molested or examined (but not raped) during some very close encounters with UFOs. All these girls were born about 9 months after the first UFO outbreak of the summer of 1947. He could not help but wonder if these young women were children of the UFO pilots from the flap of '47 being followed up on. (Book 30 pg. 184-85)

Tibetan history in the Dzyan tells of celestial fathers descending to the earth from the moon, and that some men on earth are descendants of these men. (Book 34 pg. 27) Then of course there's the Tibetan folk tales that tell of a boy with a deformed head that married the daughter of a king of heaven which we related earlier. Though no children are described from this union, the marriage of the two is worth noting in the light of the point to this section.

As we mentioned Eric Norman also notes this tendency for the gods to mate with us. He quotes Gunther Rosenberg: "There was frequent mention of union between earth women and the gods".

The Incan rulers told about the landing of their celestial ancestors and that these monarchs married their own sisters in order to keep the heirs to the crown a "pure heaven-born race, uncontaminated by any mixture of earthly mould." The blood of Incan royal mummies has been analysed and "scientists admit that the problem of their origin remains unsolved." (Book 11 pgs. 138-139) Though this particular ruling class refrained from mingling with us lowly earth creatures, the point here is that *they could have* and had to be careful so it didn't happen.

Easter Islanders Rapunui legends tell of the gods who came to them in an egg. (Book 4 pg. 121) It's worth noting that some UFO sightings describe them as shaped like an egg. Other south sea islander says they are descendants of a god "Tangalao" who came down from heaven in a gleaming egg. (Book 4 pg. 162)

Procreation breeding is often associated with the gods and mankind. Another example are Japanese emperors who were said to be descendants from the gods, and the Ainu of Hokkaido Japan claim they are children of the god Okikunumi-kamui that came from the skies and landed in Haiopira, and taught them the way to live. He also killed an evil god who also came from space and descended to earth in a "Shinta", the description of which is the same as a flying saucer. (Book 4 pg. 112, Nat. Geo. Feb. 1967 Pg. 291, 292, book 34 pg 91)

There is inside a "Chip-san" tomb a wall mural from about 2000 B.C. depicting a Japanese king welcoming seven sun discs. The word 'Chip-san' means 'the place where the Sun came down'; Similar to Ur or 'the place of descending'. (Book 34 pg. 91) This is virtually identical to Egyptian mythology that states the son of Horus descended from Ra the sun god. (Book 34 pg. 121)

The sun queen Amaterasu sent her grandson Ninigi to rule Japan, and his grandson, Jimmu Tenno was the first Japanese Emperor and indeed Tenno means heavenly monarch. Mikado (a name which now means heavenly sovereign) was a direct descendant of Amaterasu. (Book 10 pg. 107, book 34 pg. 88)

Indian Sanskrit texts talk about the gods' marriages between the gods and some marriages to us and having children. (Book 10 pg. 142)

Legends of the gods coming together with both women and men exist throughout tales of the gods in Greek, Roman, Indian, Mayan, Egyptian, North American Natives, and others; it permeates the legends. Often these kids ruled and continued on through time marrying and having more descendants, often down to modern times. (Book 23 pg. 125)

The gods that descended are never described as anything other than looking like real humans and yet always somehow more perfect, beautiful, more intelligent and with vastly superior abilities than us, and they often had with them advanced machines. Archaeologists Dr. J. Manson Valentine from Miami Florida when asked if he felt the ancient world before our era was on a par with our technology, or farther or lesser advanced, he stated unequivocally that "I think it was far beyond us." (Book 30 pg. 62)

The Orkney and Hebrides islanders tell of people that live in or under the sea who occasionally come out to live among the people and even have children with the islanders. Some of the islanders proudly trace their ancestry back to these people whose origins stem from the seas.

Quiche Mayans note that some of them were descended from the god person called Naxit (Quetzalcoatl). They also state that Quetzalcoatl was described as a white man that had come across the sea from the east. The tomb of what was said to be Quetzalcoatl's father indicated that the man was indeed white and had fair hair. No mention of him being anything other than human was noted. (Book 22 pg. 94-95)

THE INESCAPABLE CONCLUSION.

As we can see the ancients constantly spoke of people being descendants of the gods. They had children by the gods which in turn had descendants, and some of these godly lineages continue on down to this very day. If they were alien or if we were alien to them, why would they do this?

The theory of evolution has been thrust on the masses, and many people who believe this theory have written some of these source materials I refer to in this book. And some of these are certain that the gods are some aliens from distant worlds, solar systems, stars and even far away galaxies. Thus the gods on their home world have advanced through evolutionary ways and did so, far before we did, and they found us on earth a bazzilion miles from their home planet and decided to come live with us and marry us and have kids with us, build... or at least half build many cities around the world, then for no particular reason destroy our planet in many ways, and on top of this, inadvertently or deliberately destroy millions of humans, because they are so advanced apparently, and then with little or no explanation they just either returned to space or went underground. Was it worth the trip?

There is something fundamentally flawed with these assumptions. We've seen that the gods were in fact not perfect, and some died, and some fought among themselves for dominion or their brand of leadership, and yet, they have always been described as human, but just with exceptional abilities, and physiologies.

If we swallow the evolution line of reasoning, let's look at some other species. Let's pretend the most advanced and intelligent being on earth is the ass. I was going to use a donkey in this illustration because I thought a donkey was the same thing as an ass, but apparently not. So we're stuck with the ass for the purpose of this illustration. Now here on earth these asses's have begun a civilization when suddenly from the stars there arrives in space ships magnificent stallions and wonderful looking horses, maybe even a few zebras. They see us, er, the asses and decide they want to help them build civilization. The evolutionists want us to believe that both the asses's and the horses through billions of years of evolution have arrived at what they are, horses and asses. The earthly asses are in awe of the horses, and adore them and work with them to build civilization, and some of the horses marry some of the asses and they have children. Now isn't that special. Before I get to the point, if you haven't grasped it already, allow me to digress a smidge here.

It is thought that the earth houses at least 30 million different species. Ok let's say that the planet where the horses, and zebras came from also had 30 million species. If on our planet the dominant species happens to be the ass, what are the odds that the dominant species on the horse's planet would be the same or even remotely similar to an ass, such as a say a donkey or a horse: Pretty slim, maybe 30 million to one, if it happened at all. But for fun let's just say that as it happened the dominant horses species just happened to be very similar to earth's dominant species the ass. And just let's say they did marry and have kids, as ridiculous as the odds of this thing ever happening are. Do you know what these children of the horses and the asses are? They are MULES!!!!! Mules are sterile they cannot procreate, because they are descendants of two completely different <u>SPECIES!</u> Yes the horse and the ass and the donkey all look similar, well far more similar than say a spider and a fly, or an octopus and a chimpanzee. But despite the incredible similarity there is no way any of their kids are ever going to have kids of their own! There will be no descendants! PERIOD!

So if you are this evolutionists that is certain that gods by some sheer fluke looked like humans and came from space and dwelt among us and taught us and improved our evolution, or at least tried to, what are the odds they and us could have children that also had children of their own, and on down through the ages to our present time? Absolutely ZERO! Consider the spiders. There are 22,000 different species of spiders, and you know what? They all look like spiders! And you know something else? Not one of them can mate with any other species of spiders! If these so called aliens came from another planet or star or whatever, it would be like them looking like one of 22,000 species of Human types creatures coming to earth and happening on another planet with the 22,000 odd different species of Humans here (assuming evolutionary laws are equal for the spider and the human.) So what do you think are the odds then that the gods could mate with Humans and have kids that could have kids and on and on down through the ages? ZERO! So how is it possible that these gods were able to have kids with us who in turn had more kids of their own?? There is only one possibility. The gods can only be human for this to be the case. There is no other way. It is inescapable!

As screwy as those gods could be at times, in this regard I'm sure the gods knew what they were doing. This mating with us over the years was proof to us people with apparently so little brain capacity for logic, that they, the 'gods' were human! They could not possibly have descendants from these marriages if they were not the same species as us! Genetics prove only one thing here therefore, and that is that the gods HAD to be humans.

With this conclusion that the gods had to be human there is another possible reason they procreated with people here. Experiments on midges exposed to 4000 roentgens of X-rays does not cause them any organic damage and they can still reproduce, but the offspring are reduced in number and size, and the reduced capabilities are passed on to the **all** generations afterwards. (book 4 pg. 82) There is one possible way to reduce the genetic faults caused by radiation entering our earth's biosphere and reducing our genetic viability. If a "midge" that hasn't been exposed to the radiation enters the field. The gods may have been attempting to aid our viability genetically speaking because they have not been exposed to the amount of radiation we have.

THE MISSING PIECES.

Now as I mentioned before, Pindar the Greek poet in speaking of the gods said there was one race of gods and one race of men, both which came from a single mother. (Book 23 pg. 209) Do you get it now? Has the light switched on? The origin of the gods is lying there in plain sight before us. Now you can be a mule and refuse to see it or believe it, but there is no escaping it. The gods were human. Some of the ancient told us this, and some of those researchers came across this fact and they still wanted to believe that the gods were some sort of aliens to escape from a real creator God, because the gods wanted to be like God, and obviously fooled these researchers. So what happened?

Here's how this happened. I mentioned it at the beginning and you probably rolled your eyes or refused to believe it.

So I'll say it again. Pindar the Greek poet in speaking of the gods said there was one race of gods and one race of men, both which came from a single mother. Here is the explanation.

Before the great flood Eve had kids, with Adam. These two people are where all humans come from. After they ate and consumed something that gave them the knowledge of Good (ability to create) and evil, (the ability to destroy), Technology advanced and man before the flood conquered space, and colonised the planets. Through interplanetary war or just plain stupidity they blew up the planet between Mars and Jupiter, which created the asteroid belt. From evil or destruction of the fifth planet, asteroids scattered throughout the solar system and a real big one eventually hit the earth, and collapsed the protective sun filtering water canopy / shell, causing it to fall on the earth and drowning all the people on earth except Noah and his family who was warned by God of the impending doom. Noah survived, the water was pulled from earth by Mars which got knocked out of its regular orbit into a wildly erratic one and came close to the earth and pulled off the earth the excess water to make the earth inhabitable again. Meanwhile some of the sons and daughters of Adam and Eve and any Nephilim that happened to be in space at the time of the flood missed out on all the fun. Once the flood was over and the earth was inhabitable again, they came back to the earth after the flood for a look see. To their pleasant surprise, they found a few survivors, said hello and came back to the earth to live with us. After all we were the sons and daughters of Adam and Eve too. Thus the reasoning behind what the Greek Pinder said: "there was one race of gods and one race of men, both which came from a single mother." Plain as day now, right? I hope so, as I don't want to belabour the crystal clear inescapable conclusion and appear to insult your intelligence and your powers of reasoning, like the evolutionists do. Remember what the serpent said to Eve? If she ate the fruit they would be as gods. He was right, and it has screwed us up ever since! We were supposed to be as men...and women of course. Thus the gods are descendant of Eve, and that chap she hung around with named Adam, but they are not descendants of Noah, like we are, as we have already deduced.

I'll repeat a few paragraphs from my first book here, in case you don't want to buy that expensive 2 pound, 465 page, 343,000 word monster. It will help you with a third way I managed to figure out this bit of deduction we just worked our way through. I've clarified it a tiny bit too.

A Babylonian story is incredibly descriptive. A large egg came from heaven and landed in the Euphrates River. It then came to the land by the help of fishes that pushed it toward land. (This could be propulsion from under the water line causing a bubbling wake making the observers believe fish were pushing the 'egg'). The egg hatched and out came a woman named Venus. In this story she was said to have come from the antediluvian (pre-flood) world. (Book 41 pg. 109) This is pretty plain language. Yet often this and similar stories are "interpreted" rather than taken at face value. Now see how this connects to this next bit found in the same source...

A woman named Astraea is also identified as Themis (goddess of justice) or she is possibly Themis' daughter. She is said to have lived on earth before the flood. She forsook the earth just before the catastrophe (flood) occurred. This Astraea is the same as the Syrian Astarte, who is also identified as Venus! (Book 41 pg. 309) Interestingly, though Hislop deduces that these females are all the same girl, he disassociates these two events in his book and separates them by exactly 200 pages!

We see Astraea leaving earth just before the flood, though how she does this is not stated. But we then see her coming back to earth after the flood in an "egg" and landing in the Euphrates River in another legend. This therefore places the egg shaped craft to the pre flood era! Since this mid 19th century author cannot accept that anyone could physically leave the earth before the flood or for that matter return to earth after the flood, his primary assumption and goal in speaking about these legends turns into showing the symbolism of the egg and the women, not realizing he had evidence to show someone other than Noah survived from pre-flood times. After all why would he, the bible says all people on dry land died in the flood. Only knuckleheads like me would suggest otherwise.

Since space travel was something of fairytales in the 19th century, this legend telling about someone leaving the earth before the flood and returning after it was all over, was simply an impossibility to him. Therefore such a statement to him must have been meant to be allegorical, thus his only alternative was to presume since they couldn't really have left the earth, or survived the flood, then some analogies were meant by these stories, and they were not meant to be taken literally. Thus he identifies the egg as the ark of Noah and equates Themis with the spirit, apparently failing to recognize the obvious connection and similarities in these events and neglecting to ascribe any significance to them, other than allegorical lessons.

So we come to the same conclusion a few ways: through genetic constraints, and through ancient history and some legends. The gods, though they came from space after the flood...were human. If evolutionists or panspermians want to somehow say by some bizarre fluke two human species by some incredible coincidence evolved on two star systems separated by billions of miles or light years for that matter, and then met 400 million years ago so they could squash trilobites under foot with their sandals, they can go ahead and believe that. In my mind, it just can't possibly get any clearer; the gods were human and part of the same creation, sons and daughters of Adam and Eve and just happened to be in space at the time of the flood. They came back after it and thus the legends.

See Extra Bonus after Bibliography

Bibliography

Book 0 Earth, Man, & Devolution Rick Pilotte © 2007, 2008, 2017

Book 1 The Outer Space Connection by Alan & Sally Lansburg. © 1975

Book 4 Gods From Outer Space by Erich Von Daniken Bantam paperback ©1972

Book 5 Extraterrestrial Visitations from Prehistoric Times to the Present by Jacques Bergier Signet paperback ©1973

Book 6 Atlantis the Eighth Continent by Charles Berlitz Fawcett Paperback ©1984

Book 7 The Bermuda Triangle by Charles Berlitz Avon Paperback ©1974

Book 8 In Search of Ancient Mysteries. By Alan & Sally Landsburg Bantam paperback © 1974

Book 9 Scientific Creationism Edited by Dr. Henry M. Morris ©1974 /1985 Master Books

Book 10 Von Daniken's Proof by Erick Von Daniken 1977 Bantam paperback July ©1978

Book 11 We Are Not the First By Andrew Tomas Bantam Paperback ©1971

Book 12 The Secret Forces of the Pyramids by Warren Smith Zebra Paperback© 1975

Book 13 Earth Magic by Francis Hitching Kangaroo Pocket book ©1978

Book 14 Worlds in Collision by Immanuel Velikovsky ©1950 Dell Pocket book© 1973

Book 16 The Lost Continent of Mu by James Churchward ©1931 / 1950

Book 17 The 12th Planet by Zecharia Sitchin 1976 Avon Paperback ©1978

Book 19 We are the Earthquake Generation Jeffrey Goodman Ph.D. Berkley Paperback ©1979

Book 21 Timeless Earth by Peter Kolosimo Bantam paperback ©1973

Book 22 The Mysterious Unknown by Robert Charroux 1969 Corgi Paperback ©1973

Book 23 Gods and Spacemen in the Ancient West by W. Raymond Drake Signet paperback ©1974

Book 24 Without a Trace by Charles Berlitz, Ballantine paperback ©1977

Book 26 Limbo of the Lost by John William Spencer. Bantam Pocketbook ©1973

Book 27 Limbo of the Lost by John Wallace Spencer. Bantam Pocketbook ©1969

Book 29 Gods, Demons and Space Chariots by Eric Norman Lancer paperback ©1970

Book 30 Mysteries of Time and Space by Brad Steiger Dell paperback © 1974

Book 31 Secrets of Lost Atland by Robert Scrutton © 1978 Sphere paperback 1979

Book 32 Alien Meetings by Brad Steiger © 1978 Ace paperback

Book 34 Gods and Spacemen in the Ancient East by W. Raymond Drake 1968 Signet paperback Dec. ©1973

Book 35 Atlantis Rising by Brad Steiger Dell paperback ©1973

Book 37 Mysteries From Forgotten Worlds by Charles Berlitz ©1972 Granada Paperback 1983

Book 41 The Two Babylons by Rev. Alexander Hislop. First published in 1858. © 1916

Book 42 The War of Gods and Men by Zecharia Sitchin 1985 Avon Paperback © June 1985

Book 47 Flying Saucers Uncensored by Harold T. Wilkins 1955 Pyramid paperback ©Feb. 1975

Book 49 Entropy by Jeremy Rifkin 1980 Bantam paperback Oct. 1981

Book 50 Parallel Universe by Adi-Kent Thomas Jeffrey 1977 Warner Books Paperback © June 1977

Book 52 Lightning in his Hand by Inez Hunt & Wanehaw Draper 1964 A biography about Nikola Tesla

Book 53 Earth in Upheaval by Immanuel Velikovsky Pocket book paperback © 1955

Book 54 Evolution- The Fossils Say No! by Duane T. Gish Ph.D. 1978 Creation -Life Pub. Paperback

Book 56 Book of the Eskimos by Peter Freuchen's World Pub. Comp. Hardcover ©1961

Book 61 The Book of the Dead translated by Sir E. A. Wallace Budge 1960

Book 62 Strange World by Frank Edwards Ace paperback ©1964
Book 64 The Mystery of Atlantis by Charles Berlitz ©1969 Tower paperback
Book 68 Atlantis by Ignatius Donnelly 1882 (© 1976 Dover reissue)
Book 69 Realm of the Incas. Victor von Hagen Mentor paperback ©1957
Book 70 Book of the Hopi. Frank Waters. Ballantine paperback ©1963
Book 71 The Ark on Ararat by Tim LaHaye & John D. Morris Kangaroo pocket book © 1976/1977
Book 72 In Search of Noah's Ark by David Balsinger & Charles E. Sellier Sun Paperback © 1976
National Geographic Feb 1967

Internet Sources

Bell, Rosemary. Yurok Tales, Bell Books, Etna, California, 1992.

Berndt, Ronald M. and Berndt, Catherine. The Speaking Land, Inner Traditions International, Rochester, Vermont, 1994.

Bierhorst, John. The Mythology of South America, William Morrow, New York, 1988.

Bierhorst, John. Mythology of the Lenape, University of Arizona Press, Tuscon, 1995.

Carnoy, Albert J. Iranian, in Gray, v. VI, 1917.

Clark, Ella E. Indian Legends of the Pacific Northwest, University of California Press, 1953.

Dalley, Stephanie. Myths From Mesopotamia, Oxford University Press, Oxford, 1989.

Elder, John and Hertha D. Wong, 1994. Family of Earth and Sky: Indigenous Tales of Nature from around the World, Beacon Press, Boston. Reprinted in Parabola 22(1): 71-73 (Spring 1997)Erdoes, Richard and Alfonso Ortiz. American Indian Myths and Legends, Pantheon Books, New York. 1984.

Fauconnet, Max, 1968. "Mythology of Black Africa". In Guirand, Felix (ed.), New Larousse Encyclopedia of Mythology, Hamlyn, London.

Faulkner, Raymond (transl.). The Egyptian Book of the Dead, The Book of Going Forth by Day, Chronicle Books, San Francisco, 1994.

Frazer, Sir James G. Folk-Lore in the Old Testament, vol. 1, Macmillan & Co., London, 1919.

Frazer, Sir James G. The Golden Bough, Wordsworth Editions Ltd., Hertfordshire, 1993.

Frazer (also See Gaster)

Gaster, Theodor H. Myth, Legend, and Custom in the Old Testament, Harper & Row, New York, 1969. (Most of the flood stories in this work are taken from Frazer, 1919.)

Gifford, Douglas. Warriors, Gods & Spirits from Central & South American Mythology, William Collins, Glasgow, 1983.

Gifford, Edward W. and Block, Gwendoline Harris. Californian Indian Nights, University of Nebraska Press, Lincoln, 1930, 1990.

Holmberg, Uno. Finno-Ugric, Siberian, in MacCulloch, C. J. A., ed., The Mythology of All Races, v. IV, Marshall Jones Co., Boston, 1927.

Howey, M. Oldfield. The Encircled Serpent, Arthur Richmond Company, New York, 1955.

Kelsen, Hans, 1943. "The Principle of Retribution in the Flood and Catastrophe Myths", in Dundes.

Kolig, Erich, 1980. "Noah's Ark Revisited: On the Myth-Land Connection in Traditional Australian Aboriginal Thought", in Dundes.

Leon-Portilla, Miguel, 1961. "Mythology of ancient Mexico", in Kramer.

Miller, Hugh. The Testimony of the Rocks. Or, Geology in Its Bearings on the Two Theologies, Natural and Revealed. Gould and Lincoln, Boston, 1857. In MacRae, Andrew, n.d. Hugh Miller -- 19th-century creationist geologist, Sturluson, Snorri. The Prose Edda, Jean I. Young (transl.), University of California Press, Berkeley, 1954.

Vitaliano, Dorothy B. Legends of the Earth, Indiana University Press, Bloomington, 1973.

Zong In-Sob. Folk Tales from Korea, Routledge & Kegan Paul Ltd., London, 1952.

Extra Bonus

Denier's Handbook

Note originally I wrote this as a potential hand out aid for a certain political party, so you'll find some repetition of material in the book used here, but of course used in a different application.

There is an ongoing campaign to marginalize contrary opinion and even contrary science if it goes against predominant and actively promoted *theories* which are usually promoted as scientific fact or "settled science". For example the theory of evolution is pushed on students as scientific truth when in fact, not only is evolution just a theory, it is a theory that evolutionist themselves have conclusively disproven! Yeah! Evolution theory divides into three diverse and distinct branches or forms of the theory and they are; Evolution through chance, Progressive evolution, and Theistic evolution. What few people realize is that all three of these types of evolution have conclusively disproven the other two types and showed them to be completely impossible! Yet people who believe in creation are equated with delusional crackpots. Indeed evolutionists will heckle and verbally abuse creationist while they present their facts, such as was done with Dr. Henry Morris, Author of Scientific Creationism.

Without knowing who Larry Flynt was, I picked up a free movie on the side of the road called *The People Vs Larry Flynt,* because it was apparently a courtroom drama kind of movie. It turned out to be about a person who published porn magazines that always pushed the envelope on what could be printed in pictures or in comment about famous people, and thus he was constantly facing opposition and legal battles. Flynt eventually went to the Supreme Court to defend his right to free speech and expressions, versus a religious personality who wanted to sue Flynt for naughty bits said about him which were patently absurd, not to mention in bad taste. Flynt won. His right to oppose the societal norms with his own opinions or humour was a freedom that was officially guaranteed him in the Supreme Court. So it would seem this freedom goes without saying when it comes to two sides of a scientific conflict of opinion or theories. So why has any opinion or science disputing climate change and global warming been shouted down and vociferously opposed? Doesn't this seem odd if the science really isn't confirmed? Einstein said never stop asking questions; so why have people who believe the "science" of global warming or climate change stopped asking questions...what are they afraid of...or do 'they' have an agenda? There are very good reasons to question climate change and global warming as neither scenario have been proven. And what's even weirder is the supposed dire consequences of global warming or climate change haven't even been proven to be negative! There are apparently just as many pros to the scenario as cons.

It has become very unpopular to verbally contradict any beliefs, personalities or science that the media and rich influential popular personalities have coddled as their own. The media, most politicians, scientists and even ecologists have been completely duped by science that insists that what we exhale and plant life uses to grow is putting us all in danger of mortal peril. That's right carbon dioxide now referred to as CO_2 emissions, has been labelled as dangerous to life on earth, even though it is in fact essential to life. And so paradoxically we have been asked to commit suicide by limiting the amount of CO_2 created which of course would reduce plant life on the planet and consequently create worldwide famine.

If that sounds ridiculous, impossible and bizarre, then read the research which I've included here as an extra bonus. After all Atlantis, catastrophism and creation have all been actively fought against by our society as not worthy of equal time and ridiculed as unscientific; even though all have ample sound evidence that counters these popular beliefs and can be substantiated. Since any evidence that counters the global warming theory in many people's minds falls into the same category as Creation, Atlantis, catastrophism, and apparently the Easter bunny, the great pumpkin, Santa Clause and a flat earth, I think it fits in here with the other stuff in this book. No doubt conventional scientists would consider the material covered in this book as beneath their dignity to take seriously or even comment on without visible derision in their voice. So why not add to the laughter. I wonder what flat earthers think the earth looks like...a big circle? We see Jupiter revolve so fast it is obviously a sphere, so why would they think the earth is flat...Hmm ...where was I?

The belief of "global warming" or what has now been called "climate change" has gripped the world politics, and is now costing the countries of the world hundreds of billions of dollars. A "damn the torpedoes full speed ahead" mentality has gripped politicians around the globe that have been shamed into spending their constituents hard earned money on wasteful unproven hair brained schemes just to appear like they are doing something regardless of the costs; and why should they worry, it's not their money, so if they can look like they care they'll increase their chances of being re-elected. That's their bottom line.

Highly rational scientists have been called 'deniers', if they try and present any information that counters this now almost ubiquitous human caused climate change belief. They have been actively ridiculed and muzzled so that any contradictory evidence they have that overturns their chosen side, no matter how compelling it may be, is routinely ignored and not presented to the people, to the end that the population from children to societies elders are coached with completely false indoctrination. An active campaign exists to literally erase any vocalization against the status quo belief. "Deniers" are virtually treated like criminals that have escaped from the asylum that need to have their heads examined, or like perverts or scum. It's been said that any politician that ignores climate change should be in prison. Any conversation that attempts to counter global warming's lies to people who believe the nonsense just assume you are a childish imbecile and either talk over you, or ignore you because you are a stupid idiot and have no idea what you are talking about. This attitude towards people that question the science has recently been stepped up. For example the editor in chief of the Guardian Newspaper Katherine Viner has instructed her staff to stop calling it a climate change and refer to it as a climate emergency, break down or crisis. People that question are no longer to be called sceptics, but deniers, and it's not global warming any more but global heating.

I've never been any good at talking over people, and when I try I just get flustered or mad so I've given up and just figure if they don't want to hear my story, that's life. I've on occasion had people sound real interested in something I had to say, they've left the room, and come back and completely forgotten as though I never said a word. I know how Charlie Brown feels as I've felt like him pretty much all my life. However some of you reading this might find this material like a lost ammunition dump and know exactly how to use it, so I offer this as my little contribution to the hopeful return to sanity.

GRAPH OF GLOBAL TEMPERATURES MATCH CO_2 RISE.

Al Gore in his Inconvenient Truth suggests rising Carbon Dioxide (CO_2) levels causes rising global temperatures. Gore's graph shows CO_2 levels and earth temperatures, one above the other steering to the viewer to believe correlation between the two graphs is obvious. Though the link is apparently very clear, there's something rotten in Antarctica. This graph supposedly spans a time frame of 650,000 years and is based on Antarctica Ice-core data. The idea pushed is that rising CO_2 levels increases temperatures correspondingly.

However the apparent cause/effect is actually reversed, that is, the rising CO_2 levels followed rising temperatures, by between 800, and 2000 years (if the time frame of his graph can be believed). Meaning something else is causing the rise in temperatures, not CO_2, and CO_2 levels are a by-product of the system.

Gore took his graph from the June 3 1999 journal Nature, (switching the graph image left to right) and very key to the point here, is the article's graph had three parts to it, not two; CO_2, temperature and **Insolation.** (Insolation is the amount of input from the sun on a particular spot. Neither CO_2 nor temperature can change the insolation, as insolation is all light / heat intensity from the sun. The amount of insolation is determined by the angle of the sun on the spherical shape of the earth at any given point and time. On one 150,000 year span of the graph, *it's been shown that CO_2 lagged behind temperature changes by 1000-1300 years, meaning the amount of sun hitting the earth in a given area determined the temperature, and the temperature determined the amount of CO_2.* **The amount of CO_2 didn't determining the temperature, and the change in CO_2 levels were a result in the temperature changes, not the other way around.** The insolation level is the driving factor in temperature and CO_2 levels.

(Authors note. The time factor here is illogically long and the duration actually has to be compressed from 650,000 years to about 6,000 years for a linked correlation such as this to be so demonstrative [this would put the CO_2 levels rising occurring from 8-20 years after temperature rises which fits closer with solar variations and cycles] No way could such a close link be demonstrated in a graph that extends over such a long time frame as 800-2000 years as other factors could not be ruled out and no way could increased temperature and CO_2 levels so closely mirror insolation patterns without a direct link between the 3, meaning the time span has to be compressed to indicate true causal relationship revealed in the graph.)

This is one of those things that Al Gore presented in the movie that seemed so conclusive to me, until I saw the facts were deliberately transposed. He showed that there was a direct link between the global rise in CO_2 levels with ocean temperatures. The ocean held CO_2 can release about 1% of its CO_2 content into the atmosphere, which is between 60 and 90 times the concentration of the atmosphere, meaning CO_2 levels rise as the ocean slowly heat up: the more sun the faster the rise in atmospheric CO_2 concentration. The ocean contains about 8000 times the concentration of CO_2 than the atmosphere and it doesn't take much heat to release a lot of it into the atmosphere. Global CO_2 concentrations can rise in a single summer, indeed Gore showed the rising CO_2 concentrations were rising each year during what is now known as the most recent warm period directly linking CO_2 and heat. This would be the combined effect of ocean warming, forests disappearing (less CO_2 absorption) and man-made CO_2 releases, which he naturally blamed the increase CO_2 presence on manmade sources. But this is a fallacy, the ocean sources are the largest contributor to the CO_2 build-up or decline. Again we see the cause effect reversed to what Gore says, in that as the temperature rises, more CO_2 is released into the atmosphere, not the other way around. He made it appear that the rise in CO_2 was causing warmer temperatures, but it was the warmer temperatures that were heating the oceans to allow them to release more CO_2.

The conclusion is that orbital variations change insolation degrees which in turn change temperatures, followed by changes in CO_2 as the environment is altered. CO_2 levels have nothing to do with driving global temperature; it's the other way around. So to try and reduce CO_2 emissions wouldn't work to reduce the "global warming", you would have to create a shield around the earth to reduce the solar insolation to reduce the CO_2, which is completely impossible. So he's trying to have us fight an unwinnable battle, by attacking a symptom, not a cause.

Temperatures caused the change in CO_2 levels because rising temperatures causes the oceans to release CO_2; falling temperatures cause the ocean to absorb more CO_2.

So to present the idea in his graph that this increase takes between 400 and 3,000 years (based on all ice cores, and their graphs) to have a marked cause effect on the graph is baloney. The effect is visible on a yearly basis. The time scales of the ice cores are based on belief that each snow layer is one year, when in fact thousands of layers can be created in a single century [dealt with in my first book]).

THE SUN'S EFFECT

Though computer models don't include the sun, clouds or water vapour, the sun is the main contributing factor to global temperatures and clouds and water vapour are major deflectors and retainers of heat. During the early 1990's, average global temperatures did rise marginally, but this has been deduced to be caused mainly from the sun, which goes through cycles and is 98% of the driving force behind earth's warmth and climate. Piers Corbyn of Weatheraction, a company specializing in long range weather forecasting, states that 'solar charged particles impact us far more than is currently accepted, so much so he says that they are almost entirely responsible for what happens to global temperatures.'

These same solar cycles are now cooling the earth and have been since 1998 and are expected to continue the trend to between 2040 and 2053.

For 5 years from 2007-20012 a dramatic drop in sunspots were seen on the sun's surface, and this has a measurable effect here on the earth. The ice on Antarctica got thicker, and global temperatures are now cooling. The trend is so real and persistent that a mini ice age is once again considered to be a possibility, similar to how such was feared in the 60's and 70's, but which never materialized.

I've lived in Victoria for over 60 years and the 'winter' of 2016-17 is the longest sustained string of cool temperatures I can recall, lasting from November to June. Victoria might get snow once every 2 or 3 years, but this year we got it maybe 5 times. Trees were blooming late and crops were planted 6 weeks late and this season had a devastating effect on the garden culture of Victoria: as we'll see this could be the start of a long trend.

People want to blame forest fires on global warming but this too is nonsense. Forests fire have been put out as soon as possible without being allowed to burn themselves out for so long now that the forest floors have been building up combustibles that are normally burned up as forest fires which would have been caused by lightning were started. But with prolonged manmade intervention, this build-up has reached such massive proportions that the forests fires resist extinguishing and they have been becoming harder to put out. Now they have reached a point where they merge into super fires. The extent and intensity of the fires has nothing to do with CO_2 build-up, or global warming.

Solar sunspot occurrences are at the lowest ebb in nearly 400 years! A global mini ice age happened during the Maunder Minimum which occurred from the mid 17th to early 18th century when sun spots were exceedingly rare. During a 30 year span just 50 sunspots were seen when the normal number would be between 40,000 and 50,000! This caused global temperatures to drop fairly dramatically around the globe for this long stretch from 1645- 1715. During this time you could walk on the ice from Manhattan Island to Staten Island, the Thames River froze regularly every year and people could walk from Denmark across to Sweden. Eskimos were seen paddling off Britain's shores and Norway's glaciers grew as much as 100 meters a year destroying farms and villages. Snow remained at lower altitudes year round and farmlands had snow on them to late spring. Tree rings during this period were so uniform it is difficult to tell one year from another.

ANOTHER THEORY TO ACCOUNT FOR THE SYMPTOMS?

People have automatically associated long dry spells and extra forest fires with global warming. Some now have to concede this term "Global Warming" isn't correct so they call it "Climate change", though many still aren't up to date so still call it 'global warming'. Media and ill informed politicians constantly beat it into our brain that because it's settled science it has to be attacked and our hard earned cash has to be thrown at the "problem", and how dare you argue or ask questions.

Even more ludicrous, it seems now that all weather, regardless of what it is, is supposedly caused by climate change and the myth is continued by people that want us to feel guilty for breathing out carbon dioxide. But this manmade cause of climate change is just a theory that has no legs to stand on and yet we are supposedly now in a "Climate Emergency" that will kill us all in 11 years or some such nonsense if we don't throw tons of cash at it right now.

But there is another theory that is every bit as plausible to account for long dry spells and forest fires as these symptoms are not necessarily linked only with warm spells; they could in theory also be associated with long cold spells. How so?

I've seen some of the longest cold stretches in my neck of the woods in 2016-2017 and now 2018-2019, and yet some persistent nuts want us to believe the cold spells are caused by global warming despite the counterintuitive lack of logic to this premise. With the sun coming into a combination of magnetic field separations and minimal sunspots, creating what looks to be another Maunder Minimum, forest fires and crazy flood weather could also be caused by global cooling. Dry spells are not necessarily caused by global warming, but the exact opposite could occur. With a calmer and cooler sun, less evaporation would be occurring, so that cold **dry spells** could be expected from less moist cloud formation, and therefore less rain is some areas. Furthermore floods could also be expected closer to an eastern shore, caused by what clouds have formed being colder and therefore heavier and consequently dropping their moisture earlier, as they are, on average, drifting westward from the rotation of the earth. Thus Eastern coastal area land elevations could force the clouds to drop their moisture more quickly, rather than over a more widespread area, due to overall heaviness to the clouds and their inability to carry the moisture over great distances. So western shores could be dryer and more prone to forest fires and eastern coasts could be wetter and prone to floods. I don't know how good this theory is because I theorized it. I based it on my knowing some facts and creating a hypothesis based on those facts. It may or may not be valid, but I'm betting it's better than the outrageous claims that people deserve what they get in the result of forest fire because they are addicted to creating excess CO2 emissions. Truth is had there been more CO_2 the trees might have been greener, more foliated with a moister atmosphere above the forests with a higher degree of resistance to fires. And now we are being told to reduce CO2 build-up. Seriously!? This is the *LAST* thing we should be doing.

There is no correlation between CO_2 quantities emitted by human activities and the degree of global cooling or warming. There is however a direct link to temperatures on earth with solar activity and the degree of intensity of sunspots.

Some have contested the effect of sunspots on weather here on earth, because average seasonal records simply don't go back far enough to make a direct statistical link between earth temperatures and sunspots. However scientists have recently accessed Rhine river boat men records that go back for centuries which recorded things like when the river was frozen over. This data has confirmed to a 99% certainty that the relationship between solar cycles and temperatures on the Rhine are inherently linked, which of course is true for the rest of the planet.

Some have tried to suggest the little ice age had nothing to do with the sun and this Maunder Minimum was only a European or northern hemisphere issue. Well that has been shot full of holes too by a team of United Kingdom researchers which studied a peat bog near the southern tip of South America which also indicated synchronization of the little ice age in the southern hemisphere with that of the north, further confirming that the sun determines climate.

Professor Valentina Zharkova study on the inner workings of the sun from 2016 revealed that there is not just one magnetic component to the sun but two, and the interaction or lack thereof between these two fields either amplifies or dampens solar activity. Her research indicates that the two fields have recently separated and there will be no interaction between them for what will likely be the next three solar cycles, dropping the sun's magnetic field to nearly zero. This means we will likely have reduced solar activity which will last to the middle of the century, creating conditions on earth similar to the Maunder Minimum of 1645-1715 or the Dalton Minimum (approximately from 1780-1830) for the coming years between 2020 and 2053. Naturally climate scientists are trying to discredit and suppress her findings; for example they contacted the Royal Astronomical Society, demanding, behind her team's back, that they withdraw her press release. Though she offered to work with climate scientists to add their data to her results, the offer was refused.

Curiously, the CEO of Global Weather Oscillations David Dilley, research on the sun based on cycles matches Zharkova's timing for the next cooling period exactly! He's determined that each solar sub cycle lasts 230 years, the last ending in 1790 and the next cycle is due in 2020. Remarkebly he expects a huge reduction in solar activity to last 33 years ending in 2053, the exact same years Zharkova research pinpointed! He expects the cool period will be colder than the 1940's to 60's and will last about 60-100 years, then the earth will slowly warm up again, but not to the same degree it was before 1998. Amazingly other researchers, through different criteria have also concluded that the next solar minimum will start in 2019 or 2020. It may be time to invest in some ice skates and maybe even a snowmobile.

During the Maunder Minimum, winter snowfall was much heavier than previously or afterwards, and the snow came more often and stayed for months longer. Furthermore springs and summers were colder and wetter. Crop growing in Europe had to adapt to the shortened and somewhat unreliable growing season. The end of the Dalton Minimum marked the end of the "Ice Fayre" popular from the time of Elizabeth I to the mid 1830s when the little ice age was changing to the modern warm period. A renewed minimum could mean considerable food shortages and higher food costs worldwide. This coupled with the global production being outstripped by consumption for over ten years means there could be widespread famines. This reduced production is directly linked to converting crops from edible ones to ones used to make fuels.

It was inferred by Gore that **Mount Kilimanjaro glacier loss** was caused by global warming through increased CO_2 levels. This is simply not correct. Three climate changes in the last several thousand years have effected this mount, varying the glacier's size, (larger or smaller) during these periods. Ice cores indicate the glacier was actually growing from around 1 to 3 thousand years ago up until 1880 when a climate shift occurred. Gore said Dr. Lonnie Thompson predicted the mount would be ice free in ten years (or around 2015 to 2020), but this scientist only predicted the loss of Kilimanjaro ice due to ongoing and historical causes, he did not blame it on either CO_2 or global warming, but variations of climate over time. Thompson partially makes the connection of the loss of glaciations on Kilimanjaro with nearby lakes which were at one time as much as 100 meters higher. Lake Chad for example at the time of this material was just 17,000 square kilometres. A few thousand years ago this lake was between 330,000 and 438,000 square kilometres. The bottom line is less local evaporation reduces moisture and thus less snow build-up, as well as glacier shrinkage through evaporation. Simply put, drying of the surrounding air reduced the accumulation of ice. Thompson never mentioned CO_2. Reductions in the glaciations are attributed to reduced humidity, and have nothing to do with CO_2 build-up.

Actually humidity loss is an ongoing sign of global aging. Mars is known to have had oceans and they are all gone, and indeed earth's oceans levels have dropped by as much as 20 feet since 1500B.C. The earth actually has a vapour trail as it loses atmosphere to space. Ancient global climate was moister and warmer with much more forest coverage as forests retain moisture, humidity, and heat, and the global loss of tree cover is probably more the cause of humidity loss and thus reduced condensation. So cutting down forests is like speeding up the process, likened to cutting the branch we are sitting on.

Antarctica is technically a dessert with less than 6 inches of annual rainfall a year and is so devoid of humidity you can't see your breath. The reductions of Mount Kilimanjaro glaciers have been occurring slowly since 1880, long before a supposed CO_2 build-up. *The climate there is not getting warmer, but drier,* so it just won't snow. Though Gore suggested that from 1970-2005 the loss of ice was attributed to heat and CO_2 buildup, the International Journal of Climatology in 2004 stated temperature increases have not contributed to ice recession to that time.

The change in temperature on Kilimanjaro has been termed "negligible" with an average difference of a mere 0.1 Celsius in the last 50 years. The only hot air anywhere near Kilimanjaro, is Al Gore's.

LAKE CHAD EVAPORATION

Gore actually blames the shrinking of Lake Chad on CO_2 build-up too, suggesting that in 1963 'when it was full' it was the 6th largest lake in the world. But it wasn't full in 1963; that was just the lake's peak volume of the 20th century; it's been shrinking off and on for a few thousand years. At one time it was over 400,000 square Kilometres and at one time it may have been as large as 800,000 square kilometres: the largest lake in the world. It's shrunk to the current or smaller levels several times in the last thousand years and at the beginning of the 16th century Lake Chad dried up completely for a few years! Drought like the one seen at the time of Gores presentation involving Lake Chad have happened 6 times since 1400, and it has been deduced to have a potential recurrence of these minimum levels as many as three times a century. Lake Chad's Northern Pool dried up 12 times between 1975 and 1994...during the cold period!

Any accelerated shrinkage of Lake Chad recently could be contributed to more demands on the rivers that run into it from diversion and damming, as population since 1963 in the general region of the lake (Chad basin) has doubled from 13 million to 26 million people. However those that live within normal commuting distance to the lake only number 700,000. In fact were these water diversions allowed to flow into the lake instead being held in dams or reservoirs before it got into the lake, Lake Chad would be double the surface area, as about 2-3 Billion cubic meters is drawn from the flow.

In 1963 Lake Chad was its fullest in the 20th century, and Gore had to have known this to say "when it was full'. Back in 1908 the lake had shrunk so much it was down to just a northern and southern pool, nearly as small as it was when Gore showed it at its smallest. For the next 50 odd years since 1908 the lakes slowly refilled, then in the 1950's it grew rapidly and rejoined the two pools to when it reached the size it was in 1963, where Gore starts his fairy tale. Since this story was foisted on you, the lake grew, so that by 2005 it was within a meter depth of 1908 levels once again.

Some have stated that the lake had shrunk from 25,000 Km² to 1,500 km² today, but 'today' refers to the two minimums it reached, one during the 1980's when the northern 'pool' remained dry for more than a year, and the lake reached the same size back in 1973. By 2013 the lake had increased in size to 14,800 KM².

Failure to take swampland into the estimations of the lake's size also drastically plays on the numbers. Other than the usually drying and wetting cycles, which range about 4,000 KM², there has been no notable change in overall size since 1974.

There also appears to be some hidden agenda with Lake Chad with no less than NASA playing the game. NASA assembled a series of satellite photographs of Lake Chad, but careful timing and choice of photos used, made Lake Chad look like it was shrinking relentlessly. But they could have chosen different pictures over the same time period to have shown the lake was slowly expanding, the exact opposite! The months are never indicated on the picture so you are steered to believe what they want you to believe. And though knowledge of the subterfuge has become known, no attempt to modify public perception of the state of Lake Chad has been forthcoming. Scientific investigation has shown the lake has periodical fluctuations, and no support exists for the lakes disappearing any time soon. Even the climate models for the area, though varying widely, on average predict an increase in water inflow.

But the myth persists, even to the point of befuddling the odd journalist, who, despite being told by scientists the situation; they go to the Chad basin to determine the extent of the 'disaster', only to be surprised by the local fishermen complaining about the recent floods. Similarly during the Copenhagen climate change conference of 2009 when the disappearing of Lake Chad was on the agenda; the wind was taken out of the sails because of a heavy annual rainfall occurring in the Lake Chad region.

Some have accused the story tellers concerning the disappearance of Lake Chad as being construed by stakeholders who were driven by interest in drumming up international aid for the purpose of digging trenches, pipelines, and water transfers from other sources to Lake Chad. The yarn benefitted many stakeholders, middlemen, consultants, and various companies, by enabling the circulation of large sums of money across and under the table.

ICE MELTING IN THE NORTH ENDANGERING POLAR BEARS

Polar Bears, being something of an iconic Canadian National animal, have had their data manipulated to tug at your heart and purse strings. But the conclusions are based on a complete misrepresentation and twisting of the facts.

The story starts with four Polar bears that drown in an especially violent storm. This was twisted to say they died because of disappearing ice, caused by increased CO_2 levels, which supposedly melts the ice affecting the bears seal hunting and breeding habitat, thus reducing the population. This single event has been blown so out of proportion that the Center for Biological Diversity has drafted a petition to get the polar bear on the endangered list. The circus was inflated when Al Gore used a photograph of two polar bears clinging to a melting, wind sculpted, iceberg taken by Amanda Byrd in 2004. Amanda said the bears were in no danger as they were close to the coast and they can swim 100 miles. But this didn't stop Gore from using the photo to his own end and even going so far as to say they'll become extinct due to global warming. This hogwash completely ignores polar bear population data.

Summer ice has decreased by 8.59 % per ten years span for 27 years and would supposedly be gone by 2060 or sooner, and since the bears apparently need sea ice for their livelihood, this diminishing ice is considered a threat to their survival. But these claims ignore real data.

First, warming trends actually increase the bear population, not decrease it. Studies show this, and in fact during the warmer period, polar bear populations have increased in the arctic from 1970 when there was estimated to be between 5 and 10 thousand polar bears, compared to today's figure 25,000! So why do some suggest the populations of polar bears are declining? Because they take specific regions where bear populations are estimated to have declined, blow these number up to maximum estimations in their favor and apply these regional stats as though they represented the entire arctic. There are 19 regional subpopulations of polar bears, and in only 5 of those regions have the polar bear populations been said to have declined. A closer look at those five regions shows how much climate change proponents like to twist facts.

1   *Southern Beaufort* region sea population was estimated in 1986, 1988 and 1995 to be around 1800 bears with a degree of error in the range of about ±20% (meaning there were between 1440 and 2160 bears) Between 2001 and 2006 the bear estimates were put at 1526, which looks like a decline, but this too is an estimate and official confidence in numbers puts the real total somewhere between 1,211 and 1,841 bears which has an even greater degree of error than ±20%.(The earlier estimates do not have confidence numbers and in all likelihood have an even higher degree of inaccuracy) So the estimates in actuality are in all probability little changed, or at worst marginally declined, and statistically may even have marginally increased. But we'll give this one to the fear mongers.

2   *Norwegian Bay region.* Any decline in polar bear populations cannot be blamed on loss of sea ice...at least not directly, but reduced ice in the areas has reduced the number of seals taking advantage of the ice, meaning there are less seals to attract bears, so the bears probably went somewhere else where the hunting was better.

3   *Baffin Bay region.* This one should get you scratching your head. Between 1984 and 1989 the polar bear population in this region was estimated to be between 300 and 600 bears. A survey of the bears taken in this region from 1993-1997 put the declining population down to a measly 2,074 bears. How can 300-600 bears increasing to 2,074 bears 10 years later possibly be reported as a decline?! It appears to have something to do with how you report the numbers in the exact same conditions. In the earlier report their capture and population count was just limited to bears from shore fast ice and the floes off the edge of Baffin Island. In the later estimates they reported that a proportion of the population is offshore during the spring (But this was an unknown). HUH? I don't get it? It seems in one survey

they assume X % of the total bear population is off shore and uncountable, so they assume an arbitrary number is out there. There seems to be no logical explanation of the numbers arrived at and thus the cause of any computed decline is apparently shifted to a later date (2004) and the cause is apparently attributed to the hunting of the bears. Based on simulations (probably in the same conditions of the earlier surveys) they suggested that in 2004 the population was at 1600 bears which would be a decline from the 1993-1997 estimates of 2,074 bears. They say the decline was because the subpopulation was overharvested. Prior to 2004 Nunavut natives were allowed to get up to 65 bears a year. This quota was increased up to 105 per year in 2004. Why was the hunting quota increased from 65 to 105 bears in the region if the population of them is said to be declining by government counters occasionally visiting the area? Because reports from the Inuit hunters showed the polar bear population in the area had increased substantially! Furthermore no mention of CO_2 induce melting of any ice had anything to do with this weird mathematical "decrease", which is in fact a net gain from the years 1984 and 2004 of between 1,000 and 1,300 bears! Where did these guys learn their math from? Were they playing with their I-phones in math class?

4   *Kane Basin* population. (Between Canada and Greenland) This area houses just 2/3s of 1% of all the polar bears in the world, or as an undated estimated put it, a total of 164 with a ± error range of 35 bears. The area is considered a suitable habitat for the bears and could be managed if need be for a subpopulation increase. Hunting quotas are limited to just 5 on the Canadian side and 5 on the Greenland side and it appears any decline is attributable to just hunting. Hunting totals translate to between 5% and 7.8% of the total population of the bears in the region. Any decline in the bear population could be attributed solely to hunting, and if indeed there is a decrease, simply stopping bear hunts would halt any decline.

5   *Western Hudson* population. Once again these numbers are estimates with an accuracy degree of± 20%. In 1987 the population was pegged at 1,194 (or between 1,020 and 1,368) and the 2004 number estimates 935 bears in the area (or between794 and 1,026) or a decrease of about 15 bears a year. This could be counted as a genuine decline. So what's the cause? In 2004 Nunavut increased the hunting quota from 55 to 64 bears a year. Though the increase of 9 bears a year can't be considered a cause, as the quota was raised the same year as the population estimate was issued, but once again hunting quotas are based on population reports of the locals. The increase in the quota allowance is probably due to increased numbers based on local reports and not occasional visiting statisticians. But even so, if the bear subpopulation really is decreasing, a simple tweak of the hunting quotas would easily re-establish a growth in the area.

   In all five of these areas where a supposed decline in polar bear populations is reported, no mention of melting ice or CO_2 buildup was even suggested as a possible cause of declines. Any suggestion bear populations are in peril are not only exaggerations, they are a complete fabrication! But would decreasing ice cover actually be bad?
   It's been seen since 1970 that the arctic has had some ice loss after a very long period of increased ice, or no change. This is a normal fluctuation over long periods of time. The bear population nevertheless has increased from between 5 and 10,000 bears in 1970 to a fairly accurate count of 25,000 bears presently, so they are clearly not in any danger of imminent extinction, let alone an endangered species. Some might say this is because of the hunting restrictions put in place around 1975. That no doubt is part of the explanation of the increase, but polar bears are found to actually increase their populations in warmer climate, not decrease! And furthermore, these bears have survived through time when ice buildup was more or less than today. You could even use Al Gore's graphs, (the ones where he conveniently leave out the Insolation part) and his data to show that polar bears survived in interglacial periods where there was far less ice in the arctic and when the arctic was far warmer than it is today. (Oxygen isotopes, pollen, fossils and midges found in

arctic region [Canada, Russia, Norway etc.] sediment cores bear this data out.) Summer temperatures were found to have ranged between 9 and 12c, where today they average around 5c. In other areas the summer temperatures were as high as 16c compared to today's average of 6c (this data was discovered in the Fog Lake areas.) Research shows that 150 years ago the arctic was at its coldest and previously it was far warmer in the distant past. Which means any warming going on in the arctic may actually mean the area is returning to its statistical norm!

But the scaremongering continues. We were warned that global warming would cause complete ice loss in the arctic by September 2016, blaming CO_2 build-up for the loss, but the ice mass ended up being 21% greater than the 2012 low point. In 2013 arctic ice expanded by 60%.

To say Arctic ice is decreasing is false: the Northern ice hasn't declined since 1967.

CATASTROPHIC GLACIER MELTS.

Rising CO_2 level is supposedly going to melt the Himalayan glaciers to extinction by 2035 and reduce runoff water supply to people to the point of a shortage. This conclusion is at best highly slanted and at worst deliberate misinformation. Yes some glaciers melt, and they have been since the ice ages. The reports focused entirely on the few glaciers that have receded and completely ignored the glaciers that are advancing. Take for example the 30 kilometre long Gangotri glacier whose melt runoff flows into the Ganges River. For 70 years (between 1934 and 2003) the glacier receded, an average of 70 feet a year loosing 5% of its length. The next two years the retreat slowed to 38 feet a year, and since that time has been virtually at a standstill.

Canadian Glaciologist Kenneth Hewitt decided to check into these claims of disappearing glaciers and studied 6 glaciers in the region of K2, the second highest peak in the world. Of the 6 glaciers he studied, 5 were advancing and only one was in retreat. His findings indicated there was no evidence to support this conclusion. Professor Graham a glacier expert of Canada's Trent University said the conclusions were exaggerated by a factor of 25, meaning, if the glaciers were melting they speeded up the rate by 25 times signifying that in reality they might be gone as soon as the year 2750...not 2035. (However if the current solar minimum continues this could delay such glaciations melt even longer)

A Himalayan glacier specialist, John Shroder, concluded that the Intergovernmental Panel on Climate Change (IPCC) Himalayan assessment got it "Horribly wrong" and felt they were jumping to conclusions on too little data.

But not only did IPCC exaggerate the glacier reduction to give a somewhat apocalyptic conclusion, they even overstated the impact of reduced water runoff into the Ganges river by suggesting water shortages for the region. Runoff from the glacier amounts only from 3 to 4% of the water that that enters the Ganges, the rest comes from monsoons in the region.

But even if the deductions were correct for the few glaciers they found that were in retreat during the time frame they studied them, the fact is glaciers have shown variable behaviour during all the monitoring of them in the past 100 + years. True, most have retreated, some are static and some are advancing, but it's somewhat amazing we have any glaciers at all when you consider they've been slowly melting since the ice-age.(for between 3,000 and 12,000 years depending on what dating methods you use) The Himalayan glacier pattern mirrors the rest of the glaciers on the globe.

Many people now want to blame the overall glacier retreat to increased CO_2 levels globally, but where do you determine what part, if any, to blame on CO_2 when the glaciers have been in general retreat since the ice age? And that's assuming increased CO_2 levels even contribute to melting in the first place. In the Palaeozoic period, the Earth had an atmospheric CO_2 concentration estimated at 4400 parts per million (ppm), that's more than ten times the concentration of today, yet during the same time we had this CO_2 concentration of 4400 ppm, the earth also had extensive evidence of glaciations: and it's been determined that CO_2 levels and the levels of global glaciations have nothing to do with each other!

On top of fearful melts of glaciers that just aren't happening, reports of northern hemisphere snow cover declines were propagated, which were also false. Snow extent showed no decline since 1967 and five of the 6 snowiest winters on record have happened since 2003.

LACK OF MOISTURE MAY BE THE REAL CULPRIT

The effect of moisture on heat radiation is commonly observed. Moist air holds in heat at night far better than dry air. Desert temperatures commonly drop 20 to 25 degrees celsius between day and night and extremes of 40 degrees celsius swings occur in such places as the Gobi desert and Alto-Plano. In moist climates, such as coastal cities like Lima, New York, or London, the day night swing is only about 10 degrees celcius; and usually a bit less. Thus moisture has an order of magnitude far more effective than the CO_2 in retaining heat, and completely masks any possible heat retention effect from CO_2. This; however, give much greater credence to the need to preserve rain forests, or any forests, to retain moisture in our atmosphere, and to help the human caused desertification of the globe. This global disease has caused the major expansion of the Sahara and drying out of millions of square km of grass land by overgrazing in Africa, and is now causing the loss of productivity in Amazonia which, globally speaking can be catastrophic. The conversion of forest to poor quality pasture yields momentary gain and long term negative consequences. Thus one could plausibly theorize that the lack of moisture retention on land heats up the land and the air above it, and this heated air then drifts onto the oceans and warms up them, more intense storms which occur when the ocean is warmed up. But as we'll see sea surface temperature doesn't actually make a difference to storm intensity. CO_2 does not retain heat nearly as well as moisture, if it does at all. It is moisture or lack thereof on land that may be causing any perceived problems which have been blamed on minutely increased levels of CO_2 in the atmosphere. This suggests a build-up of forestation is needed, not reduction of CO_2, and as a benefit, any new forestry would thrive on the extra CO_2, creating a more humid environment. And as we'll see the extra CO_2 is already a benefit, not a detriment.

THE MAGNETIC FIELD WOULD LIKE TO WEIGH IN.

What does cause the changes in temperature? Obviously climatic swings occur seasonally by changes in insolation, from the quantity of sun light striking the surface. But globally, what causes non-seasonal long term trends? The surprise answer appears to be that a change in the magnetic field of the earth precedes temperature changes by almost exactly 3 years. If we look at measured gammas of magnetic field intensity and temperature changes offset by that three year lag, the two curves follow one another too closely to be chance. They are mirror images of one another. That begs an explanation of why this happens - does the magnetic field cause temperature change and if so HOW. Even more perplexing is what causes magnetic field gamma to change?

There also is another possibility, that both temperature and magnetic fields are being changed by some third causative change, and they are both only symptoms of that cause. We know that temperature does not cause a magnetic change, the delay precludes that. There have been numerous magnetic field N-S to S-N reversals of the magnetic field of the entire earth over geological time, and these magnetic field reversals frequently coincide with major temperature swings. In fact all of the initiations of glacial period coincide with a magnetic reversal. Thus the link of magnetic field change to temperature change is substantiated for both short and very long range events.

GREENLAND MELTING ICE CAUSING AN ICE AGE IN EUROPE.

Supposedly CO_2 build-up is causing rapid melting of ice on Greenland to potentially stop the warm Atlantic Ocean current (called the thermohaline conveyor) in its tracks, causing an ice age in Europe. First, suggesting excess heat, would cause an ice age seems counterintuitive, and frankly were there extra heat on Greenland it would also be in Europe countering the action Greenland's melting ice would cause, though oddly no one seems to have mentioned this. Gore suggests that in ancient times a huge ice lake in North

America broke an ice dam suddenly cooling down the Atlantic causing an ice age that lasted 900-1000 years. (Presumably he's talking about Lake Agassiz, which also supposedly sunk Doggerland.)

First this is only a theoretical cause of an ice age, and a lame theory at that. It suggests that the cause of the ice age...was the previous ice age, which is ludicrous.

In 1883 Krakatoa went off, and the dust from just that one volcano reduced the sunlight coming to the entire earth by 10 percent for years! Global temperatures also dropped, from just this one volcano. Immanuel Velikovsky deduced excess heat would not start and ice age, nor would excess cold! He gave a much more realistic cause of ice ages; that of many volcanoes going off in a short period of time which caused suspended particles in the atmosphere to block sun light and dropping global temperatures for long periods of time. This coupled with under water volcanoes also going off causing tremendous amounts of steam to come down as torrential rain and incredible snowstorms lasting years. There's evidence that a time existed when many volcanoes went off in the same timeframe, along with massive earthquakes, due to geologic causes, mentioned in legends, which sunk cities in the Mediterranean and around the globe .World erosion rates jumped from 20-30 tons a year to 140 tons from torrential rains, and massive snows during winters lasting continuously for years. Velikovsky's deductions have been proven correct as volcanic action has been positively linked with ice ages. (Though Velikovsky placed the ice ages in a much more recent time frame than conventional dating methods based on a variety of data. Only preconceived dating dogmas persist in placing ice ages earlier.) So it's doubtful Gores circulatory oceans streams are even the cause of even a mini ice age, let alone a contributing factor to full blown one.

Very important to the climate scenario is volcanic action in recent centuries which shows up on graphs as the cause of global temperature drops. Volcanic action in conjunction with the Maunder Minimum, drove global temperatures downward severely earth wide. After the 1830's, global volcanic action slowed down and subsequently the earth's mean temperatures slowly rose. Climate guys like to blame the industrial revolution, which I was taught in school started in 1833, as the cause of the global build-up of CO_2 (which may be true) and then blamed the CO_2 build-up for the gradual increase in global temperatures. Thus climate guys are taking the blame away from the volcanic action and the Maunder Minimum and placing it on the very slight build-up of the trace natural gas CO_2 and the industrial revolution.

But let's work on Gore's horror show about the thermohaline monster. The question becomes how much cold water would be needed to stop the northern flow of warmer currents? A computer simulation called the 'hosing experiment' showed that massive amounts of cold water could conceivably slow down the Atlantic current, but it rarely stopped it. (this experimental model by the way is vastly in Gores favor, as it wouldn't be anything like how Greenland ice would melt, which would occur relatively evenly from all coasts). The amount of water needed to nearly stop the thermohaline conveyor was found to be one million cubic meters of water per second going continually for 100 years in one general direction from off the coast of Greenland. Okay, so how much is that? It's the equivalent of 350 Niagara Falls descending from Greenland and pouring ice melt into the Atlantic for 100 years. Or put another way, this would be the equivalent of 7 times the amount of water discharged into all the oceans from all the rivers in the world, all coming off of Greenland in an obviously catastrophic meltdown of Greenland's ice.

Gore shows a map of Greenland differentiating the area where ice loss is apparently half of Greenland's total ice cover melted in a dozen years.(1992-2003) Though that entire area did have a partial melt, it's misleading to say it's all melted, but only a tiny fraction of that area is melted as is determined by mass balance studies. This adds up to about 100 cubic kilometres of ice melting every year, or the equivalent to about 1.05 (there's a decimal in there) Niagara Falls dripping off of Greenland every year, literally a 'drop in the bucket' compared to 350 Niagara Falls worth of melt needed. The math of 350 Niagara Falls would amount to 1.4 million cubic kilometres. Thus his thermohaline monster is a gross exaggeration.

But even if Greenland ice did suddenly start melting at a rate 300 times it is today to match his video figures, Greenland would run out of ice in 90 years, and the experiments showed it would take 100 years worth of ice melting at the SAME rate, just to *slow down* the thermohaline conveyor.

Most climate alarmist have realized this cataclysmic Greenland ice melt scenario is farfetched at best, so they quietly don't mention this much anymore, or if they do they hope we don't know these facts.

In 2012, arctic melting slowed and the polar summer temperatures were the coldest ever reported and stratospheric temperature six to ten mile above were near record cold temperatures, even while CO_2 was building up. By 2013 it was realized that Arctic ice had started to recover as the ice coverage had expanded by 60%.

Global warming fear mongers conveniently forgot to mention, that their own climate models indicated there might be some additional melting of Greenland ice, but not from solar heat or CO_2 build-up, but from below in the earth's mantle.

More recent analysis of Greenland ice is further making global warming advocates look, at the very least, premature, as Global Positioning Satellites show the bulk of the Greenland ice mass is getting thicker, and is slowing down its migration towards the coasts. Scientists are uncertain as to why this is happening. But if believers in manmade climate change have their way, they'll find a way to blame it on CO_2 build-up anyway.

Here's something they don't tell you...Greenland melted faster in the 1920s, and the temperatures there were warmer in the 1930's than they were during the warming period up to 1998!

ANTARCTIC ICE LOSS.

In 1978 John Mercer hypothesized that global warming could rapidly melt the West Antarctic ice sheet, raising sea level by over 16 feet (or 5 Meters). This sounded so alarming that the theory got focused on by global warming proponents. But it wasn't till around 2000 that any perceptible diminishing of this ice field was noticed which was subsequently pounced on by the green agenda. Even though it is conceded that most of the Antarctic ice mass is unchanged and thus no collapse of the Antarctic ice cover is in any way imminent, this supposed peril of an "alarming rate" of melt is still propagated.

Part of this area, called the Amundsen Sea, appears to display signs of potential 'collapse' which could conceivably melt and raise world sea levels about 5 feet over the next two centuries. Hardly alarming, nor convincing, because it is still in the hypothetical realm and scientists are wondering if the danger is even real, or just an oversimplification from a lack real data. Thorough investigation may end up proving the ice sheet has a method of equilibrium that is simply being ignored by those pushing man-made climate changes.

I've noticed a trend in all these doom and gloom forecasts: they consistently try to terrorize us with the most extreme worst case scenarios in all their forecasts and thus call for draconian measures usually costing someone a lot of money. For example they say sea level would rise so fast as to flood all coastal cities and farms causing masses of refugees. People tend to gloss over the technical talk assuming the facts are genuine, and focus on the frightening possibilities, which usually are blown way out of proportion.

Consider. This ice mass doesn't even have any instability, it has theoretically potential instability if man made global warming has any possible way of creating such a instability. The IPCC admitted they have no idea under what circumstances or conditions could cause the West Antarctic ice sheet to collapse, which hinders their ability to determine the risk of any such event happening in total or in part in the next 100 to 1000 years!

But still global warming policy makers deem the risk too great to not make any binding rules to prevent whatever that unknown factor might be that might possibly conceivably theoretically cause something to go wrong in the southern continent. It's kind of like paying massive insurance premiums on the possibility you might get hit by a meteor, which frankly is the only real possible way the Antarctic ice sheet could collapse. And there's not much we can do about that, and burning a lump of coal is not going to melt Antarctica. Perhaps volcanic action right in Antarctica or several nukes or the continent suddenly shifting could melt the ice caps, but none of these causes have anything to do with raised CO_2 levels. They say the probability of any major contribution to global sea level rise is low during the 21st century, but becomes more serious after that. Really? How do they know, when their computer models can't even predict warming trends properly for the next decade? They just blame greenhouse gasses and assume we swallow it. We'll look at the greenhouse gasses closer later on.

Here's an important bit. Most of the ice on Antarctica is sea based, so if it broke free suddenly and floated north and melted it wouldn't raise sea levels much at all, because it's just an iceberg with 90% of its mass already in the water! The only way sea level could rise, is if the land based ice slipped into the sea, or rapidly melted. But this has also been ruled out by Mercer who suggested the potential collapse, by saying that grounded ice has a very gradual melt rate and shows no history of rapid ice mass changes in the geologic past. Though global sea levels are known to have been about 6 meters higher in the last interglacial period, even this has only been theoretically tied to the ice levels of Antarctica, as no firm connection has been determined.

As it turns out Antarctica is gaining more ice than its losing! It gained 112 billion tons a year between 1992 and 2001 and an additional 82 billion tons a year from 2003 to 2008. The Antarctic sea ice increased by about 1 million cubic kilometers in 2013 alone: IPCC doesn't bother to mention stuff like this. In fact Antarctica isn't increasing sea level at all; it's been determined to be *decreasing* it by 0.23 millimeters a year! Strangely the global sea level rise is 0.27 millimeters a year (this is less than one 100th of an inch) which the IPCC initially blamed on Antarctica, but now no one knows where the rise is coming from! Even though sea ice extent hit a record low in March 2017 this probably doesn't contribute much to sea level rise, though I don't think .027 millimeters is out of the range of possibility. Sea levels have risen at a fairly consistent rate of 7 inches a century for 150 years, long before CO_2 levels began to rise in any measurable way in 1945.

There is a lot of variability in ice sheet ranges, and global warming proponents cling to the record lows to present their case. This record low was preceded just two years earlier by record ice advances. The minimum extent of Antarctic sea ice was preceded by decades of moderate sea ice growth. In fact the ice around Antarctica has been growing so much its breaking those records! During this same period Arctic ice has also been growing.

But only the recent trend in shrinking Antarctic ice was keyed in on by the global warming advocates. But ask yourself, how long can an Arctic or Antarctic ice sheet continue to grow? It eventually has to reach a limit otherwise it would grow into the tropic zones, which is just impossible. Sooner or later there has to be a counter move of the ice in an opposite direction. We've only had satellite images of the poles for a very short period, but a recent minimum in ice coverage has global warming proponents rubbing their hands with glee even though scientists say it's too soon to suggest this is anything other than normal polar fluctuations.

The conclusion is ice loss on Antarctica cannot be blamed on global warming either. Geothermal heat from under the continent is more vast than originally thought and some ice loss is due to volcanic causes. The ice loss on the western part is not new, as this phenomenon in Antarctica is within the normal range of the last 200 years.

Now consider the hype. They try and horrify you by saying Antarctica is losing as much as 36 cubic miles of ice a year! Gasp no! How serious is that? This is keyed on by global warming advocates. Well just how much ice does Antarctica have? Just the West Antarctic Ice Sheet alone contains 3.8 million cubic miles of ice. So if this area continued melting at that incredibly "alarming rate" it would take 105,555 years to lose all the ice from just the Western Antarctic ice sheet! And after losing all that ice we'ld still have the rest of the Eastern Antarctic Ice cover left! By the way the western Antarctic peninsula contains less than 10% of all the ice in Antarctica. And they say this is an "alarming rate". Get serious! When Gore made his claims, the Antarctic ice sheet had been growing for over 30 years! Even Antarctic temperature records showed no warming since records were first kept in 1957.

ELEVATED LEVELS OF CO_2 INCREASE PLANT PRODUCTIVITY

A study published in the US Geophysical Research Letters journal in conjunction with the Australian National University, discovered via satellite observations, that increased CO_2 levels correlated with an 11 % increase in foliage cover from 1982-2010 across parts of the arid areas studied in Australia, as well as North America, the Middle East and Africa. According to Commonwealth Scientific and Industrial Research Organization research scientist, Dr Randall Donohue, He stated that "Australian vegetation seems quite sensitive to CO_2 fertilization". He added "While a CO_2 effect on foliage response has long been speculated, until now it has been difficult to demonstrate,"

A CO_2 fertilization effect happens because an elevated CO_2 level helps a leaf during photosynthesis, to extract more carbon from the air or lose less water to the air, or both. Heightened CO_2 levels cause the water use of individual leaves to drop, and plants in arid environments will react by increasing their leaf count. Altered leaf coverage can be detected by satellite, especially in deserts and savannas where, generally speaking, foliage is less dense than in wetter locations.

The conclusion deemed that increased CO_2 levels will boost the foliage in dry countries and could boost forestry and agriculture in these areas. By the way this same increase in foliage would be occurring in more moist areas as well, it's just harder to prove and quantify owing to the abundance of the background greenery.

Ancient climate is known to have had CO_2 levels as high as 4,000 PPM with average CO_2 concentration at 1,200 PPM. It's also known that ancient (pre global flood) flora was lusher and grew to staggering proportions compared to today's plant life. It appears current global plant life is actually existing in a CO_2 starved environment compared to earth ancient climate, where oxygen, atmospheric pressures CO_2 and concentrations were all higher.

People don't seem to grasp just how minute a portion of the atmosphere CO_2 comprises and how minute a portion of that is human caused. If your room is 50 cubic meters of air and all the CO_2 was concentrated into just one of those cubic yards it would only be 4 100ths of that cubic meter and only 3.4% of all the CO_2 in that cubic yard would be of manmade origin. (Remember, none of the rest of the room would have any CO_2 at all...well, that is until you exhaled.) A tiny fraction of the atmosphere is manmade CO_2 or shown as a decimal, .001326% of the world's entire atmosphere is manmade CO2, and all it can do is help plants grow better. It's not toxic, harmful, or even something that needs filtering. (Unless you happen to be on Apollo 13) It is not pollution as many people seem to think it is; it's a natural part of the cycle of air that has actually been decreasing over the millennia, causing plant life to suffer stunted productivity! If anything we should be trying to create more of it, not less!

Al Gore said that CO_2 concentrations at 385 PPM were the highest concentration ever, so either he didn't do any research or "ever", means during his lifetime. Fact of the matter is CO_2 concentrations have been decreasing since before the flood, or if you believe conventional dating methods, CO_2 concentration have been on average decreasing from a High of 7,000 PPM 550 Million years BC to the current level of 385PPM.

HURRICANE KATRINA INDICATES AN ACCELERATING TREND

Gore suggested Hurricane Katrina was caused by global warming, but it is not possible in any way shape or form to attribute a single weather event to global warming or cooling. The suggestion was that this was a hurricane of intense force attributable to intensified climate differences brought on by global warming. But modern technology, satellite images, and the widespread use of personal recording devices blew the effects of the storm way out of proportion by him and the media. Far more devastating hurricanes have occurred during what were actually cooling periods on the earth, like a hurricane named Cyclone Bhola which killed between 200,000 and 1,000,000 people in 1970 and was over 100 times as deadly as Hurricane Katrina. Five other hurricanes that caused the loss of over 100,000 lives are known about and they all occurred before 1900! Gore deliberately used appalling images of the effects of Hurricane Katrina to evoke maximum emotion from audiences, yet he didn't touch these other hurricanes which were far more devastating because they occurred before his window of opportunity where world temperatures rises seemed to match his causality conclusions.

It's been suggested that hurricanes have increased in force because of growing CO_2 emissions since just the 1960's in 5 of the six major cyclone basins. This too is disproven. Satellite imaging has so improved since the 1960's that the question was asked, did the improved quality of the images create the illusion of more intensity through more clarity? Back in the 1960's there were only 2 geosynchronous satellites with 9 km resolution tracking storms and thus with just 2 of these satellites, more often than not hurricanes were observed at oblique angles. The resulting analysis of these storms based on the image quality was so varied that any given hurricane could be determined to be anywhere from a category 3, to 5 for the same storms by different analysts. Now there are at least 8 geosynchronous satellites with 4 km resolution. This upgrade was suggested to be an unfair comparison, so all the satellite images of storms over these decades were downgraded to the same quality of the images from the 1960's and it was determined that the intensity of the storms has in fact diminished in five of the six cyclone basins over this period!

A study of cyclone activity from 1760's to the 1990's showed their frequency actually decreased gradually over this time period to what was an unusually low frequency of minimal storm activity during the 1970's and 80's. The conclusion is that because of this unusual minimal active period of the 1970's and 80s, the satellite era had by chance begun at the low point of hurricane activity of the last 270 years, thus giving the illusion of increased intensity over the last 50 years, when in fact the hurricanes are simply returning to their normal intensity based on the record of the previous 270 years.

Tree rings also indicate hurricane activity via oxygen isotopes ratios, as storm isotopes are very different from normal precipitation isotopes. The study of them matched up with records of Hurricanes in the forties confirming their validity. The tree rings confirmed that the 1790's and the 1970's were times of minimal hurricane activity in the region.

Other studies based on sediment deposits from coastal lagoons in the Caribbean from a 5000 year span showed *higher or lower sea surface temperatures are not needed to influence intervals or intensity of storms*. Furthermore the time frames Gore used were far too short and unreliable to show genuine trends, as the 5000 years span showed storm intensity varied widely over time.

TORNADOES PLAUSIBLE CAUSE

However it has been shown conclusively that man can affect weather on earth detrimentally through nuclear activity.

Evidence that man can cause the earth to hit back at man with disasters was reasonably established in the early 1950's. Many atomic bombs were exploded at Frenchman's Flat in Nevada which polluted the air over the U.S. with radioactivity and with the subatomic particles of what had once been the bombs itself. That's bad enough, but then in 1953 the earth struck back. What was being noticed was a huge increase in tornadoes. By May 1953 130 had been counted; the worst year on record. Naturally the Atomic Energy Commission said "The A-bomb's effect on weather is only local in character." Then in April and then again on June 8 1953 they detonated a "very powerful A-bomb", and three days later a great wall of tornadoes formed in the skies of the Midwest, a formation like no other formation on record, killing more than four hundred person from Ohio, Pennsylvania, New York, and Massachusetts. Could that have been caused by the explosions? They studied the rainfall that fell during those tornadoes and it was unusually radioactive, in fact so radioactive "that the water could not be used for photographic purposes". The mud created by the rain was also highly radioactive. Those tornadoes were loaded with the radioactive material from those bombs a few days before, and it likely caused the tornadoes as well. (Strange Worlds by Frank Edwards 1964 page 221-223) But strangely opposition to the real danger of nuclear energy has died down while opposition to the fictional threat of more CO_2 has been ramped up because it can create taxes for the governments

296

around the globe. (All nuclear plants leak radiation and no solution to the radioactive waste exists. Jeremy Rifkin: Entropy)

AL GORE SAID THE ZIKA VIRUS WOULD SPREAD FASTER DUE TO WARMER CLIMATE.

Al Gore suggested that warmer climates in southern USA would allow the zika bearing mosquito's to flourish in higher latitudes, causing the deforming microcephaly apparently caused by this mosquito to spread to USA. Some cases of this deformity did appear to migrate to USA apparently bearing out Gore's warning. But this turns out to be just flagrant fear mongering blaming the wrong culprit.

The zika virus probably isn't causing children to be born with deformed heads but it's caused by a larvicide called Pyriproxyfen created by a Japanese subsidiary of Monsanto, which is being used on the mosquito's specifically meant to deform the larva. There had been previous outbreak of the zika virus affecting as much as 75% of local populations in South America with no birth defects resulting from the outbreaks. But in 2014 significant use of the larvicide was used, and made its way into the drinking water of the same areas where the birth defects started to occur. Argentine and Columbian scientists are saying it is not the zika virus that is causing the defects but the pesticide used on the mosquitoes that carry the virus. But people aren't listening and they are making the problem worse by using this pesticide where the zika carrying mosquitoes are found.

THE MATH.

This is a killer for CO_2 caused global warming advocates, so pay close attention. I quote Licensed Professional Geologist and Registered Environmental Assessor of California William McClenney's math.

"The oft quoted fact is that the earth is 33 degrees Celsius warmer due to the trace gases in our atmosphere. Now, since oxygen and nitrogen make up 99% of our air, which leaves only 1% of everything else. CO_2 is just 0.04%. However in that 33 degree statement, the climatologists that cooked this dish up assign 20% of the Green House Gas (GHG) effect to CO_2 and 80% to water. So let's look at that ratio for a moment. If CO_2 is responsible for 20% of GHG effect at a concentration of 0.04% in the earth's atmosphere, then dividing 20% by 0.04% we can readily calculate a thermal insulation effect to concentration ratio of 500, making it, arguably, the best insulator known to man. If, instead of 0.04% CO_2, we used pure CO_2, a concentration increase of 2,500 times, we would have the best insulator in the known universe, and since one can achieve an 8:1 compression with common air compressors, we can get an enormous amount of CO_2 in compressed insulation applications, such as between the outer and inners shells of any kind of an oven. I mean, we are talking infrared here aren't we? Isn't that what the ruckus is all about? Infrared absorption by CO_2? Now, since no one has patented CO_2 for thermal insulation purposes, either I just gave you the scoop of the energy crisis (we will call that the "Wall Street Conundrum", since no one has glommed onto this yet....), or maybe CO_2 isn't all that crash-hot of an insulator after all. And you just do have to wonder why all those Anderson Windowalls use Argon and not CO_2 between the sealed panes...... This 20% GHG factor appears to be the most egregious affect accredited to CO_2 by climate change artists. It is deeply buried in the mathematics of the "black body" calculations which most people would not look at too hard given all the high-level math. But it is there, nicely hidden.

Climatologists have some of the most sophisticated computers on the planet, and some of the most sophisticated modeling software. Using these computers, that software and that 20% GHG factor, one can easily arrive at those global warming predictions a century or more out. So with all of those exotic computers how far out can we accurately predict earth's weather?

A week, sometimes two (but rarely)? So, given we cannot predict the weather all that accurately more than a week out, we are supposed to believe predictions a century out? ...the US Government's own data on these gases... [is] that the GHG of real concern is not CO_2, it is water vapor. In its concentrated form this vapor is also known as clouds, and it is attributed 95% of GHG potential"

NOT TRUE SCIENTIFIC PROCESS.

OK pay attention...this one is important. Normally scientific methodology works with the formation of a hypothesis with evidence by some researcher to support their theory, and then other scientists try and disprove the theory. If they can't disprove it, it's considered a good theory, and possibly a proven theory. This is NOT what happened with the global warming theory. The IPCC supported the theory that increased CO_2 would cause global temperature increases and temperatures would continue increasing with human formed CO_2 added to the mix. This was termed anthropogenic global warming. But scientists that backed the theory were allowed to try to PROVE the theory, using anything that looked like evidence and even tampered with evidence if it didn't measure up to expectations and attacked anyone who challenged the theory or tried to disprove it. They reached a consensus before any proper scientific research was done!

CHANGED OUR MINDS

With the presenting of the Inconvenient Truth, Gore predicted global warming as imminent, and the BBC was originally on board at the forefront with Gore's deductions and predictions. However BBC did an about face when they analyzed the facts and the evidence a few years later. (If only North American Media would do the same) At a time when carbon dioxide emissions were continuing to increase, global temperatures were staying the same or decreasing, something climate change computer models were not predicting. Though global temperatures were rising from 1980 to 1996, since 1997 temperatures have stayed the same or declined. Climate change proponents at the time said this period of 16 years from 1997 to 2012 is too short a period to draw any conclusion from, even though they drew their conclusion of global warming from the 16 year period before that! (Prior to 1980 the fear was a mini ice age might affect the globe)

For a while Gore's *Inconvenient Truth* became part of UK's school official curriculum. But the high court of London studied the film and halted the showing of the movie to students unless certain stipulations were met, because the movie was deemed to be a form of political indoctrination, something not allowed as they are forbidden to promote partisan political views in the teaching of any subject in school. Furthermore the film was analyzed and seen to have serious errors. If teachers want to show the movie to their class, they have to clearly state that it is only one side of the argument and that if they don't, they are guilty of political indoctrination under section 406 of the education act of 1996.

Also the *inaccuracies* of the film have to be specifically mentioned and drawn to the attention of the children watching the film. In the States teachers are suspended or fired for pointing out inaccuracies in text books! Good luck on getting teachers to point out flaws in the film.

HOW DARE YOU QUESTION!

If you or former Prime Minister Harper dare question climate change and the costs of fighting it, David Suzuki thinks you and he should be put in jail. Suzuki stated "I really believe that people like the former prime minister of Canada should be thrown in jail for willful blindness," He also stated: "What I would challenge you to do is to put a lot of effort into trying to see whether there's a legal way of throwing our so-called leaders into jail because what they're doing is a criminal act,".

I've always like science stuff and one of my favorite science show host was always David Suzuki. In looking up other stuff about Suzuki of late it seems he has been led astray in some manner. He seems to assume people who push ecological agendas and the dangers they talk about have done the same amount of research into the facts that he used to do. For example he appears to assume there is some danger in genetically modified foods because there are so many people screaming against this form of food. I found this on the internet....

He insists genetically modified food is dangerous, saying "any politician or scientist who tells you these products are safe is either very stupid or lying."

Meanwhile, the government of Canada says, "after 12 years of reviewing the safety of (these) foods, Health Canada is not aware of any published scientific evidence demonstrating (these products) are any less safe than traditional foods." In my first book I showed that the ancient Sumerians with the aid of the gods created all kinds of genetically modified foods which we still use today, such as corn, bananas and others.

David Suzuki appears to have assumed the IPCC stance of human caused climate change is rock solid and hasn't investigated the science, similar to how some other scientists have been fooled into promoting this agenda until one day they checked the facts. When Suzuki was questioned by some people in Australia about other organisations conclusions contrary to the IPCC, he seemed unaware of their existence and their work. Due to my former respect of Suzuki I'm going to mail him a copy of this section of the book, in the hopes of reawakening that inquisitive spirit in Suzuki once again.

Unproven climate based agenda taxes and costs are saddling municipalities, states, provinces and indeed whole countries with billions and even trillions of dollars of expenses, just to comply with climate action legislation. It seems somewhat prudent of any politician to say "wait a minute, before I spend tax payers money on something as fishy as climate change, based on CO_2 emissions (something humans exhale to feed trees with), shouldn't we have something more to go on?" Should politicians be put in jail for daring to question this extremely costly action? Some say climate change isn't debatable. It darn well better be debatable, because your money is being used for what is a complete waste! For example people in British Columbia will be shouldering the weight to reduce this natural plant food escaping into the air so that the plants that actually like the stuff can't get at it; so we will be paying a "carbon tax" of 31% more for <u>natural</u> gas. We are paying to try and starve our plants and trees, so that *WE* can starve...and on top of that, we will have reduced timber to sell. BRILLIANT! Why don't we saw the branch we're sitting on while we're at it!? You're diligent about YOUR money, and so should your elected representatives. Stop drinking the Kool-Aid of these environmental "Eco-Nazi's" as some people have dubbed them. (Yeah it appears to be the Deniers vs. The Eco Nazi's in today's world) Indeed reducing carbon thus reducing plant growth, and using food for the purpose of fuel is truly the cause of reduced food output and potential famine or politically induced suicide worldwide. You should be really steamed about this ongoing and VERY costly deception.

Similarly John Theon a former top scientist with NASA who originally believed in global warming, upon further study became a skeptic of global warming or human caused climate change. He said "My own belief concerning anthropogenic climate change is that the models do not realistically simulate the climate system because there are many very important sub-grid scale processes that the models either replicate poorly or completely omit. Furthermore, some scientists have manipulated the observed data to justify their model results. In doing so, they neither explain what they have modified in the observations, nor do they bother to explain how they did it. They have resisted making their work transparent so that it can't be replicated independently by other scientists. Once again, this is clearly contrary to how science should be done. Thus there is no rational justification for using climate model forecasts to determine public policy." (I.E. taxing you and wasting it on nutty ideas)

The fact of the matter is computer models are breaking down as they did not predict the current cooling trend, rendering the computer models less and less reliable, if they were ever remotely sound in the first place. Even as greenhouse gasses have increased, global temperatures have been declining since 1997. Though anthropogenic climate proponents keep saying the temperatures will continue to rise...at some point, they are unable to support this claim with any evidence based on their computer models, or any evidence involving CO_2 build-up that fulfill this expectation. Some 'deniers' are starting to conclude that the failure of the temperature to rise as predicted based on CO_2 build-ups means the whole premise of global warming caused by CO_2 build-ups is therefore false. This is the point, because if the assertion that CO_2 build-up does nothing to increase temperatures, then money spent on trying to reduce CO_2 build-up is money wasted and is lining someone's pockets. The climate is just not as simple as people thought, and in fact even if the globe were warming a little it would be beneficial for crop growth and human's overall health anyway! Rising CO_2 levels have even been shown to be responsible for increased foliage growth.

James Hansen who helped put human caused climate change in the media spotlight, who by the way was under Theon at one time, has also "...called for energy industry executives to be jailed for dissenting with the man-made warming hypothesis." Hold the fort here...you should be jailed for disagreeing with an unproved *hypothesis*?!!? This is the world you are voting for if you vote green or even the status quo governments who fall for this HYPOTHESIS that CO_2 is causing global warming and therefore they need to spend billions, nay Trillions of your tax dollars chasing rainbows.

The money spent creating the Kyoto Accord plan from 1998-2003 is all considered wasted money now. Ontario wasted over 9 billion on their wind farms, and solar energy schemes which they too late realized couldn't be connected to the Ontario power grid. An Ontario Auditor general says 8 billion was wasted elsewhere on these loony climate change projects. Waste of your money and pressure on economic stability will continue to be guaranteed as long as no questioning of climate change agenda is allowed to sit on the table...money that could be better spent on paying down debt, thus reducing servicing the debt costs as well.

But it gets worse. Ignoring the scientists who insist that CO_2 has nothing to do with global climate change in any way, they arrogantly try and change CO_2 levels with dangerous methods not stopping to think what worse ecological disasters they could cause. Canada spread tons of iron filings across the Pacific Ocean to try and increase the absorption of CO_2 giving no thought as to what this might do to the chemistry of the water. US sprayed chemicals at high altitudes to create 'chemtrails' to diminish sunlight to reduce global warming. Boy is *THIS* STUPID! 'Chemtrails' are killing the trees from the top down. The truth is no one fully understands the mechanism of climate so any action done to change it could more than likely make the environment worse, not to mention a waste of money and resources.

Science is supposed to be inquisitive and test results...over and over again. Believers in manmade global warming / climate change call people that don't believe their story and question their science "Deniers" and "Flat-earthers". Those who would force us to pay taxes through the nose to prevent CO_2 from increasing want us to be believers in what they say and not question, but follow blindly. Albert Einstein said "Never stop asking questions". The science is *not* settled, and there any many problems with the science behind this theory, so you need to ask yourself why is questioning of a **theory** deemed grounds for throwing away your money on this unproven science or worse, putting you in jail because you dare question? Don't let this enforcing or indeed terrorizing of prudent questioners to get a grip on our society by voting for parties that subscribe to Carbon taxes based on unproven science. This is one reason the Libertarian party says you need to vote for freedom and vote for them this party does not fall for this CO_2 cash grab and want to axe this carbon tax or anything else based on reducing CO_2 emissions eliminated.

And what's really silly is even if CO_2 build-up were some sort of problem, the solution is ridiculously easy: Plant more trees! In fact there is very likely a correlation between deforestation and CO_2 build-up! Trees absorb CO_2 and with photosynthesis turn CO_2 back into breathable air! CO_2 is not a pollutant; it's what all creatures exhale, and what feeds us through plant production. Trying to reduce CO_2 is literally like trying to reduce population through starvation from reduced crop production.

THE FIRST BLIP ON THE RADAR.

My first clue that something was wrong with this global warming farce dawned when I first saw what has been dubbed the "hockey stick graph", which showed global temperatures slowly declining for 1000 years then suddenly increasing since the 1940's to the highest point in history due to increased CO_2 emissions. In my previous research done for my first book, I had come across climate material when I was researching dendrochronology, (tree ring dating,) so I knew there was a historical warm period and a cold period that wasn't being shown on the graph. Though at the time I couldn't remember exactly where the warm and cool periods were placed in time, I knew a genuine climate graph would not be even remotely visually similar to what was being shown on the hockey stick graph. When I later saw by chance someone (Steve

McIntyre) refuting the hockey stick graph I knew he was correct as his explanation correlated with my personal research. But I also realized something was "rotten in Denmark", and as it turns out, more rotten than I ever thought possible. Something dubbed "Climategate" gave us a window into the infamy and the apparent greed of the deception discovered through leaked emails between the scientists creating the data for promoting the global warming hypothesis.

The scientists that influence the UN's IPCC said that the world would face catastrophic warming unless trillions of dollars was spent to avert it. That already sounds suspicious. The USA alone was earmarked for 5 Trillion dollars to contribute to avert this catastrophic climate change. This dire warning was based mainly on the hockey stick graph, which has now been positively proven to be a fake! These scientists have some sort of ulterior motive because they have been deliberately faking data to eliminate the Mediaeval Warm Period and the Maunder Minimum from the graph. Many emails were uncovered that showed them agonizing over the difficulty of manipulating the data with computer programs to create the impression of slowly decreasing temperatures followed by rapidly increasing temperatures to produce the 'hockey stick' graph.

In thinking Geophysicist Dr. David Deming was a promoter of the global warming theory, one of his colleagues let down his guard. What the colleague said to Deming was presented to the US senate from an email he got from this unnamed prominent climate change researcher, which said in part "We have to get rid of the Medieval Warm Period." Leaked memos from the Climate Research Unit (CRU) showed they were aware the Medieval Warm Period was absent on the graph but kept this knowledge hidden. More than 500 scientist's climate research has been studied by investigators and they found theses scientists concluded that the existence of man-made global warming was very doubtful. They also concluded temperature increases are beneficial as sudden cooling periods have killed twice as many people as warm spells.

Further confirmation that the Hockey stick was a fabrication came from New Zealand and Australian scientists when they compared their local climate records and found that the same trick had been used on both locations data to change what was supposed to be basically a flat temperature graph into the faked ones used to compile the Hockey stick graph. In each case they could see the subterfuge was done by people influenced by the CRU.

Also found in the Climategate emails were an ongoing thread on how to avoid releasing data under freedom of information laws. The scientists were recommending to each other to delete large blocks of their climate data, which is a criminal offence when that data is requested under freedom of information laws. What and why would you want to destroy information used to prove your climate data, contrary to scientific principals, unless you wanted to hide something? Furthermore, the scientists conspired to discredit any scientists or scientific journal that published other experts questioning their data, and stopping any dissenting reports making their way into the IPCC reports. They were prepared to stop at nothing to squelch scientific debate and refuse to publish any research that disproved global warming. Even today this practice continues, calling climate science 'settled'.

Steve McIntyre's proof that the hockey stick graph was a fake was also confirmed by statistician Professor Edward Wegman who produced a report for U.S. Congress. He was really steamed at the "tightly knit group" that would collaborate with each other and peer review each other's papers in order to dominate the IPCC reports on which the future of the US and world economy could hinge. Dr. Fred Seitz of Wall Street Journal said in his 60+ years as part of the American Scientific community, he had never seen "... a more disturbing corruption of the peer-review process than the events that led to this report". (IPCC's second assessment Report: Climate change 1995)

Paleoclimate records showed large regions of the planet were considerably warmer than they are today and were so for several thousand years. Also shown was that many regions of the globe showed significant temperature drops since the 1940's, the exact opposite of what climate models predicted! Furthermore a known spike in earth temperatures that occurred between 1920 and 1940 (the same one melting Greenland ice) was removed from data used for the hockey stick graph. All post 1940 graphs showed the planet wasn't any warmer than it was centuries and millennia previous to steep increases in manmade CO_2 emissions, except of course in the Hockey Stick Graph. In fact some places on the globe during the Maunder Minimum were actually warmer than modern temperatures. Many parts of the globe are experiencing the coldest temperatures in thousands of years. One of the scientists exposed by Climategate finally admitted that the earth may have been warmer during medieval times (800-1300 AD) than now. From 1900-1940 global temperatures rose when human produced CO_2 was low and from 1940-1980 global temperatures fell while CO_2 production increased the most; the exact opposite as shown on the graph.

One other factor discovered in any data that appeared to show genuine temperature increases were found to come from weather stations that had their temperature records affected by local factors such as land development. It's a known fact that temperatures above and near cities are far warmer than at the same time out in the country because cities radiate heat. There was overwhelming evidence that the IPCC's climate data was contaminated with surface effects due to industrialization and urban development.

Though a few irate experts called for some of the scientists guilty of the collusion to be pressured to leave the CRU, little has changed and these positions have been filled by other people known to be propagandists for global warming, which is now generally called "climate change" because man-made global warming became impossible to prove in the data when countered with genuine scientific data. This is potentially the biggest scandal if not crime of the century which can literally bankrupt countries to fill pockets of people that profit from "green" technology.

Another reason they did their best to eliminate the Medieval Warm Period, is because if human industry is supposedly causing warming recently and frightful ice melts, why were the Vikings sailing around the North Atlantic to supposedly frozen places like Greenland and setting up farming communities 1,000 years ago? You saw the maps exist of Greenland with no ice, though I've not been able to determine the time they were drawn, that they were drawn at all has to be another clue of the ongoing deception.

The IPCC said that they were 97% certain that humans cause global warming but their scientists openly manipulated the key climate data of US surface temperature records. The results downgraded earlier temperatures and amplified those from recent decades, to give the appearance that the Earth has been warming far more than actual data could show. When comparisons were made between the original temperature graphs with the tampered data of IPCC, it showed that the US has actually been cooling since the Thirties, whereas the IPCC graphs showing a warming rate equivalent of more than 3 degrees Celsius per century. In actuality the earth warmed just 1/2 a degree over the past 50 years. Furthermore Meteorological Office records show that temperatures have paused and, if anything, were going down.

OTHER PROFESSORS AND SCIENTISTS DISPUTE HUMAN CAUSED GLOBAL WARMING / CLIMATE CHANGE

Many people are convinced that manmade climate change is completely false, but they are being silenced by science journals, and ignored by media and politicians who don't bother to dig into the science and instead accept what is spoon-fed them by IPCC and Gore as gospel. Those media that disagree and do manage to get heard are vilified or attacked by saying they have no authority or are not scientists. That's like arguing media people are not qualified to report on Hubble news, because they are not astronomers.

John Coleman founder of the weather channel is one such target. His 50 years in the field are discounted because he's belittled as 'just a TV weatherman' when he is in fact an accredited meteorologist. Very few of us are scientists, but that doesn't mean individuals are not allowed to assemble research material that both sides present to come to conclusions. People like Coleman and Bill Gray (Hurricane expert) are more qualified to research climate science because they are intimately acquainted with the material, so they are more prone to understand the jargon and weed through the rhetoric. Coleman is so convinced of his findings that he's not afraid to challenge a Nobel Prize, Academy Award and Emmy Award winning former Vice President of United States.

So what does Coleman say about manmade global warming and climate change?

COLEMAN INTERRUPTED.

Colman studied dozens of scientific papers and talked with numerous scientists and concluded that there was no global warming. Furthermore he said that in a decade or two, predicted temperature rises, polar melts, coastal flooding, super storm patterns, would fail to occur, and he predicted that the trend of global warming would end and a trend in global cooling would occur. He got it right, yet IPCC scientists and Gore's climate models and other global warming pushers didn't predict the global cooling that occurred after 1997. Dr Kevin Trenberth, head of the climate analysis in Colorado, wrote "The fact is we can't account for the lack of warming at the moment and it's a travesty we can't". Unexpected global cooling had global warming advocates hot under the collar and they had to change the rhetoric from "global warming" to the now more familiar term of "climate change". Their flawed computer climate models completely missed it. Never the less man is still blamed for climate change. Heaven forbid it be proven to be part of the cycles of nature!

Coleman emphatically refutes Al Gore who is not a scientist and relies heavily on computer models which are constantly shown to be inaccurate. Gore says manmade global warming caused by CO_2 from car and power plant exhaust will cause polar ice to melt, raise sea level by 20 feet, submerge islands and inundate coastal plains creating 100 million refugees around the world. However accurate readings from satellites conclude the maximum the global sea level would rise would be 7 inches over the span of a century, and that is assuming a constant rate of polar ice melt, which sadly for the climate change gurus has been shown to be cyclical and not continuous.

John Coleman learned during the 1970's to be skeptical about such alarm bells when the predicted ice ages never occurred, and doesn't accept media about global warming either. He read dozens of scientific papers, conferred with numerous scientists and concluded there is no run away climate change. He notes hundreds of other meteorologists, many with PHD's, are as certain as he is that the global warming frenzy is based on invalid science. He goes further, saying global warming is "the greatest scam in history" and "a manufactured crisis." Global warming is not something you 'believe in,' it has to stand up to the science of meteorology which is his field of expertise.

Coleman says if scientist's research conclusions aren't alarming, their work and papers gather dust and they get no research money coming their way. Several scientists worked together to drive environmental agendas, then peer reviewed each other's work to give it credibility so the conclusions wouldn't be questioned. They manipulated long term scientific data back in the late 1990's to create the illusion of rapid global warming. (This charge was proven in "Climate Gate" when these scientists' emails were leaked) More scientists of the same bent jumped into the circle to support and broaden the "research" to further enhance the slanted, bogus global warming claims. Soon they claimed to be a consensus. Their friends in government steered huge research grants their way to keep the movement going. Now their horror show has been accepted as fact and become a central issue for CNN, CBS, NBC, the Democratic Political Party, the Governor of California, school teachers and, in many cases, well informed but very gullible environmentally conscientious citizens.

Coleman maintains climate change is part of nature. Through time the earth has ranged between two climate extremes: from ice ages, to interglacial periods where the earth warms up. Interglacial periods are preferred because ice melts and life flourishes. But Gore and his crowd say man has overwhelmed nature during this interglacial period and are producing unprecedented, out of control warming. This is complete nonsense and he says the sun has everything to do with earth temperatures through solar cycles of sunspots where the globe warms when sunspots are active or the earth cools like it has since 1998 when sunspots are minimal. The IPCC finally admitted the solar cycles caused the cooling, but they said it was temporary and drastic warming would return after the cycle. He derides the IPCC: 'We are supposed to be in a panic about man-made global warming and the whole thing takes a ten year break because of the lack of Sun spots.

Digging through thousands of pages of research papers, huge IPCC documents published by the United Nations, deciphering complicated math and complex theories he concluded, "The entire global warming scientific case is based on the increase in carbon dioxide in the atmosphere from the use of fossil fuels. They don't have any other issue. Carbon Dioxide, that's it."

The focus on atmospheric carbon dioxide was started by Roger Revelle a scientist at the Scripps Oceanographic Institute. He took his research with him when he moved to Harvard and allowed his students (Al Gore was one) to help him process the data for his paper, which is how Gore got caught up in this global warming frenzy. Reveilles' paper labelled CO_2 a greenhouse gas and linked the increases in atmospheric CO_2, with global warming.

From 1958 to sometime past 2005 Charles and David Keeling measured CO_2 in the atmosphere and it rose from 315 parts per million to 385 PPM. This is a tiny fraction of our atmosphere, yet all computer models and studies designated it as a major greenhouse gas, which it simply is not, it's a trace component. And as a trace component of the atmosphere it simply cannot upset climate. It's not a pollutant, or smog, it's a naturally occurring gas. No tree or bush could be green without it. Before his death, Roger Revelle coauthored a paper cautioning that CO_2 and its greenhouse effect did not warrant extreme countermeasures. At present carbon dioxide accounts for about 390 ppm. (I've seen reports it hit 400 PPM recently)

Despite Revelles' recommendations, IPCC has attracted billions of dollars for the research to try to make the case that CO_2 is the culprit of run-away, man-made global warming. Research organizations and scientists, who are making a career out of this theory, keep cranking out the research papers. Then they endorse each other's papers, they are summarized and voted on, and viola, we are told global warming is going to kill us all unless we stop burning fossil fuels.

Coleman blames Gore's "Global warming science", for the $4 a gallon gas and shortage of world crops. How does he come to *this* conclusion? He summarizes history. Internal combustion engine and gasoline were awful polluters when they were first invented. Environmentalist originally had a very valid concern back in the 1960's when they started an attack on smog over cities caused by cars. Smog was battled with better engineering and reformulated gas that reduced emissions. The goal was to have cars emit only carbon dioxide and water vapour: two gasses known to be natural and harmless. (Carbon monoxide unfortunately is still present in exhaust and affects taxi drivers in New York so badly they are not allowed to give blood) City skies have vastly improved since the '60's. But environmentalists still like to find some demon to battle, so now they focus on harmless carbon dioxide. But carbon dioxide is not an environmental problem; they just want you to think it is.

Coleman says numerous independent research projects have been done about the greenhouse impact from carbon dioxide. These studies have proven that CO_2 is not creating a major greenhouse effect or causing an increase in temperatures. Yet environmentalists ignore these findings and claim that the burning of fossil fuels dooms the planet to run-away global warming; but it's simply a myth. Eventually environmentalists caused global warming fears to become regarded as a threat to planet Earth. This lead to a battle against fossil fuels, which has since controlled many government policies for decades, slowly changing the world we live in. Environmentalists block any drilling for oil and the building of any new refineries and pipelines, causing a perpetual gas shortage which forces gasoline prices skyward. Trying to relieve the fuel shortage lead to ethanol as an environmental fuel created from crops. The amount of acreage set aside for ethanol crops is so extreme that it has created a food shortage crisis throughout the world, which is behind the food price rises for all the grains, cereals and bread. Anyone or animal that relies on corn, soy or wheat, corn oil, soybean oil or corn syrup is affected. This has created global food shortages and high costs which have led to food riots in some third world countries. For over a dozen years food consumption has outstripped food production, leading to global reduced food stocks, which has pushed food prices higher around the planet.

Thus we see how Coleman concludes that Gore's 'global warming science' lead to $4 a gallon gas and world food shortages. Coleman's charge is verifiable too. A World Bank report blamed biofuels for the a large portion of the 140% increases in food costs between 2002 and 2008, stating that biofuels accounted for 75% of the jump in food costs during that period. Over one third of all US corn production is used to produce ethanol, and about half the vegetable oils go toward producing biodiesels. The global warming myth has actually led to the chaos we are now enduring with energy, food and gas prices. Not only have prices soared, government policy changes impact taxes, utility bills and the entire focus of government funding. *And what's really stupid is using Ethanol causes far more CO_2 emissions that does burning normal fossil fuels!*

And, now the Congress is implementing a cap and trade carbon credits policy. It all increases the public's costs. So the global warming frenzy is, indeed, threatening our civilization, but not because global warming is real; it is not, but because of the all the horrible side effects of the global warming scam. If Al Gore and his global warming scare dictate the future policy of our governments, the current economic downturn could indeed become a recession, drift into a depression and our modern civilization could fall into an abyss. And it would largely be a direct result of the entirely fictitious global warming frenzy. President Trump and a few other elected officials have been informed about these crazy claims of global warming and have been shown the true science which is why Trump and others don't take the bait and throw money at these holograms, and some Canadian politicians are fighting the carbon taxes.

Despite the negative side effects of this myth, manmade climate change has the backing of the United Nations, Gore, and Hollywood, which equals billions in backing; plus environmentalists love global warming as a tool to combat fossil fuel. USA alone pledged 5 trillion dollars to battle climate change based solely on increased CO_2. The crisis excitement got the media attention and backing because they love to tell horror stories to glue you to their broadcast. With so many media outlets on board by just accepting what's fed to them, when in theory they should be investigating the reports, they constantly propagated the global warming crisis. The very few reporters that do question get shouted down as ignorant buffoons.

So everyone, except the lunatic fringe, believes manmade global warming/ climate change...or so we are led to believe. But the media doesn't report that as of October 2016 a list of over 31,000 scientists who refute global warming was released, 9,000 of which are Ph.ds. (The internet has a field day with this fact) That dwarfs the supposed 2,500 scientists on the UN panel, and there are about 100 defectors from the UN IPCC. In the past year (circa 2015) a hundred or more scientists have issued public statements challenging global warming and more join the pushback every week. There was an International Conference of Climate Change Sceptics in New York in March of 2008 which showcased 100 power point and other types of presentations.

Conferences are now held every year. These conferences can be found online and you can view their power point presentations, and speeches. I spent about an hour or so just watching a few.

Here are some points I gleaned from watching just one online. One speaker used many official government agency graphs, that were created before the IPCC and their schemers started manipulating data and graphs to show what outcomes they wanted you to believe. ....

Obama basically force fed Climate Change costs on congress and spent 120 billion on climate issues, or about $350.00 tax dollars out of each person's pocket in the USA.

The "Waters of the US" rule allows E.P.A. to regulate all land and water uses in America. For example you are breaking the law if you catch water in a rain barrel.

Satellites indicate temperatures are fluctuating normally with no warming for over 2 decades, but global warming models and advocates blow out of proportion any fluctuations with "absurd models".

Graphs of both CO_2 levels and temperature over the same time frame clearly indicate there is no relation between the two. (The only relation that exists is ocean water temperatures which give off more CO_2 when they heat up and absorb the same when they cool, similar to a soda pop left out that releases its CO_2 as it warms up. Colder pop releases CO_2 slower than warmer pop.)

The number of days per year that weather stations record 100F on average increased from1895 to 1936 then dropped since 1936 to 2015.

Jay Lehr who helped create the EPA in the late 60's now speaks strongly against the concept of global warming, and is on a crusade to eliminate the EPA, due to the abuses of its influence and power since 1980.

Droughts have had no change over time and the graph shows a slight decrease in their numbers since 1982

Violent tornados similarly show overall average declines since 1950 peak to the present: years were 1957, 1965 and 1974 was the worst.

The Dutch have been using excessive amount of CO_2 to grow fantastic tulips for over 50 years.

Wheat rice and coarse grain production has all increased significantly since 1961 and increased CO_2 is considered a contributing factor to the increased production. Books put out that help illustrate these points are called *Climate Change Reconsidered* I and II which illustrate that increased CO_2 is a benefit to human health, wildlife, economic strength, food yield and tree and plant life flourishing.

Wildfires on average have dropped since about 1981.

Hurricane frequency and intensity climbed from about 1972 to around 1993 and have been dropping since then to a level well below the 1972 period.

Sea levels fluctuate up and down, but no perceptible change beyond the normal range of fluctuation has occurred since records started in 1910. Higher sea levels over that span would of course increase coastal flooding. Gore's alarmist videos and presentations want us to believe these coastal floods from normal sea level fluctuations are caused by the polar caps melting raising sea levels: That is hog wash. With the money he's raked in from his alarmist rhetoric, He and David Suzuki could build an island in Doggerland and have no fear of floods if they built above the highest point of sea level fluctuation...well unless a global series of Tsunamis occurred such as we chatted about in the main section of this work. They could learn how to build dikes from the Dutch and then learn how to grow tulips from them with all that extra CO_2. They probably wouldn't like living over there though because they couldn't snow the Brits likes they've done to the North Americans.

Back to Coleman; he remarked in New York that perhaps we should sue Al Gore for fraud because of his carbon credits trading scheme. The concept is that if the media won't give us a hearing and the other side will not debate us, perhaps we could use a Court of law to present our papers and our research, and, if the Judge is unbiased and understands science, we win. The media couldn't ignore that. This idea has become the basis for legal research by notable attorneys and discussion among global warming debunkers, but it's a long way from the Court room. He's very serious about this issue. "I think stamping out the global warming scam is vital to saving our wonderful way of life."

That seems fair. If people who question climate change are being threatened with jail, shouldn't the fight go to court?

Professor Bill Gray, the world's most famous hurricane expert is outraged by the belief of manmade climate change pushed on people. Though his research has been abandoned by government funds, he has spent over $100,000 of his own money to continue his research. He is convinced that global warming is "...one of the greatest hoaxes ever perpetrated on the American people" and said as much to the Unites states Senate. He deduces the belief in manmade global warming / climate change is not founded in real science but is a baby boomer "Yuppie thing". He abhors computer climate models and prefers observations and direct measurements.

Literally thousands of computer climate models have been number crunched to give various scenarios and outcomes using varying input. What is then told to the public are the worst case scenarios out of these thousands of hypothetical modeled outcomes. Furthermore programmers, almost like a game, deliberately input extreme 'what if's' into the models to get extreme outcomes, then these scenarios are called "worst case scenarios", which the media promotes as genuine alarming possible futures to add scare value to their reports. And the public buys it! This is what gets people like Bill Gray, a genuine climate scientist, furious because the models have nothing to do with real nature and they don't even include key factors like the Sun, Clouds or water vapour, the most important factors in climate and temperature!! For example one extreme worst case scenario had the globe warming by 11 Celsius. So the London Evening Standard reported that the world would "likely heat up by an average of 11°C by the end of the century!" and added ...this would melt the ice, raise sea levels threatening billions of lives. This was sheer alarmism and mass hysteria based on a deliberately extreme computer scenario that has nothing to do with reality. Gray notes that in the 1940's there were stories about global warming, then in the 1970's scientists were warning about an ice age. He states these are part of cycles and alarmists are blowing them all out of proportion. He started his crusade in the early 1990's against the global warming scares when he saw huge sums of federal money being spent on computer models instead of science that comes from direct observation: which of course would dovetail with historical records to see the systematic rhythms of nature. Instead computer modellers are deliberately tampering with historical records to make their models and graphs seem all the worse and fit their preconceived agendas. Gray also predicted "It may warm another three, five, eight years, and then it will start to cool."

These cycles can vary dramatically. Though a lot of focus has been placed on the Maunder Minimum where global temperatures varied by 2 degrees Celsius, some ancient cycles have shown a global temperature change of as much as 10-18C in as short a time frame as 10 years. If nothing else this serves to remind us that the fear mongering about potential temperature fluctuations are nothing compared to what has occurred in the earth's climate history and we need to take their dire warnings with a grain of salt.

Neil Frank, former director of the National Hurricane Center, agrees with Gray. "It's a hoax," and he says cutting carbon emissions would wind up hurting poor people. Asked if he thinks more CO_2 in the air would be a good thing. "Exactly! Maybe we're living in a carbon dioxide-starved world. We don't know." (Ancient climate evidence suggests this is actually the case)

Richard Lindzen, an MIT climate scientist has maintained for years that clouds and water vapour will counteract the greenhouse emissions of human beings. He states water vapor would increase in a warmer world because of higher rates of evaporation, and cause "negative feedbacks" countering any warming trend. "The only reason the models get such a big response is that, in models, the most important greenhouse substances, which are water vapor and clouds, act to take anything man does and make it worse," he says, whereas observations show otherwise. (Thus Lindzen speaks of water vapour and clouds being used in some computer models, but used as elements that increases global warming the very opposite of what these really factors do. If this is the case, then they have multiplied the effect of CO_2 by compounding it with clouds and water vapour in the models) Lindzen argues that the climate models can't be right, because we've already raised CO_2 and methane dramatically, and the planet simply hasn't warmed that much.

So here we have examples of clouds being used in computer models, but used to make the global warming appear worse when in fact the clouds aid in cooling; cancelling out any potential warming trends, once again showing how they use computer models to arrive at a predetermined objective.

He's correct on the water vapour countering the warming trend. One cause of the ice ages was massive volcanic action. When volcanic action increased in the oceans it caused massive evaporation which blocked out the sun for years, dropping global temperatures for decades. Snow fell constantly, even in summer times creating what we call the "ice ages".

Pablo Mauas Stated at least 98% of all climate is due solely to the sun, but it may be even more than that as it's been ascertained to a 99.99% degree of certainty that the amount of global rainfall is also due to solar influences. Initially this was nearly impossible to show but this was eventually determined by Pablo Mauas of the University of Buenos Aires. He studied the Parana River in South America (4th longest river in the world) and on a timescale of decades was able to show the river increased or decreased flow according to the number of sunspots.

German **Physicist Klaust-Eckert Puls** and Meteorologist said "...I simply parroted what the IPCC told us. One day I started checking the facts and data – first, I started with a sense of doubt, but then I became outraged when I discovered that much of what the IPCC and the media were telling us was sheer nonsense and was not even supported by any scientific facts and measurements. To this day I still feel shame that as a scientist I made presentations of their science without first checking it."

One theory scientists have put forth as the cause of the global cooling from 1940-1975 was the excessive pollution caused by the world's massive industrial build-up before governments passed clean air acts and enforced pollution controls. The pollution dimmed sunlight reducing its ability to warm the earth. Once the skies cleared the temperatures have been rising back to normal. Thus paradoxically, the very lack of pollution and any incidental CO_2 *reduction* may have caused temperatures to rise!

Henrik Svensmark, leader of the Center for Sun-climate Research of the Danish National Space center proposed a theory initiated in 1991, published in 2007 and which has since been proven. The conclusions are that the sunspots link to the solar magnetic field controls the amount of cosmic radiation reaching the earth. These rays become condensation nuclei around which water vapour forms creating clouds. The relationship between cosmic radiation (determined by sunspots) and cloud formation is a perfect match. Thus solar influences on water vapour a.k.a. clouds are the key variable in global temperature variations. None of this information was ever used in the IPCC reports, or in any of their computer models, it was ignored. All the money in the world can't change what the sun does to us on the earth; we are its benefactors and we are at its mercy.

MORE POWER

Who wins? More power in the hands of few is the bottom line. The IPCC now admits that the computer predictions for the effects of carbon emissions on global warming have been proven wrong. Furthermore they admitted that computer forecasts did not take enough notice of the natural variability of climate, consequently multiplying the effect of increased carbon emissions on world temperatures. It's been determined that IPCC officials violated standard rules of procedure and altered the data in such a way as to justify an acceptable political agenda to serve as the scientific basis for UN negotiations on restricting emissions of CO_2 and other greenhouse gases. Politicians were deliberately led to believe that mankind is responsible for warming to bring them on board with the agenda. If you can convince the world there are global problems you can give supposed moral justification to initiate a new world order of a one world government to control global problems. This is a reason U.N. set up the IPCC and the Environment Protection Agency (EPA) to promote the idea that CO_2 is the most dangerous threat to the world, when it is in fact vital to life on earth. Their next target is methane from the agricultural sector of developing countries.

FOLLOW THE MONEY

Petroleum companies wanted President Clinton and V.P. Gore to agree to the Kyoto Protocols, because the protocols would have forced huge costs on the US energy industry and energy consumers by implementations of a large hidden tax that would have lined BP and Enron's coffers with billions of dollars.

Al Gore and IPCC tried to make climate change appear to be a historic global temperature disaster. Then risk experts and their companies reaped financial rewards by defining and pricing risk, then getting the public to pay insurance premiums to protect itself from the hypothetical risk: the higher the overvalued risk, the more the corporate insurance profit. Businesses also profits from proclaiming that they are green and the word "renewable" unlocks government donations. Scientific "validity" adds weight to get the ball rolling and it figures in the game.

Trillions of your income dollars have been spent on worldwide campaigns to fix a problem that doesn't exist. Politicians and the media haven't bothered to research to see if the problem was real but just made costly policies that have been a complete waste of your tax dollars.
Why?
Dr. Tim Ball's research uncovered frightening motivation behind the manmade climate change agenda

which is too in depth to present here and which that has to be read in its entirety to be grasped. In short it puts a lot of power into the hands of the IPCC, and world governments, gives the illusion of a global problem justifying the need for a global one world government to solve the global problem, placing the ruling powers of the globe in the hands of very few. The apparent end game is to deliberately reduce global population or reduce global living standards with only the elite having any technology privileges. The charges are so alarming you just have to read Dr. Tim Ball's Book *Human Caused Global Warming* subtitled The Biggest Deception in History.

All too many politicians and media personalities just accept the rot, spoon-fed to them by the IPCC and their 'in' group of "scientists". So all I can recommend is you get in government's and the media's face and tell them to stop this nonsense, and do some damned research and spread the word so the governments can't ignore the truth any more.

REFERENCES.

Though Climate scientists refused to show their work, I'll show mine.

Material and jumping off points for internet searches:

Atlantis Rising magazine # 78, 80, 81, 85, 87, 89, 93, 94, 96, 97, 100, 101, 102, 103, 104, 107, 110, 112, 113, 114, 115, 117, 121

Nexus Magazine Volume 15 #5, V16:2, V16:6, V17:2

The internet based material is often from the jumping off stories mentioned in the above magazines. (There's no point in mentioning sites because they disappear.)

My previous research into Dendrochronology, historic climate: See my work Earth, Man, & Devolution for complete list of References, many of which are reused in this book.

Immanuel Velikovsky's works: Earth in Upheaval by Immanuel Velikovsky Pocket book paperback © 1955 Worlds in Collision by Immanuel Velikovsky ©1950 Dell Pocket book© 1973

Dr. Tim Ball: The Deliberate Corruptions of Climate Science ©2014

Dr. Tim Ball: Human Caused Global Warming. © 2017

A Few Extra Tidbits

THE STORIES BEHIND THE ART.

The cover art for my first book: In 1993 I started a painting called "Life in the Asteroid Belt" which was meant to be sort of a cool semi surreal piece using the house I was living in as my model: making it look like it had been part of a destructive blast on the fifth planet, incorporating a bit of whimsy with a girl on a bed in the kitchen. This was almost exactly how my kitchen looked with a little exaggeration on the floor deterioration, but instead of a kitchen table by the window, I put a bed nearer the observer. As I was painting it I realized it had some tie in with some of the research I was doing at the time on my first book. However I never finished the painting, because I got frustrated with it as the hands of the girl were tough for me at the time, and they got the best of me and so I crumpled up the unfinished painting in frustration and tossed it in the stove illustrated on the cover. I immediately regretted my action as it was actually a real nice painting but it was too late to pull it out of the fire. Had I just walked away from it and come back to it later which I've since learned to do, it might have been saved.

In 2012 I decided to make a card set of all my art and I had to have that painting, along with one I had lost from grade 12 when I was moved to a different group home with no chance to retrieve my art piece from the school. I wanted to include these art pieces in my card set, so I repainted them both to make my card set complete. This was after I had already published my first book and my original cover art for that book was part of it. After I painted and this time finished *Life in the Asteroid Belt* again, though only about half of its original size, I wished it could have been the cover for my first book, because the artist in me thought it was a much more artistically appealing piece. Though perhaps a little risqué, I knew I wasn't supposed to promote this book to a Christian audience originally and the art does, genuinely reflect, artistically speaking, the content of my first book. Indeed you could say this event is the central theme of the book, as I discovered that this event has played a central role in much of ancient history.

As chance would have it, because of a few costly blunders on the part of the publisher where for a time I was advertising my book which couldn't be bought through the normal channels because the original trim size become obsolete without me being properly informed, along with a few complications; I found out after I finished my 3rd edition inserts, they not only allowed me to completely replace the text of the book with my more polished third edition interior, they also allowed me to replace my old cover with my new preferred one free to make up for some of the frustrations I had experienced during the process, which I must say was very kind of them, and completely unexpected. I could not have afforded the normal costs of this change of my cover had they decided to charge me for the switch. So thanks to Trafford's kind help, my new polished and now fully illustrated edition of my first book cost me not one dime.

A funny thing happened just before it was to be placed into the publication loop. They said I had to get the artist name and consent before they could publish it. They did not realize I was the artist too, so in a sense I being told to credit myself, and give myself permission use my art. Needless to say, I had a little fun with that at their expense.

The art for this book: the front cover is based on the legends of the four suns that passed after great catastrophes. Of course some legends talk of as many as 7 suns or heavens, but descriptions of them are wanting. Also it is just easier to divide the cover into four sections. So the cover is based on the Mexican and or the Mayan four suns which they name and thus describe. They are Water sun, Fire sun, Hurricane sun and, Earthquake sun. I've not taken the time and energy to distinguish exactly which order they occurred in, though water sun would be first. However I placed them on the cover in a way that would hide the least amount of art detail.

The *back* cover is a sort of compilation of clues I found in my first book and some I found in researching stuff for this book. The area is based on a pyramid site called Teotihuacán, though I've had to foreshorten the scene to include the three main places in that location. So they appear closer together in this painting that they do in real life. I've deduced that this place was subject to a fairly substantial tsunami which demolished many of the buildings and left a build up of debris and dirt on some of the remaining structures, which would have come from the top right direction on the back cover, so I included buildings that are no longer there and took away any debris. But, I couldn't study it and be especially meticulous, as little detail would really be visible and it was not the central theme of the book anyway.

I placed two artificial globes in close proximity to each other (top right) so that a situation the ancients spoke of could be illustrated; that which was probably an electrical ark or an electrical discharge between the two bodies caused by the close proximity, something like a Jacobs' ladder or a spark one gets from a doorknob when you've walked on a charged carpet.

The yellow globe on the large pyramid is based on a mediaeval painting mentioned before. A mediaeval book illustration shows a mysterious moon like object descending to the consternation and awe of onlookers while a princess (?) turns a wheel of fortune. (**See image 24**) I used this image as an aid for the large moon descending on a pyramid on the back cover. I strongly suspect this particular globe is portrayed in religious paintings. It is a globe with a delineated equator which has a cross on top of it, and a line going up from the 'equator' to the center of the top to the point where the cross is placed.

Image 24: a mysterious moon descends

However the most spectacular shock I got when researching this piece was when I looked up the rock lapis lazuli to get the colours correct for Elysia. I happen to have a piece of lapis but wasn't positive it *was* lapis until I looked it up. Why Lapis you might ask. The Sumerians adored moon gods who dwelt in a lapis coloured moon, so I wanted to depict this moon. The shock came from the realization I got was when I looked up lapis and found that many people shape lapis stone into a sphere! Being something of an amateur rock collector, I've seen lots of neat rocks in rock hound shops. Of all the rocks I've seen I could not remember ever seeing people take the time to turn a piece of pretty rock into the shape of a sphere. Were some rock hounds aware of the Lapis Elysia connection? Eventually I did recall one time a long time ago seeing a piece of lapis in the form of a sphere, and I recalled asking the seller why it was in that shape. And he told that it was because it looked like the earth. Ok that sounded plausible.

It then suddenly dawned on me: there are many sci-fi stories of a twin earth, and I always thought this was just a vehicle for another science fiction story. I've seen sci-fi stories put forth that Jupiter was or had a duplicate earth in its orbit. I've seen it suggested that on the other side of the sun directly opposite the earth in our own orbit that there existed a duplicate earth placed in this spot for the purpose of hiding itself from us. But when I realized that Lapis Lazuli when shaped like a sphere, looks like the earth and it is how the Sumerians described the home where the gods lived, it all clicked! There *is* a "duplicate" earth in our solar system built by the preflood people. I had reached this conclusion based on my research in my first book. But to see this deduction substantiated unexpectedly with this series of clues linked with Lapis was quite an eye opener.

Earth, Man, & Devolution forgotten tidbits

(Here are a few tidbits I wrote in 2015 that I appear to have forgotten to add to the third edition of my first book and found again hidden somewhere in the computer or memory stick just before submitting this book)

EVOLUTION DECEPTION

(Would have been placed in first chapter, probably around page 24 of 3rd edition)

Ernst Haeckel (1834-1919) and his bio-genetic law may be responsible in part for WWII. How? He drew a series of embryo comparison to "prove" man and other creatures had similar embryos which pass through various evolutionary stages. Such as fish which were apparent as 'gill slits' (which in the humans actually turn into ear anatomy.) His own university colleagues put him on trial and proved in 1875 these drawing were a deliberate hoax. (microscopes today prove this further) Single-handedly he convinced all of Germany to believe in evolution. Hitler's belief in Evolution was what spurred him to try and eliminate the more inferior races. But these drawing and or his conclusions are still in the text books today lying to young people.

(Would have been inserted on around page 111 of 3rd edition)

In 1962 Mars observers saw huge flares on Mars followed by clouds forming in the area.

FLYING OR PHASING THROUGH MATTER WITNESSED

(Would have been placed on pg 333 of 3rd edition) A steward named John Sander sailing on the Queen Elizabeth in the region of the Bermuda Triangle on the way to New York from Nassau early in the morning while on deck noticed a plane at an elevation of about 600 feet about 1000 feet away flying directly towards the boat. Pointing it out to his fellow mate they watched it when suddenly about 200 feet away from the boat it plunged silently into the sea not even making a splash and just vanished right in front of them. They notified the ship and they steered toward the spot the plane disappeared but not even a oil slick existed to give away the location of the plane. This is an example of a plane caught in a power field that caused it to phase through the molecules of matter. (Book 24 pg 137)

(Would have been inserted on page 340 of 3rd edition)

Herschel, Uranus's discoverer, noticed red glowing lights on the Moon in April 1787. These have since been 'explained' as earth shine reflecting in craters. RED?

GEBAL COIN / SHEM

(would have been placed around Pg. 374 3rd edition)

I'm not one to take psychics seriously as I tend to believe some demonic forces may be working through some individuals posing as beneficial spirits and whispering in these psychics ears. The bible says to test the spirits, and it shows how to do that. Indeed other researchers have noticed people who claim to be speaking for UFO's or whatever have some definite similarities to spirit possessions. References to Edgar Cayce often came up in the research material I used for this book, and even though my dad used to talk about and refer to this 'sleeping prophet' often, I determined, that I wouldn't have this man's 'help' in creating my theories, or cheating by using his readings for substance as 'evidence'. After all how much weight can you put in something as evidence based on something people say in their sleep? So it seemed of little material value. This bit is written for the third edition so I feel I stayed true to that determination. However when gleaning through the books I used for research to find material for giants and whatever I might have missed the first time around, I stumbled on something Cayce stated that confirmed something no one else seems to have caught on to(though I might have not read enough books... so who knows). I found it in "The Bermuda Triangle by Charles Berlitz (book 7 pages 186-187) ... Cayce in 1933 is talking about a building seen in the distant past. This building has a "..."firestone" or crystal complex was kept and from which its power was diffused." I quote parts of the said pages here...

"The building above the stone was oval; or a dome wherein there could be...a portion for rolling back, so that the activity of the stars-the concentration of energies that emanate from bodies[not on earth] ...through the prisms or glass was in such a manner that it acted upon the instruments which were connected with the various modes of travel through induction methods which made much the (same) character of control as would in present day be termed remote control through radio vibrations or directions; through the kind of force impelled from the stone acted upon the motivating forces in the craft themselves."

"The building was constructed so that when the dome was rolled back there might be little or no hindrance in the direct application of power to various craft that were to be impelled through space-whether within the radius of vision or whether directed underwater or under other elements, or through other elements."

"The preparation of this stone was solely in the hands of the initiates at the time; and the entity was among those who directed the influences of the radiation which arose, in the form of rays that were invisible to the eye but acted upon the stones themselves as set in the motivating forces- whether the aircraft were lifted by the gases of the period; or whether for guiding more-of-pleasure-vehicles that may pass along closer to the earth, or crafts on the water or under the water."

"These, then, were impelled by the concentration of rays from the stones which were centered in the middle of the power station or powerhouse."

Now look again at the coin of Gebal. My drawing or interpretation of the building on the coin with the raised wall as an odd depiction of the roof in which the cone stood on thus appears based on Cayces reading, to be incorrect. Actually after drawing it I felt it might be wrong but have a difficult time figuring how a square building with a squarish superstructure could move up down or around the cone, and why would it be there at all if a craft were to land on the cone. Still the building on this coin seems to be the exact type of building Cayce was talking about, but his reading adds curious information about the building which confirms my deductions as to what the building or at least the curious stone or conical structure purpose was; some form of power source used in flight. This may be a shem, the very shem to be built on a tower of stones the bible refers to as the Tower of Babel. I might add that the finding of this coin appears to have occurred long after Cayce's dream was recorded.

ELYSIA

(Would have been inserted on around page 404 of 3rd edition)

I had previously thought Cassini had on one occasion seen a satellite by Venus, but Book 23 pg 11 says he saw it several times and the author asked could it be an immense space ship. Cassini in saw it in 1672, but not again until 1686

Abraham Scheuten (1707-89) saw a moon of Venus during its transit of the sun in 1761, as a dark spot following Venus across the sun. COOOL! I saw the transit of Venus in 2012...I'd waited for it for years... but that second item following it?...wow. that would have been a sight!

For a while this Venusian moon was a regular sight. J.H Lambert (1728-1777) had even calculated the length of time it took to orbit the planet (11 days). Yet a contemporary, Herschel, could never find the elusive moon of Venus. Some suggest they saw a distant star nearby or something on their lens...

William H. Pickering (1858-1938) felt he had found a tenth moon of Saturn and named it Themis. Pickering was no slouch...he was awarded the Lalande Prize, for scientific breakthroughs in the world of astronomy by the French Academy of Sciences. A tenth moon wasn't officially discovered until 1966, so what did HE see?

Verrier (Neptune's discoverer) in 1859 noted Mercury's orbit was so eccentric that it must be affected by another planet nearby (Vulcan)Edmond Modeste Lescarbault (1814-1894) claimed to have seen this planet transit the Sun in March 1859. No one believed it, and other credible sources saw the planet, but no one could predict when it would appear.